Beginning VB .NET 1.1 Databases: From Novice to Professional

DAN MAHARRY, JAMES HUDDLESTON, RANGA RAGHURAM, SCOTT ALLEN,
SYED FAHAD GILANI, JACOB HAMMER PEDERSEN, JON REID

Apress®

Beginning VB .NET 1.1 Databases: From Novice to Professional

ISBN (pbk): 1-59059-358-8

Distributed to the book trade in the United States by Springer-Verlag New York, LLC, 233 Spring Street, 6th Floor, New York, NY 10013 and outside the United States by Springer-Verlag GmbH & Co. KG, Tiergartenstr. 17, 69112 Heidelberg, Germany.

In the United States: phone 1-800-SPRINGER, e-mail `orders@springer-ny.com`, or visit `http://www.springer-ny.com`. Outside the United States: fax +49 6221 345229, e-mail `orders@springer.de`, or visit `http://www.springer.de`.

For information on translations, please contact Apress directly at 2560 Ninth Street, Suite 219, Berkeley, CA 94710. Phone 510-549-5930, fax 510-549-5939, e-mail `info@apress.com`, or visit `http://www.apress.com`.

The source code for this book is available to readers at `http://www.apress.com` in the Downloads section.

This book is for Jane. Her ring fits through mine, but she is my perfect fit.
—Dan Maharry

Contents at a Glance

Contents

CHAPTER 5 Creating Connections . . . 87

CHAPTER 6 Introducing Commands . . . 111

CHAPTER 14 Understanding Views and Stored Procedures 365

About the Authors

DAN MAHARRY is a writer, editor, and Web developer based in Birmingham, United Kingdom, where he lives with his fiancée, Jane. He has worked on more than forty technical books since 1997 and cowritten 10 including *Beginning ASP.NET 1.1 with Visual C# .NET* (John Wiley & Sons, 2004) and *Beginning ASP.NET Databases 1.1* (Apress, 2004). His next collaboration will cover ASP.NET 2.0. When not writing, he works as a developer for 3form Ltd. (`http://www.3form.net`), an award-winning Web publishing house also based in Birmingham. Outside of work, Dan is an avid filmmaker, film watcher, and music maker. He recently blew up a car in the name of cinema and wants to do it again. Contact him at `danm@hmobius.com`.

JAMES HUDDLESTON has worked with computers since 1974, specializing in database design and development since 1980. He has a bachelor's degree in Latin and Greek from the University of Pennsylvania and a juris doctor degree from the University of Pittsburgh. A technical reviewer of dozens of computer books, including *Beginning C# Objects* (Apress, 2004), he finds databases an endlessly fascinating area of work and almost as intellectually rewarding as his hobby, translating Homer's *Iliad* and *Odyssey* from the original Greek.

RANGA RAGHURAM has a bachelor's degree in engineering from Birla Institute of Technology and Science in Pilani, India, and a master's degree from Virginia Tech in Virginia.

SCOTT ALLEN has a master's degree in computer science from Shippensburg University. He's a Microsoft Certified Solution Developer. He regularly serves as an adjunct faculty member at various colleges in Maryland and Pennsylvania.

SYED FAHAD GILANI has more than 15 years of experience in computing. He sold his first program at the age of ten.

JACOB HAMMER PEDERSEN started programming in the early 1990s, moving gradually from Pascal to C++ to Visual Basic. In the summer of 2000 he discovered C# and has explored it happily ever since.

JON REID was editor for the C++ and Object Query Language components of the Object Data Management Group standard and has coauthored several C# books.

Acknowledgments

This isn't the first time I've revised a book based on a previous edition, but it's the first time I've been asked to translate one in its entirety, and for the trust in my ability to do so, I thank Dominic Shakeshaft at Apress. Cheers mate. Thanks also to my Special K editorial team—Kylie, Kim, and Katie—and to reviewer Mike for making sure my work never faltered without me noticing. Final thanks to Starbucks for providing the "office space" where the initial discussions for this book were held and to Stef at 3form for letting me have the time to get this done promptly. Look, Douglas, I can still see the deadline coming toward me!

Introduction

It's odd, but when you start to learn VB .NET, or any other language for that matter, one topic that's seemingly glossed over in every book is how to work with data. Fair enough, there are other topics to cover as well; Web Forms, Windows Forms, security, and file access are pretty fundamental. But once you've gotten beyond the language and asked, "So, what can I do with it?" you soon realize that almost every useful application uses (and abuses) data. Most real-world programs use data stored in relational databases, so every programmer needs to know how to access relational data. This book explains how to do this with VB .NET and ADO.NET.

We'll start at the beginning with the installations you need, and then we'll cover ADO.NET 1.1, SQL, and relational databases. Then we'll go on to more advanced topics. Finally, we'll close with a brief look ahead to ADO.NET 2.0. By the end of this book, you'll be equipped to tackle the core topics in VB .NET database programming.

Who Is This Book For?

This book is for anyone interested in how to access relational data with VB .NET. This book is targeted at programmers, managers, and even students, since only basic knowledge of VB .NET is assumed and no prior experience with relational databases or the relational database language SQL is required. We've done our best to provide comprehensive, clear descriptions of concepts and to demonstrate them with straightforward programs you can use as the basis for your own code.

What Does This Book Cover?

This book covers all the fundamentals of relational databases and ADO.NET that every VB .NET programmer needs to know and understand.

Getting Started

The aim of the first three chapters is to get you ready to tackle VB .NET programming.

- Chapter 1 explains how to install Microsoft SQL Server Desktop Engine (MSDE) and the sample databases you'll use for all the examples in this book.
- Chapter 2 takes you through the basic steps of building your first database application and then shows how you could build it using Visual Studio .NET wizards.
- Chapter 3 introduces the fundamentals of SQL, the language used to interact with all databases.

Learning ADO.NET Basics

In the next eight chapters, you'll come to discover all the key objects used to pass data to and from the data source your application is using. All the examples in these chapters are based on the command line to keep the attention on the new code rather than the form code.

- Chapter 4 introduces ADO.NET, its architecture, and the way in which it allows you to work with almost any data source with almost no changes to the same basic program.
- Chapter 5 covers the humble `Connection` object, the starting point for all conversations between application and data source, and Chapter 6 introduces commands to create, query for, update, and delete data.
- Chapters 7 and 8 shows the main receptacles for data retrieved from data sources (the `DataSet` and `DataReader` objects), the differences between them, and when each is most useful.
- Chapters 9 to 11 then put what you learned in the previous five chapters to good use, by describing how to use those principles to build Windows Forms and ASP.NET applications that access databases. You'll learn about key issues in this process of data binding and user validation.

Learning More About SQL and Relational Databases

With the basics of ADO.NET covered, the second half of the book starts by recapping and then delving deeper into the structure of a database and the language you use to communicate with it.

- Chapter 12 looks at the fundamental objects in a relational database—tables and relationships. You'll see why they're necessary; how the two work together to model information systems; and how you can create, delete, and alter them to your needs.
- Chapter 13 shows there's a great deal more to the humble query for data than was first introduced in Chapter 3 and goes off in search of more complex variations for more useful data.
- Chapters 14 and 15 go further into the structure of a database and bring four new features to your attention, each of which, used wisely, will bring improved performance and, in two cases, simpler coding to your applications. They are views, stored procedures, indexes, and constraints.
- Finally, Chapter 16 covers database security and, taking the example of SQL Server, covers the various ways to authenticate the user trying to access the data in a database and how a database then authorizes or bars access to a user. You'll also see how to administer this type of security, setting permission levels for data to be accessed at and the permission level a user or group of users has.

Advanced and Future ADO.NET Techniques

Rounding out the book, Chapters 17 to 21 introduce some of the more advanced features of ADO.NET, so you can make judgment calls about why, how, and when you should add them to your own applications. In order of appearance, these chapters cover the following:

- Using XML as a data source and format
- Handling ADO.NET exceptions in your applications
- Using database transactions to ensure the consistency of your data
- Using the events fired by the common ADO.NET objects
- Handling large data objects (images, big documents, and so on) moving in and out of your data source

Last but not least, Chapter 22 looks ahead to ADO.NET 2.0, due in late 2005, and demonstrates using the beta 1 release of Visual Studio .NET 2005 to convert ADO.NET 1.1 programs to ADO.NET 2.0. It also modifies three applications developed earlier in the book to use alternative features new in ADO.NET 2.0.

What Do You Need to Use This Book?

You can code and run many of the examples using only the command-line VB .NET compiler provided with the .NET Framework 1.1, but Visual Studio .NET 2003 is the development environment we used and the one that can run all the examples. However, Visual Basic .NET Standard Edition is adequate for almost all the examples.

Although you can use ADO.NET with any relational database, we base our examples on MSDE, because it's just as powerful as SQL Server and it's available without charge from Microsoft. In Chapter 1 we show you how to download and install both MSDE and the SQL Server documentation.

In Chapter 5 we show you how to connect to Access, DB2, Oracle, and MySQL, so you can use any of these relational database systems instead of MSDE. Of course, what data you work with will depend on which database you use, so your output will differ from the MSDE sample table data we display. Still, you should use whatever relational database system you prefer.

How to Download the Sample Code

The source code for this book is available to readers at `http://www.apress.com` in the Downloads section. Please feel free to visit the Apress Web site and download all the code there. You can also check for errata and find related titles from Apress.

CHAPTER 1

Installing MSDE

Chances are that you're already familiar with the term *data* and have some understanding that data can be stored in many formats. You can store data in a text file as a comma-separated list, or you can store it in a database such as SQL Server or Oracle. You can even store data as Extensible Markup Language (XML) documents, which is probably the biggest innovation in data storage in recent years. You can then work with this data and present it to end users in many different ways, from an application running on a local machine to a Web application viewed with a browser.

The aim of this book is to demonstrate how to work with data using VB .NET, and in order to have a common set of samples to work with, you'll start your voyage of discovery by setting up a database server and a sample database, both provided free by Microsoft. This will give you all the example data used in the book.

In this chapter, we'll cover the following topics:

- Installing Microsoft SQL Server Desktop Engine (MSDE)
- Installing the sample databases
- Installing the Microsoft SQL Server documentation
- Authentication modes
- Connecting to a database in Visual Studio .NET

Obtaining and Installing MSDE

We've chosen MSDE as the relational database management system (RDBMS) since it's available for free. MSDE is an exciting and powerful product that can be embedded in and redistributed with applications. It's the server component of SQL Server 2000, but it's limited to 25 concurrent users and doesn't include visual tools for database management and development (although you can download third-party ones if you look for them). It includes the SQL Server 2000 relational engine and storage engine. Databases and applications developed with it can be easily migrated to SQL Server 2000. If you already have SQL Server 2000 installed, feel free to use it instead of MSDE, but look through the upcoming section "Installing the Sample Databases" to see how to install the sample databases (`Northwind` and `pubs`) if they're not installed.

MSDE is provided with a number of Microsoft products, including the following:

- Microsoft Office XP (Developer Edition)
- Microsoft Visual Studio .NET (Standard, Enterprise, Architect)
- SQL Server 2000 (Standard, Enterprise, Developer Editions)

You can also download MSDE as a separate product, and that's what we'll assume you'll do. You can also install the latest sample databases and SQL Server documentation, which also applies to MSDE. We downloaded the MSDE version used in this book from `http://www.microsoft.com/sql/msde/downloads`. We downloaded the sample databases from the *Northwind and pubs Sample Databases* link from the same location. We downloaded the documentation (SQL Server Books Online) from `http://www.microsoft.com/sql/techinfo/productdoc/2000/books.asp`.

To install MSDE, perform the following steps:

1. Download `MSDE2000A.exe` from `http://www.microsoft.com/sql/msde/downloads`.
2. Run `MSDE2000A.exe`, which extracts the MSDE installation files. The License Agreement window appears. Read the license agreement, and then click I Agree.
3. The Installation Folder window appears. Specify the folder for the extracted files, and then click Finish (see Figure 1-1).

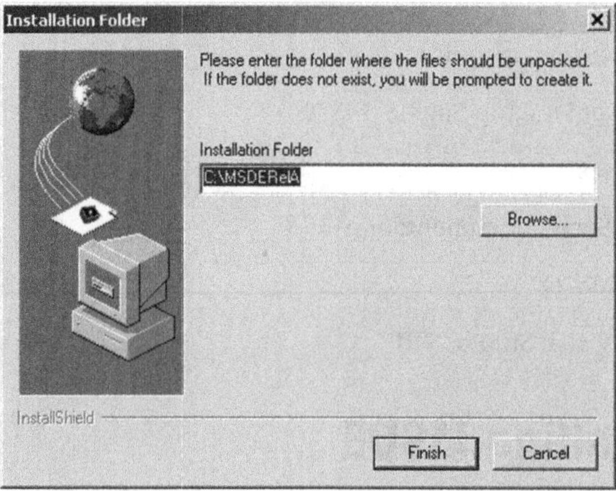

Figure 1-1. *MSDE installation's Installation Folder window*

4. If you specify a folder in step 3 that doesn't already exist, a dialog box appears and asks you to confirm that you want to create that new folder (see Figure 1-2). If this is what you intend, click Yes.

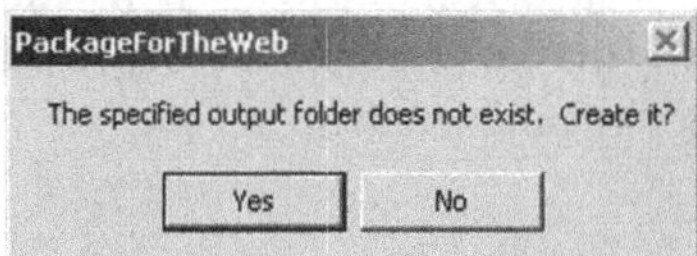

Figure 1-2. *MSDE installation's PackageForTheWeb message box*

5. A progress window appears. When the message “The package has been delivered successfully” appears, click OK.

6. The installation files are now in `C:\MSDERelA` (or wherever you put them). Open a command prompt window, and go to this directory. Run the following command, using whatever password for the system administrator (`sa`) account you prefer if you don’t want to use `password`. You may, for example, want to give the `sa` account a strong password. You can find more details on how to do this at `http://www.microsoft.com/athome/security/privacy/password.mspx`.

   ```
   setup instancename="netsdk" sapwd="password"
   ```

A progress window will display until the setup is complete. If all goes well, a Windows service named `MSSQL$NETSDK` will be created that will start automatically at Windows startup. This service is an MSDE server instance known as `(local)\netsdk` for connection purposes. By default, we chose Windows Authentication, so any user who can log onto Windows can connect to it.

■ **Note** If all doesn’t go well, you may want to refer to the following Microsoft Knowledge Base article, which deals with one reason for installation failure and how to generate a log file to identify the cause of others: `http://support.microsoft.com/default.aspx?kbid=829386`.

To start the server, from any command prompt, enter the following (see Figure 1-3):

```
net start mssql$netsdk
```

To shut it down, enter the following (see Figure 1-3):

```
net stop mssql$netsdk
```

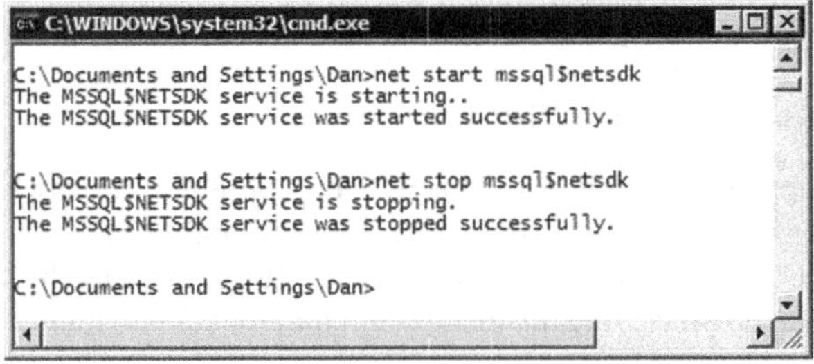

Figure 1-3. *Starting and stopping the `NETSDK` MSDE server instance*

That’s it! MSDE is installed, and you can now install the sample databases.

Installing the Sample Databases

To install the `Northwind` sample database, perform the following steps:

1. Download `SQL2000SampleDb.msi` after following the *Northwind and pubs Sample Databases* link at `http://www.microsoft.com/sql/msde/downloads`.
2. Open `SQL2000SampleDb.msi`, which extracts the sample database installation files. A welcome window appears. Click Next.
3. A License Agreement window appears. Read the license agreement, and then click the I Agree radio button. When the Next button is enabled, click it.
4. When the Choose Installation Options window appears, click Next. There is only one option, as shown in Figure 1-4, so you should go with that.

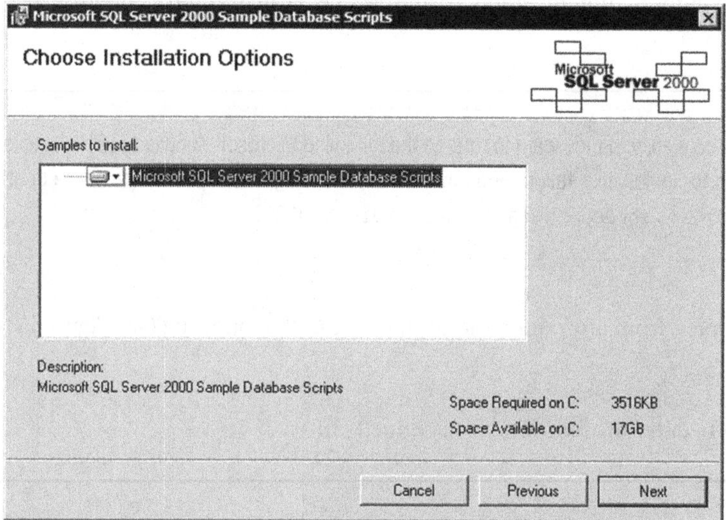

Figure 1-4. *Sample database installation's Choose Installation Options window*

5. When the Confirm Installation window appears, click Next.
6. A progress window may briefly appear, followed by the Installation Complete window. Click Close. The installation files have been extracted to (no, we're not kidding) `C:\Program Files\Microsoft SQL Server 2000 Sample Database Scripts`. Note that the sample databases haven't yet been created. Only the installation files that create them have been "installed."
7. To create (or re-create whenever you like) the `Northwind` sample database, make sure the `MSSQL$NETSDK` service is started (refer to Figure 1-3), open a command prompt window, and then go to whatever directory contains the `instnwnd.sql` file (for convenience, we copied ours to `C:\BegVBNetDb`, but that's not necessary). Then enter the following, paying attention to case (see Figure 1-5):

```
osql -E -S (local)\netsdk -i instnwnd.sql
```

Note The `-E` option connects to the MSDE instance (server) with a trusted connection, and the `-S` option specifies the server to which to connect. If you have problems getting this command to work with `(local)\netsdk`, try replacing `(local)` with the name of your machine. Thus, the command will include `-S MachineName\netsdk`.

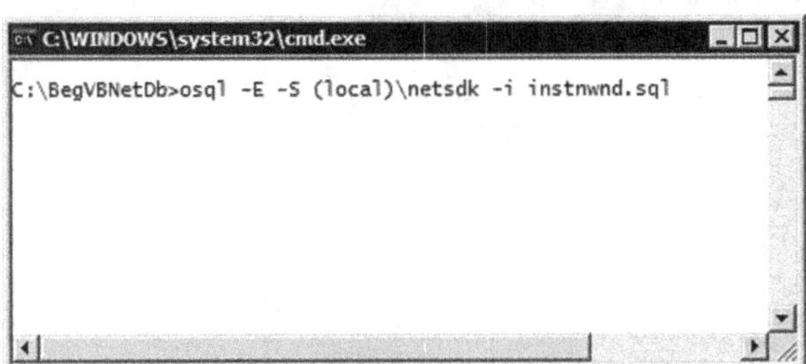

Figure 1-5. *Creating the `Northwind` sample database*

A lot of largely unintelligible output displays, eventually ending with the screen shown in Figure 1-6.

```
C:\WINDOWS\system32\cmd.exe
(1 row affected)
(1 row affected)
(1 row affected)
(1 row affected)
(1 row affected)
(1 row affected)
(1 row affected)
(1 row affected)
(1 row affected)
1> 2> 3> 4> 5> 6> 7> 8> 9> 10> 11> 12> 1> 2> 3> 4> 5> 6> 7> 1>
 8> 9> 1> 2> 3> 4> 5> 6> 7> 8> 9> 1> 2> 3> 4> 5> 6> 7> 1> 2> 3>
> 3> 4> 5> 6> 7> 8> 9> 1> 2> 3> 4> 5> 6> 7> 8> 1> 2> 3> 4> 5> 6
3> 4> 5> 6> 7> 8> 9> 10> 1>
C:\BegVBNetDb>
```

Figure 1-6. *`Northwind` sample database created*

The `Northwind` sample database is now installed in the MSDE instance `(local)\netsdk`. You can install the `pubs` sample database similarly with `osql` by using the `instpubs.sql` file.

Installing the SQL Server Documentation

To install the SQL Server documentation, perform the following steps:

1. Download `sqlbolsetup.msi` from `http://www.microsoft.com/sql/techinfo/productdoc/2000/books.asp`.
2. Open `sqlbolsetup.msi`, which extracts the documentation files. A welcome window appears. Click Next.

3. A License Agreement window appears. Read the license agreement, and then click the I Agree radio button. When the Next button is enabled, click it.

4. If you have SQL Server 2000 installed rather than MSDE, a window appears asking whether you want to upgrade the Books Online currently installed with this new version or to install them into a separate directory. Choose the separate directory, and then click Next (see Figure 1-7).

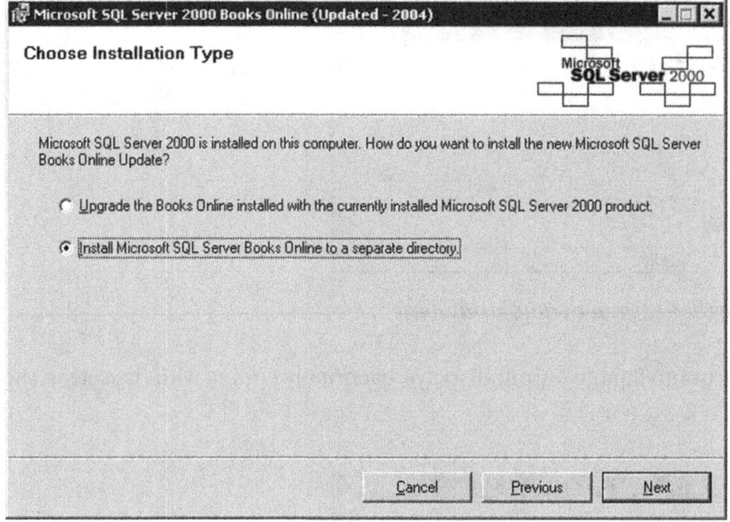

Figure 1-7. *SQL Server documentation's Choose Installation Type window*

5. When the Select Installation Folder window appears, choose the directory for it to be installed in and click Next (see Figure 1-8).

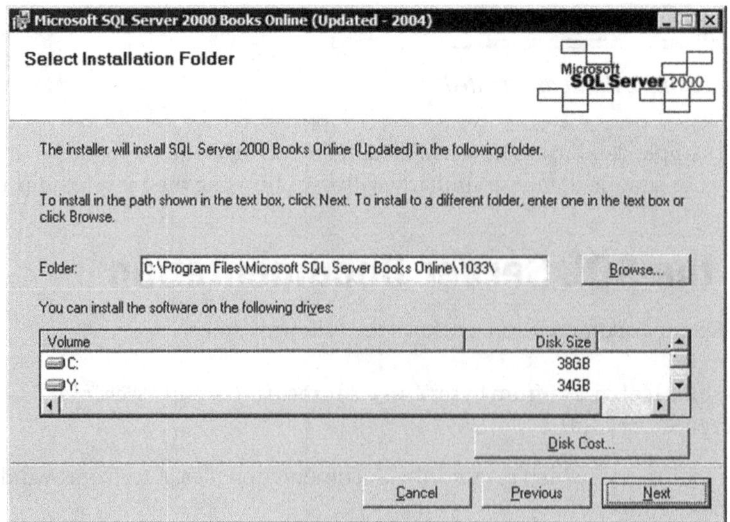

Figure 1-8. *SQL Server documentation's Select Installation Folder window*

6. When the Confirm Installation window appears, click Next.

7. A progress window appears, followed by the Installation Complete window. Click Close. The documentation files have been installed.

Microsoft SQL Server Books Online (Update 2004) is now installed. You can run it from its shortcut on the Start ➤ All Programs submenu, or, for convenience, copy the shortcut to your desktop.

Now you're ready to work with MSDE!

Introducing Authentication Modes

Before you start playing with MSDE, we'll talk a bit about who can play with it. SQL Server, and therefore MSDE, has two distinct modes for authenticating users.

- Windows Authentication
- SQL Server Authentication

■ **Tip** When we installed MSDE, we used the default security setting of Windows Authentication, since it's the more flexible and secure mode. As a rule, you should use SQL Server Authentication only when you're not connecting over a network. If you ever want to install MSDE in SQL Authentication mode, add the phrase `SECURITYMODE = SQL` to the setup command used in step 6 of the MSDE installation instructions in the "Obtaining and Installing MSDE" section.

Windows Authentication

When a database uses Windows Authentication, SQL Server validates user names and passwords through Windows security facilities. To connect to a database server with this type of authentication (known as a *trusted connection*), you must be logged onto Windows XP or Windows 2000. In most enterprise settings this will probably not be a problem, but for users on Windows 98 or earlier (or for that matter, some other operating system) this isn't possible. For such users, SQL Server Authentication is required.

SQL Server Authentication

SQL Server Authentication uses accounts that are created and stored in SQL Server itself. With SQL Server Authentication, users connecting to a database server will have two accounts: an operating system account and a SQL Server account.

With this kind of authentication, users don't need to be logged onto just Windows XP or Windows 2000, so any user with a SQL Server account can gain access. Another benefit is that a program can supply a specific user name and password in a connection string. You'll learn more about connection strings in later chapters.

Mixed Mode

What's this? We said two modes of authentication exist, and now here's a third? Not really. Mixed Mode means the database server can use both Windows Authentication and SQL Server Authentication. The benefit is that applications can connect using Windows Authentication, if available, or use SQL Server Authentication, if necessary.

Connecting with Server Explorer

You connected to your MSDE server with `osql` when you installed the sample databases. Now let's look at one way to connect with Visual Studio .NET: by using Server Explorer.

When you open Visual Studio .NET, Server Explorer is collapsed on the left (if not, press Ctrl+Alt+S to view it). Server Explorer displays a tree from which you can control just about anything on the local computer and any remote computers to which you have access. (In Visual Basic .NET Standard Edition, you can't connect to remote servers.)

Figure 1-9 shows Visual Studio .NET 2003's Server Explorer. The Visual Basic .NET Standard Edition Server Explorer displays only local data connections, but that will do just fine for these purposes.

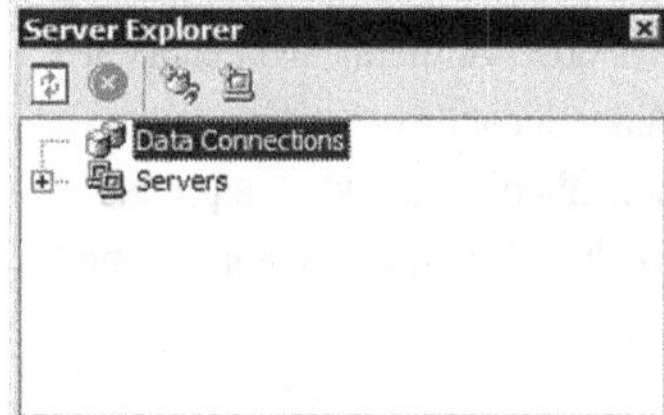

Figure 1-9. *Visual Studio .NET 2003 Server Explorer tree*

■ **Note** A big difference between Visual Studio .NET and Visual Basic .NET Standard Edition is that the Standard Edition supports only connecting to databases and viewing database details. In Visual Studio .NET you can create new databases, tables, views, stored procedures, and so on. MSDE users without Visual Studio .NET can use a tool such as Microsoft Access for visual database management. However, SQL, executed through command-line utilities or ADO.NET code, can achieve the same results. You'll eventually be comfortable enough to perform such tasks even without visual tools.

For this exercise, you're interested in the Data Connections node. Using this node, you can create and manage connections to any number of databases, located on any number of servers.

Let's create a connection to the `Northwind` database. Follow these steps:

1. Right-click the Data Connections node in the tree, and select Add Connection....
2. Enter the information from Table 1-1 into the Connection tab of the Data Link Properties dialog box (see Figure 1-10).

Table 1-1. *Connection Properties*

Property	Value
Server name	`(local)\netsdk`
Authentication	Use Windows NT Integrated Security
Database	`Northwind`

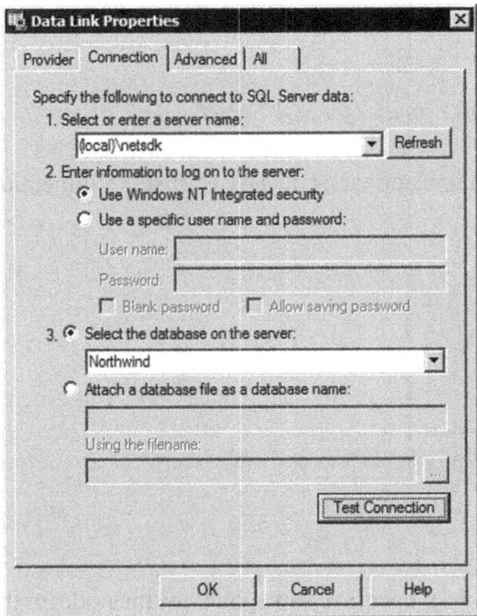

Figure 1-10. *Specifying connection properties*

3. Click the Provider tab. On this tab you can select which provider to use to connect to a database server. The default provider is Microsoft OLE DB Provider for SQL Server, which isn't an ADO.NET data provider (introduced in Chapter 4) but can connect to MSDE (see Figure 1-11).

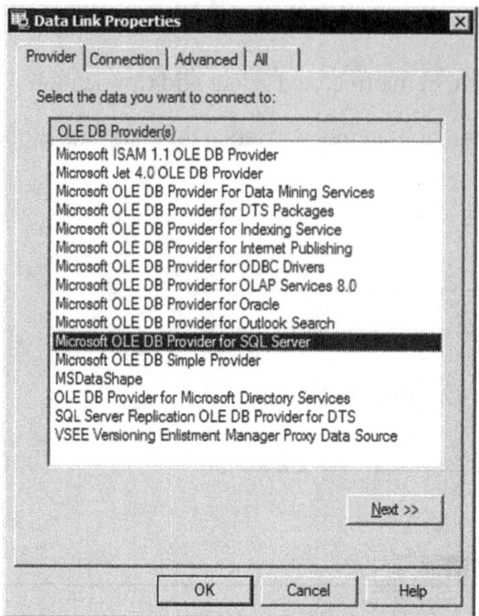

Figure 1-11. *Selecting Microsoft OLE DB Provider for SQL Server*

4. Click OK. If the SQL Server Login window appears, check Use Trusted Connection and then click OK (see Figure 1-12).

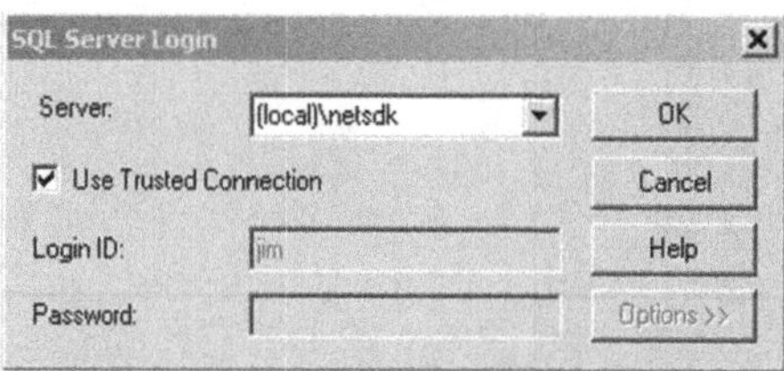

Figure 1-12. *Logging into SQL Server*

5. Expand the Database Connections node, if necessary, and you'll see the node for the new connection. Click the plus sign in front of the new node to expand it. Click the plus sign in front of the Tables node to view the tables in the `Northwind` database (see Figure 1-13).

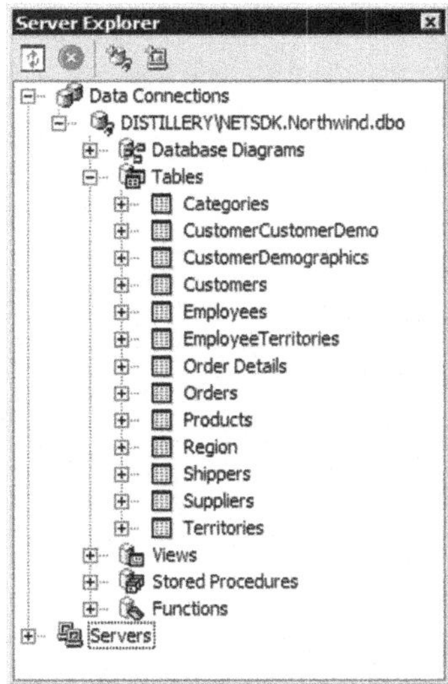

Figure 1-13. *`Northwind` tables in Server Explorer*

6. Double-click the `Employees` table to view its data (see Figure 1-14).

dbo.Employees...SDK.Northwind)

EmployeeID	LastName	FirstName	Title	TitleOfCourtesy	BirthDate	HireDate	Address
1	Davolio	Nancy	Sales Representative	Ms.	08/12/1948	01/05/1992	507 - 20th Av
2	Fuller	Andrew	Vice President, Sales	Dr.	19/02/1952	14/08/1992	908 W. Capita
3	Leverling	Janet	Sales Representative	Ms.	30/08/1963	01/04/1992	722 Moss Bay
4	Peacock	Margaret	Sales Representative	Mrs.	19/09/1937	03/05/1993	4110 Old Red
5	Buchanan	Steven	Sales Manager	Mr.	04/03/1955	17/10/1993	14 Garrett Hill
6	Suyama	Michael	Sales Representative	Mr.	02/07/1963	17/10/1993	Coventry Hou
7	King	Robert	Sales Representative	Mr.	29/05/1960	02/01/1994	Edgeham Holl
8	Callahan	Laura	Inside Sales Coordinator	Ms.	09/01/1958	05/03/1994	4726 - 11th A
9	Dodsworth	Anne	Sales Representative	Ms.	27/01/1966	15/11/1994	7 Houndstoot

Figure 1-14. *`Employees` data from Server Explorer*

Besides tables, you'll also learn about database diagrams, stored procedures, and views in this book.

Summary

In this first chapter you installed MSDE, the sample `Northwind` database, and Microsoft SQL Server Books Online. You learned about authentication modes and saw how to connect to an MSDE database with `osql` and with Visual Studio .NET's Server Explorer.

You're now ready to develop a simple application against the `Northwind` database. You'll do that in the next chapter.

CHAPTER 2

■ ■ ■

Creating a Simple Database Application

Now that you've installed your database server and looked at what's in the Northwind database, we'll walk you through the steps needed to create a basic database application using some of the powerful functionality provided by Visual Studio .NET. You won't need to look too hard at what's going on behind the scenes; instead, you'll concentrate on getting comfortable using Visual Studio .NET's built-in features. In later chapters we'll discuss the code that's generated for you by Visual Studio .NET and how to work with it to improve and refine your applications.

In this chapter, you'll learn the following:

- How to build a Windows Forms application that connects to the Northwind database and displays data from it
- How to update the database with edited data
- How to use a Visual Studio .NET wizard to do this all for you

Like any good book, the aim of this one is to teach you how the code works rather than the wizards, so we'll leave the wizards until the end, when you can see and appreciate the code they can generate on your behalf. You should then be in a position to know what you'll want to have generated and what you'll need to alter afterward to get the right results.

Creating the Application

The sample application will perform some simple but common tasks on a single table from the Northwind database. Once the application is complete, you'll know the following:

- How to display a list of last names of employees in the Northwind database
- How to display and edit information for an employee selected from the list
- How to update the edited information in the database

So, it's time to get started! In the following sections, you'll just create the project, adding to it as you progress.

Try It Out: Creating the Foundations

You'll be creating a Windows Forms application, so open Visual Studio .NET and follow these steps:

1. Create a new blank solution by clicking the *New Project* link on the Start page and then selecting the Visual Studio Solutions project type and the Blank Solution template. Alternatively, you can select File ➤ New ➤ Blank Solution... from the main menu. Name your solution `Chapter2_Examples`, specify its location (we used `C:\BegVBNetDb`), and click OK (see Figure 2-1).

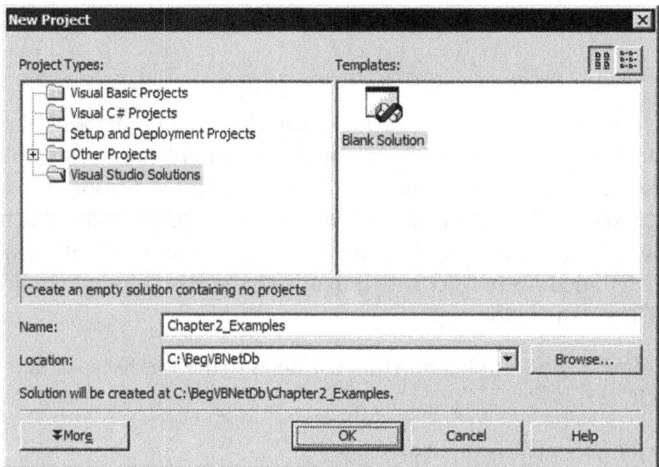

Figure 2-1. *Creating a new solution*

Note We'll use this solution structure throughout the book for the examples and in the code download. The code for each chapter will consist of one or more example projects, each contained within one chapter solution. You can obtain the code from the Downloads section of the Apress Web site (`http://www.apress.com`).

---

2. Not a lot appears to happen when you click OK. However, if you hover your mouse over Solution Explorer (normally found on the right in Visual Studio .NET), you'll see your solution listed there. Right-click the solution, and select Add ➤ New Project... from the context menu. Create a new application by selecting Visual Basic Projects and then selecting Windows Application. Name it `Employees`, and click OK.

3. In Solution Explorer, click the Show All Files icon at the top, and then expand all the nodes. You should see something like Figure 2-2.

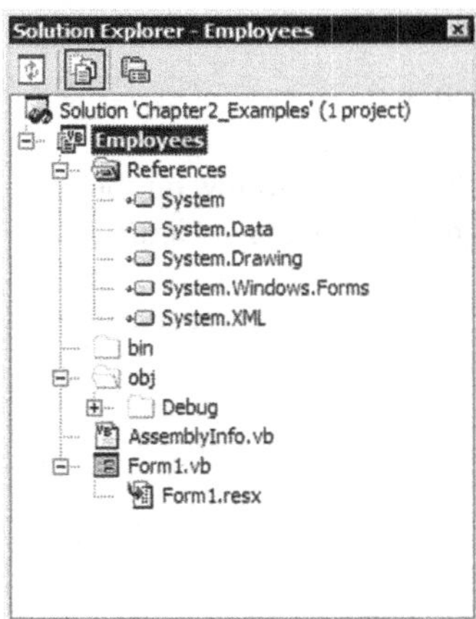

Figure 2-2. *Solution Explorer tree*

How It Works

The simple action of creating a new project has created several default files and directories. Inside the files, Visual Studio .NET has inserted some starter code.

The items in the list you'll become most acquainted with include the following:

- The `Form1.vb` file, which is the default file for a Windows form. This is where the form code resides.
- The References item, which lists namespaces. By default, Visual Studio .NET includes namespaces relating to graphical elements and data applications, because these are common parts of Windows Forms applications. As your needs become more complex, you may have to add to this list.

These two items—along with the project and solution—are the ones you use most when creating a Windows Forms application. Other types of application create slightly different files. For example, a Web Forms application will include files that relate to configuration details, global application settings, and references to namespaces with the word *Web* in them (`System.Web`, `System.Web.UI`, and so on). In contrast, when creating a console application, you see fewer items in Solution Explorer, since you're not concerned with a visual front end.

You'll now continue with the application and learn how to connect to your database. (You actually connect to the *database server*, but it's simpler to say just *database*.)

Establishing a Database Connection

To work with a database, you need to connect to it from your Windows Forms application. In Chapter 1, you saw how to create a connection to the `Northwind` database with Server Explorer, but that's not the same as creating a connection programmatically.

Try It Out: Creating a Connection

To access a database, you must first establish a connection to it.

1. Click the form to select it, and then examine the Properties window on the right. Find `(DataBindings)`. Expand it by clicking the plus sign on the left (see Figure 2-3).

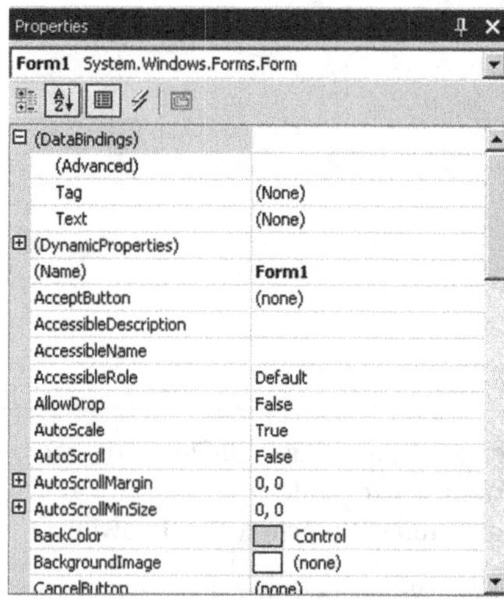

Figure 2-3. *Windows form (`DataBindings`) property*

2. Leaving the `(Advanced)` property for later, you can see two properties of the form, `Tag` and `Text`, that can be bound to data. However, if you try to assign something to them, you can't. Currently, no reference to any data exists, since you haven't yet connected your application to your database.

3. In Server Explorer, drag the connection to the `Northwind` database (that you created in Chapter 1) onto the form (see Figure 2-4). Rather than placing the connection on the form itself, Visual Studio .NET opens a tray below the form and places the connection in the tray.

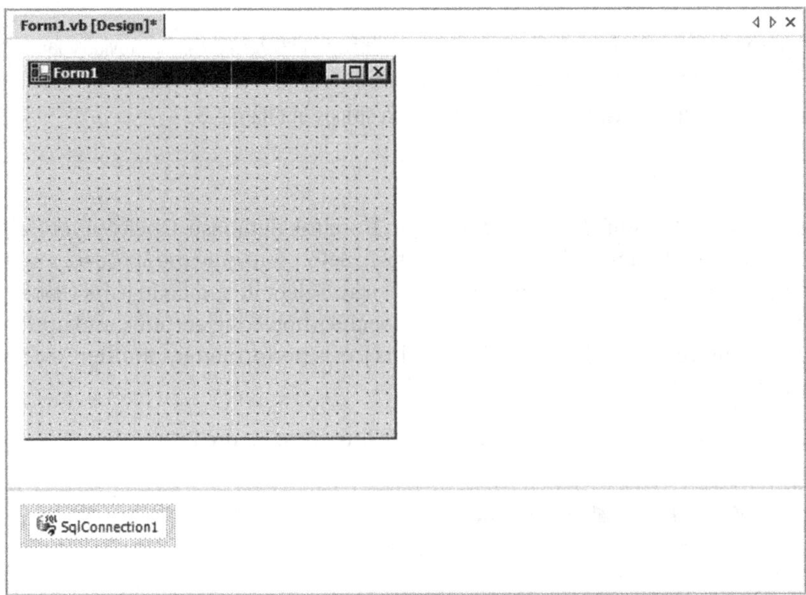

Figure 2-4. *Adding a database connection to a form*

4. Right-click the `SqlConnection1` object in the tray, and select Properties.
5. Change `(Name)` to `SqlConnectionNorthwind` (see Figure 2-5).

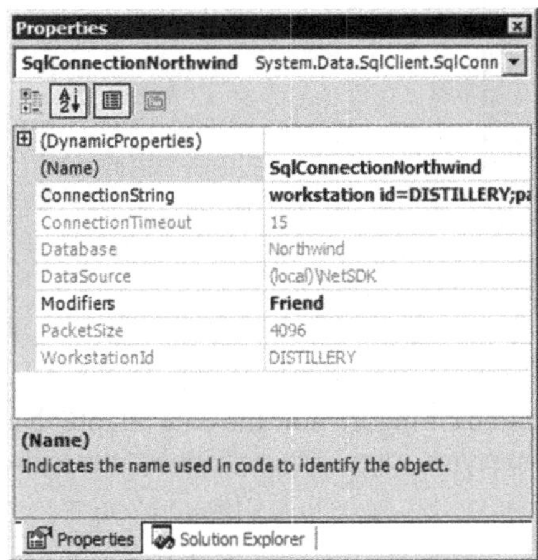

Figure 2-5. *Database connection properties*

Tip One of the other properties in the list is `ConnectionString`. A *connection string* provides parameters for establishing a database session. For now don't concern yourself too much with this, as Server Explorer generates it for you; you'll see how to write your own connection strings in Chapter 5.

---

6. The next step is to specify which data to get from the database. Open Server Explorer, and expand the Tables node of the connection. Select and drag the `Employees` table onto the form. This adds a `sqlDataAdapter` to the tray. Select it, and change its `(Name)` to `sqlDataAdapterEmployees`. A *data adapter* specifies how to select, edit, and update data. It doesn't, however, hold the data itself—this job is performed by another ADO.NET component, namely, a *dataset*.

7. Just below the properties list you'll see three links (see Figure 2-6).

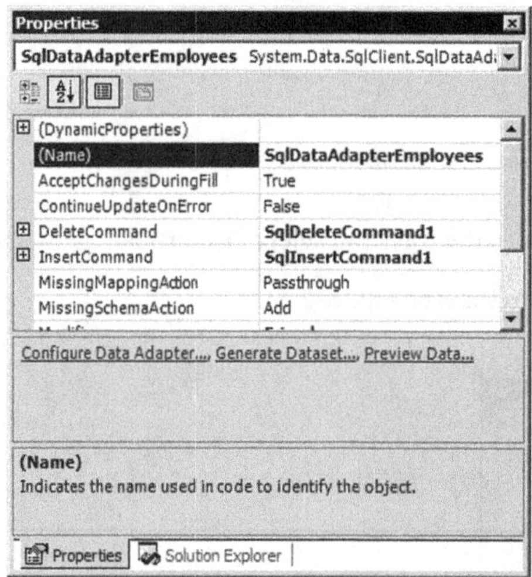

Figure 2-6. *Data adapter links*

These links are as follows:

- *Configure Data Adapter...*: Click this link to configure how the data adapter accesses the database. This was done for you when you dragged the table onto the form, so you'll leave this option alone.
- *Generate Dataset...*: This is the option in which you're interested. It will allow you to generate a dataset, which is the object that will actually contain the data from the table.
- *Preview Data...*: Clicking this link displays a window where you can preview the data.

8. Click the *Generate Dataset...* link.

9. In the dialog box, change the name from `DataSet1` to `DataSetEmployees` (see Figure 2-7) and click OK. The dataset will be added to the tray.

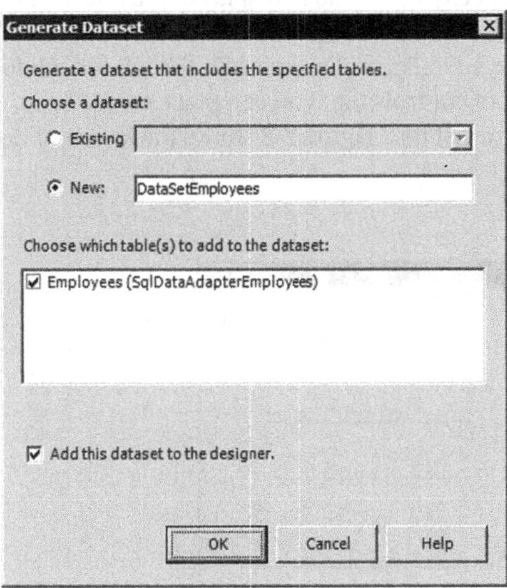

Figure 2-7. *Generate Dataset window*

How It Works

All you appear to have done so far is a lot of clicking and a bit of dragging and dropping, but don't worry, Visual Studio .NET has actually been busy writing code for you with each step. You now have the ability to connect to a database, select specific data, and work with that data using a dataset. You'll look more at data adapters and datasets in Chapter 8, where you'll learn how to code and use them.

Note that although you named the dataset `DataSetEmployees`, the designer named it `DataSetEmployees1`, so when you refer to this dataset later, you'll use `DataSetEmployees1`. If you want to change its name, you can do so in the Properties window for this dataset.

Introducing Data Binding

Now let's take some data from the database and display it using controls on a Windows form—this is what we mean by *data binding*. You have two ways to bind data to controls: *complex* and *simple* data binding. Complex data binding is supported by only a few Windows Forms controls, such as `DataGrid` and `ListBox`, and allows the control to display lists of data. Simple data binding is supported by most other Windows Forms controls, and unlike complex data binding, it allows the control to bind to only a single value at a time.

You'll use complex data binding only once in this application—to bind the data for a list of names. The rest of the controls are text boxes that use simple data binding. Let's start putting the form together.

Try It Out: Creating a User Interface

You need to create the front end for the database application, which involves a certain amount of dragging and dropping. You also need to specify what data to display in the interface controls.

1. You should have a blank form displayed in Forms Designer. To the left is a tab for the Toolbox. The Toolbox contains a list of controls that you can place on the form. You'll use five text boxes, five labels, and one list box. Figure 2-8 shows the layout of the form.

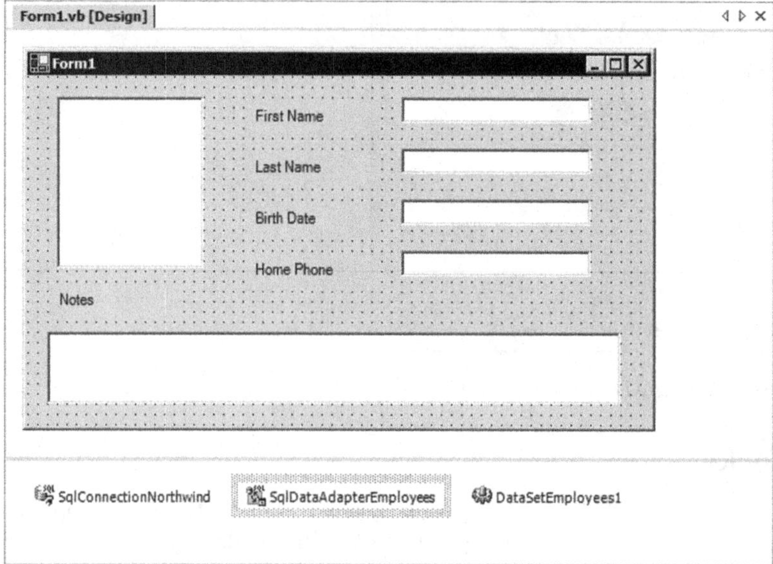

Figure 2-8. *User interface layout*

The large box is the list box. The other controls are text boxes. The text next to each text box is in a corresponding label. Add and position the controls according to Figure 2-8 by dragging and dropping them from the Toolbox onto the form.

2. Using the Properties window, set the properties of the text boxes as in Table 2-1.

Table 2-1. *Text Box Properties*

Number	Property	Value
1	`(Name)`	`TextBoxNotes`
1	`MultiLine`	`True`
2	`(Name)`	`TextBoxFirstName`
3	`(Name)`	`TextBoxLastName`
4	`(Name)`	`TextBoxBirthDate`
5	`(Name)`	`TextBoxHomePhone`

3. For each of the text boxes, clear the `Text` property.

4. For each of the labels, set the `Text` property to match the text box data.

5. Set the properties of the list box as in Table 2-2.

Table 2-2. *List Box Properties*

Property	Value	Description
(Name)	ListBoxNames	The name of the control.
`DataSource`	`DataSetEmployees1.Employees`	Identifies the dataset and table containing the data to display.
`DisplayMember`	`LastName`	The control will display the value of the `LastName` column.
`ValueMember`	`EmployeeID`	When selecting data, the control will use `EmployeeID` rather than `LastName`.

6. Select `TextBoxNotes`, and look at the top of the Properties window (see Figure 2-9). There you'll find `(DataBindings)`.

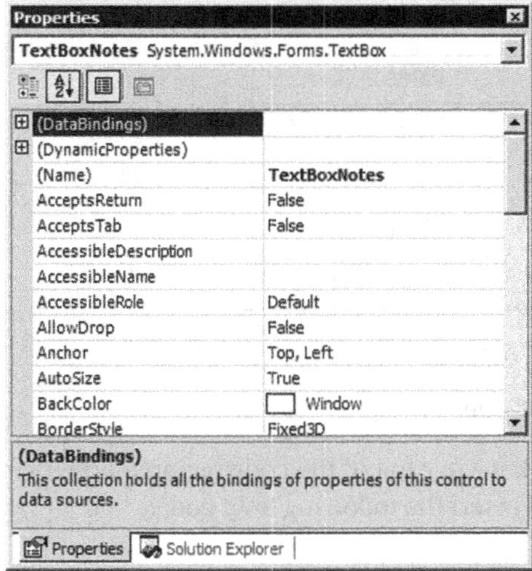

Figure 2-9. *Data bindings for* `textBoxNotes`

7. Expand this entry, and then open the `Text` property. Expand `DataSetEmployees1` and then `Employees` (see Figure 2-10). Scroll down, and select the `Notes` column.

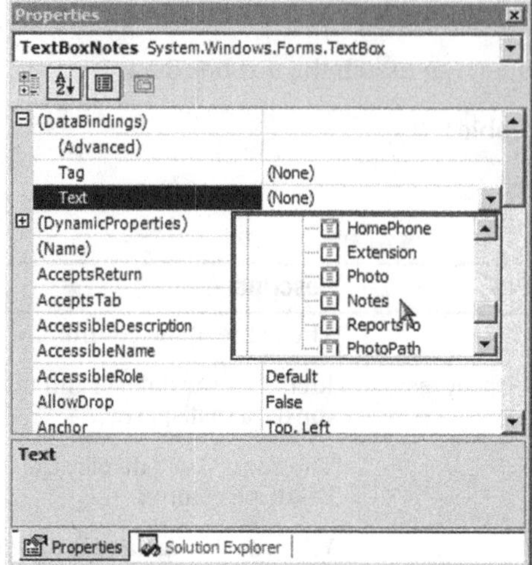

Figure 2-10. *Binding a column to a text box control*

8. Repeat steps 6 and 7 for the remaining text boxes, assigning columns to the appropriate text boxes as in Table 2-3.

Table 2-3. *Other Text Box Data Bindings*

Number	Property	Value
2	`DataBindings.Text`	`FirstName`
3	`DataBindings.Text`	`LastName`
4	`DataBindings.Text`	`BirthDate`
5	`DataBindings.Text`	`HomePhone`

9. Right-click the form, and select View Code.

10. Locate the `Form1` constructor—you'll have to expand the code region marked `Windows Form Designer generated code`—and insert the following bold code:

```
Public Sub New()
   MyBase.New()

   'This call is required by the Windows Form Designer.
   InitializeComponent()

   'Add any initialization after the InitializeComponent() call
   SqlDataAdapterEmployees.Fill(DataSetEmployees1)

End Sub;
```

11. Run the application, and you should see the `Northwind` data displayed in your Windows form, as shown in Figure 2-11.

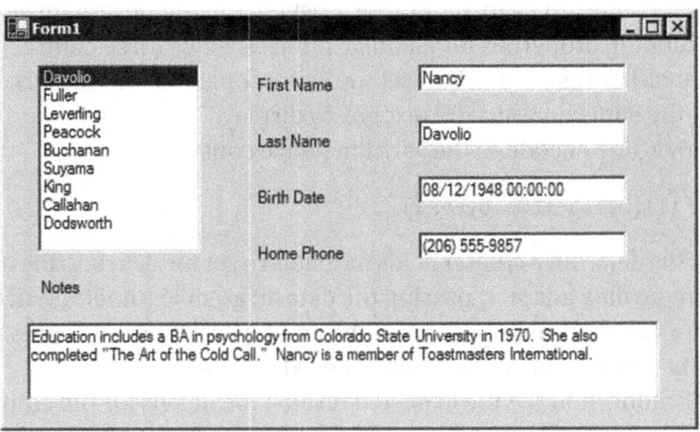

Figure 2-11. *Displaying employee data*

How It Works

You started by adding the following three ADO.NET components to the application by dragging and dropping them onto the form from Server Explorer (see Figure 2-12):

- Connection (`SqlConnectionNorthwind`)
- Data adapter (`SqlDataAdapterEmployees`)
- Dataset (`DataSetEmployees1`)

Figure 2-12. *ADO.NET objects in component tray*

You'll see these components a lot during the course of the book, so in later chapters we'll go into much more detail about them.

Note that ADO.NET uses the prefix *Sql* (for example, `SqlConnection`) for each type name. These prefixes indicate that you're working with the .NET Framework data provider for SQL Server. Had you performed all the previous steps with an Access database as the back end, the type names would have been prefixed with *OleDb* (for example, `OleDbConnection`). You'll learn more about the different data providers in Chapters 4 and 5. Aside from the way they connect to databases, and their prefixes, the components are essentially interchangeable.

After a lot of cosmetic steps where you added controls to the form and set some of their properties, you bound the list box to the `LastName` column in the `Northwind Employees` table.

First, you set the `DataSource` property. This tells the list box where it should look for its data. Remember that `DataSetEmployees1` is the ADO.NET object that stores the data. Second, you set the `DisplayMember` property, which tells the list box which column to use to fill itself.

The third property you set was ValueMember, which was bound to the table's primary key, EmployeeID. This means that when you ask the list box for the selected item in the list, you want the value of the EmployeeID column rather than that of the LastName column. (More than one employee can have same last name, but every employee must have a unique employee ID).

Next, you set the data binding properties for all the text boxes. Since these controls use simple data binding, they're rather easy to set. You set the Text property of the DataBindings collection to the column of the data you want the text box to display.

Finally, you added a single line of code to the Form1 instance constructor.

```
SqlDataAdapterEmployees.Fill(DataSetEmployees1)
```

A data adapter accesses the data, but a dataset holds the data. To get the data into the dataset, you call the Fill method on the data adapter, passing the dataset as an argument. When the application runs, the list box displays the last names of the employees in the Employees table, and the text boxes display the detail information—all achieved with one line of code!

When you run the application, you see the expected results: the details for the employee selected in the list box (Davolio) are displayed in the text boxes on the right. However, when you select another employee from the list box, nothing happens! The reason for this is that you have no link between the information displayed in the list box and what's displayed in the text boxes. You need to add this link to your code.

Try It Out: Making the Form Dynamic

To add the link, follow these steps:

1. Stay in Code view. You need to add an event handler to the ListBox control. At the top edge of the code window are two drop-down lists. From the General one on the left, select ListBoxNames, and from the Declarations one on the right, scroll down and click SelectedValueChanged.

2. The outline for the event handler will be generated and shown in the code window. Add the bold code shown in Listing 2-1 to the event handler.

Listing 2-1. *Event Handler Code*

```
Private Sub ListBoxNames_SelectedValueChanged(ByVal sender As Object, _
   ByVal e As System.EventArgs) Handles ListBoxNames.SelectedValueChanged
   If ListBoxNames.SelectedIndex <> -1 Then
      ' Clear the data bindings on the text boxes
      TextBoxFirstName.DataBindings.Clear()
      TextBoxLastName.DataBindings.Clear()
      TextBoxBirthDate.DataBindings.Clear()
      TextBoxHomePhone.DataBindings.Clear()
      TextBoxNotes.DataBindings.Clear()

      ' Add a new binding, with a new data source: the selected row
      TextBoxFirstName.DataBindings.Add("Text", _
         DataSetEmployees1.Employees.Rows(ListBoxNames.SelectedIndex), _
         "FirstName")
```

```
        TextBoxLastName.DataBindings.Add("Text", _
          DataSetEmployees1.Employees.Rows(ListBoxNames.SelectedIndex), _
          "LastName")
        TextBoxBirthDate.DataBindings.Add("Text", _
          DataSetEmployees1.Employees.Rows(ListBoxNames.SelectedIndex), _
          "BirthDate")
        TextBoxHomePhone.DataBindings.Add("Text", _
          DataSetEmployees1.Employees.Rows(ListBoxNames.SelectedIndex), _
          "HomePhone")
        TextBoxNotes.DataBindings.Add("Text", _
          DataSetEmployees1.Employees.Rows(ListBoxNames.SelectedIndex), _
          "Notes")
      End If
    End Sub
```

Run the application again. When you select an item in the list box, the values in the text boxes change, as shown in Figure 2-13.

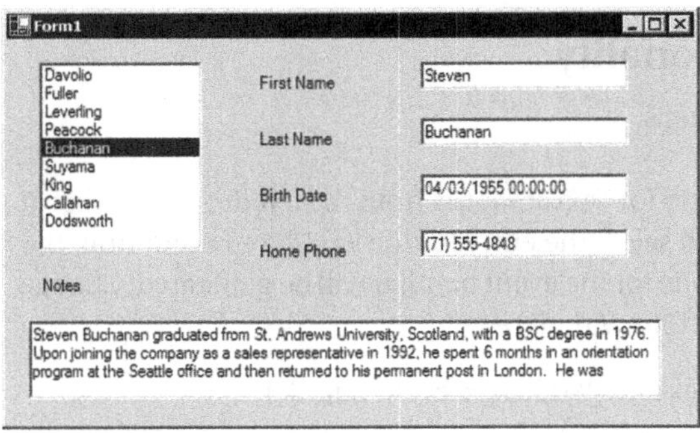

Figure 2-13. *Displaying a selected employee's data*

How It Works

You created an event handler for the `SelectedValueChanged` event of the list box. This triggers whenever a user clicks the active selection in the list box and changes it.

The event handler may look complex, but it contains only two kinds of VB .NET statements. These are repeated for each of the text boxes on the form.

```
TextBoxFirstName.DataBindings.Clear()
TextBoxFirstName.DataBindings.Add("Text", _
      DataSetEmployees1.Employees.Rows(ListBoxNames.SelectedIndex), _
      "FirstName")
```

The first statement tells the text box to remove any current data bindings. The second statement then adds a new data binding, this time with data for the currently selected row. The first parameter of the `Add` method is the name of the property you want to bind data to, namely, the `Text` property. The second parameter is the actual data the control should use. You know that the index of the selected item in the `ListBox` is the same as the row you're interested in, so you use this index to retrieve a row from the `Employees` table. The third and final parameter is the name of the column the control should use.

Now the SelectedValueChanged event first fires when the application initially runs and nothing is selected, which gives ListBoxNames.SelectedIndex a value of -1. This would raise an error as the application begins then, because DataSetEmployees1.Employees.Rows is an array and so cannot have a row with index -1. Thus you need to surround the data binding code with an if statement to circumvent this first handling of the event.

```
If ListBoxNames.SelectedIndex <> -1 Then
   ...
End If
```

Editing Data

Now that you're able to display and move around in the data, you have one last task: to edit the data and update it in the database. The editing part is simple since you're using text boxes. You'll update the database every time one of the text boxes fires the Validated event. This happens whenever a text box loses focus to another control that has the CausesValidation property set to true. This is the default for all the controls you've used in this chapter.

Try It Out: Adding Edit Functionality

To add the edit functionality, follow these steps:

1. Stay in Code view. Now select the entry for TextBoxNotes from the left drop-down list at the top edge of the code window, and select the entry for the Validated event from the right drop-down list. The skeleton code for the event handler will be generated. Change the name of the event handler to TextBox_Validated.

2. Add the following bold code to the TextBox_Validated event handler:

```
Private Sub TextBox_Validated(ByVal sender As Object, _
   ByVal e As System.EventArgs) Handles TextBoxNotes.Validated, _
   TextBoxLastName.Validated, TextBoxBirthDate.Validated, _
   TextBoxFirstName.Validated, TextBoxHomePhone.Validated

   ' Open the connection
   SqlConnectionNorthwind.Open()

   ' Update
   SqlDataAdapterEmployees.Update(DataSetEmployees1, "Employees")

   ' Refresh the data in the dataset
   SqlDataAdapterEmployees.Fill(DataSetEmployees1)

   ' Close the connection
   SqlConnectionNorthwind.Close()
End Sub
```

3. Run the application, select the third name in the list, and change the last name of that employee as shown in Figure 2-14.

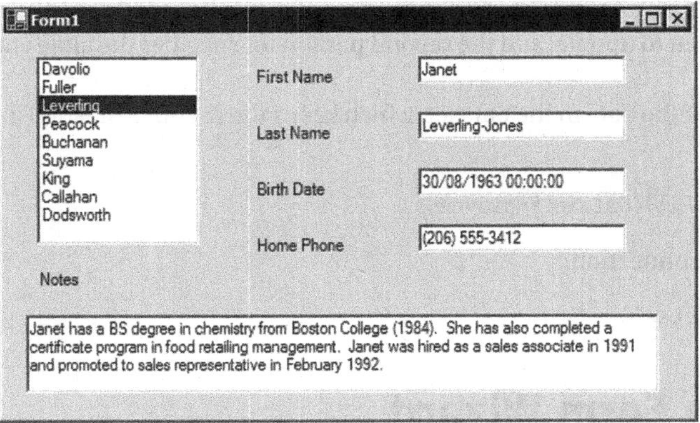

Figure 2-14. *Updating an employee's last name*

4. Hit the Tab key. This will update the database (see Figure 2-15).

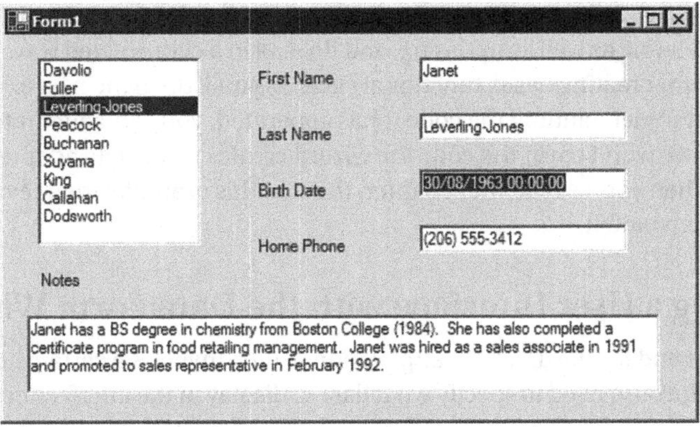

Figure 2-15. *Updated employee's last name*

How It Works

You created a single event handler, `TextBox_Validated`, which is triggered whenever a `Validated` event fires, regardless of which text boxes fired it. The first line opens the connection to the database.

```
SqlConnectionNorthwind.Open()
```

You may be surprised to learn that the connection to the database has actually been closed ever since you first called the `Fill` method on the data adapter in the instance constructor of `Form1`. The data is said to be *disconnected* from the database. This has a number of advantages over connected data, and you'll learn about this in more detail in later chapters. For now, you simply reconnect to the database in order to be able to transmit the changes to it.

The second line updates the data in the database.

```
SqlDataAdapterEmployees.Update(DataSetEmployees1, "Employees")
```

You call Update on the data adapter. The first parameter of the Update method is the dataset containing the data you want to update, and the second parameter specifies the table you want to update.

The third line refreshes the data in the dataset, which keeps the list box refreshed in case a last name was changed.

```
SqlDataAdapterEmployees.Fill(DataSetEmployees1)
```

Finally, you close the connection.

```
SqlConnectionNorthwind.Close()
```

Using the Data Form Wizard

Notice in Figure 2-15 that once you press the Tab key, the focus moved to the next text box and the list box selection was lost. Coordinating such things is beyond the scope of this simple example but is certainly needed for a robust application. Notice also that to keep the exercise short, we used only five of the thirteen columns in the Northwind database's Employees table.

Visual Studio .NET has a wizard that will automatically make all columns available, provide for inserting and deleting as well as updating, and do it all in a coordinated way. This is handy to take advantage of for creating basic, functional code, as you'll do in the next example, but remember that without understanding the code it has generated, you can't alter it to your requirements. In this case, we won't cover the code the wizard creates using data adapters and datasets until Chapter 8. When you've read that chapter, think of this example; then revisit the code here to see if you understand it.

Try It Out: Creating a User Interface with the Data Form Wizard

You need to create the front end for the database application, which involves a certain amount of dragging and dropping. You also need to specify what data to display in the interface controls.

1. Add a new VB .NET Windows application named DataFormWizard to the Chapter2_Examples solution. Select Project ➤ Add Component…, click the Data Form Wizard template, and click Open (see Figure 2-16). This starts Data Form Wizard (see Figure 2-17). Click Next.

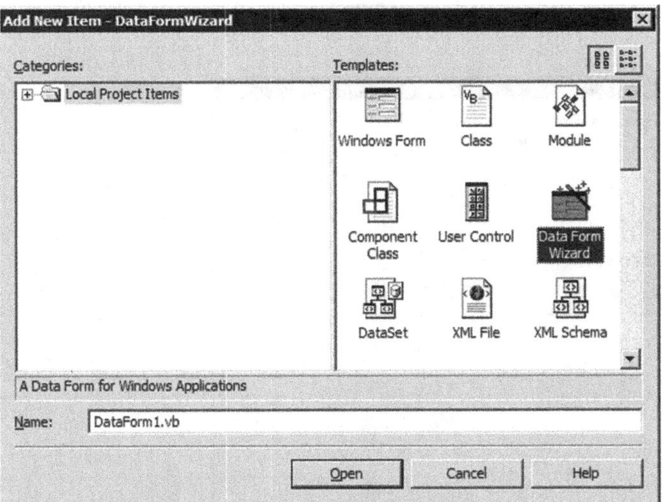

Figure 2-16. *Creating a data form with the wizard*

Figure 2-17. *Data Form Wizard's welcome window*

2. In the next window, name the new dataset `DataSet1` (see Figure 2-18). Click Next.

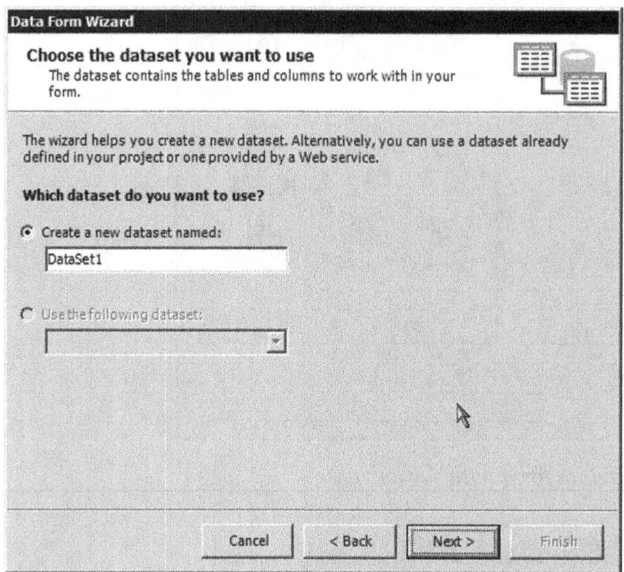

Figure 2-18. *Creating a new dataset with the wizard*

3. The connection to the `Northwind` database should be selected in the next window (see Figure 2-19). Click Next.

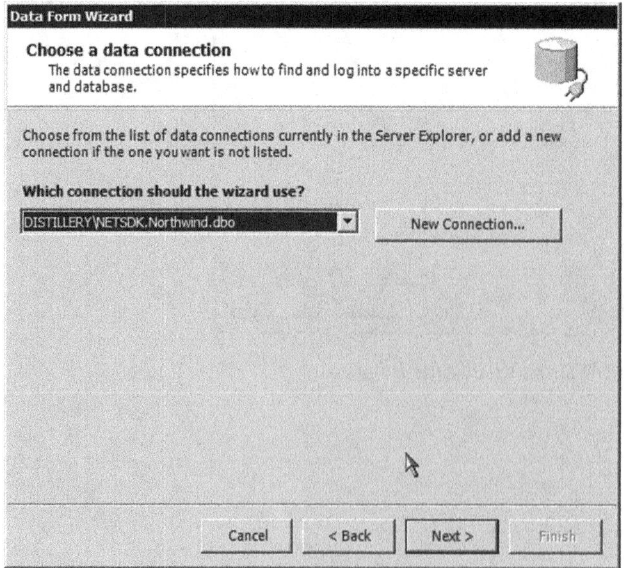

Figure 2-19. *Selecting a connection with the wizard*

4. In the next window, double-click the Employees node, and then click Next (see Figure 2-20).

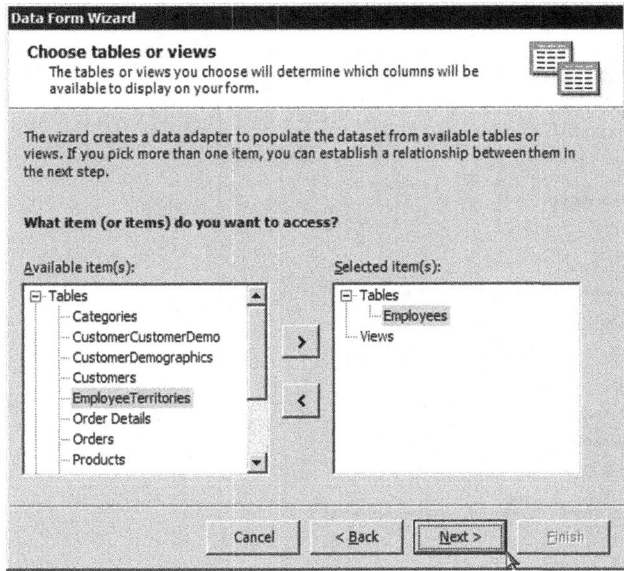

Figure 2-20. *Selecting a table with the wizard*

5. In the next window, click Next to select all the columns in the `Employees` table (see Figure 2-21).

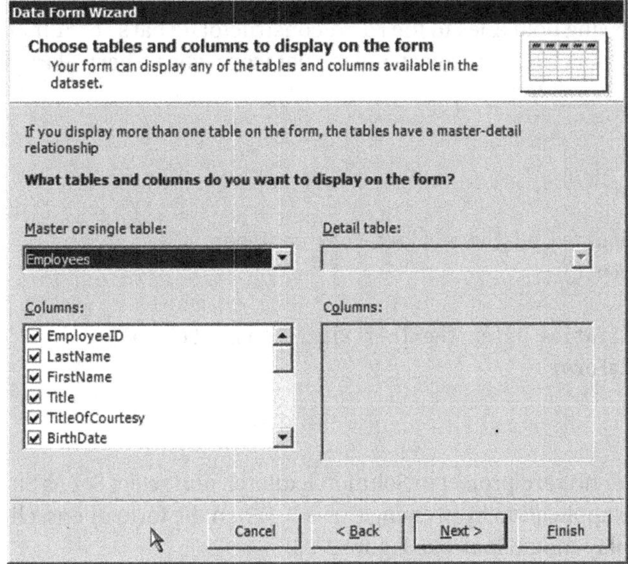

Figure 2-21. *Selecting columns with the wizard*

6. In the Choose the Display Style window, select the Single Record in Individual Controls radio button and click Finish (see Figure 2-22). The wizard exits, and the data form appears in Design view.

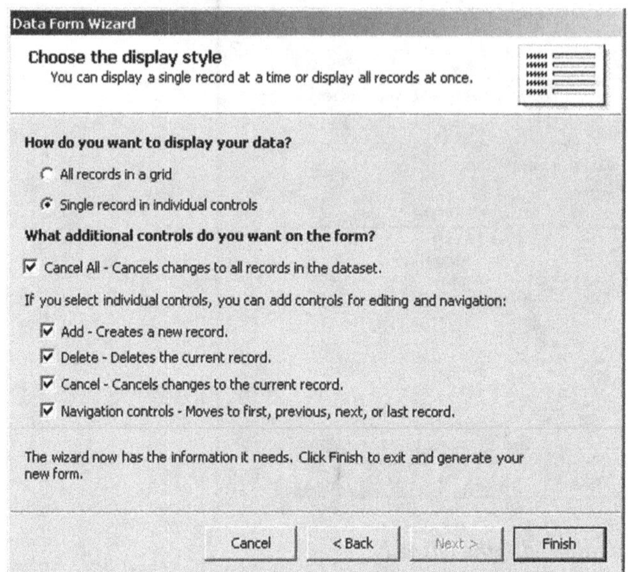

Figure 2-22. *Choosing the display style with the wizard*

7. A data form doesn't include a `Main` subroutine (although you could add one to it), so you have to do something to display it. You have several possibilities, but the easiest for now is just to add the following bold lines to the `Form1` constructor. (That's `Form1` that was generated with the `DataFormWizard` project, not the data form you've been working with in steps 2–6.)

```
Public Sub New()
    MyBase.New()

    'This call is required by the Windows Form Designer.
    InitializeComponent()

    'Add any initialization after the InitializeComponent() call
    Dim x As New DataForm1
    x.ShowDialog()
End Sub
```

8. Right-click the `DataFormWizard` project in Solution Explorer, and select Set As Startup Project. Then run the application by pressing Ctrl+F5. When the form opens, click the Load button; the display should look like Figure 2-23.

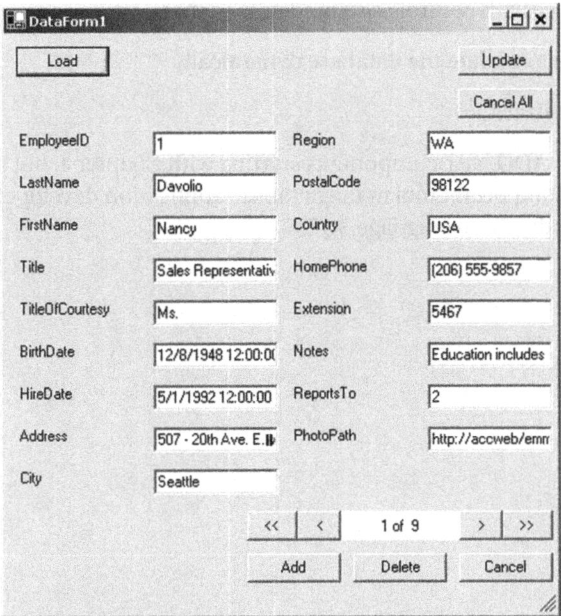

Figure 2-23. *Data form for* `Employees` *table*

■ **Tip** Notice that the address for employee 1 (Davolio) has a strange character in it. This isn't a bug in the data form but bad data in the database! (And it isn't the only place the data is unclean.) If you look at the `instnwnd.sql` file you used in Chapter 1 to create the `Northwind` database, you'll find a linefeed embedded between the street number and the apartment. A word to the wise: make sure your data is clean before debugging your programs.

Summary

In this chapter you built a simple application without looking in detail at how the code works. Instead, you relied heavily on the rapid application development (RAD) features of Visual Studio .NET. With just a few clicks and a minimal amount of coding, you created some quite powerful functionality. As you worked through the chapter, you learned the following:

- How to create a blank solution and add a Windows Forms project to it
- What Visual Studio .NET creates for you when you create a VB .NET Windows Forms application
- How to add data connectivity to your application using Server Explorer and, by a similar process, how to create a data adapter and dataset

- How to create a user interface with controls and bind data to them
- How to get your application to update the database dynamically
- How to use the Data Form Wizard

You'll learn much more about ADO.NET components starting with Chapter 4, but before you dive in, you'll look at the most important tool in the database application developer's toolkit, the international standard database language SQL.

CHAPTER 3

Introducing SQL

In the previous chapter you saw how easy it is to build a simple application using Visual Basic .NET and Visual Studio .NET that displays and modifies database data. In this chapter, we'll step away from applications and cover the basics of Structured Query Language, or SQL, if you prefer. We'll cover just enough of this quite large subject to get you to the point where you can start working with the various database objects in the .NET library. You'll then learn more about SQL in the second half of the book starting at Chapter 12.

In this chapter then, you'll learn about some of the most common elements of SQL; specifically, you'll learn about the ones that let you add, retrieve, update, and delete data from a database.

- Queries
- `INSERT` statements
- `UPDATE` statements
- `DELETE` statements
- Data types

But first an answer to the question that's probably already on your lips: Structured *what*?

What Is SQL?

If you've ever worked with relational databases, you've probably seen some SQL. SQL is the international standard database language. You can use SQL to create, retrieve, change, or delete data.

The formal definition of SQL comes from the American National Standards Institute (ANSI). It's the same as the international standard specified by the International Organization for Standardization (ISO). Transact-SQL is the dialect of SQL provided by SQL Server. Since we're using MSDE, we focus on Transact-SQL rather than standard SQL, but unless we're discussing a feature not found in standard SQL we'll refer to both simply as *SQL*. We'll use *standard SQL* when referring specifically to the ISO/ANSI version of the language. Each database vendor offers its own implementation of SQL, which conforms at some level to the standard but typically adds to it. Transact-SQL does just that, and some of the SQL used in this book may not work if you try it with a database server other than SQL Server.

Tip Relational database terminology is often confusing. For example, neither the meaning nor the pronunciation of *SQL* is crystal clear. IBM invented the language some 30 years ago and called it Structured English Query Language (SEQUEL), changing it shortly thereafter to Structured Query Language (SQL) to avoid conflict with another vendor's product. SEQUEL and SQL were both pronounced *sequel.* When the ISO/ANSI standard was adopted, it referred to the language simply as *database language SQL* and was silent on whether this was an acronym and how it should be pronounced. Today, two pronunciations are used. In the Microsoft and Oracle worlds (as well as many others), it's pronounced *sequel.* In the DB2 and MySQL worlds (among others), it's pronounced *ess cue ell.* (How one properly pronounces the name of the standard language is unclear.) We'll follow the most reasonable practice. We're working in a Microsoft environment, so we'll pronounce SQL as *sequel.* When in Rome....

Let's briefly look at the application of the previous chapter to see how it handled SQL.

If you display the properties of `SqlDataAdapterEmployees`, you'll see four of them, named `DeleteCommand`, `InsertCommand`, `SelectCommand`, and `UpdateCommand` (see Figure 3-1).

Figure 3-1. *Data adapter command properties*

The four *commands* (not a standard SQL term but an ADO.NET one) mentioned here represent a *query* and `DELETE`, `INSERT`, and `UPDATE` *statements*. (In Chapter 2 you retrieved and updated data with the data adapter but didn't insert or delete any.) In this chapter you'll look at SQL queries, data modification statements, and data types. You'll also see how queries and statements are fed into .NET programs.

Using SQL

To execute SQL, you need a way to pass it to the database manager. Various techniques are available.

- Visual Studio .NET's built-in SQL tool
- The `osql` command-line utility
- SQL Server Query Analyzer
- Custom tools

Since the minimum requirements for this book are MSDE and Visual Basic .NET Standard Edition, you'll look at all of these except SQL Server Query Analyzer. The custom tool you'll look at is one we supply with the code download and implement step by step in Appendix A. This doesn't mean you should immediately read through Appendix A (although you may if you're feeling brave); however, locating the `SqlTool.exe` file in the `Appendix A` folder of the code download may not be a bad idea.

Executing SQL from Visual Studio .NET

Both Visual Studio .NET and Visual Basic .NET Standard Edition have a tool that you used in Chapter 1 to execute SQL. Let's learn more about it.

Try It Out: Executing SQL from Visual Studio .NET

To execute SQL from Visual Studio .NET, follow these steps:

1. Open Visual Studio .NET, and navigate to Server Explorer. In Chapter 1 you created a connection to the `Northwind` database, so let's look at that connection now. Expand the Tables node, and double-click the Employees table (see Figure 3-2).

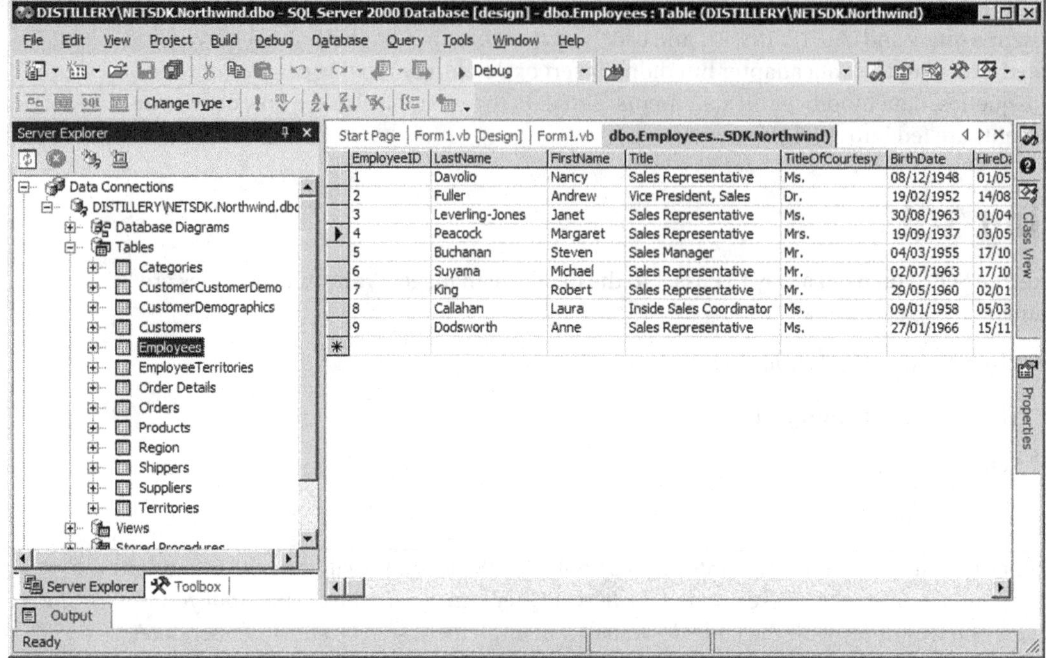

Figure 3-2. *Displaying database data with Server Explorer*

2. If you position your cursor anywhere within the data grid, the Show SQL Pane button (the one with *SQL* on it) on the Query toolbar (right-click the toolbar area, and select Query if it's not apparent) becomes enabled, so click this button; you should see the pane shown in Figure 3-3. You should now see a window above the data grid, which displays the query generated to retrieve the data.

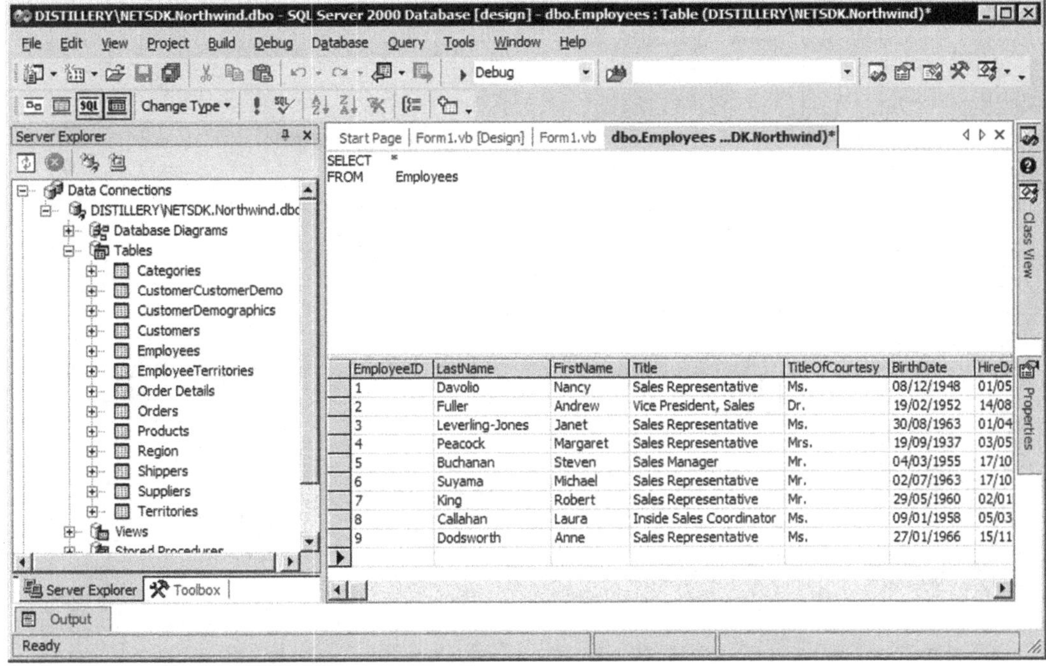

Figure 3-3. *Displaying the SQL pane*

3. To test the window, change `Employees` to `Products`, and click the Run Query icon (the one with *!* on the Query toolbar) to run the query, as shown in Figure 3-4.

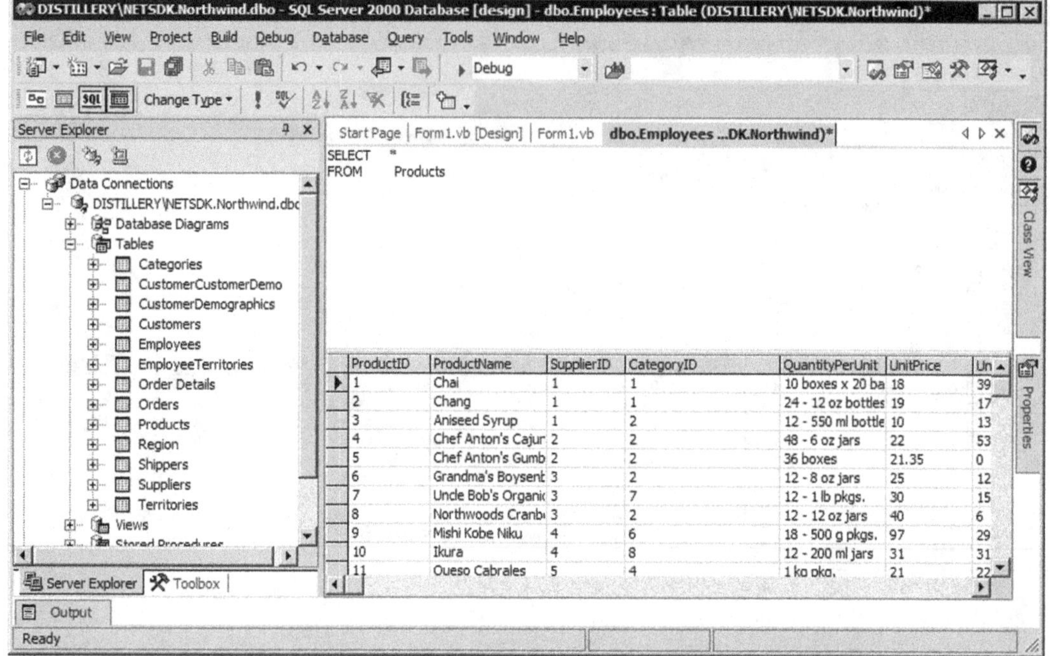

Figure 3-4. *Executing a query from the SQL pane*

How It Works

This Visual Studio .NET facility is quite powerful and lets you execute all kinds of queries and statements using SQL. Since you haven't yet looked at how SQL works, we won't cover this in detail here, but it's worth remembering that this facility exists.

Executing SQL from the Command Line

If you need to use SQL without a visual tool, you can use the `osql` utility that comes with MSDE. You can enter SQL one line at a time in a command prompt window, or you can input it from a text file. The `osql` utility is a simple but useful tool.

To use `osql`, open a command prompt window, and enter `osql` followed by appropriate arguments that specify `osql` options. Figure 3-5 lists the options, which you can obtain by running `osql /?` on a command line.

```
C:\WINDOWS\system32\cmd.exe

C:\>osql /?
usage: osql              [-U login id]          [-P password]
  [-S server]            [-H hostname]          [-E trusted connection]
  [-d use database name] [-l login timeout]     [-t query timeout]
  [-h headers]           [-s colseparator]      [-w columnwidth]
  [-a packetsize]        [-e echo input]        [-I Enable Quoted Identifiers]
  [-L list servers]      [-c cmdend]            [-D ODBC DSN name]
  [-q "cmdline query"]   [-Q "cmdline query" and exit]
  [-n remove numbering]  [-m errorlevel]
  [-r msgs to stderr]    [-V severitylevel]
  [-i inputfile]         [-o outputfile]
  [-p print statistics]  [-b On error batch abort]
  [-X[1] disable commands [and exit with warning]]
  [-O use Old ISQL behavior disables the following]
      <EOF> batch processing
      Auto console width scaling
      Wide messages
      default errorlevel is -1 vs 1
  [-? show syntax summary]

C:\>_
```

Figure 3-5. *osql options*

It's not our intention to describe all these options; we'll demonstrate the ones essential for using SQL in this book.

Try It Out: Executing SQL Using osql

To execute SQL using `osql`, follow these steps:

1. To connect to the local MSDE server, use the `-E` option to connect using a *trusted connection* (in other words, Windows Authentication) and the `-S` option followed by your server name.

   ```
   osql -E -S (local)\netsdk
   ```

■ **Tip** You can enter options in any order. You can use either a hyphen or a slash as an option indicator. Option names are case sensitive, but values associated with options aren't. For example, `-S` isn't the same option as `-s`, but `-S (local)\netsdk` is equivalent to `-S (LOCAL)\NETSDK`.

To connect to a server other than one on the local machine, simply change `(local)` to the name of the remote server. You'll find out more about connections in Chapter 5.

---

2. Now that you're connected to the server, you can enter SQL one line at a time delimited by pressing the Enter key. Once all the SQL is entered, simply type go on a separate line to execute it. Enter the following line by line:

   ```
   osql -E -S (local)\netsdk
   use northwind
   set rowcount 2
   select * from products
   go
   ```

You should see the output shown in Figure 3-6.

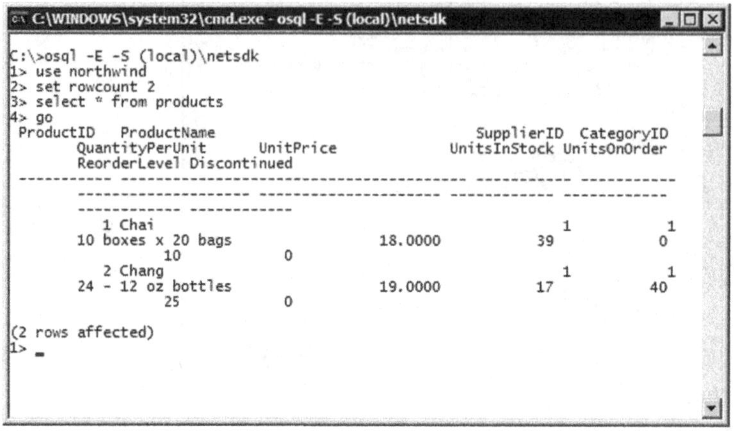

```
C:\WINDOWS\system32\cmd.exe - osql -E -S (local)\netsdk

C:\>osql -E -S (local)\netsdk
1> use northwind
2> set rowcount 2
3> select * from products
4> go
 ProductID   ProductName                              SupplierID  CategoryID
        QuantityPerUnit      UnitPrice            UnitsInStock UnitsOnOrder
        ReorderLevel Discontinued
 ----------- ---------------------------------------- ----------- -----------
        -------------------- --------------------- ------------ ------------
        ------------ ------------
           1 Chai                                               1           1
        10 boxes x 20 bags               18.0000             39           0
                  10            0
           2 Chang                                              1           1
        24 - 12 oz bottles               19.0000             17          40
                  25            0

(2 rows affected)
1> _
```

Figure 3-6. *Executing a query with osql*

3. To close the connection and exit `osql`, type `quit` and press Enter.

How It Works

Although it isn't exactly the prettiest tool, and the output isn't necessarily the easiest to read, `osql` allows you to quickly interrogate (and, in fact, do virtually anything with) a database. You can direct output to a file using the `-o` option.

In this brief example, you used `osql` to connect, with Windows Authentication, to the MSDE instance `(local)\NETSDK` created for this book. You then executed some simple SQL to retrieve just two rows from a table in the `Northwind` database. Don't worry about the actual SQL now since it merely demonstrates the tool; we'll cover most of this code soon.

To execute SQL from a file, use the `-i` option. You'd do this for more complex or repetitive operations. For example, you could have placed the four lines of code from step 2 into a file named `selectsql.sql` and then run the following:

```
osql -E -S (local)\netsdk -i selectsql.sql
```

Using the Custom Query Tool

As an additional exercise in working with VB .NET and databases, we've created a custom query application that you can use to execute the queries in this chapter. The code and an explanation of how to create this application are in Appendix A, but the working application is available in the Chapter 3 code download. Once you've worked through more of this book and feel more comfortable writing VB .NET to work with databases, you may want to revise this code and create your own version of the application.

You can execute all the SQL in this chapter, of course, with any of the tools we've mentioned, but we'll use the custom tool we build in Appendix A for the rest of the examples in this chapter. If you'd rather use `osql` or Visual Studio .NET instead, that's fine too.

Retrieving Data

In the previous chapter you used a data adapter to retrieve data from the database. The data adapter uses SQL behind the scenes. If you look again at the properties for the data adapter and expand `SelectCommand`, you'll see an entry named `CommandText` (see Figure 3-7).

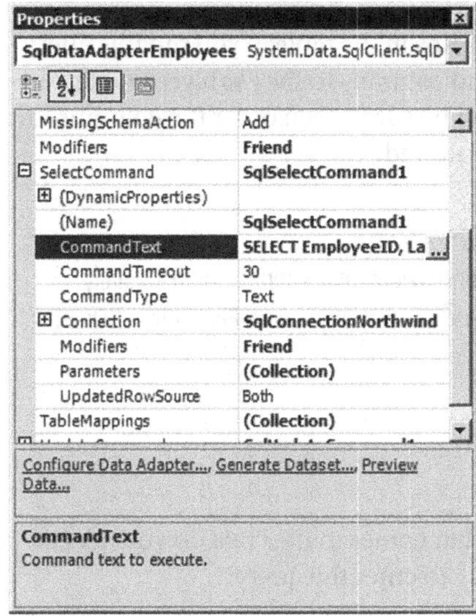

Figure 3-7. *Data adapter `SelectCommand`'s `CommandText` property*

This property contains the query that was used in the application to retrieve all the `Employees` data. Let's look at this query in more detail.

Using Queries

A query retrieves data from a database. In its simplest form, it consists of two parts.

- A `SELECT` list where the columns to be retrieved are specified
- A `FROM` clause, where the table or tables to be accessed are specified

---

■ **Tip** We've written `SELECT` and `FROM` in capital letters, simply to indicate they're SQL *keywords*. SQL isn't case sensitive, but the de facto standard is that keywords are typically written in uppercase in code.

In Transact-SQL, queries are called `SELECT` *statements*, but the ISO/ANSI standard clearly distinguishes queries from statements. The distinction is conceptually important: A query is an operation on a table that produces a table as a result; statements may (or may not) operate on tables and don't produce tables as results, so we'll call queries *queries* instead of `SELECT` *statements*. Call queries whatever you prefer, but keep in mind that queries are special elements of SQL.

Using the two keywords, SELECT and FROM, you write the simplest possible query that will get all the data from the Employees table.

```
SELECT
   *
FROM
   Employees
```

The asterisk (*) means you want to select all the columns in the table. If you run this query against the Northwind database, you'll get all the rows and columns in the Employees table. As you'll learn, using * is generally bad practice, as you can't be sure which order the columns in a table will be returned, but it's an easy query to get you started.

■ **Tip** Although most of the SQL you'll see in this book is short and sweet, statements, and especially queries, can be complex and require many lines (in extreme cases, hundreds) of code. Formatting SQL as carefully as you format VB .NET code is an excellent coding practice.

Try It Out: Writing a Simple Query

To try this query, open the Chapter3_Examples solution that comes in the code download. Hit F5 to run the SQL Tool application, and you're now ready to enter the query.

1. In the RichTextBox control at the top of the dialog box, enter the following. Leave everything in lowercase.

   ```
   select
      *
   from
      employees
   ```

2. To execute the query, press F5 or select Actions ➤ Execute.

3. The result should look something like Figure 3-8.

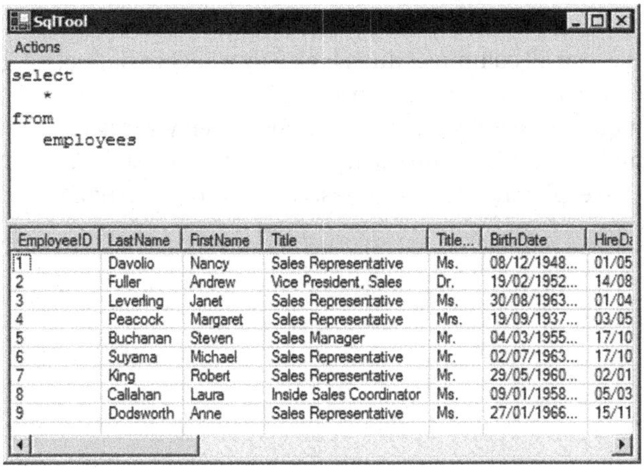

Figure 3-8. *Query result in SQL Tool*

Select the `Format statements` command by hitting F12. This colors the `SELECT` and `FROM` keywords, as well as converts them to uppercase, as in Figure 3-9.

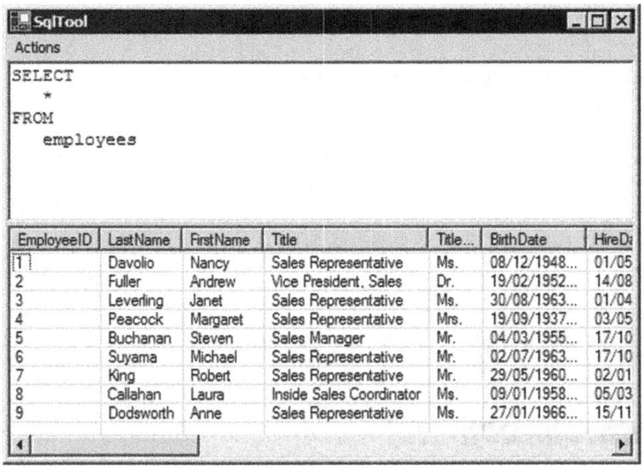

Figure 3-9. *SQL Tool formats queries and statements.*

How It Works

You asked the database to return the data for all columns, which is exactly what has happened. If you scroll to the right, you'll find all the columns in the Employees table.

Most of the time you should limit queries to only relevant columns. When you select columns you don't need, you place unnecessary strain on the network and database (another reason why using * isn't a great idea). To explicitly select columns, enter the column names after the SELECT keyword, like so:

```
SELECT
   EmployeeId,
   FirstName,
   LastName
FROM
   Employees
```

This query selects all the rows from the Employees table but only the EmployeeId, FirstName, and LastName columns. (Use the splitter between the query and result areas to expand/contract them.)

Try It Out: Selecting Specific Columns

To select specific columns, follow these steps:

1. Run the SQL Tool application, and enter the following query:

```
SELECT
   EmployeeId,
   FirstName,
   LastName
FROM
   Employees
```

2. Hit F5 to execute the query (see Figure 3-10).

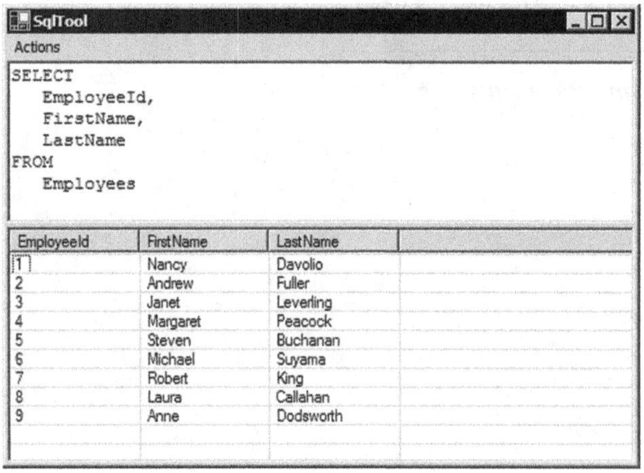

SqlTool

Actions

```
SELECT
   EmployeeId,
   FirstName,
   LastName
FROM
   Employees
```

EmployeeId	FirstName	LastName
1	Nancy	Davolio
2	Andrew	Fuller
3	Janet	Leverling
4	Margaret	Peacock
5	Steven	Buchanan
6	Michael	Suyama
7	Robert	King
8	Laura	Callahan
9	Anne	Dodsworth

Figure 3-10. *Selecting specific columns*

■ **Tip** If you still have the application running and have some text in the `RichTextBox` control, you don't have to delete it. Instead, enter the new text below the old text. Then select the new text, and hit F5. Only selected text is sent to the database. If nothing is selected, everything in the `RichTextBox` control is sent to the database.

How It Works

Figure 3-10 shows the application after the query has been run. Note that only the three columns `EmployeeId`, `FirstName`, and `LastName` are displayed.

Using the WHERE Clause

Queries may have `WHERE` clauses. The `WHERE` clause allows you to specify criteria for selecting rows. This clause can be complex, but we'll stick to a simple example for now. The syntax is as follows:

```
WHERE <column1> <operator> <column2>
```

In this clause, `<operator>` is a comparison operator (for example, =, <>, >, or <). Table 3-1, after this example, lists the comparison operators.

Try It Out: Refining Your Query

To refine your query, follow these steps:

1. Enter the following text into your application:

   ```
   SELECT
      FirstName,
      LastName,
      Country
   FROM
      Employees
   WHERE
      Country = 'USA'
   ```

2. Run the query by pressing F5, and you should see the screen shown in Figure 3-11.

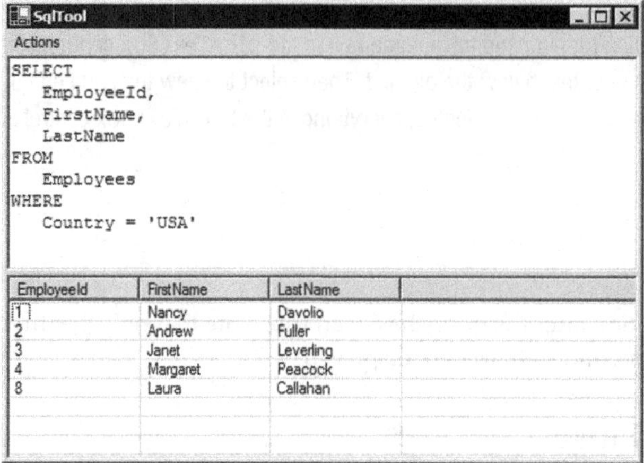

Figure 3-11. *Using the* `WHERE` *clause*

Caution SQL keywords and table and column names aren't case sensitive but string literals (enclosed in single quotes) are; hence, use `USA`, not `usa`, for this example.

How It Works

You could formulate the previous query as "Return the data for columns `FirstName`, `LastName`, and `Country` from the `Employees` table, but only for rows where the `Country` column equals *USA*."

Using the Operators of the WHERE Clause

You can use a number of different comparison operators in a `WHERE` clause (see Table 3-1).

Table 3-1. *Comparison Operators*

Operator	Description	Example
=	Equals	`EmployeeID = 1`
<	Less than	`EmployeeID < 1`
>	Greater than	`EmployeeID > 1`
<=	Less than or equal to	`EmployeeID <= 1`
>=	Greater than or equal to	`EmployeeID >= 1`
<>	Not equal to	`EmployeeID <> 1`
!=	Not equal to	`EmployeeID != 1`
!<	Not less than	`EmployeeID !< 1`
!>	Not greater than	`EmployeeID !> 1`

Tip As mentioned earlier, every database vendor has its own implementation of SQL. This discussion is specific to Transact-SQL; for example, standard SQL doesn't have the != operator and calls <> the *not equals operator*. In fact, standard SQL calls the expressions in a WHERE clause *predicates*; we'll use that term because predicates are either true or false, but other expressions don't have to be. If you work with another version of SQL, please refer to its documentation for specifics.

In addition to these operators, the LIKE operator (see Table 3-2) allows you to match patterns in character data. As with all SQL character data, strings must be enclosed in single quotes (').

Table 3-2. *LIKE Operator*

Operator	Description	Example
LIKE	Allows you to specify a pattern to search for	WHERE Title LIKE 'Sales %' selects all rows where the Title column contains a value that starts with the word *Sales* and a space.

You can use four different wildcards in the pattern (see Table 3-3).

Table 3-3. *Wildcard Characters*

Wildcard	Description
%	Any combination of characters. See the previous example.
_	Any one character. WHERE Title LIKE '_ales' selects all rows where the Title column equals *Aales, aales, Bales, bales,* and so on.
[ ]	A single character within a range [a-d] or set [abcd]. WHERE Title LIKE '[bs]ales' selects all rows where the Title column equals either the word *bales* or *sales*.
[^]	A single character not within a range [^a-d] or set [^abcd].

Sometimes it's useful to select rows where a value is unknown. When no value has been assigned to a column, the column is NULL. (This isn't the same as a column that contains the value 0 or blank.) To select a row with a column that's NULL, use the IS [NOT] NULL operator (see Table 3-4).

Table 3-4. *IS [NOT] NULL Operator*

Operator	Description	Example
IS NULL	Allows you to select rows where a column has no value.	WHERE Region IS NULL returns all rows where Region has no value.
IS NOT NULL	Allows you to select rows where a column has a value.	WHERE Region IS NOT NULL returns all rows where Region has a value.

■ **Note** You must use the IS NULL and IS NOT NULL operators (collectively called the *null predicate* in standard SQL) to select or exclude NULL column values, respectively. The following is a valid query but always produces zero rows: SELECT * FROM Employees WHERE Region = NULL. If you change = to IS, the query will return rows where regions have no value.

To select values in a range or in a set, you can use the BETWEEN and IN operators (see Table 3-5).

Table 3-5. *BETWEEN and IN Operators*

Operator	Description	Example
BETWEEN	True if a value is within a range.	WHERE Extension BETWEEN 400 AND 500 returns the rows where Extension is between 400 and 500, inclusive.
IN	True if a value is in a list. The list can be the result of a subquery.	WHERE City IN ('Seattle', 'London') returns the rows where City is either Seattle or London.

Combining Predicates

Quite often you'll need to use more than one predicate to filter your data. You can use the logical operators shown in Table 3-6.

Table 3-6. *Logical Operators*

Operator	Description	Example
AND	Combines two expressions, evaluating the complete expression as true only if both are true	WHERE (title LIKE 'Sales%' AND lastname = 'Peacock')
NOT	Negates a boolean value	WHERE NOT (title LIKE 'Sales%' AND lastname = 'Peacock')
OR	Combines two expressions, evaluating the complete expression as true if either is true	WHERE (title = 'Peacock' OR title = 'King')

When you use these operators, it's often a good idea to use parentheses to clarify the conditions. In complex queries this may be absolutely necessary.

Sorting Data

After you've filtered the data you want, you can sort the data by one or more columns and in a certain direction. Since tables are by definition unsorted, the order in which rows are retrieved by a query is unpredictable. To impose an ordering, you use the ORDER BY clause.

```
ORDER BY <column> [ASC | DESC] {, n}
```

The <column> is the column that should be used to sort the result. The {, n} syntax means you can specify any number of columns separated by commas. The result will be sorted in the order in which you specify the columns.

The following are the two sort directions:

- **ASC**: Ascending (1, 2, 3, 4, and so on).
- **DESC**: Descending (10, 9, 8, 7, and so on). If you omit the ASC or DESC keywords, the sort order defaults to ASC.

Now you've seen the following basic syntax for queries:

```
SELECT <column>
FROM <table>
WHERE <predicate>
ORDER BY <column> ASC | DESC
```

So, let's use it in an example.

Try It Out: Writing an Enhanced Query

Let's code a query that uses all this. You'll want to do the following:

- Select all the orders that have been handled by employee 5.
- Select the orders shipped to either France or Brazil.
- Display only OrderID, EmployeeID, CustomerID, OrderDate, and ShipCountry.
- Sort the orders by the destination country and the date the order was placed.

Does this sound complicated? Let's try it. Follow these steps:

1. Run the SQL Tool application, and enter the following:

```
SELECT
   OrderId,
   EmployeeId,
   CustomerId,
   OrderDate,
   ShipCountry
FROM
   Orders
WHERE
   EmployeeId = 5
   AND
   ShipCountry IN ('Brazil', 'France')
ORDER BY
   ShipCountry ASC,
   OrderDate ASC
```

2. Hit F5, and you should see output as in Figure 3-12.

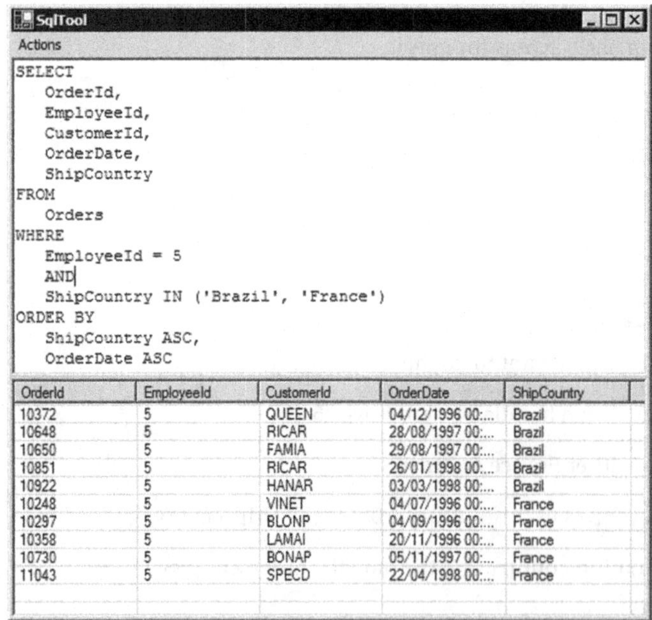

OrderId	EmployeeId	CustomerId	OrderDate	ShipCountry
10372	5	QUEEN	04/12/1996 00:...	Brazil
10648	5	RICAR	28/08/1997 00:...	Brazil
10650	5	FAMIA	29/08/1997 00:...	Brazil
10851	5	RICAR	26/01/1998 00:...	Brazil
10922	5	HANAR	03/03/1998 00:...	Brazil
10248	5	VINET	04/07/1996 00:...	France
10297	5	BLONP	04/09/1996 00:...	France
10358	5	LAMAI	20/11/1996 00:...	France
10730	5	BONAP	05/11/1997 00:...	France
11043	5	SPECD	22/04/1998 00:...	France

Figure 3-12. *Enhanced query*

How It Works

Let's look at the clauses individually. The SELECT list specifies which columns you want to use.

```
SELECT
   OrderId,
   EmployeeId,
   CustomerId,
   OrderDate,
   ShipCountry
```

The `FROM` clause specifies you want to use the `Orders` table.

```
FROM
   Orders
```

The `WHERE` clause is a bit more complicated. It consists of two predicates that individually state the following:

- `EmployeeID` must be 5.
- `ShipCountry` must be in the list Brazil and France.

As these predicates are combined with `AND`, they both must evaluate to true for a row to be included in the result.

```
WHERE
   EmployeeId = 5
   AND
   ShipCountry IN ('Brazil', 'France')
```

The `ORDER BY` clause specifies the order in which the rows are sorted. The rows will be sorted by the `ShipCountry` first and then by `OrderDate`.

```
ORDER BY
   ShipCountry ASC,
   OrderDate ASC
```

Inserting Data

The second important task you need to be able to do is add data. You do this with the `INSERT` statement. The `INSERT` statement is much simpler than a query, particularly because the `WHERE` and `ORDER BY` clauses have no meaning when inserting data and therefore aren't used.

A basic `INSERT` statement has the following parts:

```
INSERT INTO <table>
(<column1>, <column2>, ..., <columnN>)
VALUES (<value1>, <value2>, ..., <valueN>)
```

Using this syntax, let's add a new row to the `Shippers` table of the `Northwind` database. Before you insert it, let's look at the table. It has three rows (see Figure 3-13).

SqlTool

Actions

```
SELECT
    *
FROM
    Shippers
```

ShipperID	CompanyName	Phone
1	Speedy Express	(503) 555-9831
2	United Package	(503) 555-3199
3	Federal Shipping	(503) 555-9931

Figure 3-13. *Shippers data before inserting a row*

The first column, ShipperID, is an IDENTITY column, and as such you can't insert values into it explicitly—MSDE will make sure a unique value is inserted for you. Therefore, the INSERT statement will look like this:

```
INSERT INTO shippers
   (companyname, phone)
VALUES
   ('We Shred Them Before You Get Them', '555-1234')
```

Executing this statement should produce a message box reporting "1 row(s) affected." After the insert, the query will return the results in Figure 3-14. (To see the full company name, double-click the separator between the CompanyName and Phone columns.)

SqlTool

Actions

```
SELECT
    *
FROM
    Shippers
```

ShipperID	CompanyName	Phone
1	Speedy Express	(503) 555-9831
2	United Package	(503) 555-3199
3	Federal Shipping	(503) 555-9931
4	We Shred Them Before You Get Them	555-1234

Figure 3-14. *Shippers data after inserting a row*

Be careful to insert data of the correct data type. In the previous example, both the columns are the character type; therefore, you inserted strings. If one of the columns had been of integer data type, you would have inserted an integer instead. We'll describe the SQL data types in the "Using SQL Data Types" section.

Updating Data

The third important task you need to be able to do is change data. You do this with the UPDATE statement. In Chapter 2, the data adapter changed data in a database transparently, based on changes to the dataset, and you had no reason to be concerned when performing updates.

When coding UPDATE statements, however, you must be careful to include a WHERE clause, or you'll update *all* the rows in a table. In fact, you must always code an appropriate WHERE clause, or you won't change the data you intend to change. So, be careful to enter all the text in the following example before hitting F5!

■ **Tip** Should you inadvertently change something in the Northwind database, remember that you can simply re-create it using the procedure described in the section "Installing the Sample Databases" in Chapter 1.

Now that you're aware of the implications of the UPDATE statement, let's take a good look at it. In essence, it's a simple statement that allows you to update values in one or more rows and columns.

```
UPDATE <table>
SET <column1> = <value1>, <column2> = <value2>, ..., <columnN> = <valueN>
WHERE <predicate>
```

As an example, let's imagine that the company you added earlier, We Shred Them Before You Get Them, has realized that, though (unfortunately) accurate, its name isn't good for business, and it's therefore changing names to Speed of Light Delivery. To make this change in the database, you first need to locate the row with this name. More than one company could have the same name, so you shouldn't use the CompanyName column as the key. Instead you locate the correct row in the result of the previous query and make a note of the ShipperID identity column (ShipperID) value.

The primary key of the row is 4, and you can now update its CompanyName column.

```
UPDATE shippers
SET
   companyname = 'Speed of Light Delivery'
WHERE
   shipperid = 4
```

Executing this statement should produce a message box reporting "1 row(s) affected." If you retrieve the row again, you'll see that CompanyName has changed, as in Figure 3-15.

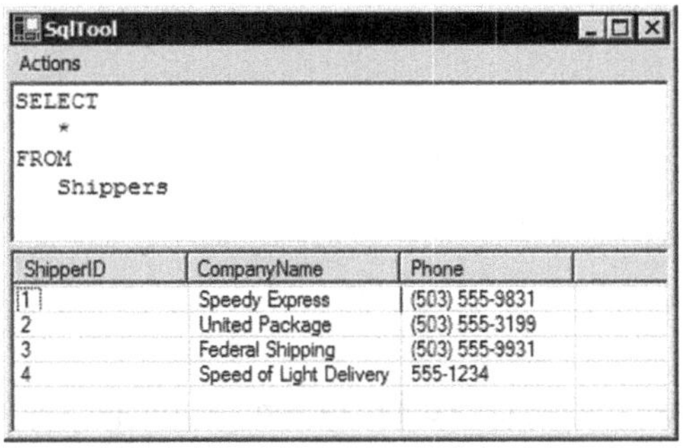

SqlTool

Actions

```
SELECT
   *
FROM
   Shippers
```

ShipperID	CompanyName	Phone
1	Speedy Express	(503) 555-9831
2	United Package	(503) 555-3199
3	Federal Shipping	(503) 555-9931
4	Speed of Light Delivery	555-1234

Figure 3-15. *Shippers data after UPDATE*

When you update more than one column, you code the SET keyword only once. For example, the following statement would change both the name and the phone of the example company:

```
UPDATE shippers
SET
   companyname = 'Speed of Light Delivery',
   phone = '555-9876'
WHERE
   shipperid = 4
```

Deleting Data

The fourth important task you need to be able to do is remove data. You do this with the DELETE statement. The DELETE statement has the same implications as the UPDATE statement; it's all too easy to delete every row (or, at least, the wrong rows) in a table by forgetting the WHERE clause, so be careful. The DELETE statement removes entire rows, and it's therefore not necessary (or possible) to specify columns. Its basic syntax is as follows (remember, the WHERE clause is optional, but without it *all* rows will be deleted):

```
DELETE FROM <table>
WHERE <predicate>
```

If Speed of Light Delivery finally gives up and goes out of business, you'd need to remove it from the Shippers table. As with the UPDATE statement, you need to determine the primary key of the row you want to remove (or recall that it's 4) and use that in the DELETE statement, like so:

```
delete from shippers
where shipperid = 4
```

Again a message box should report "1 row(s) affected." If you retrieve all the data from the Shippers table now, you'll see that Speed of Light Delivery is no longer there (see Figure 3-16).

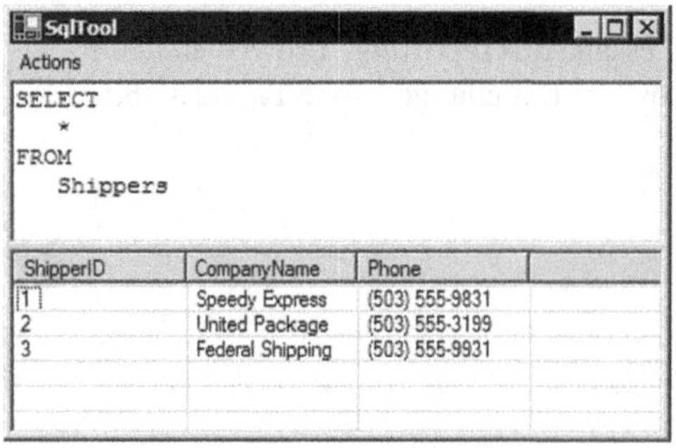

Figure 3-16. *Shippers data after deleting a row*

If you try to delete one of the three other shippers, you'll get a database error. A foreign-key relationship exists from Orders to Shippers, and MSDE enforces it, preventing deletion of Shippers rows that are referred to by Orders rows. You'll examine this in more detail in Chapter 12.

Sometimes you do need to remove every row from a table. In such cases the TRUNCATE TABLE statement may be preferable to the DELETE statement, since it performs faster. The TRUNCATE TABLE statement doesn't do any *logging* (saving each row in a log file before deleting it) to support recovery, but every row removed by DELETE is logged. See SQL Server Books Online for descriptions of both TRUNCATE TABLE and logging.

This concludes our introduction to basic SQL for retrieving, adding, changing, and removing data. Next you'll look at SQL data types.

Using SQL Data Types

In Chapter 2 you used the values of some of the columns in Employees. The reason you were able to do this relatively effortlessly is that Server Explorer had already mapped the data types of the columns in the database to types compatible with VB .NET. You can find this mapping if you open the project again.

1. Open the Chapter2_Examples solution.
2. In Solution Explorer to the right, click the Show All Files icon.
3. Double-click DataSetEmployees.xsd. This opens a window showing the *elements* of the Employees table (see Figure 3-17).

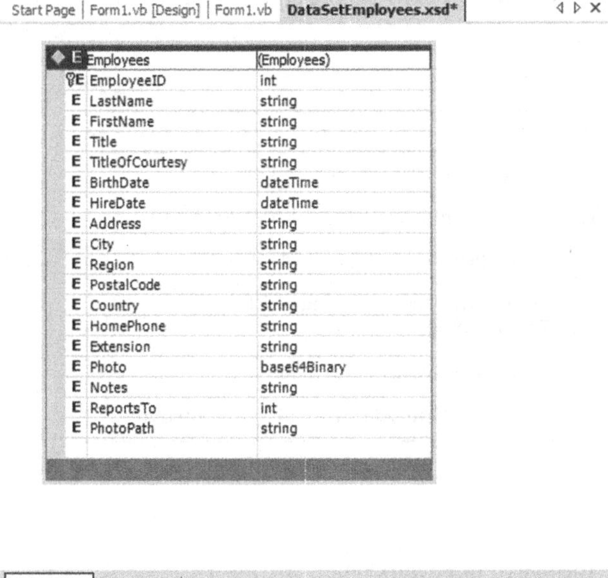

Figure 3-17. *Employees elements*

In Figure 3-17 you can see how the data has types with which VB .NET can work. These aren't, however, necessarily the same data types as the columns in the database. The following tables show the data types that are available in SQL Server and how they map to predefined VB .NET types or to a .NET Framework type (usable by any .NET language, including VB .NET).

Numeric Data Types

The eight SQL numeric data types map to VB .NET simple types (see Table 3-7).

Table 3-7. *SQL Numeric Types*

SQL Data Type	VB .NET Type	Description
`bigint`	`Long or Int64`	64-bit signed integer
`bit`	`Boolean`	Unsigned number that can be `0`, `1`, or `NULL`
`decimal`	`Decimal`	128-bit signed number
`float`	`Double`	64-bit floating-point number
`int`	`Integer or Int32`	32-bit signed integer
`real`	`Single`	32-bit floating-point number
`smallint`	`Short or Int16`	16-bit signed integer
`tinyint`	`Byte`	8-bit unsigned integer

Character String Data Types

All six SQL character string data types map to the VB .NET `String` type (see Table 3-8).

Table 3-8. *SQL Character String Data Types*

SQL Data Type	VB .NET Type	Description
`char`	`String`	Fixed-length string of 1 to 8,000 bytes
`nchar`	`String`	Fixed-length Unicode string of 1 to 4,000 bytes
`text`	`String`	Variable-length string of 1 to 2,147,483,647
`ntext`	`String`	Variable-length Unicode string of 1 to 1,073,741,823 bytes
`varchar`	`String`	Variable-length string of 1 to 8,000 bytes
`nvarchar`	`String`	Variable-length Unicode string of 1 to 4,000 bytes

Date and Time Data Types

Both SQL date and time types map to the .NET Framework type `System.Data.SqlTypes.SqlDateTime` (see Table 3-9). Note that although .NET defines `System.DateTime` with the same ability to store dates and times, it allows a different range of dates that don't map to those defined in SQL; thus, we use `SqlDateTime`.

Table 3-9. *SQL Date/Time Data Types*

SQL Data Type	VB .NET Type	Description
`datetime`	`SqlDateTime`	Date and time data from Jan. 1, 1753, through Dec. 31, 9999, accurate to 1/300th of a second
`smalldatetime`	`SqlDateTime`	Date and time data from Jan. 1, 1900, through June 6, 2079, accurate to the minute

Using Binary Data Types

All three SQL binary data types map to VB .NET `byte` arrays (see Table 3-10).

Table 3-10. *SQL Binary Data Types*

SQL Data Type	VB .NET Type	Description
`binary`	`Byte()`	Fixed-length binary data of 1 to 8,000 bytes
`image`	`Byte()`	Variable-length binary data of 0 to 2,147,483,647 bytes
`varbinary`	`Byte()`	Variable-length binary data of 1 to 8,000 bytes

Using Money Data Types

Both SQL money data types map to the .NET Framework type `System.Data.SqlTypes.SqlMoney`. (see Table 3-11). Note that although .NET also defines `Decimal` type to cover this, in general it allows a different range of dates that don't map to those defined in SQL; thus, we use `SqlMoney`.

Table 3-11. *SQL Money Data Types*

SQL Data Type	VB .NET Type	Description
`money`	`SqlMoney`	Values from -922,337,203,685,477.5808 through 922,337,203,685,477.5807
`smallmoney`	`SqlMoney`	Values from -214,748.3648 through 214,748.3647

Using Other Data Types

Three of the other five SQL data types map to types compatible with VB .NET. Two of the SQL data types aren't accessible by VB .NET (see Table 3-12).

Table 3-12. *Other SQL Data Types*

SQL Data Type	VB .NET Type	Description
`cursor`		For internal SQL Server use only
`sql_variant`	`Object`	Can hold other SQL data types
`table`		For internal SQL Server use only
`timestamp`	`Byte()`	8-byte database-unique integer
`uniqueidentifier`	`System.Guid`	128-bit globally unique integer

Summary

In this chapter you saw how to use SQL to perform the four most common tasks against a database: `SELECT`, `INSERT`, `UPDATE`, and `DELETE`. You also looked at how to use comparison and other operators to specify predicates that limit what rows are retrieved or manipulated. Finally, you surveyed the SQL data types and saw how they map to VB .NET and .NET types.

In the next chapter, you'll start looking at ADO.NET and its components, but that doesn't mean this chapter contains all the SQL you'll need for this book. Once you've come to grips with enabling these simple SQL elements within your .NET applications, you'll return in Chapter 12 to learn more SQL and database design techniques.

CHAPTER 4

What's ADO.NET?

Now that you've used SQL, MSDE, and Visual Studio .NET to create simple database applications, let's look at the final piece in the puzzle: ADO.NET. When you created the simple application in Chapter 2, you used Visual Studio .NET controls to connect to your database and work with your data. What you didn't see in detail was what Visual Studio .NET did for you behind the scenes. Underneath all the drag-and-drop functionality, Visual Studio .NET used ADO.NET objects to access and display your data. Understanding these objects is the key to building powerful database applications. Before you start building more sophisticated applications, you need to learn more about ADO.NET.

In this chapter, you'll learn the following:

- Why ADO.NET was developed
- What the core ADO.NET architecture comprises
- How to use .NET Framework data providers
- That the .NET Framework data provider is an API

Why ADO.NET?

Almost all applications require some data access. Before the .NET Framework, developers used data access technologies such as ODBC, OLE DB, and ADO in their applications; with the introduction of .NET, Microsoft created a new way to work with data, called ADO.NET. This is the only technology you need to use in .NET to access data sources, but in reality several of its predecessors are still lurking under the hood. We'll start this chapter by telling you what they are and how they fit into the grand scheme of things.

A Brief History

Back at the end of the 1980s, several big database servers and a few small ones were available to buy and use. Each used SQL (with one or two of their own proprietary extensions thrown in for good measure) to access and manipulate the data they contained, and each had their own proprietary set of programming interfaces for developers to tie their own applications into the servers. This forced a great deal of extra work onto developers, as in order to support more than one database, they would have to rewrite all their application's data access code for each database. The database vendors saw the problem and collaborated to create a common set of (*really*) low-level interfaces that all their servers would support. They called this API set Open DataBase Connectivity (ODBC).

However, writing ODBC code directly is tricky. Microsoft saw an opportunity to make things easier and wrote a set of Component Object Model (COM) components that was much easier to develop with and also let applications access data that wasn't stored in a database—something you couldn't do with ODBC. Data stored in text files, spreadsheets, and other sources could now be used as well. This new technology, called OLE DB, used ODBC to access old databases where necessary and its own code to access databases and other data sources. Based on its rapid uptake, Microsoft decided to use it as the cornerstone for its Universal Data Access (UDA) strategy.

One of the aims of UDA was to provide a more object-oriented interface to data access than the somewhat procedural one that ODBC and OLE DB presented. Thus, Data Access Objects (DAO) and Remote Data Objects (RDO) were born in 1997, and a year later ActiveX Data Objects (ADO 2.0) gave classic ASP applications access to data sources in a constantly *connected* environment. ADO was built on top of OLE DB, which means that an application can use ADO, which talks to OLE DB, which talks to ODBC, which talks to a database, if you're using older databases such as Paradox or dBASE. ADO was even simpler than OLE DB to use, however.

With the multilayered data access model and the connected nature of ADO, you could easily end up sapping server resources and creating a performance bottleneck. ADO served well, but ADO.NET is much, much better.

ADO.NET Isn't a New Version of ADO

ADO.NET is a completely new data access technology, with a new design that was built entirely from scratch. Let's first get this cleared up: ADO.NET *doesn't* stand for ActiveX Data Objects .NET. Why? It's because of many reasons, but the following are the two most important ones:

- ADO.NET is an integral part of the .NET Framework, not an external entity.
- ADO.NET *isn't* a collection of ActiveX components.

The name *ADO.NET* is analogous to ADO because Microsoft wanted developers to feel at home using ADO.NET and didn't want them to think they'd need to "learn it all over again," so it purposely named and designed ADO.NET to offer similar features implemented in a different way.

During the .NET Framework design, Microsoft realized that ADO wasn't going to fit in. ADO was available as an external package based on COM objects, requiring .NET applications to explicitly include a reference to it. In contrast, .NET applications are designed to share a single model, where all libraries are integrated into a single framework, organized into logical namespaces, and declared public to any application that wants to use them. It was wisely decided that the .NET data access technology should comply with the .NET architectural model. Hence, ADO.NET was born.

ADO.NET is designed to accommodate both connected and disconnected environments. Also, ADO.NET embraces the fundamentally important Extensible Markup Language (XML) standard (more on this in Chapter 17), much more than ADO did, since the explosion in XML use came about after ADO was developed. With ADO.NET you cannot only use XML to transfer data between applications, but you can also export data from your application into an XML file, store it locally on your system, and retrieve it later when you need to do so.

Performance usually comes with a price, but in the case of ADO.NET, the price is definitely reasonable. Unlike ADO, ADO.NET doesn't transparently wrap OLE DB providers; instead, it uses *managed data providers* that are designed specifically for each type of data source, thus leveraging their true power and adding to overall application speed and performance. It's only if the data source doesn't have its own native data provider that you must fall back to using a generic OLE DB or ODBC data provider.

ADO.NET also works in both connected and disconnected environments. You can connect to a database, remain connected while simply reading data, and then close your connection, which is a process similar to ADO. Where ADO.NET really begins to shine is in the disconnected world. If you need to edit database data, maintaining a continuous connection would be costly on the server. ADO.NET gets around this by providing a sophisticated disconnected model. Data is sent from the server and cached locally on the client. When you're ready to update the database, you can send the changed data back to the server, where updates and conflicts are managed for you.

In ADO.NET, when you retrieve data, you use an object known as a *data reader*. When you work with disconnected data, the data is cached locally in a relational data structure called a *dataset*.

ADO.NET and the .NET Framework

A dataset can hold large amounts of data in the form of tables (as `DataTable` objects), their relationships (as `DataRelation` objects), and constraints (as `Constraint` objects) in an in-memory cache, which can then be exported to an external file or to another dataset. These objects are analogous to database features (tables, relationships, and constraints), which you'll learn about in Chapters 12 and onward. Since XML support is integrated into ADO.NET, you can produce XML schemas and transmit and share data using XML documents (much more on this in Chapters 8 and 17).

Table 4-1 describes the namespaces in which ADO.NET components are grouped.

Table 4-1. *ADO.NET Namespaces*

Namespace	Description
`System.Data`	Classes, interfaces, delegates, and enumerations that define and partially implement the ADO.NET architecture
`System.Data.Common`	Classes shared by .NET Framework data providers
`System.Data.Odbc`	The .NET Framework data provider for ODBC
`System.Data.OleDb`	The .NET Framework data provider for OLE DB
`System.Data.OracleClient`	The .NET Framework data provider for Oracle
`System.Data.SqlClient`	The .NET Framework data provider for SQL Server
`System.Data.SqlServerCe`	The .NET Compact Framework data provider for SQL Server CE
`System.Data.SqlTypes`	Classes for native SQL Server data types

Since XML support has been closely integrated into ADO.NET, some ADO.NET components in the `System.Data` namespace rely on components in the `System.Xml` namespace. So, you sometimes need to include both namespaces as references in Solution Explorer.

These namespaces are physically implemented as assembly files, and if you create a new console application project in Visual Studio, references to the assemblies should automatically be created, along with the reference to the `System` assembly. However, if they're not present, simply perform the following steps to add the namespaces to your project:

1. Right-click the References item in Solution Explorer, and then click Add Reference....
2. A dialog box with a list of available references displays. Select `System.Data.dll`, `System.XML.dll`, and `System.dll` (if not already present) one by one (hold down the Ctrl key for multiple selections), and then click the Select button.
3. Click OK, and the references will be added to the project. Solution Explorer should look similar to Figure 4-1.

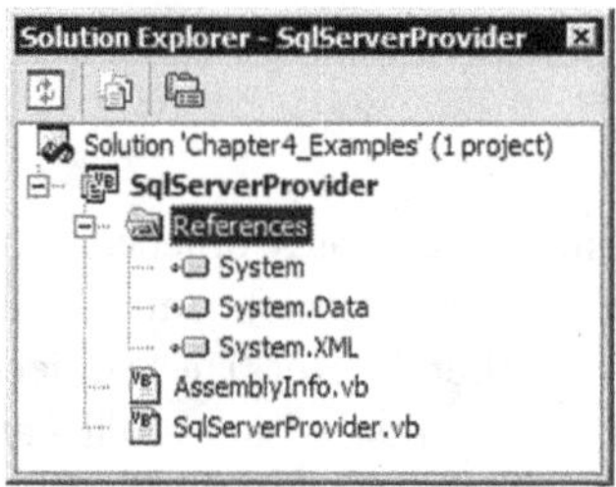

Figure 4-1. *Adding references to your project in Solution Explorer*

For those of you working from the command line, you can use the following compiler options to include the assemblies:

```
/r:System.dll /r:System.Data.dll /r:System.XML.dll
```

As you can see from Table 4-1, ADO.NET can work with older technologies such as OLE DB and ODBC. However, the SQL Server data provider communicates directly with SQL Server (versions 7.0 and newer), the most efficient form of connection, so it accesses SQL Server faster than OLE DB or ODBC. Likewise, the Oracle data provider accesses Oracle directly.

Tip It bears repeating that the quickest data provider for a data source is the one that has been specifically written for it. Failing that, you should try to use the OLE DB provider and then the ODBC provider as a last resort. We'll keep mentioning this throughout the chapter—it's that fundamental.

ADO.NET is a data access technology that's likely to be *the* primary data access technology of .NET for a long time, so learning how to use it is a worthwhile investment.

Understanding ADO.NET Architecture

Figure 4-2 presents the most important architectural features of ADO.NET. We'll discuss them in far greater detail in later chapters.

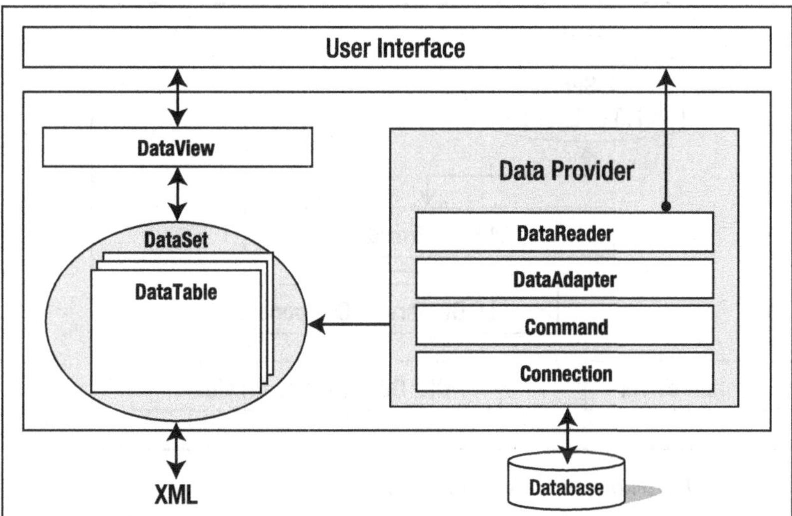

Figure 4-2. *ADO.NET architecture*

ADO.NET has two central components: data providers and datasets.

A *data provider* connects to a data source and supports data access and manipulation. You'll play with three different ones later in this chapter.

A *dataset* supports disconnected, independent caching of data in a relational fashion, updating the data source as required. A dataset contains one or more data tables. A *data table* is a row-and-column representation that provides much the same logical view as a SQL table. For example, you can store the data from the `Northwind` database's `Employees` table in a data table and manipulate the data as needed. You'll learn about datasets starting with Chapter 8.

In Figure 4-2, notice the `DataView` class (in the `System.Data` namespace). This isn't a data provider component. Data views are used primarily to bind data to Windows and Web Forms. We'll cover data views in Chapter 9.

As you saw in Table 4-1, each data provider has its own namespace. In fact, each data provider is essentially an implementation of interfaces in the `System.Data` namespace, specialized for a specific type of data source.

For example, if you use SQL Server version 7 or newer (SQL Server 2000 is actually version 8) as your database manager, you should use the SQL Server data provider (`System.Data.SqlClient`) because it's the most efficient way to work with these versions. This data provider communicates natively with SQL Server, bypassing the layers that OLE DB and ODBC connections have to use.

The OLE DB data provider supports access to older versions of SQL Server as well as to other databases, such as Access, DB2, MySQL, and Oracle. However, native data providers (such as `System.Data.OracleClient`) are preferable for performance, since the OLE DB data provider works through two other layers (the OLE DB service component and the OLE DB provider) before reaching the data source.

Figure 4-3 illustrates the difference between using the SQL Server and OLE DB data providers to access a SQL Server (version 7.0 or higher) database.

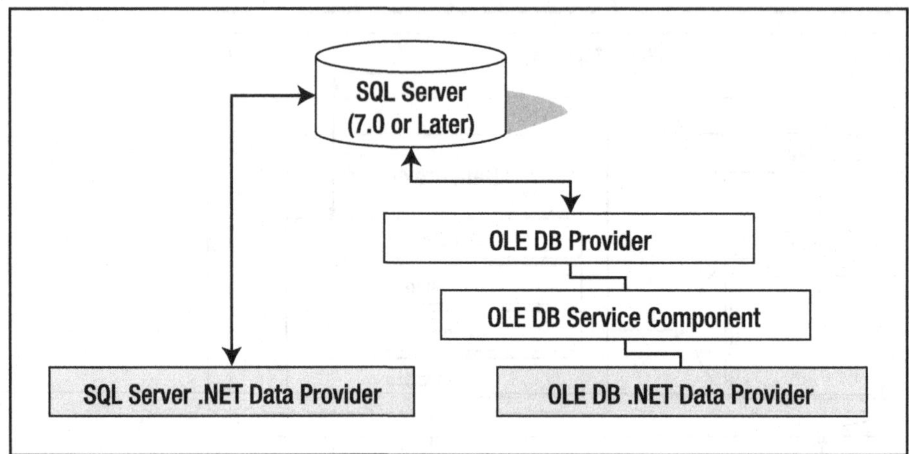

Figure 4-3. *SQL Server and OLE DB data provider differences*

If your application connects to an older version of SQL Server (6.5 or newer) or to more than one kind of database server at the same time (for example, an Access and an Oracle database connected simultaneously), only then should you choose to use the OLE DB data provider.

No hard-and-fast rules exist; you can use both the OLE DB data provider for SQL Server and the Oracle data provider (`System.Data.OracleClient`) if you want, but it's important you choose the best provider for your purpose. Given the performance benefits of the server-specific data providers, if you use SQL Server or MSDE, 99 percent of the time you should be using the `System.Data.SqlClient` classes.

Before you look at what each kind of data provider does and how it's used, you need to be clear on their core functionality. Each .NET data provider is designed to do the following two things very well:

- Provide access to data with an active connection to the data source.
- Provide data transmission to and from the independent datasets through data adapters.

Database connections are established by using the data provider's connection class (for example, `System.Data.SqlClient.SqlConnection`). Other components such as data readers, commands, and data adapters support retrieving data, executing SQL statements, and reading or writing to datasets, respectively.

As you've seen, each data provider is prefixed with the type of data source it connects to (for instance, the SQL Server data provider is prefixed with *Sql*), so its connection class is named `SqlConnection`. The OLE DB data provider's connection class is named `OleDbConnection`.

Look now at the object model of these two providers in Figure 4-4. You'll work simultaneously with different databases (Access and SQL Server) so you can see how easy it is to switch between data providers and what, if any, their main visible differences are. Note that the two data providers support the same application and share a single dataset.

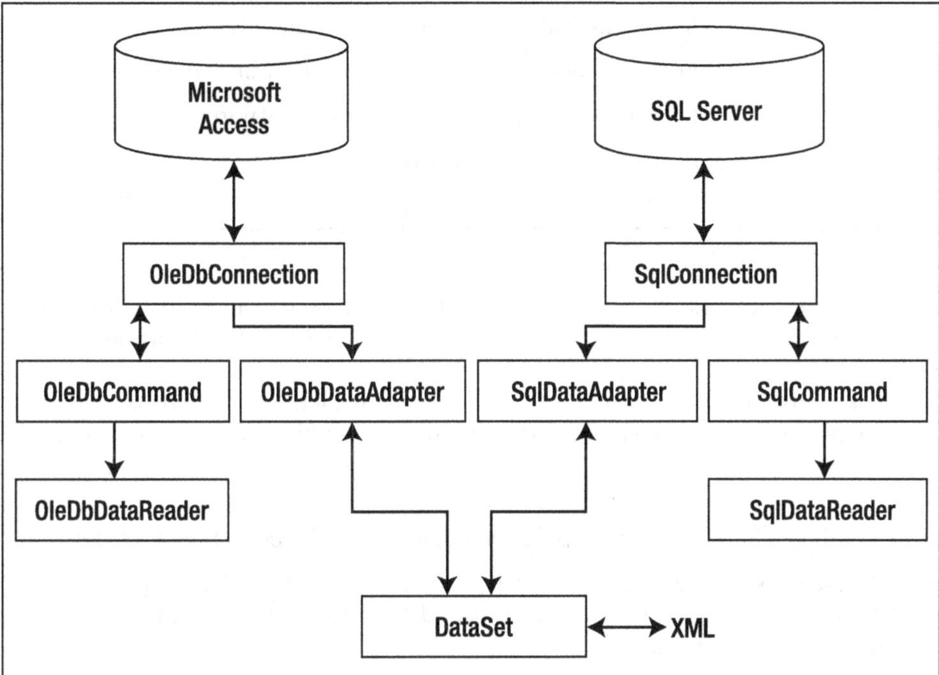

Figure 4-4. *ADO.NET concurrently using Access and SQL Server*

The OLE DB data provider belongs to the `System.Data.OleDb` namespace; the SQL Server data provider belongs to `System.Data.SqlClient`. Both data providers seem to have a similar architecture, though they're actually very different internally.

Let's see how you put the three data providers that can be used with SQL Server to work.

Using the SQL Server Data Provider

The .NET data provider for SQL Server (7.0 or newer) is located in the `System.Data.SqlClient` namespace. This data provider communicates directly with the server using its native network protocol instead of through a number of layers (the way OLE DB does).

Table 4-2 describes some important classes in the `SqlClient` namespace.

Table 4-2. *Commonly Used `SqlClient` Classes*

Classes	Description
`SqlCommand`	Executes SQL queries, statements, or stored procedures
`SqlConnection`	Represents a connection to a SQL Server database
`SqlDataAdapter`	Represents a bridge between a dataset and a data source
`SqlDataReader`	Provides a forward-only, read-only data stream of the results
`SqlError`	Holds information on SQL Server errors and warnings
`SqlParameter`	Represents a command parameter
`SqlTransaction`	Represents a SQL Server transaction

Another namespace, `System.Data.SqlTypes`, maps SQL Server data types to .NET types, both enhancing performance and making developers' lives a lot easier. We discussed this in Chapter 3.

Let's look at an example that uses the SQL Server data provider. It won't cover connections and data retrieval in detail but will familiarize you with what you'll encounter in upcoming chapters.

Try It Out: Creating a Simple Console Application Using the SQL Server Data Provider

You'll build a simple console application, which opens a connection and runs a query, using the `SqlClient` namespace against the MSDE `Northwind` database. You'll display the retrieved data in the console prompt window.

1. Open Visual Studio .NET, and create a new solution (as described in Chapter 2) named `Chapter4_Examples`.

2. Right-click the solution in Solution Explorer, select Add ➤ New Project..., create a VB .NET console application, and name the application `SqlServerProvider`. Rename `Module1.vb` to `SqlServerProvider.vb`.

3. Since you'll be creating this example from scratch, select all the code in Code view and delete it. Enter the code in Listing 4-1.

   Listing 4-1. *`SqlServerProvider` Application Source*

   ```
   Imports System
   Imports System.Data
   Imports System.Data.SqlClient
   ```

```
Module SqlServerProvider
   Sub Main()
      ' Set up connection string
      Dim ConnString As String = "server=(local)\netsdk;" & _
         "integrated security=true;database=northwind"

      ' Set up query string
      Dim CmdString As String = "SELECT * FROM employees"

      'Declare Connection and DataReader variables
      Dim Conn As SqlConnection
      Dim Reader As SqlDataReader

      Try
         'Open Connection
         Conn = New SqlConnection(ConnString)
         Conn.Open()

         'Execute Query
         Dim Cmd As New SqlCommand(CmdString, Conn)
         Reader = Cmd.ExecuteReader()

         'Display output header
         Console.WriteLine("This program demonstrates the use " & _
            "of the SQL Server Data Provider." & ControlChars.NewLine)
         Console.WriteLine("Querying database {0} with query {1}" & _
            ControlChars.NewLine, Conn.Database, Cmd.CommandText)
         Console.WriteLine("FirstName" & ControlChars.Tab & "LastName")

         'Process The Result Set
         While (Reader.Read())
            Console.WriteLine(Reader("FirstName").PadLeft(9) & _
               ControlChars.Tab & Reader(1))
         End While

      Catch ex As Exception
         Console.WriteLine("Error: {0}", ex)

      Finally
         'Close Connection
         Reader.Close()
         Conn.Close()

      End Try

   End Sub
End Module
```

4. Save the project, and then right-click the project in the Solution Explorer window. Select Properties, and set the startup object for the project to `SqlServerProvider`, as shown in Figure 4-5. Click OK.

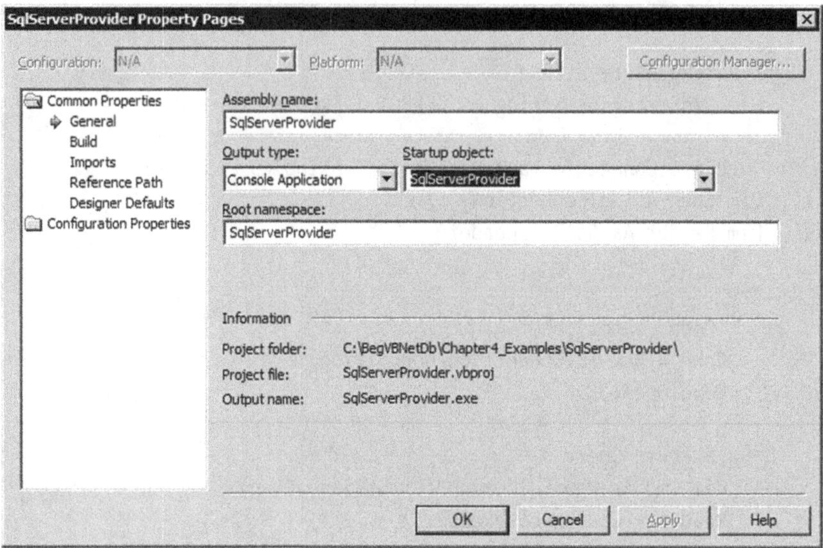

Figure 4-5. *Setting the startup object*

5. Save the project, and press Ctrl+F5 to run it. A console prompt window should appear, as shown in Figure 4-6.

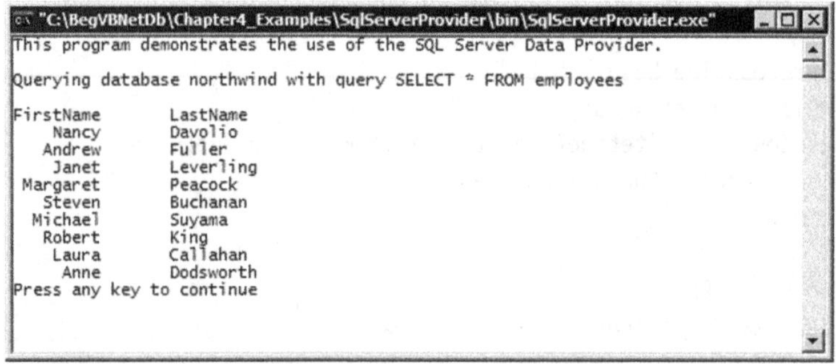

Figure 4-6. *Running the `SqlServerProvider` application*

How It Works

Let's take a look at how the code works, starting with the `Imports` directives.

```
Imports System
Imports System.Data
Imports System.Data.SqlClient
```

The reference to System.Data is actually not needed in this small program, since you don't explicitly use any of its members, but it's a good habit to always include it. The reference to System.Data.SqlClient is, of course, necessary, since you want to use the simple names of its members.

You specify the connection string with *parameters* (key-value pairs) suitable for an MSDE session.

```
' Set up connection string
Dim ConnString As String = "server=(local)\netsdk;" & _
   "integrated security=true;database=northwind"
```

The connection string contains the following parameter, which specifies Windows Authentication:

```
integrated security=true;
```

The true value is equivalent to SSPI, which stands for *Security Support Provider Interface.*

You then code the query, like so:

```
' Set up query string
Dim CmdString As String = "SELECT * FROM employees"
```

Tip The connection string is actually parsed before it's assigned to the connection's ConnectionString property, so if you want to add newlines and extra spaces for readability, that's fine. Likewise, SQL can contain extraneous newlines and spaces, so you can format it to make it more readable and maintainable.

You next declare variables for the connection and data reader, so they're available to the rest of your code. You then create the connection, like so:

```
'Declare Connection and DataReader variables
Dim Conn As SqlConnection
Dim Reader As SqlDataReader

Try
   'Open Connection
   Conn = New SqlConnection(ConnString)
```

You do this (and the rest of your database work) in a Try block to handle exceptions (in this particular case, to handle exceptions thrown by ADO.NET in response to database errors); however, in this simple example you're not interested in distinguishing them from other exceptions. Here, ADO.NET will throw an exception if the connection string parameters aren't syntactically correct, so you may as well be prepared. If you had waited until you entered the Try block to declare the connection (and data reader) variable, you wouldn't have it available in the Finally block to close the connection.

Creating the connection doesn't actually connect to the database. You need to call the Open method on the connection.

```
Conn.Open()
```

To execute the query, you first create a command object, passing its constructor the SQL statement to run and the connection on which to run it. Next, you create a data reader by calling ExecuteReader on the command object. This not only executes the query but also sets up the data reader. Note that unlike most objects, you have no way to create a data reader with a New expression.

```
'Execute Query
Dim Cmd As New SqlCommand(CmdString, Conn)
Reader = Cmd.ExecuteReader()
```

You then produce a header for your output, using connection and command properties (Database and CommandText, respectively) to get the database name and query text.

```
'Display output header
Console.WriteLine("This program demonstrates the use " & _
   "of the SQL Server Data Provider." & ControlChars.NewLine)
Console.WriteLine("Querying database {0} with query {1}" & _
   ControlChars.NewLine, Conn.Database, Cmd.CommandText)
Console.WriteLine("FirstName" & ControlChars.Tab & "LastName")
```

You retrieve all the rows in the result set by calling the data reader's Read method, which returns true if there are more rows and false otherwise. Note that the data reader is positioned immediately *before* the first row prior to the first call to Read.

```
'Process The Result Set
While (Reader.Read())
   Console.WriteLine(Reader("FirstName").PadLeft(9) & _
      ControlChars.Tab & Reader(1))
End While
```

You access each row's columns with the data reader's *indexer* (here, the SqlDataReader.Item property), which is overloaded to accept either a column name or a zero-based integer index. We're using both to demonstrate the indexer's use, but using column numbers is more efficient than using column names.

Next you handle any exceptions, quite simplistically, but at least you're developing a good habit. We'll cover exception handling much more carefully in Chapter 18.

```
Catch ex As Exception
   Console.WriteLine("Error: {0}", ex)
```

Finally, in a Finally block, you close the data reader and the connection by calling their Close methods. As a general rule, you should close things in a Finally block to be sure they get closed no matter what happens within the Try block.

```
      Finally
         'Close Connection
         Reader.Close()
         Conn.Close()

      End Try
   End Sub
End Module
```

Technically, closing the connection also closes the data reader, but closing both (in the previous order) is another good habit. A connection with an open data reader can't be used for any other purpose until the data reader has been closed.

Using the OLE DB Data Provider

Outside the .NET Framework, OLE DB is still Microsoft's high-performance data access technology. You can use it to access data stored in any format, so even in ADO.NET it plays an important role in accessing data sources that don't have their own ADO.NET data providers.

The .NET Framework data provider for OLE DB is in the namespace `System.Data.OleDb`. Table 4-3 describes some important classes in the `OleDb` namespace.Notice the similarity between the two data providers, `SqlClient` and `OleDb`. Their difference is transparent, in their implementation, but the user interface is fundamentally the same.

Table 4-3. *Commonly Used OleDb Classes*

Classes	Description
`OleDbCommand`	Executes SQL queries, statements, or stored procedures
`OleDbConnection`	Represents a connection to an OLE DB data source
`OleDbDataAdapter`	Represents a bridge between a dataset and a data source
`OleDbDataReader`	Provides a forward-only, read-only data stream of rows from a data source
`OleDbError`	Holds information on errors and warnings returned by the data source
`OleDbParameter`	class Represents a command parameter
`OleDbTransaction`	class Represents a SQL transaction

The ADO.NET OLE DB data provider requires that an OLE DB provider be specified in the connection string. Table 4-4 describes some OLE DB providers. Note that MSDASQL, the OLE DB provider for ODBC, *isn't* available in ADO.NET, since ADO.NET has its own data provider (the namespace `System.Data.Odbc`) for ODBC.

Table 4-4. *Some OLE DB Providers*

Provider	Description
DB2OLEDB	Microsoft OLE DB provider for DB2
SQLOLEDB	Microsoft OLE DB provider for SQL Server
Microsoft.Jet.OLEDB.4.0	Microsoft OLE DB provider for Access (which uses the Jet engine)
MSDAORA	Microsoft OLE DB provider for Oracle
MSDASQL	Microsoft OLE DB provider for ODBC

Let's use the OLE DB data provider to access the MSDE database, making a few straightforward changes (shown in bold in Listing 4-2) to the code in Listing 4-1. (Of course, you'd use the SQL Server data provider for real work since it's more efficient.)

Try It Out: Creating a Simple Console Application Using the OLE DB Data Provider

Follow these steps:

1. Create a new VB .NET console application named `OleDbProvider` in the `Chapter4_Examples` solution. Rename the `Module1.vb` file to `OleDbProvider.vb`. Replace the generated code with the code in Listing 4-2, which shows the changes to Listing 4-1 in bold.

Listing 4-2. *`OleDbProvider` Application Source*

```
Imports System
Imports System.Data
Imports System.Data.OleDb

Module OleDbProvider
   Sub Main()
      ' Set up connection string
      Dim ConnString As String = "provider=sqloledb;" & _
         "data source=(local)\netsdk;" & _
         "integrated security=sspi;" & _
         "database=northwind"

      ' Set up query string
      Dim CmdString As String = "SELECT * FROM employees"

      'Declare Connection and DataReader variables
      Dim Conn As OleDbConnection
      Dim Reader As OleDbDataReader
```

```
        Try
           'Open Connection
           Conn = New OleDbConnection(ConnString)
           Conn.Open()

           'Execute Query
           Dim Cmd As New OleDbCommand(CmdString, Conn)
           Reader = Cmd.ExecuteReader()

           'Display output header
           Console.WriteLine("This program demonstrates the use " & _
             "of the OleDb Data Provider." & ControlChars.NewLine)
           Console.WriteLine("Querying database {0} with query {1}" & _
             ControlChars.NewLine, Conn.Database, Cmd.CommandText)
           Console.WriteLine("FirstName" & ControlChars.Tab & "LastName")

           'Process The Result Set
           While (Reader.Read())
              Console.WriteLine(Reader("FirstName").PadLeft(9) & _
                 ControlChars.Tab & Reader(1))
           End While

        Catch ex As Exception
           Console.WriteLine("Error: {0}", ex)

        Finally
           'Close Connection
           Reader.Close()
           Conn.Close()

        End Try

     End Sub
  End Module
```

2. Since you now have two projects in your solution, you need to make this project the startup project so it runs when you hit Ctrl+F5. Right-click the project name in Solution Explorer, and then click Set As StartUp Project (see Figure 4-7).

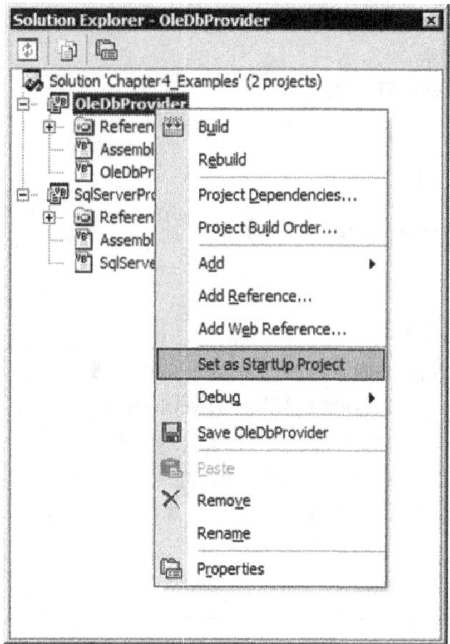

Figure 4-7. *Setting the startup project*

3. Set the startup object for this project to `OleDbProvider`, and run the application with Ctrl+F5. A console prompt window should appear, as shown in Figure 4-8.

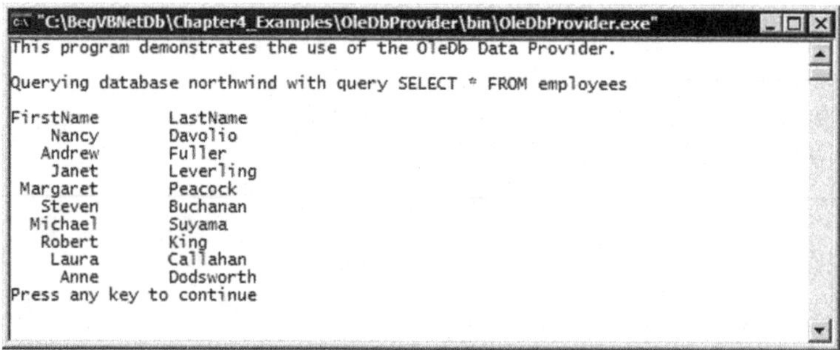

Figure 4-8. *Running the `OleDbProvider` application*

How It Works

This program does the same thing as the first example, so we'll discuss only the changes here.

You replaced `SqlClient` with `OleDb` in the third `Imports` directive.

```
Imports System.Data.OleDb
```

The connection string required the most change, since the OLE DB data provider doesn't accept the same parameters as the SQL Server data provider. In addition, it requires a `provider` parameter.

```
' Set up connection string
Dim ConnString As String = "provider=sqloledb;" & _
   "data source=(local)\netsdk;" & _
   "integrated security=sspi;" & _
   "database=northwind"
```

The remaining four lines change, so the application uses the OLE DB data provider classes for the connection, command, and data reader rather than the SQL Server data provider.

```
'Declare Connection and DataReader variables
Dim Conn As OleDbConnection
Dim Reader As OleDbDataReader

Try
   'Open Connection
   Conn = New OleDbConnection(ConnString)
   Conn.Open()

   'Execute Query
   Dim Cmd As New OleDbCommand(CmdString, OleDbConn)
   Reader = Cmd.ExecuteReader()
```

The final change was a semantic one and wasn't required by ADO.NET.

```
'Display output header
Console.WriteLine("This program demonstrates the use " & _
   "of the OleDb Data Provider." & ControlChars.NewLine)
```

Using the ODBC Data Provider

ODBC was Microsoft's original general-purpose data access technology. It's still widely used for data sources that don't have OLE DB providers or .NET Framework data providers. ADO.NET includes an ODBC data provider in the namespace `System.Data.Odbc`.

The ODBC architecture is essentially a three-tier process. An application uses ODBC functions to submit database requests. ODBC converts the function calls to the protocol (*call-level interface*) of a *driver* specific to a given data source. The driver communicates with the data source, passing any results or errors back up to ODBC. Obviously, this is less efficient than a database-specific data provider's direct communication with a database, so for performance it's preferable to avoid the ODBC data provider; it merely offers a simpler interface to ODBC but still involves all the ODBC overhead. Table 4-5 describes some important classes in the Odbc namespace.

Table 4-5. *Commonly Used Odbc Classes*

Classes	Description
OdbcCommand	Executes SQL queries, statements, or stored procedures
OdbcConnection	Represents a connection to an ODBC data source
OdbcDataAdapter	Represents a bridge between a dataset and a data source
OdbcDataReader	Provides a forward-only, read-only data stream of rows from a data source
OdbcError	Holds information on errors and warnings returned by the data source
OdbcParameter	Represents a command parameter
OdbcTransaction	Represents a SQL transaction

Let's use the ODBC data provider to access the MSDE database, making the same kind of straightforward changes (highlighted in Listing 4-3) to the code in Listing 4-1 as you did in using the OLE DB data provider.

Before you do, though, you need to create an ODBC data source—actually, you configure a DSN for use with a data source accessible by ODBC—for the Northwind database, since, unlike the SQL Server and OLE DB data providers, the ODBC data provider doesn't let you specify the server or database in the connection string. (The following works on Windows 2000 and the process is similar for other versions of Windows.)

Creating an ODBC Data Source

To create an ODBC data source, follow these steps:

1. In the Control Panel, double-click Administrative Tools.
2. In Administrative Tools, double-click Data Sources (ODBC).
3. When the ODBC Data Source Administrator window opens, click the User DSN tab and then click Add... (see Figure 4-9).

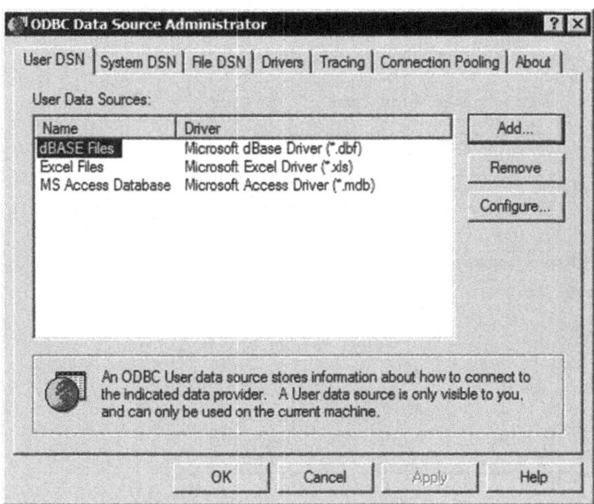

Figure 4-9. *Opening the ODBC Data Source Administrator window*

4. The Create New Data Source wizard starts. First, select the SQL Server ODBC driver; second, click Finish (see Figure 4-10).

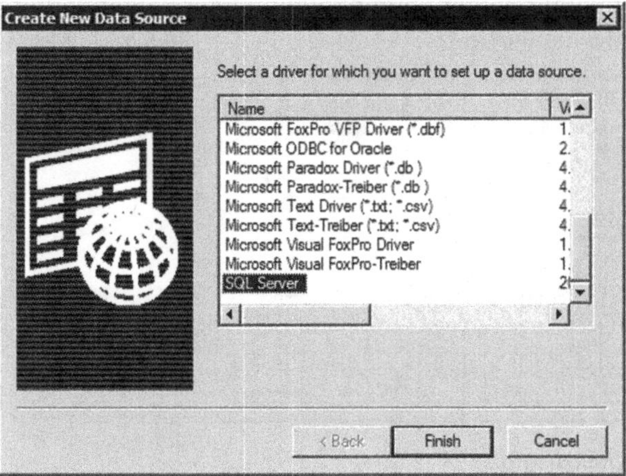

Figure 4-10. *Selecting the driver*

5. The next window prompts for the data source name and server. Fill the entries as in Figure 4-11, and then click Next.

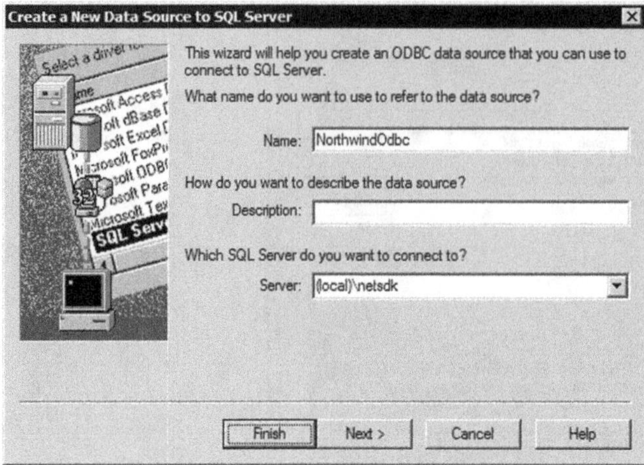

Figure 4-11. *Setting up the server and data source*

6. Accept the defaults in the authentication window by clicking Next (see Figure 4-12).

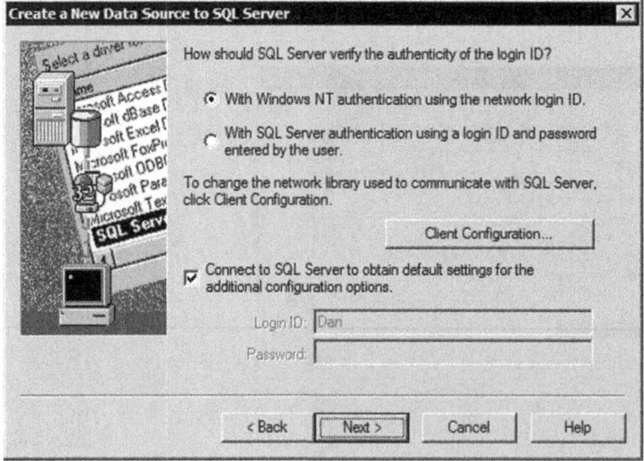

Figure 4-12. *Setting up authentication*

7. In the next window, check the Change the Default Database option, specify the `Northwind` database, and click Next (see Figure 4-13).

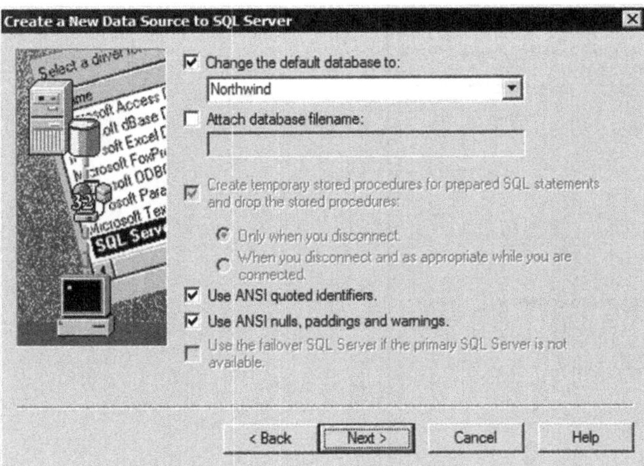

Figure 4-13. *Selecting the default database*

8. In the next window, simply click Finish (see Figure 4-14).

Figure 4-14. *Finishing the setup*

9. A confirmation window appears, describing the new data source. Click Test Data Source... (see Figure 4-15).

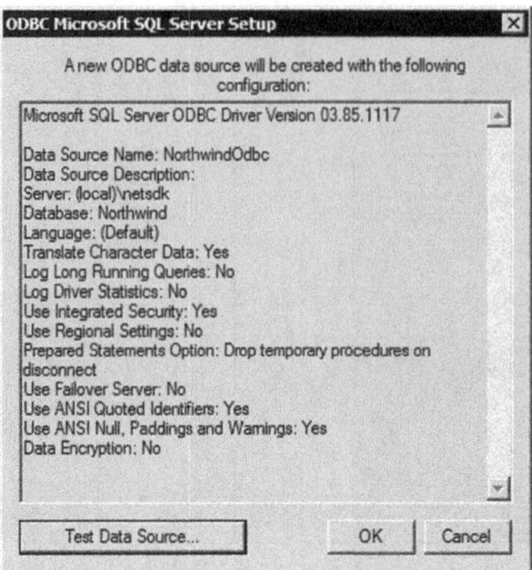

Figure 4-15. *Testing the connection*

10. A window reporting a successful test should appear (see Figure 4-16). (If it doesn't, cancel your work and *carefully* try again.) Click OK.

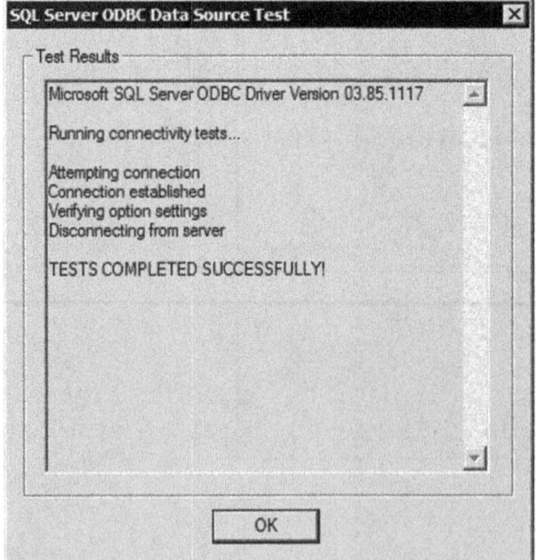

Figure 4-16. *A successful connection test*

11. When the confirmation window reappears, click OK. When the ODBC Data Source Administrator window reappears, the new data source will be on the list (see Figure 4-17).

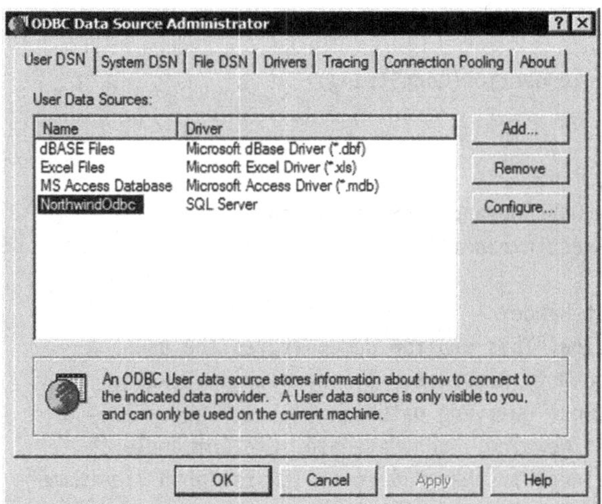

Figure 4-17. *Data source creation: new data source created*

Now that you have an ODBC data source, you can get back to programming!

Try It Out: Creating a Simple Console Application Using the ODBC Data Provider

Follow these steps:

1. Create a new VB .NET console application named `OdbcProvider` in the `Chapter4_Examples` solution. Rename the `Module1.vb` file to `OdbcProvider.vb`. Replace the generated code with the code in Listing 4-3, which shows the changes to Listing 4-1 in bold.

Listing 4-3. *`OdbcProvider` Application Source*

```
Imports System
Imports System.Data
Imports System.Data.Odbc

Module OdbcProvider
   Sub Main()
      ' Set up connection string
      Dim ConnString As String = "dsn=NorthwindOdbc"

      ' Set up query string
      Dim CmdString As String = "SELECT * FROM employees"

      'Declare Connection and DataReader variables
      Dim Conn As OdbcConnection
      Dim Reader As OdbcDataReader
```

```
        Try
            'Open Connection
            Conn = New OdbcConnection(ConnString)
            Conn.Open()

            'Execute Query
            Dim Cmd As New OdbcCommand(CmdString, Conn)
            Reader = Cmd.ExecuteReader()

            'Display output header
            Console.WriteLine("This program demonstrates the use " & _
               "of the Odbc Data Provider." & ControlChars.NewLine)
            Console.WriteLine("Querying database {0} with query {1}" & _
               ControlChars.NewLine, Conn.Database, Cmd.CommandText)
            Console.WriteLine("FirstName" & ControlChars.Tab & "LastName")

            'Process The Result Set
            While (Reader.Read())
               Console.WriteLine(Reader("FirstName").PadLeft(9) & _
                  ControlChars.Tab & Reader(1))
            End While

        Catch ex As Exception
            Console.WriteLine("Error: {0}", ex)

        Finally
            'Close Connection
            Reader.Close()
            Conn.Close()

        End Try

    End Sub
End Module
```

2. Make this project the startup by right-clicking the project name in Solution Explorer and then clicking Set As StartUp Project.

3. Set the project's startup object to `OdbcProvider`, and then run the application with Ctrl+F5. A console prompt window appears, as shown in Figure 4-18.

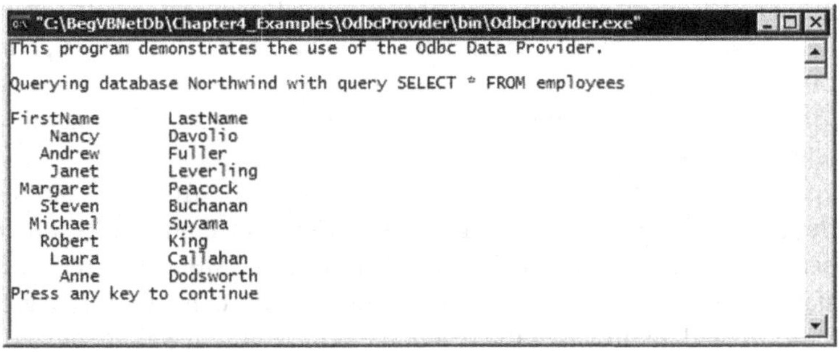

```
"C:\BegVBNetDb\Chapter4_Examples\OdbcProvider\bin\OdbcProvider.exe"
This program demonstrates the use of the Odbc Data Provider.

Querying database Northwind with query SELECT * FROM employees

FirstName       LastName
    Nancy       Davolio
   Andrew       Fuller
    Janet       Leverling
 Margaret       Peacock
   Steven       Buchanan
  Michael       Suyama
   Robert       King
    Laura       Callahan
     Anne       Dodsworth
Press any key to continue
```

Figure 4-18. *Running the* `OdbcProvider` *application*

How It Works

This was easy! You simply changed *Sql* to *Odbc* in the namespace and class names (and, of course, the output header), just as you did to modify the program to work with OLE DB. The biggest change, and the only one really deserving attention, was to the connection string.

```
' Set up connection string
Dim ConnString As String = "dsn=NorthwindOdbc"
```

The ODBC connection string isn't limited only to the DSN, but it doesn't allow blanks or newlines anywhere in the string.

■ **Tip** Each data provider has its own rules regarding both the parameters and syntax of its connection string. Consult the documentation for the provider you're using when coding connection strings.

Now that you've played with all the data providers that access SQL Server (the SQL Server CE data provider is beyond the scope of this book), let's make sure you clearly understand what a data provider is.

Data Providers Are APIs

The .NET Framework data providers, sophisticated as they are (and you'll learn plenty about exploiting their sophistication later), are simply APIs for accessing data sources, most often relational databases, in the .NET Framework. (ADO.NET is essentially one big API of which data providers are a major part.)

Newcomers to ADO.NET are often understandably confused by the Microsoft documentation. They read about `Connection`, `Command`, `DataReader`, and other ADO.NET objects, but they see no classes named `Connection`, `Command`, or `DataReader` in any of the ADO.NET namespaces. The reason is that data provider classes implement *interfaces* in the `System.Data` namespace. These interfaces define the data provider methods of the ADO.NET API.

The key concept is simple. A data provider, such as `System.Data.SqlClient`, consists of classes whose methods provide a uniform way of accessing a specific kind of data source. In this chapter you used three different data providers (SQL Server, OLE DB, and ODBC) to access the same MSDE database. The only real difference in the code was the connection string. Except for choosing the appropriate data provider, the rest of the programming was effectively the same. This is true of all ADO.NET facilities, whatever kind of data source you need to access.

The SQL Server data provider is optimized to access SQL Server and can't be used for any other RDBMS. The OLE DB data provider can access any OLE DB data source—and you used it without knowing anything about OLE DB (a major study in itself)! The ODBC data provider lets you use an even older data access technology, again without knowing anything about it. Working at such an abstract level enabled you to do a lot more, a lot more quickly, than you could have otherwise.

ADO.NET isn't just an efficient data access technology but is also an elegant one. Data providers are only one aspect of it. The art of ADO.NET programming is founded more on conceptualizing than on coding. First get a clear idea of what ADO.NET offers, and then look for the right method in the right class to make the idea a reality.

Since conceptual clarity is so important, you can view (and refer to) connections, commands, data readers, and other ADO.NET components primarily as abstractions rather than merely objects used in database programs. If you concentrate on concepts, learning when and how to use relevant objects and methods will be easy.

Summary

In this chapter, you saw why ADO.NET was developed and how it supersedes other data access technologies in the .NET Framework. We gave an overview of its architecture and then focused on one of its core components, the data provider. You built three simple examples to practice basic data provider use and experience the uniform way data access code is written, regardless of the data provider. Finally, we offered the opinion that conceptual clarity is the key to understanding and using both data providers and the rest of the ADO.NET API.

CHAPTER 5

Creating Connections

Before you can do anything useful with a database, you need to establish a *session* with the database server. You do this with an object called a *connection*, which is an instance of a class that implements the `System.Data.IDbConnection` interface for a specific data provider. In this chapter, you'll use various data providers to establish connections and look at problems that may arise and how to solve them.

By the end of this chapter, you'll learn the following:

- How to use connections
- How to specify connection strings
- How to use the most essential connection methods and properties
- How to solve common connection problems

If it makes it easier, think of the computer talking to the database by telephone. To start the conversation, the computer must first dial the right database. (The phone number is the database connection string, and the data provider is the right network.) Once the database has picked up the phone, the connection has been established. It's this connection that the `Connection` classes in this chapter model. When an application asks for information, it speaks in SQL commands, which we've mentioned before and are covered in more detail in the next chapter.

That said, back to connections.

Introducing the Data Provider Connection Classes

As you learned in Chapter 4, each data provider has its own namespace. Each has a connection class that implements the `System.Data.IDbConnection` interface. Table 5-1 summarizes the data providers supplied by Microsoft.

Table 5-1. *Data Provider Namespaces and Connection Classes*

Data Provider	Namespace	Connection Class
ODBC	`System.Data.Odbc`	`OdbcConnection`
OLE DB	`System.Data.OleDb`	`OleDbConnection`
Oracle	`System.Data.OracleClient`	`OracleConnection`
SQL Server	`System.Data.SqlClient`	`SqlConnection`
SQL Server CE	`System.Data.SqlServerCe`	`SqlCeConnection`

As you can see, the names follow a convention, using *Connection* prefixed by an identifier for the data provider. Since all connection classes implement `System.Data.IDbConnection`, the use of each one is similar. Each has additional members that provide methods specific to a particular database. You used connections in Chapter 4. Let's take a closer look at one of them: `SqlConnection` in the namespace `System.Data.SqlClient`.

Connecting to MSDE with SqlConnection

In this example, you'll connect to the MSDE `Northwind` database.

Try It Out: Using SqlConnection

Follow these steps:

1. Create a new solution named `Chapter5_Examples`.
2. Add a VB.NET console application named `Connection_Sql`. Rename the `Module1.vb` file to `Connection_Sql.vb`, and replace the generated code with the code in Listing 5-1.

Listing 5-1. *Connection_Sql*

```
Imports System
Imports System.Data
Imports System.Data.SqlClient

Module Connection_Sql

   Sub Main()
      'Connection string
      Dim connString As String = "server=(local)\netsdk; " & _
         "integrated security=true;"

      'Create connection
      Dim conn As New SqlConnection(connString)
```

```
         Try
            ' Open Connection
            conn.Open()
            Console.WriteLine("Connection Opened")
         Catch ex As SqlException
            ' Display error
            Console.WriteLine("Error: " & ex.ToString())
         Finally
            ' Close Connection
            conn.Close()
            Console.WriteLine("Connection Closed")
         End Try
      End Sub
   End Module
```

3. Set `Connection_Sql` to be the startup object, and then run it with Ctrl+F5. If the connection is successful, you'll see the output in Figure 5-1.

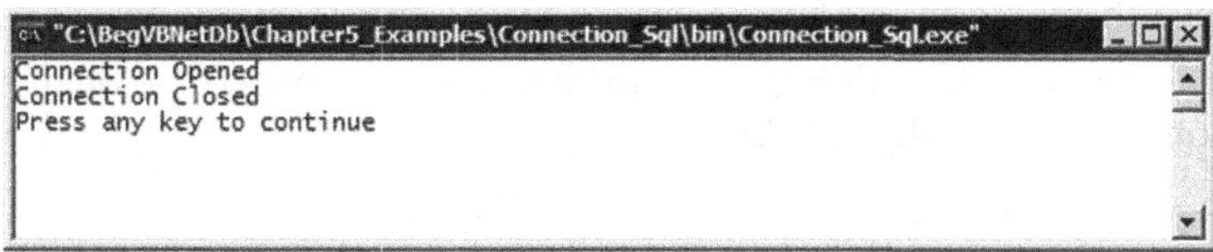

Figure 5-1. *Connecting to SQL Server*

If the connection failed, you'll see an error message much like in Figure 5-2. (You can get this by shutting down MSDE first, with `net stop mssql$netsdk` entered at a command prompt.)

```
"C:\BegVBNetDb\Chapter5_Examples\Connection_Sql\bin\Connection_Sql.exe"
Error: System.Data.SqlClient.SqlException: SQL Server does not exist or access d
enied.
   at System.Data.SqlClient.ConnectionPool.GetConnection(Boolean& isInTransactio
n)
   at System.Data.SqlClient.SqlConnectionPoolManager.GetPooledConnection(SqlConn
ectionString options, Boolean& isInTransaction)
   at System.Data.SqlClient.SqlConnection.Open()
   at Connection_Sql.Connection_Sql.Main() in C:\BegVBNetDb\Chapter5_Examples\Co
nnection_Sql\Connection_Sql.vb:line 17
Connection Closed
Press any key to continue
```

Figure 5-2. *Failed connection attempt*

Bear in mind that connections often fail for reasons having nothing to do with your code. It may be because a server isn't started, a password is wrong, or some other configuration problem exists. You'll soon look at common problems in establishing database connections.

How It Works

Let's examine the code in Listing 5-1 to understand the steps in the connection process. First, you specify the ADO.NET and the SQL Server data provider namespaces, so you can use the simple names of their members.

```
Imports System
Imports System.Data
Imports System.Data.SqlClient
```

Next, you declare the module and entry point (`Main` method) for the application.

```
Module Connection_Sql

   Sub Main()
```

Because this example is so small, you do all of your work in the `Main` method; let's look at it line by line.

The first thing you do is to create a *connection string*. A connection string consists of parameters—in other words, `key=value` pairs separated by semicolons—that specify connection information. Although some parameters are valid for all data providers, each data provider has specific parameters it will accept, so it's important to know what parameters are valid in a connection string for the data provider you're using.

```
'Connection string
Dim connString As String = "server=(local)\netsdk; " & _
   "integrated security=true;"
```

Next you create a connection (a `SqlConnection` object), passing it the connection string. This doesn't create a database session. It simply creates the object you'll use later to open a session.

```
'Create connection
Dim conn As New SqlConnection(connString)
```

Let's briefly examine each of the connection string parameters in this example. The server parameter specifies the SQL Server instance to which you want to connect.

```
server = (local)\netsdk;
```

■ **Tip** If you installed the `(local)\VSdotNET` instance of MSDE that comes with Visual Studio .NET, then you should use that name in the server clause instead.

The next clause indicates that you should use Windows Authentication to log into SQL Server.

```
integrated security = true;
```

You could alternatively use sspi instead of true, as they both have the same effect. Other parameters are available. You'll use one later to specify the database to which you want to connect.

Now you have a connection, but you still need to establish a session with the database by calling the Open method on the connection. If the attempt to open a session fails, an exception will be thrown, so you use a try statement to enable exception handling. You display a message after calling Open, but this line will be executed only if the connection was successfully opened.

```
Try
   ' Open Connection
   conn.Open()
   Console.WriteLine("Connection Opened")
```

At this stage in the code, you'd normally issue a query or perform some other database operation over the open connection. However we save that for later chapters and concentrate here on just connecting.

Next comes an exception handler in case the Open fails.

```
Catch ex As SqlException
   ' Display error
   Console.WriteLine("Error: " & ex.ToString())
```

Each data provider has a specific exception class for its error handling; SqlException is the class for the SQL Server data provider. Specific information about database errors is available from the exception, but here you're just displaying its raw contents.

When you're finished with the database, you call Close to terminate the session and then print a message to show that Close was called.

```
      Finally
         ' Close Connection
         conn.Close()
         Console.WriteLine("Connection Closed")
      End Try
   End Sub
End Module
```

You call Close within the Finally block to ensure it *always* gets called.

■ **Note** Establishing connections (database sessions) is relatively expensive. They use resources on both the client and the server. Although connections may eventually get closed, through garbage collection or by timing out, leaving one open when it's no longer needed is a bad practice. Too many open connections can slow a server down or prevent new connections from being made.

Note that you can call Close on a closed connection, and no exception will be thrown. So, your message would have been displayed if the connection had been closed earlier or even if it had never been opened. See Figure 5-2, where the connection failed but the close message was still displayed.

In one typical case, multiple calls to both Open and Close make sense. ADO.NET supports offline processing of data, even when the connection to the data provider has been closed. This pattern looks like this:

```
Try
   conn.Open()
   '
   ' Online processing here (e.g. queries) here
   '
   conn.Close()
   '
   ' offline processing here
   '
   conn.Open()  ' Reopen connection
   '
   ' Online processing(e.g., INSERT/UPDATE/DELETE) here
   '
   conn.Close() ' Reclose connection
Finally
   ' Close connection
   conn.Close()
End Try
```

The Finally block still calls Close, calling it unnecessarily if no exceptions are encountered, but this isn't a problem or expensive, and it ensures the connection will be closed. Although many programmers hold connections open until program termination, this is usually wasteful in terms of server resources. With *connection pooling*, opening and closing a connection as needed is actually more efficient than opening it once and for all.

That's it! You're finished with the first connection example. Since, however, you saw a couple possible errors, let's look at typical causes of these errors.

Debugging Connections to SQL Server

Writing the VB .NET code to use a connection is usually the easy part of getting a connection to work. Problems often lie not in the code but rather in a mismatch in the connection parameters between the client (your VB .NET program) and the database server. All appropriate connection parameters must be used and must have correct values. Even experienced database professionals often have problems getting a connection to work the first time.

More parameters are available than the ones shown here, but you get the idea. A corollary of Murphy's law applies to connections: If several things could go wrong, at least one of them will. Your goal is to check both sides of the connection to make sure all your assumptions are correct and that everything the client program specifies is matched correctly on the server.

Often the solution is on the server side. If the SQL Server instance isn't running, then the client will be trying to connect to a server that doesn't exist. If the user name and password on the client don't match the name and password of a user authorized to access the SQL Server database, then the connection will be rejected. If the database requested in the connection doesn't exist, an error will occur. If the client's network information doesn't match the server's, then the server may not receive the client's connection request, or the server response may not reach the client.

For connection problems, using the debugger to locate the line of code where the error occurs usually doesn't help—the problem almost always occurs on the call to the `Open` method. The question is, why? You need to look at the error message.

A typical error is as follows:

```
Unhandled Exception: System.ArgumentException:
   Unknown connection option in connection string: user.
```

The most likely cause for this is a simple typographical error in one of the clauses in your connection string. Make sure you've entered what you really meant to enter.

Figure 5-3 shows probably the most common message when trying to connect to SQL Server. It's the same one you saw in Figure 5-2.

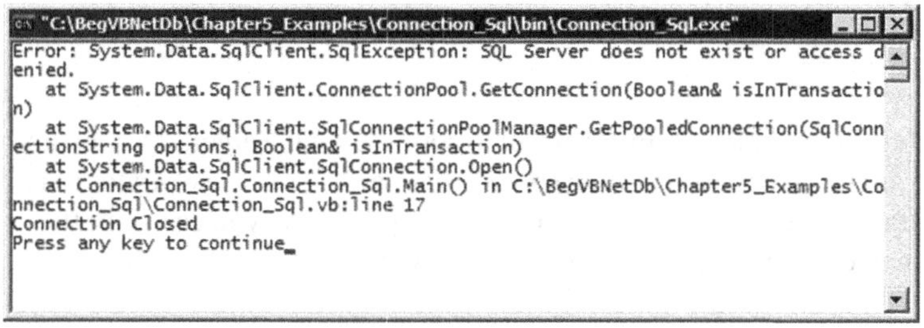

```
"C:\BegVBNetDb\Chapter5_Examples\Connection_Sql\bin\Connection_Sql.exe"
Error: System.Data.SqlClient.SqlException: SQL Server does not exist or access d
enied.
   at System.Data.SqlClient.ConnectionPool.GetConnection(Boolean& isInTransactio
n)
   at System.Data.SqlClient.SqlConnectionPoolManager.GetPooledConnection(SqlConn
ectionString options, Boolean& isInTransaction)
   at System.Data.SqlClient.SqlConnection.Open()
   at Connection_Sql.Connection_Sql.Main() in C:\BegVBNetDb\Chapter5_Examples\Co
nnection_Sql\Connection_Sql.vb:line 17
Connection Closed
Press any key to continue_
```

Figure 5-3. *Failed connection attempt*

In this case, most likely SQL Server isn't running. Restart MSDE (as explained in Chapter 1) with `net start mssql$netsdk`.

Other possible causes of this message are as follows:

- The SQL Server instance name is incorrect—you used `(local)\netsdk`, but your machine may use the `(local)\VSdotNET` instance instead. It's also possible that SQL Server was already installed as `(local)` with no instance name or is on another machine (see the next section); correct the instance name if this is the case.

- The MSDE program hasn't been installed—go back to Chapter 1 and follow the instructions there for installing MSDE.

- A security problem—your Windows login and password aren't valid on the server. This is unlikely to be the problem when talking to a `(local)` SQL Server instance, unless you installed MSDE under a different Windows login from the one you're using to write VB .NET programs.

- A hardware problem—again unlikely if you're trying to connect to a server on the same machine.

Setting Up Security and Passwords in SqlConnection

As you saw in the first chapter, you have two ways of logging into SQL Server. The first, preferred way is to use Windows integrated security, as you did in the first example. SQL Server uses your Windows login to access the database. Your Windows login must exist on the machine where SQL server is running, and your login must be authorized to access the SQL Server database or be a member of a user group that has that access.

If you don't include the `"Integrated Security = SSPI"` (or `"Integrated Security = True"` parameter in the connection string, the connection defaults to SQL Server security, which uses a separate login and password within SQL Server.

Using SQL Server Security

If you really did intend to use SQL Server security because that's how your company or department has set up access to your SQL Server (perhaps because some clients are non-Microsoft), then you need to specify a user name and password in the connection string, as shown here:

```
thisConnection.ConnectionString = _
  "server = (local)\netsdk;" & _
  "user id = sa;" & _
  "password = x1y2z3"
```

The `sa` user name is the default system administrator account for SQL Server. If a specific user has been set up, such as `george` or `payroll`, then specify that name. The password for `sa` is set when SQL Server is installed. If the user name you use has no password, you can omit the password clause entirely or specify an empty password, as follows:

```
password =;
```

However, a blank password is bad practice and should be avoided, even in a test environment.

Setting Connection String Parameters for SqlConnection

Table 5-2 summarizes the basic parameters for the SQL Server data provider connection string.

Table 5-2. *SQL Server Data Provider Connection String Parameters*

Name	Alias	Default Value	Allowed Values	Description
`Application Name`		`.NET SqlClient Data Provider`	Any string	Name of application
`AttachDBFileName`	`extended properties, Initial File Name`	None	Any path	Full path of an attachable database file
`Connect Timeout`	`Connection Timeout`	`15`	`0–32767`	Seconds to wait to connect

Table 5-2. *SQL Server Data Provider Connection String Parameters (Continued)*

Name	Alias	Default Value	Allowed Values	Description
`Data Source`	`Server, Address, Addr, Network Address`	None	Server name or network address	Name of the target SQL Server instance
`Encrypt`		`false`	`true`, `false`, `yes`, `no`	Specifies whether to use SSL encryption
`Initial Catalog`	`Database`	None	Any database that exists on server	Database name
`Integrated Security`	`Trusted_Connection`	`false`	`true, false, yes, no, sspi`	Specifies the authentication mode
`Network Library`	`Net`	`dbmssocn`	`dbnmpntw, dbmsrpcn, dbmsadsn, dbmsgnet, dbmslpcn, dbmsspxn, dbmssocn`	Network `.dll`
`Packet Size`		8192	Multiple of 512	Network packet size in bytes
`Password`	`PWD`	None	Any string	Password if not using Windows Authentication
`Persist Security Info`		`false`	`true`, `false`, `yes`, `no`	Specifies whether sensitive information should be passed back after connecting
`User ID`	`UID`		None	User name if not using Windows Authentication
`Workstation ID`		Local computer name	Any string	Workstation connecting to SQL Server

The Alias column in Table 5-2 gives alternate parameter names. For example, you can specify the server using any of the following:

```
data source = (local)\netsdk
server = (local)\netsdk
address = (local)\netsdk
addr = (local)\netsdk
network address = (local)\netsdk
```

Understanding Connection Pooling

One low-level detail that's worth noting—even though you shouldn't change it—is *connection pooling*. Recall that creating connections is expensive in terms of memory and time. With pooling, a closed connection isn't immediately destroyed but is kept in memory in a pool of unused connections. If a new connection request comes in that matches the properties of one of the unused connections in the pool, then the unused connection is used for the new database session.

Creating a totally new connection over the network can take seconds whereas reusing a pooled connection can happen in milliseconds; it's much faster to use pooled connections. The connection string has parameters that can change the size of the connection pool or even turn off connection pooling. The default values (for example, connection pooling is on by default) are appropriate for the vast majority of applications. See the SQL Server Books Online for details.

Improving Your Use of Connection Objects

The code in the first sample program was simple so you could concentrate on how connections work. Let's enhance it a bit.

Using the Connection String in the Connection Constructor

You created the connection and specified the connection string in separate steps. Since you always have to specify a connection string, you can use an overloaded version of the constructor that takes the connection string as an argument.

```
'Create connection
Dim conn As New SqlConnection( _
   "server=(local)\netsdk;integrated security=true;")
```

This constructor sets the `ConnectionString` property when creating the `SqlConnection` object.

Displaying Connection Information

Connections have several properties that provide information about the connection. Most of these properties are read-only, since their purpose is to display rather than set information. (You set connection values in the connection string.) These properties are often useful when debugging, to verify that the connection properties are what you expect them to be.

Here, we'll describe the connection properties common to most data providers. The complete list of properties and methods is available in the SQL Server Books Online. Later, you'll see some of the properties specific to other data providers.

Try It Out: Displaying Connection Information

Follow these steps:

1. Add a VB .NET console application named `Display`, and rename `Module1.vb` to `Display.vb`.

2. Replace the code in `Display.vb` with that in Listing 5-2.

Listing 5-2. *Display.vb*

```
Imports System
Imports System.Data
Imports System.Data.SqlClient

Module Display

   Sub Main()
      'Connection string
      Dim connString As String = "server=(local)\netsdk; " & _
         "integrated security=sspi;"

      'Create connection
      Dim conn As New SqlConnection(connString)

      Try
         ' Open Connection
         conn.Open()
         Console.WriteLine("Connection Opened")

         ' Display connection properties
         Console.WriteLine("Connection Properties")
         Console.WriteLine("- ConnectionString : {0}", _
            conn.ConnectionString)
         Console.WriteLine("- Database : {0}", _
            conn.Database)
         Console.WriteLine("- DataSource : {0}", _
            conn.DataSource)
         Console.WriteLine("- ServerVersion : {0}", _
            conn.ServerVersion)
         Console.WriteLine("- State : {0}", conn.State)
         Console.WriteLine("- WorkstationId : {0}", _
            conn.WorkstationId)

      Catch ex As SqlException
         ' Display error
         Console.WriteLine("Error: " & ex.ToString())
      Finally
         ' Close Connection
         conn.Close()
         Console.WriteLine("Connection Closed")
      End Try
   End Sub
End Module
```

3. Make it the startup project, set `Display` to be the startup object, and then run it with Ctrl+F5. If the connection is successful, you'll see output like that shown in Figure 5-4.

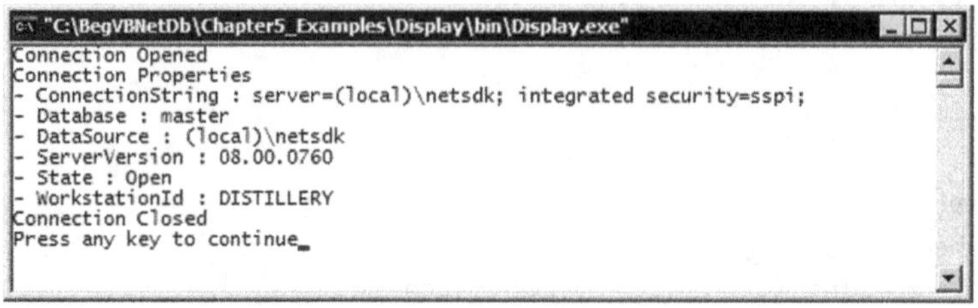

```
"C:\BegVBNetDb\Chapter5_Examples\Display\bin\Display.exe"
Connection Opened
Connection Properties
- ConnectionString : server=(local)\netsdk; integrated security=sspi;
- Database : master
- DataSource : (local)\netsdk
- ServerVersion : 08.00.0760
- State : Open
- WorkstationId : DISTILLERY
Connection Closed
Press any key to continue_
```

Figure 5-4. *Displaying SQL Server connection information*

How It Works

The `ConnectionString` property can be both read and written. Here you display it.

```
Console.WriteLine("- ConnectionString : {0}", _
   conn.ConnectionString)
```

You'll see the value you assigned to it, including the whitespace, in the verbatim string.

What's the point? Well, it's handy when debugging connections to verify that the connection string really contains the values you thought you assigned. For example, if you're trying out different connection options, you may have different connection string parameters in the program. You may have commented out one intending to use it later but forgot about it. Displaying the `ConnectionString` property helps to see that a parameter is missing.

The next statement displays the `Database` property. Since each SQL Server instance has several databases, this property shows which one you're initially using when you connect.

```
Console.WriteLine("- Database : {0}", _
   conn.Database)
```

In this program, it displays the following, since you didn't specify a database in the connection string and were connected to the default database, which for this MSDE instance is `master`:

```
Database: master
```

If you wanted to connect to the `Northwind` database, then you'd need to specify the `Database` parameter. For example:

```
'Connection string
Dim connString As String = _
   "server=(local)\netsdk;" & _
   "integrated security=sspi;" & _
   "database=Northwind;"
```

Again, this is a handy property to display for debugging purposes. If you get an error saying that a particular table doesn't exist, often the problem isn't that the table doesn't exist but that it isn't in the database to which you're connected. Displaying the `Database` property helps you to find that kind of error quickly.

TIP If you specify a database in the connection string that doesn't exist on the server, you may see the error: "System.Data.SqlClient.SqlException: Cannot open database requested in login 'Northwind'. Login fails." This can happen if you didn't run the script to create the Northwind sample database when installing MSDE.

You can change the database currently used on a connection with the ChangeDatabase method. You'll see a good use for that method in Chapter 6.

The next statement displays the DataSource property, which gives the server instance name for SQL Server database connections.

```
Console.WriteLine("- DataSource : {0}", _
   conn.DataSource)
```

In this program it displays the same SQL Server instance name you've used in all the examples so far.

```
DataSource: (local)\netsdk
```

The utility of this again is mainly for debugging purposes.

The ServerVersion property displays the server version information.

```
Console.WriteLine("- ServerVersion : {0}", _
   conn.ServerVersion)
```

It shows the version of MSDE you installed in Chapter 1. (Your version may differ.)

```
ServerVersion: 08.00.0760
```

The version number is useful for debugging. This information actually comes from the server, so it indicates the connection is working.

The State property indicates whether the connection is open or closed.

```
Console.WriteLine("- State : {0}", conn.State)
```

Since you display this property after the Open call, it shows that the connection is open.

```
State: Open
```

You've been displaying your own message that the connection is open, but this property contains the current state. If the connection is closed, then the State property would be Closed.

The WorkstationId property is specific to SQL Server but is handy for debugging, so it deserves mention.

```
Console.WriteLine("- WorkstationId : {0}", _
   conn.WorkstationId)
```

The workstation ID is a string identifying the client computer. It defaults to the computer name. Our computer is named DISTILLERY, but yours, of course, will be different.

```
WorkstationId: DISTILLERY
```

What makes this useful for debugging is that the SQL Server tools on the server can display which workstation ID issued a particular command. If you don't know which machine is causing a problem, you can modify your programs to display the `WorkstationId` property and compare them to the workstation IDs displayed on the server.

You can also set this property with the workstation ID connection string parameter as follows, so if you want all the workstations in, say, Building B to show that information on the server, you can indicate that in the program:

```
'Connection string
Dim connString As String = _
   "server=(local)\netsdk; " & _
   "integrated security=sspi;" & _
   "workstation id = Building B;"
```

That completes the discussion of the fundamentals of connecting to SQL Server. Now let's look at connecting with other data providers.

Connecting to Microsoft Access with OleDbConnection

As you saw in the previous chapter, you use the OLE DB data provider to work with any OLE DB–compatible data store. Microsoft provides OLE DB data providers for SQL Server, Microsoft Access (Jet), Oracle, and a variety of other database and data file formats.

If a native data provider is available for a particular database or file format (such as the `SqlClient` data provider for SQL Server), then it's generally better to use it rather than the generic OLE DB data provider. This is because OLE DB introduces an extra layer of indirection between the VB .NET program and the data source.

One common database format for which no native data provider exists is the Microsoft Access database (`.mdb` file) format, also known as the Jet database engine format, so in this case you need to use the OLE DB (or the ODBC) data provider.

Try It Out: Connecting to Access with the OLE DB Data Provider

Follow these steps:

1. Copy the Microsoft Access `Northwind.mdb` file to your development directory (use `c:\begvbnetdb`), or note the full path name to the file for use in the connection string. By default, you'll find it at `C:\Program Files\Microsoft Office\OFFICE11\SAMPLES\northwind.mdb`.

2. Create a new VB.NET console application named `AccessConnect`, and rename `Module1.vb` to `AccessConnect.vb`.

3. Replace the code in `AccessConnect.vb` with that in Listing 5-3. This is basically the same code as `Display.vb`, with the changed code in bold.

Listing 5-3. *AccessConnect.vb*

```
Imports System
Imports System.Data
Imports System.Data.OleDb

Module AccessConnect

   Sub Main()
      'Connection string
      Dim connString As String = _
         "provider= microsoft.jet.oledb.4.0; " & _
         "data source=c:\begvbnetdb\northwind.mdb;"

      'Create connection
      Dim conn As New OleDbConnection(connString)

      Try
         ' Open Connection
         conn.Open()
         Console.WriteLine("Connection Opened")

         ' Display connection properties
         Console.WriteLine("Connection Properties")
         Console.WriteLine("- ConnectionString : {0}", _
            conn.ConnectionString)
         Console.WriteLine("- Database : {0}", _
            conn.Database)
         Console.WriteLine("- DataSource : {0}", _
            conn.DataSource)
         Console.WriteLine("- ServerVersion : {0}", _
            conn.ServerVersion)
         Console.WriteLine("- State : {0}", conn.State)

      Catch ex As OleDbException
         ' Display error
         Console.WriteLine("Error: " & ex.ToString())
      Finally
         ' Close Connection
         conn.Close()
         Console.WriteLine("Connection Closed")
      End Try
   End Sub
End Module
```

4. Make it the startup project, set AccessConnect to be the startup object, and then run it with Ctrl+F5. If the connection is successful, you'll see output like that shown in Figure 5-5.

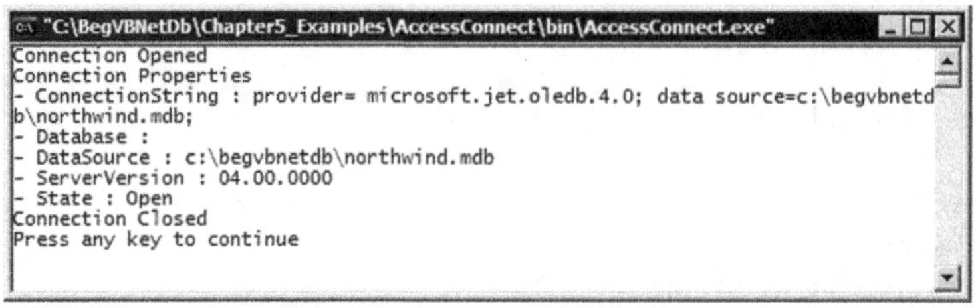

```
"C:\BegVBNetDb\Chapter5_Examples\AccessConnect\bin\AccessConnect.exe"
Connection Opened
Connection Properties
- ConnectionString : provider= microsoft.jet.oledb.4.0; data source=c:\begvbnetd
b\northwind.mdb;
- Database :
- DataSource : c:\begvbnetdb\northwind.mdb
- ServerVersion : 04.00.0000
- State : Open
Connection Closed
Press any key to continue
```

Figure 5-5. *Displaying Access connection information*

How It Works

We'll discuss only the differences between this example and the previous ones.

The first step is to reference the OLE DB data provider namespace, System.Data.OleDb.

```
Imports System.Data.OleDb
```

Next, you specify the connection string. Instead of the server parameter, you use Provider and Data Source. You can't use the Integrated Security parameter with OLE DB.

```
'Connection string
Dim connString As String = _
   "provider= microsoft.jet.oledb.4.0; " & _
   "data source=c:\begvbnetdb\northwind.mdb;"
```

Next, you create an OleDbConnection object instead of a SqlConnection object.

```
'Create connection
Dim conn As New OleDbConnection(connString)
```

Note that you omitted the WorkstationId property in your display. The OLE DB data provider doesn't support it.

This is the pattern for accessing any data source with any .NET data provider. Specify the connection string with parameters specific to the data provider. Use the appropriate objects from the data provider namespace. Use only the properties and methods provided by that data provider.

Now let's access some other major RDBMSs. All can be used with the OLE DB and ODBC data providers, but all also have their own native data providers, which you'll use. You'll start with Oracle, since Microsoft supplies its own .NET data provider for Oracle as part of the .NET Framework.

Connecting to Oracle

Both Microsoft and Oracle supply a .NET Framework data provider for Oracle. You'll use `System.Data.OracleClient`, the Microsoft-supplied data provider.

■ **Tip** You must download and install the .NET data provider for Oracle before you can run this example. You can find the installer at `http://www.microsoft.com/downloads/release.asp?ReleaseID=40032` or at `http://www.oracle.com/technology/software/tech/windows/odpnet/index.html`. The Microsoft data provider for Oracle isn't part of the .NET Framework core assembly file, so you must explicitly reference it. Also, Oracle supplies different data providers for Oracle 9*i* and Oracle 10*g*. They're backward, but not forward, compatible and, of course, must be explicitly referenced.

Try It Out: Connecting to Oracle with System.Data.OracleClient

Follow these steps:

1. Add a VB .NET console application named `OracleConnect`, and rename the `Module1.vb` file to `OracleConnect.vb`.

2. Replace the code in `OracleConnect.vb` with that in Listing 5-4. The code in bold shows the changes from the code in Listing 5-3. Change the connection string parameter values to reflect your server name, user ID, and password.

Listing 5-4. *OracleConnect.vb*

```
Imports System
Imports System.Data
Imports System.Data.OracleClient

Module OracleConnect

   Sub Main()
      'Connection string
      Dim connString As String = _
         "server = o92; " & _
         "uid = scott;" & _
         "password = tiger;"

      'Create connection
      Dim conn As New OracleConnection(connString)
```

```
        Try
            ' Open Connection
            conn.Open()
            Console.WriteLine("Connection Opened")

            ' Display connection properties
            Console.WriteLine("Connection Properties")
            Console.WriteLine("- ConnectionString : {0}", _
               conn.ConnectionString)
            Console.WriteLine("- ServerVersion : {0}", _
               conn.ServerVersion)
            Console.WriteLine("- State : {0}", conn.State)

        Catch ex As OracleException
            ' Display error
            Console.WriteLine("Error: " & ex.ToString())
        Finally
            ' Close Connection
            conn.Close()
            Console.WriteLine("Connection Closed")

        End Try
    End Sub
End Module
```

3. Add a reference to the Oracle data provider assembly (`System.Data.OracleClient.dll`) to the project. Right-click the References item. Click Add Reference.... Navigate to `System.Data.OracleClient.dll`, and double-click it. Click OK.

4. Make this the startup project and `OracleConnect` the startup object, and run it with Ctrl+F5. If the connection is successful, you'll see output like that shown in Figure 5-6.

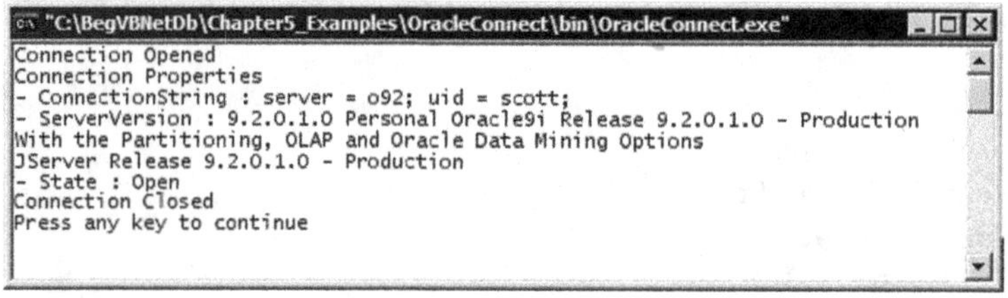

```
"C:\BegVBNetDb\Chapter5_Examples\OracleConnect\bin\OracleConnect.exe"
Connection Opened
Connection Properties
- ConnectionString : server = o92; uid = scott;
- ServerVersion : 9.2.0.1.0 Personal Oracle9i Release 9.2.0.1.0 - Production
With the Partitioning, OLAP and Oracle Data Mining Options
JServer Release 9.2.0.1.0 - Production
- State : Open
Connection Closed
Press any key to continue
```

Figure 5-6. *Connecting to Oracle with the `System.Data.OracleClient` data provider*

How It Works

Except for the connection string and use of `Oracle` as the type name prefix, this code is basically like the earlier examples.

Note that you omitted the `Database` and `WorkstationId` properties in the display. The `OracleClient` data provider doesn't support them.

■ **Tip** If you're working from the command line, use the compiler option `-r:System.Data.OracleClient.dll` when compiling this application to include the reference to the Oracle data provider rather than following step 3 of the previous example.

Connecting to DB2

IBM supplies a .NET Framework data provider for DB2 in namespace `IBM.Data.DB2`.

■ **Note** With version 8.2, DB2 includes the .NET Framework data provider, named `IBM.Data.DB2`—note the unconventional use of uppercase—in assembly file `IBM.Data.DB2.dll`. It's analogous to the SQL Server data provider but uses *DB2* instead of *Sql* as the prefix for type names. Like every data provider, it has some connection string parameters and methods of its own, but otherwise it operates exactly as you'd expect. Since `IBM.Data.DB2` isn't part of the .NET Framework Class Library, you need to explicitly add a reference for its assembly to your project.

Try It Out: Connecting to DB2 with IBM.Data.DB2

Follow these steps:

1. Add a VB .NET console application named `Db2Connect`, and rename the `Module1.vb` file to `Db2Connect.vb`.

2. Replace the code in `Db2Connect.vb` with that in Listing 5-5. The code in bold shows the changes from the code in Listing 5-4.

Listing 5-5. *Db2Connect.vb*

```
Imports System
Imports System.Data
Imports IBM.Data.DB2

Module Db2Connect

   Sub Main()
      'Connection string
      Dim connString As String = _
         "database = sample;"

      'Create connection
      Dim conn As New DB2Connection(connString)
```

```
        Try
            ' Open Connection
            conn.Open()
            Console.WriteLine("Connection Opened")

            ' Display connection properties
            Console.WriteLine("Connection Properties")
            Console.WriteLine("- ConnectionString : {0}", _
                conn.ConnectionString)
            Console.WriteLine("- Database : {0}", _
                conn.Database)
            Console.WriteLine("- ServerVersion : {0}", _
                conn.ServerVersion)
            Console.WriteLine("- State : {0}", conn.State)

        Catch ex As DB2Exception
            ' Display error
            Console.WriteLine("Error: " & ex.ToString())
        Finally
            ' Close Connection
            conn.Close()
            Console.WriteLine("Connection Closed")

        End Try

    End Sub
End Module
```

3. Add a reference to the DB2 data provider assembly (`IBM.Data.DB2.dll`) to the project. Right-click the References item. Click Add Reference.... Navigate to `IBM.Data.DB2.dll`, and double-click it. Click OK.

4. Make this the startup project and `Db2Connect` the startup object, and run it with Ctrl+F5. If the connection is successful, you'll see output like that shown in Figure 5-7.

```
"C:\BegVBNetDb\Chapter5_Examples\Db2Connect\bin\Db2Connect.exe"
Connection Opened
Connection Properties
- ConnectionString : database = sample;
- Database : SAMPLE
- ServerVersion : 08.02.0000
- State : Open
Connection Closed
Press any key to continue
```

Figure 5-7. *Connecting to DB2 with the `IBM.Data.DB2` data provider*

How It Works

Except for the connection string and use of `DB2` as the type name prefix, this code is just like the earlier examples.

Note that you omitted the `WorkstationId` property in the display. The `IBM.Data.DB2` data provider doesn't support it.

■ **Tip** From the command line, you used the compiler option (note the quotes) `-r:"c:\program files\ibm\sqllib\bin\netf11\ibm.data.db2.dll"` to include the DB2 data provider when compiling your application. Your path may differ depending on where DB2 was installed.

Connecting to MySQL

MySQL supplies a .NET Framework data provider for its RDBMS in the namespace `MySql.Data.MySqlClient`.

■ **Note** The MySQL data provider is an open-source product that you can download from `http://dev.mysql.com/downloads/connector/net/1.0.html`. It's analogous to the SQL Server data provider but uses *MySql* instead of *Sql* as the prefix for type names. Like every data provider, it has some connection string parameters and methods of its own, but otherwise it operates as you'd expect. `MySql.Data.MySqlClient` isn't part of the .NET Framework Class Library, so you need to explicitly add a reference for its assembly to your project.

Try It Out: Connecting to MySql with MySql.Data.MySqlClient

Follow these steps:

1. Add a VB .NET console application named `MySqlConnect`, and rename the `Module1.vb` file to `MySqlConnect.vb`.

2. Replace the code in `MySqlConnect.vb` with that in Listing 5-6, changing the `user id` and `password` parameter values appropriately. The code in bold shows the changes from the code in Listing 5-5.

Listing 5-6. *MySqlConnect.cs*

```
Imports System
Imports System.Data
Imports MySql.Data.MySqlClient

Module MySqlConnect

   Sub Main()
      'Connection string
      Dim connString As String = _
         "Database=Test;" & _
         "Data Source=localhost;" & _
         "User Id=root;" & _
         "Password=secpas"

      'Create connection
      Dim conn As New MySqlConnection(connString)

      Try
         ' Open Connection
         conn.Open()
         Console.WriteLine("Connection Opened")

         ' Display connection properties
         Console.WriteLine("Connection Properties")
         Console.WriteLine("- ConnectionString : {0}", _
            conn.ConnectionString)
         Console.WriteLine("- Database : {0}", _
            conn.Database)
         Console.WriteLine("- DataSource : {0}", _
            conn.DataSource)
         Console.WriteLine("- ServerVersion : {0}", _
            conn.ServerVersion)
         Console.WriteLine("- State : {0}", conn.State)

      Catch ex As MySqlException
         ' Display error
         Console.WriteLine("Error: " & ex.ToString())
      Finally
         ' Close Connection
         conn.Close()
         Console.WriteLine("Connection Closed")
      End Try
   End Sub
End Module
```

3. Add a reference to the MySQL data provider assembly (`MySql.Data.dll`) to the project. Right-click the References item. Click Add Reference.... Then click Browse..., navigate to `MySql.Data.dll`, and then double-click it. Click OK.

4. Make this the startup project and `MySqlConnect` the startup object, and run it with Ctrl+F5. If the connection is successful, you'll see output like that shown in Figure 5-8.

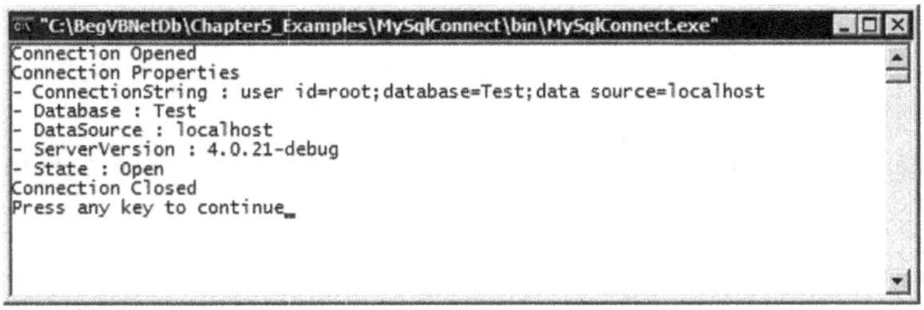

```
"C:\BegVBNetDb\Chapter5_Examples\MySqlConnect\bin\MySqlConnect.exe"
Connection Opened
Connection Properties
- ConnectionString : user id=root;database=Test;data source=localhost
- Database : Test
- DataSource : localhost
- ServerVersion : 4.0.21-debug
- State : Open
Connection Closed
Press any key to continue
```

Figure 5-8. *Connecting to MySQL with the* `MySql.Data.MySqlClient` *data provider*

How It Works

Except for the connection string and use of `MySql` as the type name prefix, this code is just like the earlier examples.

Note that you omitted the `WorkstationId` property in the display. The `MySql.Data.MySqlClient` data provider doesn't support it.

■ **Tip** From the command line, you used the compiler option `-r:" C:\Program Files\MySQL AB\Connector .NET\bin\.NET 1.1"` (note the quotes and spaces). Your path may differ depending on where the data provider was installed.

Summary

In this chapter, you looked at connections using various data providers. You learned about connection strings and connection string parameters, and you saw how to open and close connections.

You examined different security options for SQL Server and other data sources and also saw how to display information about the connection after it's established, using the properties of a connection.

You saw how to handle exceptions generated by connection errors and learned to close the connection in the `finally` block of the exception handler to ensure that the connection is closed in all cases.

Finally, you looked at specific examples of connecting to different data sources, including the following:

- SQL Server
- Microsoft Access
- Oracle
- DB2
- MySQL

In the next chapter, you'll look at ADO.NET *commands* and see how to use them to access data.

CHAPTER 6

Introducing Commands

Once you've established a connection to the database, you want to start interacting with it and getting it doing something useful for you. You may need to add, update, or delete some data, or perhaps modify the database in some other way. Whatever the task, it will inevitably involve a *command*.

In this chapter, we'll explain commands, which are objects that encapsulate the SQL for the action you want to perform and that provide methods for submitting it to the database. Each data provider has a command class that implements the `System.Data.IDbCommand` interface.

In this chapter, you'll learn how to do the following:

- Create commands
- Associate commands with connections
- Use connection methods that apply to commands
- Use command properties and methods
- Set command text
- Execute commands
- Process command results
- Use commands with different data providers

We'll use the SQL Server data provider (`System.Data.SqlClient`) in most of our examples. Its command is named `SqlCommand`. Then, at the end of the chapter, we'll touch on using commands with other data providers.

So then, let's get started by learning how to create a command.

Creating a Command

You can create a command either using the `SqlCommand` constructor or using methods that create the object for you. Let's look at the first of these alternatives.

Try It Out: Creating a Command with a Constructor

In this example you'll create a SqlCommand object but not yet do anything with it.

1. Open Visual Studio .NET, and create a new blank solution called Chapter6_Examples.
2. Within the new solution, create a new VB .NET Console Application project named CommandExampleSql. Rename Module1.vb to CommandExampleSql.vb.
3. Replace the code in CommandExampleSql.vb with that in Listing 6-1.

Listing 6-1. *CommandExampleSql (First Version)*

```
Imports System
Imports System.Data
Imports System.Data.SqlClient

Module CommandExampleSql

   Sub Main()
      'Create Connection object
      Dim connString As String = "server=(local)\netsdk; " & _
         "integrated security=sspi;"
      Dim thisConnection As New SqlConnection(connString)

      'Create Command object
      Dim thisCommand As New SqlCommand
      Console.WriteLine("Command Created")

      Try
         ' Open Connection
         thisConnection.Open()
         Console.WriteLine("Connection Opened")

      Catch ex As SqlException
         ' Display error
         Console.WriteLine("Error: " & ex.ToString())
      Finally
         ' Close Connection
         thisConnection.Close()
         Console.WriteLine("Connection Closed")
      End Try
   End Sub
End Module
```

4. Set CommandExampleSql to be the program's startup object, and then run it without debugging (Ctrl+F5). You should see the output in Figure 6-1.

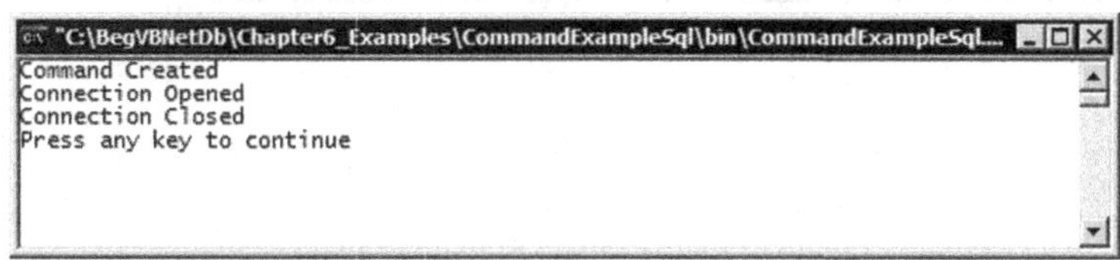

Figure 6-1. *CommandExampleSql (first version)*

How It Works

You create a SqlCommand object using the default constructor, and print a message indicating you've created it.

```
'Create Command object
Dim thisCommand As New SqlCommand
Console.WriteLine("Command Created")
```

In this example, the command is empty. It isn't associated with a connection, and it doesn't have its text (in other words, SQL) set. You can't do much with it here, so let's move on and look at how you can associate it with your connection.

Associating a Command with a Connection

For your commands to be executed against the database of your choice, each command must be associated with a connection to that particular database. You do this by setting the Connection property of the command, and in order to save resources, multiple commands can use the same connection. You have a couple of ways to set this association up, so let's try them in the sample program.

Try It Out: Setting the Connection Property

To set the connection property, follow these steps:

1. Add the following bold code to the Try block of Listing 6-1.

```
Try
   ' Open Connection
   thisConnection.Open()
   Console.WriteLine("Connection Opened")

   ' Connect Command To Connection
   thisCommand.Connection = thisConnection
   Console.WriteLine("Created Command On Connection")

Catch ex As SqlException
```

2. Run it (Ctrl+F5). You should see the output in Figure 6-2.

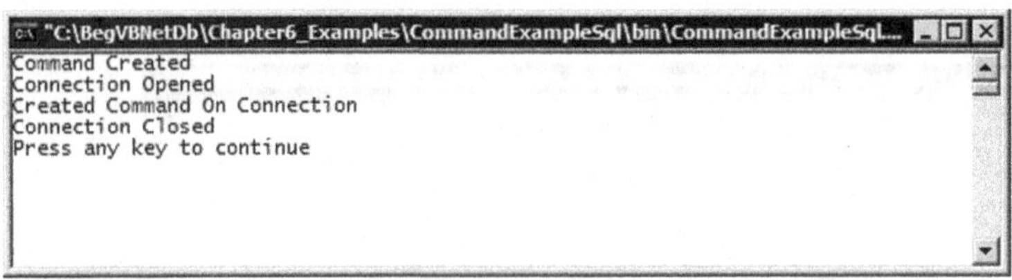

Figure 6-2. *CommandExampleSql (second version)*

How It Works

As you saw in the previous example, you start the code by creating the connection and command.

```
'Create Connection object
Dim connString As String = "server=(local)\netsdk; " & _
   "integrated security=sspi;"
Dim thisConnection As New SqlConnection(connString)

'Create Command object
Dim thisCommand As New SqlCommand
```

At this point, both the connection and command exist, but they aren't associated with each other in any way. It's only when you assign the connection to the command's `Connection` property that they become associated.

```
' Connect Command To Connection
thisCommand.Connection = thisConnection
```

The actual assignment occurs after the call to `thisConnection.Open` in this particular example, but you could have done it before calling `Open`; the connection doesn't have to be open for the `Connection` property of the command to be set.

As mentioned earlier, you have a second option for associating a connection with a command; calling the connection's `CreateCommand` method will return a new command with the `Connection` property set to that connection.

```
' create SqlCommand
Dim thisCommand As SqlCommand = thisConnection.CreateCommand()
```

This block of code is equivalent to the previous one; in both cases you end up with a command associated with your connection. It's also just one line of code, because you don't have to assign the `Connection` property.

You still need one more thing in order to use the command, and that's the text of the command. Let's see how to set that next.

Assigning Text to a Command

Every command has the property `CommandText`, which holds the SQL to execute. You can assign to this property directly or specify it when constructing the command. Let's look at these alternatives.

Try It Out: Setting the CommandText Property

To set the `CommandText` property, follow these steps:

1. Modify the `Try` block with the following bold code:

```
Try
   ' Open Connection
   thisConnection.Open()
   Console.WriteLine("Connection Opened")

    ' Connect Command To Connection
    thisCommand.Connection = thisConnection

    ' Associate SQL with Command
    thisCommand.CommandText = "SELECT COUNT(*) FROM Employees"
    Console.WriteLine("Ready to execute : {0}", _
       thisCommand.CommandText)

 Catch ex As SqlException
```

2. Run it (Ctrl+F5). You should see the output in Figure 6-3.

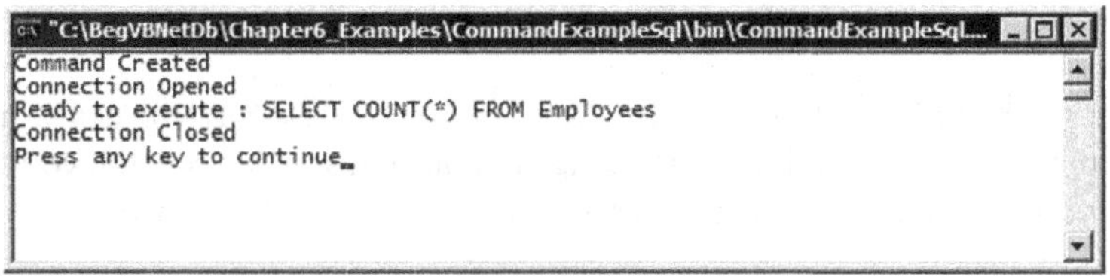

```
"C:\BegVBNetDb\Chapter6_Examples\CommandExampleSql\bin\CommandExampleSql...
Command Created
Connection Opened
Ready to execute : SELECT COUNT(*) FROM Employees
Connection Closed
Press any key to continue_
```

Figure 6-3. *CommandExampleSql (third version)*

How It Works

`CommandText` is just a string, so you can print it with `Console.WriteLine` just like any other string. The SQL, `"SELECT COUNT(*) FROM Employees"`, will return the number of employees in the `Northwind Employees` table when you're ready.

Note You must set both the `Connection` and the `CommandText` properties of a command before the command can be executed.

You can set both of these properties when you create the command with yet another variation of its constructor, as shown here:

```
'Create Command object
Dim thisCommand As New SqlCommand _
   ("SELECT COUNT(*) FROM Employees", thisConnection)
```

This is equivalent to the previous code that assigns each property explicitly. This is the most commonly used variation of the `SqlCommand` constructor, and you'll use this one for the rest of the chapter.

Executing Commands

Commands aren't much use unless you can execute them, so let's look at that now. Commands have several different methods for executing SQL. The differences between these methods depend on the results you expect from the SQL code. Queries return rows of data, but statements don't. You determine which method to use by considering what you expect to be returned (see Table 6-1).

Table 6-1. *Command Execution Methods*

If the Command Is Going to Return...	You Should Use...
Nothing. (It isn't a query.)	`ExecuteNonQuery`
A single value.	`ExecuteScalar`
Zero or more rows.	`ExecuteReader`
XML. (You'll learn more about this in Chapter 17.)	`ExecuteXmlReader`

The SQL code you just used in the example, `"SELECT COUNT(*) FROM Employees"`, should return one value, the number of employees. Looking at Table 6-1, you can see that you should use the `ExecuteScalar` method of `SqlCommand` to return this one result. Let's try it.

Try It Out: Using the ExecuteScalar Method

To use the `ExecuteScalar` method, follow these steps:

1. Add a new VB .NET Console Application project named `CommandExampleScalar` to your open solution, `Chapter6_Examples`. Rename `Module1.vb` to `CommandExampleScalar.vb`.

2. Replace the code in `CommandExampleScalar.vb` with the code in `CommandExampleSql.vb`.

3. Modify the code in `CommandExampleScalar.vb` as indicated by the bold lines in Listing 6-2.

Listing 6-2. *CommandExampleScalar*

```
Imports System
Imports System.Data
Imports System.Data.SqlClient

Module CommandExampleScalar

  Sub Main()
    'Create Connection object
    Dim thisConnection As New SqlConnection _
      ("server=(local)\netsdk;" & _
       "integrated security=sspi;" & _
       "database=northwind")

    'Create Command object
    Dim thisCommand As New SqlCommand _
      ("SELECT COUNT(*) FROM Employees", thisConnection)

    Try
      ' Open Connection
      thisConnection.Open()
      Console.WriteLine("Connection Opened")

      ' Execute Query
      Console.WriteLine("Number of Employees : {0}", _
        thisCommand.ExecuteScalar())

    Catch ex As SqlException
      ' Display error
      Console.WriteLine("Error: " & ex.ToString())
    Finally
      ' Close Connection
      thisConnection.Close()
      Console.WriteLine("Connection Closed")

    End Try

  End Sub
End Module
```

4. Make it the startup project, and then run it (Ctrl+F5). You should see the output in Figure 6-4.

```
"C:\BegVBNetDb\Chapter6_Examples\CommandExampleScalar\bin\CommandExampleS...
Connection Opened
Number of Employees : 9
Connection Closed
Press any key to continue
```

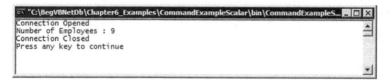

Figure 6-4. *CommandExampleScalar*

How It Works

ExecuteScalar takes the CommandText property and sends it to the database using the command's Connection property. It returns the result (9) as a single object, which you display with Console.WriteLine.

This is pretty simple to follow, but it's worth noting this really is simpler than you'll usually have it because Console.WriteLine takes any kind of object as its input. In fact, ExecuteScalar's return type is object, the superclass of all types in the .NET Framework, which makes perfect sense when you remember that a database can hold any type of data. So, if you want to assign the returned object to a variable of a specific type (Integer, for example), the object must be cast to the specific type. Now Visual Basic .NET will do this cast to an Integer for you, but if the types aren't compatible, the system will generate a runtime error that indicates an invalid cast, and you'll have to cast it explicitly.

The following is an example that demonstrates this idea. In it, you store the result from ExecuteScalar in the variable count, implicitly casting it to the specific type Integer.

```
Dim thisCommand As New SqlCommand _
   ("SELECT COUNT(*) FROM Employees", thisConnection
Dim count As Integer = thisCommand.ExecuteScalar
Console.WriteLine("Number of Employees : {0}", count)
```

If you're sure the type of the result will always be an Integer (a safe bet with COUNT(*)), then the previous code is safe. However, if you left the implicit cast in place and changed the CommandText of the command to the following:

```
SELECT FirstName FROM Employees WHERE LastName='Davolio'
```

then ExecuteScalar would return the string Nancy instead of an integer, and you'd get this exception:

```
Unhandled Exception: System.InvalidCastException:
Cast from string "Nancy" to type Integer is not valid.
```

because you can't cast a string to an Integer (unless of course the string contains just numbers, which someone's first name shouldn't contain).

Another problem may occur if a query actually returns multiple rows where you thought it would return only one; for example, what if there were multiple employees with the last name Davolio? In this case, ExecuteScalar just returns the first row of the result and ignores the rest. If you use ExecuteScalar, make sure you not only expect but actually get a single value returned.

Executing Commands with Multiple Results

For queries where you're expecting multiple rows and columns to be returned, use the command's ExecuteReader method.

ExecuteReader returns a data reader, an instance of the SqlDataReader class that you'll study in the next chapter. Data readers have methods that allow you to read successive rows in result sets and retrieve individual column values.

We'll leave the details of data readers for the next chapter, but for comparison's sake, we'll give a brief example here of using the ExecuteReader method to create a SqlDataReader from a command to display query results.

Try It Out: Using the ExecuteReader Method

To use the ExecuteReader method, follow these steps:

1. Add a new VB .NET Console Application project named CommandExampleReader to your solution, Chapter6_Examples. Rename Module1.vb to CommandExampleReader.vb.
2. Replace the code in CommandExampleReader.vb with the code in Listing 6-3.

Listing 6-3. *CommandExampleReader*

```
Imports System
Imports System.Data
Imports System.Data.SqlClient

Module CommandExampleReader

   Sub Main()
      'Create Connection object
      Dim thisConnection As New SqlConnection _
         ("server=(local)\netsdk;" & _
          "integrated security=sspi;" & _
          "database=northwind")

      'Create Command object
      Dim thisCommand As New SqlCommand _
         ("SELECT FirstName, LastName FROM Employees", _
          thisConnection)

      Try
         ' Open Connection
         thisConnection.Open()
         Console.WriteLine("Connection Opened")

         ' Execute Query
         Dim thisReader As SqlDataReader = thisCommand.ExecuteReader()
```

```
            While (thisReader.Read())
               Console.WriteLine("Employee: {0} {1}", _
                  thisReader.GetValue(0), thisReader.GetValue(1))
            End While

         Catch ex As SqlException
            ' Display error
            Console.WriteLine("Error: " & ex.ToString())
         Finally
            ' Close Connection
            thisConnection.Close()
            Console.WriteLine("Connection Closed")

         End Try
      End Sub
   End Module
```

3. Make it the startup project and CommandExampleReader the startup object, and then run it (Ctrl+F5). You should see the output in Figure 6-5, displaying the first and last names of all nine employees.

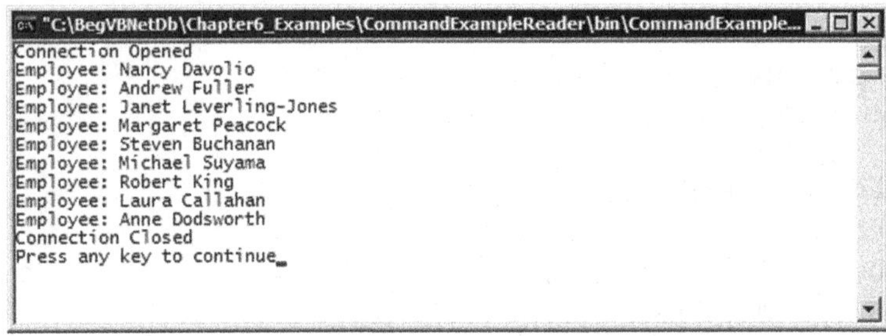

Figure 6-5. *CommandExampleReader*

How It Works

In this example you've used the ExecuteReader method to retrieve and then output the first and last names of all the employees in the Employees table. As with ExecuteScalar, ExecuteReader takes the CommandText property and sends it to the database using the connection from the Connection property.

When you used the ExecuteScalar method, you produced only a single scalar value. In contrast, using ExecuteReader returned a SqlDataReader object.

```
' Execute Query
Dim thisReader As SqlDataReader = thisCommand.ExecuteReader()

While (thisReader.Read())
   Console.WriteLine("Employee: {0} {1}", _
      thisReader.GetValue(0), thisReader.GetValue(1))
End While
```

The SqlDataReader object has a Read method that gets each row in turn and a GetValue method that gets the value of a column in the row. The particular column whose value it retrieves is given by the integer parameter indicating the index of the column. Note that GetValue uses a zero-based index, so the first column is column zero, the second column is column one, and so on. Since the query asked for two columns, FirstName and LastName, these are the columns numbered 0 and 1 in this query result.

Executing Statements

The ExecuteNonQuery method of the command executes SQL statements instead of queries. Let's try it.

Try It Out: Using the ExecuteNonQuery Method

To use the ExecuteNonQuery method, follow these steps:

1. Add a new VB .NET Console Application project named CommandExampleNonQuery to your solution, Chapter6_Examples. Rename Module1.vb to CommandExampleNonQuery.vb.
2. Replace the code in CommandExampleNonQuery.vb with the code in Listing 6-4.

Listing 6-4. *CommandExampleNonQuery*

```
Imports System
Imports System.Data
Imports System.Data.SqlClient

Module CommandExampleNonQuery

   Sub Main()
      'Create Connection object
      Dim thisConnection As New SqlConnection _
         ("server=(local)\netsdk;" & _
          "integrated security=sspi;" & _
          "database=northwind")

      'Create Command objects
      Dim scalarCommand As New SqlCommand _
         ("SELECT COUNT(*) FROM Employees", thisConnection)
      Dim nonqueryCommand As SqlCommand = _
         thisConnection.CreateCommand()

      Try
         ' Open Connection
         thisConnection.Open()
         Console.WriteLine("Connection Opened")
```

```
            ' Execute Scalar Query
            Console.WriteLine("Before INSERT, Number of Employees = {0}", _
               scalarCommand.ExecuteScalar())

            ' Set up and execute INSERT Command
            nonqueryCommand.CommandText = _
               "INSERT INTO Employees (Firstname,Lastname) " & _
               "VALUES ('Aaron','Aardvark')"
            Console.WriteLine("Executing {0}", nonqueryCommand.CommandText)
            Console.WriteLine("Number of rows affected : {0}", _
               nonqueryCommand.ExecuteNonQuery())

            ' Execute Scalar Query Again
            Console.WriteLine("After INSERT, Number of Employees = {0}", _
               scalarCommand.ExecuteScalar())

            ' Set up and execute DELETE Command
            nonqueryCommand.CommandText = _
               "DELETE FROM Employees WHERE " & _
               "Firstname='Aaron' AND Lastname='Aardvark'"
            Console.WriteLine("Executing {0}", nonqueryCommand.CommandText)
            Console.WriteLine("Number of rows affected : {0}", _
               nonqueryCommand.ExecuteNonQuery())

            ' Execute Scalar Query Again
            Console.WriteLine("After DELETE, Number of Employees = {0}", _
               scalarCommand.ExecuteScalar())

         Catch ex As SqlException
            ' Display error
            Console.WriteLine("Error: " & ex.ToString())
         Finally
            ' Close Connection
            thisConnection.Close()
            Console.WriteLine("Connection Closed")

         End Try
      End Sub
   End Module
```

3. Make it the startup project and `CommandExampleNonQuery` the startup object, and then run it (Ctrl+F5). You should see the output in Figure 6-6.

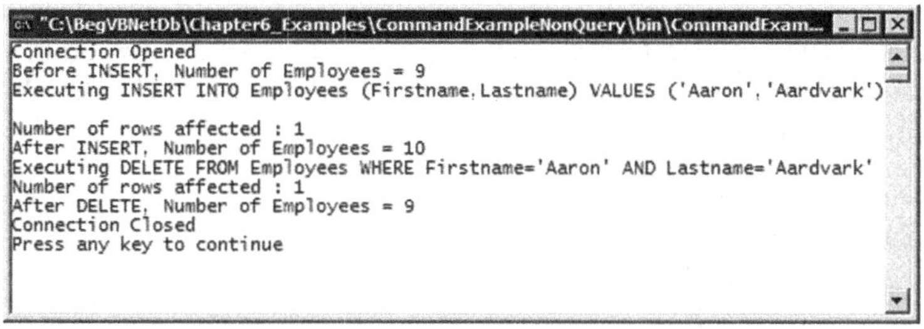

```
"C:\BegVBNetDb\Chapter6_Examples\CommandExampleNonQuery\bin\CommandExam...
Connection Opened
Before INSERT, Number of Employees = 9
Executing INSERT INTO Employees (Firstname,Lastname) VALUES ('Aaron','Aardvark')

Number of rows affected : 1
After INSERT, Number of Employees = 10
Executing DELETE FROM Employees WHERE Firstname='Aaron' AND Lastname='Aardvark'
Number of rows affected : 1
After DELETE, Number of Employees = 9
Connection Closed
Press any key to continue
```

Figure 6-6. *CommandExampleNonQuery*

How It Works

In this program you actually create and use two commands. The first is selectCommand, which encapsulates a SELECT COUNT(*) query to count the rows in the Employees table, as you did in an earlier example. You'll use this command several times to monitor the number of rows as you insert and delete employees. The command text of selectCommand stays constant, so you initialize the command text using the variant of the SqlCommand constructor that sets its CommandText and Connection properties at the time you create selectCommand itself.

```
'Create Command objects
Dim scalarCommand As New SqlCommand _
   ("SELECT COUNT(*) FROM Employees", thisConnection)
```

Next, you create another command named nonqueryCommand. This will be used for executing the INSERT and DELETE commands. Since the command text of this object won't remain constant (you'll change the text when you switch from INSERT to DELETE), you'll set the command text for these commands just before you execute the commands. The only property you'll initialize when constructing nonqueryCommand is the Connection property; the CreateCommand() method of the Connection object is an easy way to do this.

```
Dim nonqueryCommand As SqlCommand = _
   thisConnection.CreateCommand()
```

The first nonquery operation performed after you open the connection is an INSERT to add a row to the table. You're going to prove this has worked by keeping track of the number of rows in the table, so first you need to open the connection, and then you use selectCommand to display the number of rows in the table before you modify anything.

```
' Open Connection
thisConnection.Open()
Console.WriteLine("Connection Opened")

' Execute Scalar Query
Console.WriteLine("Before INSERT, Number of Employees = {0}", _
   scalarCommand.ExecuteScalar())
```

Note that you called ExecuteScalar to execute the query, using the command text and connection as initialized when selectCommand was created. Next you create the command text for the insert and assign it to the CommandText property of nonqueryCommand. Then display the text on the console.

```
' Set up and execute INSERT Command
nonqueryCommand.CommandText = _
   "INSERT INTO Employees (Firstname,Lastname) " & _
   "VALUES ('Aaron','Aardvark')"
Console.WriteLine("Executing {0}", nonqueryCommand.CommandText)
```

Note that you haven't executed the command yet. You do this in the next line with a call to ExecuteNonQuery.

```
Console.WriteLine("Number of rows affected : {0}", _
   nonqueryCommand.ExecuteNonQuery())
```

ExecuteNonQuery returns an Integer indicating how many rows were affected by the command. Since you want to display the number of affected rows, you put the call to ExecuteNonQuery within the call to Console.WriteLine so you don't have to store the result in a temporary variable but instead use it directly. Again you use the scalar command to display the number of rows, this time after the INSERT operation.

```
' Execute Scalar Query Again
Console.WriteLine("After INSERT, Number of Employees = {0}", _
   scalarCommand.ExecuteScalar())
```

Now you want to restore the table to its original state, so you need a DELETE statement to delete the employee you just inserted. You'll reuse nonqueryCommand and modify the CommandText property to hold a DELETE statement.

```
' Set up and execute DELETE Command
nonqueryCommand.CommandText = _
   "DELETE FROM Employees WHERE " & _
   "Firstname='Aaron' AND Lastname='Aardvark'"
Console.WriteLine("Executing {0}", nonqueryCommand.CommandText)
```

Now you execute the DELETE statement with ExecuteNonQuery the same way you executed INSERT and again use selectCommand to display the results.

```
Console.WriteLine("Number of rows affected : {0}", _
   nonqueryCommand.ExecuteNonQuery())

' Execute Scalar Query Again
Console.WriteLine("After DELETE, Number of Employees = {0}", _
   scalarCommand.ExecuteScalar())
```

As we said, when INSERT, UPDATE, or DELETE execute, they affect some number of rows in the database; the return value from ExecuteNonQuery indicates how many rows were affected.

If this number comes back zero when you didn't expect it to do so, then maybe you specified the WHERE clause of the SQL statement incorrectly. For example, if you mistype the WHERE clause for the DELETE statement in the previous program, you may see the output shown in Figure 6-7.

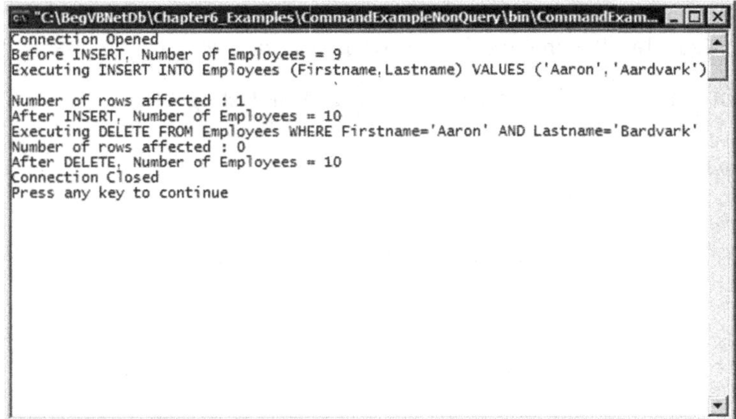
Connection Opened
Before INSERT, Number of Employees = 9
Executing INSERT INTO Employees (Firstname,Lastname) VALUES ('Aaron','Aardvark')

Number of rows affected : 1
After INSERT, Number of Employees = 10
Executing DELETE FROM Employees WHERE Firstname='Aaron' AND Lastname='Bardvark'
Number of rows affected : 0
After DELETE, Number of Employees = 10
Connection Closed
Press any key to continue

Figure 6-7. *Misspelling* Aardvark

We misspelled *Aardvark* as *Bardvark*, so it didn't find any rows to delete. The number of employees remaining after the DELETE is ten, not nine as expected. If you fix this error and rerun the program, you insert one more row but then delete two, as shown in Figure 6-8.

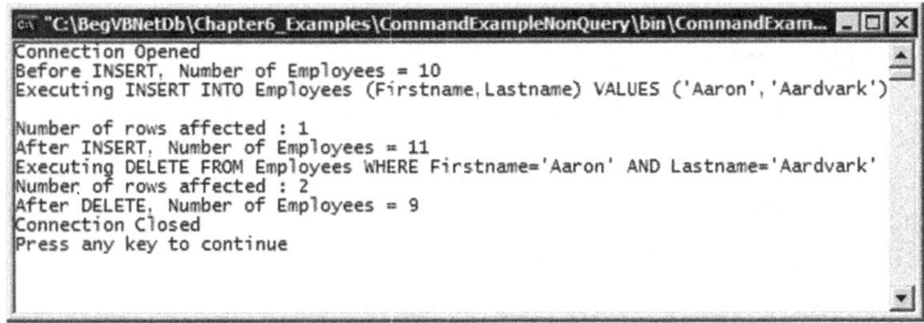
Connection Opened
Before INSERT, Number of Employees = 10
Executing INSERT INTO Employees (Firstname,Lastname) VALUES ('Aaron','Aardvark')

Number of rows affected : 1
After INSERT, Number of Employees = 11
Executing DELETE FROM Employees WHERE Firstname='Aaron' AND Lastname='Aardvark'
Number of rows affected : 2
After DELETE, Number of Employees = 9
Connection Closed
Press any key to continue

Figure 6-8. *Correcting* Aardvark

This is because the second row was left behind when the previous DELETE failed to find it.

Creating Tables

Of course, adding data to and removing data from your tables aren't the only nonqueries you'll end up sending to your server. Often you'll need to create a table or other database object from your program, such as creating a temporary table to hold some data as part of your application processing on the server.

Such operations use the CREATE statement and are part of the Data Definition Language (DDL). This is distinguished from the Data Manipulation Language (DML), which includes INSERT, UPDATE, and DELETE.

You use ExecuteNonQuery to execute DDL as well as DML. Let's check it out.

Try It Out: Using ExecuteNonQuery for CREATE TABLE

The aim of this example is to create a table called `MyTmpTable` and insert some data into it by executing a `CREATE TABLE` statement on the tempdb database.

1. Add a new VB .NET Console Application project called `CommandExampleCreate` to your solution, `Chapter6_Examples`. Rename `Module1.vb` to `CommandExampleCreate.vb`.
2. Replace the code in `CommandExampleCreate.vb` with the code in Listing 6-5.

Listing 6-5. *CommandExampleCreate*

```
Imports System
Imports System.Data
Imports System.Data.SqlClient

Module CommandExampleCreate

   Sub Main()
      'Create Connection object
      Dim thisConnection As New SqlConnection _
         ("server=(local)\netsdk;" & _
          "integrated security=sspi;" & _
          "database=tempdb")

      'Create Command object
      Dim nonqueryCommand As SqlCommand = _
         thisConnection.CreateCommand()

      Try
         ' Open Connection
         thisConnection.Open()
         Console.WriteLine("Connection Opened")

         ' Execute NonQuery To Create Table
         nonqueryCommand.CommandText = _
            "CREATE TABLE MyTmpTable (COL1 integer)"
         Console.WriteLine("Executing {0}", _
            nonqueryCommand.CommandText)
         Console.WriteLine("Number of rows affected : {0}", _
            nonqueryCommand.ExecuteNonQuery())

         ' Execute NonQuery To Insert Data
         nonqueryCommand.CommandText = _
            "INSERT INTO MyTmpTable VALUES (37)"
         Console.WriteLine("Executing {0}", _
            nonqueryCommand.CommandText)
         Console.WriteLine("Number of rows affected : {0}", _
            nonqueryCommand.ExecuteNonQuery())
```

```
        Catch ex As SqlException
            ' Display error
            Console.WriteLine("Error: " & ex.ToString())
        Finally
            ' Close Connection
            thisConnection.Close()
            Console.WriteLine("Connection Closed")

        End Try

    End Sub
End Module
```

3. Make this the startup project and CommandExampleCreate the startup project, and then run it (Ctrl+F5). You should see the output in Figure 6-9.

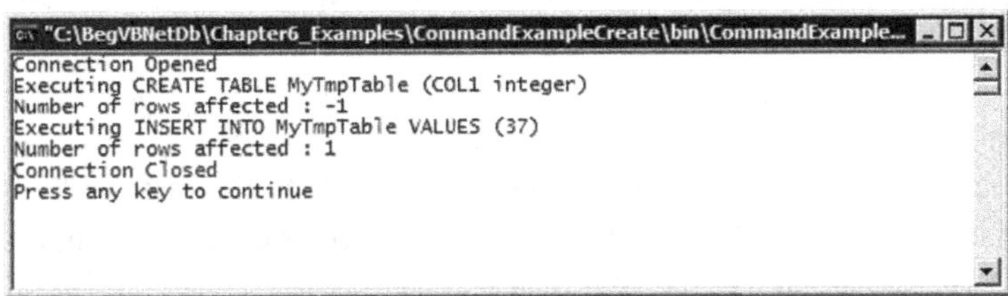

Figure 6-9. *CommandExampleCreate*

How It Works

You repeat the style from the previous example, using CreateCommand to create a command named nonqueryCommand associated with the connection at create time.

```
'Create Command object
Dim nonqueryCommand As SqlCommand = _
   thisConnection.CreateCommand()
```

You have two tasks to do in this example—creating the table and then filling it with some data—so that's two commands you need to issue. As before, you'll need to change the CommandText property for each of these tasks before you execute the commands. First, you execute the CREATE TABLE statement.

```
' Execute NonQuery To Create Table
nonqueryCommand.CommandText = _
   "CREATE TABLE MyTmpTable (COL1 integer)"
Console.WriteLine("Executing {0}", _
   nonqueryCommand.CommandText)
Console.WriteLine("Number of rows affected : {0}", _
   nonqueryCommand.ExecuteNonQuery())
```

ExecuteNonQuery returns a negative one (-1) when executing DDL such as CREATE TABLE, since creating a new table doesn't affect any rows of existing tables. So you see the CREATE TABLE being executed, and the return value is -1.

Second, you execute the INSERT statement to put some data into the table.

```
' Execute NonQuery To Insert Data
nonqueryCommand.CommandText = _
   "INSERT INTO MyTmpTable VALUES (37)"
Console.WriteLine("Executing {0}", _
   nonqueryCommand.CommandText)
Console.WriteLine("Number of rows affected : {0}", _
   nonqueryCommand.ExecuteNonQuery())
```

The insert affects one row, so ExecuteNonQuery returns a positive one (1).

ExecuteNonQuery also returns -1 if you give it a query to execute. This is because you haven't changed any rows. However, don't use ExecuteNonQuery for queries; you'll want to look at the result set (or scalar value), and ExecuteReader or ExecuteScalar are the methods to use for this.

Note Note that because you created MyTmpTable in the tempdb temporary database, it will disappear the next time SQL Server is restarted. That's OK for this table; you were just using it as an example. However, don't use the tempdb database for any data you really want to be permanent.

Creating Databases

The previous example created a table in the tempdb database, which is always present in SQL Server for temporary tables. This is handy for incidental work, but it's often more convenient to create a whole database for your application rather than new tables in a database that already exists.

As it turns out, this is easy enough to program in ADO.NET; you just execute the Transact-SQL CREATE DATABASE statement. You have a chicken-and-egg problem, however, in that you can't connect to the database until the database exists. This is one reason why connections have a ChangeDatabase method. Let's see how it's used.

Try It Out: Creating a Database and Using It

To create a database and use it, follow these steps:

1. Add a new VB .NET Console Application project named CommandExampleCreateDb to your solution, Chapter6_Examples. Rename Module1.vb to CommandExampleCreateDb.vb.

2. Replace the code in CommandExampleCreateDb.vb with the code in Listing 6-6, which is identical to Listing 6-5 except for the bold lines.

Listing 6-6. *CommandExampleCreateDb*

```
Imports System
Imports System.Data
Imports System.Data.SqlClient

Module CommandExampleCreateDb

   Sub Main()
      'Create Connection object
      Dim thisConnection As New SqlConnection _
         ("server=(local)\netsdk;" & _
          "integrated security=sspi;" & _
          "database=tempdb")

      'Create Command object
      Dim nonqueryCommand As SqlCommand = _
         thisConnection.CreateCommand()

      Try
         ' Open Connection
         thisConnection.Open()
         Console.WriteLine("Connection Opened")

         ' Execute NonQuery To Create Database
         nonqueryCommand.CommandText = _
            "CREATE DATABASE MyDb"
         Console.WriteLine("Executing {0}", _
            nonqueryCommand.CommandText)
         Console.WriteLine("Number of rows affected : {0}", _
            nonqueryCommand.ExecuteNonQuery())

         ' Switch to MyDb
         Console.WriteLine("Database created, now switching")
         thisConnection.ChangeDatabase("MyDb")


         ' Execute NonQuery To Create Table
         nonqueryCommand.CommandText = _
            "CREATE TABLE MyTmpTable (COL1 integer)"
         Console.WriteLine("Executing {0}", _
            nonqueryCommand.CommandText)
         Console.WriteLine("Number of rows affected : {0}", _
            nonqueryCommand.ExecuteNonQuery())
```

```
            ' Execute NonQuery To Insert Data
            nonqueryCommand.CommandText = _
               "INSERT INTO MyTmpTable VALUES (37)"
            Console.WriteLine("Executing {0}", _
               nonqueryCommand.CommandText)
            Console.WriteLine("Number of rows affected : {0}", _
               nonqueryCommand.ExecuteNonQuery())

         Catch ex As SqlException
            ' Display error
            Console.WriteLine("Error: " & ex.ToString())
         Finally
            ' Close Connection
            thisConnection.Close()
            Console.WriteLine("Connection Closed")

         End Try
      End Sub
   End Module
```

3. Make this the startup project and `CommandExampleCreateDb` the startup object, and then run it (Ctrl+F5). You should see the output shown in Figure 6-10.

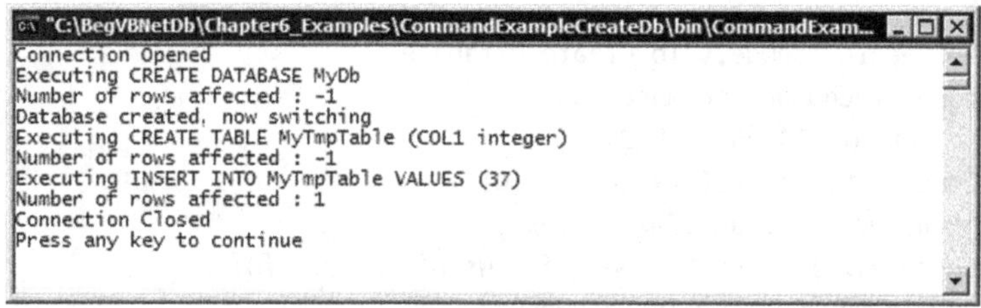

Figure 6-10. *CommandExampleCreateDb*

How It Works

This example works almost exactly the same as the previous one. The new addition is creating the database and switching to the newly created database within VB .NET without having to open a new connection. When the database is created, the current database is the one specified when you opened the connection (in this case `tempdb`, since you didn't change that part of the code).

```
Dim thisConnection As New SqlConnection _
   ("server=(local)\netsdk;" & _
    "integrated security=sspi;" & _
    "database=tempdb")
```

If you don't specify the `Database` parameter in the connection string, then the default database, `master`, becomes the current database. However, the current database is irrelevant when you issue the `CREATE DATABASE` command.

```
' Execute NonQuery To Create Database
nonqueryCommand.CommandText = _
   "CREATE DATABASE MyDb"
Console.WriteLine("Executing {0}", _
   nonqueryCommand.CommandText)
```

If you're creating this on your local machine, you can actually see the program pause and hear your disk drive work as it creates the new file to contain the new database. Immediately after creating the database, you switch to the new database.

```
' Switch to MyDb
Console.WriteLine("Database created, now switching")
thisConnection.ChangeDatabase("MyDb")
```

Now when the `CREATE TABLE` command is executed to create `MyTmpTable`, the table is created in `MyDatabase`, not `tempdb`.

```
' Execute NonQuery To Create Table
nonqueryCommand.CommandText = _
   "CREATE TABLE MyTmpTable (COL1 integer)"
Console.WriteLine("Executing {0}", _
   nonqueryCommand.CommandText)
Console.WriteLine("Number of rows affected : {0}", _
   nonqueryCommand.ExecuteNonQuery())
```

For temporary tables, just use the `tempdb` database. If you need to create permanent tables, it's a good idea to put them in their own database. However, though it's possible to create databases in SQL Server this way, databases are usually not created in programs. Databases, even small ones, aren't trivial matters.

Setting Command Parameters

When the server executes a SQL query or statement, all the information needed by the server must be contained within the string in the `CommandText` property. So if you want to insert some numbers into a column, you must specify the numbers as part of the string for the `INSERT` command, like so:

```
INSERT INTO MyTmpTable VALUES (1)
INSERT INTO MyTmpTable VALUES (2)
INSERT INTO MyTmpTable VALUES (3)
INSERT INTO MyTmpTable VALUES (4)
```

It'd get very tedious very quickly if you had to write out a separate `INSERT` for every value, so it'd be great if you could generate them all within a function. Fortunately, this is pretty simple. `CommandText` is a `string`, so you could build the string for the text by converting the variable containing the value you want to insert into the database into a string, like this:

```
Try
   ' Open Connection
   thisConnection.Open()
   Console.WriteLine("Connection Opened")

   For i As Integer = 1 To 4
      nonqueryCommand.CommandText = _
         "INSERT INTO MyTmpTable VALUES (" & i & ")"

      Console.WriteLine("Executing {0}", _
         nonqueryCommand.CommandText)
      Console.WriteLine("Number of rows affected : {0}", _
         nonqueryCommand.ExecuteNonQuery())
   Next i
End Try
```

This approach to building the command text with normal string operations works just fine for simple `INSERT` statements and does the job with relatively few lines of code as well. However, it can get complicated to maintain, especially if you need to insert values into multiple columns, each of different types. Also, for data types (for example, byte arrays containing binary data) this method doesn't work correctly (for example, `ToString` returns the name of the type rather than the data itself for many reference types).

A better way to handle these more complex cases is to use *command parameters*, which have the following advantages:

- The mapping between the variables in your code and the place where they're used in SQL is clearer and more readable.
- The conversion between VB .NET types and SQL data types is cleaner and more correct with parameters. As you'll see, parameters let you use the type definitions that are specific to a particular ADO.NET data provider to ensure that your program variables are mapped to the correct SQL data types.
- Parameters let you use the `Prepare` method, which can make your code run faster. This is described in more detail in the "How It Works" section of the following example.
- Parameters are used extensively in more advanced programming techniques, such as when using stored procedures (see Chapter 14) and working with irregular data (see Chapter 21).

A parameter is a placeholder in the command text where a value will be substituted. In SQL Server *named parameters* are used; these begin with `@` followed by the parameter name with no intervening space. So then, in the following `INSERT` statement, `@MyName` and `@MyNumber` are both parameters:

```
INSERT INTO MyTable VALUES (@MyName, @MyNumber)
```

■ **Note** Some data providers use the standard SQL *parameter marker*, a question mark (?), instead of named parameters. You'll look at this when you look at other data providers' commands in the "Using Commands with Other Data Providers" section.

Try It Out: Using Command Parameters and the Prepare Method

Follow these steps:

1. Add a new VB .NET Console Application project named CommandExampleParameters to your solution, Chapter6_Examples. Rename Module1.vb to CommandExampleParameters.vb.
2. Replace the code in CommandExampleParameters.vb by copying the code from the previous example, CommandExampleCreateDB.vb. Change the module to CommandExampleParameters, and edit the Try block with the bold code in Listing 6-7.

Listing 6-7. *Modifications for CommandExampleParameters*

```
Try
    ' Open Connection
    thisConnection.Open()
    Console.WriteLine("Connection Opened")

    ' Execute NonQuery To Create Table
    nonqueryCommand.CommandText = _
       "CREATE TABLE MyTable " & _
       "(MyName VARCHAR (30), MyNumber integer)"
    Console.WriteLine("Executing {0}", _
       nonqueryCommand.CommandText)
    Console.WriteLine("Number of rows affected : {0}", _
       nonqueryCommand.ExecuteNonQuery())

    ' Create INSERT statement with named parameters
    nonqueryCommand.CommandText = _
       "INSERT INTO MyTable VALUES (@MyName, @MyNumber)"

    ' Add Parameters to Command Parameters collection
    nonqueryCommand.Parameters.Add("@MyName", SqlDbType.VarChar, 30)
    nonqueryCommand.Parameters.Add("@MyNumber", SqlDbType.Int)

    ' Prepare command for repeated execution
    nonqueryCommand.Prepare()
```

```
         ' Data to be inserted
         Dim names() As String = {"Zach", "Sarah", "John", "Donald"}
         For i As Integer = 0 To 3
            nonqueryCommand.Parameters("@MyName").Value = names(i)
            nonqueryCommand.Parameters("@MyNumber").Value = i
            Console.WriteLine("Executing {0}", _
               nonqueryCommand.CommandText)
            Console.WriteLine("Number of rows affected : {0}", _
               nonqueryCommand.ExecuteNonQuery())
         Next i

         Catch ex As SqlException
             ' Display error
             Console.WriteLine("Error: " & ex.ToString())
         Finally
            ' Close Connection
            thisConnection.Close()
            Console.WriteLine("Connection Closed")
     End Try
```

3. Make this the startup project and CommandExampleParameters the startup object, and then run it (Ctrl+F5). You should see the output in Figure 6-11.

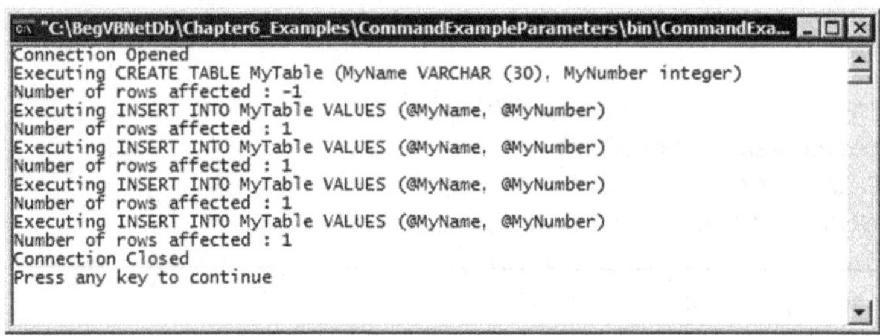

Figure 6-11. *CommandExampleParameters*

How It Works

The general outline of this example is similar to the first example that created a table in tempdb and inserted a row into the table. Other than that, you created a table with two columns instead of one and changed class names, and the rest of the code up to setting the text for the first INSERT is the same as in previous examples. Here's where you first specify the parameters @MyName and @MyNumber inside the text of the INSERT statement:

```
' Create INSERT statement with named parameters
nonqueryCommand.CommandText = _
   "INSERT INTO MyTable VALUES (@MyName, @MyNumber)"
```

Next you need to add these parameters to the command's Parameters collection. Parameters is a property that's a collection of SqlParameter objects. You use the collection's Add method to add new members to the collection.

```
' Add Parameters to Command Parameters collection
nonqueryCommand.Parameters.Add("@MyName", SqlDbType.VarChar, 30)
nonqueryCommand.Parameters.Add("@MyNumber", SqlDbType.Int)
```

Each SqlParameter object has a name that must match a name used in the command text and a type that's specified by the System.Data.SqlDbType enumeration. SqlDbType lets you specify a SQL Server–specific data type for columns, as discussed back in Chapter 3. This helps ensure correct type conversion when variables from your VB .NET program are substituted for the parameters. Next you call the command's Prepare method. Prepare lets the database server know that a command with parameters is going to be repeated several times, so it can precompile the command at the server, resulting in faster execution and less memory usage.

```
' Prepare command for repeated execution
nonqueryCommand.Prepare()
```

The Prepare method isn't a requirement for using parameters, but it's a good idea if you're going to execute the same command multiple times with the only change to the command being different values for the parameter variables. Be aware that not every database and data provider supports the preparing SQL for execution, but SQL Server and the SqlClient data provider do.

With the parameters set up, it's just a matter of inserting the various data values as required. You have four names in an array, so names(0) is Zach, names(1) is Sarah, and so on. You use a For loop and set the @MyName parameter to a name from the names() array and the @MyNumber parameter to an integer from the loop index for each iteration through the loop. By assigning the Value property of the parameter, you tell the system to convert the value from the variable in the program to the appropriate text to substitute into the INSERT statement.

```
' Data to be inserted
Dim names() As String = {"Zach", "Sarah", "John", "Donald"}
For i As Integer = 0 To 3
   nonqueryCommand.Parameters("@MyName").Value = names(i)
   nonqueryCommand.Parameters("@MyNumber").Value = i
```

Next you display the command text.

```
Console.WriteLine("Executing {0}", _
   nonqueryCommand.CommandText)
```

Notice that it prints the parameter name rather than the actual substituted value. For each iteration of the loop, you get this:

```
INSERT INTO MyTable VALUES (@MyName, @MyNumber)
```

This is because the parameter substitution doesn't actually change the command text string; instead, parameters are substituted at the time the command is executed at the server, which is the next step.

```
   Console.WriteLine("Number of rows affected : {0}", _
      nonqueryCommand.ExecuteNonQuery())
Next i
```

When the command is actually executed, the server substitutes Zach for @MyName and 0 for @MyNumber on the first iteration, Sarah for @MyName and 1 for @MyNumber on the next iteration, and so on. Each of the four times the command is executed, one row is affected. The result is the same as if you had executed the literal commands.

```
INSERT INTO MyTable VALUES ('Zach', 0)
INSERT INTO MyTable VALUES ('Sarah', 1)
INSERT INTO MyTable VALUES ('John', 2)
INSERT INTO MyTable VALUES ('Donald', 3)
```

After you finish inserting the data, you close the connection. This example finishes your look at how commands are used with the SQL Server data provider. The SqlCommand class has a few more methods and properties, but they're beyond the scope of this book. You'll finish this chapter with a look at how the commands are used with other data providers.

Using Commands with Other Data Providers

The OLE DB and ODBC data providers have commands, OleDbCommand and OdbcCommand, and both act very much the same as SqlCommand. Let's look at a couple of examples.

Try It Out: Using OleDbCommand

This example accesses a Northwind database, but this time it accesses the one that comes with Microsoft Access (Northwind.mdb).

1. Add a new VB .NET Console Application project named CommandOleDbQuery to your solution, Chapter6_Examples. Rename Module1.vb to CommandOleDbQuery.vb.

2. Replace the code in CommandOleDbQuery.vb with the code in Listing 6-8.

Listing 6-8. *CommandOleDbQuery*

```
Imports System
Imports System.Data
Imports System.Data.OleDb

Module CommandOleDbQuery

   Sub Main()
      'Create Connection object
      Dim thisConnection As New OleDbConnection _
         ("Provider=Microsoft.Jet.OLEDB.4.0;" & _
          "Data Source=C:\BegVbNetDb\northwind.mdb")
```

```
         'Create Command object
         Dim thisCommand As New OleDbCommand _
            ("SELECT ProductID, ProductName FROM Products", _
             thisConnection)

         Try
            ' Open Connection
            thisConnection.Open()
            Console.WriteLine("Connection Opened")

            ' Execute Query
            Dim thisReader As OleDbDataReader = thisCommand.ExecuteReader()

            While (thisReader.Read())
               Console.WriteLine("Product: {0} {1}", _
                  thisReader.GetValue(0), thisReader.GetValue(1))
            End While

         Catch ex As OleDbException
            ' Display error
            Console.WriteLine("Error: " & ex.ToString())
         Finally
            ' Close Connection
            thisConnection.Close()
            Console.WriteLine("Connection Closed")
         End Try
      End Sub
   End Module
```

3. Make this the startup project and CommandOleDbQuery the startup object, and then run it (Ctrl+F5). You should see the output in Figure 6-12.

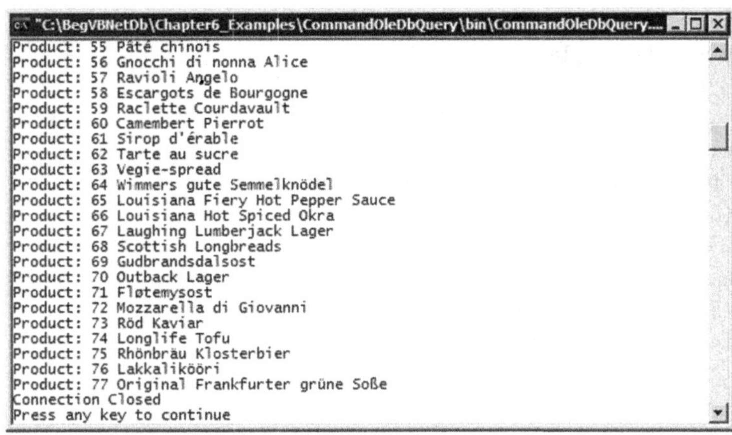

Figure 6-12. *CommandOleDbQuery*

How It Works

The code in this example is similar to the CommandExampleReader example (Listing 6-3), using System.Data.OleDb instead of System.Data.SqlClient and changing the query and formatting for the new table. You construct OleDbCommand in the same way as SqlCommand, specifying the command text and connection.

```
'Create Command object
Dim thisCommand As New OleDbCommand _
   ("SELECT ProductID, ProductName FROM Products", _
    thisConnection)
```

The SQL accepted by the Microsoft Access (Jet) engine has some differences from Transact-SQL, but for basic operations they're the same.

Now let's try an example with the ODBC data provider. You'll discover once again that only a few differences between it and the SQL Server data provider exist.

Try It Out: Using OdbcCommand

For this example, you'll base the code on the command parameters example you created earlier (CommandExampleParameters.vb).

1. Add a new VB .NET Console Application project named CommandOdbcExample to your solution, Chapter6_Examples. Rename Module1.vb to CommandOdbcExample.vb.
2. Replace the code in CommandOdbcExample.vb by copying the code from CommandExampleParameters.vb and making the changes given by the bold code in Listing 6-9.

Listing 6-9. *CommandOdbcExample*

```
Imports System
Imports System.Data
Imports System.Data.Odbc

Module CommandOdbcExample

   Sub Main()
      'Create Connection object
      Dim thisConnection As New OdbcConnection _
         ("dsn=NorthwindOdbc")

      'Create Command object
      Dim nonqueryCommand As OdbcCommand = _
         thisConnection.CreateCommand()
```

```
Try
   ' Open Connection
   thisConnection.Open()
   Console.WriteLine("Connection Opened")

   ' Execute NonQuery To Create Table
   nonqueryCommand.CommandText = _
      "CREATE TABLE MyTable " & _
      "(MyName VARCHAR (30), MyNumber integer)"
   Console.WriteLine("Executing {0}", _
      nonqueryCommand.CommandText)
   Console.WriteLine("Number of rows affected : {0}", _
      nonqueryCommand.ExecuteNonQuery())

   ' Create INSERT statement with ? unnamed parameters
   nonqueryCommand.CommandText = _
      "INSERT INTO MyTable VALUES (?, ?)"

   ' Add Parameters to Command Parameters collection
   nonqueryCommand.Parameters.Add("@MyName", OdbcType.VarChar, 30)
   nonqueryCommand.Parameters.Add("@MyNumber", OdbcType.Int)

   ' Prepare command not supported in ODBC
   ' nonqueryCommand.Prepare()

   ' Data to be inserted
   Dim names() As String = {"Zach", "Sarah", "John", "Donald"}
   For i As Integer = 1 To 4
      nonqueryCommand.Parameters("@MyName").Value = names(i - 1)
      nonqueryCommand.Parameters("@MyNumber").Value = i
      Console.WriteLine("Executing {0}", _
         nonqueryCommand.CommandText)
      Console.WriteLine("Number of rows affected : {0}", _
         nonqueryCommand.ExecuteNonQuery())
   Next i

   ' Check to see the data we inserted
   nonqueryCommand.CommandText = _
      "SELECT MyName, MyNumber FROM MyTable"
   Dim thisReader As OdbcDataReader = nonqueryCommand.ExecuteReader()

   While (thisReader.Read())
      Console.WriteLine("Name and Number: {0} {1}", _
         thisReader.GetValue(0), thisReader.GetValue(1))
   End While
```

```
            ' Close the reader so we can execute another command
            thisReader.Close()

            ' Drop Temporary table
            nonqueryCommand.CommandText = "DROP TABLE MyTable"
            nonqueryCommand.ExecuteNonQuery()

        Catch ex As OdbcException
            ' Display error
            Console.WriteLine("Error: " & ex.ToString())
        Finally
            ' Close Connection
            thisConnection.Close()
            Console.WriteLine("Connection Closed")
        End Try
    End Sub
End Module
```

3. Make it the startup project, and then run it (Ctrl+F5). You should see the output in Figure 6-13.

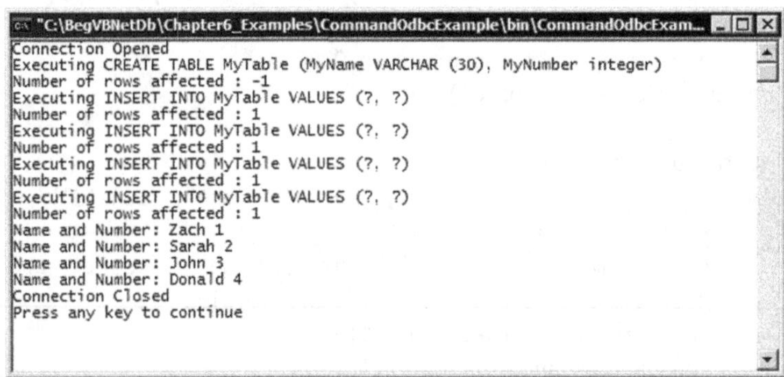

Figure 6-13. *CommandOdbcExample*

How It Works

Again you see the differences in the names of the data provider objects OdbcConnection and OdbcCommand as well as in the connection string.

Command parameters are an area where several differences exist among the data providers. The ODBC provider doesn't support named parameters; instead it uses unnamed parameters indicated in the text of the command by the standard SQL question mark.

```
' Create INSERT statement with ? unnamed parameters
nonqueryCommand.CommandText = _
   "INSERT INTO MyTable VALUES (?, ?)"
```

Unnamed parameters are position dependent; the first parameter added will be associated with the first question mark, and so on, in order. Here you do the Add operation; note the names are used here, but they're ignored when substituting into the command text:

```
' Add Parameters to Command Parameters collection
nonqueryCommand.Parameters.Add("@MyName", OdbcType.VarChar, 30)
nonqueryCommand.Parameters.Add("@MyNumber", OdbcType.Int)
```

Note you use the OdbcType enumeration that lists the ODBC data provider types; the SqlDbType used in CommandExampleParameters.vb is specific to SQL Server, even though the same basic types are supported.

```
' Prepare command not supported in ODBC
' nonqueryCommand.Prepare()
```

SQL Server doesn't support the Prepare method through an ODBC connection, so you don't call it here; as stated earlier, it's optional. This is an optimization issue; it doesn't affect the program except potentially in performance.

The insertion loop is the same as in the earlier example.

```
' Data to be inserted
Dim names() As String = {"Zach", "Sarah", "John", "Donald"}
For i As Integer = 1 To 4
   nonqueryCommand.Parameters("@MyName").Value = names(i - 1)
   nonqueryCommand.Parameters("@MyNumber").Value = i
   Console.WriteLine("Executing {0}", _
      nonqueryCommand.CommandText)
   Console.WriteLine("Number of rows affected : {0}", _
      nonqueryCommand.ExecuteNonQuery())
Next i
```

You added a DataReader to check on the data you inserted; note that it's an OdbcDataReader.

```
' Check to see the data we inserted
nonqueryCommand.CommandText = _
   "SELECT MyName, MyNumber FROM MyTable"
Dim thisReader As OdbcDataReader = nonqueryCommand.ExecuteReader()
```

You also added a DROP TABLE statement to get rid of the table, since it's supposed to be temporary. Note that you have to close the data reader first.

```
' Close the reader so we can execute another command
thisReader.Close()

' Drop Temporary table
nonqueryCommand.CommandText = "DROP TABLE MyTable"
nonqueryCommand.ExecuteNonQuery()
```

That finishes the ODBC example and the chapter as well. Let's summarize.

Summary

In this chapter, you learned the following:

- What an ADO.NET command is and does
- How to create a command
- How to associate a command with a connection
- How to set command text
- When to use the different command execution methods
- How to use `ExecuteScalar` for queries that return single values
- How to use `ExecuteReader` to process result sets
- How to use `ExecuteNonQuery` for DML and DDL
- How to create databases and tables using `ExecuteNonQuery`
- What command parameters are and how to use them
- How to use commands, specifically `OleDbCommand` and `OdbcCommand`, with other data providers

In the next chapter, you'll look in more depth at data readers, which you created in some of the examples in this chapter with a call to `ExecuteReader`. Data readers give you the results of a SQL query that returns more than one item of data.

CHAPTER 7

Introducing Data Readers

You've seen how connection and command objects fit into an application's interaction with a data source. Now it's time to begin looking in depth at what you can do with the results once a command has been executed. You've seen that statements produce no result and that some queries produce only single "scalar" values. In general, though, the queries you'll send to a data source in your applications will return several pieces of data, collectively known as a *result set*.

One of the methods we've used to deal with result sets in previous chapters is to employ a data reader to access the data directly from the database. The other is to store the result set locally in a dataset. You'll learn more about datasets in the next chapter and employ your time here looking at data readers in more detail. As you progress, you'll gradually learn how they're used, and you'll learn their importance in ADO.NET programming.

In particular, you'll see how to use data readers to do the following:

- Retrieve query results
- Get information with ordinal and column name indexers
- Get result set information
- Get schema information
- Process multiple result sets

As you'll see, the data reader isn't far removed from previous ADO objects, and it has pros and cons when compared with a dataset. The key is to understand what it's especially good for and use it appropriately. Let's start with a wide view. . .

Understanding Data Readers in General

The third component of a data provider then, in addition to connections and commands, is the *data reader*. Once you've connected to a database and queried it, you need some way to read the result set. This is where the data reader enters.

If you're from an ADO background, an ADO.NET data reader is like an ADO forward-only/ read-only client-side recordset, but it's not a COM object.

Data readers are objects that implement the `System.Data.IDataReader` interface. A data reader is a fast, unbuffered, forward-only, read-only connected stream of data that retrieves data on a per-row basis. Alternatively, you could say that it reads one row at a time as it loops through a result set.

You can't directly instantiate a data reader; instead, you create one with the ExecuteReader method of a command. For example, the following line of code shows a call made to ExecuteReader on an OLE DB command (thisCommand):

```
Dim thisReader As OleDbDataReader = thisCommand.ExecuteReader()
```

When you need to query a database—for instance, if you queried the Northwind Employees table with the OLE DB data provider—the ExecuteReader method would be called to create an OleDbDataReader instance for the query. Once at your disposal, you can use this data reader to access the result set.

Tip One point that we'll discuss further in the next chapter is choosing a data reader vs. a dataset. The general rule is to always use a data reader for simply retrieving data. If all you need to do is display data, all you need to use in most cases is a data reader.

We'll now demonstrate basic data reader usage with a few examples. The first example is the most basic; it simply uses a data reader to loop through a result set.

Let's say you've successfully established a connection with the database, a query has been executed for results, and everything seems to be going fine—what now? The next sensible thing to do would be to retrieve the records and then possibly display them. You know that the ExecuteReader method returns a data reader instance for you to use. So now, you start reading.

The following console application illustrates how to use a SqlDataReader and shows you how to loop through a result set to retrieve rows.

Try It Out: Looping Through a Result Set

To loop through a result set, follow these steps:

1. In Visual Studio .NET, create a new blank solution named Chapter7_Examples.
2. Add a VB .NET console application named DataLooper, and rename the Module1.vb file to DataLooper.vb.
3. Replace the code in DataLooper.vb with that in Listing 7-1.

Listing 7-1. *DataLooper.vb*

```
Imports System
Imports System.Data
Imports System.Data.SqlClient
```

```
Module DataLooper

   Sub Main()
      'Create Connection object
      Dim thisConnection As New SqlConnection _
         ("server=(local)\netsdk;" & _
          "integrated security=sspi;" & _
          "database=northwind")

      'Create Command object
      Dim thisCommand As New SqlCommand _
         ("SELECT ContactName FROM Customers", _
          thisConnection)

      Try
         ' Open Connection
         thisConnection.Open()
         Console.WriteLine("Connection Opened")

         ' Execute Query
         Dim thisReader As SqlDataReader = thisCommand.ExecuteReader()

         While (thisReader.Read())
            Console.WriteLine("Name: {0}", thisReader(0))
         End While

         'Close DataReader
         thisReader.Close()

      Catch ex As SqlException
         ' Display error
         Console.WriteLine("Error: " & ex.ToString())
      Finally
         ' Close Connection
         thisConnection.Close()
         Console.WriteLine("Connection Closed")
      End Try
   End Sub
End Module
```

4. Set `DataLooper` as the project's startup object, and then run it with Ctrl+F5. You should see the output in Figure 7-1.

```
"C:\BegVBNetDb\Chapter7_Examples\DataLooper\bin\DataLooper.exe"
Name: Alejandra Camino
Name: Jonas Bergulfsen
Name: Jose Pavarotti
Name: Hari Kumar
Name: Jytte Petersen
Name: Dominique Perrier
Name: Art Braunschweiger
Name: Pascale Cartrain
Name: Liz Nixon
Name: Liu Wong
Name: Karin Josephs
Name: Miguel Angel Paolino
Name: Anabela Domingues
Name: Helvetius Nagy
Name: Palle Ibsen
Name: Mary Saveley
Name: Paul Henriot
Name: Rita Müller
Name: Pirkko Koskitalo
Name: Paula Parente
Name: Karl Jablonski
Name: Matti Karttunen
Name: Zbyszek Piestrzeniewicz
Connection Closed
Press any key to continue_
```

Figure 7-1. *DataLooper*

How It Works

Let's walk through the code and see what you've created. You began your program with the usual set of instructions, including importing commonly used namespaces, setting up the connection details, and creating a query for your database, as shown in the following code:

```
Imports System
Imports System.Data
Imports System.Data.SqlClient

Module DataLooper

    Sub Main()
        'Create Connection object
        Dim thisConnection As New SqlConnection _
            ("server=(local)\netsdk;" & _
             "integrated security=sspi;" & _
             "database=northwind")

        'Create Command object
        Dim thisCommand As New SqlCommand _
            ("SELECT ContactName FROM Customers", _
             thisConnection)

        Try
            ' Open Connection
            thisConnection.Open()
            Console.WriteLine("Connection Opened")
```

In the past few chapters, we've gone over connections and the commands quite extensively. Since you're already familiar with the two objects and their usage, let's get straight down to the intricacies of using a data reader.

If you recall from the discussion just before this example, a `SqlDataReader` class is an abstract class and can't be instantiated explicitly. For this reason, you obtain an instance of a `SqlDataReader` by executing the `ExecuteReader` method of `SqlCommand`. You do this with the following line of code:

```
' Execute Query
Dim thisReader As SqlDataReader = thisCommand.ExecuteReader()
```

Once you have a reader attached to the active connection, you can loop through each row of the returned data reader, provided that it isn't empty, and retrieve values column by column. To do this, you need to make a call to the `Read` method of `SqlDataReader`, which returns `true` if a "next" row is available and advances the cursor or returns `false` if another row isn't available. Since `Read` advances the cursor to the next available record, you have to call it each time manually. So for this purpose, you use the following `While` loop in the example to do the job:

```
While (thisReader.Read())
```

Once you call the `Read` method, the next row is returned as a collection and stored in the `SqlDataReader` object itself. To access data from a specific column, you can use a number of methods (we'll cover these in the next section), but for this application you used the ordinal indexer lookup method, giving the column number to the reader to retrieve values (just as you'd give an index to an array of integers perhaps). Since in this case you chose a single column from the `Customers` table while querying the database, only the "zeroth" (0th) indexer is accessible, so you use the following line of code to display each record one by one:

```
Console.WriteLine("Name: {0}", thisReader(0))
```

To be able to use the connection for another purpose or to run another query on the database, it's important you call the `Close` method of `SqlDataReader` to close the reader explicitly. This is because, once the reader is attached to an active connection, the connection remains busy fetching data for the reader and remains unusable for another purpose until the reader has been detached from it. The following line shows this being done after you've looped through the result set and you're done using the data reader:

```
'Close DataReader
thisReader.Close()
```

Once the connection has been used, it's closed explicitly in the `Finally` clause. If for some reason you don't close the connection, the garbage collector will. However, remember, sometimes you may have pending queries or transactions lined up in a queue, and closing the connection explicitly makes sure they're all processed and executed before the application ends. The garbage collector won't do this; it'll just collect unreferenced objects, and you may end up losing some of the changes you made to the data since the queue wouldn't be processed. It's advisable that you close the connection explicitly with the `Close` method.

```
Finally
   ' Close Connection
   thisConnection.Close()
   Console.WriteLine("Connection Closed")
End Try
```

Using Ordinal Indexers

In the previous example, we mentioned using ordinal indexers when retrieving column data from the database. You'll look at the same code snippet again and learn more about it. However, to avoid any kind of confusion, you'll consider only the piece of code where the actual index has been referenced.

```
thisReader(0)
```

Does this look familiar? If you've ever used arrays, this line shouldn't be foreign to you. This is one of the ways you can request that a data reader fetch data, and this method of fetching data is called the *ordinal indexer method*. The indexer you pass to the data reader object is actually an item property, and the return value is an object.

Compared to column name indexing, which you'll learn about in the next section, this method is faster simply because the reader doesn't have to find the column from the row but jumps right to it with the index provided, saving time, energy, and resources. The following example demonstrates this more clearly.

Try It Out: Using Ordinal Indexers

Let's compare ordinal indexing to a real-world example; say you're standing in a street of 50 houses and you have to find someone named John Hook. All you're aware of is his name, and you don't know which house is his. To find him, you'll have to individually check each house. Wouldn't it be a lot easier if you knew his address instead and stepped right to it? Sure it would! That's just what ordinal indexing is.

Let's consider a small console application that uses the ordinal indexer lookup method and later compare the results with that of the field name indexing method, which we'll cover in the next section.

To be able to start and execute your program, perform the following steps:

1. Add a VB .NET console application named `OrdinalIndexer`, and rename the `Module1.vb` file to `OrdinalIndexer.vb`.

2. Replace the code in `OrdinalIndexer.vb` with that in Listing 7-2.

Listing 7-2. *OrdinalIndexer*

```
Imports System
Imports System.Data
Imports System.Data.SqlClient

Module OrdinalIndexer

   Sub Main()
      'Create Connection object
      Dim thisConnection As New SqlConnection _
         ("server=(local)\netsdk;" & _
          "integrated security=sspi;" & _
          "database=northwind")

      'Create Command object
      Dim thisCommand As New SqlCommand _
         ("SELECT CompanyName, ContactName FROM Customers " & _
          "WHERE ContactName LIKE 'M%'", thisConnection)

      Try
         ' Open Connection
         thisConnection.Open()
         Console.WriteLine("Connection Opened")

         ' Execute Query
         Dim thisReader As SqlDataReader = thisCommand.ExecuteReader()

         Console.WriteLine("{0}  {1}", _
            "Company Name".PadLeft(25), _
            "Contact Name".PadLeft(25))

         While (thisReader.Read())
            Console.WriteLine("{0} | {1}", _
               thisReader(0).ToString().PadLeft(25), _
               thisReader(1).ToString().PadLeft(25))
         End While

         'Close DataReader
         thisReader.Close()
```

```
            Catch ex As SqlException
               ' Display error
               Console.WriteLine("Error: " & ex.ToString())
         Finally
               ' Close Connection
               thisConnection.Close()
               Console.WriteLine("Connection Closed")
            End Try
         End Sub
      End Module
```

3. Make this the startup project and the startup object, and run it with Ctrl+F5. You should see the output in Figure 7-2.

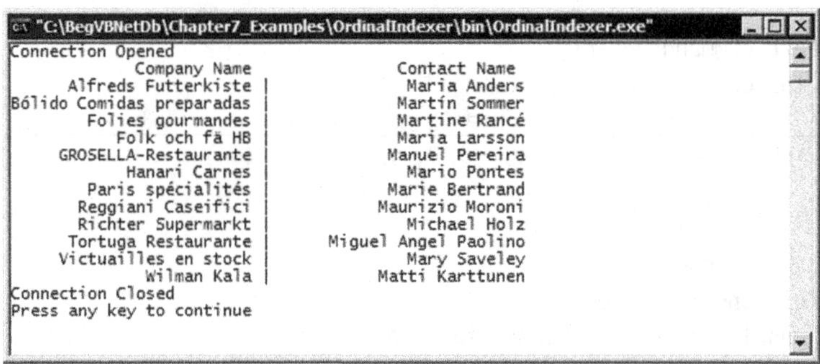

Figure 7-2. `OrdinalIndexer`

How It Works

Since you've looked at the connection details for examples such as this in earlier chapters, we won't dwell on that here. Let's move onto the data reader–specific code.

For this example, you queried the `Customers` table for the columns `CompanyName` and `ContactName`, where contact names begin with the letter *M*.

```
'Create Command object
Dim thisCommand As New SqlCommand _
   ("SELECT CompanyName, ContactName FROM Customers " & _
    "WHERE ContactName LIKE 'M%'", thisConnection)
```

Since two columns were selected by your query, the returned data would also comprise a collection of rows from only these two columns, thus allowing access to only two possible data reader indexers, 0 and 1.

The SQL query itself defines which column is accessed through index 0 and index 1. In this case, `CompanyName` is named first and is thus accessed through index 0, so `ContactName` comes under index 1. This of course makes sense, but it should also ring a few warning bells. Ordinal indexers may be faster than the column name indexers you'll see in the next example, but they also work blind. If you can't guarantee the order of the columns selected in the query or use the wildcard (*) in a query, you may not be retrieving the content you think you are. Try switching around the two column names in the SQL query, and run the program again to see what we mean.

You call on the ordinal indexers in a While loop, fetching values of the two columns for you, as the cursor advances to a new row in the dataset every time a call to the Read method is made. Since the returned value is an object, you need to explicitly convert the value into a string so that you can use the PadLeft function for displaying the output in an organized manner.

```
While (thisReader.Read())
   Console.WriteLine("{0} | {1}", _
      thisReader(0).ToString().PadLeft(25), _
      thisReader(1).ToString().PadLeft(25))
End While
```

After retrieving column values, you explicitly close the reader to free or unbind your connection or any other resource and close the connection in the Finally block.

```
'Close DataReader
thisReader.Close()
..
' Close Connection
thisConnection.Close()
```

Using Column Name Indexers

It's true that most of the time we don't really keep track of column numbers and prefer retrieving values by their respective column names, simply because it's much easier to remember them by their names, which also makes the code more self-documenting.

You perform column name indexing by passing a column name to the data reader, as opposed to the ordinal indexer method. This has many advantages. For instance, it means you can change the order of the SQL query and your code won't produce unexpected results. It won't prevent errors from being raised if you remove columns from a query and continue to reference them, but, then again, neither will using ordinal indexers.

On the downside, as we noted in the previous example, column name indexers are slightly slower than ordinal indexers. This is because .NET must reconcile the column name with an index first and then use that to get the value required.

The following code snippet retrieves the same columns (CompanyName and ContactName) that the last example did, using the column name indexer method:

```
Console.WriteLine("{0} | {1}", _
   thisReader("CompanyName").ToString().PadLeft(25), _
   thisReader("ContactName").ToString().PadLeft(25))
```

You can use this code snippet with the example you saw for the ordinal indexer method by performing the following steps:

1. Open the code for the previous example, and search for the following lines of code:

   ```
   Console.WriteLine("{0} | {1}", _
      thisReader(0).ToString().PadLeft(25), _
      thisReader(1).ToString().PadLeft(25))
   ```

2. Replace these lines with the following ones:

```
Console.WriteLine("{0} | {1}", _
   thisReader("CompanyName").ToString().PadLeft(25), _
   thisReader("ContactName").ToString().PadLeft(25))
```

3. Save the project, and execute it. This will produce the same result that you saw for the ordinal indexer method.

The next section may prove to be a much better approach for most cases.

Using Typed Accessor Methods

You've probably noticed how simple it is to retrieve data from any OLE DB–specific data source using the OLE DB data provider, or even from a SQL Server back end using the SQL Server data provider, but has it occurred to you that the string or the integer values you retrieve would probably not be represented the same way in the database? It could simply be a `varchar`, a `text`, an `nvarchar`, or a `numeric` value stored in the database that you conveniently retrieve and use without knowing what's really going on behind the scenes. It's true that SQL supports retrieving column data in various data formats by simply requesting it in that type.

When a data reader returns a value from a data source, the resulting value is retrieved and stored locally in a .NET Framework type rather than the original data source type. This in-place type conversion feature is a trade-off between consistency and speed, so to give some control over the data being retrieved, the data reader exposes typed accessor methods that you can use if you know the specific type of the value being returned.

Typed accessor methods all begin with a `Get`, take an ordinal for data retrieval, and are type safe; VB .NET won't allow you to get away with unsafe casts. These methods turn out to be faster than both the ordinal and the column name indexer methods. Being faster than column name indexing seems only logical as the typed accessor methods take ordinals for referencing; however, we need to explain how it's faster than ordinal indexing. This is because even though both techniques take in a column number, the conventional ordinal indexing method needs to look up the data type of the result and then eventually go through a type conversion. On the contrary, the overhead of looking up the schema is disregarded in the case of typed accessor calls.

For almost all data types supported by SQL Server or by OLE DB–specific databases (since some databases support data types such as Oracle's `VARCHAR2`, in contrast to `varchar` in SQL Server), respective .NET Framework types and typed accessor methods are available.

Table 7-1 should give you a brief idea of when to use typed accessors and with what data type. You'll first consider SQL Server data types, their corresponding .NET Framework types, typed accessors, and special SQL Server–specific typed accessor methods designed particularly for returning objects of type `System.Data.SqlTypes`.

Table 7-1. *SQL Server Accessor Types*

SQL Server Data Types	.NET Framework Type	.NET Framework Typed Accessor	SqlType Typed Accessor
bigint	Int64	GetInt64	GetSqlInt64
binary	Byte[]	GetBytes	GetSqlBinary
bit	Boolean	GetBoolean	GetSqlBit
char	String or Char[]	GetString or GetChars	GetSqlString
datetime	DateTime	GetDateTime	GetSqlDateTime
decimal	Decimal	GetDecimal	GetSqlDecimal
float	Double	GetDouble	GetSqlDouble
image or long varbinary	Byte[]	GetBytes	GetSqlBinary
int	Int32	GetInt32	GetSqlInt32
money	Decimal	GetDecimal	GetSqlMoney
nchar	String or Char[]	GetString or GetChars	GetSqlString
ntext	String or Char[]	GetString or GetChars	GetSqlString
numeric	Decimal	GetDecimal	GetSqlDecimal
nvarchar	String or Char[]	GetString or GetChars	GetSqlString
real	Single	GetFloat	GetSqlSingle
smalldatetime	DateTime	GetDateTime	GetSqlDateTime
smallint	Int16	GetInt16	GetSqlInt16
smallmoney	Decimal	GetDecimal	GetSqlDecimal
sql_variant	Object	GetValue	GetSqlValue
long varchar	String or Char[]	GetString or GetChars	GetSqlString
timestamp	Byte[]	GetBytes	GetSqlBinary
tinyint	Byte	GetByte	GetSqlByte
uniqueidentifier	Guid	GetGuid	GetSqlGuid
varbinary	Byte[]	GetBytes	GetSqlBinary
varchar	String or Char[]	GetString or GetChars	GetSqlString

And now you'll look at some available OLE DB data types, their corresponding .NET Framework data types, and their typed accessor methods (see Table 7-2).

Table 7-2. *OLE DB Accessor Types*

OLE DB Type	.NET Framework Type	.NET Framework Typed Accessor
DBTYPE_I8	Int64	GetInt64
DBTYPE_BYTES	Byte[]	GetBytes
DBTYPE_BOOL	Boolean	GetBoolean
DBTYPE_BSTR	String	GetString
DBTYPE_STR	String	GetString
DBTYPE_CY	Decimal	GetDecimal
DBTYPE_DATE	DateTime	GetDateTime
DBTYPE_DBDATE	DateTime	GetDateTime
DBTYPE_DBTIME	DateTime	GetDateTime
DBTYPE_DBTIMESTAMP	DateTime	GetDateTime
DBTYPE_DECIMAL	Decimal	GetDecimal
DBTYPE_R8	Double	GetDouble
DBTYPE_ERROR	ExternalException	GetValue
DBTYPE_FILETIME	DateTime	GetDateTime
DBTYPE_GUID	Guid	GetGuid
DBTYPE_I4	Int32	GetInt32
DBTYPE_LONGVARCHAR	String	GetString
DBTYPE_NUMERIC	Decimal	GetDecimal
DBTYPE_R4	Single	GetFloat
DBTYPE_I2	Int16	GetInt16
DBTYPE_I1	Byte	GetByte
DBTYPE_UI8	UInt64	GetValue
DBTYPE_UI4	UInt32	GetValue
DBTYPE_UI2	UInt16	GetValue
DBTYPE_VARCHAR	String	GetString
DBTYPE_VARIANT	Object	GetValue
DBTYPE_WVARCHAR	String	GetString
DBTYPE_WSRT	String	GetString

To see typed accessor methods in action, let's now look at a console application that uses them. For this example, you'll use the `Products` table from the `Northwind` database.

Table 7-3 shows the data design of the table. Note that the data types given in the table will be looked up for their corresponding typed methods from Tables 7-1 and 7-2 so you can use them correctly in your application.

Table 7-3. *`Northwind` `Products` Table Data Types*

Column Name	Data Type	Length	Allow Nulls?
`ProductID` (unique)	`int`	4	No
`ProductName`	`nvarchar`	40	No
`SupplierID`	`int`	4	Yes
`CategoryID`	`int`	4	Yes
`QuantityPerUnit`	`nvarchar`	20	Yes
`UnitPrice`	`money`	8	Yes
`UnitsInStock`	`smallint`	2	Yes
`UnitsOnOrder`	`smallint`	2	Yes
`ReorderLevel`	`smallint`	2	Yes
`Discontinued`	`bit`	1	No

Try It Out: Using Typed Accessor Methods

To use typed accessor methods, follow these steps:

1. Add a VB .NET console application named `TypedMethods`, and rename the `Module1.vb` file to `TypedMethods.vb`.

2. Replace the code in `TypedMethods.vb` with that in Listing 7-3.

Listing 7-3. *TypedMethods*

```
Imports System
Imports System.Data
Imports System.Data.SqlClient

Module TypedMethods

   Sub Main()
      'Create Connection object
      Dim thisConnection As New SqlConnection _
         ("server=(local)\netsdk;" & _
          "integrated security=sspi;" & _
          "database=northwind")
```

```
         'Sql Query
         Dim sql As String = _
            "SELECT ProductName, UnitPrice, " & _
                 "UnitsInStock, Discontinued " & _
            "FROM Products"

         'Create Command object
         Dim thisCommand As New SqlCommand _
            (sql, thisConnection)

         Try
            ' Open Connection
            thisConnection.Open()
            Console.WriteLine("Connection Opened")

            ' Execute Query
            Dim thisReader As SqlDataReader = thisCommand.ExecuteReader()

            ' Fetch Data
            While (thisReader.Read())
               Console.WriteLine("{0} | {1} | {2} | {3}", _
               thisReader.GetString(0).PadLeft(32), _
               thisReader.GetDecimal(1), _
               thisReader.GetInt16(2), _
               thisReader.GetBoolean(3))
            End While

            'Close DataReader
            thisReader.Close()

         Catch ex As SqlException
            ' Display error
            Console.WriteLine("Error: " & ex.ToString())
         Finally
            ' Close Connection
            thisConnection.Close()
            Console.WriteLine("Connection Closed")
         End Try
      End Sub
   End Module
```

3. Make this the startup project and `TypedMethods` the startup object, and run it with Ctrl+F5. You should see the output in Figure 7-3.

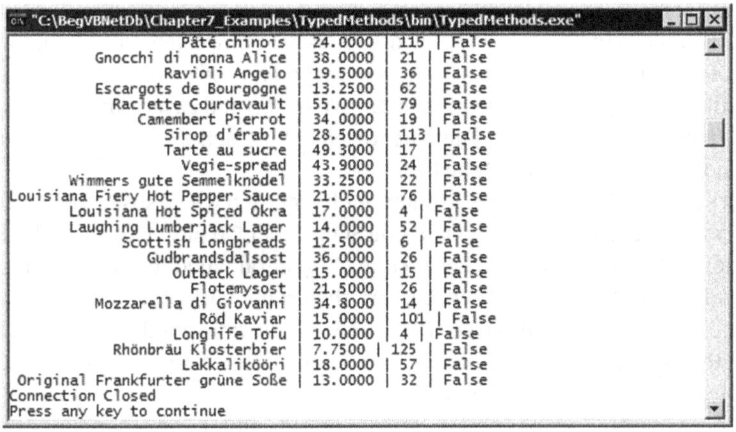

```
"C:\BegVBNetDb\Chapter7_Examples\TypedMethods\bin\TypedMethods.exe"
                      Pâté chinois | 24.0000 | 115 | False
             Gnocchi di nonna Alice | 38.0000 | 21 | False
                     Ravioli Angelo | 19.5000 | 36 | False
             Escargots de Bourgogne | 13.2500 | 62 | False
                Raclette Courdavault | 55.0000 | 79 | False
                   Camembert Pierrot | 34.0000 | 19 | False
                      Sirop d'érable | 28.5000 | 113 | False
                      Tarte au sucre | 49.3000 | 17 | False
                       Vegie-spread | 43.9000 | 24 | False
           Wimmers gute Semmelknödel | 33.2500 | 22 | False
Louisiana Fiery Hot Pepper Sauce | 21.0500 | 76 | False
          Louisiana Hot Spiced Okra | 17.0000 | 4 | False
         Laughing Lumberjack Lager | 14.0000 | 52 | False
               Scottish Longbreads | 12.5000 | 6 | False
                  Gudbrandsdalsost | 36.0000 | 26 | False
                      Outback Lager | 15.0000 | 15 | False
                        Flotemysost | 21.5000 | 26 | False
            Mozzarella di Giovanni | 34.8000 | 14 | False
                       Röd Kaviar | 15.0000 | 101 | False
                      Longlife Tofu | 10.0000 | 4 | False
              Rhönbräu Klosterbier | 7.7500 | 125 | False
                      Lakkalikööri | 18.0000 | 57 | False
  Original Frankfurter grüne Soße | 13.0000 | 32 | False
Connection Closed
Press any key to continue
```

Figure 7-3. *TypedMethods*

How It Works

After establishing a connection, you query the `Products` table for `ProductName`, `UnitPrice`, `UnitsInStock`, and `Discontinued`.

```
'Sql Query
Dim sql As String = _
   "SELECT ProductName, UnitPrice, " & _
          "UnitsInStock, Discontinued " & _
   "FROM Products"
```

The reason for our choice of columns was to deal with different kinds of data types and show how you could use relevant typed methods to obtain the correct results.

After obtaining a data reader (and executing the query) with `ExecuteReader`, you come to the part where you used the typed accessor methods.

```
' Fetch Data
While (thisReader.Read())
   Console.WriteLine("{0} | {1} | {2} | {3}", _
   thisReader.GetString(0).PadLeft(32), _
   thisReader.GetDecimal(1), _
   thisReader.GetInt16(2), _
   thisReader.GetBoolean(3))
End While
```

Tallying with the tables, given earlier, for native data types, you can see that you can access an `nvarchar`, a `money`, a `smallint`, and a `bit` data type in SQL Server by using the `GetString`, `GetDecimal`, `GetInt16`, and the `GetBoolean` accessor methods, respectively.

This technique is fast and completely type safe. By this we mean that the implicit conversions from native data types to the .NET Framework types are completely safe and handled, thus leveraging speed and performance. Also, if a typed method is used incorrectly—for example, with a noncompatible data type—an exception is thrown for invalid casts. For instance, if you try using the `GetString` method on a `bit` data type instead of using the `GetBoolean` method, a "Specified cast is not valid" exception will be thrown.

Talking about speed and performance, remember how much we've stressed using the right provider for a specific database? If you're using SQL Server 7.0 or newer, the .NET Framework has much more to offer. Along with these relatively general typed methods (you can use these typed methods with any version of SQL Server), the Framework offers optimized typed methods specifically designed for SQL Server 7 and newer. You can spot these typed methods by the addition of the phrase *Sql* in the middle. For instance, the `GetString` method's SQL Server 7 (and newer) counterpart is `GetSqlString`.

You can use these methods just like other typed methods, but it's worth mentioning that they return types in the `System.Data.SqlTypes` namespace. For instance, the `GetSqlString` method returns an object of type `System.Data.SqlTypes.SqlString` and not of type `System.String`, which the `GetString` method returns.

Getting Data About Data

So far all you've learned to do is retrieve data from the data source. Once you have a populated data reader in your hands, you can do a lot more. You're exposed to a number of useful methods that you can use for retrieving schema information or retrieving information directly related to the returned data. Table 7-4 describes these metadata functions and properties of the data reader.

Table 7-4. *Data Reader Metadata Properties and Methods*

Method or Property Name	Description
`Depth`	A property that gets the depth of nesting for the current row
`FieldCount`	A property that holds the number of columns in a result set
`GetDataTypeName`	A method that accepts an index and returns a string containing the name of the column data type
`GetFieldType`	A method that accepts an index and returns the .NET Framework type of the object
`GetName`	A method that accepts an index and returns the name of the specified column
`GetOrdinal`	A method that accepts a column name and returns the column index
`HasRows`	A property that indicates the `DataReader` contains one or more rows

Let's look at a sample application that utilizes some of these methods and properties.

Try It Out: Getting Information About a Result Set with a Data Reader

To get information about a result set with a data reader, follow these steps:

1. Add a VB .NET console application named `ResultSetInfo`, and rename the `Module1.vb` file to `ResultSetInfo.vb`.
2. Replace the code in `ResultSetInfo.vb` with that in Listing 7-4.

Listing 7-4. *ResultSetInfo*

```
Imports System
Imports System.Data
Imports System.Data.SqlClient

Module ResultSetInfo

   Sub Main()
      'Create Connection object
      Dim thisConnection As New SqlConnection _
         ("server=(local)\netsdk;" & _
          "integrated security=sspi;" & _
          "database=northwind")

      'Create Command object
      Dim thisCommand As New SqlCommand _
         ("SELECT ContactName, ContactTitle FROM Customers " & _
          "WHERE ContactName LIKE 'M%'", thisConnection)

      Try
         ' Open Connection
         thisConnection.Open()
         Console.WriteLine("Connection Opened")

         ' Execute Query
         Dim thisReader As SqlDataReader = thisCommand.ExecuteReader()

         ' Get column names
         Console.WriteLine("Column Names: {0} | {1}", _
            thisReader.GetName(0).PadLeft(11), _
            thisReader.GetName(1))

         ' Get column data types
         Console.WriteLine("Data types: {0} | {1}", _
            thisReader.GetDataTypeName(0).PadLeft(13), _
            thisReader.GetDataTypeName(1))
```

```
            Console.WriteLine()

            While (thisReader.Read())
               ' Get column values for all rows
               Console.WriteLine("{0} | {1}", _
                  thisReader.GetString(0).PadLeft(25), _
                  thisReader.GetString(1))
            End While

            ' Get number of columns
            Console.WriteLine()
            Console.WriteLine("Number of columns in a row: {0}", _
               thisReader.FieldCount)

            ' Get info about each column
            Console.WriteLine("'{0}' has index {1} and type {2}", _
               thisReader.GetName(0), _
               thisReader.GetOrdinal("ContactName"), _
               thisReader.GetFieldType(0))

            Console.WriteLine("'{0}' has index {1} and type {2}", _
               thisReader.GetName(1), _
               thisReader.GetOrdinal("ContactTitle"), _
               thisReader.GetFieldType(1))

            'Close DataReader
            thisReader.Close()

         Catch ex As SqlException
            ' Display error
            Console.WriteLine("Error: " & ex.ToString())
         Finally
            ' Close Connection
            thisConnection.Close()
            Console.WriteLine("Connection Closed")
         End Try
      End Sub
   End Module
```

3. Make this the startup project and `ResultSetInfo` the startup object, and run it with Ctrl+F5. You should see the output in Figure 7-4.

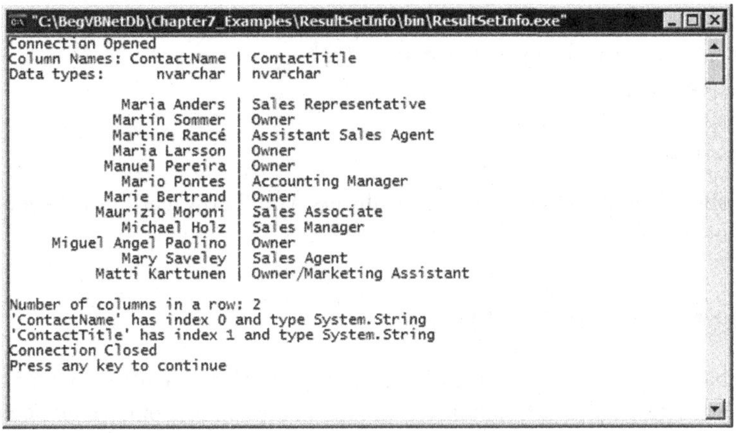

```
"C:\BegVBNetDb\Chapter7_Examples\ResultSetInfo\bin\ResultSetInfo.exe"
Connection Opened
Column Names: ContactName | ContactTitle
Data types:      nvarchar | nvarchar

          Maria Anders | Sales Representative
         Martín Sommer | Owner
         Martine Rancé | Assistant Sales Agent
         Maria Larsson | Owner
        Manuel Pereira | Owner
          Mario Pontes | Accounting Manager
        Marie Bertrand | Owner
       Maurizio Moroni | Sales Associate
          Michael Holz | Sales Manager
   Miguel Angel Paolino | Owner
          Mary Saveley | Sales Agent
       Matti Karttunen | Owner/Marketing Assistant

Number of columns in a row: 2
'ContactName' has index 0 and type System.String
'ContactTitle' has index 1 and type System.String
Connection Closed
Press any key to continue
```

Figure 7-4. *ResultSetInfo*

How It Works

The `GetName` method gets a column name by its index. This method returns information *about* the result set, so it can be called before the first call to `Read`.

```
' Get column names
Console.WriteLine("Column Names: {0} | {1}", _
   thisReader.GetName(0).PadLeft(11), _
   thisReader.GetName(1))
```

The `GetDataTypeName` method returns the database data type of a column. It too can be called before the first call to `Read`.

```
' Get column data types
Console.WriteLine("Data types: {0} | {1}", _
   thisReader.GetDataTypeName(0).PadLeft(13), _
   thisReader.GetDataTypeName(1))
```

The `FieldCount` property of the data reader contains the number of columns in the result set. This is useful for looping through columns without knowing their names or other attributes.

```
' Get number of columns
Console.WriteLine()
Console.WriteLine("Number of columns in a row: {0}", _
   thisReader.FieldCount)
```

Finally, we demonstrate how the GetOrdinal and GetFieldType methods are used. The former returns a column index based on its name; the latter returns the .NET type. These are the converses of GetName and GetDataTypeName, respectively.

```
' Get info about each column
Console.WriteLine("'{0}' has index {1} and type {2}", _
   thisReader.GetName(0), _
   thisReader.GetOrdinal("ContactName"), _
   thisReader.GetFieldType(0))
```

So much for obtaining information about result sets. You'll now learn how to get information about schemas.

Getting Data About Tables

The term *schema* has several meanings in relational databases. Here, we use it to refer to the design of a data structure, particularly a database table. A table consists of rows and columns, and each column can have a different data type. The columns and their attributes (data type, length, and so on) make up the table's schema.

To retrieve schema information easily, you can call the GetSchemaTable method on a data reader. As the name suggests, this method returns a System.Data.DataTable object, which is a representation (schema) of the table queried and contains a collection of rows and columns in the form of DataRow and DataColumn objects. These rows and columns are returned as collection objects by the properties Rows and Columns of the DataTable class.

However, here's where a slight confusion usually occurs. Data columns aren't column values but are column definitions (also called *column schemas*) that represent and control the behavior of individual columns. The object can be looped through by using a column name indexer and can tell you a lot about the dataset. Let's begin with a practical demonstration of the GetSchemaTable method.

Try It Out: Getting Schema Information

To get schema information, follow these steps:

1. Add a VB .NET console application named SchemaTable, and rename the Module1.vb file to SchemaTable.vb.
2. Replace the code in SchemaTable.vb with that in Listing 7-5.

Listing 7-5. *SchemaTable*

```
Imports System
Imports System.Data
Imports System.Data.SqlClient

Module SchemaTable
```

```
Sub Main()
   'Create Connection object
   Dim thisConnection As New SqlConnection _
      ("server=(local)\netsdk;" & _
       "integrated security=sspi;" & _
       "database=northwind")

   'Sql Query
   Dim sql As String = _
      "SELECT * FROM Employees"

   'Create Command object
   Dim thisCommand As New SqlCommand _
      (sql, thisConnection)

   Try
      ' Open Connection
      thisConnection.Open()
      Console.WriteLine("Connection Opened")

      ' Execute Query
      Dim thisReader As SqlDataReader = thisCommand.ExecuteReader()

      ' Get schema table for employees table
      Dim schema As DataTable = thisReader.GetSchemaTable()

      ' Display each row in the schema table
      ' Each row describes a column in the employees table
      For Each row As DataRow In schema.Rows
         For Each col As DataColumn In schema.Columns
            Console.WriteLine(col.ColumnName & " = " & _
               row(col).ToString())
         Next
         Console.WriteLine("---------------")
      Next


      'Close DataReader
      thisReader.Close()

   Catch ex As SqlException
      ' Display error
      Console.WriteLine("Error: " & ex.ToString())
```

```
            Finally
               ' Close Connection
               thisConnection.Close()
               Console.WriteLine("Connection Closed")
            End Try
         End Sub
      End Module
```

3. Make this the startup project and SchemaTable the startup object, and run it with Ctrl+F5. You should see the output in Figure 7-5.

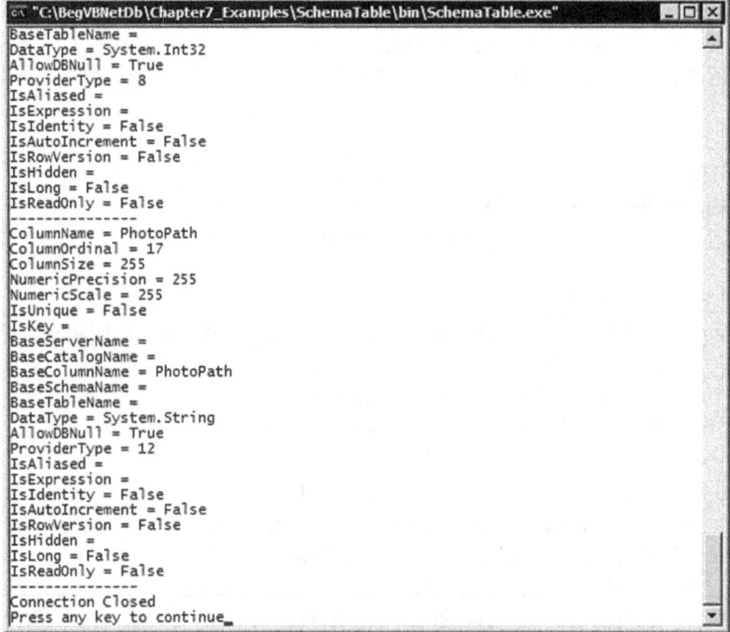

Figure 7-5. *SchemaTable*

How It Works

Other than connection similarities, the code is quite different from the code you saw earlier. When the call to the GetSchemaTable method is made (as follows), a populated instance of a data table is returned. You can use a data table to represent a complete table in a database, either in the form of a table that represents its schema or in the form of a table that holds all its original data for offline use.

```
' Get schema table for employees table
Dim schema As DataTable = thisReader.GetSchemaTable()
```

In this example, once you grab hold of a schema table, you retrieve a collection of rows through the Rows property of DataTable and a collection of columns through the Columns property of the DataTable. (You can use the Rows property to add a new row into the table altogether or remove one, and you can use the Columns property for adding or deleting an existing column—we'll cover this in Chapter 8.) Each row returned by the table describes one column in the original table, so for each of these rows, you traverse through the column's schema information one by one, using a nested for each loop.

```
' Display each row in the schema table
' Each row describes a column in the employees table
For Each row As DataRow In schema.Rows
   For Each col As DataColumn In schema.Columns
      Console.WriteLine(col.ColumnName & " = " & _
         row(col).ToString())
   Next
   Console.WriteLine("---------------")
Next
```

Notice how you used the ColumnName property of the DataColumn object to retrieve the current schema name in the loop, and then you retrieved the value related to that schema by using the familiar indexer-style method that uses the DataRow object. The DataRow accepts a number of overloaded indexers, and this is only one of the few ways of doing it. You can also access the column schema separately if you give a schema name to the DataRow object, for example, like this:

```
Console.WriteLine("Null value allowed: " & col.AllowDBNull)
```

The previous line displays whether the column supports null values (in other words, whether the AllowDBNull property of the data column is true [allowed] or false).

Using Multiple Result Sets with a Data Reader

Sometimes you may really want to get a job done quickly and also want to query the database with two or more queries at the same time. As well as this, you wouldn't want the overall application performance to suffer in any way either by instantiating more than one command or data reader or by exhaustively using the same objects over and over again, adding to the code as you go.

So, is there a way you can get a single data reader to loop through multiple result sets? Yes, data readers have a method, NextResult, that advances the reader to the next result set. Let's try it.

Try It Out: Handling Multiple Result Sets

To handle multiple result sets, follow these steps:

1. Add a VB .NET console application named MultipleResults, and rename the Module1.vb file to MultipleResults.vb.

2. Replace the code in MultipleResults.vb with that in Listing 7-6.

Listing 7-6. *MultipleResults*

```
Imports System
Imports System.Data
Imports System.Data.SqlClient

Module MultipleResults

   Sub Main()
      'Create Connection object
      Dim thisConnection As New SqlConnection _
         ("server=(local)\netsdk;" & _
          "integrated security=sspi;" & _
          "database=northwind")

      'Sql Query 1
      Dim sql1 As String = _
         "SELECT CompanyName, ContactName " & _
         "FROM Customers WHERE CompanyName LIKE 'A%'"

      'Sql Query 2
      Dim sql2 As String = _
         "SELECT FirstName, LastName " & _
         "FROM Employees"

      'Combine queries
      Dim sql As String = sql1 & sql2

      'Create Command object
      Dim thisCommand As New SqlCommand _
         (sql, thisConnection)

      Try
         ' Open Connection
         thisConnection.Open()
         Console.WriteLine("Connection Opened")

         ' Execute Query
         Dim thisReader As SqlDataReader = thisCommand.ExecuteReader()
```

```
            ' Loop through result sets
            Do
               ' Fetch Data
               While (thisReader.Read())
                  Console.WriteLine("{0} | {1}", _
                  thisReader(0), _
                  thisReader(1))
               End While
               Console.WriteLine("".PadLeft(60, "="))
            Loop While (thisReader.NextResult())

            'Close DataReader
            thisReader.Close()

         Catch ex As SqlException
            ' Display error
            Console.WriteLine("Error: " & ex.ToString())
         Finally
            ' Close Connection
            thisConnection.Close()
            Console.WriteLine("Connection Closed")
         End Try
      End Sub
   End Module
```

3. Make this the startup project and `MultipleResults` the startup object, and run it with Ctrl+F5. You should see the output in Figure 7-6.

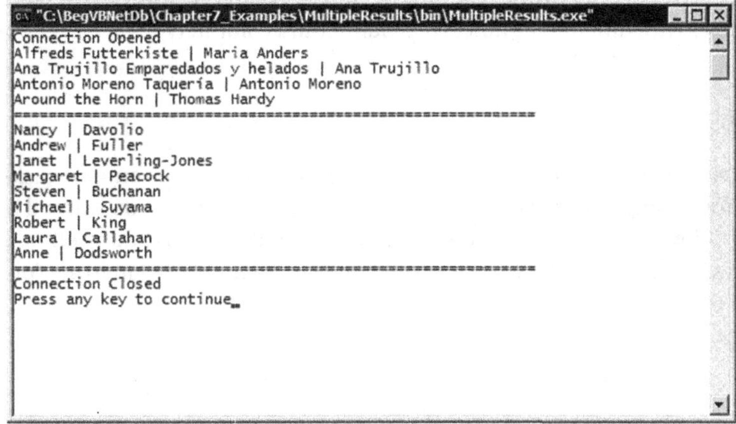

Figure 7-6. *MultipleResults*

How It Works

This program is essentially the same as the first, DataLooper (Listing 7-1). Here, you define two separate queries and then combine them.

```
'Combine queries
Dim sql As String = sql1 & sql2
```

■ **Caution** Some RDBMSs require an explicit character as a separator between multiple queries, but SQL Server requires only whitespace before subsequent SELECT keywords, which you have because of the verbatim strings.

The only other change is how you loop through the result sets. You nest the loop inside one that retrieves rows inside one that moves through result sets.

```
' Loop through result sets
Do
   ' Fetch Data
   While (thisReader.Read())
      Console.WriteLine("{0} | {1}", _
      thisReader(0), _
      thisReader(1))
   End While
   Console.WriteLine("".PadLeft(60, "="))
Loop While (thisReader.NextResult())
```

We chose only two character-string columns per query to simplify things. Extending this to handle result tables with different numbers of columns and column types is straightforward.

Summary

In this chapter you learned how to use data readers to perform a variety of common tasks, from simply looping through single result sets to handling multiple result sets. You learned how to retrieve values for columns by column name and index and learned about the methods available for handling values of different data types. You also learned how to get information about result sets and get schema information.

CHAPTER 8

Introducing Datasets and Data Adapters

In the previous chapter you saw how to use data readers to access database data in a connected, forward-only, read-only fashion. Often, this is all you want to do, and a data reader suits your purposes perfectly.

In this chapter, you'll look at the alternative object for accessing data, the *dataset*. Unlike data readers, which are objects of data provider-specific classes that implement the `System.Data.IDataReader` interface, datasets are objects of the class `System.Data.DataSet`, a distinct ADO.NET component used by all data providers. Datasets are completely independent of and disconnected from data sources. Their fundamental purpose is to provide a relational view of data stored in an in-memory cache.

Note In yet another somewhat confusing bit of terminology, the class is named `DataSet`, but the generic term is spelled *dataset* (when one expects *data set*). Why Microsoft does this is unclear, especially since *data set* is the more common usage outside ADO.NET. Nonetheless, we'll follow the .NET convention and call `DataSet` objects *datasets*.

So, if a dataset isn't connected in any way to a database, then how do you populate it with data and save its data back to the database? This is where *data adapters* come in. Think of data adapters as bridges between datasets and data sources. Without a data adapter, a dataset can't access any kind of data source. The data adapter takes care of all connection details for the dataset, populates it with data, and updates the data source.

In this chapter, we'll cover the following:

- Datasets and data adapters
- How data is stored in a dataset with data tables, data rows, and data columns
- How to get different views of the data in a dataset
- How to manipulate data in a dataset

- How to persist changes in the dataset back to the original data source
- Working with datasets and XML
- Typed and untyped datasets

Understanding the Object Model

We'll start this chapter with a quick presentation of all the new objects you'll need to understand in order to work with datasets and data adapters. You'll start by looking at the difference between datasets and data readers and then move on to look in more detail at how data is structured within a dataset and how a dataset works in collaboration with a data adapter.

Datasets vs. Data Readers

If you simply want to read and display data, then you need to use only a data reader, as you saw in the previous chapter, particularly if you're working with large quantities of data. In situations where you need to loop through thousands or millions of rows, you want a fast sequential reader (reading a single row from the result set at one time), and the data reader does this job in an efficient way.

If you need to manipulate the data in any way and then update the database, then you need to use a dataset. A data adapter fills a dataset by using a data reader, and with a dataset, additional resources are needed to save data for disconnected use. That is, data is retrieved from a data source and saved in the dataset, and then the connection is broken so you just work with the local copy of the data. You need to think about whether you really need a dataset; otherwise, you'll just be wasting resources. Unless you need to update the data source or use other dataset features such as reading and writing to XML files, exporting database schemas, and creating XML views of a database, you should use a data reader.

Introducing Datasets

The notion of a dataset in ADO.NET is a big step in the world of multitiered database application development. When retrieving or modifying large amounts of data, maintaining an open connection to a data source while waiting for users to make requests is an enormous waste of precious resources.

Datasets help tremendously here, because they enable you to store and modify large amounts of data in a local cache, view the data as tables, and process the data in an *offline* mode (in other words, disconnected from the database).

Let's look at an example. Imagine you're trying to connect to a remote database server over the Internet for detailed information about some business transactions. You search on a particular date for all available transactions, and the results are displayed. Behind the scenes, your application creates a connection with the data source, joins a couple of tables, and retrieves the results. Suppose you now want to edit this information and add or remove details. Whatever the reason, your application will go through the same cycle over and over again: creating a new connection, joining tables, and retrieving data. Not only is there overhead in creating a new connection each time, but you may be doing a lot of other redundant work, especially if you're dealing with the same data. Wouldn't it be better if you could connect to the data source once, store the data locally in a structure that resembles a relational database, close the connection, modify the local data, and then propagate the changes to the data source when the time is right?

This is exactly what the dataset is designed to do. A dataset stores relational data as collections of *data tables*. You met data tables briefly in the previous chapter when a `System.Data.DataTable` object was used to hold schema information. In that instance, and in every other one when you use data tables and a dataset, the dataset acts as the container for data tables, and the data tables contain both the data you've asked for and the metadata describing the structure of the data retrieved.

Figure 8-1 shows the dataset architecture.

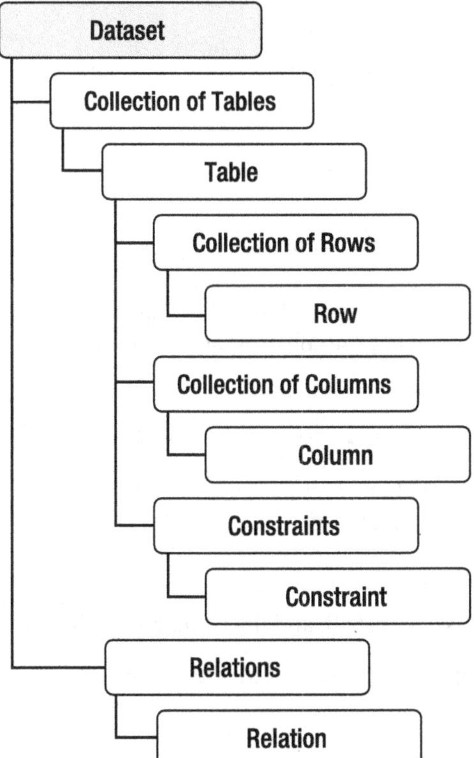

Figure 8-1. *Dataset architecture*

The architecture mirrors the logical design of a relational database. You'll see how to use data tables, data rows, and data columns in this chapter, but we'll leave relationships and constraints until Chapter 12, when we'll introduce their database and SQL equivalents.

Introducing Data Adapters

When you first instantiate a dataset, it contains no data. You obtain a populated dataset by passing it to a data adapter, which takes care of connection details and is a component of a data provider. A dataset isn't part of a data provider. It's like a bucket, ready to be filled with water, but it needs an external pipe to let the water in. In other words, the dataset needs a data adapter to populate it with data and to support access to the data source.

Each data provider has its own data adapter in the same way that it has its own connection, command, and data reader. Figure 8-2 depicts the interactions between the dataset, data adapter, and data source.

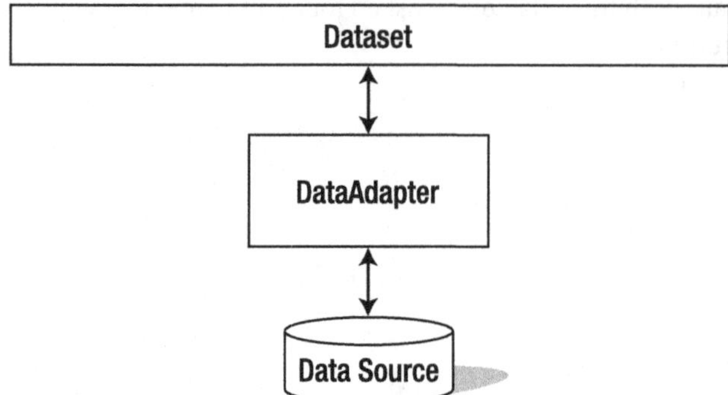

Figure 8-2. *Interactions between dataset, data adapter, and data source*

The data adapter constructor is overloaded. You can use any of the following to get a new data adapter. We're using the SQL Server data provider, but the constructors for the other data providers are analogous.

```
Dim da As New SqlDataAdapter
Dim da As New SqlDataAdapter(SqlCommand cmd)
Dim da As New SqlDataAdapter(String sql, SqlConnection conn)
Dim da As New SqlDataAdapter(String sql, String connstring)
```

So, you can create a data adapter in four ways:

- You can use its parameterless constructor (assigning SQL and the connection later).
- You can pass its constructor a command object (here, `cmd` is a `SqlCommand` object).
- You can pass a SQL string and a connection.
- You can pass a SQL string and a connection string.

You'll see all this working in action shortly. For now, we'll move on and show how you use data tables, data columns, and data rows. You'll use these in upcoming sections.

Introducing Data Tables, Data Columns, and Data Rows

A data table is an instance of the class `System.Data.DataTable`. It's conceptually analogous to a relational table. As shown in Figure 8-1, a data table has collections of data rows and data columns. You can access these nested collections via the `Rows` and `Columns` properties of the data table.

A data table can represent a stand-alone independent table, either inside a dataset—as you'll see in this chapter—or as an object created by another method, as you saw in the previous chapter when a data table was returned by calling the method `GetSchemaTable` on a data reader.

A data column represents the schema of a column within a data table and can then be used to set or get column properties. For example, you could use it to set the default value of a column by assigning a value to the DefaultValue property of the data column.

You obtain the collection of data columns using the data table's Columns property, whose indexer accepts either a column name or a zero-based index; see the following example (where dt is a data table):

```
Dim col As DataColumn = dt.Columns("ContactName")
Dim col As DataColumn = dt.Columns(2)
```

A data row represents the data in a row. You can programmatically add, update, or delete rows in a data table. To access rows in a data table, you use the Rows property, whose indexer accepts a zero-based index (for example, where dt is a data table).

```
Dim row As DataRow = dt.Rows(2)
```

That's enough theory for now. It's time to do some coding and see how these objects work together in practice!

Working with Datasets and Data Adapters

The first order of the day is to create a dataset; .NET gives you two options.

```
Dim ds As new DataSet()
Dim ds As new DataSet("MyDataSet")
```

If you use the parameterless constructor, the dataset name defaults to NewDataSet. If you need more than one dataset, it's good practice to use the other constructor and name it explicitly. However, you can always change the dataset name by setting its DataSetName property.

You can populate a dataset in one of two ways.

- Using a data adapter
- Reading from an XML document

In this chapter, you'll use data adapters. You'll learn how to populate a dataset from an XML document in Chapter 17.

Try It Out: Populating a Dataset with a Data Adapter

In this example, you'll create a dataset, populate it with a data adapter, and then display its contents.

1. Create a new blank solution named Chapter8_Examples.
2. Add a VB .NET console application named PopDataset, and rename the Module1.vb file to PopDataset.vb.
3. Replace the code in PopDataset.vb with that in Listing 8-1.

Listing 8-1. *PopDataset*

```
Imports System
Imports System.Data
Imports System.Data.SqlClient

Module PopDataSet

   Sub Main()
      'Create Connection object
      Dim thisConnection As New SqlConnection _
         ("server=(local)\netsdk;" & _
          "integrated security=sspi;" & _
          "database=northwind")

      'Sql Query
      Dim sql As String = _
         "SELECT ProductName, UnitPrice " & _
         "FROM Products " & _
         "WHERE UnitPrice < 20"

      Try
         ' Open Connection
         thisConnection.Open()
         Console.WriteLine("Connection Opened")

         ' Create Data Adapter
         Dim da As New SqlDataAdapter(sql, thisConnection)

         ' Create and fill Dataset
         Dim ds As New DataSet
         da.Fill(ds, "products")

         ' Get Data Table
         Dim dt As DataTable = ds.Tables("products")

         'Display Data
         For Each row As DataRow In dt.Rows
            For Each col As DataColumn In dt.Columns
               Console.WriteLine(row(col))
            Next
            Console.WriteLine("".PadLeft(20, "="))
         Next

      Catch ex As SqlException
         ' Display error
         Console.WriteLine("Error: " & ex.ToString())
```

```
        Finally
            ' Close Connection
            thisConnection.Close()
            Console.WriteLine("Connection Closed")
        End Try
    End Sub
End Module
```

4. Set PopDataset as the project's startup object, and then run it with Ctrl+F5. You should see the output in Figure 8-3.

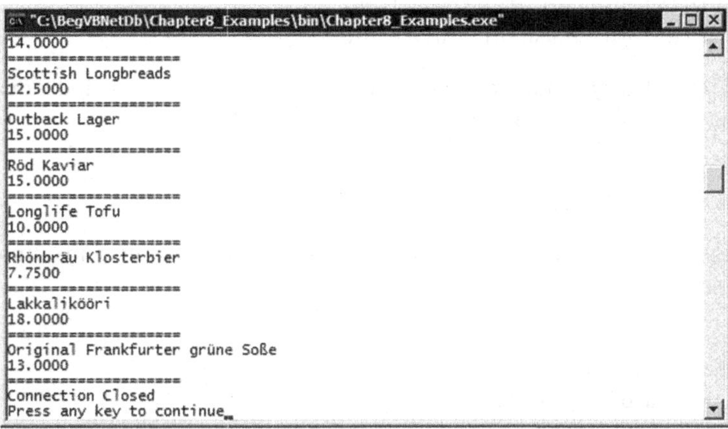

Figure 8-3. *PopDataset*

How It Works

After defining a query and opening a connection, you create and initialize a data adapter.

```
' Create Data Adapter
Dim da As New SqlDataAdapter(sql, thisConnection)
```

You then create the dataset.

```
' Create and fill Dataset
Dim ds As New DataSet
```

At this stage, all you have is an empty dataset. The key line is where you use the Fill method on the data adapter to execute the query, retrieve the data, and populate the dataset.

```
da.Fill(ds, "products")
```

The Fill method uses a data reader internally to access the table schema and data and then uses them to populate the dataset.

Note that this method isn't just used for filling datasets. It has a number of overloads and can also be used for filling an individual data table without a dataset, if needed.

If you don't provide a name for the table to the Fill method, it will automatically be named *Tablen*, where *n* starts as an empty string (the first table name is simply Table) and increments every time a new table is inserted into the dataset. It's better practice to explicitly name data tables, but here it doesn't really matter.

If the same query is run more than once on the dataset that already contains data then Fill updates the data, skipping the process of redefining the table based on the schema.

It's worth mentioning here that the following code would have produced the same result. Instead of passing the SQL and connection to the data adapter's constructor, you could have set its SelectCommand property with a command that you created with the appropriate SQL and connection. The two are equivalent, as the SqlDataAdapter assumes that both the SQL string and SqlCommand object represent a SELECT query and sets SelectCommand with their contents.

```
' Create Data Adapter
Dim da As New SqlDataAdapter(sql, thisConnection)
da.SelectCommand = New SqlCommand(sql, thisConnection)
```

With a populated dataset at your disposal, you can now access the data in individual data tables. (The dataset contains only one data table.)

```
' Get Data Table
Dim dt As DataTable = ds.Tables("products")
```

Finally, you use nested For Each loops to access the columns in each row and output their data values to the screen.

```
'Display Data
For Each row As DataRow In dt.Rows
   For Each col As DataColumn In dt.Columns
      Console.WriteLine(row(col))
   Next
   Console.WriteLine("".PadLeft(20, "="))
Next
```

Filtering and Sorting in a DataSet

In the previous example, you saw how to extract data from a dataset. However, if you're working with datasets, then the chances are that you're going to want to do more with the data than merely displaying it. Often, you'll want to dynamically filter or sort the data. In the following example, you'll see how you can use data rows to do this.

Try It Out: Dynamically Filtering and Sorting Data in a Dataset

Follow these steps:

1. Add a VB .NET console application named FilterSort, and rename the Module1.vb file to FilterSort.vb.

2. Replace the code in FilterSort.vb with that in Listing 8-2.

Listing 8-2. *FilterSort*

```
Imports System
Imports System.Data
Imports System.Data.SqlClient

Module FilterSort

   Sub Main()
      'Create Connection object
      Dim thisConnection As New SqlConnection _
         ("server=(local)\netsdk;" & _
          "integrated security=sspi;" & _
          "database=northwind")

      ' Sql Query 1
      Dim sql1 As String = _
         "SELECT * FROM Customers "

      ' Sql Query 2
      Dim sql2 As String = _
         "SELECT * FROM Products " & _
         "WHERE UnitPrice < 10"

      ' Combine Queries
      Dim sql As String = sql1 & sql2

      Try
         ' Create Data Adapter
         Dim da As New SqlDataAdapter
         da.SelectCommand = New SqlCommand(sql, thisConnection)

         ' Create and fill Dataset
         Dim ds As New DataSet
         da.Fill(ds, "customers")

         ' Get the Data Tables Collection
         Dim dtc As DataTableCollection = ds.Tables

         ' Get and Display First Data Table
         ' 1. Display header
         Console.WriteLine("Results From Customers Table")
         Console.WriteLine("CompanyName".PadRight(25) & _
            " | ContactName")
```

```
            ' 2. Set display filter
            Dim filter1 As String = "Country = 'Germany'"

            ' 3. Set sort
            Dim sort1 As String = "CompanyName ASC"

            ' 4. Display filtered and sorted data
            For Each row As DataRow In _
               dtc("Customers").Select(filter1, sort1)
               Console.WriteLine("{0} | {1}", _
                  row("CompanyName").ToString().PadRight(25), _
                  row("ContactName"))
            Next

            ' Get and Display Second Data Table
            ' 1. Display header
            Console.WriteLine("========================")
            Console.WriteLine("Results from Products Table")
            Console.WriteLine("ProductName".PadRight(31) & _
               " | UnitPrice")

            ' 2. Display Data
            For Each row As DataRow In dtc(1).Rows
               Console.WriteLine("{0} | {1}", _
                  row("ProductName").ToString().PadRight(31), _
                  row("unitprice"))
            Next

         Catch ex As SqlException
            ' Display error
            Console.WriteLine("Error: " & ex.ToString())
         Finally
            ' Close Connection
            thisConnection.Close()
            Console.WriteLine("Connection Closed")
         End Try
      End Sub
   End Module
```

3. Make this the startup project and `FilterSort` the startup object, and run it with Ctrl+F5. You should see the output in Figure 8-4.

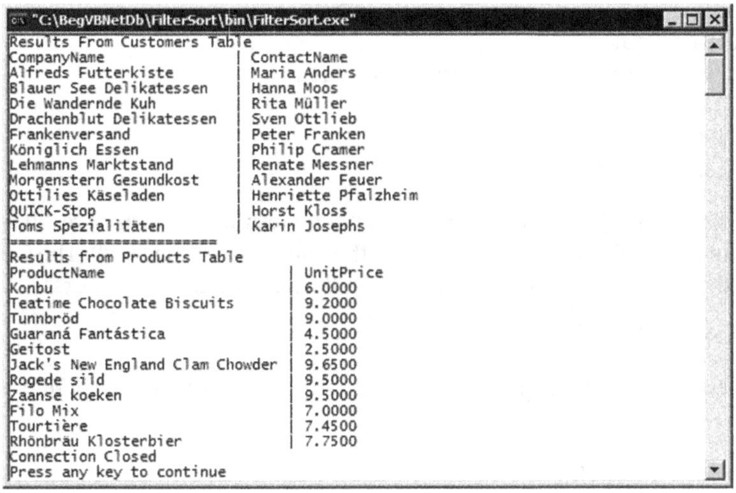

```
"C:\BegVBNetDb\FilterSort\bin\FilterSort.exe"
Results From Customers Table
CompanyName                 | ContactName
Alfreds Futterkiste         | Maria Anders
Blauer See Delikatessen     | Hanna Moos
Die Wandernde Kuh           | Rita Müller
Drachenblut Delikatessen    | Sven Ottlieb
Frankenversand              | Peter Franken
Königlich Essen             | Philip Cramer
Lehmanns Marktstand         | Renate Messner
Morgenstern Gesundkost      | Alexander Feuer
Ottilies Käseladen          | Henriette Pfalzheim
QUICK-Stop                  | Horst Kloss
Toms Spezialitäten          | Karin Josephs
========================
Results from Products Table
ProductName                       | UnitPrice
Konbu                             | 6.0000
Teatime Chocolate Biscuits        | 9.2000
Tunnbröd                          | 9.0000
Guaraná Fantástica                | 4.5000
Geitost                           | 2.5000
Jack's New England Clam Chowder   | 9.6500
Rogede sild                       | 9.5000
Zaanse koeken                     | 9.5000
Filo Mix                          | 7.0000
Tourtière                         | 7.4500
Rhönbräu Klosterbier              | 7.7500
Connection Closed
Press any key to continue
```

Figure 8-4. *FilterSort*

How It Works

You create a connection and then code and combine two queries.

```
'Create Connection object
Dim thisConnection As New SqlConnection _
   ("server=(local)\netsdk;" & _
    "integrated security=sspi;" & _
    "database=northwind")

' Sql Query 1
Dim sql1 As String = _
   "SELECT * FROM Customers "

' Sql Query 2
Dim sql2 As String = _
   "SELECT * FROM Products " & _
   "WHERE UnitPrice < 10"

' Combine Queries
Dim sql As String = sql1 & sql2
```

You create a dataset and a data adapter assigning the `SelectCommand` property of the data adapter a command that encapsulates the query and connection (for internal use by its `Fill` method).

```
' Create Data Adapter
Dim da As New SqlDataAdapter
da.SelectCommand = New SqlCommand(sql, thisConnection)

' Create and fill Dataset
Dim ds As New DataSet
```

You then fill the dataset. Each query returns a separate result set, and each result set is stored in a separate data table (in the order in which the queries were specified). The first table is explicitly named `customers`; the second will be given the default name `customers1`.

```
da.Fill(ds, "customers")
```

You get the data table collection from the dataset `Tables` property for ease of reference later.

```
' Get the Data Tables Collection
Dim dtc As DataTableCollection = ds.Tables
```

As part of displaying the first data table, you declare two strings.

```
' 2. Set display filter
Dim filter1 As String = "Country = 'Germany'"

' 3. Set sort
Dim sort1 As String = "CompanyName ASC"
```

The first string is a *filter expression* that specifies row selection criteria. It's syntactically the same as a SQL `WHERE` clause predicate. You want only rows where the `Country` column equals `"Germany"`. The second string specifies your sort criteria and is syntactically the same as a SQL `ORDER BY` specifier, giving a data column name and sort sequence.

You use a `For Each` loop to display the rows selected from the data table, passing the filter and sort strings to the `Select` method of the data table. This particular data table is the one named `Customers` in the data table collection.

```
' 4. Display filtered and sorted data
For Each row As DataRow In _
   dtc("Customers").Select(filter1, sort1)
   Console.WriteLine("{0} | {1}", _
      row("CompanyName").ToString().PadRight(25), _
      row("ContactName"))
Next
```

Here you obtain a reference to a single data table from the collection (the `dtc` object) using the table name that you specified when creating the dataset. The overloaded `Select` method does an internal search on the data table, filters out rows not satisfying the selection criterion, sorts the result as prescribed, and finally returns an array of data rows. You access each column in the row, using the column name in the indexer.

It's important to note that you could have achieved the same result—much more efficiently—had you simply used a different query for the `Customer` data.

```
SELECT * FROM Customers
WHERE Country = 'Germany'
ORDER BY CompanyName
```

This would be ideal in terms of performance, but it'd be feasible only if the data you needed were limited to these specific rows in this particular sequence. However, if you were building a more elaborate system, it may be better to pull all the data once from the database (as you do here) and then filter and sort it in different ways. ADO.NET's rich suite of methods for manipulating datasets and their components gives you a broad range of techniques for meeting specific needs in an optimal way.

■ **Tip** In general, try to exploit SQL, rather than code VB .NET procedures, to get the data you need from the database. Database servers are optimized to perform selections and sorts, as well as other things. Queries can be far more sophisticated and powerful than the ones you've been playing with in this chapter. By carefully (and creatively) coding queries to return *exactly* what you need, you not only minimize resource demands (on memory, network bandwidth, and so on) but also reduce the code you must write to manipulate and format result set data.

The loop through the second data table is interesting mainly for its first line

```
For Each row As DataRow In dtc(1).Rows
```

which uses an ordinal index. Since you didn't rename the second data table (you could have done so with its `TableName` property), it was better to use the index rather than the name (`customers1`), since a change to the name in the `Fill` call would require you to change it here, an unlikely thing to remember to do, if the case ever arose.

Comparing FilterSort to PopDataset

In the first example, `PopDataset` (Listing 8-1), you saw how simple it is to get data into a dataset. The second example, `FilterSort` (Listing 8-2), was just a variation, demonstrating how multiple result sets are handled and how to filter and sort data tables. However, the two programs have one major difference. Did you notice it?

`FilterSort` doesn't explicitly open a connection! In fact, it's the first (but won't be the last) program you've written that doesn't. Why doesn't it?

The answer is simple but *very* important. The `Fill` method *automatically* opens a connection if it's not open when `Fill` is called. It then closes the connection after filling the dataset. However, if a connection is open when `Fill` is called, it uses that connection and *doesn't* close it afterward.

So, although datasets are completely independent of databases (and connections), just because you're using a dataset doesn't mean you're running disconnected from a database. If you want to run disconnected, use datasets, but don't open connections before filling them (or, if a connection is open, close it first). Datasets in themselves don't imply either connected or disconnected operations.

You left the standard connection close method in the `Finally` block. Since it can be called without error on a closed connection, it presents no problems if called unnecessarily but definitely guarantees that the connection will be closed, whatever may happen in the `Try` block.

Note If you want to prove this for yourself, simply open the connection in `FilterSort` before calling `Fill` and then display the value of the connection's `State` property. It will be `Open`. Comment out the `Open` call, and run it again. `State` will be closed.

Using Data Views

In the previous example, you saw how to dynamically filter and sort data contained by a data table using the `Select` method. However, ADO.NET has another approach for doing much the same thing and more, *data views*. A data view (an instance of class `System.Data.DataView`) enables you to create dynamic views of the data stored in an underlying data table, reflecting all the changes made to its content and the ordering. This differs from the `Select` method, which returns an array of data rows whose contents reflect the changes to data values but not the data ordering.

Note A *data view* is a dynamic representation of the contents of a data table. Like a SQL view, it doesn't actually hold data.

Try It Out: Refining Data with a Data View

We won't cover all aspects of data views here, as they're beyond the scope of this book. However, to show how it can be used, we'll present a short example that uses a data view to dynamically sort and filter an underlying data table.

1. Add a VB .NET console application named `DataViewExample`, and rename the `Module1.vb` file to `DataViewExample.vb`.

2. Replace the code in `DataViewExample.vb` with that in Listing 8-3.

Listing 8-3. *`DataViewExample`*

```
Imports System
Imports System.Data
Imports System.Data.SqlClient

Module DataViewExample
```

```
   Sub Main()
      'Create Connection object
      Dim thisConnection As New SqlConnection _
         ("server=(local)\netsdk;" & _
          "integrated security=sspi;" & _
          "database=northwind")

      ' Sql Query
      Dim sql As String = _
         "SELECT ContactName, Country " & _
         "FROM Customers"

      Try
         ' Create Data Adapter
         Dim da As SqlDataAdapter = New SqlDataAdapter
         da.SelectCommand = New SqlCommand(sql, thisConnection)

         ' Create and fill Dataset
         Dim ds As New DataSet
         da.Fill(ds, "Customers")

         ' Get The Data Table
         Dim dt As DataTable = ds.Tables("Customers")

         ' Create Data View
         Dim dv As New DataView(dt, _
            "country = 'Germany'", _
            "country", _
            DataViewRowState.CurrentRows)

         ' Display Data In Data View
         For Each row As DataRowView In dv
            For i As Integer = 0 To dv.Table.Columns.Count - 1
               Console.Write(row(i).PadRight(20))
            Next
            Console.WriteLine()
         Next

      Catch ex As SqlException
         ' Display error
         Console.WriteLine("Error: " & ex.ToString())
      Finally
         ' Close Connection
         thisConnection.Close()
         Console.WriteLine("Connection Closed")
      End Try
   End Sub
End Module
```

3. Make this the startup project and startup object, and run it with Ctrl+F5. You should see the output in Figure 8-5.

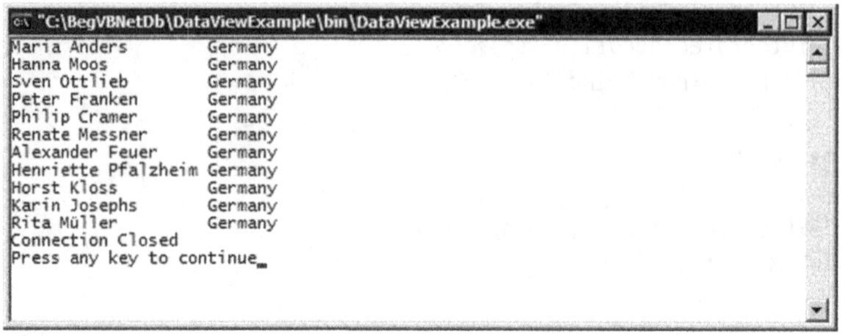

```
"C:\BegVBNetDb\DataViewExample\bin\DataViewExample.exe"
Maria Anders          Germany
Hanna Moos            Germany
Sven Ottlieb          Germany
Peter Franken         Germany
Philip Cramer         Germany
Renate Messner        Germany
Alexander Feuer       Germany
Henriette Pfalzheim   Germany
Horst Kloss           Germany
Karin Josephs         Germany
Rita Müller           Germany
Connection Closed
Press any key to continue
```

Figure 8-5. *DataViewExample*

How It Works

This program is basically the same as the other examples, so we'll focus on its use of a data view. You create a new data view and initialize it by passing four parameters to its constructor.

```
' Create Data View
Dim dv As New DataView(dt, _
   "country = 'Germany'", _
   "country", _
   DataViewRowState.CurrentRows)
```

The first parameter is a data table, the second is a filter for the contents of the data table, the third is the sort column, and the fourth specifies the types of rows to include in the data view.

System.Data.DataViewRowState is an enumeration of states that rows can have in a data view's underlying data table. Table 8-1 summarizes the states.

Table 8-1. *Data View Row States*

DataViewRowState **Members**	**Description**
Added	A new row
CurrentRows	Current rows including unchanged, new, and modified ones
Deleted	A deleted row
ModifiedCurrent	The current version of a modified row
ModifiedOriginal	The original version of a modified row
None	None of the rows
OriginalRows	Original rows, including unchanged and deleted
Unchanged	A row that hasn't been modified

Every time a row is added, modified, or deleted, its row state changes to the appropriate one in Table 8-1. This is useful if you're interested in retrieving, sorting, or filtering specific rows based on their state (for example, all new rows in the data table or all rows that have been modified).

You then loop through the rows in the data view.

```
' Display Data In Data View
For Each row As DataRowView In dv
   For i As Integer = 0 To dv.Table.Columns.Count - 1
      Console.Write(row(i).PadRight(20))
   Next
   Console.WriteLine()
Next
```

Just as a data row represents a single row in a data table, a *data row view* (perhaps it would have been better to call it a *data view row*) represents a single row in a data view. You retrieve the filtered and the sorted column data for each data row view and output it to the console.

As this simple example suggests, data views offer a powerful and flexible means of dynamically changing what data one works with in a data table.

Modifying Data in a Dataset

In the following sections, you'll work through a practical example showing a number of ways to update data in data tables programmatically. Note that here you'll just modify the data in the dataset but not update the data in the database. You'll see in the "Propagating Changes to a Data Source" section how to persist changes to a dataset in the original data source.

Note Changes you make to a dataset aren't automatically propagated to a database. To save the changes in a database, you need to connect to the database again and explicitly perform the necessary updates.

Try It Out: Modifying a Data Table in a Dataset

Follow these steps:

1. Add a VB .NET console application named `ModifyDataTable`, and rename the `Module1.vb` file to `ModifyDataTable.vb`.

2. Replace the code in `ModifyDataTable.vb` with that in Listing 8-4.

Listing 8-4. *ModifyDataTable*

```
Imports System
Imports System.Data
Imports System.Data.SqlClient

Module ModifyDataTable

   Sub Main()
      'Create Connection object
      Dim thisConnection As New SqlConnection _
         ("server=(local)\netsdk;" & _
          "integrated security=sspi;" & _
          "database=northwind")

      ' Sql Query
      Dim sql As String = _
         "SELECT * FROM Employees " & _
         "WHERE Country = 'UK'"

      Try
         ' Create Data Adapter
         Dim da As New SqlDataAdapter
         da.SelectCommand = New SqlCommand(sql, thisConnection)

         ' Create and fill Dataset
         Dim ds As New DataSet
         da.Fill(ds, "Employees")

         ' Get the Data Table
         Dim dt As DataTable = ds.Tables("Employees")

         ' Display Rows Before Changed
         Console.WriteLine("Before altering the dataset")
         For Each row As DataRow In dt.Rows
            Console.WriteLine("{0} | {1} | {2}", _
               row("FirstName").ToString().PadRight(10), _
               row("LastName").ToString().PadRight(10), _
               row("City"))
         Next

         ' FirstName column should be nullable
         dt.Columns("firstname").AllowDBNull = True

         ' Modify city in first row
         dt.Rows(0)("City") = "Birmingham"
```

```
            ' Add A Row
            Dim newRow As DataRow = dt.NewRow()
            newRow("firstname") = "Edna"
            newRow("lastname") = "Everage"
            newRow("titleofcourtesy") = "Dame"
            newRow("city") = "Sydney"
            newRow("country") = "Australia"
            dt.Rows.Add(newRow)

            ' Display Rows After Alteration
            Console.WriteLine("=========")
            Console.WriteLine("After altering the dataset")
            For Each row As DataRow In dt.Rows
               Console.WriteLine("{0} | {1} | {2}", _
                  row("FirstName").ToString().PadRight(10), _
                  row("LastName").ToString().PadRight(10), _
                  row("City"))
            Next

            ' Code for updating the database would be here

         Catch ex As SqlException
            ' Display error
            Console.WriteLine("Error: " & ex.ToString())
         Finally
            ' Close Connection
            thisConnection.Close()
            Console.WriteLine("Connection Closed")
         End Try
      End Sub
   End Module
```

3. Make this the startup project and the startup object, and run it with Ctrl+F5. You should see the output in Figure 8-6.

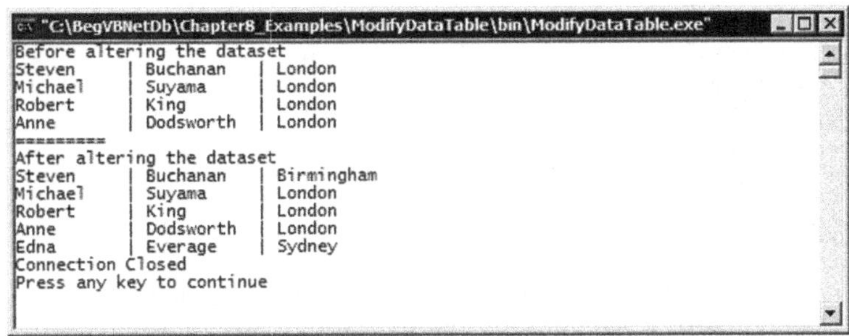

Figure 8-6. *ModifyDataTable*

How It Works

As before, you use a single data table from the dataset.

```
' Get the Data Table
Dim dt As DataTable = ds.Tables("Employees")
```

Next, you display the data in the table before making any changes.

```
' Display Rows Before Changed
Console.WriteLine("Before altering the dataset")
For Each row As DataRow In dt.Rows
   Console.WriteLine("{0} | {1} | {2}", _
      row("FirstName").ToString().PadRight(10), _
      row("LastName").ToString().PadRight(10), _
      row("City"))
Next
```

Now let's alter a few things. First, you can see an example of how you can change the schema information. You select the `FirstName` column, whose `AllowNull` property is set to `False` in the database, and you change it—just for the purposes of demonstration—to `True`.

```
' FirstName column should be nullable
dt.Columns("firstname").AllowDBNull = True
```

Note that you could have used an ordinal index (for example, `dt.Columns(1)`) if you knew what the index for the column was, but using * to select all columns makes this less reliable since the position of a column may change if the database table schema changed.

Your second alteration is modifying a record using the same technique. You simply select the appropriate row and set its columns to whatever values you want, consistent with the column data types, of course. The following line shows the `City` column of the first row of the dataset being changed to *Birmingham*:

```
' Modify city in first row
dt.Rows(0)("City") = "Birmingham"
```

Next you add a new row to the data table, like so:

```
' Add A Row
Dim newRow As DataRow = dt.NewRow()
newRow("firstname") = "Edna"
newRow("lastname") = "Everage"
newRow("titleofcourtesy") = "Dame"
newRow("city") = "Sydney"
newRow("country") = "Australia"
dt.Rows.Add(newRow)
```

The `NewRow` method creates a data row (a `System.Data.DataRow` instance). You use the data row's indexer to assign values to its columns. Finally, you add the new row to the data table, calling the `Add` method on the data table's `Rows` property, which references the rows collection.

Note that you don't provide a value for EmployeeID since it's an IDENTITY column. If you persisted the changes to the database, then SQL Server would automatically provide a value for it.

Updating data sources requires learning more about data adapter methods and properties. Let's take a look at these now.

Propagating Changes to a Data Source

You've seen how a data adapter populates a dataset's data tables. What you haven't looked at yet is how a data adapter updates and synchronizes a data source with data from a dataset. It has three properties that support this (analogous to its SelectCommand property that supports queries).

- UpdateCommand
- InsertCommand
- DeleteCommand

We'll describe each of these properties briefly and then put them to work.

Using the UpdateCommand Property

The UpdateCommand property of the data adapter holds the command used to update the data source when the data adapter's Update method is called.

For example, to update the City column in the Employees table with the data from a data table, one approach is to write code such as the following (where da is the data adapter, dt is the data table, conn is the connection, and ds is the dataset):

```
' Create command to update Employees City column
Dim updateSql As String = _
   "UPDATE Employees " & _
   "SET City = '" & dt.Rows(0)("City") & "'" & _
   "WHERE EmployeeId = '" & dt.Rows(0)("EmployeeId") & "'"
da.UpdateCommand = New SqlCommand(updateSql, conn)

// Update Employees table
da.Update(ds, "employees")
```

This isn't very pretty—or useful. Basically, you coded an UPDATE statement and embedded two data column values for the first row in a data table in it. It's valid SQL, but that's its only virtue and it's not much of one, since it updates only one database row, the row in Employees corresponding to the first data row in the employees data table.

Another approach works for any number of rows. Recall from the CommandExampleParameters program in Chapter 6 how you used command parameters for INSERT statements. You can use them in any query or data manipulation statement. Let's recode the previous example with command parameters.

Try It Out: Propagating Dataset Changes to a Data Source

Follow these steps:

1. Add a VB .NET console application named PropagateChanges, and rename the Module1.vb file to PropagateChanges.vb.

2. Replace the code in PropagateChanges.vb with that in Listing 8-5. This is a variation on ModifyDataTable in Listing 8-4, with the nullability and insertion logic removed since they're irrelevant here. The changes are marked in bold text.

Listing 8-5. *PropagateChanges*

```
Imports System
Imports System.Data
Imports System.Data.SqlClient

Module PropagateChanges

   Sub Main()
      'Create Connection object
      Dim thisConnection As New SqlConnection _
         ("server=(local)\netsdk;" & _
          "integrated security=sspi;" & _
          "database=northwind")

      ' Sql Select Query
      Dim sql As String = _
         "SELECT * FROM Employees " & _
         "WHERE Country = 'UK'"

      ' Sql Update Statement
      Dim updateSql As String = _
         "UPDATE Employees " & _
         "SET City = @City " & _
         "WHERE EmployeeId = @EmployeeId"

      Try
         ' Create Data Adapter
         Dim da As New SqlDataAdapter
         da.SelectCommand = New SqlCommand(sql, thisConnection)

         ' Create and fill Dataset
         Dim ds As New DataSet
         da.Fill(ds, "Employees")
```

```
' Get the Data Table
Dim dt As DataTable = ds.Tables("Employees")

' Display Rows Before Changed
Console.WriteLine("Before altering the dataset")
For Each row As DataRow In dt.Rows
   Console.WriteLine("{0} | {1} | {2}", _
      row("FirstName").ToString().PadRight(10), _
      row("LastName").ToString().PadRight(10), _
      row("City"))
Next

' Modify city in first row
dt.Rows(0)("City") = "Birmingham"

' Display Rows After Alteration
Console.WriteLine("==========")
Console.WriteLine("After altering the dataset")
For Each row As DataRow In dt.Rows
   Console.WriteLine("{0} | {1} | {2}", _
      row("FirstName").ToString().PadRight(10), _
      row("LastName").ToString().PadRight(10), _
      row("City"))
Next

' Update Employees
' 1. Create Command
Dim UpdateCmd As New SqlCommand(updateSql, thisConnection)

' 2. Map Parameters
' 2.1 City
UpdateCmd.Parameters.Add("@city", _
   SqlDbType.NVarChar, 15, "city")

' 2.2 EmployeeId
Dim idParam As SqlParameter = _
   UpdateCmd.Parameters.Add("@employeeId", _
   SqlDbType.Int, 4, "employeeid")
idParam.SourceVersion = DataRowVersion.Original

' Update employees
da.UpdateCommand = UpdateCmd
da.Update(ds, "employees")
```

```
            Catch ex As SqlException
               ' Display error
               Console.WriteLine("Error: " & ex.ToString())
            Finally
               ' Close Connection
               thisConnection.Close()
               Console.WriteLine("Connection Closed")
            End Try
        End Sub
    End Module
```

3. Make this the startup project and the startup object, and run it with Ctrl+F5. You should see the output in Figure 8-7.

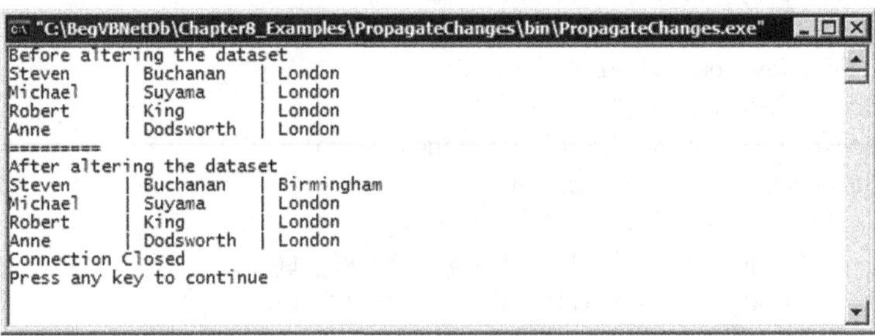

Figure 8-7. *PropagateChanges*

How It Works

You added an UPDATE statement in the string variable updateSql to the code.

```
' Sql Update Statement
Dim updateSql As String = _
   "UPDATE Employees " & _
   "SET City = @City " & _
   "WHERE EmployeeId = @EmployeeId"
```

You replaced the update comment in the Try block with quite a bit of code. Let's look at it piece by piece. Creating a command is nothing new, but notice that you use the variable containing the update SQL statement (updateSql), not the query one (sql).

```
' Update Employees
' 1. Create Command
Dim UpdateCmd As New SqlCommand(updateSql, thisConnection)
```

Then you configure the command parameters. The @city parameter is mapped to a data column named city. Note that you don't specify the data table, but you must be sure the type and length are compatible with this column in whatever data table you eventually use.

```
' 2.1 City
UpdateCmd.Parameters.Add("@city", _
   SqlDbType.NVarChar, 15, "city")
```

Next, you configure the @employeeid parameter, mapping it to a data column named employeeid. Unlike @city, which by default takes values from the current version of the data table, you want to make sure that @employeeid gets values from the version *before* any changes. Although it doesn't really matter here, since you didn't change any employee IDs, it's a good habit to specify the original version for primary keys, so if they do change, the correct rows are accessed in the database table. Note also that you save the reference returned by the Add method so you can set its SourceVersion property. Since you didn't need to do anything else with @city, you didn't have to save a reference to it.

```
' 2.2 EmployeeId
Dim idParam As SqlParameter = _
   UpdateCmd.Parameters.Add("@employeeId", _
   SqlDbType.Int, 4, "employeeid")
idParam.SourceVersion = DataRowVersion.Original
```

Finally, you set the data adapter's UpdateCommand property with the command to update the Employees table so it will be the SQL the data adapter executes when you call its Update method. You then call Update on the data adapter to propagate the change to the database. Here you had only one change, but since the SQL is parameterized, the data adapter will look for all changed rows in the employees data table and submit updates for all of them to the database.

```
' Update employees
da.UpdateCommand = UpdateCmd
da.Update(ds, "employees")
```

If you check with Server Explorer or the SQL Tool application, you'll see the update has been propagated to the database. The city for employee Steven Buchanan is now Birmingham, not London.

Using the InsertCommand Property

The data adapter uses the InsertCommand property for inserting rows into a table. Upon calling the Update method, all rows added to the data table would be searched for and propagated to the database.

Let's again modify ModifyDataTable (Listing 8-4) to propagate its new row to the database.

Try It Out: Propagating New Dataset Rows to a Data Source

Follow these steps:

1. Add a VB .NET console application named PropagateAdds, and rename the Module1.vb file to PropagateAdds.vb.

2. Replace the code in PropagateAdds.vb with that in Listing 8-6. This is a variation on ModifyDataTable in Listing 8-4, with the nullability and update logic removed since they're irrelevant here. The changes to the original code are in bold.

Listing 8-6. *PropagateAdds*

```
Imports System
Imports System.Data
Imports System.Data.SqlClient

Module PropagateAdds

   Sub Main()
      'Create Connection object
      Dim thisConnection As New SqlConnection _
         ("server=(local)\netsdk;" & _
          "integrated security=sspi;" & _
          "database=northwind")

      ' Sql Query
      Dim sql As String = _
         "SELECT * FROM Employees " & _
         "WHERE Country = 'UK'"

      Dim insertSql As String = _
         "INSERT INTO Employees " & _
         "(firstname, lastname, titleofcourtesy, city, country)" & _
         " VALUES " & _
         "(@firstname, @lastname, @titleofcourtesy, @city, @country)"

      Try
         ' Create Data Adapter
         Dim da As New SqlDataAdapter
         da.SelectCommand = New SqlCommand(sql, thisConnection)

         ' Create and fill Dataset
         Dim ds As New DataSet
         da.Fill(ds, "Employees")

         ' Get the Data Table
         Dim dt As DataTable = ds.Tables("Employees")

         ' Display Rows Before Changed
         Console.WriteLine("Before altering the dataset")
         For Each row As DataRow In dt.Rows
            Console.WriteLine("{0} | {1} | {2}", _
               row("FirstName").ToString().PadRight(10), _
               row("LastName").ToString().PadRight(10), _
               row("City"))
         Next
```

```
            ' Add A Row
            Dim newRow As DataRow = dt.NewRow()
            newRow("firstname") = "Edna"
            newRow("lastname") = "Everage"
            newRow("titleofcourtesy") = "Dame"
            newRow("city") = "Sydney"
            newRow("country") = "Australia"
            dt.Rows.Add(newRow)

            ' Display Rows After Alteration
            Console.WriteLine("=========")
            Console.WriteLine("After altering the dataset")
            For Each row As DataRow In dt.Rows
               Console.WriteLine("{0} | {1} | {2}", _
                  row("FirstName").ToString().PadRight(10), _
                  row("LastName").ToString().PadRight(10), _
                  row("City"))
            Next

            ' Insert employees
            ' 1. Create command
            Dim insertCmd As New SqlCommand(insertSql, thisConnection)

            ' 2. Map parameters
            insertCmd.Parameters.Add("@firstname", _
               SqlDbType.NVarChar, 10, "firstname")
            insertCmd.Parameters.Add("@lastname", _
               SqlDbType.NVarChar, 20, "lastname")
            insertCmd.Parameters.Add("@titleofcourtesy", _
               SqlDbType.NVarChar, 25, "titleofcourtesy")
            insertCmd.Parameters.Add("@city", _
               SqlDbType.NVarChar, 15, "city")
            insertCmd.Parameters.Add("@country", _
               SqlDbType.NVarChar, 15, "country")

            ' 3. Insert employees
            da.InsertCommand = insertCmd
            da.Update(ds, "Employees")

         Catch ex As SqlException
            ' Display error
            Console.WriteLine("Error: " & ex.ToString())
         Finally
            ' Close Connection
            thisConnection.Close()
            Console.WriteLine("Connection Closed")
         End Try
      End Sub
   End Module
```

3. Make this the startup project and the startup object, and run it with Ctrl+F5. You should see the output in Figure 8-8.

```
"C:\BegVBNetDb\Chapter8_Examples\PropagateAdds\bin\PropagateAdds.exe"
Before altering the dataset
Steven      | Buchanan    | Birmingham
Michael     | Suyama      | London
Robert      | King        | London
Anne        | Dodsworth   | London
==========
After altering the dataset
Steven      | Buchanan    | Birmingham
Michael     | Suyama      | London
Robert      | King        | London
Anne        | Dodsworth   | London
Edna        | Everage     | Sydney
Connection Closed
Press any key to continue
```

Figure 8-8. *PropagateAdds*

How It Works

You added an INSERT statement in the string variable insertSql to the code.

```
Dim insertSql As String = _
   "INSERT INTO Employees " & _
   "(firstname, lastname, titleofcourtesy, city, country)" & _
   " VALUES " & _
   "(@firstname, @lastname, @titleofcourtesy, @city, @country)"
```

You replaced the update comment in the try block with quite a bit of code. Let's look at it piece by piece. Creating a command is nothing new, but notice that you use the variable containing the INSERT SQL statement (insertSql), not the query one (sql).

```
' Insert employees
' 1. Create command
Dim insertCmd As New SqlCommand(insertSql, thisConnection)
```

Then you configure the command parameters. The five columns for which you'll provide values are each mapped to a named command parameter. You don't supply the primary key value since it's generated by SQL Server, and the other columns are nullable, so you don't have to provide values for them. Note that all the values are current values, so you don't have to specify the SourceVersion property.

```
' 2. Map parameters
insertCmd.Parameters.Add("@firstname", _
   SqlDbType.NVarChar, 10, "firstname")
insertCmd.Parameters.Add("@lastname", _
   SqlDbType.NVarChar, 20, "lastname")
insertCmd.Parameters.Add("@titleofcourtesy", _
   SqlDbType.NVarChar, 25, "titleofcourtesy")
insertCmd.Parameters.Add("@city", _
   SqlDbType.NVarChar, 15, "city")
insertCmd.Parameters.Add("@country", _
   SqlDbType.NVarChar, 15, "country")
```

Finally, you set the data adapter's InsertCommand property with the command to insert into the Employees table so it will be the SQL the data adapter executes when you call its Update method. You then call Update on the data adapter to propagate the change to the database. Here you added only one row, but since the SQL is parameterized, the data adapter will look for all new rows in the employees data table and submit inserts for all of them to the database.

```
' 3. Insert employees
da.InsertCommand = insertCmd
da.Update(ds, "Employees")
```

If you check with Server Explorer or the SQL Tool application, you'll see the new row has been propagated to the database. Dame Edna Everage is now in the Employees table.

Using the DeleteCommand Property

You use the DeleteCommand property to execute SQL DELETE statements. As you learned in Chapter 3, DELETE statements can potentially wipe out all the data in a table by mistake, so you have to make sure these are written correctly. The same is true of DELETE and data tables, so be careful.

Let's again modify ModifyDataTable (Listing 8-4) to propagate its new row to the database.

Try It Out: Propagating New Dataset Rows to a Data Source

Follow these steps:

1. Add a VB .NET console application named PropagateDeletes, and rename the Module1.vb file to PropagateDeletes.vb.

2. Replace the code in PropagateDeletes.vb with that in Listing 8-7. This is a variation on ModifyDataTable in Listing 8-4, with irrelevant logic removed. The new code is marked in bold.

Listing 8-7. *PropagateDeletes*

```
Imports System
Imports System.Data
Imports System.Data.SqlClient

Module PropagateDeletes

   Sub Main()
      'Create Connection object
      Dim thisConnection As New SqlConnection _
         ("server=(local)\netsdk;" & _
          "integrated security=sspi;" & _
          "database=northwind")
```

```
' Sql Query
Dim sql As String = _
   "SELECT * FROM Employees " & _
   "WHERE Country = 'Australia'"

Dim deleteSql As String = _
   "DELETE FROM Employees " & _
   "WHERE EmployeeId = @employeeid"

Try
   ' Create Data Adapter
   Dim da As New SqlDataAdapter
   da.SelectCommand = New SqlCommand(sql, thisConnection)

   ' Create and fill Dataset
   Dim ds As New DataSet
   da.Fill(ds, "Employees")

   ' Get the Data Table
   Dim dt As DataTable = ds.Tables("Employees")

   ' Display Rows Before Changed
   Console.WriteLine("Before altering the dataset")
   For Each row As DataRow In dt.Rows
      Console.WriteLine("{0} | {1} | {2}", _
         row("FirstName").ToString().PadRight(10), _
         row("LastName").ToString().PadRight(10), _
         row("City"))
   Next

   ' Delete Employees
   ' 1. Create Command
   Dim deleteCmd As New SqlCommand(deleteSql, thisConnection)

   ' 2. Map Parameters
   deleteCmd.Parameters.Add("@employeeid", _
      SqlDbType.Int, 4, "employeeid")

   ' 3. Select Employees
   Dim filter1 As String = _
      "firstname = 'Edna' and lastname = 'Everage'"

   ' 4. Delete Employees From Local DataTable
   For Each row As DataRow In dt.Select(filter1)
      row.Delete()
   Next
```

```
            ' 5. Propagate deletions to database
            da.DeleteCommand = deleteCmd
            da.Update(ds, "employees")

            ' Display Rows After Alteration
            Console.WriteLine("=========")
            Console.WriteLine("After altering the dataset")
            For Each row As DataRow In dt.Rows
               Console.WriteLine("{0} | {1} | {2}", _
                  row("FirstName").ToString().PadRight(10), _
                  row("LastName").ToString().PadRight(10), _
                  row("City"))
            Next

         Catch ex As SqlException
            ' Display error
            Console.WriteLine("Error: " & ex.ToString())
         Finally
            ' Close Connection
            thisConnection.Close()
            Console.WriteLine("Connection Closed")
         End Try
      End Sub
   End Module
```

3. Make this the startup project and the startup object, and run it with Ctrl+F5. You should see the output in Figure 8-9.

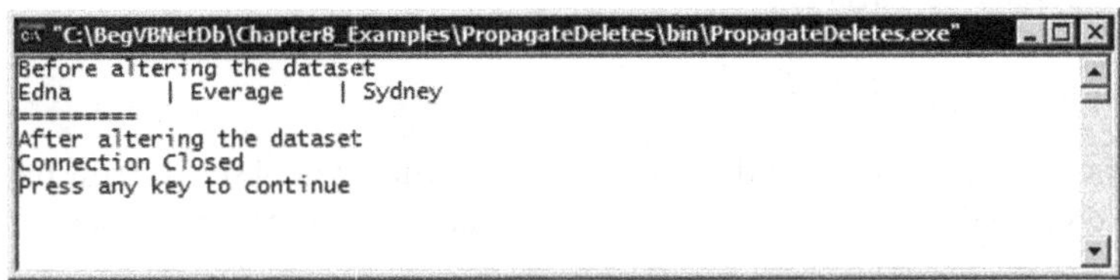

Figure 8-9. *PropagateDeletes*

How It Works

You added a DELETE statement in the string variable deleteSql to the code.

```
Dim deleteSql As String = _
   "DELETE FROM Employees " & _
   "WHERE EmployeeId = @employeeid"
```

You inserted the delete code ahead of the display. After creating a command and mapping a parameter, like so:

```
' Delete Employees
' 1. Create Command
Dim deleteCmd As New SqlCommand(deleteSql, thisConnection)

' 2. Map Parameters
deleteCmd.Parameters.Add("@employeeid", _
   SqlDbType.Int, 4, "employeeid")
```

you select the row to delete and delete it. Actually, you select all rows for employees named Edna Everage, since you don't know (or care about) their employee IDs. Although you expect only one row to be selected, you use a loop to delete all the rows. (If you ran the PropagateInserts program multiple times, you'd have more than one row that matches these selection criteria.)

```
' 3. Select Employees
Dim filter1 As String = _
   "firstname = 'Edna' and lastname = 'Everage'"

' 4. Delete Employees From Local DataTable
For Each row As DataRow In dt.Select(filter1)
   row.Delete()
Next
```

Finally, you set the data adapter's DeleteCommand property with the command to delete from the Employees table so it will be the SQL the data adapter executes when you call its Update method. You then call Update on the data adapter to propagate the changes to the database. Whether you delete one row or several, your SQL is parameterized, and the data adapter will look for all deleted rows in the employees data table and submit deletes for all of them to the database.

```
' 5. Propagate deletions to database
da.DeleteCommand = deleteCmd
da.Update(ds, "employees")
```

If you check with Server Explorer or the SQL Tool application, you'll see the row has been removed from the database. Dame Edna Everage is no longer in the Employees table.

Understanding Command Builders

Although straightforward, it's a bit of a hassle to code SQL statements for the UpdateCommand, InsertCommand, or DeleteCommand properties, so each data provider has its own *command builder*. If a data table corresponds to a single database table, then you can use a command builder to automatically generate the appropriate UpdateCommand, InsertCommand, and DeleteCommand properties for a data adapter. This is all done transparently when a call is made to the data adapter's Update method.

To be able to dynamically generate INSERT, DELETE, and UPDATE statements, the command builder uses the data adapter's SelectCommand property to extract metadata for the database table. If any changes are made to the SelectCommand property after invoking the Update method, you should call the RefreshSchema method on the command builder to refresh the metadata accordingly.

To create a command builder, you create an instance of the data provider's command builder class, passing a data adapter to its constructor. For example, the following code creates a SQL Server command builder:

```
Dim da As new SqlDataAdapter
Dim cb As new SqlCommandBuilder(da)
```

Note For a command builder to work, the `SelectCommand` data adapter property must contain a query that returns either a primary key or a unique key for the database table. If none is present, an `InvalidOperation` exception is generated, and the commands aren't generated.

Let's convert the `PropagateAdds` application in Listing 8-6 to use a command builder.

Try It Out: Using SqlCommandBuilder

Follow these steps:

1. Add a VB .NET console application named `PropagateAddsBuilder`, and rename the `Module1.vb` file to `PropagateAddsBuilder.vb`.
2. Replace the code in `PropagateAddsBuilder.vb` with that in Listing 8-8. This is a variation on `PropagateAdds` in Listing 8-6. The changes are marked in bold.

Listing 8-8. *PropagateAddsBuilder*

```
Imports System
Imports System.Data
Imports System.Data.SqlClient

Module PropagateAddsBuilder

   Sub Main()
      'Create Connection object
      Dim thisConnection As New SqlConnection _
         ("server=(local)\netsdk;" & _
          "integrated security=sspi;" & _
          "database=northwind")

      ' Sql Query
      Dim sql As String = _
         "SELECT * FROM Employees " & _
         "WHERE Country = 'UK'"
```

```
Try
   ' Create Data Adapter
   Dim da As New SqlDataAdapter
   da.SelectCommand = New SqlCommand(sql, thisConnection)

   ' Create Command Builder
   Dim cb As New SqlCommandBuilder(da)

   ' Create and fill Dataset
   Dim ds As New DataSet
   da.Fill(ds, "Employees")

   ' Get the Data Table
   Dim dt As DataTable = ds.Tables("Employees")

   ' Display Rows Before Changed
   Console.WriteLine("Before altering the dataset")
   For Each row As DataRow In dt.Rows
      Console.WriteLine("{0} | {1} | {2}", _
         row("FirstName").ToString().PadRight(10), _
         row("LastName").ToString().PadRight(10), _
         row("City"))
   Next

   ' Add A Row
   Dim newRow As DataRow = dt.NewRow()
   newRow("firstname") = "Edna"
   newRow("lastname") = "Everage"
   newRow("titleofcourtesy") = "Dame"
   newRow("city") = "Sydney"
   newRow("country") = "Australia"
   dt.Rows.Add(newRow)

   ' Display Rows After Alteration
   Console.WriteLine("==========")
   Console.WriteLine("After altering the dataset")
   For Each row As DataRow In dt.Rows
      Console.WriteLine("{0} | {1} | {2}", _
         row("FirstName").ToString().PadRight(10), _
         row("LastName").ToString().PadRight(10), _
         row("City"))
   Next

   ' Insert employees
   da.Update(ds, "Employees")
```

```
      Catch ex As SqlException
         ' Display error
         Console.WriteLine("Error: " & ex.ToString())
      Finally
         ' Close Connection
         thisConnection.Close()
         Console.WriteLine("Connection Closed")
      End Try
   End Sub
End Module
```

3. Make this the startup project and the startup object, and run it with Ctrl+F5. You should see the output in Figure 8-10.

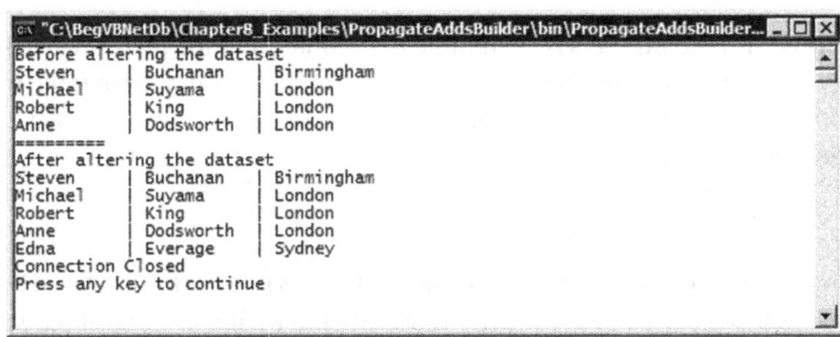

Figure 8-10. *PropagateAddsBuilder*

How It Works

The most interesting things to note aren't the line (yes, just one plus a comment) you added as much as what you replaced. The single statement

```
' Create Command Builder
Dim cb As New SqlCommandBuilder(da)
```

made all the following code unnecessary:

```
Dim insertSql As String = _
   "INSERT INTO Employees " & _
   "(firstname, lastname, titleofcourtesy, city, country)" & _
   " VALUES " & _
   "(@firstname, @lastname, @titleofcourtesy, @city, @country)"

' 1. Create command
Dim insertCmd As New SqlCommand(insertSql, thisConnection)
```

```
' 2. Map parameters
insertCmd.Parameters.Add("@firstname", _
   SqlDbType.NVarChar, 10, "firstname")
insertCmd.Parameters.Add("@lastname", _
   SqlDbType.NVarChar, 20, "lastname")
insertCmd.Parameters.Add("@titleofcourtesy", _
   SqlDbType.NVarChar, 25, "titleofcourtesy")
insertCmd.Parameters.Add("@city", _
   SqlDbType.NVarChar, 15, "city")
insertCmd.Parameters.Add("@country", _
   SqlDbType.NVarChar, 15, "country")

' 3. Insert employees
da.InsertCommand = insertCmd
```

Obviously, using command builders is preferable to manually coding SQL; however, remember that they work only on single tables and that the underlying database table must have a primary or unique key. Also, the data adapter `SelectCommand` property must have a query that includes the key columns.

■ **Note** Though all five of the data providers in the .NET Framework Class Library have command builder classes, no class or interface exists in the `System.Data` namespace that defines them. So, if you want to learn more about command builders, the best place to start is the description for the builder in which you're interested. The `System.Data.DataSet` class and the `System.Data.IDataAdapter` interface define the underlying components that command builders interact with, and their documentation provides the informal specification for the constraints on command builders.

Understanding Concurrency

You've seen that updating a database with datasets and data adapters is relatively straightforward. However, things have been oversimplified; you've been assuming that no other changes have been made to the database while you've been working with disconnected datasets.

Imagine two separate users trying to make conflicting changes to the same row in a dataset and then trying to propagate these changes to the database. What happens? How does the database resolve the conflicts? Which row gets updated first, or second, or at all? The answer is unclear. As with so many real-world database issues, it all depends on a variety of factors. However, ADO.NET provides a fundamental level of concurrency control that's designed to prevent update anomalies.

Basically, a dataset marks all added, modified, and deleted rows. If a row is propagated to the database but has been modified by someone else since the dataset was filled, the data manipulation operation for the row is ignored. This technique is known as *optimistic concurrency* and is essentially the job of the data adapter. When the `Update` method is called, the data adapter attempts to reconcile all changes. This works well in an environment where users seldom contend for the same data.

This type of concurrency is different from what's known as *pessimistic concurrency*, which *locks* rows upon modification (or sometimes even on retrieval) to avoid conflicts. Most database managers use some form of locking to guarantee data integrity.

Disconnected processing with optimistic concurrency is essential to successful multitier systems. How to employ it most effectively given the pessimistic concurrency of RDBMSs is a thorny problem. Don't worry about it, but keep in mind that many issues exist, and the more complex your application, the more likely you'll have to become an expert in concurrency.

We'll leave the issue of concurrency here because it's a big topic that gets complicated after a little research. The point is that you're now aware of this fundamental problem that will occur when the number of users simultaneously accessing a data source increases. If you want to read more on this subject, Wayne Plourde has a nice article on implementing a simple .NET concurrency solution at `http://www.15seconds.com/issue/030604.htm` that can take you further. Microsoft, meanwhile, has a more general discussion about database concurrency issues at `http://msdn.microsoft.com/library/en-us/vbcon/html/vbtskPerformingOptimisticConcurrencyChecking.asp`.

Using Datasets and XML

XML is the fundamental medium for data transfer in the .NET environment. In fact, XML technologies are a major foundation for ADO.NET. Datasets organize data internally as XML and have a variety of methods for reading and writing in XML. For example:

- You can import and export the structure of a dataset as an XML schema using `System.Data.DataSet`'s `ReadXmlSchema` and `WriteXmlSchema` methods.
- You can read the data (and, optionally, the schema) of a dataset from and write it to an XML file with `ReadXml` and `WriteXml`. This can be useful when exchanging data with another application or making a local copy of a dataset.
- You can bind a dataset to an XML document (an instance of `System.Xml.XmlDataDocument`). The dataset and data document are *synchronized*, so either ADO.NET or XML operations can be used to modify it.

Let's look at one of these in action, copying a dataset to an XML file.

■ **Note** If you're unfamiliar with XML, don't worry. ADO.NET doesn't require any detailed knowledge of it. Of course, the more you know, the better you can understand what's happening transparently, so we've provided a short primer on XML in Appendix B.

Try It Out: Extracting a Dataset to an XML File

You can preserve the contents and schema of a dataset in one XML file using the dataset's `WriteXml` method or in separate files using `WriteXml` and `WriteXmlSchema`. `WriteXml` is overloaded, and in this example we'll show a version that extracts both data and schema.

1. Add a VB .NET console application named `WriteXML`, and rename the `Module1.vb` file to `WriteXML.vb`.

2. Replace the code in `WriteXML.vb` with that in Listing 8-9.

Listing 8-9. *WriteXML*

```
Imports System
Imports System.Data
Imports System.Data.SqlClient

Module WriteXML

   Sub Main()
      'Create Connection object
      Dim thisConnection As New SqlConnection _
         ("server=(local)\netsdk;" & _
          "integrated security=sspi;" & _
          "database=northwind")

      ' Sql Query
      Dim sql As String = _
         "SELECT ProductName, UnitPrice FROM Products"

      Try
         ' Create Data Adapter
         Dim da As New SqlDataAdapter
         da.SelectCommand = New SqlCommand(sql, thisConnection)

         ' Create and fill Dataset
         Dim ds As New DataSet
         da.Fill(ds, "products")

         ' Extract DataSet to XML file
         ds.WriteXml("c:\begvbnetdb\chapter8_examples\productstable.xml")

      Catch ex As SqlException
         ' Display error
         Console.WriteLine("Error: " & ex.ToString())
      Finally
         ' Close Connection
         thisConnection.Close()
         Console.WriteLine("Connection Closed")
      End Try
   End Sub
End Module
```

3. Make this the startup project and the startup object, and run it with Ctrl+F5. You should see the output in Figure 8-11.

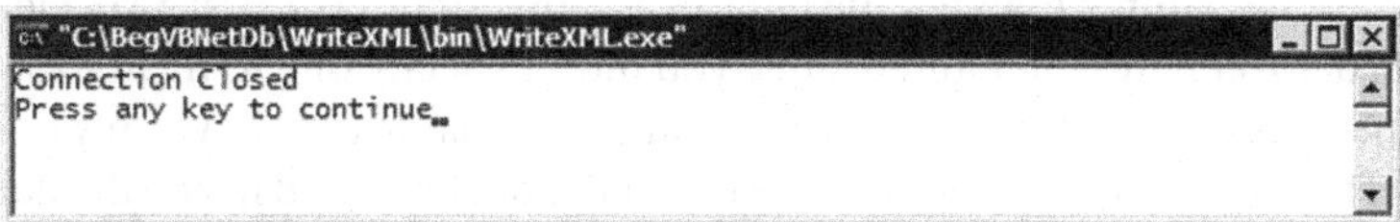

Figure 8-11. *WriteXML*

4. Not much seems to have happened, but that's because you wrote to a file rather than to the screen. Right-click the solution, select Add ➤ Add Existing Item..., and double-click `productstable.xml` in the list that appears. You should see the display in Figure 8-12.

Tip XML files are plain text. If you compiled from a command prompt, simply open the `productstable.xml` file in any editor, or use the `type` or `more` command, to view it.

---

productstable.xml

```
<?xml version="1.0" standalone="yes"?>
<NewDataSet>
  <products>
    <ProductName>Chai</ProductName>
    <UnitPrice>18.0000</UnitPrice>
  </products>
  <products>
    <ProductName>Chang</ProductName>
    <UnitPrice>19.0000</UnitPrice>
  </products>
  <products>
    <ProductName>Aniseed Syrup</ProductName>
    <UnitPrice>10.0000</UnitPrice>
  </products>
  <products>
    <ProductName>Chef Anton's Cajun Seasoning</ProductName>
    <UnitPrice>22.0000</UnitPrice>
  </products>
  <products>
    <ProductName>Chef Anton's Gumbo Mix</ProductName>
    <UnitPrice>21.3500</UnitPrice>
  </products>
  <products>
```

XML Data

Figure 8-12. *`productstable.xml` file displayed in Visual Studio*

How It Works

This program is just like the others. The only change was replacing the usual console display loop with the method call to write the XML file.

```
' Extract DataSet to XML file
ds.WriteXml("c:\begvbnetdb\chapter8_examples\productstable.xml")
```

You gave the full path for the XML file to place it in the solution directory. Had you given only the filename, it would have been placed in the `bin\Debug` subdirectory under the `WriteXml` project directory.

Note that the XML has simply mapped the dataset as a hierarchy. The first XML element `<NewDataSet>` is the dataset name (defaulted since you didn't specify one to the dataset constructor). The next element, `<products>`, uses the data table name (you have only one data table since you used only one query to populate the dataset), and it's nested inside the dataset element. The data column elements, `<productname>` and `<unitprice>`, are nested inside this element.

The data for each column appears (as plain text) between the *start tag* (for example, `<productname>`) and the *end tag* (for example, `</productname>`) for each column element. Note that the elements named for the data table actually represent individual rows, not the whole table. So, each pair of column elements are contained within the start tag `<products>` and end tag `</products>` for each row.

If you scroll to the bottom of the XML file, you'll find the end tag `</NewDataSet>` for the dataset.

XML is fundamental to ADO.NET. You'll see more of it in Chapter 17.

Understanding Typed and Untyped Datasets

Before we end the chapter, we need to broach the subject of typed datasets. Thus far, all the datasets you've used have been untyped. They were created simply as instances of `System.Data.DataSet`. There's nothing incorrect about this at all, but sometimes creating a dataset as a .NET type can be advantageous.

An untyped dataset has no built-in schema. The schema is only implicit. It grows as you add tables and columns to the dataset, but these objects are exposed as collections rather than as XML schema elements.

However, as you learned in the previous section, you can explicitly export a schema for an untyped dataset with `WriteXmlSchema` (or `WriteXml`).

A typed dataset, then, is one that's derived from `System.Data.DataSet` and uses an XML Schema (typically in an `.xsd` file) when declaring the dataset class. Information from the schema (tables, columns, and so on) is extracted, generated as VB .NET code, and compiled, so the new dataset class is an actual .NET type with appropriate objects and properties.

Untyped and typed datasets are equally valid, but typed datasets have many advantages; in particular, because they are typed, they make it easier to spot errors when using them. Visual Studio .NET also offers extensive support for creating and using them (good IntelliSense functionality in this case) when you decide to use them.

Let's see an example. Suppose you retrieved the `Customers` table from the `Northwind` database and wanted to find out the value of the company name field in the first row of the table now sitting in the first data table of your dataset. If you used an untyped dataset, you'd need to write this:

```
Console.WriteLine(ds.Tables(0).Rows(0)("CompanyName"))
```

If you used a typed dataset, you'd write this:

```
Console.WriteLine(ds.Customers(0).CompanyName)
```

As you can see, the code for the typed dataset is easier to read but requires more preparation. You would have to retrieve the schema for the customer table first and then generate a class from that using the `xsd.exe` utility. That class defines the typed dataset you then use with the data adapter. The complete routine is described in the .NET SDK at `http://msdn.microsoft.com/library/en-us/vbcon/html/cpcongeneratingstronglytypeddataset.htm` if you don't have a copy of Visual Studio .NET and at `http://msdn.microsoft.com/library/en-us/vbcon/html/vburfcreatingadotypeddatasetsfromexistingschemainvisualstudio.asp` if you do.

Technically speaking, typed datasets are faster and more efficient than untyped datasets, because typed datasets have a defined schema, and when they're populated with data, runtime type identification and conversion isn't necessary, since this has been taken care of at compile time. Untyped datasets do a lot more work to do every time a result set is loaded.

However, typed datasets aren't always the best choice. If you're dealing with data that isn't basically well defined, whose definition dynamically changes, or is only of temporary interest, the flexibility of untyped datasets outweighs the many benefits of typed ones. For more information on typed datasets, refer to `http://www.awprofessional.com/articles/article.asp?p=30593`.

Summary

In this chapter, you learned the basics of datasets and data adapters. A dataset is a relational representation of data that has a collection of data tables, with each data table having collections of data rows and data columns. A data adapter is an object that controls how data is loaded into a dataset and how changes to the dataset data are propagated back to the data source.

You studied techniques to fill and access datasets, how to filter and sort data tables, and noted that though datasets are database-independent objects, disconnected operation isn't the default mode. You learned how to propagate data modifications back to databases with parameterized SQL, how the issues of simultaneous user access may affect the way you write code, and the data adapter's `UpdateCommand`, `InsertCommand`, and `DeleteCommand` properties. Finally, you saw how command builders can simplify single-table updates and how using typed datasets combine data with the XML schema, which defines it to make multiple-table access easier as long as those tables don't change themselves in the meantime.

In the next chapter, you'll start working with form-based applications, as we've now covered the basics of database interaction in .NET and it's time to leave console applications behind. You'll learn how to use the data you've queried for by binding it to controls and that these techniques apply equally to Windows Forms and Web Forms.

CHAPTER 9

Building Windows Forms Applications

Recall the simple Windows Forms database application that you developed in Chapter 2? Since then, you've looked at using data access techniques, getting used to terms such as *connection strings*, *data readers*, and *datasets*, and using these items in console applications. You'll now return to the visual side of database applications and visit the world of Windows Forms applications.

Applications can deliver data to users in numerous ways, but it's important to consider the most effective mode of delivery. Windows Forms offer many benefits; they're easy to use, simple to implement, and can transparently iterate through database data. They're also better looking and more user friendly than dull console windows.

This chapter will introduce Windows Forms database applications. You'll see how Window Forms controls can bind to data and support interaction with a database. Specifically, you'll look at the following:

- Simple data binding
- Complex data binding
- How data binding works
- Different types of data structures, including arrays, data tables, datasets, and data views
- How a data grid works and how to use this powerful control in applications

We'll demonstrate data binding with various controls, including `Label`, `TextBox`, `ListBox`, and `DataGrid`.

Let's start by looking at data binding.

What's Data Binding?

The term *data binding* has a literal meaning when it comes to Windows Forms applications. It refers to the technique of interfacing elements of a data source with a graphical interface, such as using a `TextBox` control to bind to a single value from a column.

ADO.NET provides a neat data binding infrastructure for graphical controls to seamlessly bind themselves to almost any structure that contains data. This means that the data source can be anything from an array of values to a set of rows; in fact, it can be anything (such as class `System.Data.DataView`) that implements the `System.Collections.IEnumerable` interface.

Using data binding in applications essentially reduces the amount of code you have to write for retrieving data from databases. It's true that using data objects in code provides greater control over data, but data binding can achieve the same results if used properly.

You can bind Windows Forms controls to data in the following two ways:

- Simple data binding
- Complex data binding

Performing Simple Data Binding

This type of data binding is a one-to-one association between an individual control property and a single element of a data source. You can use it for controls that show only one value at a time. For example, you can bind the `Text` property of a `TextBox` control to a `DataTable` column. If the underlying data source is modified, the control's `Refresh` method updates the bound value, reflecting any changes.

To get comfortable with the idea, let's code a small Windows Forms application that uses simple data binding to bind two `TextBox` controls to two different columns of the `Northwind` database's `Employees` table.

Try It Out: Coding the First Simple Data Binding Application

In this application, you'll bind two values to two text boxes to display the first and last names of an employee.

1. In Visual Studio .NET, create a new solution named `Chapter9_Examples`.
2. Add a VB .NET Windows application named `DataBinding`.
3. You should now be in Design view. In the Toolbox, either double-click the `TextBox` control twice to produce two text boxes that you can position on the form or drag two `TextBox` controls onto the form. Make your form look similar to the one in Figure 9-1.

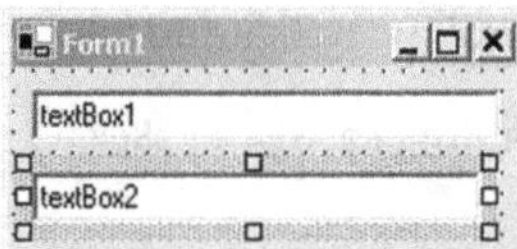

Figure 9-1. *DataBinding text boxes*

4. Press F7 to go to Code view. Add the following `Imports` directive:

```
Imports System.Data.SqlClient
```

5. Go back to Design view by clicking the Design tab or by pressing Shift+F7, and double-click the form (but outside the text boxes) to go to the underlying code. Your cursor should now be positioned in the Form1_Load method, which was added when you double-clicked the form. Add the following code:

```
Private Sub Form1_Load(ByVal sender As System.Object, _
   ByVal e As System.EventArgs) Handles MyBase.Load
   'Create Connection object
   Dim thisConnection As New SqlConnection _
      ("server=(local)\netsdk;" & _
      "integrated security=sspi;" & _
      "database=northwind")

   ' Sql Query
   Dim sql As String = _
      "SELECT * FROM Employees"

   ' Create Data Adapter
   Dim da As New SqlDataAdapter(sql, thisConnection)

   ' Create and fill Dataset
   Dim ds As New DataSet
   da.Fill(ds, "Employees")

   ' Bind to firstname column of the employees table
   TextBox1.DataBindings.Add("text", ds, "employees.firstname")

   ' Bind to lastname column of the employees table
   TextBox2.DataBindings.Add("text", ds, "employees.lastname")
End Sub
```

6. Run the code with Ctrl+F5, and after the program compiles, you should see the form in Figure 9-2.

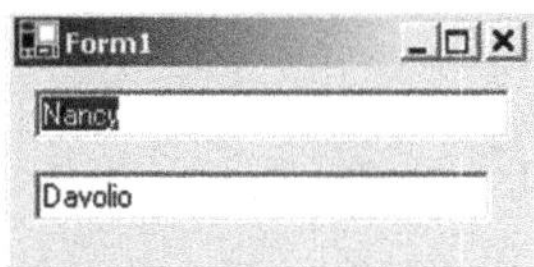

Figure 9-2. *DataBinding text boxes bound to data columns*

How It Works

When the application is first created, Visual Studio .NET automatically generates a lot of code for you, which exists for the most part to handle all the initialization for you. You're mainly concerned with the Form1_Load method that you created when you double-clicked the form in Design view, since that's the method called when the form is first displayed.

Your first task is to establish a connection with the database and fill a newly created dataset with the result set. Once you have all the data fetched, you perform the actual bindings with the following lines of code:

```
' Bind to firstname column of the employees table
TextBox1.DataBindings.Add("text", ds, "employees.firstname")

' Bind to lastname column of the employees table
TextBox2.DataBindings.Add("text", ds, "employees.lastname")
```

Each data-bound control in a Windows Forms application maintains a list of bindings for all its data-bound properties. The bindings are in a property named `DataBindings`, which holds a collection of type `ControlBindingsCollection` (more on this later in the "Understanding Data Binding: Behind the Scenes" section). This collection can contain a number of individual control property bindings, with each binding added using the `Add` method.

Since a text box is capable of displaying only one value at a time, you bind its `Text` property to the `FirstName` column of the `Employees` table using the `Add` method. The `Add` method has the following parameters:

- The name of the control property to bind to
- The data source
- A string identifying the data source member to bind to

Since you're using a dataset as the data source, the data member is a data column in a data table. In the example, the last parameter is used to bind the `Text` property to the `firstname` and the `lastname` data columns of the `employees` data table.

Performing Complex Data Binding

Unlike simple data binding, complex data binding is an association between the control and one or more data elements of the data source. You can perform this type of binding with controls that allow more than one value to be displayed at one time, such as a data grid or a data list.

The next example is a Windows Forms application, using a data grid, which displays all columns of the `Northwind` database's `Customers` table.

Try It Out: Coding the First Complex Data Binding Application

Follow these steps:

1. Add a VB .NET Windows application named `ComplexBinding`.
2. Add a `DataGrid` control from the Toolbox. Your form should look similar to the one shown in Figure 9-3.

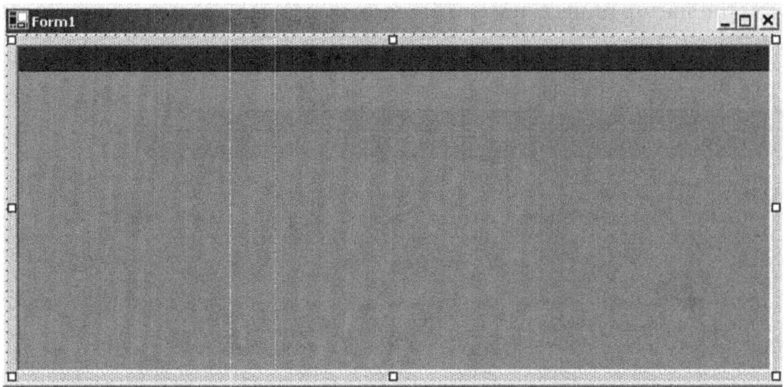

Figure 9-3. *ComplexBinding data grid*

3. Press F7 to go to Code view. Add the following `Imports` directive:

```
Imports System.Data.SqlClient
```

4. Double-click the form to go to the underlying code. Your cursor should now be positioned in the `Form1_Load` method. Add the following code:

```
Private Sub Form1_Load(ByVal sender As System.Object, _
   ByVal e As System.EventArgs) Handles MyBase.Load
   'Create Connection object
   Dim thisConnection As New SqlConnection _
      ("server=(local)\netsdk;" & _
      "integrated security=sspi;" & _
      "database=northwind")

   ' Sql Query
   Dim sql As String = _
      "SELECT * FROM Customers"

   ' Create Data Adapter
   Dim da As New SqlDataAdapter(sql, thisConnection)

   ' Create and fill Dataset
   Dim ds As New DataSet
   da.Fill(ds, "Customers")

   ' Bind the data table to the data grid
   DataGrid1.SetDataBinding(ds, "Customers")
End Sub
```

5. Make this the startup project, and run the code with Ctrl+F5. You should see the form in Figure 9-4.

Form1

CustomerID	CompanyNa	ContactName	ContactTitle	Address	City	Region
ALFKI	Alfreds Futter	Maria Anders	Sales Repres	Obere Str. 57	Berlin	(null)
ANATR	Ana Trujillo E	Ana Trujillo	Owner	Avda. de la C	México D.F.	(null)
ANTON	Antonio More	Antonio More	Owner	Mataderos 2	México D.F.	(null)
AROUT	Around the H	Thomas Hard	Sales Repres	120 Hanover	London	(null)
BERGS	Berglunds sn	Christina Ber	Order Admini	Berguvsvägen	Luleå	(null)
BLAUS	Blauer See D	Hanna Moos	Sales Repres	Forsterstr. 57	Mannheim	(null)
BLONP	Blondesddsl	Frédérique Ci	Marketing Ma	24, place Klé	Strasbourg	(null)
BOLID	Bólido Comid	Martín Somm	Owner	C/ Araquil, 67	Madrid	(null)
BONAP	Bon app'	Laurence Leb	Owner	12, rue des B	Marseille	(null)
BOTTM	Bottom-Dollar	Elizabeth Lin	Accounting M	23 Tsawasse	Tsawassen	BC
BSBEV	B's Beverage	Victoria Ashw	Sales Repres	Fauntleroy Ci	London	(null)
CACTU	Cactus Comi	Patricio Simp	Sales Agent	Cerrito 333	Buenos Aires	(null)
CENTC	Centro comer	Francisco Ch	Marketing Ma	Sierras de Gr	México D.F.	(null)

Figure 9-4. *ComplexBinding data grid bound to data table*

How It Works

Just like the previous example, this example goes through a similar progression, with Visual Studio .NET automatically generating code for you and doing the main initialization for the DataGrid control. Your interest, again, lies with the Form1_Load method where you insert code to render data from a table, using the data grid.

Once you've established a connection with the data source, you populate a dataset from the Customers table using a data adapter. Next, you need to bind the DataGrid control to the newly populated dataset. You do so by using the following line of code:

```
DataGrid1.SetDataBinding(ds, "Customers")
```

The SetDataBinding method of the DataGrid control accepts two parameters: the data source object and a string literal that describes a data member in the data source. Here, a data source can be any object that's capable of holding data, such as an array or a data table. The data member describes what element to bind to the control. In the case, you used a dataset as the data source, and the Customers data table contained in the dataset as a data member.

A call to the SetDataBinding method binds all columns of the Customers data table to the DataGrid control at runtime, which renders the data in the style of a spreadsheet.

You previously used the DataBindings collection property to add bindings to the control. You could use this method in the code if you were to bind the DataSource property of the control to the Customers data table. The following line of code is an alternative to using the SetDataBinding method:

```
DataGrid1.DataBindings.Add("datasource", ds, "Customers")
```

This syntax is particularly useful if you need to add more bindings for other individual properties of the control.

You'll learn more about the DataGrid control and the advantages of using a SetDataBinding method later in the "Using Data Grids" section.

Understanding Data Binding: Behind the Scenes

In the previous few sections you saw running examples of Windows Forms applications using data-bound controls. But how does all this work? How do controls *really* bind themselves? To answer these questions, we'll give you some insight into the data binding mechanism and show how it works.

The Windows data-bound controls (such as a Label, a Button, or a TextBox) are able to bind to data because of the functionality made available by the Binding class (System.Windows.Forms.Binding), which is provided by the .NET Framework. This class is responsible for creating a simple binding between a single control property and a data element in a data source. Have a look at the following code:

```
TextBox1.DataBindings.Add("text", ds, "employees.firstname")
```

This line was taken from the first example in the chapter. Recall that we mentioned that the DataBindings property of a control (any class that derives from the System.Windows.Forms.Control class) returns a ControlBindingsCollection object, which is a collection of Binding objects, each of which can be added by using the Add method. This means that a data-bound control can have a collection of bindings, each associated with a different property of the control; for example, you could bind the Text property of a Label control to a single column in a table and, at the same time, bind its ForeColor property to an array of different color values, completely unrelated to the table.

The Add method has two overloads: one that takes a single Binding object and another that implicitly creates an instance of a Binding object by calling the Binding class constructor (the one you used in the previous examples).

The Binding class constructor takes three parameters. The first parameter can be the name of a property of a control, such as the Text property of a TextBox control or the DataSource property of a DataGrid control.

The second parameter of the Binding class constructor can be an instance of the DataSet, DataTable, DataView, or DataViewManager class or any class that implements the System.Collections.IList interface. You'll look at a number of examples using different data sources later in the "Understanding Types of Data Sources" section.

The third parameter describes a data member from a data source. It's a string literal that must resolve into a scalar value, such as a data column in a data table.

If you'd rather declare a Binding object explicitly, the following code is an example of what your code would look like if you were to bind the Text property of a TextBox control to a data element in a table:

```
Dim newBind As New Binding("text", ds, "employees.firstname")
TextBox1.DataBindings.Add(newBind)
```

This approach could be useful in situations where you'd like to bind two or more controls to the same data element. For example, if you have a Label control and a TextBox control in a Windows Forms application and you'd like to bind both of these controls to the same column in a table, for whatever reason, you could create one Binding object and add that to the ControlBindingsCollection of each of the controls by calling the Add method.

The following code describes one such scenario of binding the `Text` property of the two controls to the same column in the `Employees` table, assuming you already have a `Label` control and a `TextBox` control on your Windows Forms application:

```
Dim newBind As New Binding("text", ds, "employees.firstname")
TextBox1.DataBindings.Add(newBind)
Label1.DataBindings.Add(newBind)
```

Note that when you use a dataset as a data source for binding your control, you actually are binding to a data view invisibly, behind the scenes. Recall from the discussion in the previous chapter that data views are specifically designed for providing different views of the data stored in an underlying data table, so they're useful when it comes to data binding Windows Forms controls.

A data view can allow two or more controls to be bound to the same data source, thus allowing each bound control to have a different view of data altogether. For instance, one control could display all available rows in a table (using as a `DataGrid` control), and another could display selected data.

Similarly, a bound `DataRow` object is actually a `DataRowView` object that provides a customizable view.

Synchronizing Controls with a Data Source

Data binding is a powerful feature, allowing your application to make the most of rendering data dynamically and making it simple to synchronize bound controls with the underlying data source.

Suppose you build a Windows Forms–based application that uses a couple of `TextBox` controls to bind to the same data source, each control bound to a different column in a table. Realistically, the data source will probably have more than one row, such as how the `Employees` table in the `Northwind` database holds a number of rows. In the first example of simple data binding, you bound a couple of text boxes to the data source and displayed only one row (the first row from the result set, to be precise). Most likely, you'd want to allow the user to navigate back and forth through the available rows using Next and Back buttons. For this to happen, your controls will need to be synchronized so that they display the correct data from the current row, as they're currently bound to two different columns.

The `System.Windows.Forms` namespace includes an abstract class for this purpose. A *binding manager* is an instance of a class that derives from the abstract `BindingManagerBase` class.

The binding manager enables greater control over the data being displayed by bound controls, which are bound to the same data source, by maintaining the current position of the row pointer. This means that whenever a data source evaluates a list of data elements, the binding manager supervises and keeps track of the ordinal position of the current row in the data source. Also, the binding manager fires events to notify the application if the current position in the data source has changed.

The two fundamental properties of a binding manager are Position and Current. Position is a zero-based integer value that describes an ordinal position of the rows being read in the data source. With the Position property, you can programmatically advance the row pointer to move onto the next row and vice versa. The Current property returns the data object at the current position in the data source.

The two concrete binding managers are CurrencyManager and PropertyManager. CurrencyManager is specifically designed for data sources that implement IList (or the interfaces, such as IListSource and IBindingList, that are based on it), such as Array, DataSet, and DataTable. It sounds a bit odd, but bear with it; this CurrencyManager has nothing to do with money. The PropertyManager, on the other hand, is returned for a data source that's neither a list nor a collection but is a single property of another object or is a single value. Note that you can use it only for maintaining the Current property of the object. Trying to use the Position property will have no effect, since the data source isn't a list but a single value.

You can't create an instance to the BindingManagerBase class directly because it's an abstract base class, but you can obtain instances to its derived classes by calling the BindingContext property of a Windows form, which returns an instance of an appropriate binding manager type, depending on the type of data source being used.

Every Windows form groups all bindings defined by its child controls into a collection called BindingContext. This collection returns an appropriate binding manager for the specified data source and data member.

Let's now look at a simple example that illustrates how to use a binding manager. The application will extend beyond the use of a couple of TextBox controls by introducing two buttons, Next and Back, that you'll use for navigating through the data source.

Try It Out: Creating a Simple Application Using a Binding Manager

Follow these steps:

1. Add a VB .NET Windows application named BindingManagerEx.

2. In Design view, drag two TextBox controls and two Button controls from the Toolbox onto the form. Change the Text property of one button to << Back. Change the text of other button to Next >>. Your form should look similar to Figure 9-5.

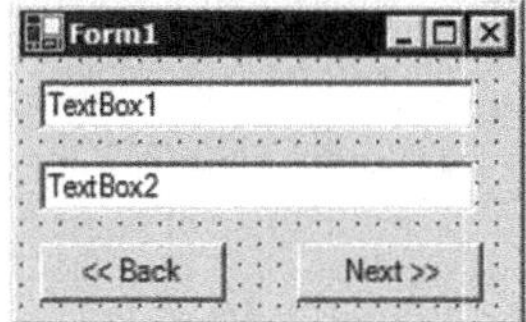

Figure 9-5. *BindingManagerEx buttons*

3. Change the (Name) property of one button to buttonBack and the other button to buttonNext.

4. In the Toolbox, click the Data tab and drag a `DataSet` control onto the form. You should see the window in Figure 9-6.

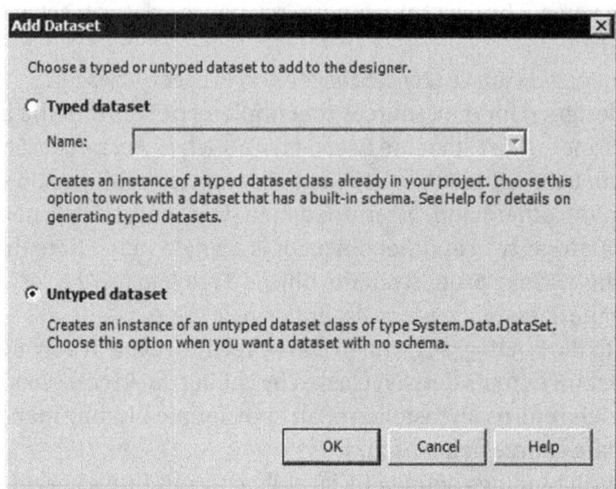

Figure 9-6. *`BindingManagerEx`: Adding a dataset*

5. Choose Untyped Dataset, and click OK. This will create a dataset in the component tray.

6. Press F7 to go to Code view. Add the following `Imports` directive:

```
Imports System.Data.SqlClient
```

7. Add the following field to the `Form1` class declaration.

```
' Declare a binding manager field
Private bMgr As BindingManagerBase
```

8. Press Shift+F7 to go to Design mode. Double-click the form, and you'll be taken to the underlying code for the `Form1_Load` method. Add the following code to the method:.

```
Private Sub Form1_Load(ByVal sender As System.Object, _
   ByVal e As System.EventArgs) Handles MyBase.Load
   'Create Connection object
   Dim thisConnection As New SqlConnection _
      ("server=(local)\netsdk;" & _
       "integrated security=sspi;" & _
       "database=northwind")

   ' Sql Query
   Dim sql As String = _
      "SELECT * FROM Employees"

   ' Create Data Adapter
   Dim da As New SqlDataAdapter(sql, thisConnection)
```

```
    ' Fill Dataset
    da.Fill(DataSet1, "Employees")

    ' Bind to firstname column of the employees table
    TextBox1.DataBindings.Add("text", DataSet1, "employees.firstname")

    ' Bind to lastname column of the employees table
    TextBox2.DataBindings.Add("text", DataSet1, "employees.lastname")

    ' Create the Binding Manager
    bMgr = Me.BindingContext(DataSet1, "Employees")
End Sub
```

9. Return to Design view, and double-click the Next button. Place the following code in the `buttonNext_Click` method:.

```
' Point to the next row and refresh the text box
bMgr.Position += 1
```

10. Return to Design view, and double-click the Back button. Place the following code in the `buttonBack_Click` method:

```
' Point to the previous row and refresh the text box
bMgr.Position -= 1
```

11. Make this the startup project, and run the code with Ctrl+F5. You should see the form in Figure 9-7.

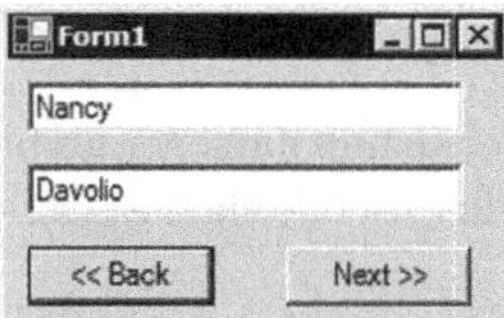

Figure 9-7. *BindingManagerEx running*

How It Works

This code is similar to the first example you saw in this chapter, with the exception of the binding manager used to navigate through the data source. Since this example is a mere upgrade of the one you saw earlier, we can safely skip details regarding simple data binding techniques and move onto the part where you've actually used the binding manager to do the job.

After declaring a `BindingManagerBase` field, the next thing you do is get a suitable binding manager from the `BindingContext` property of the form. This happens in the following line of code:

```
bMgr = Me.BindingContext(DataSet1, "Employees")
```

In this case, `BindingContext` returns an instance of a `CurrencyManager` since a `DataSet` implements the `IListSource` interface. With a binding manager at hand, you can now manage all data bindings in the Windows Forms application that various controls set on the specified data source.

The next step is to implement the navigational buttons. The buttonNext_Click method is called every time the Next button is clicked. The body of the method includes a single line of code, as follows, that basically increments the position of the current row in the data source by incrementing the value returned by the Position property of the binding manager:

```
' Point to the next row and refresh the text box
bMgr.Position += 1
```

Similarly, the buttonBack_Click method is called every time the Back button is clicked. This method uses a single line of code, as follows, to decrement the position of the current row in the data source by decrementing the value returned by the Position property of the binding manager:

```
' Point to the previous row and refresh the text box
bMgr.Position -= 1
```

Understanding Types of Data Sources

Earlier in the chapter you learned that a set of interfaces exists that can be derived from, and any class that implements any one of these interfaces is eligible for use with bound controls, as a valid data source.

Coming back to the same list of interfaces, you'll spend the following sections studying some available classes that implement these interfaces and see how they can be used with data that's bound to controls.

Binding to Arrays

In most cases, an Array is best suited to storing and retrieving consistent data. Arrays have runtime support for manipulating data and are easy to work with in the code via the ICollection interface.

At times you may want to display the contents of an array in a TextBox control. For example, you may have details of cars stored in an array and would like to display the data to a potential customer in a text box. Let's take a look at a quick example.

Try It Out: Building a Simple Application That Binds to an Array

Follow these steps:

1. Add a VB .NET Windows application named Arrays.

2. In Design view, drag a TextBox control from the Toolbox onto the form. Double-click the form, and enter the following code in the Form1_Load method. Your form should look similar to Figure 9-8.

```
Private Sub Form1_Load(ByVal sender As System.Object, _
   ByVal e As System.EventArgs) Handles MyBase.Load
   Dim carDetails() As String = _
      {"Ferrari", "Red", "F355", "1965", "£125,000"}
   TextBox1.DataBindings.Add("text", carDetails, "")
End Sub
```

3. Make this the startup project, and run the code with Ctrl+F5. You should see the form in Figure 9-8.

Figure 9-8. *Arrays: Binding a text box to an array*

How It Works

The code shows an array of strings bound to the `Text` property of the `TextBox` control. You pass `""` to the `Add` method since the array doesn't have data members or a navigation path that could be further resolved into a single scalar value. Ideally, this parameter should be used for a `DataSet` or a `DataTable` since they can be navigated through a set of tables or columns.

To be able to iterate through the array, you can use the `Position` property of the binding manager for the purpose. However, you'll have to pass `""` as the data member of the `BindingContext` property since it's an array and has no member objects. You could do this with the following code:

```
Dim bMgr As BindingManagerBase = Me.BindingContext(carDetails, "")
```

Binding to Data Tables

The `DataTable` class implements the `IListSource` interface. As you may recall, a `DataTable` either can be accessed from within a `DataSet` or can exist as an independent object, consisting of rows and columns. You'll consider the latter case for the time being.

A `DataTable` is another good example of a data source, and it's a typical one, since it can be used for both simple and complex binding examples. To bind a `DataTable` to a control, you have two options. You can bind the whole table to a control that supports complex binding (a control that can display more than one row at one time), or you can bind a single column to a control that supports simple binding.

Let's look at an example of an application that implements both simple and complex bound controls.

Try It Out: Building a Simple Application That Binds to a Data Table

Follow these steps:

1. Add a VB .NET Windows application named `DataTableBinding`.

2. In Design view, add two `TextBox` controls and a `ListBox` control to the form. Your form should look similar to Figure 9-9.

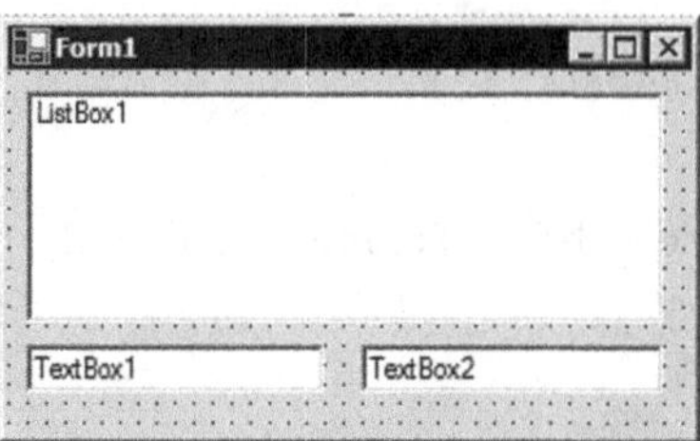

Figure 9-9. *`DataTableBinding`: Form layout*

3. Click the Data tab in the Toolbox, and drag a `DataSet` control onto the form. In the window that appears, select Untyped Dataset, and click OK.

4. Press F7 to go to Code view. Add the following `Imports` directive:

```
Imports System.Data.SqlClient
```

5. In Design view, double-click the form, and add the following code to the `Form1_Load` method:

```
Private Sub Form1_Load(ByVal sender As System.Object, _
   ByVal e As System.EventArgs) Handles MyBase.Load

   'Create Connection object
   Dim thisConnection As New SqlConnection _
      ("server=(local)\netsdk;" & _
       "integrated security=sspi;" & _
       "database=northwind")

   ' Sql Query
   Dim sql As String = _
      "SELECT FirstName, LastName FROM Employees"

   ' Create Data Adapter
   Dim da As New SqlDataAdapter(sql, thisConnection)

   ' Fill DataSet and Create DataTable
   da.Fill(DataSet1, "Employees")
   Dim dt As DataTable = DataSet1.Tables("Employees")

   ' Complex bind a listbox control at design time to
   ' display values from the firstname data column
   ListBox1.DataSource = dt
   ListBox1.DisplayMember = "FirstName"
```

```
    ' Bind to firstname column of the employees table
    TextBox1.DataBindings.Add("text", dt, "FirstName")

    ' Bind to lastname column of the employees table
    TextBox2.DataBindings.Add("text", dt, "LastName")
End Sub
```

6. Make this the startup project, and run the code with Ctrl+F5. You should see the form in Figure 9-10.

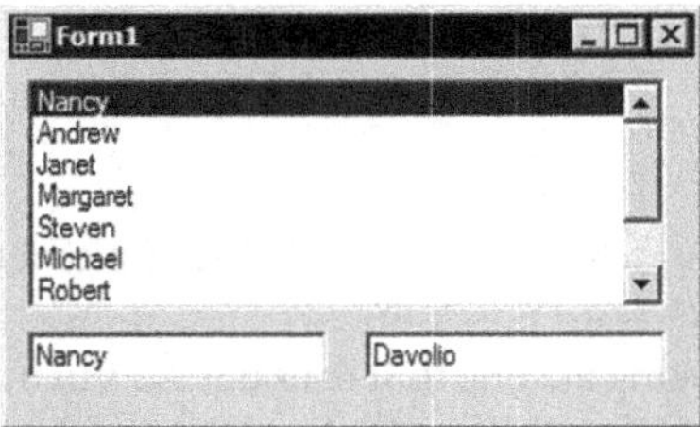

Figure 9-10. *DataTableBinding running*

How It Works

In this example you have a ListBox control bound to a DataTable object extracted from a populated DataSet, as shown in the following code:

```
Dim dt As DataTable = DataSet1.Tables("Employees")

' Complex bind a listbox control at design time to
' display values from the firstname data column
ListBox1.DataSource = dt
ListBox1.DisplayMember = "FirstName"
```

You bound the ListBox control at design time by setting its DataSource and DisplayMember properties. The DataSource property takes a collection object as a data source, such as a DataTable or a DataSet. The DisplayMember property takes a data member from within the data source for filling the ListBox with data. In the example, since you have a DataTable object as a data source, the DisplayMember property takes a column name for binding to the control.

Similarly, the text boxes are bound to the DataTable by adding bindings to the DataBindings collection and providing the column names from the DataTable as data members.

```
' Bind to firstname column of the employees table
TextBox1.DataBindings.Add("text", dt, "FirstName")

' Bind to lastname column of the employees table
TextBox2.DataBindings.Add("text", dt, "LastName")
```

Caution You used a select list to retrieve specific columns from the `Employees` table not only because it's best practice (asking only for what you need) but also because the `DisplayMember` property is case sensitive. Had you used a * instead of the column names, the column names would have been `FirstName` and `LastName`, and you would have had to provide the display member as `FirstName`. Further, had you spelled it in the select list as `firstName` instead of `firstname`, the `DisplayMember` argument would have had to be `firstName`! In general, select only the columns you need and keep in mind that although SQL isn't case sensitive, some ADO.NET features are. Whatever case you use for table and column names, use the same case when the names are contained in strings.

Binding to Datasets

The most flexible data source in the toolkit is the dataset. `System.Data.DataSet` implements the `System.ComponentModel.IListSource` interface.

Throughout the rest of this chapter, you'll be looking at code that uses datasets to navigate through tables and rows, not only because it's easier to handle but also because data binding is quick and straightforward. When we discussed datasets in detail in the previous chapter, you discovered that they could be used to store relational data disconnected from a data source. This makes them great candidates for being sources for data-bound controls. Indeed, you've already seen a brief example of this in the first exercise of this chapter. Rather than repeating ourselves, we'll move straight onto binding to datasets through data views.

Binding to Data Views

The `DataView` class implements the `System.ComponentModel.ITypedList` interface and presents a customizable view of a data table. Binding to a `DataView` object is as simple as binding to a `DataTable` object since a `DataView` provides a dynamic view of the contents of a data table. In fact, using a data view can provide further control over the data you display by implementing custom sorts and filters.

Try It Out: Building a Simple Application That Binds to a Data View

Follow these steps:

1. Add a VB .NET Windows application named `DataSetBind`.
2. In Design view, add two `TextBox` controls to the form. Your form should look similar to Figure 9-11 (or indeed Figure 9-1).

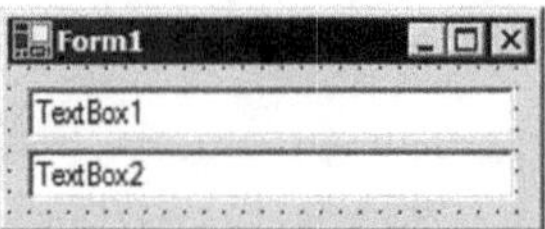

Figure 9-11. *DataViewBind: Form layout*

3. Click the Data tab in the Toolbox, and drag a `DataSet` control onto the form. In the window that appears, select Untyped Dataset, and click OK.

4. Press F7 to go to Code view. Add the following `Imports` directive:

```
Imports System.Data.SqlClient
```

5. In Design view, double-click the form, and add the following code to the `Form1_Load` method:

```
Private Sub Form1_Load(ByVal sender As System.Object, _
   ByVal e As System.EventArgs) Handles MyBase.Load

   'Create Connection object
   Dim thisConnection As New SqlConnection _
      ("server=(local)\netsdk;" & _
       "integrated security=sspi;" & _
       "database=northwind")

   ' Sql Query
   Dim sql As String = _
      "SELECT * FROM Employees"

   ' Create Data Adapter
   Dim da As New SqlDataAdapter(sql, thisConnection)

   ' Fill Dataset and Get Data Table
   da.Fill(DataSet1, "Employees")
   Dim dt As DataTable = DataSet1.Tables("Employees")

   ' Create a DataView with Filter and Sort Order
   Dim dv As New DataView(dt, _
      "Country='UK'", "FirstName", _
      DataViewRowState.CurrentRows)

   ' Bind TextBox1 to FirstName column of the Employees table
   TextBox1.DataBindings.Add("text", dv, "FirstName")

   ' Bind TextBox2 to LastName column of the Products table
   TextBox2.DataBindings.Add("text", dv, "LastName")
End Sub
```

6. Make this the startup project, and run the code with Ctrl+F5. You should see the output in Figure 9-12.

Figure 9-12. *DataViewBind running*

How It Works

You use a DataView object to simply filter and sort the contents of a data table, and then you display them in the controls.

```
' Fill Dataset and Get Data Table
da.Fill(DataSet1, "Employees")
Dim dt As DataTable = DataSet1.Tables("Employees")

' Create a DataView with Filter and Sort Order
Dim dv As New DataView(dt, _
   "Country='UK'", "FirstName", _
   DataViewRowState.CurrentRows)
```

As with the previous examples, you first fill a dataset with data. The next step is to create a data table to represent the table in which you're interested. You then refine the data using the data view to select the first name column of all employees based in the United Kingdom from the table in the data table.

The next step is to bind to the text boxes.

```
' Bind TextBox1 to FirstName column of the Employees table
TextBox1.DataBindings.Add("text", dv, "FirstName")

' Bind TextBox2 to LastName column of the Products table
TextBox2.DataBindings.Add("text", dv, "LastName")
```

Using Data Grids

The DataGrid control is one of the most powerful Windows Forms controls (and indeed it also exists as a Web Forms control, too, as you'll see in the next chapter). A DataGrid control resembles a spreadsheet in its appearance. Like the name suggests, it provides you with a scrollable grid of rows and columns, completely customizable for displaying data in a number of ways and accessing data just the way you want.

To add to the flavor, you can use it with almost any data source, such as an Array or a DataSet, as long as it implements either the IList interface or the IListSource interface. You can provide a modifiable, formatted user interface of a DataSet from the most humble appearance, such as displaying a single table at one time, to the most superior, displaying related tables in a parent-child fashion. (You'll find out a lot more about parent-child tables and relationships in Chapter 12.)

You can bind the DataGrid to a data source using the DataSource and the DataMember properties at design time, or you can use the SetDataBinding method at runtime. The difference between runtime and design-time binding is that with design-time binding, you can't reset the DataSource and the DataMember properties once they've been set. On the other hand, using the SetDataBinding method, you can set a data source at runtime, switching between sources when desired. Also, in most cases, the object to which you want to bind doesn't exist until runtime. This is true for structures such as an Array, which typically needs to be instantiated and populated at runtime. For this reason, it's a good idea to bind objects programmatically at runtime, rather than binding them at design time.

Previously, you used a `DataGrid` for data binding. You'll now look at a simple application that binds a data grid to a dataset and displays data in a parent-child fashion, showing related data in two tables.

Try It Out: Binding a Data Grid to Show Data in a Parent-Child Relationship

Follow these steps:

1. Add a VB .NET Windows application named `MultiTableDataGrid`.
2. In Design view, add a `DataGrid` control to the form. Your form should look similar to Figure 9-13.

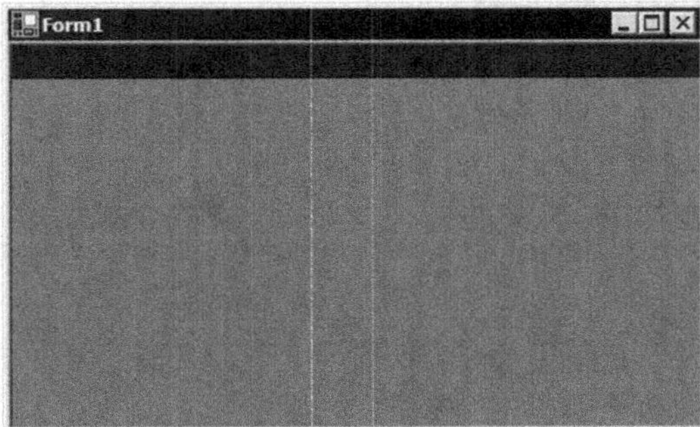

Figure 9-13. *`MultiTableDataGrid` layout*

3. In the Toolbox, click the Data tab and drag a `DataSet` control onto the form, and again choose Untyped Dataset in the window that appears.
4. Press F7 to go to Code view. Add the following `Imports` directive:

```
Imports System.Data.SqlClient
```

5. In Design mode, double-click the form, and add the following code to the `Form1_Load` method:

```
Private Sub Form1_Load(ByVal sender As System.Object, _
   ByVal e As System.EventArgs) Handles MyBase.Load

   'Create Connection object
   Dim thisConnection As New SqlConnection _
      ("server=(local)\netsdk;" & _
       "integrated security=sspi;" & _
       "database=northwind")
```

```
    ' Sql Queries
    Dim sql1 As String = _
       "SELECT * FROM Employees "

    Dim sql2 As String = _
       "SELECT * FROM Orders"

    Dim sql As String = sql1 & sql2

    ' Create Data Adapter
    Dim da As New SqlDataAdapter(sql, thisConnection)

    ' Map Default table names to Employees and Orders
    da.TableMappings.Add("Table", "Employees")
    da.TableMappings.Add("Table1", "Orders")

    ' Fill Dataset
    da.Fill(DataSet1)

    ' Create a relation between the two tables
    Dim dr As New DataRelation( _
       "EmployeeOrders", _
       DataSet1.Tables(0).Columns("EmployeeId"), _
       DataSet1.Tables(1).Columns("EmployeeId"))
    DataSet1.Relations.Add(dr)

    ' Bind the data to the grid at runtime
    DataGrid1.SetDataBinding(DataSet1, "Employees")
End Sub
```

6. Make this the startup project, and run the code with Ctrl+F5. You should see the form in Figure 9-14 after clicking the plus sign next to the second employee.

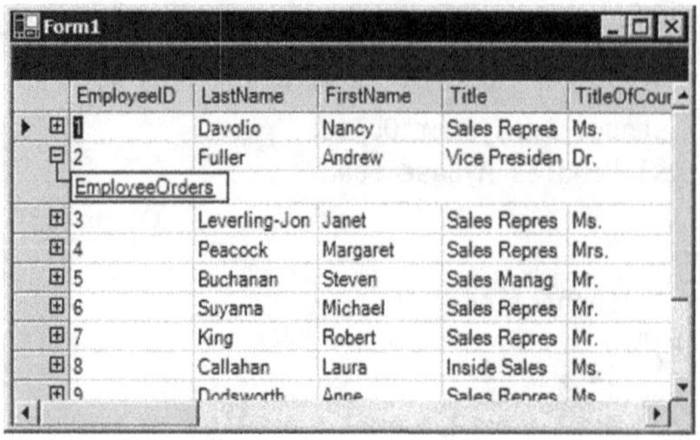

EmployeeID	LastName	FirstName	Title	TitleOfCour
1	Davolio	Nancy	Sales Repres	Ms.
2	Fuller	Andrew	Vice Presiden	Dr.
EmployeeOrders				
3	Leverling-Jon	Janet	Sales Repres	Ms.
4	Peacock	Margaret	Sales Repres	Mrs.
5	Buchanan	Steven	Sales Manag	Mr.
6	Suyama	Michael	Sales Repres	Mr.
7	King	Robert	Sales Repres	Mr.
8	Callahan	Laura	Inside Sales	Ms.
9	Dodsworth	Anne	Sales Repres	Ms.

Figure 9-14. *MultiTableDataGrid: Employee list*

7. Click the *EmployeeOrders* link, and you should see the form in Figure 9-15, displaying the orders for the selected employee.

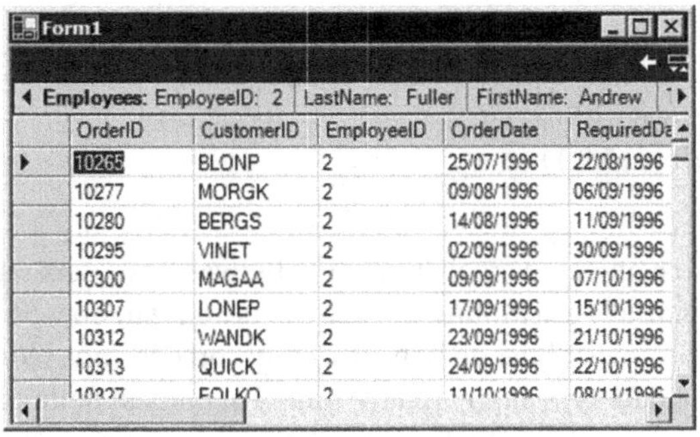

Figure 9-15. *MultiTableDataGrid: Related orders*

How It Works

The DataGrid can present data from the two tables in a very organized manner. What's good about a DataGrid is that it allows you to navigate through related tables with ease. After clicking the plus sign on the side of a row that contains related data in a distinct table, a hyperlink appears, leading you to yet another table (the related table) for displaying all available related rows. Let's see how the code managed to do so.

In the Form1_Load method, you submitted two queries.

```
' Sql Queries
Dim sql1 As String = _
   "SELECT * FROM Employees "

Dim sql2 As String = _
   "SELECT * FROM Orders"

Dim sql As String = sql1 & sql2
```

Next, you filled the DataSet with the data from two result sets returned, but before calling the Fill method, you mapped custom table names to the default table names (Table and Table1) provided by the data adapter and added these mapped names to the data adapter's table mappings collection. This ensures that the data table named (by default) Table in the dataset can be referenced as employees; the one named Table1 can be referenced as orders. Note that this is just for your convenience and isn't mandatory.

```
' Map Default table names to Employees and Orders
da.TableMappings.Add("Table", "Employees")
da.TableMappings.Add("Table1", "Orders")

' Fill Dataset
da.Fill(DataSet1)
```

The next two statements illustrate a DataRelation object being used for relating two distinct tables inside a DataSet.

```
' Create a relation between the two tables
Dim dr As New DataRelation( _
   "EmployeeOrders", _
   DataSet1.Tables(0).Columns("EmployeeId"), _
   DataSet1.Tables(1).Columns("EmployeeId"))
DataSet1.Relations.Add(dr)
```

In ADO.NET, you use a DataRelation object to create a relation between two data tables in a dataset. This so-called relation (it is actually a *relationship* and has nothing to do with the relational database concept of a relation) is established between common columns (corresponding columns must have the same data type but can have different names) belonging to two distinct tables, which logically relate the tables. We'll cover relationships between tables in Chapter 12.

After a relationship has been defined programmatically, it's added to the Relations collection of the dataset. The next thing you do is bind the employees data table to the DataGrid control.

```
' Bind the data to the grid at runtime
DataGrid1.SetDataBinding(DataSet1, "Employees")
```

Once the data grid is bound, it automatically searches for all tables related to the bound data table and presents the data in a scrollable grid form.

A data grid is a great way of quickly prototyping your applications, because it does a lot of work for you. It's also simple to update the data source using a bound DataGrid control, and that's just what you'll explore next.

Updating a Data Source Using a Data Grid

Until now, all you've learned to do is display data using data-bound controls. It's time you see how modified data in a bound control can be propagated to the data source using very little code.

In the previous chapters you discovered how to use DataCommand, DataAdapter, and CommandBuilder objects to update data in the data source, and we've discussed when to use which object. Based on that knowledge, you'll use a SqlDataAdapter and a SqlCommandBuilder in a simple application that binds a DataSet object to a DataGrid control. The example illustrates how easy it is to apply the techniques of updating the data source that you used in a console application in a Windows Forms application.

Try It Out: Updating a Data Source with a Bound Data Grid

Follow these steps:

1. Add a VB .NET Windows application named DataGridUpdate.

2. Add a `DataGrid` control and a `Button` control to the form. Change the `Text` property of your button to `Update` and the name of the button to `buttonUpdate`. Your form should look similar to the one shown in Figure 9-16.

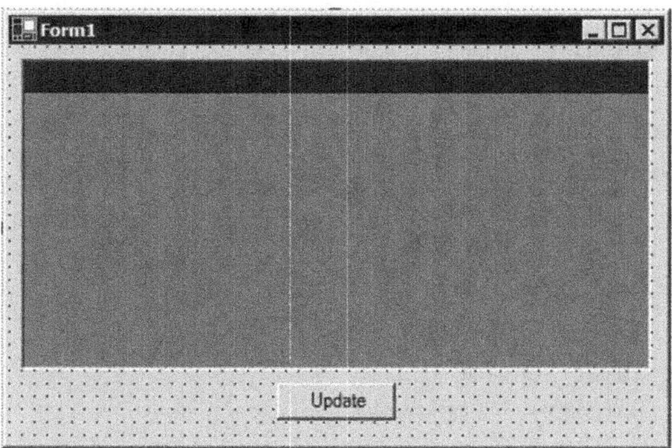

Figure 9-16. *`DataGridUpdate` layout*

3. Add a `DataSet` control to the form, selecting Untyped Dataset when prompted.

4. Now choose a `SqlCommand` control from the Toolbox, and drag it onto the form. This will create a `SqlCommand` object reference in your application named `sqlCommand1`.

5. Press F7 to go to the Code view. Add the following `Imports` directive:

```
Imports System.Data.SqlClient
```

6. Add the following fields to the `Form1` class declaration:

```
Private cb As SqlCommandBuilder
Private da As SqlDataAdapter
```

7. In Design mode, double-click the form, and add the following code to the `Form1_Load` method:

```
Private Sub Form1_Load(ByVal sender As System.Object, _
   ByVal e As System.EventArgs) Handles MyBase.Load

   'Create Connection object
   Dim thisConnection As New SqlConnection _
      ("server=(local)\netsdk;" & _
       "integrated security=sspi;" & _
       "database=northwind")

   ' Sql Query
   Dim sql As String = _
      "SELECT * FROM Employees "
```

```
    ' Create a Command
    SqlCommand1 = New SqlCommand(sql, thisConnection)

    ' Create SqlDataAdapter
    da = New SqlDataAdapter
    da.SelectCommand = SqlCommand1

    ' Create SqlCommandBuilder object
    cb = New SqlCommandBuilder(da)

    ' Fill Dataset
    da.Fill(DataSet1, "Employees")

    ' Bind the data to the grid at runtime
    DataGrid1.SetDataBinding(DataSet1, "Employees")
End Sub
```

8. Back in Design mode, double-click the Update button. Add the following code to the `buttonUpdate_Click` method:

```
Private Sub buttonUpdate_Click(ByVal sender As System.Object, _
    ByVal e As System.EventArgs) Handles buttonUpdate.Click

    da.Update(DataSet1, "Employees")

End Sub
```

9. Make this the startup project, and run the code with Ctrl+F5. You should see the form in Figure 9-17.

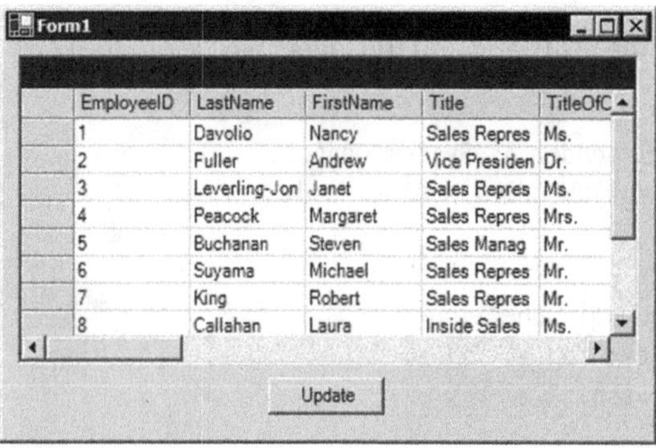

Figure 9-17. *DataGridUpdate running*

How It Works

To be able to use a SqlCommandBuilder object, you create a SqlCommand object and pass it to the SqlDataAdapter object (recall that you learned how to use a SqlCommandBuilder in the previous chapter). The following code shows a SqlCommand object being created and passed to the SqlDataAdapter you created for filling the DataSet:

```
' Create a Command
SqlCommand1 = New SqlCommand(sql, thisConnection)

' Create SqlDataAdapter
da = New SqlDataAdapter
da.SelectCommand = SqlCommand1
```

You then created a SqlCommandBuilder object. You used a SqlCommandBuilder so that you don't have to explicitly code update, insert, or delete statements, since the command builder will generate SQL for you.

```
' Create SqlCommandBuilder object
cb = New SqlCommandBuilder(da)
```

Next, you filled the DataSet with data and bound it to your DataGrid control.

```
' Fill Dataset
da.Fill(DataSet1, "Employees")

' Bind the data to the grid at runtime
DataGrid1.SetDataBinding(DataSet1, "Employees")
```

Clicking the Update button updates the data source. The buttonUpdate_Click method has only one line of code, which does all the work for you.

```
da.Update(DataSet1, "Employees")
```

This line calls the Update method of the data adapter, which in turn uses the command builder to generate suitable SQL from the metadata it collects.

Using a data grid for modifying tabular data is extremely simple. It has built-in functionality for notifying different events that are launched every time data in the grid changes.

Summary

In this chapter, we discussed various ways to fetch data automatically from an external data source, be it an array, a database, a dataset, or any data structure capable of storing and retrieving data. You also saw how Windows Forms controls offer built-in support for binding to data sources and retrieving and modifying them. The main topics covered in this chapter were as follows:

- Understanding what data binding is
- Understanding the types of data-bound controls (simple and complex binding)

- Synchronizing controls with a data source
- Understanding the types of bindable data sources
- Using a data grid for data binding
- Updating data sources with bound controls

In the next chapter, you'll meet the Web equivalents to a lot of these controls, as you look into ASP.NET and the world of Web Forms.

CHAPTER 10

Using ASP.NET

ASP.NET is the featured Microsoft technology for building Web applications. You can deploy these applications on a Web server, for the entire Internet to reach, or perhaps on an intranet, for just the workers in your department. With the .NET Compact Framework you even get support for cell phones and other mobile devices. ASP.NET is so rich in functionality that it can't be covered in a single book, let alone a single chapter. Bearing this in mind, this chapter will focus on an important topic for database development: data binding with the `DataGrid` Web Forms control. By the end of the chapter you should have a solid understanding of the following data grid features:

- Performing basic data binding
- Paging rows
- Selecting a row to detail
- Customizing the column display
- Editing rows
- Deleting rows
- Sorting rows

Along the way you'll build a simple ASP.NET Web application and learn a few of the differences between Windows Forms and Web Forms development.

Understanding the Basics

You first need to understand some of the basic ground rules for the technology you'll be using.

Visual Studio .NET provides a similar environment for developing Web Forms applications as it does for Windows Forms applications. You can drag and drop controls onto Web Forms applications, double-click to handle events, and right-click controls to set properties. Most of the techniques you've learned for Windows Forms applications are also applicable to Web Forms applications developed with ASP.NET. Web Forms applications work in a slightly different manner under the covers, however, so being aware of these differences can help you build better Web applications.

A Web browser will request a Web form using the Hypertext Transfer Protocol (HTTP) network protocol. HTTP is a stateless protocol, meaning each request has no knowledge of any of the previous requests or information pertinent to the user's session on the Web site. Instead, the Web application has the burden of managing the user's session state; for example, it must remember the items in a customer's shopping cart as they move from Web form to Web form. Managing state yourself makes building Web applications a little more complicated than a traditional form application, but fortunately ASP.NET provides a feature-rich infrastructure to ease the burden.

Web Forms also pander their output format to the software and hardware on which they will be displayed. Windows forms render themselves graphically using the native controls and user interface elements of the operating system. Web Forms, on the other hand, render themselves using Hypertext Markup Language (HTML), Wireless Markup Language (WML), XML, and script: all text formats. Although a text format may sound limiting, you can actually reach a larger variety of clients using Web Forms. Web browsers on Linux, Solaris, and cell phones can translate the textual representation of a Web form into a graphical display for the host platform.

Understanding Web Forms

Throughout the chapter you'll uncover more nuances in Web Forms programming, but you already have enough information now to begin your first simple application.

Try It Out: Creating Your First Web Forms Project

You'll use Visual Studio .NET 2003 to create a new ASP.NET Web application. If you're using VB .NET or a different version of Visual Studio .NET, you may see a few minor details that differ from our figures, but you'll be able to follow the examples without a problem.

You'll be adding functionality to this project through a series of examples in this chapter that will show you more about how ASP.NET can work with data. Let's start by creating the project.

1. Open Visual Studio .NET, and create a new blank solution called `Chapter10_Examples`.

2. Add a new VB .NET ASP.NET project to the solution by selecting File ➤ Add Project ➤ New Project.... Select Visual Basic Projects, click the ASP.NET Web Application icon, specify Location as `http://localhost/WebDataGrid`, and click OK, as in Figure 10-1.

3. As shown in Figure 10-1, the project creation dialog box takes on a slightly different look when selecting a Web application instead of a Windows application. Instead of finding a drive location for the new project, you need to enter an HTTP location. Internet Information Services (IIS), Microsoft's Web server, will process and serve your ASP.NET Web Forms application, so the form must be located in a directory managed by IIS. Visual Studio .NET will set up the application's IIS environment for you. All you need to do is give it a name—and make sure that IIS is already running. In this example you simply create the project on the local machine, and Visual Studio .NET configures IIS to accept the new project named `WebDataGrid`.

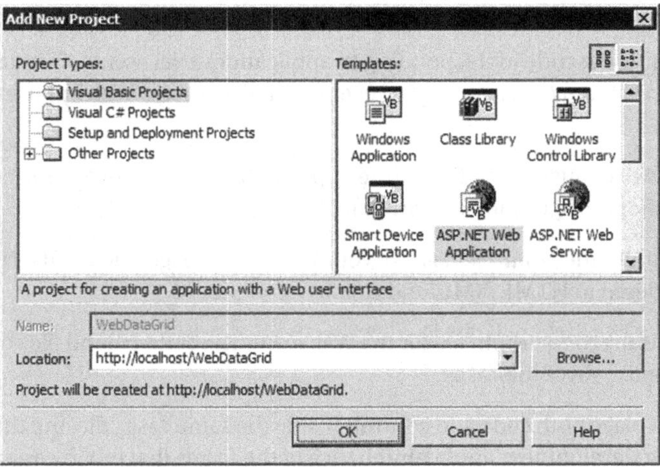

Figure 10-1. *Creating the `WebDataGrid` project*

Tip You control IIS with the Internet Services Manager. IIS should have been installed as part of your Windows environment. If it is, you can get to its documentation by going to `http://localhost/iisHelp` in any browser.

---

4. Once you click OK, your hard drive will get busy spinning, and eventually you'll have the basic building blocks of a Web application ready to go.

How It Works

Let's take a look at what Visual Studio .NET has created for you. When Visual Studio .NET displays your new project, you may notice some file types you don't recognize in Solution Explorer. Click the Show All Files icon, and expand the `WebForm1.aspx` item. Solution Explorer will appear as in Figure 10-2.

Figure 10-2. *`WebDataGrid` items expanded*

The following are important items specific to Web applications:

- `Global.asax` contains the code for responding to application-level events (for example, the `Application_Start` and `Application_End` events that fire when a Web application begins and ends).
- `Web.config` is an XML configuration file for the application. This file contains security, debugging, and other configuration information.
- `WebForm1.aspx` contains the *visual elements* of your Web Forms page, such as the controls and text to be rendered in HTML, XML, and so on.
- `WebForm1.aspx.vb` is the *code-behind* file for the Web form. The code-behind file contains the application logic to drive the `.aspx`.

Technically, you can place both code and controls inside the same `.aspx` file, but the separation makes the ongoing development and maintenance of the forms that much easier. For example, it allows a Web page designer to adjust the look and feel of a Web page independently of the programmer who is writing the code to implement the page's functionality. The `.aspx` file contains the control tags, HTML, and script sent to the Web browser, and the code-behind file contains VB .NET code in a class.

Later in the chapter we'll discuss how the ASP.NET runtime binds these two pieces together when a client requests the form using a Web browser. For now, let's add some functionality to the application.

Try It Out: Designing the Web Form

Once Visual Studio .NET has finished creating all the files in the project, it automatically opens the Web form `.aspx` page and displays it in Design view, which, by default, starts off in Grid Layout mode. This mode allows the precise placement of the visual elements on your Web form using X and Y coordinates in much the same way controls are arranged in Windows form development.

An alternate layout mode is Flow Layout mode in which controls are arranged top to bottom as you add them to the form. Instead of having precise control over the placement of controls, flow layout lets the client's Web browser arrange the controls to match the user's environment as best it can; this is a good choice when you're trying to reach as many different types of clients as possible.

1. You'll work in Flow Layout mode, so the first thing to do is switch over from Grid Layout mode. Right-click the form, and select Properties from the context menu. In the Property Pages dialog box (Figure 10-3), change the Page Layout option to FlowLayout and click OK.

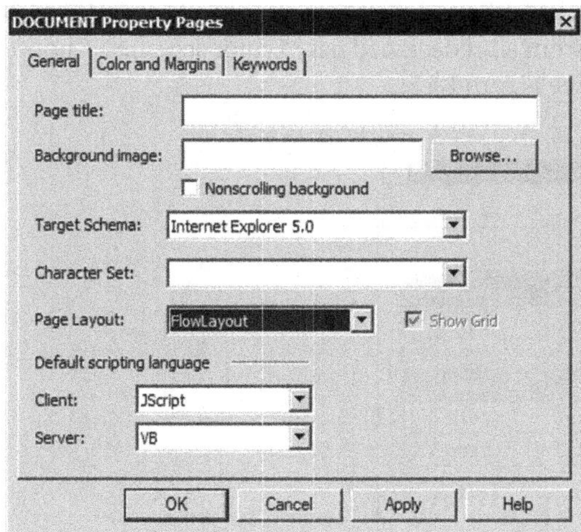

Figure 10-3. *Changing page layout*

2. When you're working with Web forms in Design view, Visual Studio .NET adds two sections to the Toolbox window, called Web Forms and HTML, which contain the ASP.NET and HTML controls you can place on your Web form.

   You'll be using the `DataGrid` control from the Web Forms Toolbox (see Figure 10-4). Make sure the Web Forms horizontal divider is selected, and within that pop-up group, double-click the `DataGrid` control. You'll see a data grid appear on the previously empty form.

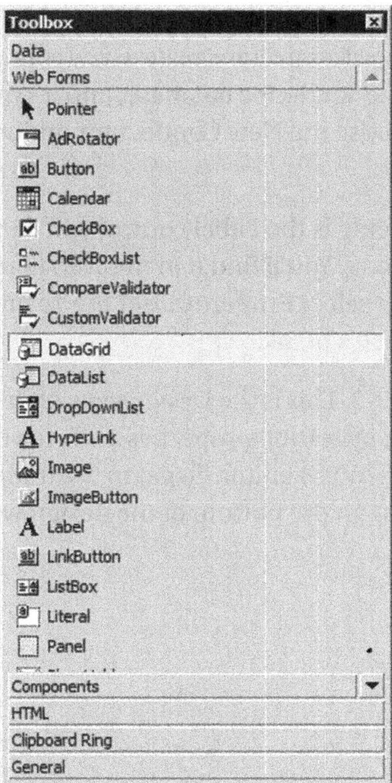

Figure 10-4. *Web Forms Toolbox*

3. Let's add some styling to the control. Right-click the data grid and select Auto Format... from the context menu to pick from a predesigned list of color schemes. Choose the Simple3 format, and click OK (see Figure 10-5).

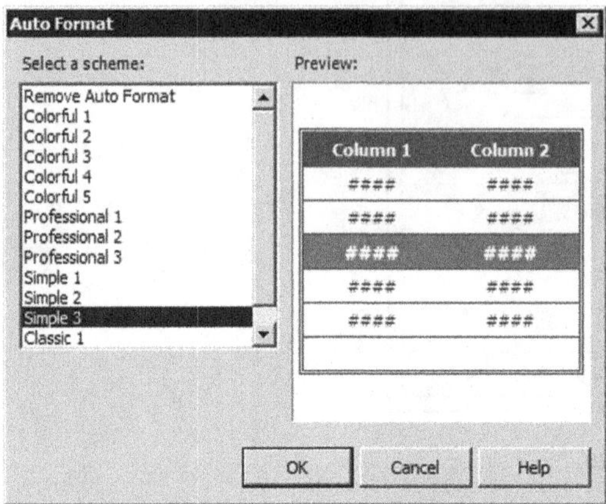

Figure 10-5. *Selecting an Auto Format style*

4. The next control you'll put on the form is a `SqlConnection`. You'll find it under the Data tab of the Toolbox. Double-click it to add it to the form, and you'll notice it appears in the component tray. This is because the `SqlConnection` won't be visible to users who access your application.

5. Click the `SqlConnection`, and find the `ConnectionString` property. Select the blank box next to it, and a drop-down list will appear containing a list of all the database connections you have defined in Server Explorer and an option will appear to create a new connection. Back in Chapter 1, you created a connection to the `Northwind` database, and it's this that you'll select from the list. If it doesn't appear, choose the New Connection option and follow the steps in Chapter 1 to create it.

6. The last control to go on the form for the time being is the Label control you'll use to display error messages if anything should go wrong. You'll find it in the Web Forms tab of the Toolbox. Right-click the `Label` control, and select Properties. Set the `id` property to `ErrorLabel` and clear the `Text` property so that it's blank.

7. So far the Web form looks like the one in Figure 10-6. This is the Design view of the form. From here you can continue to tweak the design by setting properties and viewing the results in the What You See Is What You Get (WYSIWYG) editor. To get to the underlying source for the `.aspx` page, click the HTML button on the bottom of the design window.

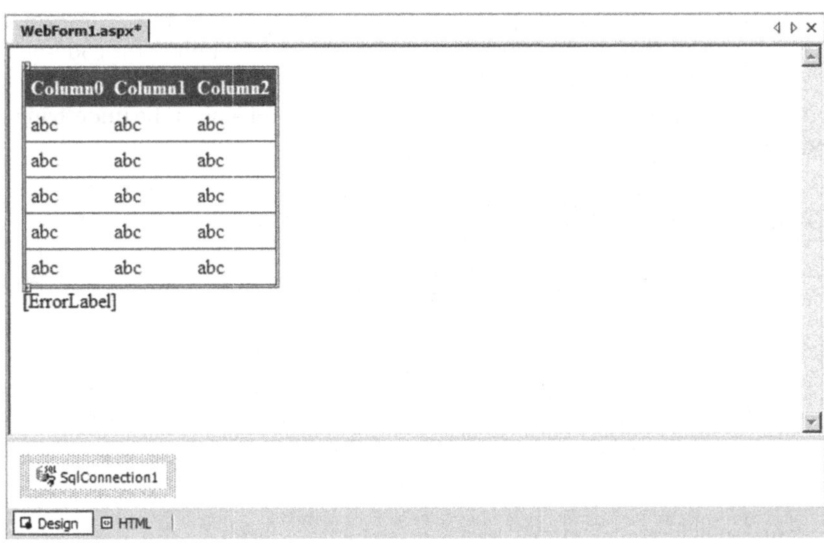

Figure 10-6. *`WebForm1` layout*

How It Works

Let's walk through what you've created and examine some of the code that's generated automatically for you by Visual Studio .NET.

■ **Tip** You may recall back in step 2 you learned that you can add both HTML controls and Web Forms controls to your Web form—let's take a quick look at what we meant by that. *HTML controls* are simple static controls, each control mapping to an equivalent HTML element. These controls are useful when you want to place, for example, a label on the page and not modify the contents when the page executes. By adding a `Runat="Server"` clause in the HTML of the page, though, you can interact with the controls on the server. This comes in handy when migrating a Web application already in place to ASP.NET, replacing old HTML directly with the equivalent control.

On the other hand, Web Forms controls, also known as *server controls*, are accessible by default from the code-behind VB .NET code, meaning you can change a server control's appearance and populate the control with data specific to each incoming request. These controls reside in the `System.Web.UI.WebControls` namespace.

You've added two controls to the page, a DataGrid and a SqlConnection. However, the SqlConnection won't be displayed on the screen and so is dealt with only in the code-behind for the page and not the HTML determining how it looks on the screen. To see that this is so, you can click the HTML tab at the bottom of the design window and look at the underlying .aspx source code (see Figure 10-7).

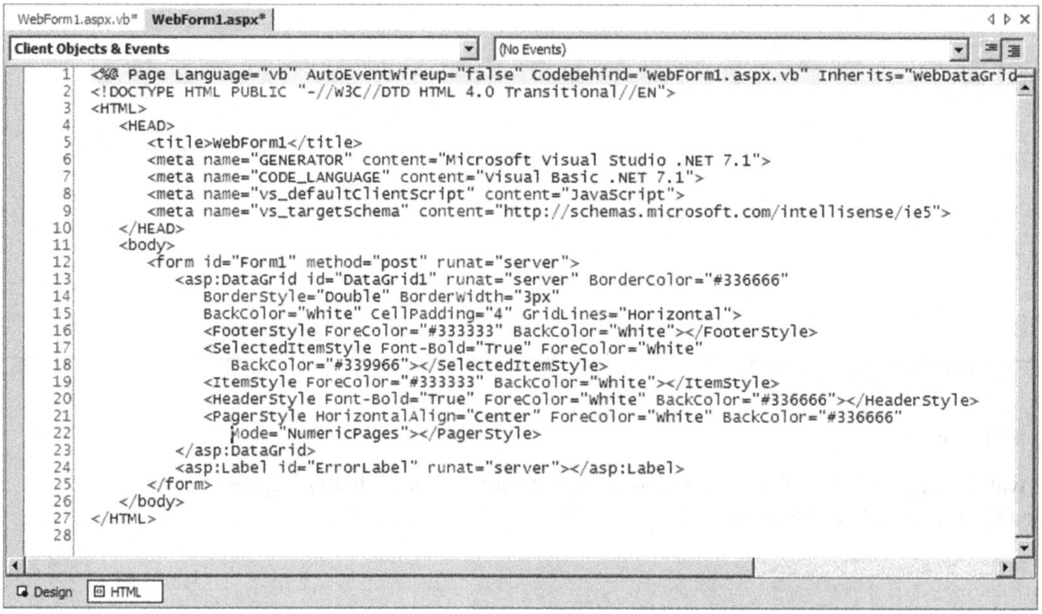

WebForm1.aspx.vb* WebForm1.aspx*

Client Objects & Events | (No Events)

```
<%@ Page Language="vb" AutoEventWireup="false" Codebehind="WebForm1.aspx.vb" Inherits="WebDataGrid
<!DOCTYPE HTML PUBLIC "-//W3C//DTD HTML 4.0 Transitional//EN">
<HTML>
   <HEAD>
      <title>WebForm1</title>
      <meta name="GENERATOR" content="Microsoft Visual Studio .NET 7.1">
      <meta name="CODE_LANGUAGE" content="Visual Basic .NET 7.1">
      <meta name="vs_defaultClientScript" content="JavaScript">
      <meta name="vs_targetSchema" content="http://schemas.microsoft.com/intellisense/ie5">
   </HEAD>
   <body>
      <form id="Form1" method="post" runat="server">
         <asp:DataGrid id="DataGrid1" runat="server" BorderColor="#336666"
            BorderStyle="Double" BorderWidth="3px"
            BackColor="White" CellPadding="4" GridLines="Horizontal">
            <FooterStyle ForeColor="#333333" BackColor="White"></FooterStyle>
            <SelectedItemStyle Font-Bold="True" ForeColor="White"
               BackColor="#339966"></SelectedItemStyle>
            <ItemStyle ForeColor="#333333" BackColor="White"></ItemStyle>
            <HeaderStyle Font-Bold="True" ForeColor="White" BackColor="#336666"></HeaderStyle>
            <PagerStyle HorizontalAlign="Center" ForeColor="White" BackColor="#336666"
               Mode="NumericPages"></PagerStyle>
         </asp:DataGrid>
         <asp:Label id="ErrorLabel" runat="server"></asp:Label>
      </form>
   </body>
</HTML>
```

Design | HTML

Figure 10-7. *WebForm1 HTML view*

Let's walk through this code.

```
<%@ Page Language="vb"
    AutoEventWireup="false"
    Codebehind="WebForm1.aspx.vb"
    Inherits="WebDataGrid.WebForm1"%>
```

The beginning of the file contains the @ Page directive. This gives the ASP.NET engine processing instructions for the .aspx, including the following:

- The source language for the file
- Where to find the corresponding code-behind file
- Whether you'll manually assign event handlers for the page in your own code (AutoEventWireup)
- The name of the VB .NET class (declared in the code-behind file) with the logic for this page (Inherits)

Following the page directive, the head of the HTML page contains meta tags declaring the server- and client-side languages being used and the application generating the code.

```
<HEAD>
   <title>WebForm1</title>
   <meta name="GENERATOR" Content="Microsoft Visual Studio .NET 7.1">
   <meta name="CODE_LANGUAGE" Content="Visual Basic .NET 7.1">
   <meta name="vs_defaultClientScript" content="JavaScript">
   <meta name="vs_targetSchema"
      content="http://schemas.microsoft.com/intellisense/ie5">
</HEAD>
```

The body of the HTML page contains the code for the DataGrid and Label controls you've pulled onto the form (see Listing 10-1).

Listing 10-1. *Body of WebDataGrid HTML Page*

```
<body>
   <form id="Form1" method="post" runat="server">
      <asp:DataGrid id="DataGrid1" runat="server" BorderColor="#336666"
         BorderStyle="Double" BorderWidth="3px" BackColor="White"
         CellPadding="4" GridLines="Horizontal">
         <FooterStyle ForeColor="#333333" BackColor="White"></FooterStyle>
         <SelectedItemStyle Font-Bold="True" ForeColor="White"
            BackColor="#339966"></SelectedItemStyle>
         <ItemStyle ForeColor="#333333" BackColor="White"></ItemStyle>
         <HeaderStyle Font-Bold="True" ForeColor="White"
            BackColor="#336666"></HeaderStyle>
         <PagerStyle HorizontalAlign="Center" ForeColor="White"
            BackColor="#336666" Mode="NumericPages"></PagerStyle>
      </asp:DataGrid>
      <asp:Label id="ErrorLabel" runat="server"></asp:Label>
   </form>
</body>
```

Server control tags (such as <asp:DataGrid>) contain all the color and style attributes for the control. The Simple3 template you used to autoformat the grid set all these properties for you. Notice also that the nested properties will control the appearance of the column header, footer, and selected item.

The most important attributes in the server control tag are the runat and id attributes. Setting runat="server" tells ASP.NET to execute the control on the server, before the page goes to the client, allowing you to manipulate the control in VB .NET, and id allows you to give the control a name with which you can access it from within your code. Let's look at the code itself now.

Viewing the Code-Behind File

The easiest way to view the code behind the form is to right-click the form (in Design view or in the Solution Explorer window) and select View Code from the context menu (or press F7). Visual Studio .NET has generated all the code in this file, but you'll be adding your own code throughout the rest of the chapter. It starts with a class declaration for the page. The class here is derived from the System.Web.UI.Page class. The Page class represents the .aspx form and provides a number of methods, properties, and events you'll use in the course of writing the data grid application.

```
Public Class WebForm1
    Inherits System.Web.UI.Page
```

The next section of code, between the #region markers, is managed by the designer. The three Protected fields—sqlConnection1, DataGrid1, and ErrorLabel—represent the components you dropped onto the form earlier. The ASP.NET runtime will initialize these variables to reference the form components when the user requests the page; you'll learn more about this subject in the "Understanding the ASP.NET Page Life Cycle" section.

The two methods here, Page_Init() and InitializeComponent(), are responsible for initializing variables and event handlers. You can see that in the latter the connection string you created back in step 5 is given to the sqlConnection1 member. You won't be changing any of the code in this section.

```
#Region " Web Form Designer Generated Code "

   'This call is required by the Web Form Designer.
   <System.Diagnostics.DebuggerStepThrough()> _
   Private Sub InitializeComponent()
      Me.SqlConnection1 = New System.Data.SqlClient.SqlConnection
      '
      'SqlConnection1
      '
      Me.SqlConnection1.ConnectionString = _
      "workstation id=DISTILLERY;packet size=4096;" & _
      "integrated security=SSPI;data source=""" & _
      "(local)\NetSDK"";persist security info=False;" & _
      "initial catalog=Northwind"
   End Sub

   Protected WithEvents DataGrid1 As System.Web.UI.WebControls.DataGrid
   Protected WithEvents SqlConnection1 As _
      System.Data.SqlClient.SqlConnection
   Protected WithEvents ErrorLabel As System.Web.UI.WebControls.Label

   'NOTE: The following placeholder declaration is required by the Web
   'Form Designer. Do not delete or move it.
   Private designerPlaceholderDeclaration As System.Object

   Private Sub Page_Init(ByVal sender As System.Object, _
      ByVal e As System.EventArgs) Handles MyBase.Init
        'CODEGEN: This method call is required by the Web Form Designer
        'Do not modify it using the code editor.
        InitializeComponent()
   End Sub

#End Region
```

Finally, Page_Load is an event handler that the runtime will call after the page is initialized and the member variables reference the controls. In later examples you'll use this method to perform the data binding.

```
Private Sub Page_Load(ByVal sender As System.Object, _
   ByVal e As System.EventArgs) Handles MyBase.Load
        'Put user code to initialize the page here
End Sub

End Class
```

Binding Data to a Data Grid

The first task is to bind some data that you'll pull from the Northwind database to the DataGrid control that you've added to our form. As you want to have the data display on the screen when the page is loaded, you'll tie this data binding into the Page_Load event, but it's perfectly possible to leave it until a user has clicked a button on the page first.

Try It Out: Binding Data

It's the Page_Load method that lets you set up objects before the page generates any HTML output, and it's this method in which you'll do the data binding.

You don't need to add any more controls to the form itself, so all you need do is add to the code-behind in WebForm1.aspx.vb.

1. Add an Imports directive for the System.Data.SqlClient namespace at the top of the file. This will give you access to the SQL Server .NET data provider.

2. The way to bind data to a data grid is straightforward, but it's good practice to write it as a method that you can call more than once. Indeed, you'll see later in the chapter how this provides you with some flexibility when adding additional functionality. With the method written, all you need do then is call it from Page_Load, with the following code:

```
Private Sub BindDataGrid()
   ' Sql Query
   Dim sql As String = _
      "SELECT FirstName, LastName, Title, Extension " & _
      "FROM Employees"

   Dim thisCommand As New SqlCommand(sql, SqlConnection1)

   Try
      ' Open Connection
      sqlConnection1.Open()

      ' Run Query and get Data Reader
      Dim thisReader As SqlDataReader = thisCommand.ExecuteReader()
```

```
        ' Attach Reader to DataGrid and Bind
        DataGrid1.DataSource = thisReader
        DataGrid1.DataBind()

    Catch ex As Exception
        ' Display error
        ErrorLabel.Text = "Error: " & ex.ToString()

    Finally
        sqlConnection1.Close()
    End Try
End Sub

Private Sub Page_Load(ByVal sender As System.Object, _
    ByVal e As System.EventArgs) Handles MyBase.Load
        BindDataGrid()
End Sub
```

3. Build, and run with Ctrl+F5. Visual Studio .NET will compile the code-behind file, launch Internet Explorer, and navigate the browser to the `.aspx` page, giving you the display in Figure 10-8.

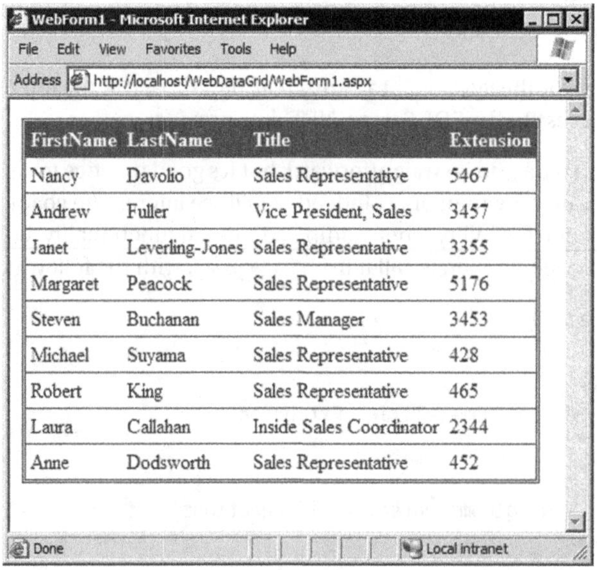

WebForm1 - Microsoft Internet Explorer

File Edit View Favorites Tools Help

Address http://localhost/WebDataGrid/WebForm1.aspx

FirstName	LastName	Title	Extension
Nancy	Davolio	Sales Representative	5467
Andrew	Fuller	Vice President, Sales	3457
Janet	Leverling-Jones	Sales Representative	3355
Margaret	Peacock	Sales Representative	5176
Steven	Buchanan	Sales Manager	3453
Michael	Suyama	Sales Representative	428
Robert	King	Sales Representative	465
Laura	Callahan	Inside Sales Coordinator	2344
Anne	Dodsworth	Sales Representative	452

Done Local intranet

Figure 10-8. *WebDataGrid running*

GETTING ASP.NET TALKING TO MSDE

If you try to run this page and instead get an error saying that the login failed for your machine's ASPNET account, this is because MSDE doesn't recognize that account. To fix this, open a command window and type the following three commands, replacing MACHINE with the name of your computer:

```
osql -E -S (local)\NETSDK -C -Q "sp_grantlogin 'MACHINE\ASPNET'"
osql -E -S (local)\NETSDK -d database ➥
   -Q "sp_grantdbaccess 'MACHINE\ASPNET'"
osql -E -S (local)\NETSDK -d database ➥
   -Q "sp_addrolemember 'db_owner', 'MACHINE\ASPNET'"
```

The commands and their responses will look like the following screen. For reference, our computer is called DISTILLERY, and we're granting access to the NORTHWIND database. You'll find a bigger discussion of this fix at http://asp.net/Forums/ShowPost.aspx?tabindex=1&PostID=268887.

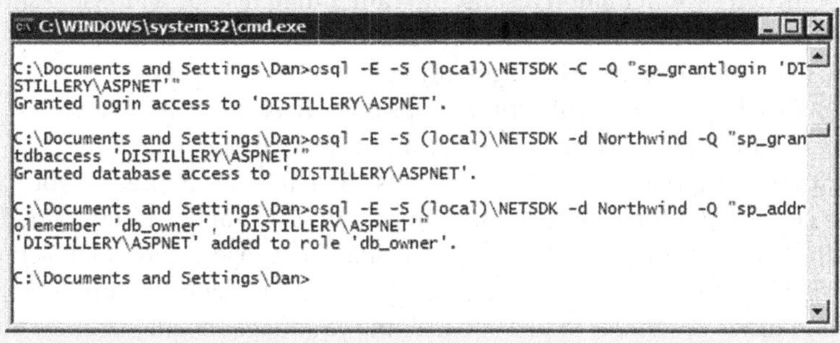

How It Works

If you look at BindDataGrid again, you'll find that all but the penultimate two lines of the method look decidedly familiar. All they're doing is creating a DataReader object that contains the data returned from the query you sent to Northwind. It's the following two calls to the data grid that actually do all the hard work:

```
' Attach Reader to DataGrid and Bind
DataGrid1.DataSource = thisReader
DataGrid1.DataBind()
```

The first call sets the DataSource property of the data grid to the data reader.

■ **Tip** Note that a data grid's data source could be a data view, an array, or indeed any object that implements the System.Collections.IEnumerable interface. You saw this in Chapters 8 and 9.

The actual binding takes place when you invoke the `DataBind` method of the data grid. Just like a Windows Forms data grid, the Web Forms data grid can display all the query results using the column names as headers.

Note also that you used mixed case for the column names in the SQL query as a convenient way to display capitalized column headings. Try putting all the column names in the query in lowercase to see what effect it has on the data grid: all the column headers will be in lowercase. This isn't necessarily the most professional way to do things, but it's a simple expedient for the example's purposes.

The first data grid example is easy to get running, but it doesn't have much functionality. Throughout the rest of the chapter you'll add the ability to edit, delete, and sort rows in the data grid, as well as look at some of the additional differences in Web programming. The first feature you'll add is the ability to page the results.

Paging in a Data Grid

If you've ever used a Web-based search engine, then you've probably come across the scenario where your query has returned several million results, but rather than display all those results on one page, the page shows them in groups of 10, 50, or 100 at a time. Chances are you'll find what you're looking for in the first two or three pages anyway.

This act of breaking up a large set of results into groups that are easier to handle and adding controls for the user to navigate through these groups is known as *paging*.

Paging is important in Web applications for two reasons. First, it's nice to present your users with manageable chunks of information. If the `Employees` table of `Northwind` contained 5,000 rows, throwing all 5,000 items into the Web browser would create a long page of information. Second, the time needed to download the entire data for 5,000 rows could be quite a while. Even as broadband usage continues to pick up, keeping your pages small increases the perceived performance of the application. Showing only 50 rows at once is faster for the client than waiting for all 5,000 rows to appear.

Try It Out: Data Grid Paging

You can enable paging in a data grid in several ways, but they all amount to setting the data grid's `AllowPaging` property to `true`.

- Right-click the data grid, and select Properties to open the Properties window and set `AllowPaging` to `True`.
- Add the attribute to the `@ Page` server control tag in the `.aspx` (`AllowPaging="True"`).
- If paging depends on some user preference setting (some users may want paged results, others may not), you could conditionally set the property in the `Page_Load` method using this:

  ```
  DataGrid1.AllowPaging = FindThisUsersPagingPreference()
  ```

- Set the property using the data grid's Property Builder.

In this example, you'll use the Property Builder. This tool categorizes the wide selection of properties for a data grid into functional tabs, and it's handy to know how to use it. You'll use it a few more times in this chapter before you finish.

1. Switch to Design view, and right-click the data grid. Select Property Builder… from the context menu. When the dialog box appears, click Paging in the left column (see Figure 10-9).

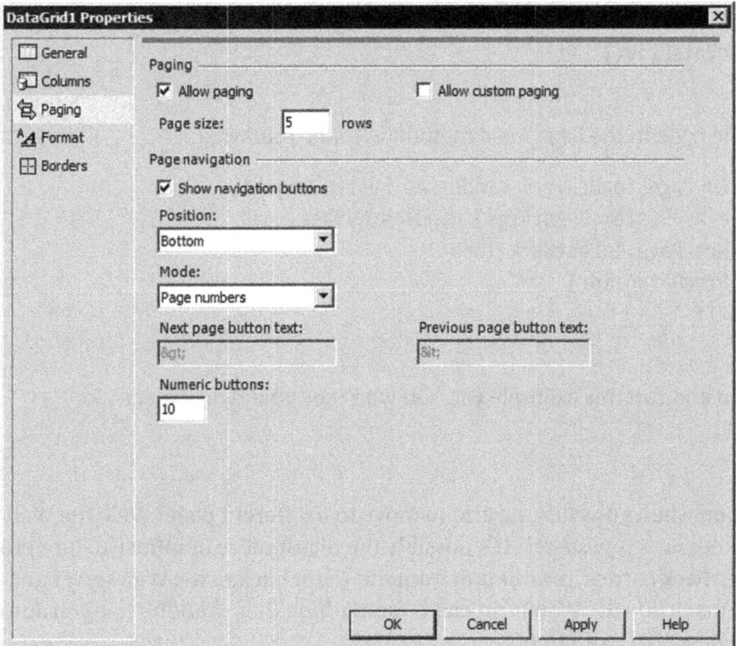

Figure 10-9. *Data grid Properties dialog box*

2. As shown in Figure 10-9, set the `AllowPaging` property to `true` by selecting the Allow Paging check box. Set the Page Size option (the number of rows to display per page) to *5*. You can leave the location and the type of page navigation controls (next and previous hyperlinks vs. page-numbered hyperlinks) for the data grid at their defaults. However, if you wanted to provide your own custom navigation bar for moving among the pages, you'd clear the Show Navigation Buttons check box. Click OK.

3. With the data now separated into pages, you have to teach the data grid what to do when someone chooses to change the page. You do this by creating an event handler for the `PageIndexChanged` event.

4. To assign an event handler, switch to the code-behind for the page. Just underneath the tab for `WebForm1.aspx.vb`, you'll see two drop-down boxes. Select the entry for `DataGrid1` in the left box and then the `PageIndexChanged` event in the right box. Visual Studio .NET inserts an empty event handler for it into the code. All you need to do is add the following bold lines:

```
Private Sub DataGrid1_PageIndexChanged(ByVal source As Object, _
   ByVal e As System.Web.UI.WebControls.DataGridPageChangedEventArgs) _
   Handles DataGrid1.PageIndexChanged
      DataGrid1.CurrentPageIndex = e.NewPageIndex
      BindDataGrid()
End Sub
```

5. Replace the code in the `Page_Load` method with the following:

```
Private Sub Page_Load(ByVal sender As System.Object, _
   ByVal e As System.EventArgs) Handles MyBase.Load
      If Not Page.IsPostBack Then
         BindDataGrid()
      End If
End Sub
```

6. Don't build and run this example yet. You won't see what you expect.

How It Works

So what will happen when you click the grid to move to a different page? Well, the Web form performs what's known as a *postback*. It's possibly the nicest piece of infrastructure provided by ASP.NET. A postback carries information from the client back to the Web server and allows you to handle events inside the Web form class—something that wouldn't happen automatically over the stateless HTTP protocol.

The `PageIndexChanged` event handler takes an argument of type `DataGridPageChangedEventArgs` containing the new page number to use in the `NewPageIndex` property. If you simply assign this value to the grid's `CurrentPageIndex` property and rebind the data, the data grid is smart enough to extract and display the rows for the new page. The grid then packages the rows as HTML and sends them back to the client.

You may remember you also had a call to `BindDataGrid` in the `Page_Load` method. Now you don't want to execute it again in `Page_Load` when a postback event occurs because the event handler will handle binding if needed. You need to check whether the page has been loaded as a result of a postback, because if it was, you'd end up binding to the data grid twice.

Fortunately, you inherit a property, `IsPostBack`, from the `System.Web.UI.Page` class to tell you if you're in a postback. That's why you modified the `Page_Load` method.

Combining a Data Grid and Dataset

Although the `SqlDataReader` class is the best choice for performance, it now has a limitation. If you compile and execute the code you have so far, you'll get the error shown in Figure 10-10.

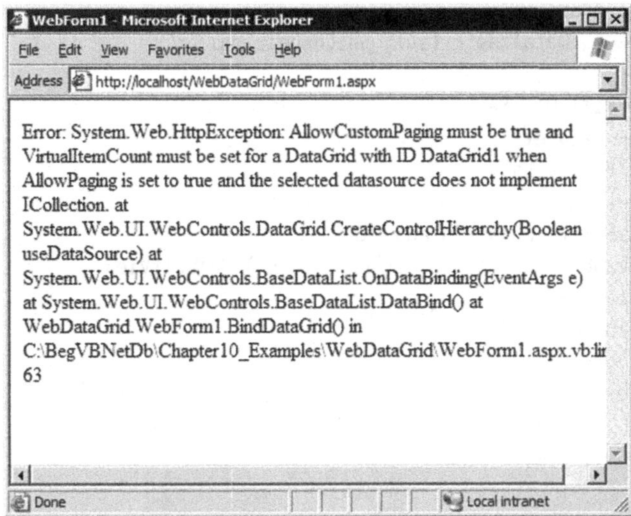

Figure 10-10. *WebDataGrid error*

Although the `DataSource` property of the data grid accepts any object implementing `IEnumerable`, paging requires the data source object to implement `ICollection`, which `SqlDataReader` doesn't. Both the `ICollection` and `IEnumerable` interfaces allow the grid to loop through each row in the result set, but `ICollection` provides a count of the total number if items in the result set, and `IEnumerable` doesn't.

The grid uses this count to determine the total number of pages required. You could perform some custom paging calculations to replace the pieces of `ICollection` that would do this automatically, but you'll take an alternate route and replace the data reader with a data view.

Try It Out: Binding to a Data View

All of the changes you need to switch from a data reader to a data view are in the `BindDataGrid` method.

1. Replace the existing version of `BindDataGrid` with the following code. Notice you're using the same query as before, but you now populate a dataset with the result set instead of retrieving it with a data reader.

```
Private Sub BindDataGrid()

   ' Sql Query
   Dim sql As String = _
      "SELECT FirstName, LastName, Title, Extension " & _
      "FROM Employees"

   Try
      ' Open Connection
      SqlConnection1.Open()
```

```
            ' Create Data Adapter
            Dim da As New SqlDataAdapter(sql, SqlConnection1)

            ' Create and fill DataSet
            Dim ds As New DataSet
            da.Fill(ds, "Employees")

            ' Attach DataSet to DataGrid and Bind
            DataGrid1.DataSource = ds.Tables("Employees").DefaultView
            DataGrid1.DataBind()
         Catch ex As Exception
            ' Display error
            ErrorLabel.Text = "Error: " & ex.ToString()
         Finally
            SqlConnection1.Close()
         End Try

      End Sub
```

How It Works

The reworked BindDataGrid pulls the data from the Northwind database into a data table in a dataset. The data grid's DataSource property is then set to the DefaultView of that data table. Note that it's the DefaultView property (a data view) of the data table rather than the data table itself that implements ICollection and allows the data grid to perform paging calculations for you.

Using a dataset will turn out to have several other advantages for you, as you'll see later, but right now, let's make sure it actually works. You should now be able to build and execute the form without errors. As shown in Figure 10-11, the form will display five rows with hyperlink page numbers to click and see the rest.

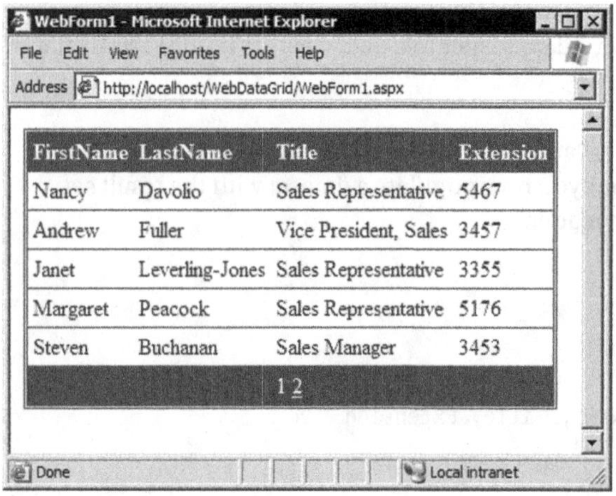

Figure 10-11. *Revised WebDataGrid running*

The next step in the application is to build in a small caching feature, but before you do that it'll help a lot if you take a step back and look at how the ASP.NET runtime processes the page. This background information will allow you to make some more improvements to the application in addition to caching.

Understanding the ASP.NET Page Life Cycle

The first time a request arrives for an `.aspx` page, the ASP.NET runtime combines the `.aspx` page with the class in the code-behind file and creates a new class. The runtime dynamically compiles this new class and caches the result to service future requests. Figure 10-12 depicts the life cycle.

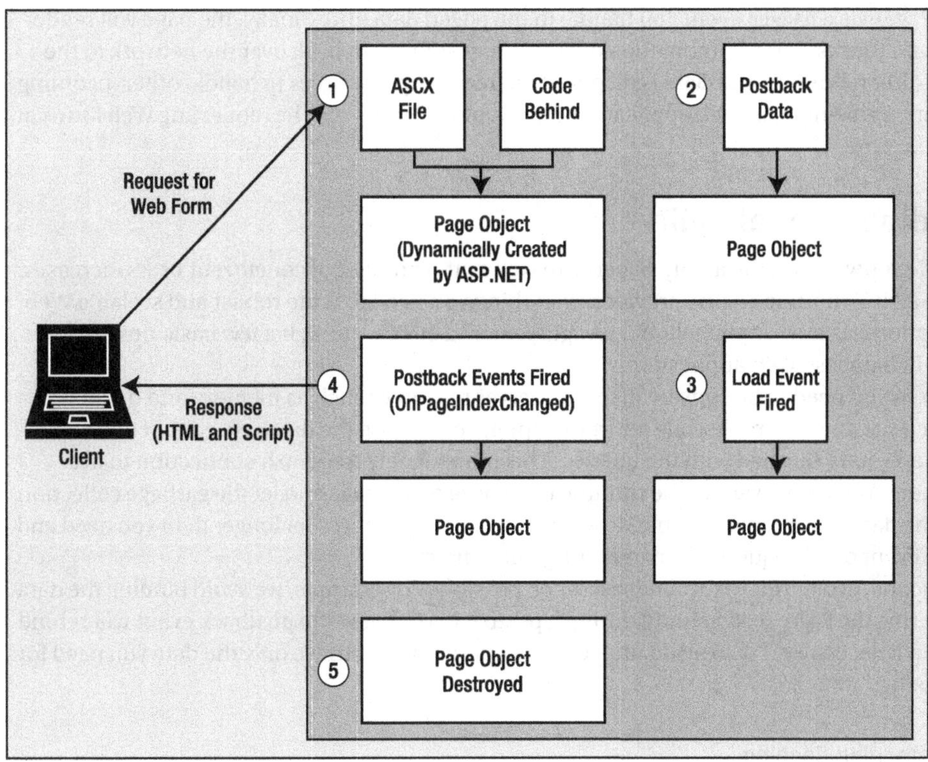

Figure 10-12. *ASP.NET page life cycle*

For each request, the runtime will instantiate a new instance of this class. This means when a user requests the paged data grid you built and then clicks a new page number, a new instance of the dynamically generated class services the request—you don't have the same instance of the class you used for the initial request. This is a primary difference between Web Forms and Windows Forms. In Windows Forms, the same class can continue to handle events for a user during the entire life of the application.

To help cover these seams, the ASP.NET runtime will repopulate the form's controls on postback with all the properties just as they appeared on the client. So, for instance, a check box control marked *checked* on the client and then posted to the Web server will have its `Checked` property set to `true`, instead of the default value of `false`. ASP.NET refers to this process as restoring the *view state.*

After restoring the view state, the runtime fires the `Load` event, and the code can perform any initialization you need. Once this step is complete, any postback events are fired, such as the `OnPageIndexChanged` event you handle in the paged data grid. Finally, the page will render itself, and the result is a combination of HTML and script sent back over the network to the client. After rendering, the class is disposed of, freeing up resources to handle other incoming requests. Remember, in Web applications, thousands of users may be requesting Web forms at the same time.

Building for Scalability

Scalable software has the ability to perform well as the number of concurrent users increases. The ASP.NET runtime engine provides everything you need to write robust and scalable Web applications, as long as you follow a few guidelines. Let's go through a few basic tips for scalability in database Web applications.

First, you need to be conservative with server resources such as memory and database connections. In the sample code for this chapter, you'll close the database connection explicitly when you're finished with the queries. This immediately frees up a connection to use elsewhere. You could wait for the runtime to dispose of the page and let the garbage collection close the database connection, but doing so only holds a resource for longer than you need and may prevent other requests from executing immediately.

Second, avoid trips to the database when possible. For example, we avoid binding the data grid during the `Page_Load` method during a postback. We know the postback event will rebind the data if necessary. Try to avoid unnecessary queries, and retrieve only the data you need for processing.

Understanding Caching

Like any programming guidelines however, one must often be traded off against the other, and it's left to you to determine the balance for your own application. The balance between the two recommendations we've given for example applies when you start to think about caching data you've pulled from the database. Caching a query result in memory on the server uses more memory resources; on the other hand, it also saves a trip to the database. Evaluating these types of trade-offs correctly can help the performance of your application.

For example, once you query the Employees table and send the results to the client in a paged data grid, you can assume the client is probably going to examine more rows. If you simply reload the dataset from memory instead of from the database, you can save a trip to the database. Caching the dataset sounds like a good idea, particularly since you have a small number of rows in the table. If the Employees table contained thousands of rows, you may use too much memory for caching and actually hurt server performance. Evaluating these trade-offs usually requires you to factor in the number of users you support, the hardware your application runs on, and even how users navigate through the application.

Many techniques for caching are available in ASP.NET. In this example you'll use the Session object. The Session object allows you to store data specific to each client. ASP.NET creates a new session when a client first navigates to your site. After a specified amount of inactivity (20 minutes is the default), ASP.NET will clear a user's session contents to conserve resources.

You can configure ASP.NET to store session contents in memory (the default option and also the fastest option) or even in a SQL Server database. Although storing the results of a database query in a database may sound strange, if the original query is particularly complicated, you still may see a performance gain. Also, remember you could store multiple queries in the same dataset.

Try It Out: Using a Session

Follow these steps:

1. First, update the BindDataGrid method with the code in Listing 10-2. We've highlighted new and changed code in bold. Notice the method takes a Boolean parameter to force a refresh of the dataset from the database instead of the session cache.

Listing 10-2. *Revised BindDataGrid*

```
Private Sub BindDataGrid(ByVal refresh As Boolean)
   Dim ds As New DataSet

   ' Locate dataset
   If refresh Or Session("Employees") Is Nothing Then

      ' Sql Query
      Dim sql As String = _
         "SELECT FirstName, LastName, Title, Extension " & _
         "FROM Employees"

      Try
         ' Open Connection
         SqlConnection1.Open()
```

```
            ' Create Data Adapter
            Dim da As New SqlDataAdapter(sql, SqlConnection1)

            ' Fill DataSet
            da.Fill(ds, "Employees")

            ' Save dataset in Session state
            Session("Employees") = ds

         Catch ex As Exception
            ' Display error
            ErrorLabel.Text = "Error: " & ex.ToString()
         Finally
            SqlConnection1.Close()
         End Try
      Else
         ds = CType(Session("Employees"), DataSet)
      End If

      ' Attach DataSet to DataGrid and Bind
      DataGrid1.DataSource = ds.Tables("Employees").DefaultView
      DataGrid1.DataBind()
   End Sub
```

2. Add a second version of `BindDataGrid` (see Listing 10-3). This parameterless version forwards the call to the Boolean `BindDataGrid` without requesting a refresh of the dataset from the database. This will allow you to bind a data grid without always specifying a refresh parameter.

Listing 10-3. *Parameterless BindDataGrid*

```
Private Sub BindDataGrid()
   BindDataGrid(False)
End Sub
```

3. In the `Page_Load` method, add a `true` argument to the call to `BindDataGrid`. This ensures the most recent data is retrieved when the page is first loaded. `DataGrid1_PageIndexChanged` can remain the same and pull data from the `Session` cache.

```
Private Sub Page_Load(ByVal sender As System.Object, _
   ByVal e As System.EventArgs) Handles MyBase.Load
      If Not Page.IsPostBack Then
         BindDataGrid(True)
      End If
End Sub
```

How It Works

You've now overloaded the BindDataGrid method, creating two versions with different signatures. The first now has a boolean parameter (or *flag*) to force a refresh of the session contents, because one other big danger in caching data is showing your user out-of-date results when someone else has changed the underlying data. The best data to cache is static data; trying to cache rapidly changing information may show incorrect results.

Notice that you first test the Session collection (an instance of the HttpSessionState class) to see if an item named employees exists. If this returns Nothing, or if the refresh flag is set, you need to query the database and populate a new dataset to store in the session. During Page_Load, you force a refresh to ensure the user sees the most current data, but during processing of the OnPageIndexChanged event, you allow the page to use a cached copy of the data and save yourself a trip to the database.

Selecting a Row

So far, so good—the data grid has done everything you've asked of it so far, but it's not the be-all, end-all of simple data retrieval. Indeed, it's just not suited to displaying some types of data, be it for practical or aesthetic reasons. Take, for instance, the Notes field in Northwind's Employees table, which contains some additional facts and background information about staff stored as free-form text.

Rather than displaying this text directly in the data grid, which would clutter the screen up quite a bit, you'll implement a more elegant solution and allow users to select the row containing the employee they want to know more about. When they do select a row, the Notes about that employee will appear in a separate area of the Web form.

Adding a select capability to the data grid is similar to the steps you just used in adding paging. First, you'll adjust the data grid properties and then add an event handler. You'll also need to add some more user interface elements to display the employee's notes.

Try It Out: Adding a Detail Display

Follow these steps:

1. Return to the property builder once more by right-clicking the DataGrid control in Design view and selecting Property Builder....

2. Select Columns. Under the list of available columns, expand the Button Column node and move a Select node into the list of selected columns. Change the Button type to PushButton, and leave the defaults for all other settings. This will give you a column of buttons for the user to click when selecting a row.

3. Check the Create Columns Automatically at Run Time check box. If you fail to do this, the grid will display only your columns of check boxes. The Property Builder should look like Figure 10-13. Click OK.

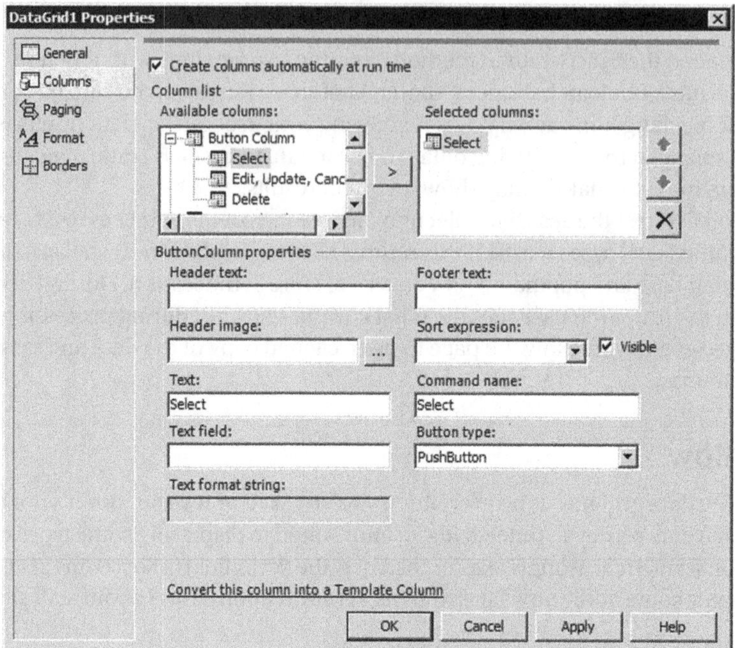

Figure 10-13. *Adding a button column to a data grid with Property Builder*

4. Drag a `Panel` Web control from the Toolbox onto the form. A panel is a container for other controls, which will come in handy when you want to show and hide the detail information display. Set the panel's `Visible` property to `False`. Instead of hiding and displaying all the controls individually, you'll just hide and display the panel control (and therefore all its contents as well) instead.

5. Widen the panel on the form to 250 × 50 pixels. Add an HTML `Table` to it from the HTML section of the Toolbox. It should have one column and two rows.

6. Drag a `Label` control from the Web Forms section of the Toolbox to the second row of the table. You'll use it to display the notes. In keeping with the color scheme, you'll adjust the layout and color properties of the two new controls so the Design view of the updated form looks like Figure 10-14.

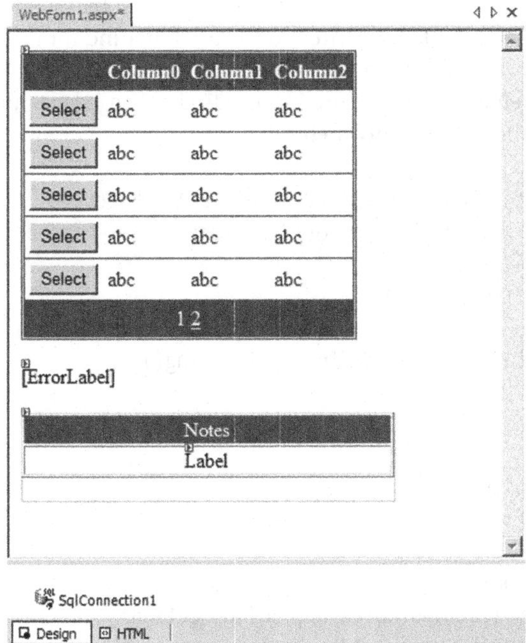

Figure 10-14. *WebDataGrid with panel*

The `.aspx` for this section of the page should contain the code in Listing 10-4.

Listing 10-4. *WebDataGrid Panel .aspx Code*

```
<asp:Panel id="Panel1" runat="server" Visible="False"
   Width="250px" Height="50px">
   <TABLE id="Table1" cellSpacing="1" cellPadding="1"
      width="300" border="1">
      <TR>
         <TD style="COLOR: white; BACKGROUND-COLOR: #336666"
            align="center">
            Notes
         </TD>
      </TR>
      <TR>
         <TD align="center">
            <asp:Label id="Label1" runat="server">Label</asp:Label>
         </TD>
      </TR>
   </TABLE>
</asp:Panel>
```

7. The event you want to catch when a user has selected a row is the SelectedIndexChanged event, so you need to create a handler for it. Switch to the code-behind for the page. Just underneath the tab for WebForm1.aspx.vb, you'll see two drop-down boxes. Select the entry for DataGrid1 in the left box and then the SelectedIndexChanged event in the right box. Add the following code to the empty method:

```
Private Sub DataGrid1_SelectedIndexChanged(ByVal sender As Object, _
   ByVal e As System.EventArgs) Handles DataGrid1.SelectedIndexChanged

   ' Get Index of Selected Item
   Dim key As String = _
      DataGrid1.DataKeys(DataGrid1.SelectedIndex).ToString()

   ' Sql Query For Notes Field
   Dim NotesSql As String = _
      "SELECT Notes FROM Employees " & _
      "WHERE EmployeeId = @EmployeeId"

   ' Create Command and add parameter
   Dim NotesCommand As New SqlCommand(NotesSql, SqlConnection1)
   NotesCommand.Parameters.Add("@EmployeeId", key)

   Try
      ' Open Connection
      SqlConnection1.Open()

      ' Run query and get data reader
      Dim NotesReader As SqlDataReader = NotesCommand.ExecuteReader()

      ' If there's data, make it visible
      If NotesReader.Read() Then
         Label1.Text = NotesReader("Notes").ToString()
         Panel1.Visible = True
      End If

      ' Close datareader
      NotesReader.Close()
```

```
Catch ex As Exception
        ' Display error
        ErrorLabel.Text = "Error: " & ex.ToString()

Finally
        ' Close connection
        SqlConnection1.Close()

     End Try
  End Sub
```

Making It Work

The first step in the event handler is finding the EmployeeID of the employee to detail. You haven't needed to access this in this example yet, so you'll have to add EmployeeID to the query in BindDataGrid.

```
' Sql Query
Dim sql As String = _
  "SELECT EmployeeId, FirstName, LastName, Title, Extension " & _
  "FROM Employees"
```

The EmployeeID field will now be bound to the grid with the other information, but how do you retrieve the ID of the selected employee from the grid? You actually have several ways to achieve this, but one of the safest approaches is to use the DataKeys collection of the data grid. This property is specifically designed to hold the primary key values for each row as they appear in the grid. All you need to do is to give the data grid the name of the field containing the key values, in this case EmployeeID. You add the following bold code to the BindDataGrid method, just after assigning the DataSource property:

```
' Attach DataSet to DataGrid and Bind
DataGrid1.DataSource = ds.Tables("Employees").DefaultView
DataGrid1.DataKeyField = "EmployeeId"
DataGrid1.DataBind()
```

You can retrieve the correct ID to use from DataKeys by using the SelectedIndex property of the data grid. Once you've retrieved the results of the query, you simply need to set the Label control's Text property to display the notes and then unhide the Panel control. The grid will automatically highlight the selected row for you using the SelectedItem style property. The resulting display should look like Figure 10-15.

Note that EmployeeID is now also shown in the grid, even though it's of no real use to the user. In the "Using Bound Columns" section, you'll look at keeping EmployeeID from being displayed in the data grid and use the column only to populate the DataKeys collection.

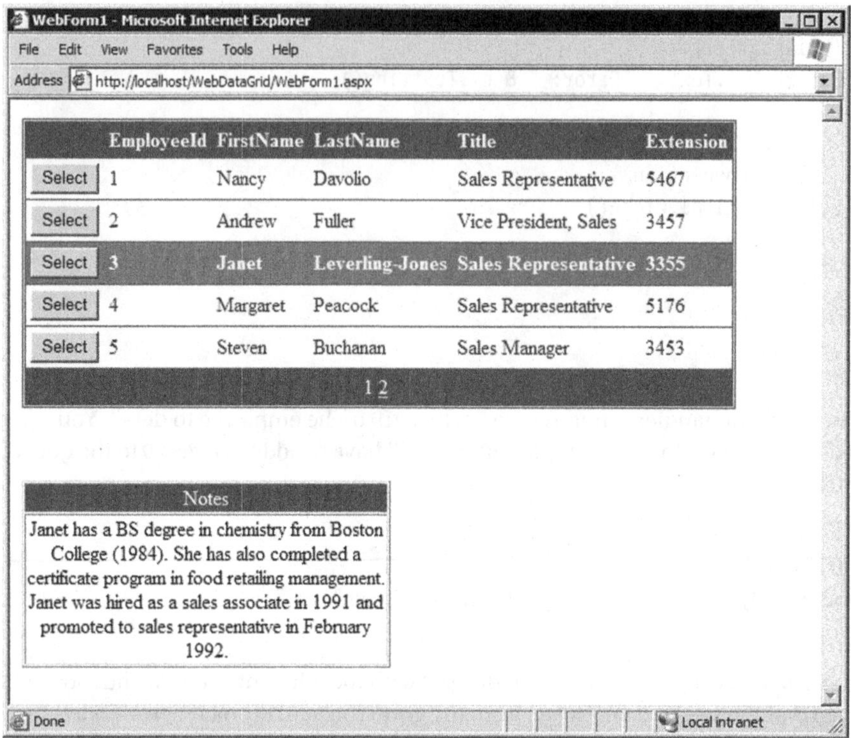

Figure 10-15. *Displaying* `Notes` *for a selected employee*

Tweaking the View State

If you build and run the page now, you'll see that everything seems to be working fine. However, a problem exists that's easy to re-create. Select a row on the first page (say, row two) and then move to page two. Without some additional code, you'll see that the data grid will still think the second row on this new page is the one that has been selected, which it isn't. If you had selected the fifth row, this would have been even more awkward because page two doesn't have a fifth row to display.

The problem lies in that when ASP.NET rebuilds the data grid as a form is posted back, it simply re-creates the whole of a server control's view state unless told otherwise. Consider that when a row is selected, you don't call `BindDataGrid` in the respective event handler, because nothing in the data grid has changed. The data grid can continue to use the same information you sent during the initial page request. The data grid saved the initial information in the view state, and the runtime restored this information during the initialization step of the postback request. During rendering, the data grid simply rewrote the HTML, with some slight adjustments to the formatting for the selected row.

What you need to do is reset the `SelectedIndex` property of the data grid to -1, meaning no row is selected, and then rehide the detail panel. The updated code for the `DataGrid1_PageIndexChanged` event handler for the paging event is as follows:

```
Private Sub DataGrid1_PageIndexChanged(ByVal source As Object, _
   ByVal e As System.Web.UI.WebControls.DataGridPageChangedEventArgs) _
   Handles DataGrid1.PageIndexChanged
      DataGrid1.CurrentPageIndex = e.NewPageIndex
      DataGrid1.SelectedIndex = -1
      Panel1.Visible = False
      BindDataGrid()
End Sub
```

You're starting to see a fairly functional database application emerge. However, you have still some cosmetic problems. For instance, the column names use the name of the database field instead of a friendly name. In the next section, you'll look at how to customize the columns of the data grid.

Using Bound Columns

Bound columns give you more control over the look of the columns in a data grid. Instead of letting the data grid create, name, and format columns automatically, you can explicitly specify the columns for the grid to use.

Try It Out: Adding Bound Columns

Follow these steps:

1. You begin again with the Property Builder dialog box for the grid by right-clicking the data grid, selecting PropertyBuilder..., and selecting Columns. Uncheck the Create Columns Automatically at Run Time check box.

2. From the Available columns list, move a Bound Column node into the Selected columns list for each column you need to display. For each column you set the Header text to the text you prefer (for instance, *First Name*) and the Data Field to the database column to bind to (*FirstName*). Move a bound column node over for First Name, Last Name, Title, and Phone.

3. You'll now add the staff's hire dates to the grid to demonstrate how you can format a column automatically. Add `HireDate` to the query in the `BindDataGrid` method.

   ```
   Dim sql As String = _
      "SELECT EmployeeId, FirstName, LastName, " & _
      "Title, Extension, HireDate " & _
      "FROM Employees"
   ```

4. Back in the Property Builder, add another bound column for the Hire Date and set the Data Formatting Expression option to `{0:d}`. This is the same format specifier as used in the Format method of the `String` class. It indicates a short date format and will exclude the time of day in the output. Check the Read Only check box as well (see Figure 10-16). You'll see why in the "Editing a Data Grid" section.

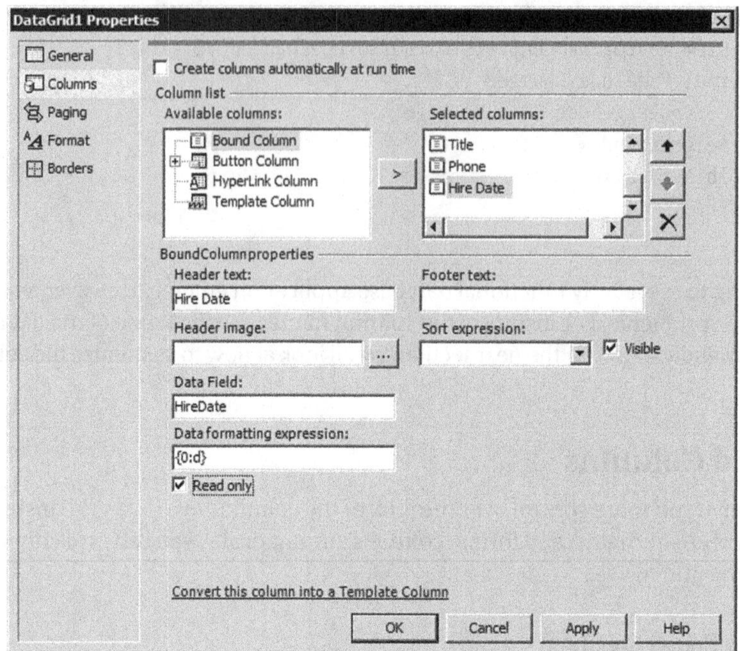

Figure 10-16. *Adding a read-only column*

5. Last but not least, you'll alter the button column in the grid to use your own image rather than a button. Select the Select column in the Selected Columns list box and change `Button Type` to `LinkButton` and `Text` to `<img border=0 src=magnify.gif>`. (You'll find this image in the code download in the Chapter 10 solution.)

Behind the scenes, the Property Builder has been turning your bound instructions into their corresponding code within the `<asp:datagrid>` controls tags.

```
<asp:datagrid id="DataGrid1" runat="server" GridLines="Horizontal"
   CellPadding="4" BackColor="White" BorderWidth="3px" PageSize="5"
   BorderStyle="Double" BorderColor="#336666" AllowPaging="True"
   AutoGenerateColumns="False">

   <FooterStyle ForeColor="#333333" BackColor="White"></FooterStyle>
   <SelectedItemStyle Font-Bold="True" ForeColor="White"
      BackColor="#339966"></SelectedItemStyle>
   <ItemStyle ForeColor="#333333" BackColor="White"></ItemStyle>
   <HeaderStyle Font-Bold="True" ForeColor="White"
      BackColor="#336666"></HeaderStyle>
```

```
    <Columns>
       <asp:ButtonColumn Text="&lt;img border=&quot;0&quot;
          src=&quot;magnify.gif&quot;&gt;" CommandName="Select">
       </asp:ButtonColumn>
       <asp:BoundColumn DataField="firstname" HeaderText="First Name">
       </asp:BoundColumn>
       <asp:BoundColumn DataField="lastname" HeaderText="Last Name">
       </asp:BoundColumn>
       <asp:BoundColumn DataField="Title" HeaderText="Title">
       </asp:BoundColumn>
       <asp:BoundColumn DataField="Extension" HeaderText="Phone">
       </asp:BoundColumn>
       <asp:BoundColumn DataField="HireDate" ReadOnly="True"
          HeaderText="Hire Date" DataFormatString="{0:d}">
       </asp:BoundColumn>
    </Columns>

    <PagerStyle HorizontalAlign="Center" ForeColor="White"
       BackColor="#336666" Mode="NumericPages">
    </PagerStyle>
 </asp:datagrid>
```

6. Rebuild, and run the new version of `WebDataGrid`. It should now look like Figure 10-17.

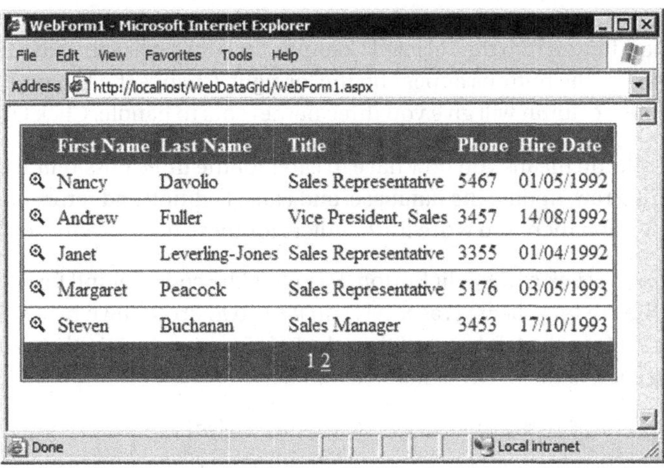

Figure 10-17. *Revised* `WebDataGrid`

How It Works

This example has two interesting items to note. First, you didn't specify a column for the `EmployeeID` field, but it's still a part of the query. You need `EmployeeID` when a user clicks to see more details about an employee, so you still include this field in the query and assign `EmployeeID` to the `DataKeyField` property of the data grid. However, since you now have control over which columns from the dataset appear, and since an internal identifier may not be of much value to the user, you simply don't provide a column to display `EmployeeID`.

Second, you slightly changed the `ButtonColumn`. Instead of displaying a push button for selecting a row, you now display a link button. In addition, you changed the `Text` property of the column to write an HTML image tag. This gave the grid a slightly fancier look with a custom icon (a magnifying glass).

Editing a Data Grid

So far, you've worked with the `DataGrid` control purely as a means to view the data already stored in a database, but you can use it to edit and update data as well.

Try It Out: Adding Editing Capability

To trigger the data grid's inline editing facilities, you'll add another button to the right of each row so users can indicate which row they want to alter.

1. Open the Property Builder dialog box for the data grid once again. In the dialog box, go to the Available Columns area and expand the Button Column node. Then move an Edit, Update, Cancel button into the Selected Columns list. You'll place this new column at the end of the list so the buttons appear on the far right. Change the Button type to PushButton. The new column will give you three new events to handle. Click OK.

   This new button column means you now have to cater for the three possibilities you've given the user: edit a row, update the database, and cancel editing and return to read-only mode. The next job then is to write the handlers for these three events.

2. First, you'll deal with a click of the Edit button. Switch to the code-behind for the page. Just underneath the tab for `WebForm1.aspx.vb`, you'll see two drop-down boxes. Select the entry for `DataGrid1` in the left box and then the `EditCommand` event in the right box. Add the following code to the newly generated handler:

   ```
   Private Sub DataGrid1_EditCommand(ByVal source As Object, _
      ByVal e As System.Web.UI.WebControls.DataGridCommandEventArgs) _
      Handles DataGrid1.EditCommand
         DataGrid1.EditItemIndex = e.Item.ItemIndex
         BindDataGrid()
   End Sub
   ```

3. Repeat step 2 to create a handler for the `CancelCommand` event, and add the following code to handle the Cancel button:

```
Private Sub DataGrid1_CancelCommand(ByVal source As Object, _
   ByVal e As System.Web.UI.WebControls.DataGridCommandEventArgs) _
   Handles DataGrid1.CancelCommand
      DataGrid1.EditItemIndex = -1
      BindDataGrid()
End Sub
```

4. You need to code an UPDATE statement for the data grid, using the values from the text box controls in the edited row. Follow the steps to create the handler for the UpdateCommand event in step 2, and add the following code:

```
Private Sub DataGrid1_UpdateCommand(ByVal source As Object, _
   ByVal e As System.Web.UI.WebControls.DataGridCommandEventArgs) _
   Handles DataGrid1.UpdateCommand

   ' Get Index of Selected Item
   Dim key As String = _
      DataGrid1.DataKeys(DataGrid1.EditItemIndex).ToString()

   ' Sql Query For Notes Field
   Dim UpdateSql As String = _
      "UPDATE Employees SET " & _
         "firstname = @firstname, " & _
         "lastname = @lastname, " & _
         "title = @title, " & _
         "extension = @extension " & _
      "WHERE EmployeeId = @employeeid"

   ' Create Command and add parameter
   Dim UpdateCommand As New SqlCommand(UpdateSql, SqlConnection1)
   UpdateCommand.Parameters.Add("@employeeid", key)
   UpdateCommand.Parameters.Add("@firstname", _
      CType(e.Item.Cells(1).Controls(0), TextBox).Text)
   UpdateCommand.Parameters.Add("@lastname", _
      CType(e.Item.Cells(2).Controls(0), TextBox).Text)
   UpdateCommand.Parameters.Add("@title", _
      CType(e.Item.Cells(3).Controls(0), TextBox).Text)
   UpdateCommand.Parameters.Add("@extension", _
      CType(e.Item.Cells(4).Controls(0), TextBox).Text)

   Try
      ' Open Connection
      SqlConnection1.Open()
```

```
            ' Run the Update Command
            UpdateCommand.ExecuteNonQuery()
         Catch ex As Exception
            ' Display error
            ErrorLabel.Text = "Error: " & ex.ToString()

         Finally
            ' Close connection
            SqlConnection1.Close()

         End Try
         DataGrid1.EditItemIndex = -1
         BindDataGrid(True)
      End Sub
```

5. Build and run the Web form with Ctrl+F5. Click the Edit button in the fourth row to see Figure 10-18.

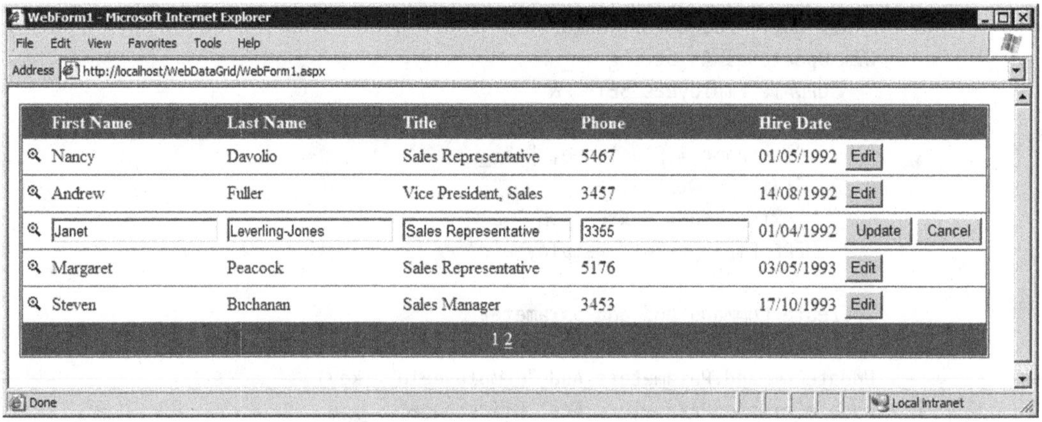

Figure 10-18. *WebDataGrid with editing buttons*

How It Works

When you click the Edit button, the DataGrid1_EditCommand method is invoked, and you can find out which row is selected from the DataGridCommandEventArgs parameter. Making the row into a set of editable text boxes is then a matter of updating the data grid's EditItemIndex property and rebinding the data to update the new edit controls. The data grid will then provide an edit box for each column in the row, with the exception of Hire Date, because you marked this column as read-only.

Once a row is in edit mode, the user can change the values in each text box and click either Cancel or Update. These are the other two events you handle. For a cancel event, you just need to reset the data grid's EditItemIndex property to –1, indicating no row is being edited, and then rebind the data to ensure the data grid reflects this.

To handle the update event, the first step is retrieving the EmployeeID to update from the DataKeys collection.

```
Dim key As String = _
   DataGrid1.DataKeys(DataGrid1.EditItemIndex).ToString()
```

Then, to get the updated field values, you use the DataGridCommandEventArgs parameter. As you saw earlier, this parameter contains an Item property representing the currently selected row in the data grid. Item is a reference to a DataGridItem object. Previously you used the ItemIndex property of DataGridItem to simply see which row the user clicked, but this time you need to dig a little deeper.

The DataGridItem contains a Cells collection, and one cell exists for each column in the grid. The first cell (Cells(0)) is the select column with the magnifying glass. The second cell (Cells(1)) is the first name column—and so on for each column. You must visit each cell containing a value you need and extract the contents of the edited text box.

Each cell contains a property named Controls. This collection contains all the child controls in the cell. For bound columns in a data grid, the text box is always the only control in the collection; thus you use Controls(0) to retrieve a reference to the text box. You cast the object returned from the Controls collection to a TextBox and then extract the Text property.

```
UpdateCommand.Parameters.Add("@firstname", _
   CType(e.Item.Cells(1).Controls(0), TextBox).Text)
UpdateCommand.Parameters.Add("@lastname", _
   CType(e.Item.Cells(2).Controls(0), TextBox).Text)
UpdateCommand.Parameters.Add("@title", _
   CType(e.Item.Cells(3).Controls(0), TextBox).Text)
UpdateCommand.Parameters.Add("@extension", _
   CType(e.Item.Cells(4).Controls(0), TextBox).Text)
```

Before you leave the DataGrid1_UpdateCommand method you have to reset the EditItemIndex property to force the grid out of edit mode. Then you have to bind the data source again, forcing a refresh by passing true to BindDataGrid so the refresh will pick up the new values from the database and reset the cached dataset in the Session.

Finally, you need to modify the DataGrid1_PageIndexChanged event handler one more time. You need to ensure that edit mode is canceled if the user changes pages in the middle of an edit. This will prevent the same problem discussed earlier when a row is selected and the page is changed. The following code shows the updated method. Add the following bold line to the method:

```
Private Sub DataGrid1_PageIndexChanged(ByVal source As Object, _
   ByVal e As System.Web.UI.WebControls.DataGridPageChangedEventArgs) _
   Handles DataGrid1.PageIndexChanged
      DataGrid1.CurrentPageIndex = e.NewPageIndex
      DataGrid1.SelectedIndex = -1
      DataGrid1.EditItemIndex = -1
      Panel1.Visible = False
      BindDataGrid()
End Sub
```

In the next section you'll allow the user to also edit the hire date but with a new type of column: a *template* column.

Using Template Columns

A template column affords you the highest level of control over a data grid column's appearance. It's completely up to you as the developer to determine when and how to display data from the data source using a *data binding expression.* You could, for example, combine the first name and last name columns into a single column using a template column. To demonstrate, you'll use a template column to display the hire date.

Try It Out: Using a Template Column

Follow these steps:

1. Open the Property Builder for the data grid again, and select the Hire Date column in the list of Selected Columns. Click the Convert This Column into a Template Column link. Click OK.

2. You'll modify the Template Column directly in HTML view. Visual Studio .NET has already coded for the static view of the date, but you'll add the template for editing the date. Add the following bold code to the `asp:TemplateColumn` element:

```
<asp:TemplateColumn HeaderText="Hire Date">
<ItemTemplate>
   <asp:Label runat="server" Text=
      '<%# DataBinder.Eval(Container, "DataItem.HireDate", "{0:d}") %>'>
   </asp:Label>
</ItemTemplate>
<EditItemTemplate>
   <asp:Calendar ID="Calendar1" Runat="server" BorderColor="#336666"
      ShowGridLines="True" NextPrevFormat="ShortMonth"
      VisibleDate='<%# DataBinder.Eval(Container, "DataItem.HireDate") %>'
      SelectedDate=
         '<%# DataBinder.Eval(Container, "DataItem.HireDate") %>'>
      <TitleStyle ForeColor="White" BackColor="#336666"></TitleStyle>
   </asp:Calendar>
</EditItemTemplate>
</asp:TemplateColumn>
```

3. The grid is now set up to edit `HireDate`, but you need to adjust the event handler for the Update button so that it will update the `HireDate` column as well. Modify the `UpdateCommand` handler with the following bold code:

```
Private Sub DataGrid1_UpdateCommand(ByVal source As Object, _
   ByVal e As System.Web.UI.WebControls.DataGridCommandEventArgs) _
   Handles DataGrid1.UpdateCommand

   ' Get Index of Selected Item
   Dim key As String = _
      DataGrid1.DataKeys(DataGrid1.EditItemIndex).ToString()
```

```
    ' Sql Query For Notes Field
    Dim UpdateSql As String = _
       "UPDATE Employees SET " & _
          "firstname = @firstname, " & _
          "lastname = @lastname, " & _
          "title = @title, " & _
          "extension = @extension, " & _
          "hiredate = @hiredate " & _
       "WHERE EmployeeId = @employeeid"

    ' Create Command and add parameter
    Dim UpdateCommand As New SqlCommand(UpdateSql, SqlConnection1)
    UpdateCommand.Parameters.Add("@employeeid", key)
    UpdateCommand.Parameters.Add("@firstname", _
       CType(e.Item.Cells(1).Controls(0), TextBox).Text)
    UpdateCommand.Parameters.Add("@lastname", _
       CType(e.Item.Cells(2).Controls(0), TextBox).Text)
    UpdateCommand.Parameters.Add("@title", _
       CType(e.Item.Cells(3).Controls(0), TextBox).Text)
    UpdateCommand.Parameters.Add("@extension", _
       CType(e.Item.Cells(4).Controls(0), TextBox).Text)
    UpdateCommand.Parameters.Add("@hiredate", _
    CType(e.Item.Cells(5).FindControl("Calendar1"), Calendar).SelectedDate)

    Try
       ' Open Connection
       SqlConnection1.Open()

       ' Run the Update Command
       UpdateCommand.ExecuteNonQuery()

    Catch ex As Exception
       ' Display error
       ErrorLabel.Text = "Error: " & ex.ToString()

    Finally
       ' Close connection
       SqlConnection1.Close()

    End Try

    DataGrid1.EditItemIndex = -1
    BindDataGrid(True)
End Sub
```

4. Run with Ctrl+F5. When you try to edit a column, a `Calendar` control will appear in place of the date for you to choose another one (see Figure 10-19).

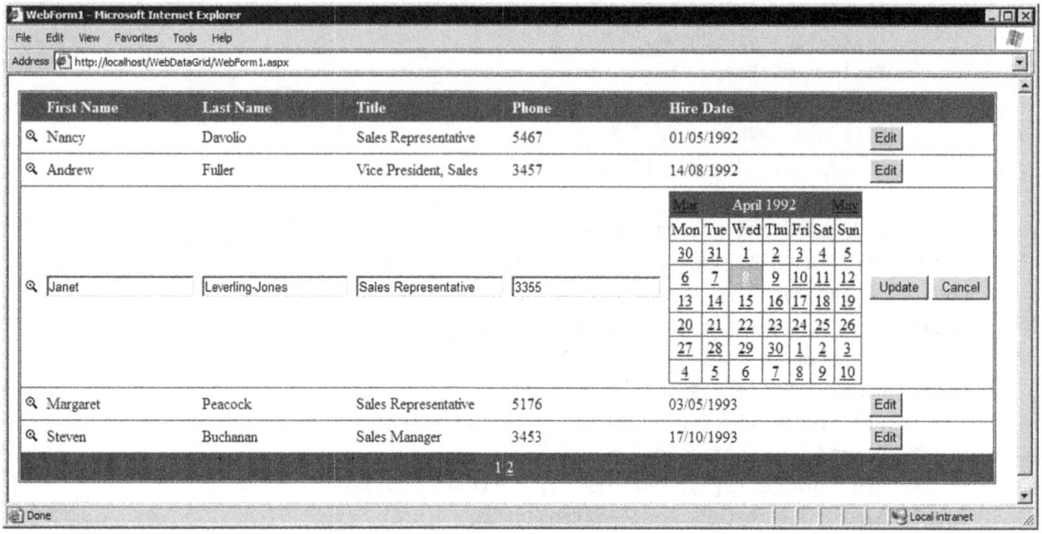

Figure 10-19. *Calendar control provided for editing*

How It Works

Every template column is composed of one or more item templates. In this example, you use an `ItemTemplate` and an `EditItemTemplate`, but `HeaderTemplates` and `FooterTemplates` exist as well. The `ItemTemplate` controls the appearance of the data during normal viewing, and the `EditItemTemplate` controls the view when the item is in edit mode.

For the item template, you've used a simple `Label` control, and for the edit template, you've used a `Calendar` control. While the regular display for the hire date will look the same as when the column was a bound column, the edit display will look entirely different, albeit somewhat ungainly. (As an exercise you may like to try to improve the aesthetics.)

It's possible to insert any amount of text, HTML, and server-side controls into a template to achieve the desired result. When you're ready to display data from the data source, you'll need to use a data binding expression.

As you can see from the previous `.aspx` code snippet, data bindings use a special expression format. You always place the expression between the delimiters: <%# and %>.

```
<asp:Label runat="server" Text=
   '<%# DataBinder.Eval(Container, "DataItem.HireDate", "{0:d}") %>'>
</asp:Label>
```

Inside these delimiters you use the static `Eval` method of the `DataBinder` class; this method was designed for just this purpose. `Eval` has two required parameters: first the container and then the expression to evaluate against the container. For a data grid, the container is always the `Container`. The expression is the field name to use, in this case `DataItem.HireDate`.

In the previous example you set the Label control's Text property to the result of a data binding expression. For the calendar control, you need to set both the SelectedDate and VisibleDate properties to make sure the hire date is both highlighted and visible in the monthly calendar.

Updating the employee hire date value uses the same basic logic to extract the date value from the Calendar control but with one slight difference—you can't be exactly sure where the Calendar control actually appears in the cell's Control collection. To get a reference to the calendar then, you use the cell's FindControl method and pass it the ID of the calendar control, as shown in the following expression:

```
UpdateCommand.Parameters.Add("@hiredate", _
   CType(e.Item.Cells(5).FindControl("Calendar1"), Calendar).SelectedDate)
```

Deleting Rows

With what you've learned in this chapter, you should find adding the ability to delete a row an almost familiar task, and indeed it is. Again, the data grid provides you with a lot of help to achieve this.

Try It Out: Deleting Rows

Follow these steps:

1. In Design view, right-click the data grid and open the Property Builder again. Click Columns, expand the Button Column node, and move a Delete button into the list of Selected Columns. Click OK.

2. Now you'll deal with a click of the Delete button. Switch to the code-behind for the page. Just underneath the tab for WebForm1.aspx.vb, you'll see two drop-down boxes. Select the entry for DataGrid1 in the left box and then the DeleteCommand event in the right box. Add the following code to the newly generated handler:

```
Private Sub DataGrid1_DeleteCommand(ByVal source As Object, _
   ByVal e As System.Web.UI.WebControls.DataGridCommandEventArgs) _
   Handles DataGrid1.DeleteCommand

   DataGrid1.SelectedIndex = -1
   Panel1.Visible = False
   DataGrid1.EditItemIndex = -1

   ' Get Index of Selected Item
   Dim key As String = DataGrid1.DataKeys(e.Item.ItemIndex).ToString()

   ' Sql Query For Notes Field
   Dim DeleteSql As String = _
      "DELETE FROM Employees " & _
      "WHERE employeeid = @employeeid"
```

```
        ' Create command and add parameter
        Dim DeleteCommand As New SqlCommand(DeleteSql, SqlConnection1)
        DeleteCommand.Parameters.Add("@employeeid", key)

        Try
            ' Open Connection
            SqlConnection1.Open()

            ' Run delete command
            DeleteCommand.ExecuteNonQuery()

        Catch ex As Exception
            ' Display error
            ErrorLabel.Text = "Error: " & ex.ToString()

        Finally
            ' Close connection
            SqlConnection1.Close()

        End Try

        BindDataGrid(True)
    End Sub
```

3. Run with Ctrl+F5. You'll be able to delete from the `Employees` table any employee who has taken no orders. If they have, however, deleting them without first deleting their orders would violate referential integrity, and you'll get an error.

Caution So what happens if you delete the only entry on a page and it calls `BindDataGrid(true)`? Well, ASP.NET attempts to reload that page, which now no longer exists, so it presents an invalid page index error. To fix this, you need to update the data grid's `CurrentPageIndex` property. We'll leave this as an exercise for you to complete.

How It Works

The event handler for the `Delete` button is quite straightforward. First, you set the data grid back to its original state by resetting `SelectedIndex` and `EditItemIndex` and making the `Notes` panel invisible again.

```
DataGrid1.SelectedIndex = -1
Panel1.Visible = False
DataGrid1.EditItemIndex = -1
```

Second, you grab the `EmployeeID` of the row to be deleted from the `DataKeys` collection, as you've done before, and build a `DELETE` statement.

```
' Get Index of Selected Item
Dim key As String = DataGrid1.DataKeys(e.Item.ItemIndex).ToString()

' Sql Query For Notes Field
Dim DeleteSql As String = _
   "DELETE FROM Employees " & _
   "WHERE employeeid = @employeeid"
```

Third, you create the SqlCommand object and build your parameter collection for it.

```
' Create command and add parameter
Dim DeleteCommand As New SqlCommand(DeleteSql, SqlConnection1)
DeleteCommand.Parameters.Add("@employeeid", key)
```

Finally, you execute the query and force a refresh while rebinding the data grid.

```
Try
   ' Open Connection
   SqlConnection1.Open()

   ' Run delete command
   DeleteCommand.ExecuteNonQuery()

Catch ex As Exception
   ' Display error
   ErrorLabel.Text = "Error: " & ex.ToString()

Finally
   ' Close connection
   SqlConnection1.Close()

End Try

BindDataGrid(True)
```

Sorting a Data Grid

The final feature to add to the data grid is the ability to sort the rows by any column.

Try It Out: Adding Sorting to a Data Grid

Follow these steps:

1. Adding the ability to sort begins with, as you may have guessed by now, the Property Builder dialog box. In the General section of the dialog box, check the Allow Sorting check box. Doing this will change the column headings into hyperlinks that will raise the OnSortCommand when they're clicked.

2. For each bound column, specify a Sort Expression matching the Data Field. For example, set the Sort Expression for the First Name column to `firstname`, the Last Name column to `lastname`, and so on. When you've finished, click OK.

3. Now you'll deal with a click of the sort links. Switch to the code-behind for the page. Just underneath the tab for `WebForm1.aspx.vb`, you'll see two drop-down boxes. Select the entry for `DataGrid1` in the left hand and then the `SortCommand` event in the right box. Add the following code to the newly generated handler. Notice that you modify the data binding code to accept a sort expression and simply forward the sort expression to this method for processing.

```
Private Sub DataGrid1_SortCommand(ByVal source As Object, _
   ByVal e As System.Web.UI.WebControls.DataGridSortCommandEventArgs) _
   Handles DataGrid1.SortCommand
      DataGrid1.SelectedIndex = -1
      Panel1.Visible = False
      DataGrid1.EditItemIndex = -1
      BindDataGrid(e.SortExpression)
End Sub
```

4. `BindDataGrid` won't accept a sort expression until you update it. You'll overload it with two new versions. A caller will now be able to pass no parameters, just a refresh flag, just a sort expression, or both a refresh flag and a sort expression. Replace the two `BindDataGrid` methods with the following code:

```
Private Sub BindDataGrid()
   BindDataGrid(False, "")
End Sub

Private Sub BindDataGrid(ByVal refresh As Boolean)
   BindDataGrid(refresh, "")
End Sub

Private Sub BindDataGrid(ByVal sortExpression As String)
   BindDataGrid(False, sortExpression)
End Sub

Private Sub BindDataGrid(ByVal refresh As Boolean, _
   ByVal sortExpression As String)

   Dim ds As New DataSet
   If refresh Or Session("Employees") Is Nothing Then
      ' Sql Query
      Dim sql As String = _
         "SELECT EmployeeId, FirstName, LastName, " & _
         "Title, Extension, HireDate " & _
         "FROM Employees"
```

```
        Try
           ' Open Connection
           SqlConnection1.Open()

           ' Create Data Adapter
           Dim da As New SqlDataAdapter(sql, SqlConnection1)

           ' Fill DataSet
           da.Fill(ds, "Employees")

           ' Save DataSet in Session State
           Session("Employees") = ds

        Catch ex As Exception
           ' Display error
           ErrorLabel.Text = "Error: " & ex.ToString()
        Finally
           SqlConnection1.Close()
        End Try
     Else
        ds = CType(Session("Employees"), DataSet)
     End If

     ' Create sorted view of data
     Dim dv As DataView = ds.Tables("Employees").DefaultView

     If sortExpression <> "" Then
        dv.Sort = sortExpression
     End If

     ' Bind data grid to sorted view
     DataGrid1.DataSource = dv
     DataGrid1.DataKeyField = "EmployeeId"
     DataGrid1.DataBind()
  End Sub
```

5. Run with Ctrl+F5. Click any column heading to sort that column in ascending order. Figure 10-20 shows a sort by last name.

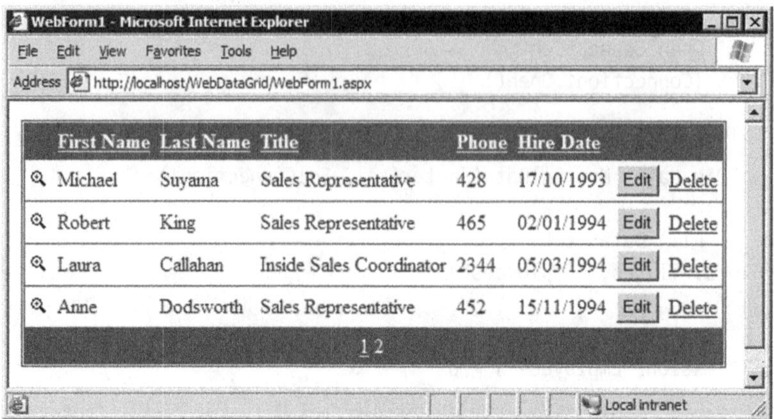

Figure 10-20. *Sorting by columns*

How It Works

When you click a column heading and raise a `SortCommand` event, its handler takes two parameters. One is the source, and the other is of type `DataGridSortCommandEventArgs`. One of the properties of this parameter is a string, `SortExpression`. You can specify a sort expression for each bound column and template column in the data grid. The sort expression passed in the event handler parameter is the sort expression given to the column. For example, you gave the `Last` Name column the sort expression `lastname`. When a user clicks on the Last Name header, this is the sort expression used by the event handler.

If you don't specify a sort expression for a bound column, the column doesn't display with a hyperlink and isn't sortable. You can specify any string for the sort expression; however, to make programming easier, you used a sort expression compatible with the `DataView`'s `Sort` property. This property accepts a column name followed by `ASC` for an ascending sort or `DESC` for a descending sort. If the sort order isn't specified, ascending is the default.

Summary

In this chapter we demonstrated how powerful ASP.NET, and in particular the Web Forms `DataGrid` control, are for online database applications. Using just a small amount of code, you wrote an application that lets you select, edit, delete, update, and sort rows in a data grid. You also saw how to control rendering of data using bound columns and how to use data binding expressions inside template columns.

Along the way you learned some of the differences between Web Forms and Windows Forms programming. You'll build on what you learned in this chapter when you study validation controls and ASP.NET data input next.

CHAPTER 11

■ ■ ■

Validating Web User Input

Data validation is important in any application. Making sure data conforms to required constraints is vital to data integrity. Before inserting data into a database, you need to make sure that the user has entered all the necessary information, that all dates are valid, that all numbers are within valid ranges, and that all other checks take place to guarantee the data conforms to both the database definition and the business rules.

In Web applications, data validation is as important as in Windows applications, but it has a different twist. Over the Internet, a user will enter information into a Web form and then post that to a server, which provides the opportunity to validate the data twice: once on the client side and once on the server side. This allows you to quickly respond to errors detected on the client and still preserve a high level of security on the server.

ASP.NET provides a number of validation controls that facilitate validation on both sides of the network. These controls are the main focus of this chapter, which will cover the following topics:

- Using the ASP.NET validation controls: `RequiredFieldValidator`, `RangeValidator`, `CompareValidator`, and `RegularExpressionValidator`
- Creating custom client- and server-side validations with the `CustomValidator`
- Displaying validation error messages in detail and in summary

You'll build a Web Forms page to validate and insert new employees into the `Northwind` database. You'll also learn some additional tips for server-control data binding. Before getting into validation control details, however, we'll build a simple application to demonstrate how the controls work.

Try It Out: Creating a Validation Example

For the first example you'll create an ASP.NET Web application named `WebDataValidation`.

1. Open Visual Studio .NET, and create a new blank solution called `Chapter11_Examples`.
2. Add a new ASP.NET project called `WebDataValidation` to the solution by selecting File ➤ Add Project ➤ New Project.... (see Figure 11-1). As you saw in the previous chapter, Visual Studio .NET will take care of configuring IIS to support the new application.

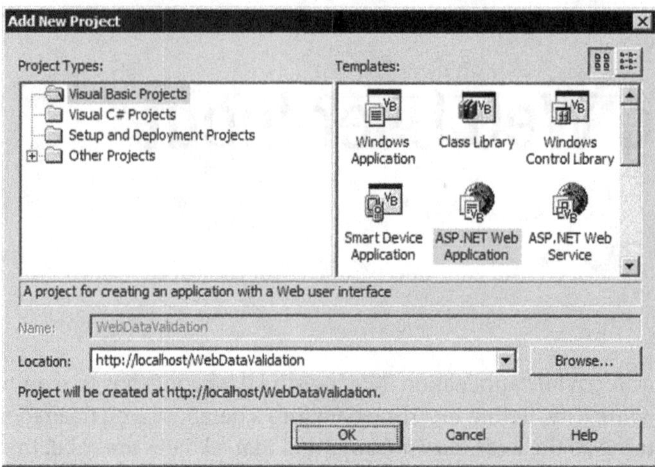

Figure 11-1. *Creating `WebDataValidation`*

3. Once the new application is set up, switch the layout mode of `WebForm1.aspx` from GridLayout to FlowLayout by right-clicking the empty form, selecting Properties from the context menu, and changing the `PageLayout` property.

4. You'll begin by placing four controls from the Web Forms section of the Toolbox onto the form. First, place a `TextBox` control and give it an `(ID)` of `FirstNameTextBox`, one `RequiredFieldValidator` (`FirstNameRequiredFieldValidator`), and two `Button` controls (`SubmitButton` and `CancelButton`).

5. For `CancelButton`, find the `CausesValidation` property in the Properties window for the button and set it to `false`. Set its `Text` property to `Cancel`. Set the `Text` property of `SubmitButton` to `Submit`.

6. The `RequiredFieldValidator` control forces the user to enter text into the control associated with the validator. In this case, it's the text box. To link the validator with text box then, select the validator, find the `ControlToValidate` property, and select `FirstNameTextBox` from the drop-down list. First Name is now a required field in the form. Set the validator's `ErrorMessage` property to `First Name Is Required` as well.

7. In Design view, drag the controls around, and add some Hypertext Markup Language (HTML) so the form looks like Figure 11-2. Notice how you can see the `RequiredFieldValidator` error message displayed on the form. This is the position the error message will appear in if validation fails.

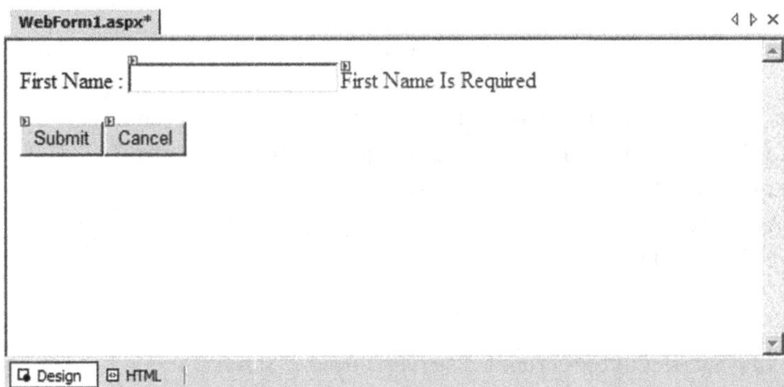

Figure 11-2. *WebDataValidation layout*

8. For this first example, you don't need to place much code into the code-behind file. Double-click the SubmitButton control, and add the following code to the event handler given by the integrated development environment (IDE):

```
Private Sub SubmitButton_Click(ByVal sender As System.Object, _
   ByVal e As System.EventArgs) Handles SubmitButton.Click
      If Page.IsValid Then
         ' Process input here
      End If
End Sub
```

9. Switch back to Design view of the form, and double-click the Cancel button. Add the following code to the new event handler for the click event:

```
Private Sub CancelButton_Click(ByVal sender As System.Object, _
   ByVal e As System.EventArgs) Handles CancelButton.Click
      FirstNameTextBox.Text = ""
End Sub
```

10. Build and run the Web page. Enter a name, and click Submit. Nothing will happen. Clicking Cancel meanwhile will remove the name from the text box. Now click Submit again. This time the validator will display an error message that tells you to type a first name in the box.

How It Works

So far, the page isn't doing very much, but you've already laid the foundations for a useful page. Switch to HTML view, and you'll see in the <body> of the page the new button validation property and validator control.

```
<body>
   <form id="Form1" method="post" runat="server">
   <p>First Name :
      <asp:TextBox id="FirstNameTextBox" runat="server"></asp:TextBox>
      <asp:RequiredFieldValidator id="FirstNameRequiredFieldValidator"
         runat="server" ErrorMessage="First Name Is Required"
         ControlToValidate="FirstNameTextBox">
      </asp:RequiredFieldValidator>
   </p>
   <p>
      <asp:Button id="SubmitButton" runat="server" Text="Submit">
      </asp:Button>
      <asp:Button id="CancelButton" runat="server" Text="Cancel"
         CausesValidation="False">
      </asp:Button>
   </p>
   </form>
</body>
```

By default, whenever a button is clicked on a Web form, it's validated, but by setting the Cancel button's `CausesValidation` property to `false`, you can override this. On this page, clicking Cancel will clear all the fields on the form, so you don't have to validate any of the fields when the user clicks this button. The only field on the form is the text box at the moment so when a user clicks the Cancel button, you simply clear the control and allow the user to start anew.

Although the event handler for the Submit button currently performs no activity in the database, clicking Submit will cause the form to validate its contents against whatever validation checks are in place. In this case, it's just the `RequiredFieldValidator`, so the text box is checked for content. If something has been typed in, it will pass the page as valid; if not, it will raise the error given by its `ErrorMessage` property.

Before the end of the chapter, you'll be inserting the information from the form into `Northwind` in the `SubmitButton_Click` handler, but for now, notice that you check the `IsValid` property of the base class performing any action. If `IsValid` returns a value of `true`, you can be certain all of the validation checks were successful. Notice that this also means the form validation takes place before the code in the event handler.

Technically, the `RequiredFieldValidator` fails when the value in the associated control matches the value of the `InitialValue` property of the `RequiredFieldValidator`. If you want to make sure the user changes some default value placed into the control, set the control's `Text` value and the `InitialValue` property of the `RequiredFieldValidator` to the same value. In other words, the `ControlToValidate` doesn't need to be empty to fail a validation; it simply needs to contain the same value as the `InitialValue` of the `RequiredFieldValidator`, which in this example is empty.

As another example, suppose you wanted to make sure the First Name text box first appeared on the form with the text *No Name* appearing inside. You could set the `InitialValue` property of the `RequiredFieldValidator` control and the `Text` property of the `TextBox` control to the string `No Name`. This will allow the string to appear on the form but force the user to change the value in the text box before the form will pass its validation checks.

Performing Web Validation

With the first example of using an ASP.NET validation control under your belt, we'll take a minute to discuss how to validate data on both the client and server sides, how ASP.NET controls work in both situations, and how to apply that knowledge to your Web Forms applications.

Enabling Client-Side Validation

If a user's browser (or other Web client) is capable and configured to execute client-side script—for example, JavaScript—validation will occur on the client before the browser posts the data to the server. Internet Explorer 4.0 and newer can perform client-side validation if scripting is enabled.

Client-side validation provides the user with quick feedback since the validation code is executed on the client machine. By default, whenever the user clicks a button on the form, the script executes the validation checks for each validation control on the form. If *any* of the validation controls on a form fails, the script cancels the postback to the server and displays error messages on the form. This behavior creates a quick turnaround time for users since they don't wait on a server round-trip to discover errors. It also helps save resources on the server since you won't waste time processing a request with invalid information. For these two reasons, client-side validations are a good feature to offer in a Web application.

Disabling Client-Side Validation

Every good rule of thumb deserves an exception though, and there are times when you'll want to avoid client-side validation checks. We have seen one such example in our first form. By setting the `CausesValidation` property of a `Button` to `false` you can disable all validation checks when a user clicks that particular button. This is useful when you have a button control that does not require validation checks, such as a cancel button or a refresh button. Likewise, if a client-side check is likely to be unacceptably slow—for example, because the form requires checking against a long list on the server.

If you want to disable client-side validation for a specific validation control, you can set the control's `EnableClientScript` property to `false`.

Enabling Server-Side Validation

When a button is clicked by a user and a button-click event is fired, a postback is initiated. All data requiring validation is then validated by ASP.NET on the server side. It's possible, however, to completely disable a validation control by setting its `Enabled` property to `false`.

Of course, you should always perform validation checks on the server, even if the client supports validation. Not executing server-side checks leaves your application code vulnerable to malicious users who may circumvent client-side validations in an effort to break into or damage your servers. For situations where you are verifying passwords or product activation codes, it's vital that you validate these items on the server. Simply put, you can never trust the data in an incoming request and must always validate on the server.

Understanding Validation in the Page Life Cycle

The previous chapter talked about the typical ASP.NET page life cycle. After a request arrives, the server instantiates an object built from the code-behind logic and the ASPX file. The ASP.NET runtime then initializes this object, restores the view state of the server controls, and fires the `Load` event, which you typically handle with the `Page_Load` method. Once these steps are complete, the runtime will execute all the enabled server validation controls. It's possible to force validation again programmatically later, but we'll leave this topic for the time being. If any of the controls fail, the page's `IsValid` property will test `false`. Finally, the engine fires the postback event (such as a button-click event), and then it renders and disposes of the page. Validation is already complete by the time you reach a click event in your code-behind file.

■ **Note** When validation fails, the normal flow of execution continues. You need to check the `IsValid` property to know if a validation check failed.

One of the great features of the built-in validation controls is how they will keep your server-side and client-side validation checks synchronized. When modifying an existing application, it's sometimes easy to update half of the validation code and not the other. The server validation controls keep this logic packaged into a single component.

So then, the validation controls take care of validation on both the server and the client unless you tell them otherwise. Except for a few situations, this validation is recommended. In the next section, you'll learn about the rest of the ASP.NET validation controls.

With a better understanding of the theory and mechanics behind validation controls, let's move on to an overview of the controls provided by the .NET Framework.

Using the ASP.NET Validation Controls

ASP.NET provides six validation-related controls (in namespace `System.Web.UI.WebControls`), and although they each check something different, they all work in much the same way as the `RequiredFieldValidator` control you saw earlier (see Table 11-1).

Table 11-1. *ASP.NET Validation Controls*

Control Name	Description
`RequiredFieldValidator`	Shown earlier. Makes the input control a required field.
`CompareValidator`	Compares the value in a control against a constant value or the value in another input control.
`RangeValidator`	Checks that the value in a control is within a range of values.
`RegularExpressionValidator`	Matches the value in an input control against a pattern.
`CustomValidator`	Performs user-defined validation on an input control.
`ValidationSummary`	Summarizes error messages for a form in a Web page, message box, or both.

All these validation controls, with the exception of the `ValidationSummary` class, derive from the `BaseValidator` class, giving them common methods and properties. Indeed, you're already familiar with two key points concerning them that you must not forget.

- Validation controls execute when the user clicks a `Button` control, be it a HTML button server control or an `<ASP:..` button server control such as the `LinkButton` or `ImageButton`.
- Validation controls must have the `ControlToValidate` property set before rendering the page, or the control throws a `System.Web.HttpException`. The one exception to this rule is the `CustomValidator` component, which doesn't need to be tied to a specific control to validate.

The standard controls you can associate a validator with are `TextBox`, `ListBox`, `DropDownList`, and `RadioButtonList`. You can also validate some HTML controls, including `HtmlInputText`, `HtmlInputFile`, `HtmlSelect`, and `HtmlTextArea`.

You saw the `RequiredFieldValidator` control in the first sample program, so let's move on to examine the rest of the controls.

Using the RangeValidator Control

The next control you'll use, the `RangeValidator` control, ensures the value inside a control stays within a specified range. For example, you may need to restrict the value of an input box between 0 and 100 to represent a percentage. Alternately, in this example you'll restrict input in a text box to a range of dates. The date must be within one week (plus or minus) of the current date.

Try It Out: Using the RangeValidator Control

Follow these steps:

1. Continuing to build on the first example Web form, add an additional `TextBox` control, and set the `(ID)` property to `HireDateTextBox`.
2. Drag a `RangeValidator` control onto the form beside the `HireDateTextBox` control. Set the `(ID)` property to `HireDateValidator`. Set the `ControlToValidate` property to `HireDateTextBox`, and set the `Type` property to `Date`. Set the `ErrorMessage` to `The hire date must be within one week of today's date`. The form should now look like Figure 11-3.

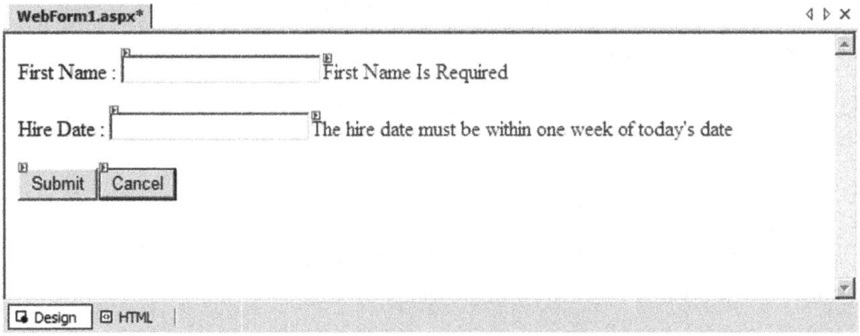

Figure 11-3. *Revised `WebDataValidation` layout*

3. Change the Display property of the RangeValidator from Static to Dynamic.

4. Drag a RequiredFieldValidator control beside the RangeValidator. Set its (ID) property to HireDateRequiredFieldValidator, and set the ControlToValidate to the HireDateTextBox. The error message for this control is Hire Date is required.

5. Right-click the form, select View Code, and add the following code to the form's Page_Load function:

```
Private Sub Page_Load(ByVal sender As System.Object, _
   ByVal e As System.EventArgs) Handles MyBase.Load
   If Not Page.IsPostBack Then
      Dim NextWeek As DateTime = DateTime.Today.Add(TimeSpan.FromDays(7))
      Dim LastWeek As DateTime = _
         DateTime.Today.Subtract(TimeSpan.FromDays(7))
      HireDateValidator.MaximumValue = NextWeek
      HireDateValidator.MinimumValue = LastWeek
   End If
End Sub
```

6. You also need to add a line of code to clear the HireDateTextBox control when the Cancel button is clicked.

```
Private Sub CancelButton_Click(ByVal sender As System.Object, _
   ByVal e As System.EventArgs) Handles CancelButton.Click
      FirstNameTextBox.Text = ""
      HireDateTextBox.Text = ""
End Sub
```

7. Build and run the page. Try to raise the two possible errors for HireDateTextBox on your own. Remember that validation will fail for a given input control if the value of the control doesn't convert into the Type property of the RangeValidator. For instance, an invalid (unconvertible) string will generate a validation error, as shown in Figure 11-4.

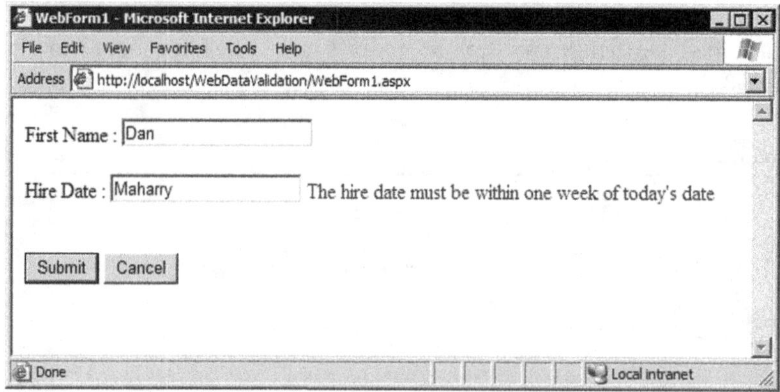

Figure 11-4. *WebDataValidation range error*

How It Works

In the previous example you created a text box in which you require a date be added that's neither seven days more nor less than today's date. To enforce this, you tied two validation controls to the form and tied them to the HireDateTextBox. Behind the scenes, the HTML looks like this:

```
<P>Hire Date :
   <asp:TextBox id="HireDateTextBox" runat="server"></asp:TextBox>
   <asp:RangeValidator id="HireDateValidator" runat="server"
      ErrorMessage="The hire date must be within one week of today's date"
      ControlToValidate="HireDateTextBox" Type="Date" Display="Dynamic">
   </asp:RangeValidator>
   <asp:RequiredFieldValidator id="HireDateRequiredFieldValidator"
      runat="server" ErrorMessage="Hire Date is required"
      ControlToValidate="HireDateTextBox">
</asp:RequiredFieldValidator></P>
```

Without the RequiredFieldValidator, users don't have to type a value into the HireDateTextBox control, but if they do, it must be in a proper date format and in the specified range. The RangeValidator will make this range check for you. Why not just use the RangeValidator by itself? You shouldn't do this simply because this control will not validate the contents of an input control if the control is empty, and thus you need the RequiredFieldValidator.

When multiple validation controls reference an input, all the validation checks must pass for the field to be valid. On the other hand, you need to be careful if you do use multiple Validator controls that they don't contradict each other. For example, two RangeValidators referencing a text box with one specifying a range of 0 to 50 and the other a range of 100 to 150 will always fail that text box, and IsValid will return false for the page. By definition, the value in the text box will always be outside the given range of at least one of the checks.

Remember also that the RangeValidator has a Type property. This property can take one of the following values: String, Integer, Double, Date, or Currency. If the value the RangeValidator is examining isn't of the type expected, it will first try to convert the value into the correct type. If it can't do this, the validation will fail automatically.

Your requirement was to force a user to enter a date within one week of the current system time. Obviously, you can't enter a MinimumValue and MaximumValue at design time, so you need to set these properties when the page is executed and thus alter the Page_Load handler. Fortunately, validation controls, like all the Web Forms server controls, are available as member variables in the code-behind page, so you can set the range limits programmatically.

```
Private Sub Page_Load(ByVal sender As System.Object, _
   ByVal e As System.EventArgs) Handles MyBase.Load
   If Not Page.IsPostBack Then
      Dim NextWeek As DateTime = DateTime.Today.Add(TimeSpan.FromDays(7))
      Dim LastWeek As DateTime = _
         DateTime.Today.Subtract(TimeSpan.FromDays(7))
      HireDateValidator.MaximumValue = NextWeek
      HireDateValidator.MinimumValue = LastWeek
   End If
End Sub
```

Using the CompareValidator Control

The third control you'll use is the `CompareValidator` control, which compares the value of an input control to either a constant value (possibly from a database) or the value in another input control. If the former, you can specify the constant in the `ValueToCompare` property. If the latter, you specify the ID of the control containing the value you want for comparison in the `ControlToCompare` property.

■ **Note** You don't want to set both the `ControlToCompare` property and the `ValueToCompare` property. If this happens, however, the `ControlToCompare` property takes precedence, and the only validation will happen against the value in the second control.

Like the `RangeValidator`, the `CompareValidator` has a `Type` property you can set to `String`, `Integer`, `Double`, `Date`, or `Currency`. The value in or pointed at by the `ControlToValidate` property must convert to this type for validation to succeed.

Try It Out: Using the CompareValidator Control

To demonstrate the `CompareValidator`, you'll use the scenario of setting a password. When the user types a password into the box, the letters will display as asterisks. Since it's difficult for users to know if they made a typing mistake, users are generally given two input controls: one to enter the password and another to confirm the password. These input values have to match for a valid password.

1. Drag two Web Forms `TextBox` controls onto the form. Set the `(ID)` properties to `PasswordTextBox` and `ConfirmPasswordTextBox`, and set the `TextMode` properties on both controls to `Password`.

2. Drag a `CompareValidator` onto the form. Set the `(ID)` property to `PasswordCompareValidator`. Set the `ErrorMessage` property to the string `Passwords do not match`. Set the `ControlToValidate` to `ConfirmPasswordTextBox`, and set the `ControlToCompare` to `PasswordTextBox`. The form should now look like Figure 11-5.

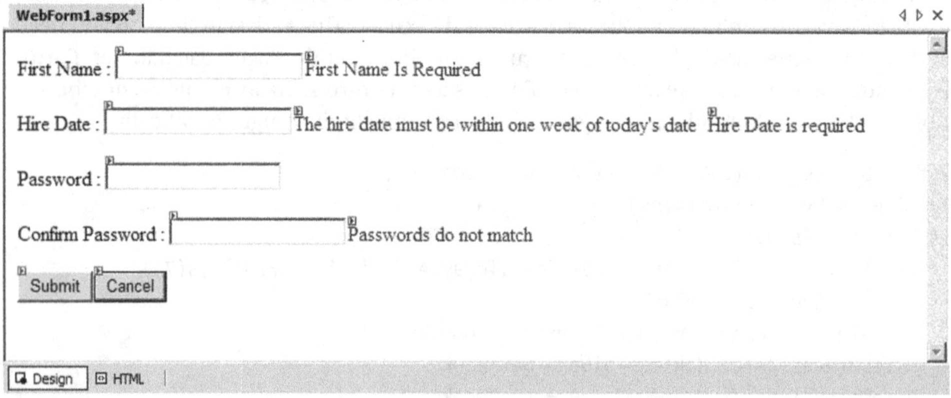

WebForm1.aspx*

First Name : First Name Is Required

Hire Date : The hire date must be within one week of today's date Hire Date is required

Password :

Confirm Password : Passwords do not match

Submit Cancel

Design HTML

Figure 11-5. *WebDataValidation with compare validator*

3. Build and run the page. Experiment with different strings to see what passes as valid.

How It Works

If you enter text into both of the password `TextBox` controls, the `CompareValidator` will perform a validation check. The validator will first try to convert the contents of the `TextBox` to the `Type` specified by the `Type` property of the validator. In this example, you left the `Type` as the default of `String`, but you can also select `Integer`, `Double`, `Date`, and `Currency`.

The `CompareValidator` control also has an `Operator` property to describe the type of comparison to perform. You've left this property at the default setting of `Equal`, but you can also perform greater-than and less-than comparisons.

Notice you haven't placed a `RequiredFieldValidator` on either of the password input controls. This will allow the user to complete the form with an empty password. However, it also exposes the problem that `CompareValidator` will compare an empty string in the Confirm Password text box with a nonempty string in the Password text box and not raise an error (although the same isn't true the other way round).

Using the RegularExpressionValidator Control

The previous validator control for which ASP.NET predetermines the functionality is the `RegularExpressionValidator` control. This powerful control allows you to make sure the input of a certain control matches a certain pattern such as a phone number or e-mail address in the correct format. It also follows the same rules you've seen for the previous controls. For instance, it won't fail validation on an empty input control, and you specify the control to validate using the `ControlToValidate` property.

You must give the pattern to check the input against in the `ValidationExpression` property as a *regular expression*, which, while powerful, uses a flexible but somewhat cryptic syntax. For example, the regular expression `*.vb` will match the strings `webform1.vb` and `myform.vb` but not the string `myform.vbx`. You may recognize this as one of the specifiers from a File Open or File Save dialog box. You probably use regular expressions quite a few times a day without realizing it.

■ **Tip** You won't work through the regular expression (RegEx) syntax here, as it'd take quite some time, but needless to say, if you want to go deeply into it, the .NET documentation has a large section devoted to RegExes.

You can't do justice to the full capabilities of regular expressions in this chapter, so instead of covering how to design your own regular expressions, you'll work with some of the expressions built into the `RegularExpressionValidator`.

Try It Out: Using the RegularExpressionValidator Control

For this example, you'll add a control to the Web form for a user to enter a Web address and use a `RegularExpressionvalidator` to ensure the string entered by the user is a proper HTTP URL.

1. Drag a new `TextBox` control onto the form. Give it an `(ID)` of `PhotoUrlTextBox`.
2. Drag a `RegularExpressionValidator` onto the form. Give it an `(ID)` of `PhotoUrlRegularExpressionValidator` and the `ErrorMessage` `This is not a valid URL.` Your form should now look like Figure 11-6.

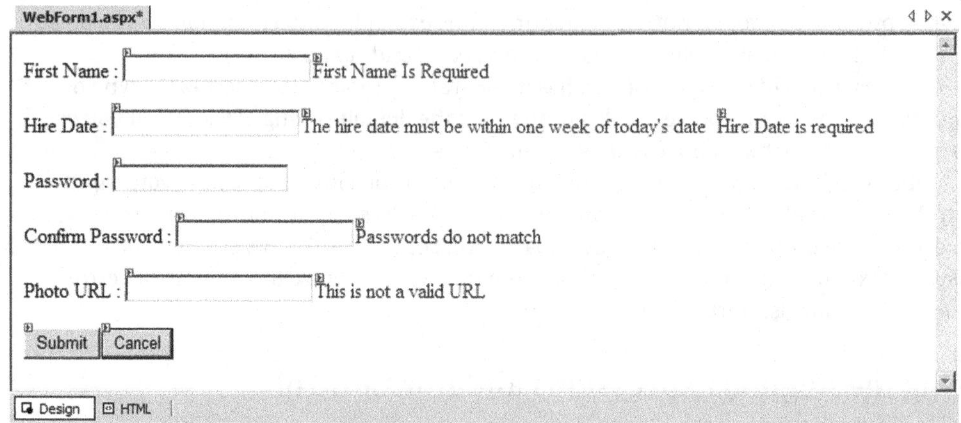

Figure 11-6. *`WebDataValidation` with regular expression validator*

3. You now need to set a control to validate and an expression with which to validate it. Right-click the new validator, and open the Properties dialog box. Choose PhotoUrlTextBox from the drop-down for `ControlToValidate`. Find the `ValidationExpression` property, and click the ellipsis to enter the Regular Expression Editor (see Figure 11-7). The dialog box contains a variety of predefined regular expressions to validate phone numbers, postal codes, and more. You can also enter a custom regular expression or build on one of the predefined items. Select Internet URL, and click OK.

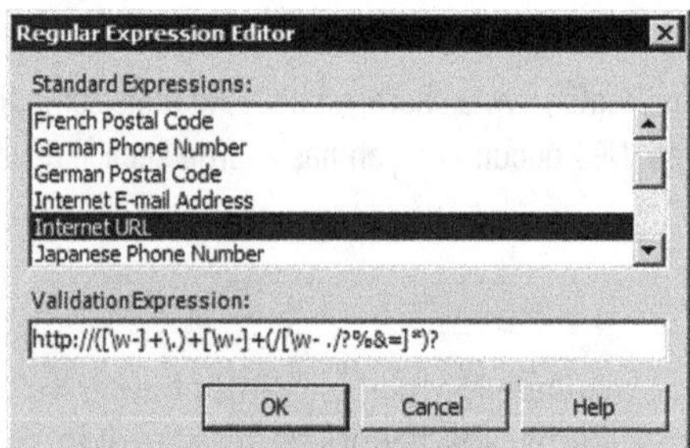

Figure 11-7. *Regular Expression Editor*

4. Build the page, and run it. Try to enter some values into the new text box, and see what's valid. The predefined regular expression will force you to enter a URL of the form `http://computer.domain`.

Using the CustomValidator Control

If none of the validation controls we've covered so far provides the check you need on your page, it's time to write your own validation logic in a CustomValidator control. A custom validator is useful in a number of circumstances, including the following:

- The validation requires a database query.
- The validation requires a mathematical expression beyond a simple comparison.
- The validation requires the inspection of multiple input controls.

CustomValidator objects obey most of the rules that govern the other validation controls, with the exception that the need to set the ControlToValidate property is optional. You have free rein in the validation code to gather and analyze any information required to declare the page valid.

Try It Out: Using the CustomValidator Control

As an example, let's assume that the image URL you introduced in the previous example points to a JPG format file. Although this validation is also possible to achieve with a custom regular expression, you can demonstrate a straightforward CustomValidator for the same result.

1. Drag a CustomValidator from the Toolbox onto the form next to the RegularExpressionValidator and set its (Id) to PhotoUrlCustomValidator. Set the ControlToValidate property to PhotoUrlTextBox, and the ErrorMessage property to the string Unsupported file format.
2. Now set the ClientValidationFunction to validate_photoformat. This is the name of the function you'll write in the next step.
3. Switch to HTML view, and place the following JavaScript block at the top of the page's HTML <body>. This is the client-side validation routine for the CustomValidator control.

```
<body>
   <script language="javascript">
      function validate_photoformat(oSrc, args)
      {
         args.IsValid = false;
         if(args.Value)
         {
            var length = args.Value.length;
            var endsWith = args.Value.substr(length - 3, 3);
            if(endsWith == "jpg")
            {
               args.IsValid = true;
            }
         }
      }
   </script>
   <form id="Form1" method="post" runat="server">
```

4. Now switch to WebForm1.aspx.vb, and select the PhotoUrlCustomValidator control in the left drop-down box near the top of the window. Select the ServerValidate event entry from the right drop-down box, and add the following code to the empty event handler that's generated for you:

```
Private Sub PhotoUrlCustomValidator_ServerValidate( _
   ByVal source As Object, ByVal args As _
   System.Web.UI.WebControls.ServerValidateEventArgs) Handles _
   PhotoUrlCustomValidator.ServerValidate
      args.IsValid = False
      If args.Value <> "" Then
         Dim length As Integer = args.Value.Length
         Dim endsWith As String = args.Value.Substring(length - 3)
         If endsWith = "jpg" Then
            args.IsValid = True
         End If
      End If
   End Sub
```

5. Build and run the page. You'll find that the URLs in PhotoUrlTextBox must now end with jpg. It's not perfect, however; for example, http://www.apress.com/images/myjpg will be considered valid by this code.

How It Works

When you use a CustomValidator, you must supply code for both client- and server-side validation. The client-side code takes the shape of a JavaScript function placed directly into the .aspx page between <script> and </script> tags and sent directly to a client's Web browser for execution as needed. The server-side code is housed inside the validator's ServerValidate event handler and is written in VB .NET.

First, let's review the ClientValidationFunction property. This property is specific to the CustomValidator and allows you to give the name of a function existing in client-side script to act as your client-side validation routine.

```
<asp:CustomValidator id="PhotoUrlCustomValidator" runat="server"
   ErrorMessage="Unsupported file format"
   ControlToValidate="PhotoUrlTextBox"
   ClientValidationFunction="validate_photoformat">
</asp:CustomValidator>
```

If this property isn't set, you can still perform a server-side validation. You implemented this function in client-side script by adding code to the ASPX file inside a script tag.

The name of the function must match the value of the ClientValidationFunction property, and it must take two arguments.

```
function validate_photoformat(oSrc, args)
```

The second variable passed to the function (args) is the primary variable here. It's a collection with two members.

- The IsValid member (which you have to set) indicates if the validation has passed or failed.
- The Value member contains the text from the control you need to validate. If no control was specified with the ControlToValidate property of the CustomValidator, the Value property contains an empty string.

The code here is quite simple to follow. You start by assuming that the control isn't valid until you prove otherwise.

```
args.IsValid = false;
```

If no Value exists to check against, it remains invalid, and you leave the function. If it does have a value, you just extract the last three characters and see if they're jpg. If so, you say the value in the control is valid. If not, then it isn't.

```
if (args.Value != null)
{
   int length = args.Value.Length;
   string endsWidth = args.Value.Substring(length - 3);
   if (endsWidth == "jpg")
   {
      args.IsValid = true;
   }
}
```

The code in the server-side validation isn't very different from the JavaScript version. The method accepts two arguments, with the second of type ServerValidateEventArgs containing the important IsValid and Value properties.

Note that if you want to write your own client-side routines, you need to write them in JavaScript, PerlScript, or some other scripting language that can be placed inside <script> tags.

Using the ValidationSummary Control

The last control to cover in this chapter doesn't actually do any validation itself but does interact with all the validation controls you've covered. The ValidationSummary control, then, lets you display all the validation errors in a single location of the Web form in a number of different formats.

It takes only a few simple steps to achieve this behavior.

1. Add a ValidationSummary control to the form.
2. Choose how to display the errors by setting the DisplayMode property of the control to List, BulletList, or SingleParagraph. You probably want to try each of these settings to see which looks best with your form layout.
3. Set the Display property for each control to None if you don't want the validation controls themselves to display errors on the form. This will force the ErrorMessage to display only inside the ValidationSummary control.

Try It Out: Creating the Validation Example in Full

In this example, we've taken the set of controls and validators created in the previous examples and added a new drop-down list control to select an employee's manager, another text box to allow the user to specify a date of birth for the new employee, the validation controls to go with them, and, most important, a `ValidationSummary` control that will display all the validation error messages for the form. Rather than add the code step by step, however, to keep the length of this example down, we've prepared a new `.aspx` page for you to use and will just highlight key elements. You'll find it in the code download for this chapter as `SummaryForm.aspx`.

There are two key differences between this example and the previous one aside from the extra controls.

1. Each of the validator controls has had its `Display` property set to `None`, as indicated by their error messages being enclosed in braces ([ ]) on the form.

2. We've placed a `ValidationSummary` control on the right side of the form with the `DisplayMode` property set to `List` (see Figure 11-8). In HTML mode, the control looks like this:

```
<asp:ValidationSummary
   id="EmployeeValidationSummary"
   runat="server"
   DisplayMode="List">
</asp:ValidationSummary>
```

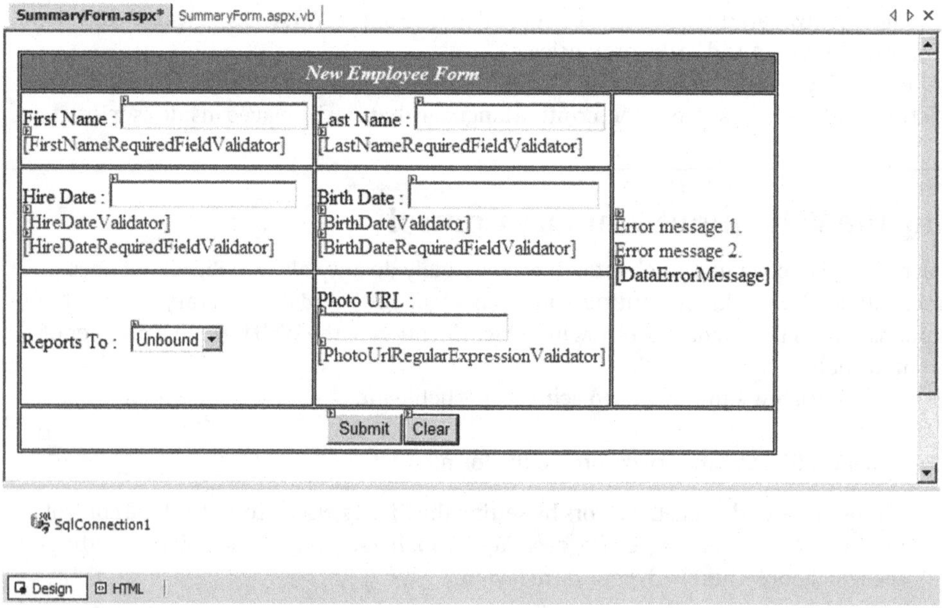

Figure 11-8. *SummaryForm layout*

That's actually all the code you need to use the ValidationSummary control (the runtime will automatically place error messages inside the control for you), but before you can run the page, you'll need to make sure that sqlConnection1 is pointing at your copy of the Northwind database. Alter its ConnectionString property accordingly.

Now build and run the page. If you launch the form and click Submit without entering any values, you should see the Web page in Figure 11-9. Notice that all the validation errors appear in the validation summary, but unfortunately you see no indication of which fields have produced the errors. This will place the burden on the user to find the input controls with the invalid values. In the next section you'll try to improve the error feedback.

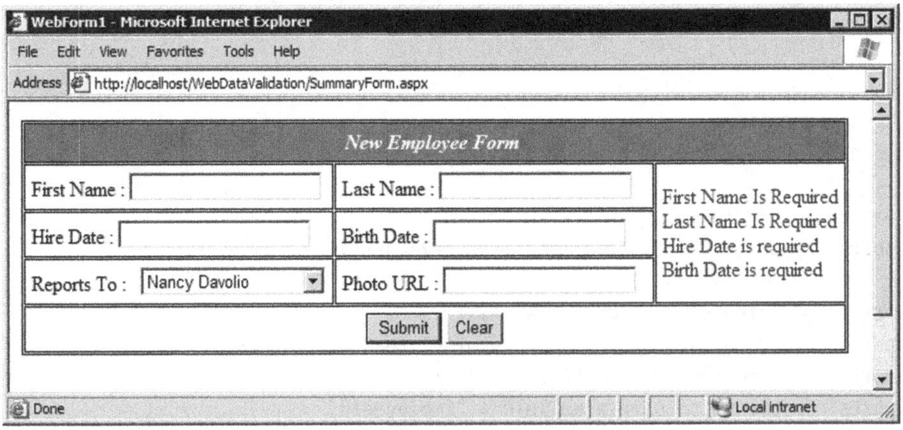

Figure 11-9. *SummaryForm running*

How It Works

The majority of SummaryForm.aspx is simply the previous example rearranged a bit so that the effect of the ValidationSummary control is a bit more obvious than it would be otherwise. Besides this control on the right of the form, you'll notice that you now have a drop-down control for the user to select the employee's manager in the bottom-left corner of the form. To populate this, you'll call a method to create a list of employees from the Employees table in the Northwind database and copy those names into the control. You need this to occur before the page is rendered, so you call this method from within the Page_Load event handler.

```
Private Sub Page_Load(ByVal sender As System.Object, _
   ByVal e As System.EventArgs) Handles MyBase.Load
   If Not Page.IsPostBack Then

      ' Fill Drop Down Box
      BindReportToDropDown()
```

While this behavior seems unrelated to validation, it's a good example of the data binding capability of Web Forms controls, and it offers an example of how you can help the user avoid validation errors by forcing a selection from a list of good values. By not allowing the user to make a mistake, you've improved the quality of the user experience with your application.

The method to bind the data to the drop-down list is as follows:

```
Private Sub BindReportToDropDown()
   ' Query string
   Dim sql As String = _
      "SELECT EmployeeID, " & _
      "FirstName + ' ' + LastName As Name " & _
      "FROM Employees"

   'Create Command and Reader
   Dim ReportsToCommand As New SqlCommand(sql, SqlConnection1)
   Dim ReportsToReader As SqlDataReader

   Try
      ' Open Connection
      SqlConnection1.Open()

      ' Get data in DataReader
      ReportsToReader = ReportsToCommand.ExecuteReader()

      ' Attach and bind data to drop down list
      ReportsToDropDownList.DataSource = ReportsToReader
      ReportsToDropDownList.DataTextField = "Name"
      ReportsToDropDownList.DataValueField = "EmployeeId"
      ReportsToDropDownList.DataBind()
   Catch ex As Exception
      DataErrorMessage.Text = ex.ToString()
   Finally
      ReportsToReader.Close()
      SqlConnection1.Close()
   End Try
End Sub
```

Note that you've retrieved both the name and employee ID from the database. The list of names will be displayed in the `DropDownList` (as given by setting `DataTextField`), and the corresponding IDs will be the value returned by the list when a name is selected (as given by setting `DataValueField`). This distinction between display and value comes in handy when you examine the new code to insert an employee record into the database. The `ReportsTo` field in the `Employees` table holds the ID, rather than the name, of the new hire's boss, so the code will need to extract the `EmployeeId` of the selected manager to generate the correct `INSERT` statement for you. Thanks to this little trick, you can easily pull the `EmployeeId` using the value field of the selected item in the `DropDownList`.

The following code shows the updated event handler invoked when the user clicks the Submit button on the form:

```
Private Sub SubmitButton_Click(ByVal sender As System.Object, _
   ByVal e As System.EventArgs)
   If Page.IsValid Then

      ' Query string
      Dim sql As String = _
         "INSERT INTO Employees( " & _
         "FirstName, LastName, HireDate, " & _
         "BirthDate, ReportsTo, PhotoPath) " & _
         "VALUES" & _
         "(@FirstName, @LastName, @HireDate,
         "@BirthDate, @ReportsTo, @PhotoURL)"

      'Create Command
      Dim SubmitCommand As New SqlCommand(sql, SqlConnection1)

      ' Set up parameters
      SubmitCommand.Parameters.Add("@FirstName", FirstNameTextBox.Text)
      SubmitCommand.Parameters.Add("@LastName", LastNameTextBox.Text)
      SubmitCommand.Parameters.Add("@HireDate", HireDateTextBox.Text)
      SubmitCommand.Parameters.Add("@BirthDate", BirthDateTextBox.Text)
      SubmitCommand.Parameters.Add("@ReportsTo", _
         ReportsToDropDownList.SelectedItem.Value)
      SubmitCommand.Parameters.Add("@PhotoURL", PhotoUrlTextBox.Text)

      Try
         ' Open Connection
         SqlConnection1.Open()

         ' Run Insert query
         SubmitCommand.ExecuteNonQuery()

      Catch ex As Exception
         DataErrorMessage.Text = ex.ToString()
      Finally
         SqlConnection1.Close()
         ClearFields()
      End Try
   End If
End Sub
```

The last line of the handler makes a call to the helper method `ClearFields`. This short method simply clears each of the text boxes and the drop-down list in the form. It is also called when the `Clear` button is clicked.

```
Private Sub ClearButton_Click(ByVal sender As Object, _
   ByVal e As System.EventArgs) Handles ClearButton.Click
      ClearFields()
End Sub

Private Sub ClearFields()
   FirstNameTextBox.Text = ""
   LastNameTextBox.Text = ""
   HireDateTextBox.Text = ""
   BirthDateTextBox.Text = ""
   PhotoUrlTextBox.Text = ""
   ReportsToDropDownList.SelectedIndex = 0
End Sub
```

Using Inline and Summary Errors

You may or may not have noticed during the chapter that all the validation controls have an additional property named `Text`. When no `ValidationSummary` control is present on a `Form`, the runtime will use the `Text` property (if present) to display an error message on the form instead of the `ErrorMessage` property. However, when a `ValidationSummary` control is present on the form, the `ErrorMessage` text displays in the `ValidationSummary` area, but the `Text` property still displays inline where the validation control exists on the form. You use this behavior to indicate the input controls failing validation.

For each validation control on `SummaryForm.aspx`, set the `Display` property to `Static` and the `Text` to an asterisk. When you execute the form and validation errors occur, you get the display shown in Figure 11-10. Each input control with an error is marked with an asterisk, which helps the user locate the problem data. In this figure, the Submit button has been clicked without entering any data.

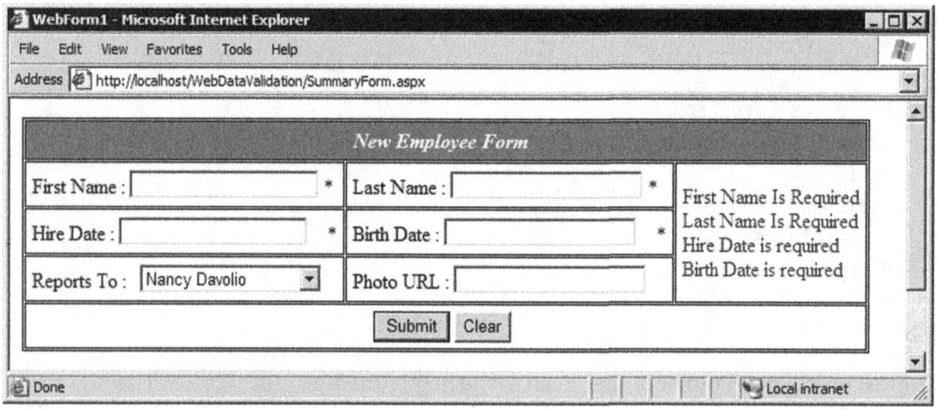

Figure 11-10. *SummaryForm with errors*

As you can see, the `ValidationSummary` control is useful for collecting validation errors into a single location on the `WebForm` control. Remember to use the `ErrorMessage` and `Text` properties of your validation control to control the placement of your error messages while letting the user know where to correct the errors.

Performing Programmatic Validation

If the need arises, you can force validation checks to occur in addition to those that run automatically. For example, you may want to populate a form with information during initialization and need to check that it will validate. In the `Page_Load` handler, you may want to check the `IsValid` property of the page to see if the initialized data validates. Without adding an additional step, however, a call to `IsValid` produces the error shown in Figure 11-11.

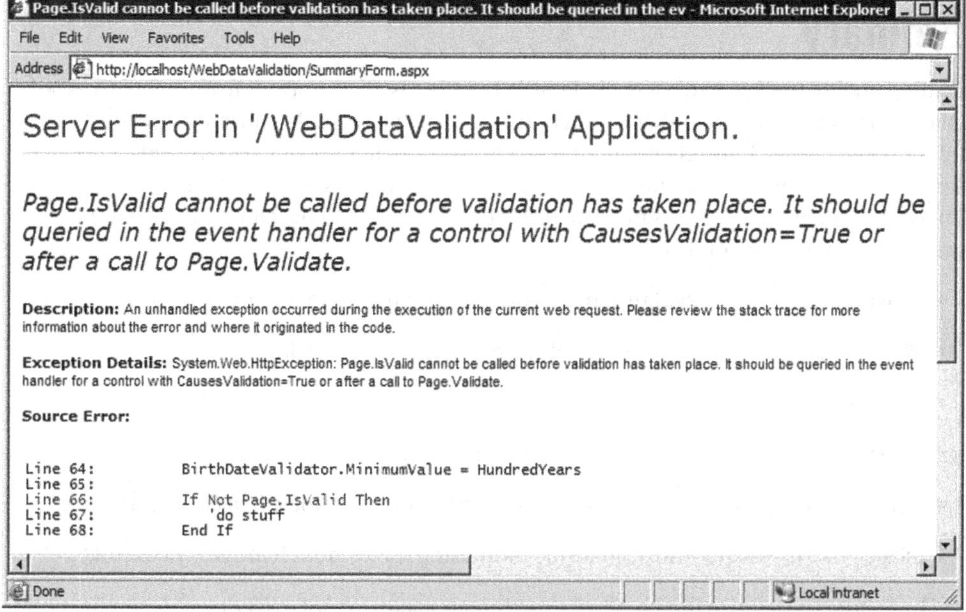

Figure 11-11. *SummaryForm premature IsValid error*

Calling the `Validate` method of the `Page` before checking the `IsValid` property will fix the exception shown in Figure 11-11. This is the same method used by the ASP.NET runtime when a user clicks a `Button` control with the `CausesValidation` property set to `true`. If you place this call in the `Page_Load` method as follows, any validation errors will appear on the first page view for the user:

```
Private Sub Page_Load(ByVal sender As System.Object, _
   ByVal e As System.EventArgs) Handles MyBase.Load

   If Not Page.IsPostBack Then
         ' Initialize form

         Page.Validate()
         If Not Page.IsValid Then
            'do stuff
         End If

      End If
   End Sub
```

Summary

Providing quality feedback to users on data entry errors is an important feature for any type of application. You learned how Web applications are special cases, because you can perform validation logic on both the client and the server. The validation controls covered is this chapter will give you the capability to perform these validations inside a neatly designed framework where you can customize the validation logic if need be. During this chapter you saw how to perform the following:

- Use the `RequiredFieldValidator` to require a user to enter data into a field.
- Use the `RangeValidator` to restrict data to a range of valid values.
- Use the `CompareValidator` to compare the values of two input controls.
- Use the `RegularExpressionValidator` to match input to a pattern.
- Implement custom server-side and client-side validation logic in a `CustomValidator`.
- Place error messages into a single location using the `ValidationSummary` control.

The features covered in this chapter are extremely useful for ASP.NET database applications. In Chapter 15, you'll see how to use database constraints as another mechanism to ensure only valid data enters a database.

CHAPTER 12

Working with Tables and Relationships

Well done for making it this far! By doing so, you have now learned about all the basic .NET classes, objects, techniques, and problems that you'll use and face when working with databases in your applications, whether they're based on the command line, Windows Forms, or the Web. .NET code is the main focus of this book, but that doesn't mean you have nothing else to learn. In Chapter 1 you briefly learned about the structure of a database, and you know that a relational database uses tables to store and manage data in an organized way. In the next few chapters, you'll look in more detail at the structure of a database and the various elements you'll use to get the most from the database that your code is using.

In this chapter, we'll start from scratch and teach you how to design tables and how to define relationships between tables. Specifically, we'll cover the following:

- Creating and deleting tables
- Using primary and foreign keys
- Understanding referential integrity
- Understanding normalization and denormalization

Tables and the relationships between them are fundamental items in a database. No matter how well you code an application, if the group of tables and the relationships you set up between them aren't well designed, problems will arise because the database and the application have to work around the bad design.

Working with Tables

As mentioned a moment ago, *tables* are the fundamental structure in a relational database. All the data you add to a database are stored in tables, including system information such as user information and even the details of the relationships between tables.

Every table has zero or more *rows* and one or more *columns*. Each column (or *attribute*) represents a piece of information, and each row represents one instance of the object or event that the table is modeling. For example, in the `Employees` table in the `Northwind` database, each row is an instance of an employee, and the `LastName` column in that table represents the last name of each employee.

Each column in a table is strongly typed, just like every field in VB .NET, but there are some differences between SQL data types and VB .NET types. This is why SQL data types are mapped to specific .NET types in the `System.Data` namespace rather than the ones you usually use.

Creating a Table

Let's start by creating a table with a few columns. You can do this in two ways.

- By using a visual tool that generates and executes a `CREATE TABLE` statement for you
- By manually coding a `CREATE TABLE` statement

In the following example, you'll use Server Explorer to create a table named `test_Employees` in the `Northwind` database. Note that this table name is prefixed with `test_` to distinguish it from the `Employees` table.

Try it Out: Creating a Table Using Server Explorer

Follow these steps:

1. Open Server Explorer, expand the `Northwind` connection, right-click the Tables node, and click New Table.
2. In the window that opens, enter the information shown in Figure 12-1. We've specified three columns: `EmployeeId` of type `int`, `LastName` of type `varchar(30)`, and `BirthDate` of type `datetime`. You can choose the data type by clicking a Data Type cell and picking it from the drop-down list. Note that the BirthDate column has Allow Nulls checked. This means that rows can be inserted without birth date values (in other words, you may not know the birth date).

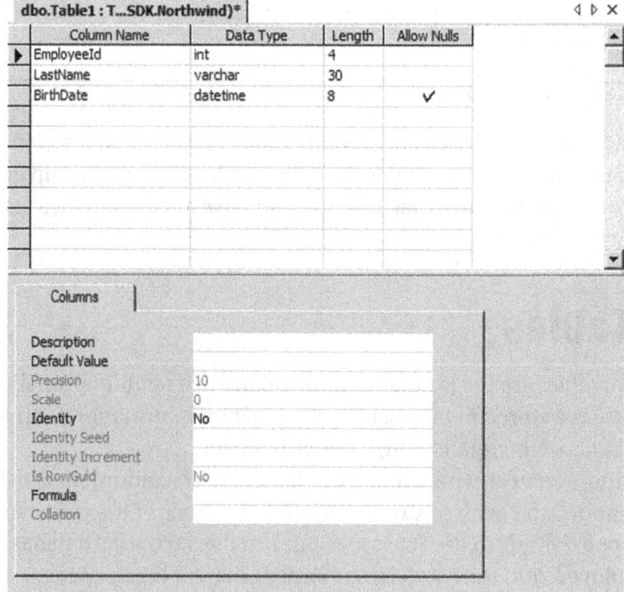

Figure 12-1. *Defining a table in Server Explorer*

3. Click the Save icon on the toolbar. When prompted for a name for the table, enter `test_Employees` and then click OK (see Figure 12-2).

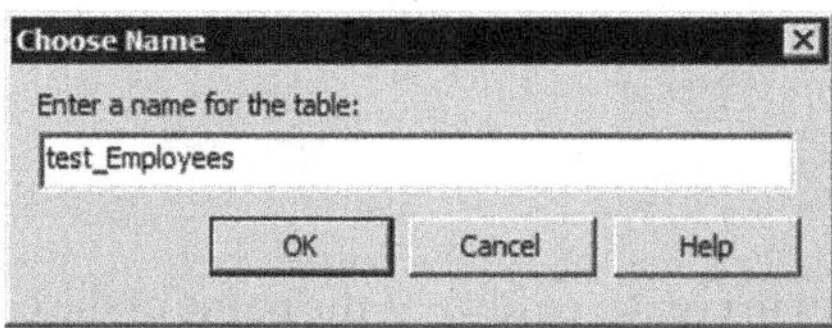

Figure 12-2. *Naming a table in Server Explorer*

How It Works

If all has gone well, Visual Studio .NET has created a new table as requested. Now, to verify that the table was saved, expand the Tables node in Server Explorer. It should appear as in Figure 12-3, with the column names you specified.

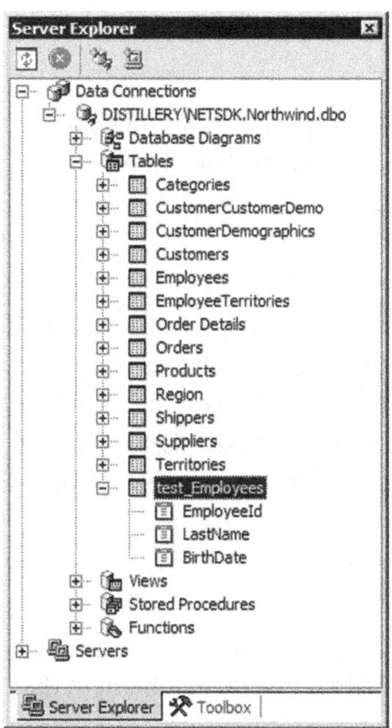

Figure 12-3. *`test_Employees` columns in Server Explorer*

Now that you've seen how to create tables in a database using Server Explorer, we'll teach you how to do it using SQL.

Try It Out: Creating a Table Using SQL

Tables are created with SQL using the `CREATE TABLE` statement. The simplest form of this statement is as follows:

```
CREATE TABLE tablename
   (
   column1 datatype1 nullspec1,
   column2 datatype2 nullspec2,
   ...,
   columnn datatypen nullspecn
   )
```

where `tablename` is the name of the table you want to create, `column1` is the name of the column, `datatype1` is the data type of `column1`, and `nullspec1` specifies whether the column should allow null values.

To create a table similar to the one you saw in the previous section using the `CREATE TABLE` statement, use the following SQL to create a `test_Employees` table:

```
CREATE TABLE test_Employees
   (
   EmployeeID int NOT NULL,
   LastName varchar(30) NOT NULL,
   BirthDate datetime NULL
   )
```

While most parts of this syntax are intuitive, notice that the null specifications for columns are either `NULL` or `NOT NULL`. Also note that a database can have only one table with the same name, which is why you renamed the table in this example.

■ **Note** Actually, table names in SQL Server are composed of three parts, and it's the combination that must be unique within a database. For simplicity you've avoided the issue by using a unique table name. Further, though you can use mixed case for table and column names, and SQL Server accepts this as the spelling for these database objects, SQL references to database objects *aren't case sensitive*. For example, you can refer to table `test_Employees` as `test_employees` (or even `Test_employeeS`); this also applies to column names.

When a table is created using Server Explorer, behind the scenes a `CREATE TABLE` statement is issued against the database. You can also explicitly issue the `CREATE TABLE` statement in the following ways:

- A stored procedure (which we'll cover in Chapter 14)
- The SQL tool built into Visual Studio .NET (as you saw in Chapter 3)
- An application, such as the one you'll build later in the chapter
- Query Analyzer, if you've installed the full SQL Server rather than just MSDE
- The `osql` command-line tool (which you also saw in Chapter 3)

Adding Rows to a Table

After creating a table, you can add rows to it in several ways. You'll explore two of these ways in this chapter.

- Server Explorer
- A VB .NET application

Let's add rows using Server Explorer.

Try It Out: Adding Rows to a Table with Server Explorer

To add rows to a table with Server Explorer, do this:

1. In Server Explorer, right-click the `test_Employees` table and select Retrieve Data from Table. This presents you with a data grid where you can add rows. Add the row for Lister, as shown in Figure 12-4.

dbo.test_Emplo...SDK.Northwind)

EmployeeId	LastName	BirthDate
1	Lister	11/07/1964

Figure 12-4. *Adding a row to `test_Employees` with Server Explorer*

How It Works

When you enter values for a new row, the row isn't actually added until all data has been entered and you move to another row. Then Server Explorer creates an `INSERT` statement in the background and runs that statement against the table. If all the data entered is consistent with the column data types, the row is inserted into the table.

To add another row to `test_Employees` using SQL, you could code the following:

```
INSERT INTO test_Employees
   (
   EmployeeId,
   LastName,
   BirthDate
   )
VALUES (2, 'Rimmer', '03/28/1960')
```

Or you could use this, since when you provide all values, the column list is optional:

```
INSERT INTO test_Employees
VALUES (2, 'Rimmer', '03/28/1960')
```

Note, however, that using the column list is definitely the best practice. It allows you to understand which value is being added to which column.

Dropping a Table

Dropping a table from the database will completely remove it from the database and will lose all the data and dependency relationships. You can drop a table with Server Explorer by right-clicking the table and selecting Delete. You can also drop a table with the following SQL:

```
DROP TABLE tablename
```

where `tablename` is the name of the table to drop from the database.

Now that you can create and drop tables with relative ease, create the columns, and choose the data types you want to use, you'll move on to the really exciting and powerful features of relational databases.

Specifying Table Relationships

In the first part of this chapter you learned how to create a single table. So far in this book, the information you've worked with in a table has been about a single entity and attribute—for example, an employee's last name, first name, phone number, and so on. But consider that the information is never used in isolation.

- Employees are employed by companies.
- Companies sell products to customers.
- Customers make orders for products.
- Orders are dealt with by employees, and so on.

The point we're making here is that the objects you'll model in a database relate to each other. The previous four bullets each describe a relationship between two entities you can describe in a table, and you can use a database to model and keep track of the relationships between entities modeled in a database.

In Chapter 7, you saw two tables that contained related information—the employees in one table took the orders stored in the other table. Any table can be related to another if a relationship exists between the two sets of information you want to track.

You can have many tables in a relational database, all containing related data. Looking at the tables in the `Northwind` database, there are many possible connections between tables, some of which have indeed been set up as relationships. For example, one sales rep in a company may have generated many orders, which have been placed by quite a few companies. These companies may, however, have placed many different orders. The parts on the orders may have come from different suppliers, but chances are that each supplier can supply more than one part to the Northwind Traders company. Already you can probably see some groups of entities—employees, customers, orders, and suppliers. In the `Northwind` example, many more tables exist that help to relate the data, using different types of relationships.

The following three types of relationship exist:

- One-to-one
- Many-to-one
- One-to-many

If you have two tables related in a database, then it's intuitive to think that you need rules in order to ensure that changes to the first table won't make data in the second table inconsistent. This is where keys and constraints play a big role. In the next section of the chapter, you'll look at keys and constraints and the benefits they bring to relational databases.

Understanding Keys and Constraints

Two main types of keys are used in database: *primary keys* and *foreign keys.*

Constraints are important for validating data. For example, if you were storing ages in a table, then someone who accidentally hit the minus sign before typing in an age could create all sorts of problems. A constraint that checked for positive ages would avoid this sort of error.

Understanding Primary Keys

Let's take a closer look at the original `Employee` table in the `Northwind` database. The first column is `EmployeeID`. The IDs range from 1 to 9, and each employee has a unique `EmployeeID` assigned to him or her. A column or a combination of columns that uniquely identifies each row in a table is called the *primary key.* Additionally, no part of a primary key can have a null value. `EmployeeID` uniquely identifies each employee and is the primary key of the `Employees` table. On the other hand, the `LastName` column can't be specified as the primary key since more than one employee could have the same last name.

To specify the primary key for a table using Visual Studio .NET, follow these steps:

1. In Server Explorer, right-click the `test_Employee` table in the `Northwind` database and select Design Table.
2. Right-click the column you want to be the primary key and select Set Primary Key, or select the column and click the Set Primary Key icon (the key icon) in the table's toolbar.

Whichever method you choose, the column that now holds the primary key is marked with a key symbol, as shown in Figure 12-5, where we've selected `EmployeeId` as the primary key.

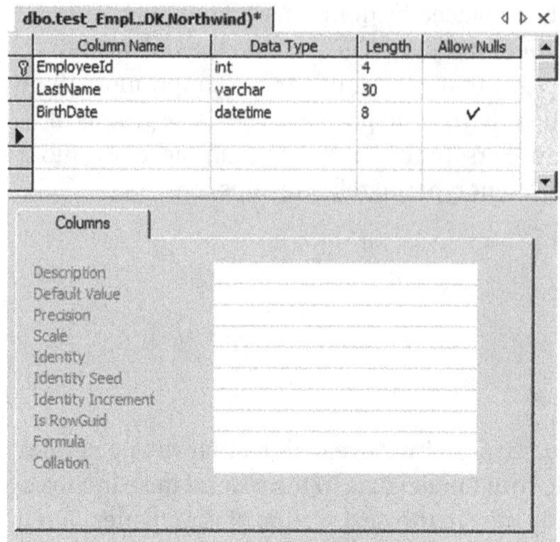

Figure 12-5. *Specifying a primary key*

When using SQL, you can add a primary key at design time with the following by simply adding the keywords `PRIMARY KEY` to the column definition:

```
CREATE TABLE test_Employees
   (
   EmployeeID int NOT NULL PRIMARY KEY,
   LastName varchar(30) NOT NULL,
   BirthDate datetime NULL
   )
```

Understanding Foreign Keys

A *foreign key* is a column or a combination of columns that matches the primary key (or, in most RDBMSs including SQL Server, any unique key) of another table. To better understand what this means, let's examine the `Orders`, `Order Details`, `Employees`, and `Products` tables. Figure 12-6 shows the tables with their columns.

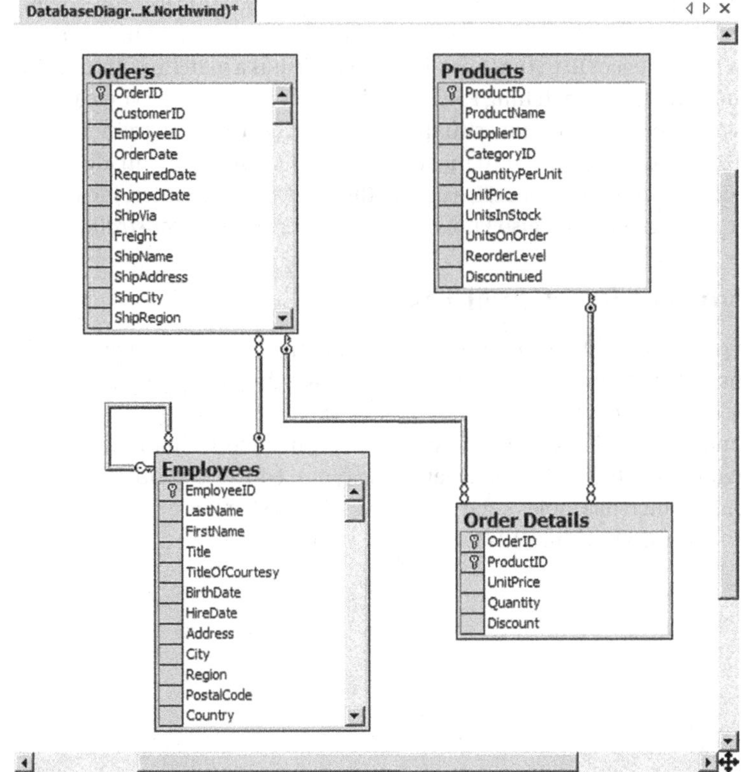

Figure 12-6. *Some* `Northwind` *table relationships*

Say you want to determine which employee generated an order for a given product. On-screen, you just ask the database or the information, but behind the scenes, the database needs to work through four steps to figure it out on your behalf.

1. First it finds the `ProductID` for the named product in the `Products` table.
2. Then it looks at the `Order Details` table and finds the `OrderID` for the order containing the `ProductID` discovered in step 1.
3. Then it scans the `Orders` table for the `EmployeeID` that corresponds to the `OrderID` found in step 2.
4. Finally, it looks at the `Employees` table and discovers the name of the employee corresponding to the `EmployeeID` found in step 3.

We've intuitively explained the concept of the foreign key in the preceding example. The ProductID column in the Order Details table references the ProductID primary key of the Products table. This guarantees that each ProductID in the Order Details table has a matching ProductID in the Products table. If you can't find a matching ProductID in the Products table, you can't figure out what the product is. You can eliminate situations such as these by constraining the ProductID column in the Order Details table with the foreign key. If an attempt is made to insert a row for which no corresponding ProductID exists in the Products table, then the database will produce an error. Foreign keys are also known as *referential integrity constraints.*

Understanding Types of Relationships

Relationships specify that one table relates to another table. Relationships ensure integrity and reduce the data redundancy. You enforce relationships by matching the foreign key of one table with the primary key of another table.

As mentioned, three main types of relationship exist: one-to-one, one-to-many, and many-to-many. To understand the differences between these types, consider another MSDE sample database named pubs, which has tables such as employee, publishers, pub_info, titles, titleauthor, and authors, as shown in Figure 12-7.

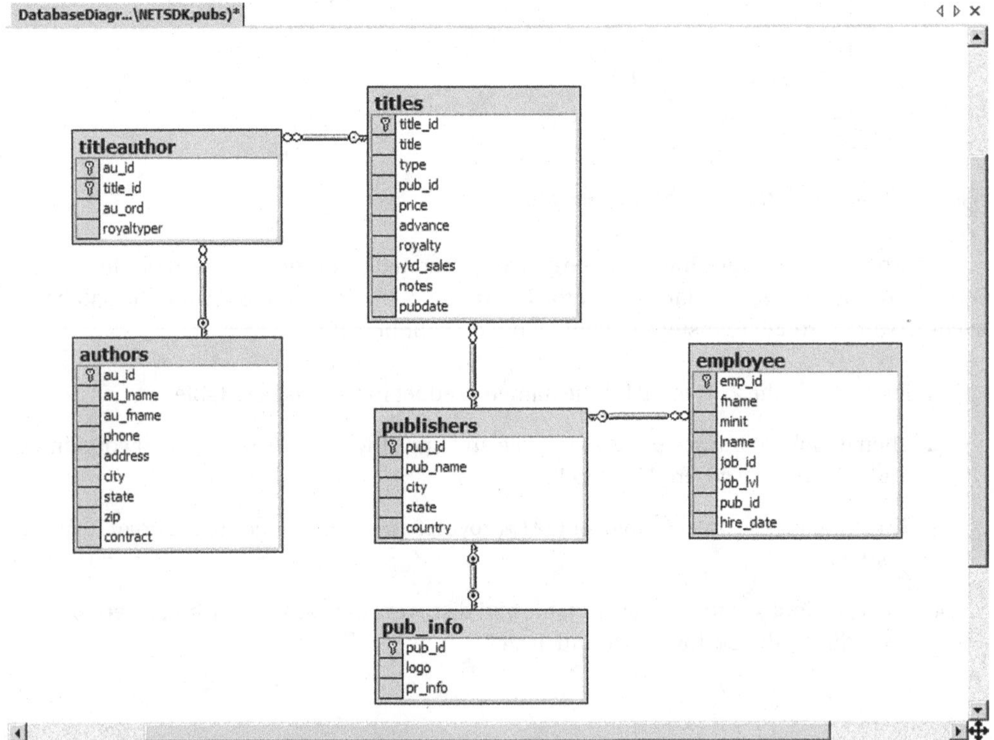

Figure 12-7. *Some pubs table relationships*

From Figure 12-7, you can see that the following is true:

- `employee` contains employee information, including the ID of the publisher for which the employees work.
- `publishers` contains publisher information.
- `pub_info` contains the publisher's logo.
- `titles` contains book information, including the ID of the publisher.
- `authors` contains author information, including the ID of the publisher for which the employees work.
- `titleauthor` contains both the author and title IDs.

The tables in Figure 12-7 all have varying types of relationships to each other. The following list explains the different types more clearly:

One-to-one relationships: In a one-to-one relationship, a row in table A has exactly one matching row in table B, and vice versa. The relationship between the `publishers` and `pub_info` tables is a one-to-one relationship—each publisher in the `publishers` table has only one logo, so only one related row is in the `pub_info` table. In Figure 12-7, the one-to-one relationship is shown with a key on both sides of the relationship.

One-to-many relationships: In a one-to-many relationship, one row in table A can have many matching rows in table B. But any one row in table B can have only one matching row in table A. The relationship between the `publishers` and `employee` tables is a one-to-many relationship. One publisher can have many employees.

Many-to-many relationships: In a many-to-many relationship, a row in table A can have many matching rows in table B, and vice versa. The relationship between the `titles` and `authors` table is a many-to-many relationship. Several authors can write one title, and one author can write several titles. A many-to-many relationship is created by a third table (here, `titleauthor`), sometimes called a *junction table.*

The primary key of a junction table consists of the foreign keys to both table A and table B. The many-to-many relationship here is actually defined by two one-to-many relationships, from `titles` and `authors` to `titleauthor`.

Now that you have an understanding of relationships and the different types of keys, let's look at what they mean in terms of relational databases in this example.

Understanding Referential Integrity

Once you define a relationship between tables, you need to enforce *referential integrity* (RI) between the tables. RI exists when all foreign key values in the child table match primary key values in the parent table.

Enforcing RI is essential to prevent inconsistent data from being entered into a database. Let's look at an example to demonstrate the point.

Try It Out: Enforcing Referential Integrity

You can verify the RI violation by opening the `Order Details` table in the `Northwind` database and inserting a row with `OrderID` of `20000` and `ProductID` of `77`. You'll get the error message in Figure 12-8.

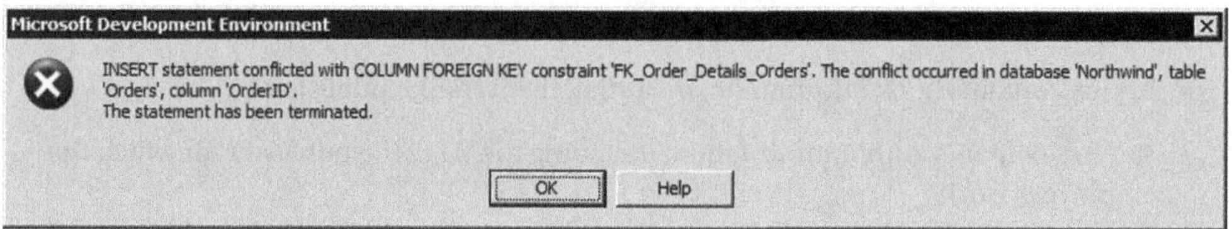

Figure 12-8. *Violating RI*

How It Works

When you attempted to add a row with `OrderID` of `20000` and `ProductID` of `77` to `Order Details`, SQL Server enforced the foreign key constraint between `Orders` and `Order Details`. Since an `Order` with `OrderID` of `20000` doesn't exist, an error was raised.

Understanding Database Diagrams

Database diagrams show tables and their relationships. Relationships among tables can easily be specified and conceptualized in database diagrams. A large database with many tables can have several diagrams; for example, a `Sales` diagram and an `Invoicing` diagram can show only the tables and the relationships relevant to `Sales` and `Invoicing`, respectively. Database diagrams are objects in a SQL Server database just like tables and stored procedures are.

■ **Note** Database diagrams aren't part of either the relational model or standard SQL. SQL Server provides them as database objects, but other RDBMSs don't. Check your RDBMS to see if it offers a similar database design facility.

Let's try defining relationships using a database diagram.

Try It Out: Defining Relationships Using a Database Diagram

Let's create a database diagram to show the `Orders`, `Order Details`, and `Products` tables in the `Northwind` database and the relationships between them.

■ **Tip** This feature isn't available in Visual Basic .NET Standard Edition, but Microsoft Access offers it, and the procedure in Access is similar to that for Visual Studio .NET.

Follow these steps:

1. In Server Explorer, right-click Database Diagrams and select New Diagram.
2. The screen that pops up will list all the tables in the database. Select `Order Details`, `Orders`, and `Products`, as shown in Figure 12-9, and click Add.

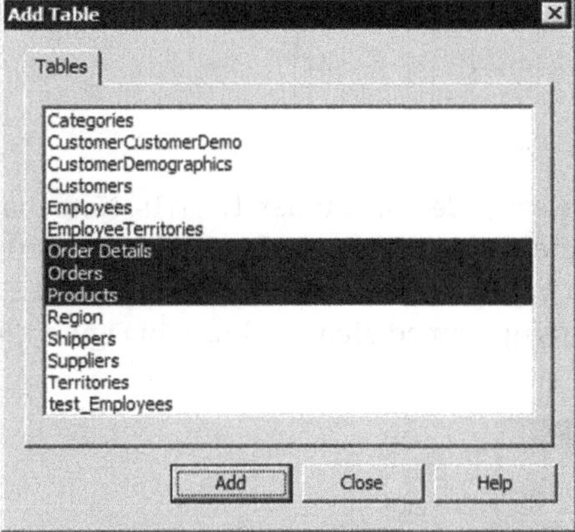

Figure 12-9. *Adding tables to a database diagram*

3. The tables selected will be added to the diagram, and the table names will be removed from the list. Click Close in the dialog box, and the relationships between them will be added to the diagram. You'll now remove a relationship line and learn how to define the relationship. To remove a relationship, right-click a relationship, and select Delete Relationship from Database (see Figure 12-10). Delete the relationship between `Orders` and `Order Details`.

Figure 12-10. *Deleting a relationship*

4. Now let's redefine the relationship between `Orders` and `Order Details`. Note that the `OrderID` column is the primary key of the `Orders` table and a foreign key in the `Order Details` table. Drag the `OrderID` column from the `Order Details` table to the `Orders` table. The Create Relationship dialog box pops up immediately, as shown in Figure 12-11.

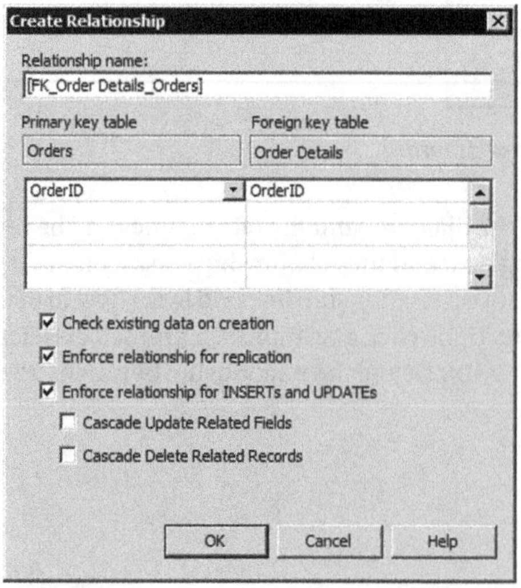

Figure 12-11. *Create Relationship window*

■ **Note** The Orders table is listed as the primary key table, and Order Details is listed as the foreign key table. The primary key (OrderID) of the parent table is listed in the left pane, and the foreign key (again, OrderID) in the child table is listed in the right pane. A relationship will be created between the tables based on these keys. The name of this relationship is [FK_Order Details_Orders]. The relationship requires that that every OrderID value in the Order Details table must also exist in the Orders table.

---

5. Check both the cascade-related boxes, and then click OK to create the relationship.
6. Click the Save icon in the toolbar to save the relationship. You'll be asked to specify a name for the diagram. Name the diagram Sales. Click OK.
7. When the Save window appears, click Yes.

You can access a saved diagram from Server Explorer by double-clicking the diagram node after expanding the Database Diagrams node.

How It Works

In this exercise, you defined a relationship by linking the primary key and foreign keys. When a relation is set, RI is enforced. You can change the relationships between the tables in the diagram and add more tables to it if you want.

The Order Details table has a *composite* primary key, which is the combination of the OrderID and ProductID columns. So, you can associate a given order with a given ProductID only once, but you can associate it with any or all (or no) products.

If you think about it, this makes sense, because in a single order you wouldn't list a product a thousand times over; you'd list it once and specify the quantity ordered.

Understanding Constraints

A primary key is one kind of *constraint* on a table. So is a foreign key. Other constraints can be specified for a table and its columns. Constraints are typically used for validation and for ensuring data integrity; in Chapter 15 you'll look at constraints in detail. The following is a brief list of them:

- NOT NULL: When a column is specified to be NOT NULL, null values can't be assigned to that column. This means that either the column must have a default value or the user will be forced to enter a value for it before the row is inserted into the table.
- UNIQUE: A unique constraint on a table requires that values for a column or set of columns are unique. It can be specified in addition to the primary key, which by definition is unique.
- DEFAULT: When a default constraint is specified on a column, a default value is generated if no value is supplied for that column.
- CHECK: The check constraint checks if the value of the column satisfies a certain criterion.

Understanding Normalization

Normalization is a technique for minimizing redundant data in a logical database design. Normalized designs are less subject to update anomalies because they (ideally) keep each data item in only one place. Normalized database designs usually reduce data storage demands, typically enhancing the performance data manipulation operations while making query processing more complicated. These trade-offs must be carefully evaluated in terms of the required performance profile of a database. Often, a database design needs to be *denormalized* to adequately satisfy operational needs.

Normalizing a logical database design involves a set of formal processes to separate the data into multiple, related tables. The result of each process is referred to as a *normal form*. Five normal forms have been identified in theory, but most of the time third normal form (3NF) is as far as one needs to go in practice. Since to be in 3NF a *relation* (the formal term and more precise concept for what SQL calls a table) must already be in second normal form (2NF), and 2NF requires a relation to be in first normal form (1NF). Let's look briefly at what these normal forms mean.

First normal form (1NF) means that all column values are *scalar*; in other words, they have a single value that can't be further decomposed in terms of the data model. For example, although individual characters of a string can be accessed through a procedure that decomposes the string, the characters aren't accessible *by name* in SQL, so, as far as the data model is concerned, they aren't part of the model. Likewise, in a table with a manager column and a column containing a list of employees who work for a given manager, the manager and the list would be accessible by name but the individual employees wouldn't be. All relations—and SQL tables—are by definition in 1NF since the lowest level of accessibility by name (known as the table's *granularity*) is the column level, and, as you've just seen, column values are scalars in SQL.

Second normal form (2NF) requires that *attributes* (the formal term for SQL columns) that aren't parts of keys be *functionally dependent* on a key that uniquely identifies them. Functional dependence basically means that for a given key value only one value exists in a table for a column or set of columns. For example, if a table contained employees and their titles, and more than one employee could have the same title (very likely), a key that uniquely identified employees wouldn't uniquely identify titles, so the titles wouldn't be functionally dependent on a key of the table. To put the table into 2NF, you'd create a separate table for titles—with its own unique key—and replace the title in the original table with the key from the new table. Note how this reduces data redundancy. The titles themselves now appear only once in the database. Only their keys appear in other tables, and key data isn't considered redundant (though, of course, it requires columns in other tables and data storage).

Third normal form (3NF) extends the concept of functional dependence to *full functional dependence*. Essentially, this means that all nonkey columns in a table are uniquely identified by the whole primary key, not just part of the primary key. For example, if you revised the 1NF `managers-employees` table to have three columns (`managername`, `employeeid`, and `employeename`) instead of two, and you defined the composite primary key as `managername` + `employeeid`, the table would be in 2NF (since `employeename`, the nonkey column, is dependent on the primary key), but it wouldn't be in 3NF since `employeename` is uniquely identified by part of the primary key (`employeeid`). Creating a separate table for employees and removing `employeename` from `managers-employees` would put the table into 3NF. Note that even though this table is now normalized to 3NF, the database design is still not as normalized as it should be. Creating another table for managers, using an ID shorter than the manager's name, though not required for normalization here, is definitely the better approach and would be needed for a real-world database.

Database design (even of small databases) is an art more than a science, and applying normalization wisely is always important. On the other hand, normalization inherently increases the number of tables and therefore the number of joins required to retrieve data. *Denormalizing* one or more tables, by intentionally providing redundant data to reduce the complexity of joins and get quicker query response times, may be necessary. With either normalization or denormalization, the goal is to control redundancy so that the database design adequately (and ideally, optimally) supports the actual use of the database.

Working with SQL in VB .NET

Up until now you've seen how to access databases using Server Explorer. You'll now submit SQL from a VB .NET application against the `Northwind` database.

Try It Out: Creating a SQL Statement Processor

Follow these steps:

1. Create a solution named `Chapter12_Examples`. Then, add a VB .NET Windows application named `StatementProcessor` to the solution.

2. Change the name of the form to `StatementProcessor.vb`.

3. Add a text box named `SqlStatement` and a button named `ExecuteButton`.

4. Add another text box named `ResultBox` to see the result of the execution.

5. Set the `MultiLine` property of the text boxes to `True`, and clear their text properties.

6. Add two labels with the text shown Figure 12-12.

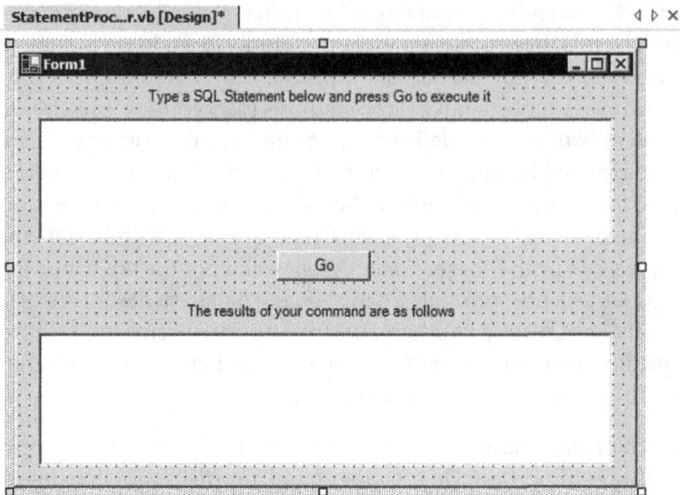

Figure 12-12. *StatementProcessor layout*

7. Add the following Imports directive to the `StatementProcessor.vb` file:

```
Imports System.Data.SqlClient
```

8. Add a `SqlConnection` to the form from the Data tab of the Toolbox. Set its `ConnectionString` property to that for the `Northwind` database.

9. Double-click `ExecuteButton` and add the following code to the `ExecuteButton_Click` method:

```
Private Sub ExecuteButton_Click(ByVal sender As System.Object, _
   ByVal e As System.EventArgs) Handles ExecuteButton.Click
   ' Get SQL Query from textbox
   Dim sql As String = SqlStatement.Text

   ' Create Command object
   Dim NewCommand As New SqlCommand(sql, SqlConnection1)

   Try
      ' Open Connection
      SqlConnection1.Open()

      ' Execute Command
      NewCommand.ExecuteNonQuery()
```

```
        ' Display Result Message
        ResultBox.Text = "SQL executed successfuly"

    Catch ex As Exception
        ' Display error message
        ResultBox.Text = ex.ToString()

    Finally
        ' Close Connection
        SqlConnection1.Close()

    End Try
End Sub
```

10. Before running the application, delete (in Server Explorer) the `test_Employees` table that you created earlier, as you'll be re-creating it.

11. Run the application with Ctrl+F5. In the upper text box, enter the `CREATE TABLE` statement as shown in Figure 12-13, and then click the Execute Command button. After a pause you should see the text *SQL executed successfully* in the lower text box.

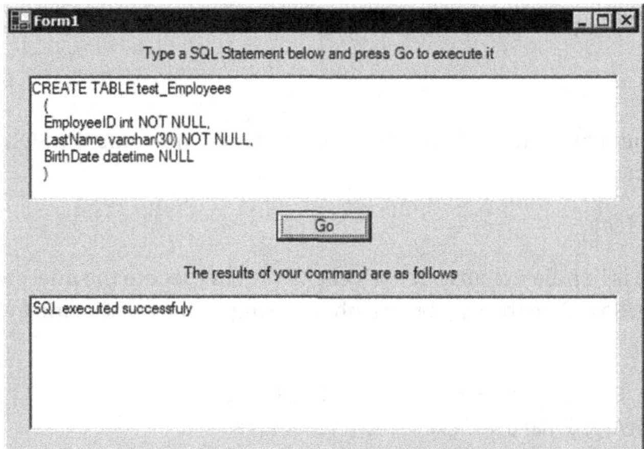

Figure 12-13. *`StatementProcessor` running*

12. Verify whether the table exists in the `Northwind` database by right-clicking the Tables node in Server Explorer and selecting Refresh. You'll see that the `test_Employees` table has been created with three columns, as shown in Figure 12-14.

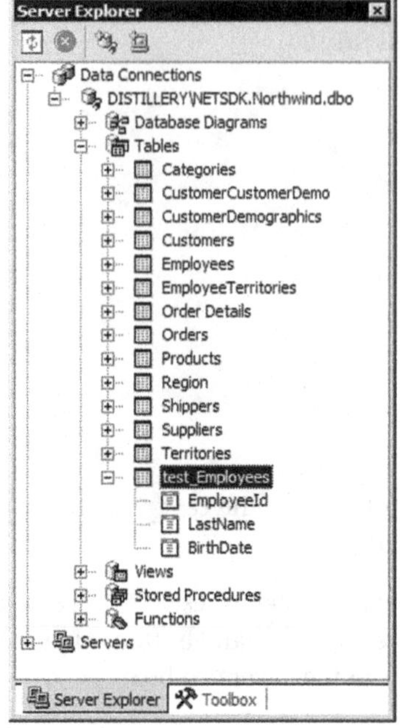

Figure 12-14. *Table* `test_Employees` *in Server Explorer*

How It Works

We've covered all the code here many times before. First, you start by including the SQL Server data provider in your project.

```
Imports System.Data.SqlClient
```

Second, all you need do is handle `ExecuteButton`'s click event to execute the query written in the `SqlStatement` text box. So create the `SqlCommand` object using the given SQL and available `SqlConnection` object.

```
Private Sub ExecuteButton_Click(ByVal sender As System.Object, _
   ByVal e As System.EventArgs) Handles ExecuteButton.Click
   ' Get SQL Query from textbox
   Dim sql As String = SqlStatement.Text

   ' Create Command object
   Dim NewCommand As New SqlCommand(sql, SqlConnection1)
```

With the SqlCommand object created, you just open the connection and call ExecuteNonQuery to run it. As we know, ExecuteNonQuery can return an integer representing the number of rows affected by an INSERT, UPDATE, or DELETE operation, but in this case, you choose not to catch the return value since you're creating a table and not inserting, updating, or deleting rows.

```
    Try
      ' Open Connection
      SqlConnection1.Open()

      ' Execute Command
      NewCommand.ExecuteNonQuery()
```

If all goes well, you display a success message in the result text box. If not, any error message is shown in the result text box instead.

```
      ' Display Result Message
      ResultBox.Text = "SQL executed successfully"

    Catch ex As Exception
      ' Display error message
      ResultBox.Text = ex.ToString()
```

Finally, you close the connection.

```
    Finally
      ' Close Connection
      SqlConnection1.Close()

    End Try
End Sub
```

That's it! You've created a useful little tool for executing SQL statements. Now let's see how you can add rows to your table using the application you've just built.

Try It Out: Adding Rows to a Table

Recall that initially you used Server Explorer to insert rows, but this time you'll use your application to submit your SQL. All you have to do is to execute an INSERT statement against the test_Employees table. To do this, follow these steps:

1. Enter the statement to insert a row for the employee Rimmer, as shown in Figure 12-15.

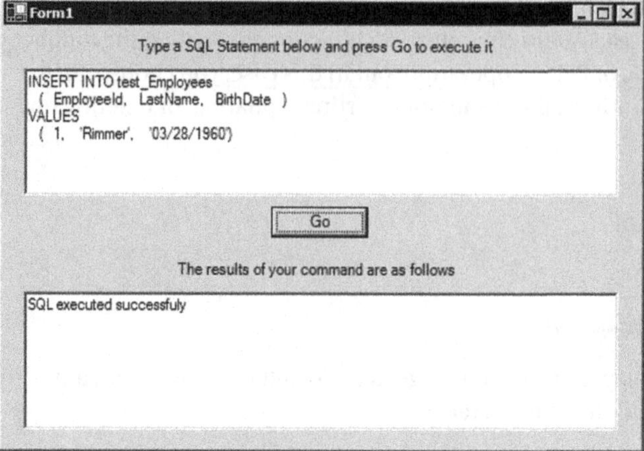

Figure 12-15. *Inserting a row into `test_Employees`*

2. You can verify that the row was added with Server Explorer.

3. Now let's try to add another row with the same `EmployeeId`. While it doesn't make sense for two different employees to have the same ID, the `test_Employees` table will at this time allow it, as shown in Figure 12-16. You can verify that the row was added with Server Explorer.

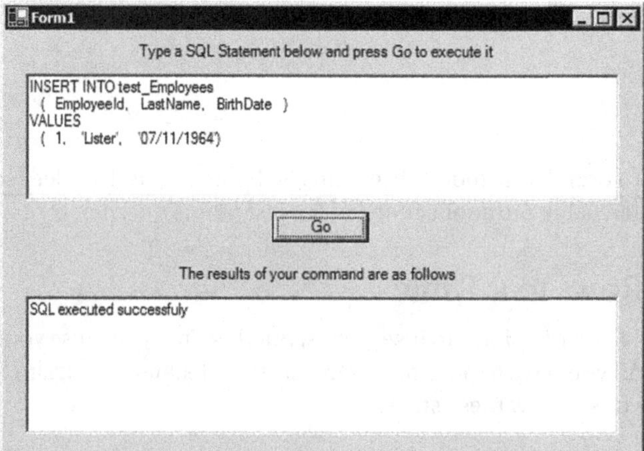

Figure 12-16. *Inserting a duplicate row into `test_Employees`*

How It Works

At the moment, no constraint on `test_Employees` enforces uniqueness, so you're allowed to create multiple rows with the same `EmployeeId`. To prevent two rows from having the same `EmployeeId`, you must specify `EmployeeId` as the primary key of `test_Employees`. If you try to apply this to the table in its current state, you'll get an error, because there are duplicate `EmployeeIds` in the table and because a primary key must be unique.

Let's look at how you can test primary and foreign key constraints, as well as how to drop tables using SQL.

Try It Out: Testing the Primary Key Constraint

Follow these steps:

1. In `StatementProcessor`, delete all the rows in `test_Employees` with the following SQL statement:

   ```
   TRUNCATE TABLE test_Employees
   ```

2. In Server Explorer, right-click `test_Employees`, and select Design Table. In the design grid that appears, right-click the `EmployeeId` row and select Set Primary Key.
3. Click the Save icon to save the change to the table design, and then close the design window.
4. In `StatementProcessor`, add an employee to the table for `employeeid 1` using the following statement. (Note that you can omit the column list since you're providing values for all columns in the order in which the columns are defined in the table.)

   ```
   INSERT INTO test_Employees
   VALUES (1, 'Rimmer', '03/28/1960')
   ```

5. Add another employee with a different last name and birth date but the same `EmployeeId`.

   ```
   INSERT INTO test_Employees
   VALUES (1,'Lister', '07/11/1964')
   ```

If the constraint is being enforced, then you won't be able to enter duplicate data into the table, and you'll get the error message in Figure 12-17.

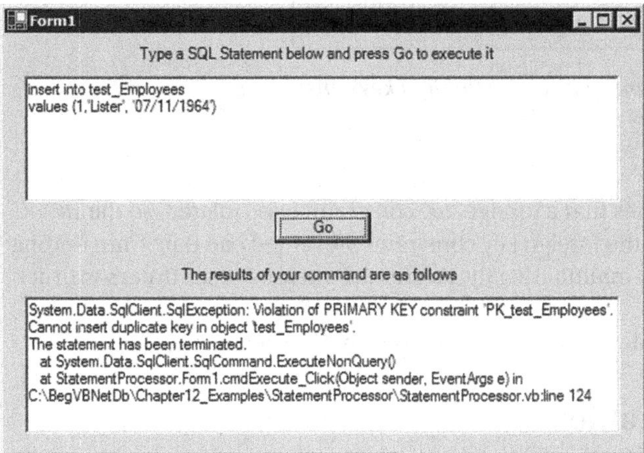

Figure 12-17. *Preventing a duplicate row in `test_employees`*

How It Works

As you expected, an error message was given. The error message indicates that the primary key constraint has been violated by attempting to insert a second employee with an `employeeid` of 1.

Now let's see an example where a foreign key constraint is violated.

Try It Out: Testing the Foreign Key Constraint (Referential Integrity)

Notice from the earlier example involving the `Order Details` table in the `Northwind` database that it's a child of the `Orders` table. This relationship requires that for every order in the `Order Details` table, that order must also exist in the parent `Orders` table. Let's try to violate this relationship and see what kind of error you encounter.

1. In `StatementProcessor`, enter the `INSERT` statement as shown in Figure 12-18 and notice the resulting error message. (Note that you enclose the table name in double quotes because it contains an embedded blank. This is standard SQL. Transact-SQL also accepts square brackets in place of double quotes.)

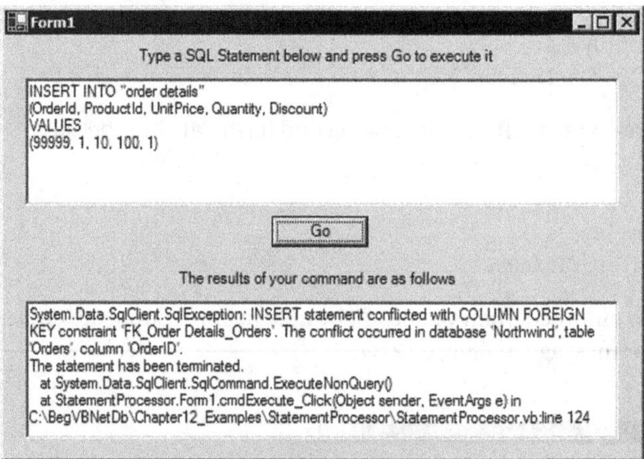

Figure 12-18. *Enforcing referential integrity (foreign key constraints)*

How It Works

As you can see, the message indicates that a foreign key constraint was violated, so the `INSERT` statement wasn't successful. Thus, the foreign key constraint prevented bad data from finding its way into the `Order Details` table, maintaining the referential integrity of the `Orders` to `Order Details` parent-child relationship.

Let's do one last example and delete (in SQL, *drop*) the table you added.

Try It Out: Dropping a Table

Let's try to drop the `test_Employees` table, regardless of how many rows it may have.

1. In StatementProcessor, enter the DROP statement as shown in Figure 12-19.

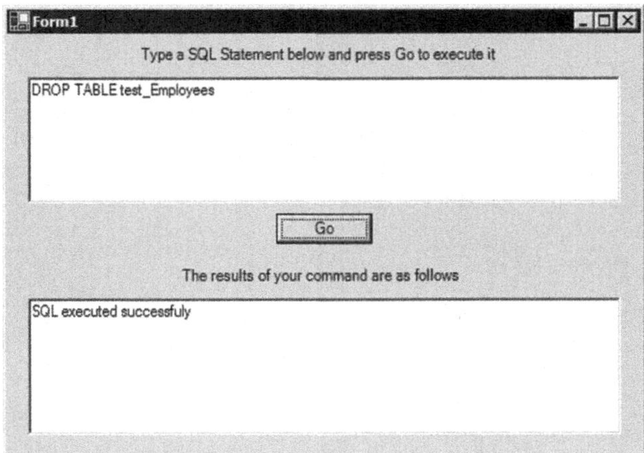

Figure 12-19. *Dropping a table*

How It Works

You can verify that the table has been deleted from the Northwind database with Server Explorer. Note that you didn't receive a single warning message telling you that you were about to make a significant change to your database. The statement was simply executed. Remember that care must be exercised when issuing the DROP TABLE statement as it completely removes both the table definition and its data. If you accidentally drop a table, the only way to restore it is from a backup of the database.

Summary

In this chapter you took some significant steps in furthering your understanding of relational databases. The ability to establish relationships between tables gives you a lot of flexibility and power. As you worked through the chapter, you did the following:

- You learned how to create and drop tables.
- You learned what primary keys and foreign keys are and how they're used to define relationships among tables. You also learned about the different types of relationships and how to define them using database diagrams.
- You learned how to normalize tables during database design and why normalization and denormalization are important.
- You learned how to add rows to a table using Server Explorer and use a VB .NET application.
- You learned about error messages that are generated when primary key and foreign key constraints are violated.

In the next chapter you'll move from SQL statements to revisit SQL queries and experiment with more advanced query facilities.

CHAPTER 13

Learning More About Queries

In the previous chapter, you started looking in more detail at the various elements that make up a database. You saw that databases use tables and constraints to model relationships between the objects being modeled within them and that each table contains rows that contain the actual data pertaining to individual objects. In this chapter, you'll continue learning more about databases with a more detailed look at the SQL queries you've used to pull information from the database into your applications.

You've used SQL queries—those SQL statements beginning with the keyword `SELECT`—almost everywhere since Chapter 3, but they've been very simple, returning a number of columns given a certain condition. In fact, SQL has a wide variety of functions and constructs for querying beyond those you've seen, and although we'll demonstrate some more of the most common variants, we won't cover all the possible permutations in one chapter. To give you an indication of how much there is to the `SELECT` statement, whole books have been dedicated to just that. They sell quite well, too.

Focusing back on this book meanwhile, you'll learn about the following features of SQL queries:

- `DISTINCT` keyword
- Subqueries
- `GROUP BY` clause
- Aggregate functions
- `CASE` expressions
- Date functions
- Joins

Before diving in, you'll rewrite the VB .NET application from the previous chapter to run queries and display their results. Then you'll practice coding various types of queries against the `Northwind` database.

Building the Northwind Query Application, Part II

The revised application is similar to the one in Chapter 12, but it differs in how it handles result sets returned from queries. In Chapter 12, you used DDL statements such as CREATE TABLE and DML statements such as INSERT that don't return rows. You used the ExecuteNonQuery method on a command. With queries, though, you may get zero, one, or many rows, containing one or more columns of data. Let's see how to revise the application to handle any number of rows and columns.

Try It Out: Extending the Northwind SQL Application

Follow these steps:

1. Create a solution named Chapter13_Examples.
2. Add a VB .NET Windows application, named QueryProcessor, to it.
3. Rename Form1.vb to QueryProcessor.vb. Change its Text property to QueryProcessor, and then add two labels, a multiline text box, a button, and a list view so that the form looks like Figure 13-1.

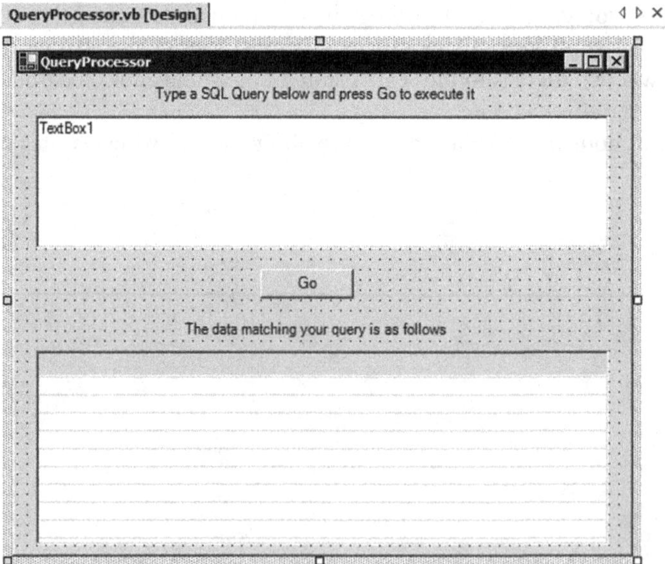

Figure 13-1. *QueryProcessor layout*

4. Name the text box SqlStatement, the Go button ExecuteButton, and the list view ResultBox.

5. Set the View property of the list view to Details so that the results will be displayed with column headers. Set the GridLines property to True.

6. Add the following Imports directive to the QueryProcessor.vb file since you'll be using the SqlClient data provider:

```
Imports System.Data.SqlClient
```

7. Return to Design view, and add a SqlConnection to the form from the Data tab of the Toolbox. Set its ConnectionString property to that for the Northwind database.

8. Now double-click the Go button. Add the following code to the ExecuteButton_Click method:

```
Private Sub ExecuteButton_Click(ByVal sender As System.Object, _
   ByVal e As System.EventArgs) Handles ExecuteButton.Click

   ' Clear list view column headers and items
   ResultBox.Columns.Clear()
   ResultBox.Items.Clear()

   ' Get SQL Query from textbox
   Dim sql As String = SqlStatement.Text

   ' Create Command object
   Dim NewQuery As New SqlCommand(sql, SqlConnection1)

   Try
      ' Open Connection
      SqlConnection1.Open()

      ' Execute Command and Get Data
      Dim NewReader As SqlDataReader = NewQuery.ExecuteReader()

      ' Get column names for list view from data reader
      For i As Integer = 0 To NewReader.FieldCount - 1
         Dim header As New ColumnHeader
         header.Text = NewReader.GetName(i)
         ResultBox.Columns.Add(header)
      Next

      ' Get rows of data and show in list view
      While NewReader.Read()
         ' Create list view item
         Dim NewItem As New ListViewItem
```

```
            ' Specify text and subitems of list view
            NewItem.Text = NewReader.GetValue(0).ToString()
            For i As Integer = 1 To NewReader.FieldCount - 1
               NewItem.SubItems.Add(NewReader.GetValue(i).ToString())
            Next

            ' Add item to list view items collection
            ResultBox.Items.Add(NewItem)
         End While

         'Close Data Reader
         NewReader.Close()

      Catch ex As SqlException
         ' Create an error column header
         Dim ErrorHeader As New ColumnHeader
         ErrorHeader.Text = "SQL Error"
         ResultBox.Columns.Add(ErrorHeader)

         ' Add Error List Item
         Dim ErrorItem As New ListViewItem(ex.Message)
         ResultBox.Items.Add(ErrorItem)

      Catch ex As Exception
         ' Create an error column header
         Dim ErrorHeader As New ColumnHeader
         ErrorHeader.Text = "Error"
         ResultBox.Columns.Add(ErrorHeader)

         ' Add Error List Item
         Dim ErrorItem As New ListViewItem("An error has occurred")
         ResultBox.Items.Add(ErrorItem)

      Finally
         SqlConnection1.Close()
      End Try
   End Sub
```

9. Run it with Ctrl+F5. If you enter the query in Figure 13-2, you should see the result shown in the figure.

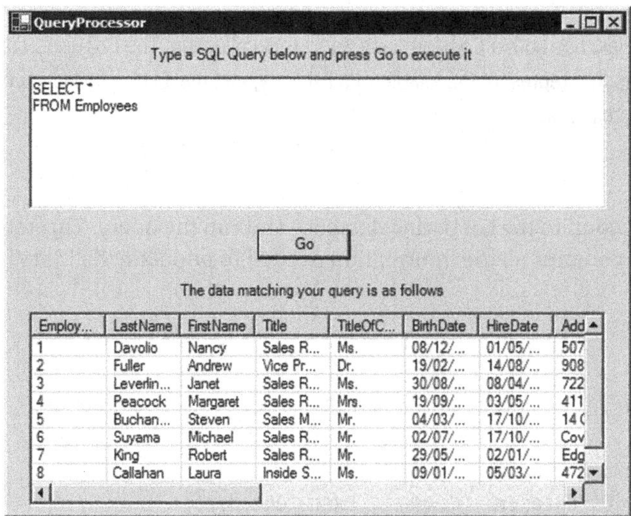

Employ...	LastName	FirstName	Title	TitleOfC...	BirthDate	HireDate	Add
1	Davolio	Nancy	Sales R...	Ms.	08/12/...	01/05/...	507
2	Fuller	Andrew	Vice Pr...	Dr.	19/02/...	14/08/...	908
3	Leverlin...	Janet	Sales R...	Ms.	30/08/...	08/04/...	722
4	Peacock	Margaret	Sales R...	Mrs.	19/09/...	03/05/...	411
5	Buchan...	Steven	Sales M...	Mr.	04/03/...	17/10/...	14 (
6	Suyama	Michael	Sales R...	Mr.	02/07/...	17/10/...	Cov
7	King	Robert	Sales R...	Mr.	29/05/...	02/01/...	Edg
8	Callahan	Laura	Inside S...	Ms.	09/01/...	05/03/...	472

Figure 13-2. *QueryProcessor: Executing a query*

How It Works

Most of the code here should be familiar to you now, but we'll still run through it for practice. You start by clearing the column captions and the rows in the list view. This is needed because you'll be using the application to execute diverse SQL queries and statements, and each will return different results. You therefore clear the list view completely before repopulating it with a new result. Then you create a new `SqlCommand` object that contains the SQL from the `SqlStatement` text box.

```
Private Sub ExecuteButton_Click(ByVal sender As System.Object, _
   ByVal e As System.EventArgs) Handles ExecuteButton.Click

   ' Clear list view column headers and items
   ResultBox.Columns.Clear()
   ResultBox.Items.Clear()

   ' Get SQL Query from textbox
   Dim sql As String = SqlStatement.Text

   ' Create Command object
   Dim NewQuery As New SqlCommand(sql, SqlConnection1)
```

■ **Note** Remember that a list view has both a Columns and an Items collection. The Columns collection contains ColumnHeader objects that represent the header of a list view, and the Items collection contains ListViewItem objects that represent data.

Then you open a connection to the Northwind database and run the query. This returns a SqlDataReader object that contains all the information needed to populate the ListView control.

```
Try
   ' Open Connection
   SqlConnection1.Open()

   ' Execute Command and Get Data
   Dim NewReader As SqlDataReader = NewQuery.ExecuteReader()
```

The next few lines of code read the column names of the data reader and display them as headers in the list view. To do this, you iterate through the columns of the data reader until you reach FieldCount, the number of columns in the data reader. Note that the Columns collection is zero-based, though, so columns are numbered from 0 (zero) to FieldCount - 1.

Then, a ColumnHeader object represents each column of the list view. For each column in the data reader, a corresponding column header is created in the list view. The data reader's GetName method returns the name of the column at a specified index. This name is used as the name of the list view's column. Finally, the column header is added to the Columns collection of the list view, as follows, so that the list view will have a corresponding column for each column in the data reader.

```
   ' Get column names for list view from data reader
   For i As Integer = 0 To NewReader.FieldCount - 1
      Dim header As New ColumnHeader
      header.Text = NewReader.GetName(i)
      ResultBox.Columns.Add(header)
   Next
```

Following this, you iterate through the rows of the data reader, creating a ListViewItem object for each row. To start, you set its Text property to the value of the first column of the data reader. Given the example SQL query, that's EmployeeId, so Text would be 1, 2, and so on.

```
   ' Get rows of data and show in list view
   While NewReader.Read()
      ' Create list view item
      Dim NewItem As New ListViewItem

      ' Specify text and subitems of list view
      NewItem.Text = NewReader.GetValue(0).ToString()
```

The first column of the ListView has an index of zero. The second column of a ListView is called the first SubItem, the third column is the second SubItem, and so on. You now iterate through the columns in the data reader's current row, grab the value contained therein, and add it as a `SubItem` to the `ListViewItem`. Note that you start from the second column of the data reader (`index=1`) because you already used the first column in the `ListViewItem`'s `Text` property.

```
         For i As Integer = 1 To NewReader.FieldCount - 1
            NewItem.SubItems.Add(NewReader.GetValue(i).ToString())
         Next
```

Once the `ListViewItem` object contains all the contents of the row in the data reader, you add it to the `Items` collection of the list view.

```
         ' Add item to list view items collection
         ResultBox.Items.Add(NewItem)
      End While
```

After looping through all the rows, you close the data reader.

```
      'Close Data Reader
      NewReader.Close()
```

You've included two `Catch` clauses here to differentiate between an error in the SQL query and another error occurring. Both work in the same way, creating a new column in the list view and displaying the error inside that.

```
   Catch ex As SqlException
      ' Create an error column header
      Dim ErrorHeader As New ColumnHeader
      ErrorHeader.Text = "SQL Error"
      ResultBox.Columns.Add(ErrorHeader)

      ' Add Error List Item
      Dim ErrorItem As New ListViewItem(ex.Message)
      ResultBox.Items.Add(ErrorItem)

   Catch ex As Exception
      ' Create an error column header
      Dim ErrorHeader As New ColumnHeader
      ErrorHeader.Text = "Error"
      ResultBox.Columns.Add(ErrorHeader)

      ' Add Error List Item
      Dim ErrorItem As New ListViewItem("An error has occurred")
      ResultBox.Items.Add(ErrorItem)
```

Finally, you close the connection.

```
   Finally
      SqlConnection1.Close()
   End Try
End Sub
```

Now that you've created an application that will execute and display results conveniently, you'll learn more about writing queries.

Writing More SQL Query Syntax

It's highly important for any serious database programmer to master SQL, and with this in mind you'll expand your knowledge of SQL query syntax. For the rest of this chapter, you'll query the `Northwind` database in a variety of ways using the `QueryProcessor` application.

Using DISTINCT

The `DISTINCT` keyword is used in a query to exclude duplicate values from the result set. It can be used only once in the select list of a query. If multiple columns are selected, `DISTINCT` eliminates rows where the combination of all the column values are identical.

Say you want to find the `ProductID`s against which orders have been placed. `DISTINCT` certainly helps you with this type of query.

Try It Out: Querying Using DISTINCT

To query using `DISTINCT`, follow these steps:

1. Enter the following query into the `QueryProcessor` application, and click Execute:

```
SELECT
   ProductId
FROM
   [Order Details]
```

2. All the product IDs that have an order placed against them are returned (see Figure 13-3).

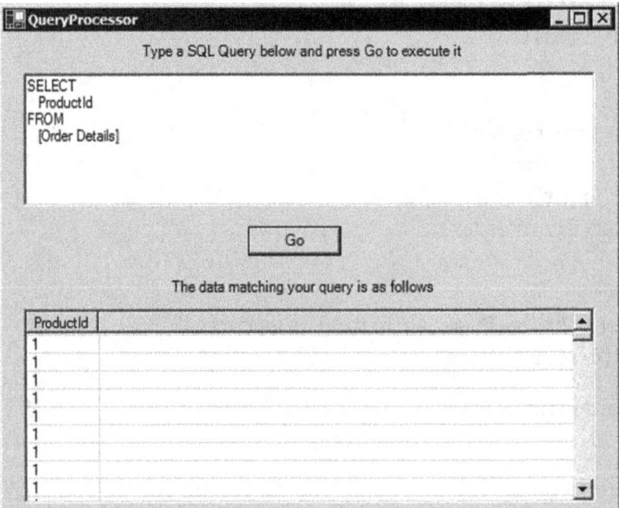

Figure 13-3. *Querying product IDs without the `DISTINCT` keyword*

Now change the query to include DISTINCT.

```
SELECT DISTINCT
   ProductId
FROM
   [Order Details]
```

3. You should see the result in Figure 13-4. The product IDs are returned but without duplicates.

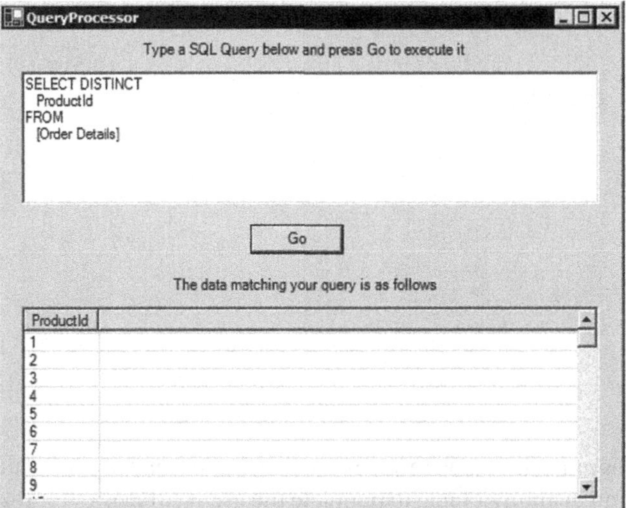

Figure 13-4. *Using the DISTINCT keyword*

How It Works

You know that Order Details contains ProductIDs for various orders and that Products has a list of products available for sale. Obviously, different orders can contain the same ProductID, so you use DISTINCT to eliminate duplicates and get a simple list of product IDs.

Using Subqueries

Subqueries are queries embedded in other queries that use the result of the subquery as part of their own retrieval logic. You can use subqueries in many contexts to create sophisticated queries. If you keep in mind that all queries are simply operations on tables that produce a single table (a result set, called a *derived table* in standard SQL), understanding subqueries will not be difficult. Let's look at some of their typical uses.

Using IN

The IN operator (the IN predicate in standard SQL) determines if the value of a specific column matches a list of values. The list must be of a data type compatible with the column to be matched and may be composed of either literals separated by commas or the result set from a subquery, but not both. The following is some example syntax:

```
SELECT
   column1, column2, ..., columnN
FROM
   table1
WHERE
   columnX IN (1, 10, 14)
```

Here, the list contains three integer literals. The matching column (`columnX`, which is some column in the table but not necessarily one in the select list) must be of a numeric data type for this list to be compatible. Only the rows in `table1` whose `columnX` value is 1, 10, or 14 will be selected.

```
SELECT
   column1, column2, ..., columnN
FROM
   table1
WHERE
   columnX IN
     (
      SELECT
         column1
      FROM
         table2
     )
```

This query accomplishes much the same result as the first, but instead of a list of literals it uses the values from a column in another table to populate the list. If `column1` of `table2` had only the values 1, 10, and 14, this would have the same effect as the first query. Of course, if other values occurred in `table2`, they would also occur in the list, and the outer query probably wouldn't produce the same result set as the first query. (A subquery is often referred to as an *inner query*, and the query that contains it is referred to as an *outer query*.)

You have many, many variations on how you can code subqueries. Since they *are* queries, all the clauses and other keywords available for queries can be used in them. Our goal here is to simply show the straightforward pattern they follow and, in this case, to demonstrate how they can be used to replace a list of literals.

Now let's look more closely at the `IN` predicate itself. For example, you may want to get a list of all orders entered by employees with IDs of 1 and 6.

Try It Out: Using the IN Predicate

To use the `IN` predicate, do this:

1. Enter the following query into the `QueryProcessor` application, and execute it. You should see the results shown in Figure 13-5. (Scroll down, and you'll see that only rows where `EmployeeID` equals 1 or 6 are selected.)

```
SELECT
   *
FROM
   Orders
WHERE
   EmployeeId IN (1, 6)
ORDER BY
   EmployeeId
```

■ **Tip** Recall that `SELECT *` is actually bad practice in real-world programming. Best practice is to specify explicitly the columns to select. We'll use `SELECT *` for simplicity, but you should use a select list in serious applications.

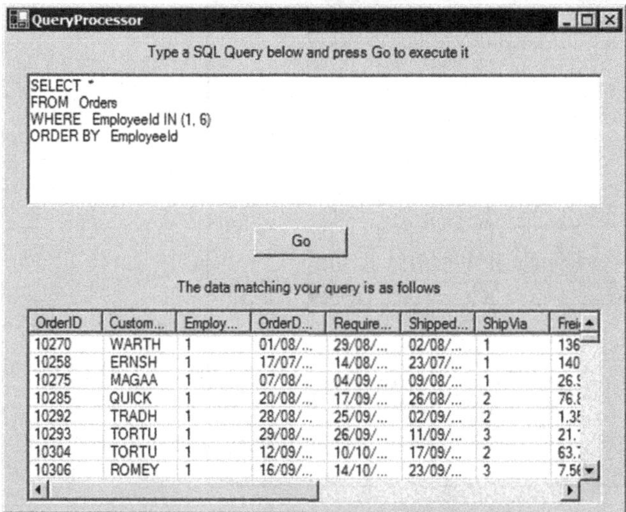

Figure 13-5. *Using the IN predicate*

How It Works

Here, you use a list of literal values with the `IN` operator. The following `WHERE` clause specifies that only rows where `EmployeeID` equals either 1 or 6 should be retrieved:

```
WHERE
   EmployeeId IN (1, 6)
```

The keyword `NOT`, used in used in conjunction with `IN`, selects rows that don't match any value in a list. Let's say you need to get a list of all orders that have been entered by employees other than the ones with IDs of 1 or 6.

Try It Out: Using the NOT IN Predicate

To use the `NOT IN` predicate, do this:

1. Enter the following query into the `QueryProcessor` application, and execute it. You should see the results shown in Figure 13-6.

```
SELECT
   *
FROM
   Orders
WHERE
   EmployeeId NOT IN (1, 6)
ORDER BY
   EmployeeId
```

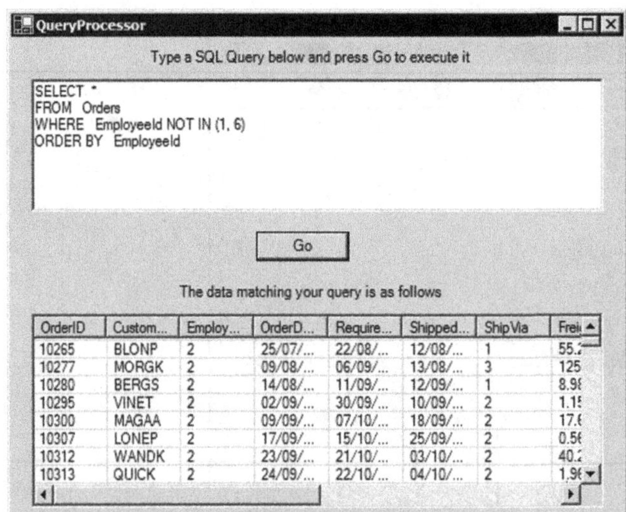

Figure 13-6. *Using the NOT IN predicate*

How It Works

Here, you use the same list of literal values with the `IN` operator. The following `WHERE` clause specifies that only rows where `EmployeeID` doesn't equal either 1 or 6 should be retrieved:

```
WHERE
   EmployeeId NOT IN (1, 6)
```

You can use functions along with the IN operator. For example, the SUBSTRING function returns a portion of a string. You could use this instead of the LIKE predicate if you needed to find all the employees whose last name begins with a *D* or an *S*.

Try It Out: Using a Function with the IN Predicate

To use a function with the IN predicate, do this:

1. Enter the following query into the QueryProcessor application, and execute it. You should see the results shown in Figure 13-7.

```
SELECT
   *
FROM
   Employees
WHERE
   SUBSTRING (lastname, 1, 1) IN ('D', 'S')
```

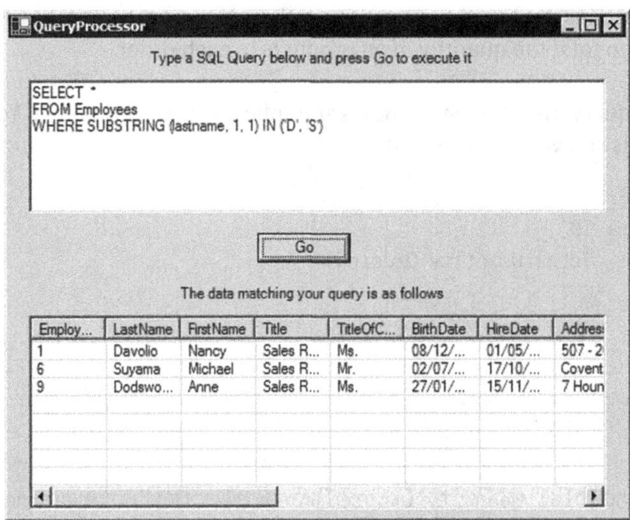

Figure 13-7. *Using a function with the IN predicate*

How It Works

Here, you use a list of literal values with the IN operator, but instead of matching a column against them, you match the result of a function applied against a column value. The following WHERE clause specifies that only rows where the first character of the employee's last name is either *D* or *S* should be retrieved:

```
WHERE
   SUBSTRING (lastname, 1, 1) IN ('D', 'S')
```

In the SUBSTRING function, the first argument specifies the character data type column (or other string expression) from which you want to extract a substring. The second argument specifies the position where you want to begin extracting the substring. In this case, by specifying 1, you start the extract at the first character. The third argument specifies the number of characters you want to extract. In this case, by specifying 1, you extract one character.

The net effect of this function is that, for each row in the table, the first character of the LastName column is extracted by the function. Then the substring is compared to the list. If it matches an entry in the list, the row is selected.

Using GROUP BY

The GROUP BY clause groups rows sharing common values for the purpose of calculating an aggregate. Often you'll want to generate reports from the database with summary figures for a particular column or set of columns. For example, you may want to find out the total quantity for each order from the Order Details table.

Try It Out: Using the GROUP BY Clause

The Order Details table contains the list of products for each order and the quantity of each product ordered. You need to total the quantity of all products in each order.

1. Enter the following query into the QueryProcessor application, and execute it. You should see the results shown in Figure 13-8.

```
SELECT
   OrderId AS 'Order ID',
   SUM(Quantity) AS 'Total Quantity Ordered'
FROM
   [Order Details]
GROUP BY
   OrderId
```

■ **Tip** The literals Order ID and Total Quantity Ordered provide *aliases* for the columns. (In SQL Server you could use square brackets instead of the standard SQL single quotes.) Neither alias is required, but when using functions it's typical to specify an alias. Otherwise the column heading would have been blank (or sum(quantity), depending on your RDBMS). We added the alias for OrderID to demonstrate how you can specify explicit column names in SQL. This is better practice than relying on whatever spelling may automatically be used based on the column name in the database or the query.

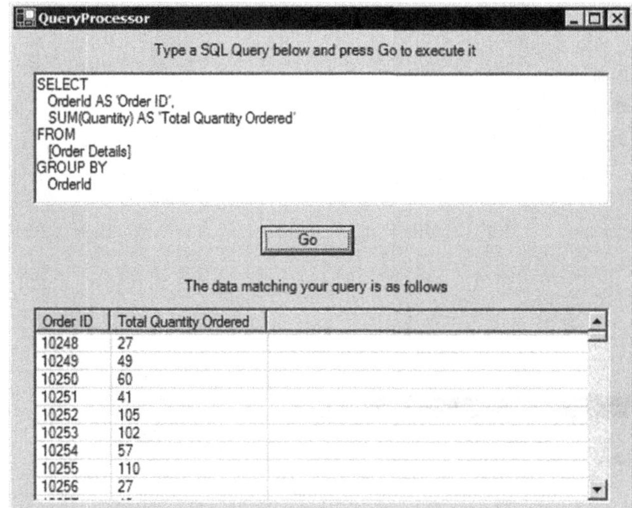

Figure 13-8. *Using the* `GROUP BY` *clause*

How It Works

You use the `SUM` function to total the `Quantity` column of the `Order Details` table by `OrderID`. The alias provides a custom column header for the total.

```
SUM(Quantity) AS 'Total Quantity Ordered'
```

Using Other Aggregates

SQL has several built-in functions that aggregate the values of a column. Aggregate functions return a single value. For example, you can use the aggregate functions to calculate the total number or average value of orders placed. You can find the order with the least value or the most expensive order. Aggregate functions, as their name indicates, work on a set of records and then calculate the appropriate aggregated value. `SUM`, `MIN`, `MAX`, `AVG`, and `COUNT` are the frequently used aggregate functions.

Let's assume you want to find the minimum, maximum, and average number of items of each product from the `Order Details` table.

Try It Out: Using the MIN, MAX, and AVG Functions

To use these functions, do this:

1. Enter the following query into the `QueryProcessor` application, and execute it. You should see the results shown in Figure 13-9.

```
SELECT
   ProductId,
   MIN(Quantity) AS 'Minimum',
   MAX(Quantity) AS 'Maximum',
   AVG(Quantity) AS 'Average'
FROM
   [Order Details]
GROUP BY
   ProductId
ORDER BY
   ProductId
```

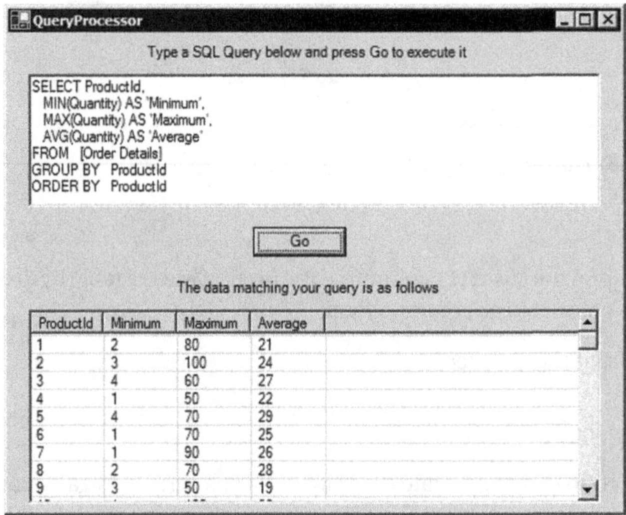

Figure 13-9. *Using the* `MIN`*,* `MAX`*, and* `AVG` *functions*

How It Works

You used the `MIN` and `MAX` functions to find the minimum and maximum values and the `AVG` function to calculate the average value.

```
SELECT
   ProductId,
   MIN(Quantity) AS 'Minimum',
   MAX(Quantity) AS 'Maximum',
   AVG(Quantity) AS 'Average'
FROM
   [Order Details]
```

Since you wanted the results listed by product, you used the GROUP BY clause.

```
GROUP BY
   ProductId
ORDER BY
   ProductId
```

From the result set you see that product 1 had a minimum order quantity of 2, a maximum order quantity of 80, and an average order quantity of 21.

■ **Note** You used an ORDER BY clause to assure the results were in product ID sequence. Some RDBMSs would have inferred this sequence from the GROUP BY clause, but SQL Server doesn't. In general, unless you explicitly use ORDER BY, the sequence of the rows in a result set can't be predicted.

Using Datetime Functions

Although the SQL standard defines a DATETIME data type and its components YEAR, MONTH, DAY, HOUR, MINUTE, and SECOND, it doesn't dictate how an RDBMS makes this data available. Each RDBMS offers a suite of functions that extract parts of DATETIMEs. Let's look at some examples of Transact-SQL datetime functions.

Try It Out: Using Transact-SQL Date and Time Functions

To use Transact-SQL date and time functions, do this:

1. Enter the following query into the QueryProcessor application, and execute it. Widen the first two columns, and you should see the results shown in Figure 13-10.

```
SELECT
   CURRENT_TIMESTAMP          AS [Standard DateTime],
   GETDATE()                  AS [Transact-SQL DateTime],
   DATEPART(YEAR, GETDATE()) AS [DATEPART Year],
   YEAR(GETDATE())            AS [YEAR function],
   DATEPART(HOUR, GETDATE()) AS [HOUR]
```

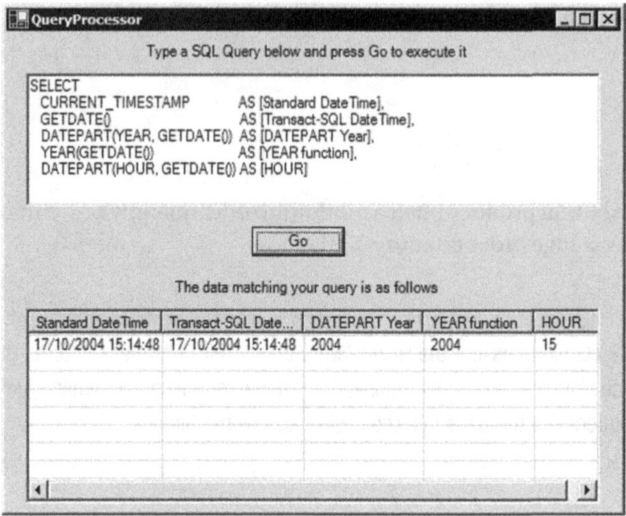

Figure 13-10. *Handling dates and times in Transact-SQL*

How It Works

You used a nonstandard version of a query, omitting the FROM clause, to display the current date and time and individual parts of them. The first two columns in the select list give the complete date and time.

```
CURRENT_TIMESTAMP         AS [Standard DateTime],
GETDATE()                 AS [Transact-SQL DateTime],
```

The first line uses the CURRENT_TIMESTAMP value function of standard SQL; the second uses the GETDATE function of Transact-SQL. They're equivalent in effect, both returning the complete current date and time. (Note that the output format is specific to your RDBMS.)

The next two lines each provide the current year. The first uses the Transact-SQL DATEPART function; the second uses the Transact-SQL YEAR function. Both take a datetime argument and return the integer year. The DATEPART function's first argument specifies what part of a datetime to extract. Note that Transact-SQL doesn't provide a date specifier for extracting a complete date, and it doesn't have a separate DATE function.

```
DATEPART(YEAR, GETDATE()) AS [DATEPART Year],
YEAR(GETDATE())           AS [YEAR function],
```

The final line gets the current hour. The Transact-SQL DATEPART function must be used here since no HOUR function is analogous to the YEAR function. Note that Transact-SQL doesn't provide a time specifier for extracting a complete time, and it doesn't have a separate TIME function.

```
DATEPART(HOUR, GETDATE()) AS [HOUR]
```

You can format dates and times and alternative functions for extracting and converting them in various ways. Dates and times can also be added and subtracted and incremented and decremented. How this is done is RDBMS-specific, though all RDBMSs comply to a reasonable extent with the SQL standard in how they do it. Whatever RDBMS you use, you'll find that dates and times are the most complicated data types to use. But, in all cases you'll find that functions (typically a richer set of them than in Transact-SQL) are the basic tools for working with dates and times.

■ **Tip** When providing date and time input, character string values are typically expected; for example, `6/28/2004` would be the appropriate way to specify the value for a column holding the current date from the example. However, RDBMSs store datetimes in system-specific encodings. When you use date and time data, read the SQL manual for your database carefully to see how to best handle it.

Using CASE Expressions

The `CASE` expression allows an alternative value to be displayed depending on the value of a column. For example, a `CASE` expression can provide *Texas* in a result set for rows that have the value *TX* in the `state` column. Let's take a look at the syntax of the `CASE` expression. It has two different forms: the simple `CASE` and the searched `CASE`.

This is the simple `CASE` syntax, where the `ELSE` part is optional:

```
CASE <case operand>
   WHEN <when operand> THEN
      <when result>
   ELSE
      <else result>
END
```

The `CASE` keyword is followed by a column name or expression that's to be tested against the operand (a scalar value) following the `WHEN` keyword. If `<case operand>` has the same value as `<when operand>`, `<when result>` is used; otherwise, `<else result>` is used as the selection list value.

Try It Out: Using a Simple CASE Expression

To use a simple `CASE` expression, do this:

1. Enter the following query into the `QueryProcessor` application, and execute it. You should see the results as in Figure 13-11.

```
SELECT DISTINCT
  YEAR(OrderDate) AS NumYear,
   CASE YEAR(OrderDate)
      WHEN 1998 THEN
         'Last year'
      ELSE
         'Prior year'
   END AS LabYear
FROM
   Orders
```

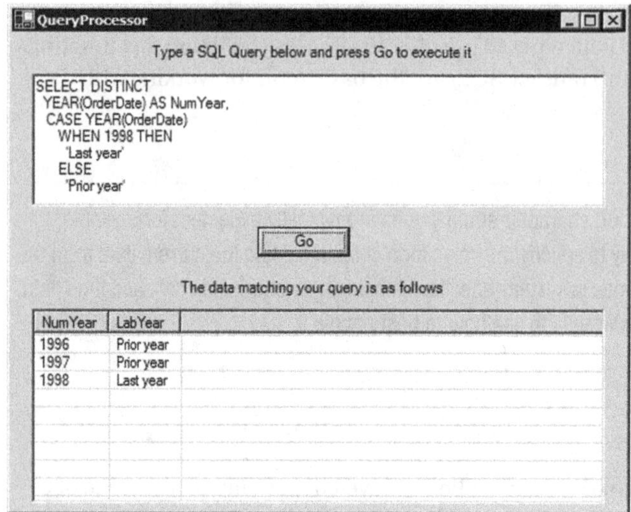

Figure 13-11. *Using a simple CASE expression*

How It Works

You're simply labeling years as either *Last year* or *Prior year* depending on whether they were 1998 (the last year for orders in this version of the `Northwind` database) or earlier (in this database none are later than 1998). The first two lines get a list of the distinct years (in the `Orders` table).

```
SELECT DISTINCT
  YEAR(OrderDate) AS NumYear,
```

Note that you specify an alias `NumYear`, but since it doesn't include blanks, you don't have to enclose it in single quotes (or brackets).

The next item in the select list (note that a `CASE` expression is used just like a column name or function call) is a simple `CASE` expression where you provide the result of the `YEAR` function applied to the order date as the `<case operand>`, the numeric literal 1998 as the `<when operand>`, and two strings to label the last year and the prior years, depending on whether the year is 1998 (in other words, whether it matches the `<when operand>`).

```
CASE YEAR(OrderDate)
   WHEN 1998 THEN
     'Last year'
   ELSE
     'Prior year'
END AS LabYear
```

Note that since a `CASE` expression is merely another member of a select list, you can (and do) give it an alias, `LabYear`.

Let's modify the `CASE` expression to get an idea of how flexible it can be.

Try It Out: Using a More Complex Simple CASE Expression

For a more complex simple [sic] CASE expression, try this:

1. Enter the following query into the QueryProcessor application, and execute it. You should see the results as in Figure 13-12.

```
SELECT DISTINCT
   YEAR (OrderDate) AS NumYear,
   CASE YEAR (OrderDate)
      WHEN 1998 THEN
         STR (YEAR (OrderDate))
      ELSE
         CASE YEAR (OrderDate)
            WHEN 1997 THEN
               'Prior year'
            ELSE
               'Earlier'
         END
   END AS LabYear
FROM
   Orders
```

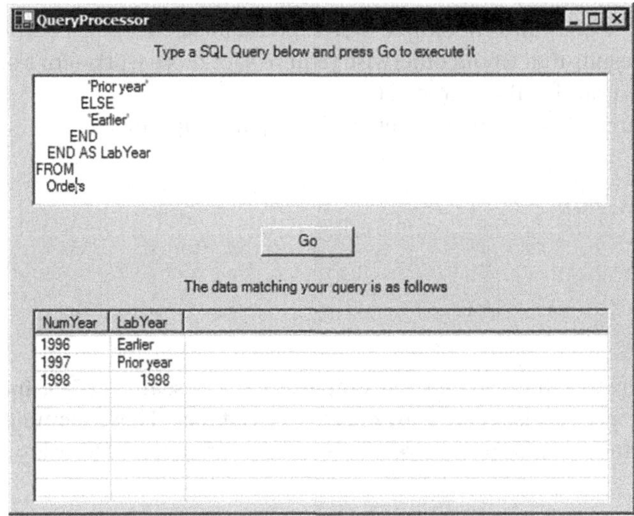

Figure 13-12. *Using a more complex simple CASE expression*

How It Works

You do a couple interesting things here. First, you change the label for the last year to the year itself rather than a string, showing that the <when operand> can be a data value (here, in fact, the result of a function applied to a column).

```
WHEN 1998 THEN
   STR (YEAR (OrderDate))
```

Note that you use the STR function to convert the integer returned by YEAR to a string, since you're planning to use strings for the alternative labels, and a CASE expression must return values of a single data type.

You then nest a CASE expression inside the original ELSE (they can also be nested in the WHEN part) to support labeling the other years separately. You label 1997 as *Prior year* and all others as *Earlier*.

```
   ELSE
      CASE YEAR (OrderDate)
         WHEN 1997 THEN
            'Prior year'
         ELSE
            'Earlier'
      END
END AS LabYear
```

Many other variations are possible. The simple CASE expression can be quite complex. Exploit it to achieve query results that would otherwise require a lot more work—for both you and the database! Now, let's examine the searched CASE.

The following is the searched CASE syntax, where the ELSE part is optional:

```
CASE
   WHEN <search condition> THEN
      <when result>
   ELSE
      <else result>
END
```

Note the differences between the searched and simple CASEs. The searched CASE has no <case operand>, and <when operand> is replaced by <search condition>. These seemingly minor changes add an enormous amount of power. Let's modify the simple CASE example to demonstrate.

Try It Out: Using a Searched CASE Expression

To use a searched CASE expression, do this:

1. Enter the following query into the QueryProcessor application, and execute it. You should see the results as in Figure 13-13.

```
SELECT DISTINCT
   YEAR(OrderDate) AS NumYear,
   CASE
      WHEN
         YEAR(OrderDate) =
            (
            SELECT
               MAX(YEAR(OrderDate))
            FROM
               Orders
            )
      THEN
        'Last year'
      ELSE
        'Prior year'
   END AS LabYear
FROM
   Orders
```

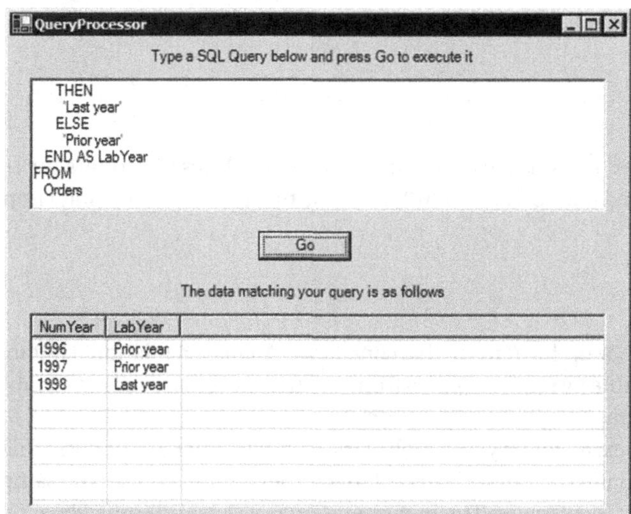

Figure 13-13. *Using a searched* CASE *expression*

How It Works

The original query, though it worked, was severely limited in that it works correctly only if 1998 is really the last year for orders. You corrected this flaw with a searched CASE. Now the query will do the right thing whatever years are in the Orders table! You replace the numeric literal, `<when operand>`, like so:

```
WHEN 1998 THEN
```

with a predicate (which can be just as complex as any predicate in a WHERE clause), like so:

```
YEAR(OrderDate) =
   (
   SELECT
       MAX(YEAR(OrderDate))
   FROM
      Orders
   )
```

This predicate includes a subquery. Remember, subqueries are simply queries embedded in other queries. Here, one is embedded in a CASE expression rather than in an IN predicate (as demonstrated earlier in the chapter). The value returned by the subquery is the maximum year in the Orders table, so whenever you run the query, you'll get the correct last year—without ever having to know what it is.

■ **Note** Complex queries are a normal part of database applications. The more you learn about SQL, the better you'll be able to exploit its considerable power. All major RDBMSs have *very* intelligent query optimizers that can find efficient access paths for even complex queries. You should code whatever complexity you need, relying on the optimizer to do its job; however, even simple queries can sometimes be inefficient, depending on how they're coded. In addition to learning SQL, learn whatever tool your RDBMS offers to analyze query access paths.

You've merely scratched the surface of the many, many facilities SQL offers for coding complex, highly sophisticated queries. Let's now look at the most (but far from only) important one.

Using Joins

Most queries require information from more than one table. A *join* is a relational database operation that produces a table by retrieving data from two (not necessarily distinct) tables and matching their rows according to a *join specification.*

Different types of joins exist, which you'll look at individually, but keep in mind that every join is a *binary* operation; that is, one table is joined to another, which may be the same table since tables can be joined to themselves. The join operation is a rich and somewhat complex topic. The next sections will cover the basics, using the Northwind database.

Using Inner Joins

An inner join is the most frequently used join. It returns only rows that satisfy the join specification. Although in theory any relational operator (such as > or <) can be used in the join specification, almost always the equality operator (=) is used. Joins using the equality operator are called *natural joins.*

The basic syntax for an inner join is as follows:

```
SELECT
   <select list>
FROM
   left-table INNER JOIN right-table
   ON
   <join specification>
```

Notice that `INNER JOIN` is a binary operation, so it has two operands, `left-table` and `right-table`, which may be base tables or anything (for example, a table produced by a subquery or by another join) that can be queried. The `ON` keyword begins the join specification, which can contain anything that could be used in a `WHERE` clause.

Let's look at an example, where you retrieve a list of orders, the IDs of the customers who placed them, and the last name of the employees who took them.

Try It Out: Writing an Inner Join

To write an inner join, do this:

1. Enter the following query into the `QueryProcessor` application, and execute it. You should see the results as in Figure 13-14.

```
SELECT
   Orders.OrderId,
   Orders.CustomerId,
   Employees.LastName
FROM
   Orders INNER JOIN Employees
   ON
   Orders.EmployeeId = Employees.EmployeeId
```

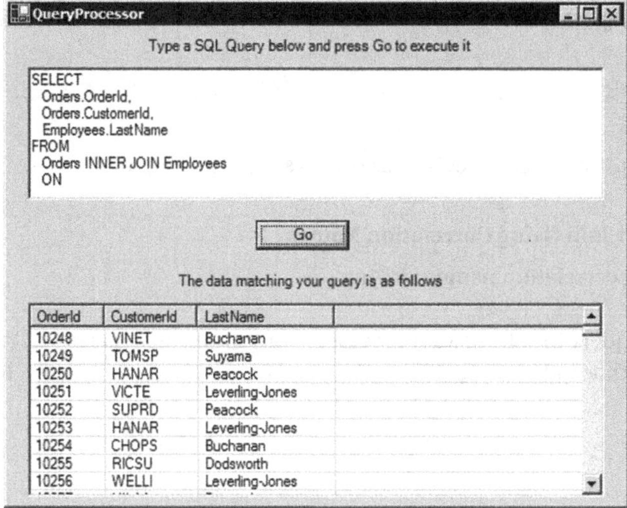

Figure 13-14. *Coding an inner join*

How It Works

Let's start with the select list.

```
SELECT
   Orders.OrderId,
   Orders.CustomerId,
   Employees.LastName
```

Since you're selecting columns from two tables, you need to identify which table a column comes from, which you do by prefixing the table name and a dot (.) to the column name. This is known as *disambiguation*, or removing ambiguity so the database manager knows which column to use. Though this has to be done only for columns that appear in both tables, best practice is to qualify all columns with their table names.

The following `FROM` clause specifies both the tables you're joining and the kind of join you're using:

```
FROM
   Orders INNER JOIN Employees
```

It also specifies the criteria for joining them.

```
   ON
   Orders.EmployeeId = Employees.EmployeeId
```

The inner join on `EmployeeId` produces a table composed of three columns: `OrderId`, `CustomerId`, and `LastName`. The data is retrieved from rows in `Orders` and `Employees` where their `EmployeeId` columns have the same value. Any rows in `Orders` that don't match rows in `Employees` are ignored and vice versa. (This isn't the case here, but you'll see an example soon.) An inner join always produces only rows that satisfy the join specification.

■ **Note** Columns used for joining don't have to appear in the select list. In fact, `EmployeeID` isn't in the select list of the example query.

Joins can be quite complicated. Let's revise this one to simplify things a bit.

Try It Out: Writing an Inner Join Using Correlation Names

To write an inner join using correlation names, do this:

1. Enter the following query into the `QueryProcessor` application, and execute it. You should see the results as in Figure 13-15.

```
SELECT
   o.OrderId,
   o.CustomerId,
   e.LastName
FROM
   Orders o INNER JOIN Employees e
   ON
   o.EmployeeId = e.EmployeeId
```

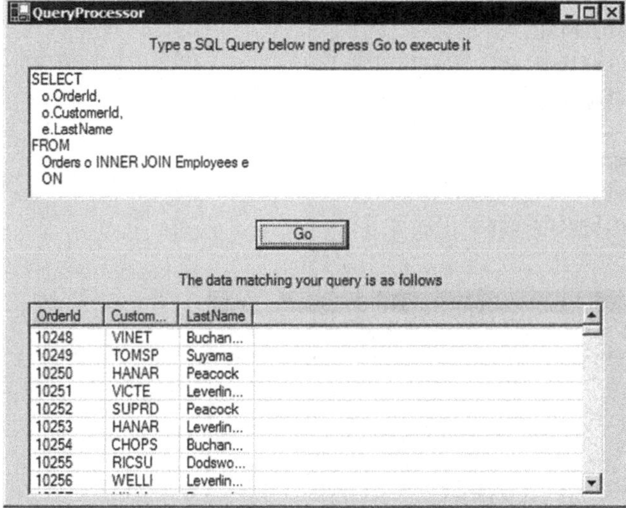

Figure 13-15. *Coding an inner join using correlation names*

How It Works

You've simplified the table references by providing a *correlation name* for each table. This is somewhat similar to providing column aliases, but correlation names are intended to be used as alternative names for tables. Column aliases are used more for labeling than for referencing columns.

```
FROM
   Orders o INNER JOIN Employees e
```

You can now refer to `Orders` as `o` and to `Employees` as `e`. Correlation names can be as long as table names and can be in mixed case, but obviously the shorter they are, the easier they are to code. You used the correlation names in both the select list and the `ON` clause.

```
SELECT
   o.OrderId,
   o.CustomerId,
   e.LastName
FROM
   Orders o INNER JOIN Employees e
   ON
   o.EmployeeId = e.EmployeeId
```

Let's do another variation, so you can see how to use correlation names and aliases together.

Try It Out: Writing an Inner Join Using Correlation Names and Aliases

To write an inner join using correlation names and aliases, do this:

1. Enter the following query into the `QueryProcessor` application, and execute it. You should see the results as in Figure 13-16.

```
SELECT
   o.OrderId    AS OrderID,
   o.CustomerId AS CustomerID,
   e.LastName   AS Employee
FROM
   Orders o JOIN Employees e
   ON
   o.EmployeeId = e.EmployeeId
```

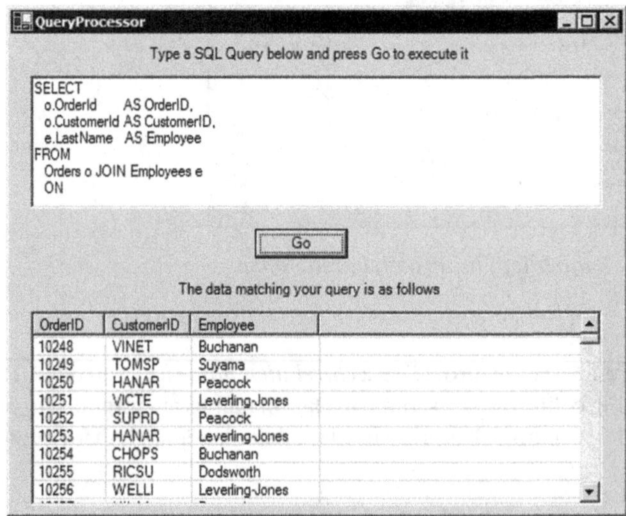

Figure 13-16. *Coding an inner join using correlation names and aliases*

How It Works

You simply add aliases for each column in the select list. This produced more customized column headings. It has no effect on the rest of the query.

```
SELECT
   o.OrderId    AS OrderID,
   o.CustomerId AS CustomerID,
   e.LastName   AS Employee
```

You also remove the keyword INNER from the join operator, just to see that it's optional. It's better practice to use it, since it clearly distinguishes inner joins from *outer joins*, which you'll look at soon.

```
FROM
   Orders o JOIN Employees e
```

As the next example of inner joins, you'll look at their original—but deprecated—syntax. You may see this frequently in legacy code, and it still works with most RDBMSs, but the SQL standard may not allow it in the future.

Try It Out: Writing an Inner Join Using the Original Deprecated Syntax

To write an inner join using the original deprecated syntax, do this:

1. Enter the following query into the QueryProcessor application, and execute it. You should see the results as in Figure 13-17.

```
SELECT
   o.OrderId    AS OrderID,
   o.CustomerId AS CustomerID,
   e.LastName   AS Employee
FROM
   Orders o, Employees e
WHERE
   o.EmployeeId = e.EmployeeId
```

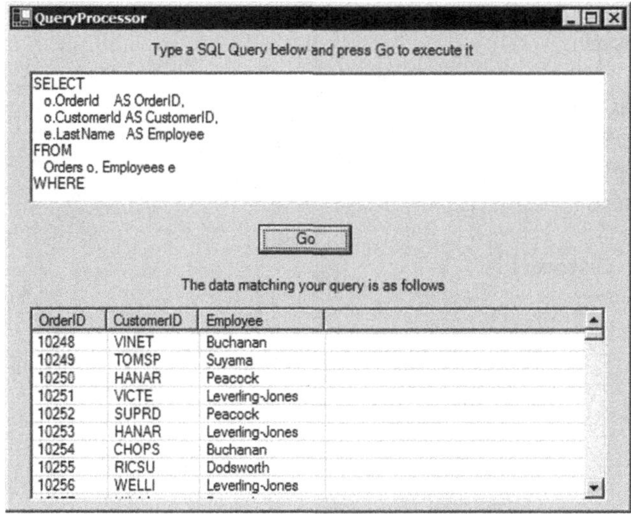

Figure 13-17. *Coding an inner join using original syntax*

How It Works

Note the differences in how you specify the join operator with a comma, instead of `INNER JOIN`, and how you used a `WHERE`, instead of an `ON`, clause.

```
FROM
   Orders o, Employees e
WHERE
   o.EmployeeId = e.EmployeeId
```

This syntax was the only one available until the 1992 SQL standard. Any number of tables could be specified, separated by commas. All join predicates had to be specified in a single `WHERE` clause. Although you haven't seen an example, in the new syntax each join is a distinct operation on two tables and has its own `ON` clause, so joining more than two tables requires multiple join operators, each with its own `ON` clause. The new syntax is preferred not only because the old syntax may someday be unsupported, but also because it forces you to specify precisely (and think clearly about) what joins you need.

As the final inner join example, you'll see how to perform joins on more than two tables with the new syntax.

Try It Out: Writing an Inner Join of Three Tables

You'll replace the customer ID with the customer name. To get it, you have to access the `Customers` table. Enter the following query into the `QueryProcessor` application, and execute it. If you widen the `CustomerName` column, you should see the results in Figure 13-18.

```
SELECT
   o.OrderId     AS OrderID,
   c.CompanyName AS 'Customer Name',
   e.LastName    AS Employee
FROM
   Orders o INNER JOIN Employees e
   ON
      o.EmployeeId = e.EmployeeId
      INNER JOIN Customers c
      ON
         o.CustomerId = c.CustomerId
```

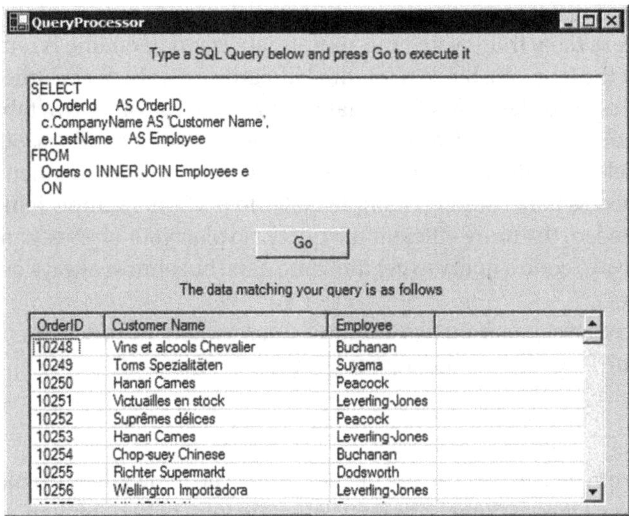

Figure 13-18. *Coding an inner join of three tables*

How It Works

First, you modified the select list, replacing `CustomerID` from the `Orders` table with `CompanyName` from the `Customers` table.

```
SELECT
   o.OrderId      AS OrderID,
   c.CompanyName AS 'Customer Name',
   e.LastName     AS Employee
```

Second, you added a second inner join, as always with two operands: the table produced by the first join and the base table `Customers`. You can use parentheses to enclose joins and make them clearer when you use multiple joins (although you didn't do it here). Furthermore, since joins produce tables, their results can also be associated with correlation names for reference in later joins and even in the select list, but such complexity is beyond the scope of this discussion.

```
FROM
   Orders o INNER JOIN Employees e
   ON
      o.EmployeeId = e.EmployeeId
      INNER JOIN Customers c
      ON
         o.CustomerId = c.CustomerId
```

What happens is this: The result of the first join, which matched orders to employees, is matched against the `Customers` table from which the appropriate customer name is retrieved for each matching row from the first join. Since referential integrity exists between `Orders` and both `Employees` and `Customers`, all `Orders` rows have matching rows in the other two tables.

How the database actually satisfies such a query depends on a number of things, but joins are such an integral part of relational database operations that query optimizers are themselves optimized to find efficient access paths among multiple tables to perform multiple joins. However, the fewer joins needed, the more efficient the query, so plan your queries carefully. Usually you have several ways to code a query to get the same data, but almost always only one of them is the most efficient.

Now you know how to retrieve data from two or more tables—when the rows match. What about rows that don't match? That's where outer joins come in.

Using Outer Joins

Outer joins return *all* rows from (at least) one of the joined tables even if rows in one table don't match rows in the other. Three types of outer joins exist: left outer join, right outer join, and full outer join. The terms *left* and *right* refer to the operands on the left and right of the join operator. (Refer to the basic syntax for the inner join, and you'll see why we called the operands `left-table` and `right-table`.) In a left outer join, all rows from the left table will be retrieved whether they having matching rows in the right table. Conversely, in a right outer join, all rows from the right table will be retrieved whether they have matching rows in the left table. In a full outer join, all rows from both tables are returned.

■ **Tip** Left and right outer joins are logically equivalent. It's always possible to convert a left join into a right join by changing the operator and flipping the operands or a right join into a left with a similar change. So, only one of these operators is actually needed. Which one you choose is basically a matter of personal preference, but a useful rule of thumb is to use either left or right, but not both in the same query. The query optimizer won't care, but humans find it much easier to follow a complex query if the joins always go in the same direction.

When is this useful? Quite frequently. In fact, whenever a parent-child relationship exists between tables, despite the fact that referential integrity is maintained, some parent rows may not have related rows in the child table. (And, though we didn't mention it earlier, child rows may be allowed to have null foreign key values and therefore not match any row in the parent table.) This situation doesn't exist in the original `Orders` and `Employees` data, so you'll have to add some data before you can see the effect of outer joins.

You need to add an employee so you have a row in the `Employees` table that doesn't have related rows in `Orders`. To keep things simple, you'll provide data only for the columns that aren't nullable.

Try It Out: Adding an Employee with `QueryProcessor`

To add an employee with `QueryProcessor`, do this:

1. Enter the following SQL into the QueryProcessor application, and execute it. You should see the (lack of) results, as in Figure 13-19.

```
INSERT INTO Employees
   (FirstName, LastName)
VALUES
   ('Dave', 'Arnold')
```

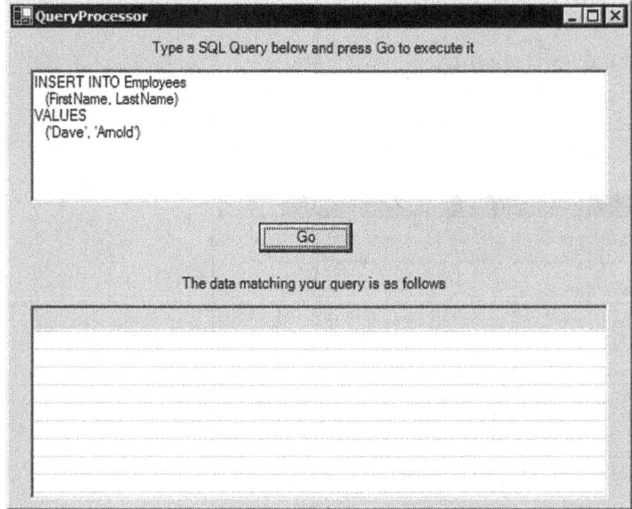

Figure 13-19. *Adding an employee with QueryProcessor*

How It Works

Although QueryProcessor isn't really designed to handle SQL statements, it submits them to the database. Since statements don't return result sets, you have no output to display. You submit a single INSERT statement, providing the two required columns for the Employees table. Of the other columns, EmployeeID is an IDENTITY column, so you can't provide a value for it, and the rest are nullable, so you don't need to provide values for them.

```
INSERT INTO Employees
   (FirstName, LastName)
VALUES
   ('Dave', 'Arnold')
```

You now have a new employee, Dave Arnold, who has never taken an order.

Now, let's say you want a list of all orders taken by all employees—but this list must include *all* employees, even those who haven't taken any orders.

Try It Out: Using LEFT OUTER JOIN

To use LEFT OUTER JOIN, do this:

1. Enter the following SQL into the `QueryProcessor` application, and execute it. You should see the results as in Figure 13-20.

```
SELECT
   e.FirstName,
   e.LastName,
   o.OrderId
FROM
   Employees e LEFT OUTER JOIN Orders o
   ON
      e.EmployeeId = o.EmployeeId
ORDER BY
   2, 1
```

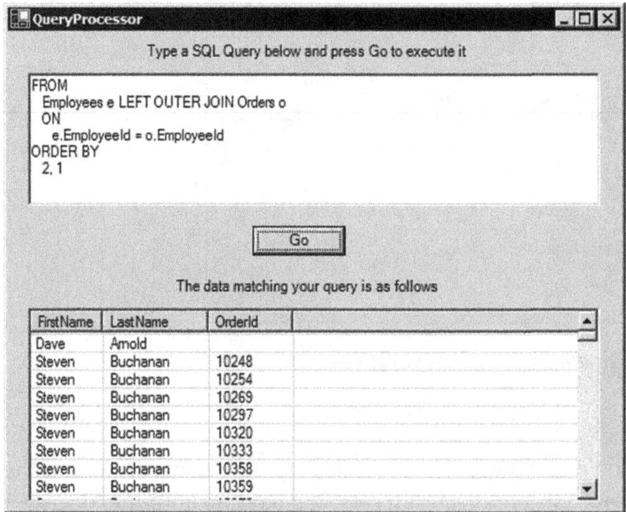

Figure 13-20. *Coding a left outer join*

How It Works

Had you used an inner join you would have missed the row for the new employee. (Try it to see for yourself.) The only new SQL in the `FROM` clause is the join operator itself.

```
FROM
   Employees e LEFT OUTER JOIN Orders o
```

You also added an `ORDER BY` clause, to sort the result set by first name within last name, to see that the kind of join has no effect on the rest of the query, and to see an alternate way to specify columns, by position number within the select list rather than by name. This technique is convenient and may be the only way to do it for columns that are produced by expressions (for example, by the `SUM` function).

```
ORDER BY
   2, 1
```

Note that the OrderID column for the new employee is blank. This is because the column is NULL, since no value exists for it. The same holds true for any columns from the table that don't have matching rows (in this case, the right table).

You can obtain the same result by placing the Employees table on the right and the Orders table on the left of the join operator and changing the operator to RIGHT OUTER JOIN. (Try it!) Remember to flip the correlation names, too.

The keyword OUTER is optional and is typically omitted. Left and right joins are *always* outer joins.

Using Other Joins

The SQL standard also provides for FULL OUTER, UNION, and CROSS JOINs (and even NATURAL JOIN, basically an inner join using equality predicates), but these are much less used and beyond the scope of this book. We won't provide examples, but this section contains a brief summary of them.

A FULL OUTER join is like a combination of both the LEFT and RIGHT OUTER joins. All rows from both tables will be retrieved, even if they have no related rows in the other table.

A UNION join is unlike outer joins in that it doesn't match rows. Instead, it creates a table that has all the rows from both tables. For two tables, it's equivalent to the following query:

```
SELECT
   *
FROM
   table1
UNION ALL
   SELECT
      *
   FROM
      table2
```

The tables must have the same number of columns, and the data types of corresponding columns must be compatible (able to hold the same types of data).

A CROSS join combines all rows from both tables. It doesn't provide for a join specification, since this would be irrelevant. It produces a table with all columns from both tables and as many rows as the product of the number of rows in each table. The result is also known as a *Cartesian product*, since that's the mathematical term for associating each element (row) of one set (table) with all elements of another set. For example, if there are five rows and five columns in table A and ten rows and three columns in table B, the cross join of A and B would produce a table with fifty rows and eight columns. This join operation is not only virtually inapplicable to any real-world query, but it's also a potentially very expensive process for even small real-world databases. (Imagine using it for a production tables with thousands or even millions of rows.)

Summary

In this chapter, you learned how to construct more sophisticated queries using the following SQL features:

- The DISTINCT keyword to eliminate duplicates from the result set
- Subqueries, which are queries embedded in other queries
- The IN predicate, using lists of literals and lists returned by subqueries
- Aggregate functions such as MIN, MAX, SUM, and AVG
- The GROUP BY clause for categorizing aggregates
- CASE expressions for providing column values based on logical tests
- Functions for accessing the components of the datetime data type
- Inner, outer, and other joins

You've now looked in closer detail at all the elements of a database that were used in previous chapters. As a result, the next few chapters will sail you into uncharted database territory. You'll start by learning about two more important database objects that build upon your knowledge of tables and SQL queries: views and stored procedures.

CHAPTER 14

Understanding Views and Stored Procedures

In this chapter you'll learn about *views* and *stored procedures*. Views are named queries that produce *viewed tables* (to use the standard SQL definition) that can be used in much the same way as the tables (or other views) on which they're based. Stored procedures are routines known to the database manager that allow you to package SQL in an optimal fashion for reuse.

Both have many advantages. In this chapter, you'll look at the following:

- What a view is and how to create one
- What a stored procedure is and how to create one
- How to provide input to and handle output from a stored procedure
- How to use views and stored procedures in VB .NET programs

Using Views

Views are often used for security to limit access to data. You can create views that don't include columns (and rows) containing sensitive information, thereby hiding the data from users. This is important, but it's only one aspect of the view concept.

The fundamental purpose of views is to provide convenient perspectives on data, minimizing what users need to know to get the information they want. Views allow you to hide not just data but database complexity. Since they're queries, and queries are operations on tables that produce a single table, you can specify whatever complicated operations you need (for example, joining tables and performing calculations) yet present the end results as just another (viewed) table. Unlike a base table, a view doesn't actually contain data. For this reason views are often called *virtual tables*.

The following are some common uses for views:

- **Joining multiple tables so they look like a single table**: You can use views to join both tables and other views. Querying against such views is much simpler than working with the base tables themselves.
- **Restricting users to specific rows**: Views can be highly selective. Users can be restricted to only those views that expose the data they're allowed to see.

- **Restricting users to specific columns:** Only the columns in a view's select list are exposed. Even the column names can be changed so the nature of the underlying data is clarified or disguised.
- **Aggregating information:** Views can summarize data, thus providing more precise information while hiding details.

Let's look at the views that are already in the `Northwind` database. In Server Explorer, expand the Views node. You'll see the views in Figure 14-1.

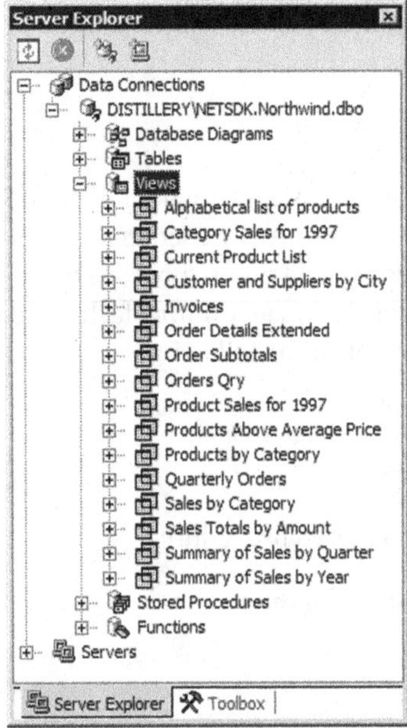

Figure 14-1. *Northwind views*

You can open a view by right-clicking it and selecting Retrieve Data from View. You can see the query behind the view by right-clicking the view and selecting Design View.

You can create views in an MSDE database in two ways.

- Using Server Explorer
- Executing the `CREATE VIEW` statement

If you're using a full SQL Server instance, you can also use its Query Analyzer to execute the `CREATE VIEW` statement or its Enterprise Manager to create views. In any case (or database), you can write a VB .NET program to execute the `CREATE VIEW` statement.

Since you're using MSDE, you'll look at using Server Explorer first, before looking at the `CREATE VIEW` statement itself.

Try It Out: Creating and Using a View from Server Explorer

Let's create a simple view and use it in Server Explorer. Since, as explained before, a view is a saved query, you'll define a query involving the `Employees` and `Orders` tables.

1. In Server Explorer, right-click the Views node and select New View.
2. A dialog pops up and lists all the tables in the database. Select the `Orders` and `Employees` tables, and then click Add and then click Close. The tables that are selected will be placed in a diagram pane. Check the boxes next to EmployeeID, LastName, and FirstName in `Employees` and OrderID in `Orders`. As you check the columns, notice that they're added to the query in the third pane. Right-click anywhere outside the diagram components, and select Run. The screen should appear as in Figure 14-2.

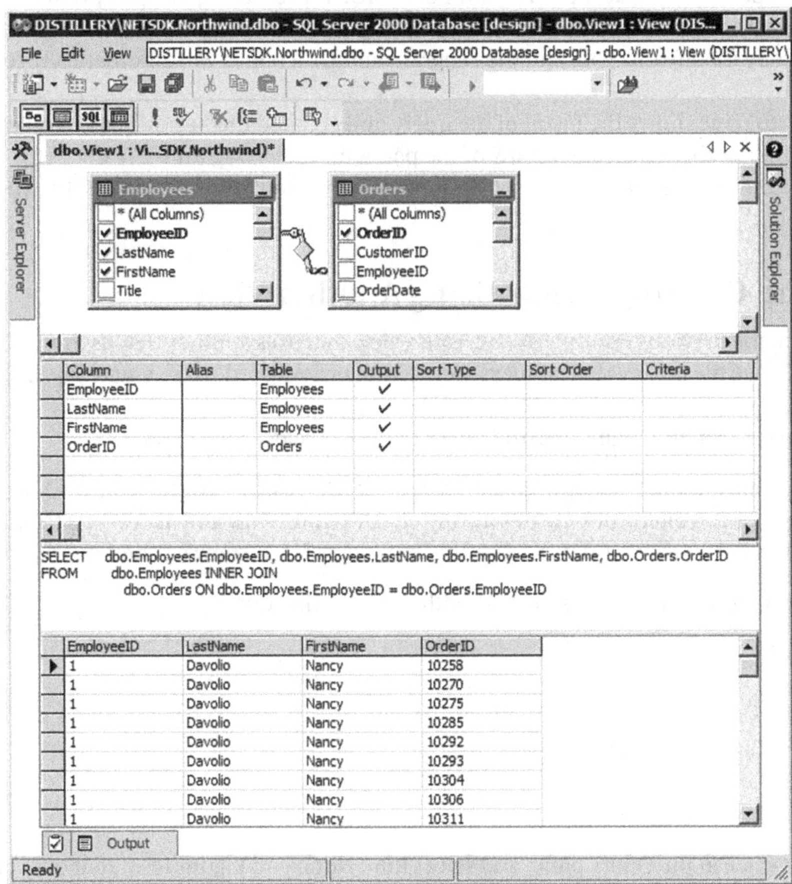

Figure 14-2. *Creating a view with Server Explorer*

3. Save the view by clicking the Save icon. A window pops up and asks you to name the view. Name it `EmployeesAndOrders`, and then click `OK`. Behind the scenes a `CREATE VIEW` statement is executed to create the view.

How It Works

The dialog box is divided into four panes. The Diagram pane shows the tables, their columns, and the relationship between the tables. In this case, a one-to-many relationship exists between `Employees` and `Orders`.

The second pane is called the Grid pane, and it shows the columns selected in the query. Since you checked `EmployeeID`, `LastName`, `FirstName`, and `OrderId`, they appear in the column headed `Column`, with their tables in the column headed `Table`. Notice that the `Output` column is checked; this means that the corresponding column in the table will be listed in the query output.

The third pane is the Query pane. It shows the SQL representing the query that makes up the view. As you add or remove tables or columns, this pane will display the modified SQL. You can also directly modify the SQL, and the Diagram and Grid panes will automatically reflect the changes.

The fourth pane shows the result of the query and is called the Results pane. You can see the data in the view by right-clicking any of the panes and selecting Run.

Let's see how to use the `EmployeesAndOrders` view to obtain information for the employee with ID 1 only.

Try It Out: Creating a View Using Another View

Expanding on the previous example, let's create a view that uses another view as though it were a table. You'll use the `EmployeesAndOrders` view but select only orders for employee 1.

1. In Server Explorer, right-click the Views node and select New View.

2. When the Add Table dialog appears, click Close. Don't select any tables. (The View tab at the top of this dialog box creates a copy of an existing view and allows you to alter it afterward. You won't use it in this book, but it's useful to know it's there.)

3. In the Query pane, replace the SQL with the following query:

```
SELECT
   *
FROM
   EmployeesAndOrders
WHERE
   EmployeeId = 1
```

4. Right-click in the Query pane, and select Run. Notice (in Figure 14-3) that only orders for employee 1 are returned.

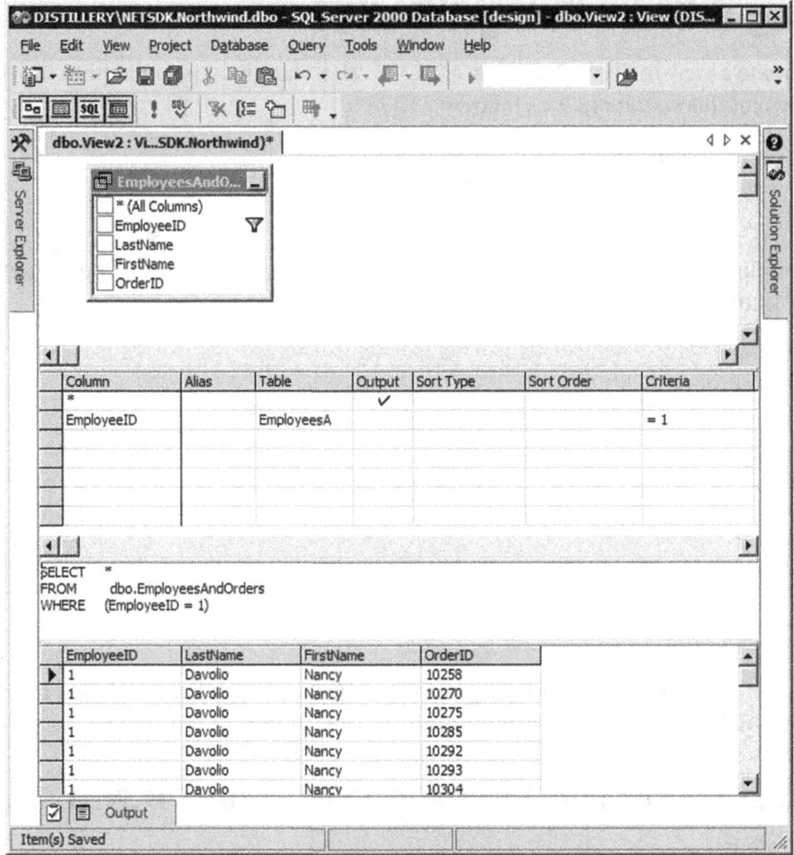

Figure 14-3. *Creating a view based on a view*

5. Save the view as `EmployeesAndOrders_1`. You can use this view like a table. Double-click it in Server Explorer, and observe that the results are always displayed for employee 1.

How It Works

You used the `EmployeesAndOrders` view to create another view. While the `EmployeesAndOrders` view gets all orders taken by all employees, the `EmployeesAndOrders_1` view selects only orders taken by employee 1.

You can also create ad hoc queries (that is, queries that aren't saved) using `EmployeesAndOrders` to obtain information about other employees as well, but only with the information for the columns that are in the view.

Creating a View Using VB .NET

When you create a view in Server Explorer, a `CREATE VIEW` statement is run behind the scenes. The basic form of this statement is as follows:

```
CREATE VIEW <view name>
AS
<query>
```

For example, the `EmployeesAndOrders_1` view could have been created using the following `CREATE VIEW` statement:

```
CREATE VIEW
   EmployeesAndOrders_1
AS
SELECT
   EmployeeId,
   LastName,
   FirstName,
   OrderId
FROM
   EmployeesAndOrders
```

Now you'll use a custom VB .NET program to create views. You'll also see how to access a view from VB .NET and display the results.

Try It Out: Creating and Accessing a View from VB .NET

Follow these steps:

1. Create a new solution named `Chapter14_Examples`.
2. Add a VB .NET Windows application named `ViewsAndSPs` to the solution. Rename `Form1.vb` to `ViewsAndSPs.vb`. Change the `Text` property of the form to `Views and Stored Procedures`.
3. Add a `TabControl` control, and click the *Add Tab* link in the Properties pane twice to create two tab pages. Change their text to `Views` and `StoredProcedures`.
4. To the Views page add buttons, text boxes, and a list view, as shown in Figure 14-4. Name the controls and set their properties as in Table 14-1. (You'll design the Stored Procedures page later in the chapter.)

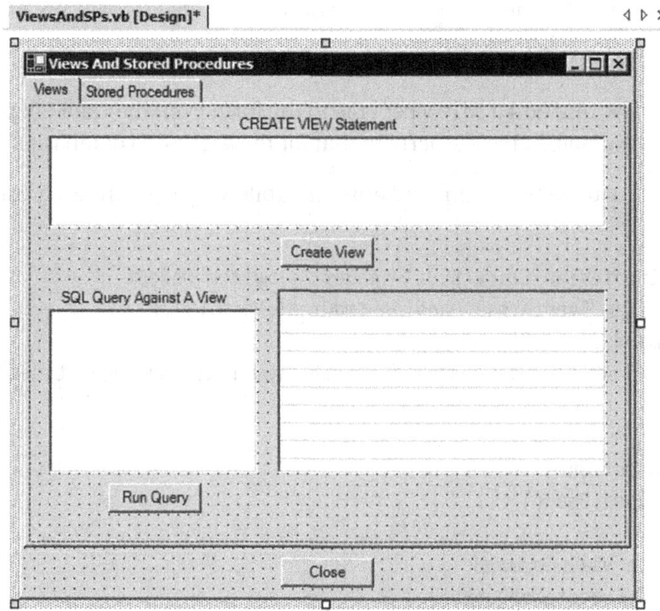

Figure 14-4. *ViewsAndSPs tab page layout*

Table 14-1. *Views Tab Page Attributes*

Control	Name	Remarks
TabControl	tabControl1	Add two pages to the TabPages property, and specify the Text property as Views and Stored Procedures, respectively.
Label	label1	Text: CREATE VIEW statement.
TextBox	txtCreateView	To type in the SQL statement to create a view. Set the Multiline property to True.
Button	cmdCreateView	Text: Create View. To execute the statement in txtCreateView.
Label	label2	Text: Querying a View
TextBox	txtSQL	For queries against views. Set the Multiline property to True.
ListView	lvwViewRS	To show the data retrieved by the view. Set the GridLines property to True and the View property to Details.
Button	cmdQueryView	Text: Run Query. To execute the query typed in txtSQL.
Button	cmdClose	Text: Close. To close the form.

5. Add an `Imports` directive for the SQL Server data provider to the `ViewsAndSPs.vb` file.

```
Imports System.Data.SqlClient
```

6. Return to Design view, and add a `SqlConnection` to the form from the Data tab of the Toolbox. Set its `ConnectionString` property to that for the `Northwind` database.

7. Double-click the Create View button, and enter the following code in its click event handler:

```
Private Sub cmdCreateView_Click(ByVal sender As System.Object, _
   ByVal e As System.EventArgs) Handles cmdCreateView.Click
   ' Create Command
   Dim ViewCommand As New SqlCommand(txtCreateView.Text, SqlConnection1)

   Try
      ' Open Connection
      SqlConnection1.Open()

      ' Run Create View Command
      ViewCommand.ExecuteNonQuery()

      ' Display success message
      MessageBox.Show("View was created successfully")

   Catch ex As SqlException
      ' Display error message
      MessageBox.Show("Could not create the view. " & _
         ex.Message)
   Catch ex As Exception
      ' Display error message
      MessageBox.Show("An application error occurred." & _
         ex.ToString())
   Finally
      ' Close Connection
      SqlConnection1.Close()
   End Try
End Sub
```

8. Double-click the Run Query button, and enter the following code in its click event handler:

```
Private Sub cmQueryView_Click(ByVal sender As System.Object, _
   ByVal e As System.EventArgs) Handles cmQueryView.Click
   ' Clear list view control
   lvwViewRS.Columns.Clear()
   lvwViewRS.Items.Clear()

   ' Create Command
   Dim QueryCommand As New SqlCommand(txtSQL.Text, SqlConnection1)
```

```
    Try
       ' Open Connection
       SqlConnection1.Open()

       ' Execute Command and Get Data
       Dim NewReader As SqlDataReader = QueryCommand.ExecuteReader()

       ' Get column names for list view from data reader
       For i As Integer = 0 To NewReader.FieldCount - 1
          Dim header As New ColumnHeader
          header.Text = NewReader.GetName(i)
          lvwViewRS.Columns.Add(header)
       Next

       ' Get rows of data and show in list view
       While NewReader.Read()
          ' Create list view item
          Dim NewItem As New ListViewItem

          ' Specify text and subitems of list view
          NewItem.Text = NewReader.GetValue(0).ToString()
          For i As Integer = 1 To NewReader.FieldCount - 1
             NewItem.SubItems.Add(NewReader.GetValue(i).ToString())
          Next

          ' Add item to list view items collection
          lvwViewRS.Items.Add(NewItem)
       End While

       ' Close data reader
       NewReader.Close()

    Catch ex As SqlException
       ' Display error message
       MessageBox.Show("Could not create the view. " & _
          ex.Message)
    Catch ex As Exception
       ' Display error message
       MessageBox.Show("An application error occurred." & _
          ex.ToString())
    Finally
       ' Close Connection
       SqlConnection1.Close()
    End Try
 End Sub
```

9. Build and run the project with Ctrl+F5. In the text box below `CREATE VIEW Statement`, enter the following statement, and click Create View:

```
CREATE VIEW EmployeesAndOrders_2
AS
SELECT
   e.EmployeeID,
   e.LastName,
   e.FirstName,
   o.OrderID
FROM
   Employees e INNER JOIN Orders o
   ON
      e.EmployeeId = o.EmployeeId
WHERE
   e.EmployeeId = 2
```

You'll get a confirmation message saying the view was created successfully.

10. In Server Explorer, refresh the Views node and you'll see the EmployeesAndOrders_2 node.

11. Now let's test the view itself. Recollect that a view can be queried like a table. In the text box captioned *Querying a View*, enter the following query, and click the Execute button:

```
SELECT
   *
FROM
   EmployeesAndOrders_2
```

You'll see the result of the query as in Figure 14-5.

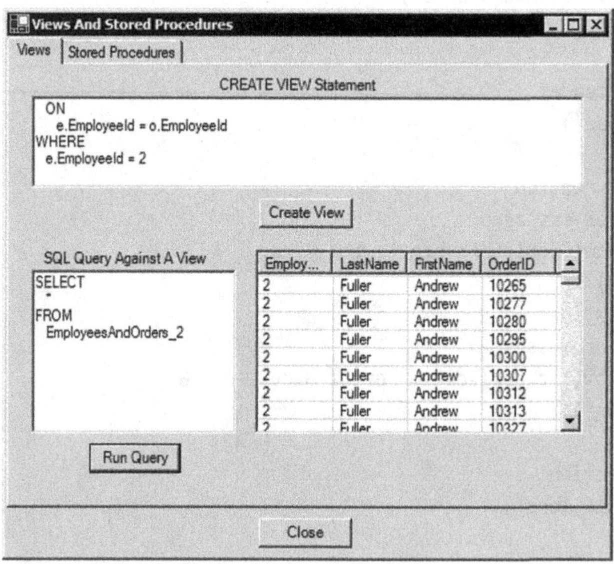

Figure 14-5. *Querying* `EmployeesAndOrders_2`

How It Works

Since most of the code should be familiar to you by now from discussions in previous chapters, we'll go over only the main points here. First, you coded a CREATE VIEW statement, which defined a view containing EmployeeID, LastName, FirstName, and OrderId. When you clicked the Create View button, the statement was submitted by the ExecuteNonQuery method and the view was created.

```
   ' Create Command
   Dim ViewCommand As New SqlCommand(txtCreateView.Text, SqlConnection1)

...

   ' Run Create View Command
   ViewCommand.ExecuteNonQuery()
```

After creating the view, you tested it by coding a query against it and clicking the Execute button. Since queries return datasets, you used the ExecuteReader method to get a data reader.

```
   ' Create Command
   Dim QueryCommand As New SqlCommand(txtSQL.Text, SqlConnection1)

...

   ' Execute Command and Get Data
   Dim NewReader As SqlDataReader = QueryCommand.ExecuteReader()
```

You populated the list view header with the data reader column names and then looped through the rows in the data reader and displayed them, closing the data reader at the end of the loop. Since the EmployeesAndOrders_2 view filters the data, only rows for employee 2 are displayed.

```
' Get column names for list view from data reader
For i As Integer = 0 To NewReader.FieldCount - 1
   Dim header As New ColumnHeader
   header.Text = NewReader.GetName(i)
   lvwViewRS.Columns.Add(header)
Next

' Get rows of data and show in list view
While NewReader.Read()
   ' Create list view item
   Dim NewItem As New ListViewItem

   ' Specify text and subitems of list view
   NewItem.Text = NewReader.GetValue(0).ToString()
   For i As Integer = 1 To NewReader.FieldCount - 1
      NewItem.SubItems.Add(NewReader.GetValue(i).ToString())
   Next
```

```
   ' Add item to list view items collection
   lvwViewRS.Items.Add(NewItem)
End While

' Close data reader
NewReader.Close()
```

You've seen how to create views and use them in queries, but there's more to views that's beyond our concern in this book. For example, some views are updatable, and others aren't. Also, some views enforce constraints, but others don't. Unless you're performing updates, you typically don't have to know whether you're accessing data through a table or view. Even then you don't need to know as long as the view is updatable.

Using Stored Procedures

Stored procedures are callable modules executed by the database manager. Most RDBMSs have supported them for years, but many required they be written in a language (C and Java are the most common) other than SQL. Today, the SQL standard and most RDBMSs support stored procedures coded purely in SQL and have enhanced SQL to include procedural statements, such as `IF` and `WHILE`, and even structured exception handling. With this added functionality, stored procedures have become an extremely important part of database programming. Providing reusable, optimized code, they can significantly improve system performance and reliability while reducing the time and cost of both development and operation. They're essentially a precompiled version of the SQL queries and commands you've been using up to now, and because they're precompiled, they execute faster than commands you include in your .NET code.

Stored procedures can have *parameters* that can be used for input or output. They also return a single integer status code and can return one or more result sets. They can be called from client programs or other stored procedures. They are powerful, indeed, and are becoming the preferred mode of database programming, particularly for multitier applications and Web services, since (among their many benefits) they can dramatically reduce network traffic between clients and database servers.

You'll learn how to create different kinds of stored procedures using Server Explorer and then learn how to use them in VB .NET applications. You'll begin by creating a stored procedure that has no parameters. This kind of stored procedure is most often used to execute predefined queries.

Try It Out: Creating and Executing a Stored Procedure with No Parameters

Suppose that you want a result set showing the employee ID and last name for all employees of Northwind Traders. Let's code a stored procedure to provide this. (You'll refine this stored procedure, adding parameters, later.)

■ **Note** To run this example, you must have Visual Studio .NET Professional or higher. If you have Visual Basic .NET Standard Edition, skip to the next "Try It Out" section.

Follow these steps:

1. In Server Explorer, expand the `Northwind` connection, right-click the Stored Procedures node, and click New Stored Procedure.

2. You'll be presented with a window as in Figure 14-6.

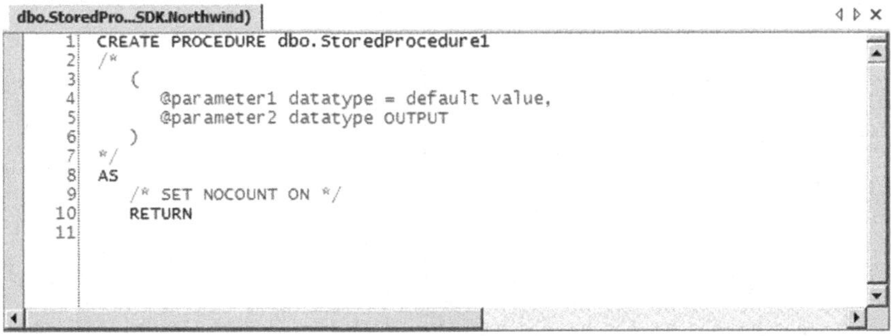

dbo.StoredPro...SDK.Northwind)

```
CREATE PROCEDURE dbo.StoredProcedure1
/*
	(
		@parameter1 datatype = default value,
		@parameter2 datatype OUTPUT
	)
*/
AS
	/* SET NOCOUNT ON */
	RETURN
```

Figure 14-6. *Stored procedure skeleton SQL*

The /* and */ symbols delimit comments and code inside them is ignored by the database engine. They're used to comment out more than one line of code. (A pair of hyphens, --, is the standard SQL single-line comment delimiter. Anything from the dashes through the end of the line is a comment and is ignored.)

Replace the skeleton with the following:

```
CREATE PROCEDURE dbo.Select_AllEmployees
AS
   SELECT
      EmployeeId,
      LastName
   FROM
      Employees
RETURN
```

3. Save the stored procedure by clicking the Save icon. Notice that under the Stored Procedures node in Server Explorer, there's a new Select_AllEmployees node.

4. Now let's execute the stored procedure. Right-click the Select_AllEmployees node in Server Explorer, and click Run Stored Procedure. An output window, as shown in Figure 14-7, appears and shows the results of the stored procedure execution. Scroll down to the bottom, and notice that the last line says `@RETURN_VALUE = 0`. Stored procedures return a value of zero by default. But this can be changed, as you'll see in a later example.

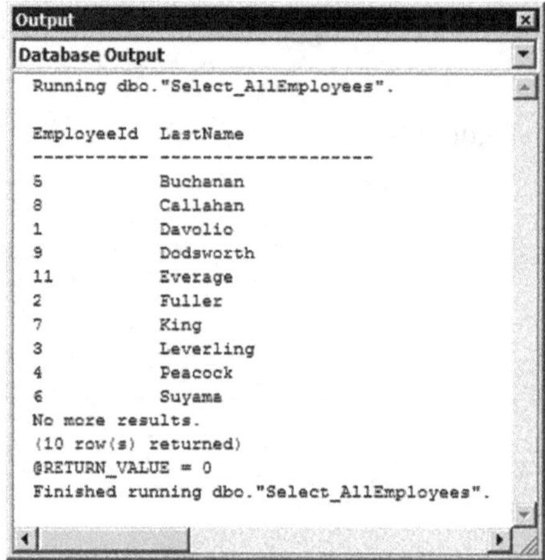

Figure 14-7. *Output from `sp_SelectAllEmployees`*

How It Works

This is a simple stored procedure. In a `CREATE PROCEDURE` statement, you specify the name of the stored procedure; the `dbo` prefix indicates that only user accounts with database owner privileges may run the stored procedure. It also stops the database looking first in the master database for the stored procedure and saves you a bit more time. Then the `AS` keyword separates the signature (the procedure's name and parameter list, but here you define no parameters) of the stored procedure from its body (the SQL that makes up the procedure).

```
CREATE PROCEDURE dbo.Select_AllEmployees
AS
```

After `AS`, the procedure body has just two components, a query and a `RETURN` statement.

```
   SELECT
      EmployeeId,
      LastName
   FROM
      Employees
RETURN
```

The `RETURN` statement signifies that the stored procedure has completed its work. That's it; after you saved the stored procedure, you executed it. It ran and produced a result set, the list of all employees, displayed in the Output window.

To modify an existing stored procedure, right-click its node, select Edit Stored Procedure, and then make changes in the editor that appears. Note that the `ALTER PROCEDURE` statement is used.

If you expand the new node, you'll see nodes for the two columns in its query's select list.

■ **Note** You'll often see stored procedures with names beginning with `sp_` or `xp_`. The prefix `sp_` is a Transact-SQL convention that typically indicates that the stored procedure is coded in SQL. The prefix `xp_` is also used to indicate that the stored procedure isn't written in SQL. (However, not all `sp_` stored procedures provided by SQL Server are written in SQL either.) In general, you don't need to add these.

Try It Out: Using an Alternative Method for Creating a Stored Procedure

If you don't have Visual Studio .NET Professional, you can still use Server Explorer to create stored procedures, by submitting SQL as you did in Chapter 3. Let's walk through the steps briefly.

1. In Server Explorer, expand the connection to the `Northwind` database.
2. Double-click any table, for example, `Employees`. Once the data grid is displayed, click the Show SQL Pane icon on the toolbar.
3. Replace the SQL with the following:

```
CREATE PROCEDURE dbo.Select_AllEmployees
AS
   SELECT
      EmployeeId,
      LastName
   FROM
      Employees
RETURN
```

4. Click the Run Query icon to execute the `CREATE PROCEDURE` statement, and the new stored procedure is created. You'll get a small confirmation dialog box reporting success. Click OK.
5. Right-click the Stored Procedures node in Server Explorer, and click Refresh. A node for the new stored procedure appears in the tree (see Figure 14-8).
6. Now let's execute the stored procedure. Right-click the Select_AllEmployees node in Server Explorer, and click Run Stored Procedure. An output window (refer to Figure 14-7) appears, showing the results of the stored procedure execution. Scroll down to the bottom, and notice that the last line says `@RETURN_VALUE = 0`. Stored procedures return a value of zero by default. But you can change this, as you'll see in a later example.

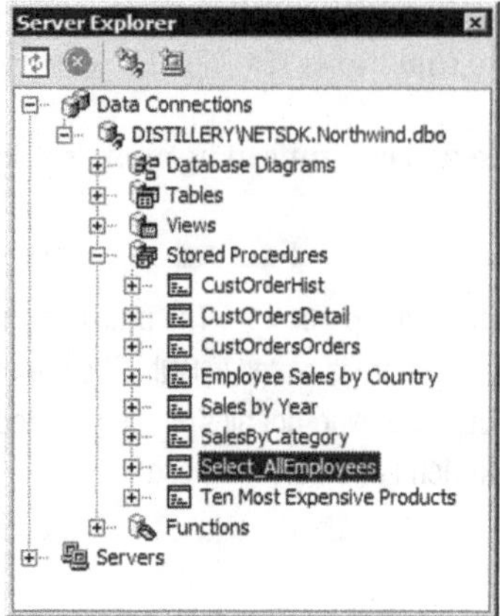

Figure 14-8. *Server Explorer tree including* `Select_AllEmployees`

How It Works

All you did was execute a `CREATE PROCEDURE` statement. See the preceding "How It Works" for an explanation of what it does.

If you expand the new node, you'll see nodes for the two columns in its query's select list.

For each of the other stored procedures you create in this chapter, if you don't have Visual Studio .NET Professional, you'll need to follow these steps to create each new stored procedure, as the code in the later examples depends on them.

Let's move on to look at some more stored procedures.

Try It Out: Creating and Executing a Stored Procedure with a RETURN Value

In this example the stored procedure will return 1 if the number of orders is greater than 100 and 2 otherwise. An application calling this stored procedure could test the return value and display an appropriate message to the user. (Since there are more than 800 orders, you expect a return value of 1.)

1. Create a stored procedure with the following SQL:

```
CREATE PROCEDURE dbo.Orders_MoreThan100
AS
   DECLARE @orders int

   SELECT
      @orders = COUNT(*)
   FROM
      Orders

   IF @orders > 100
      RETURN 1
   ELSE
      RETURN 2
```

2. If you try to run the stored procedure the same way you ran the first one, by right-clicking it in the Server Explorer tree and then clicking Run Stored Procedure, you won't get what you expect (see Figure 14-9).

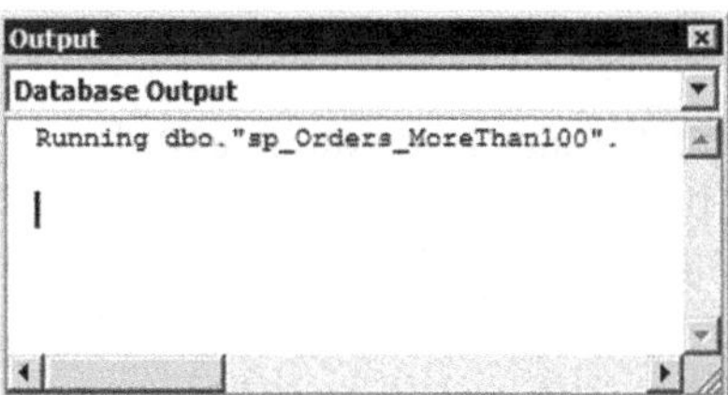

Figure 14-9. *Trying to run `Order_MoreThan100`*

3. Notice that you can't expand the Stored Procedures node in the tree. Unlike `Select_AllEmployees`, it has no items for display, so the only output was the message that the procedure was running.

4. Open the Tables node in Server Explorer, and double-click Orders. Click the SQL icon and replace the code in the editor pane with the following:

```
DECLARE @rc int
EXEC @rc = orders_morethan100
SELECT @rc
```

5. Click the Run Query icon to execute the stored procedure. You should get the same output as in Figure 14-10. The return value appears as though it were the first and only column in a single-row result set.

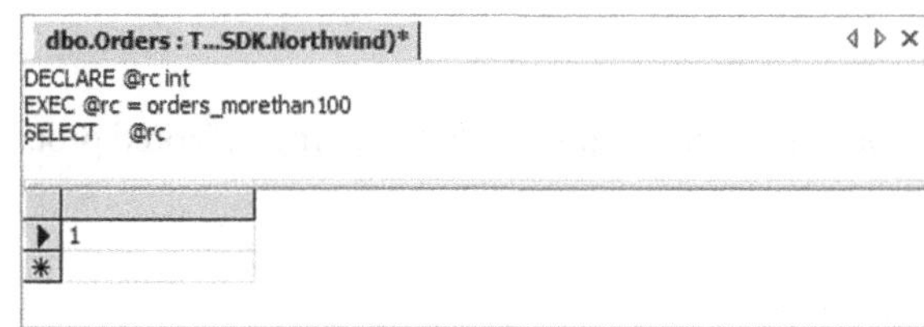

Figure 14-10. *Correctly displaying `Orders_MoreThan100` output*

How It Works

You begin by creating a stored procedure called `Orders_MoreThan100` that has no parameters.

```
CREATE PROCEDURE dbo.Orders_MoreThan100
AS
```

In the procedure body (following the `AS` keyword) you first declare an integer variable called `@orders` to hold the number of orders. (In Transact-SQL, local variable names begin with `@`.)

```
DECLARE @orders int
```

Then, within a query select list, you assign a value to the variable with the COUNT function.

```
SELECT
   @orders = COUNT(*)
FROM
   Orders
```

Finally, you code an IF statement that returns 1 if the value of the variable @Orders is greater than 100, and 2 if the value is less than or equal to 100.

```
IF @orders > 100
   RETURN 1
ELSE
   RETURN 2
```

Since the only item in the select list is a local variable, there are no columns per se for output, so you have to write some code to capture the return value and display it. The code is straightforward. First you declare a local variable to hold the return value after the procedure terminates.

```
DECLARE @rc int
```

Then you execute the stored procedure with an EXECUTE (short form: EXEC) statement, assigning the return value to the local variable.

```
EXEC @rc = orders_morethan100
```

Finally, you display the value of the local variable. (This use of SELECT is a Transact-SQL extension to standard SQL, a query requiring no FROM clause.) Note that since you're executing a query, you get a result set, here with only one value in it. That's why the output has one row with one column.

```
SELECT @rc
```

Now let's now look at a stored procedure that accepts an input argument. Stored procedures that accept input are very useful.

Note The term *parameter* refers to a variable declared between parentheses before the AS keyword in stored procedure declaration. An *argument* is a value passed as input to a procedure and stored in an *input parameter* for use within the procedure. Stored procedures can also declare *local variables* that aren't parameters and output parameters that aren't associated with arguments. Parameters and local variables exist only while the procedure is executing.

Try It Out: Creating and Executing a Stored Procedure with an Input Parameter

In the following example, the stored procedure accepts an employee number and returns a list of orders taken by that employee.

1. Create a stored procedure with the following SQL:

```
CREATE PROCEDURE dbo.Orders_ByEmployeeId
   @employeeid int
AS
   SELECT
      OrderId,
      OrderDate
   FROM
      Orders
   WHERE
      EmployeeId = @employeeid
RETURN
```

2. Execute the procedure. Since it requires an `EmployeeID` as an input parameter, you'll be prompted for it (see Figure 14-11).

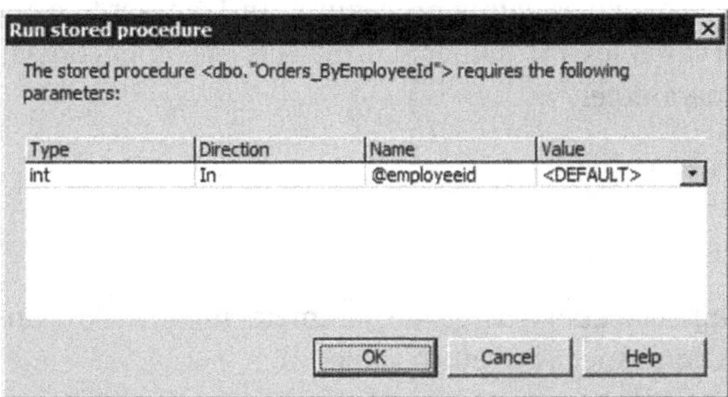

Figure 14-11. *Prompting for `Orders_ByEmployeeID` input*

Observe the columns in Figure 14-11. The data type, direction, and name of the parameter are displayed. The direction `In` means the parameter is an input parameter. Enter 2 in the Value column, and click OK.

The stored procedure will return the output in Figure 14-12.

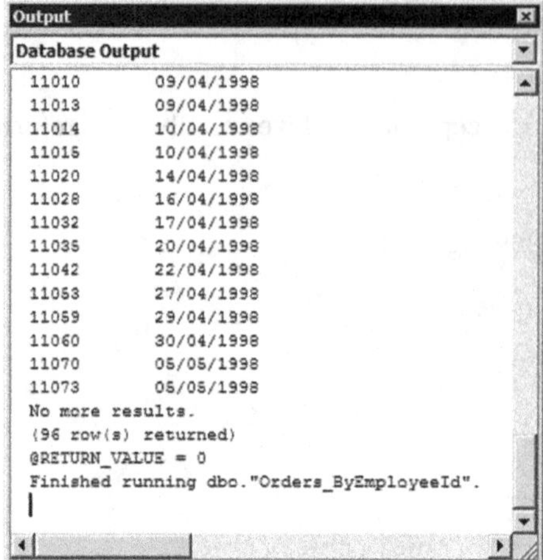

Figure 14-12. *Output of* `Orders_ByEmployeeID` *for employee 2*

How It Works

When you create the stored procedure, you specify an input parameter. Parameters are declared between the stored procedure name and the `AS` keyword (much like declaring VB .NET method parameters). The line `@employeeid int` specifies the name of the parameter, `@employeeid`, and its data type, `int`. Parameters are local variables within procedures. In Transact-SQL they're preceded by `@`, just as declared local variables are. (Other SQL dialects use other conventions.) By default, a parameter is an input parameter.

```
CREATE PROCEDURE dbo.Orders_ByEmployeeId
   @employeeid int
AS
```

The body of the procedure comprises a query, using the parameter in the `WHERE` clause, and a `RETURN` statement. Notice that you don't specify a return value.

```
   SELECT
      OrderId,
      OrderDate
   FROM
      Orders
   WHERE
      EmployeeId = @employeeid
RETURN
```

In Transact-SQL, a stored procedure can have up to 2,100 parameters, but typically only a few are used.

The `RETURN` statement can return only a single integer value. What if you need to return more than one value or a value that's not an integer? You could use a result set, but the overhead of generating and processing it for only one row is likely to be less efficient than using output parameters.

Try It Out: Executing a Stored Procedure with Input and Output Parameters

Say you want to find the earliest date and the latest date that a given employee placed an order, as indicated by `OrderDate` in `Orders`. You could write a stored procedure that takes an employee ID as an input parameter and return the dates as columns in a query. But you can be a bit more efficient by using two output parameters.

1. Create a stored procedure with the following SQL:

```
CREATE PROCEDURE dbo.Dates_ByEmployeeId
   @employeeid int ,
   @edate      datetime = NULL OUTPUT,
   @ldate      datetime = NULL OUTPUT
AS
   SELECT
      @edate = MIN(OrderDate),
      @ldate = MAX(OrderDate)
   FROM
      Orders
   WHERE
      EmployeeId = @employeeid
RETURN
```

2. Run the stored procedure from the SQL pane as in the previous example but using the following SQL. You should see the result in Figure 14-13.

```
DECLARE
   @earliest datetime,
   @latest   datetime
EXEC Dates_ByEmployeeId 2, @earliest output, @latest output
SELECT @earliest, @latest
```

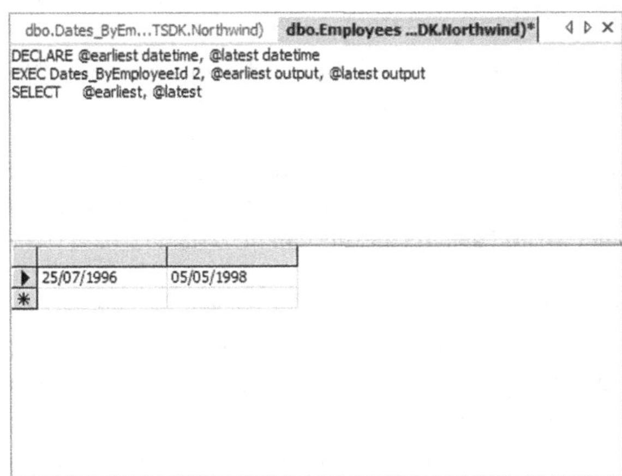

Figure 14-13. *Displaying output parameters*

How It Works

You specify one input parameter (@employeeid) of type int and two output datetime parameters (@edate and @ldate). You'll pass an employee ID to the stored procedure as an input argument and pass back the earliest and latest order dates for the employee in the output parameters. Though not absolutely required, you default the output parameters to nulls (= null) before you specify that they're output parameters (output). Parameters need to be initialized before use. By explicitly defaulting the output parameters to null, you make it somewhat easier to code and invoke the procedure. (Input parameters can also be given default values.)

```
CREATE PROCEDURE dbo.Dates_ByEmployeeId
   @employeeid int ,
   @edate      datetime = NULL OUTPUT,
   @ldate      datetime = NULL OUTPUT
AS
```

In the body of the procedure, you assign values to the output parameters by using the MIN and MAX functions on OrderDate.

```
   SELECT
      @edate = MIN(OrderDate),
      @ldate = MAX(OrderDate)
   FROM
      Orders
   WHERE
      EmployeeId = @employeeid
```

You executed the procedure with a variation on the previous example, which captured and displayed the return code. You declared two local variables to hold the returned dates.

```
DECLARE
   @earliest datetime,
   @latest   datetime
```

You executed the procedure, passing it an integer argument for the employee ID and specifying the local variables as the recipients of the two output parameters.

```
EXEC Dates_ByEmployeeId 2, @earliest output, @latest output
```

Finally, you displayed the results using the Transact-SQL extension to a standard SQL query.

```
SELECT @earliest, @latest
```

In this example, two output values were returned. In a more complex problem, several input parameters can be supplied to a stored procedure, and several output parameters, a RETURN value other than zero (if needed), and also result sets can be returned.

■ **Note** The syntax for creating and executing stored procedures differs slightly depending on what dialect of SQL an RDBMS supports. Even in Transact-SQL you'll have additional provisions for declaring and accessing parameters that may be useful to know about depending on what your procedures need to do. We've presented the most generic (and most often used) syntax, but consult your SQL documentation for the details of how best to define and call stored procedures.

Working with Stored Procedures in VB .NET

You've learned about stored procedures using Server Explorer. Now you'll explore them using VB .NET. You'll extend the `ViewsAndSPs` application you developed earlier in the chapter to handle stored procedures.

Try It Out: Setting Up a VB .NET Project to Execute Stored Procedures

Perform this step:

1. Earlier in this chapter, you created a form with two tabs, one for views and another for stored procedures. Select the Stored Procedures tab and add buttons, text boxes, and a list view as shown in Figure 14-14 and described in Table 14-2.

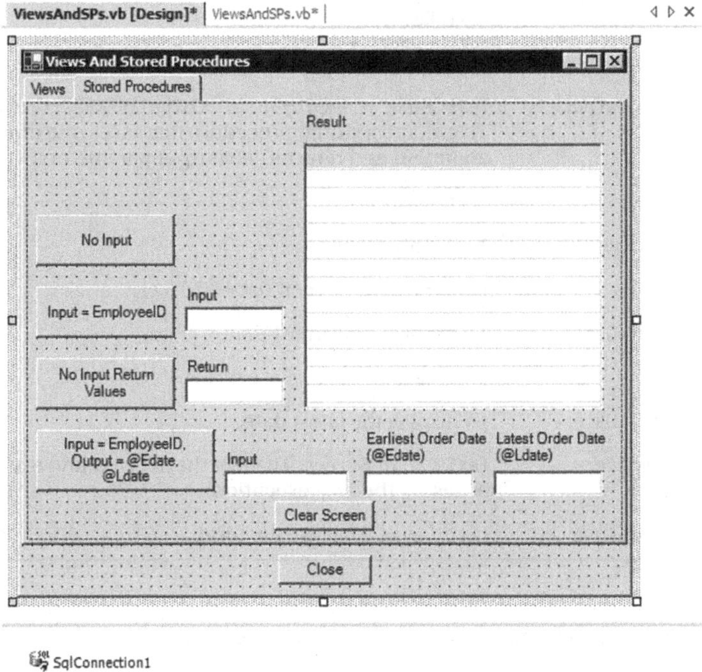

Figure 14-14. *Stored Procedures tab page layout*

Table 14-2. *ViewsAndSPs Tab Page Attributes*

Control	Name	Remarks
Label		Text: Result.
ListView	LvwRS	To display results. Set the GridLines property to True and the View property to Details.
Button	cmdNoInput	Text: No-Input. To execute a stored procedure without any input parameters.
Button	cmdInput	Text: Input = EmployeeID. To execute a stored procedure by supplying one input parameter.
Label		Text: Input
TextBox	txtEmpId1	To supply the employee ID argument.
Button	cmdReturn	Text: No-Input RETURN values. To execute a stored procedure that returns values using the RETURN statement.
Label		Text: Return.
TextBox	txtReturn	To display the value from the RETURN statement.
Button	cmdOutput	Text: Input = Employee ID, Output = @Edate, @Ldate. To execute a stored procedure that takes one input argument and returns two output parameters.
Label		Text: Input.
TextBox	txtEmpId2	To supply the input.
Label		Text: Earliest Order Date (@EDate).
TextBox	txtEDate	To display the earliest date.
Label		Text: Latest Order Date (@Ldate).
TextBox	txtLDate	To display the latest date.
Button	cmdClear	Text: Clear Screen. To clear the list view and text boxes for the next execution.
Button	cmdClose	Text: Close. To close the form.

Now let's try to execute the stored procedures one at a time.

Try It Out: Executing a Stored Procedure with No Input Parameters from VB .NET

You want to execute Select_AllEmployees, which takes no input and returns a list of all employees. You need to write code behind the cmdNoInput button to execute this stored procedure and display the results in the list view to its right.

1. Add the following code to the click event handler for the No Input button:

```
Private Sub cmdNoInput_Click(ByVal sender As System.Object, _
   ByVal e As System.EventArgs) Handles cmdNoInput.Click
   ' Clear list view control
   lvwRS.Columns.Clear()
   lvwRS.Items.Clear()

   ' Create Command
   Dim NoInputCommand As SqlCommand = SqlConnection1.CreateCommand()
   NoInputCommand.CommandType = CommandType.StoredProcedure
   NoInputCommand.CommandText = "Select_AllEmployees"

   Try
      ' Open Connection
      SqlConnection1.Open()

      ' Execute Command and Get Data
      Dim NewReader As SqlDataReader = NoInputCommand.ExecuteReader()

      ' Get column names for list view from data reader
      For i As Integer = 0 To NewReader.FieldCount - 1
         Dim header As New ColumnHeader
         header.Text = NewReader.GetName(i)
         lvwRS.Columns.Add(header)
      Next

      ' Get rows of data and show in list view
      While NewReader.Read()
         ' Create list view item
         Dim NewItem As New ListViewItem

         ' Specify text and subitems of list view
         NewItem.Text = NewReader.GetValue(0).ToString()
         For i As Integer = 1 To NewReader.FieldCount - 1
            NewItem.SubItems.Add(NewReader.GetValue(i).ToString())
         Next

         ' Add item to list view items collection
         lvwRS.Items.Add(NewItem)
      End While

      ' Close data reader
      NewReader.Close()
```

```
      Catch ex As SqlException
         ' Display error message
         MessageBox.Show("Could not create the view. " & _
            ex.Message)
      Catch ex As Exception
         ' Display error message
         MessageBox.Show("An application error occurred." & _
            ex.ToString())
      Finally
         ' Close Connection
         SqlConnection1.Close()
      End Try
   End Sub
```

2. Build and run the solution with Ctrl+F5. Click the No Input button to see the results as shown in Figure 14-15.

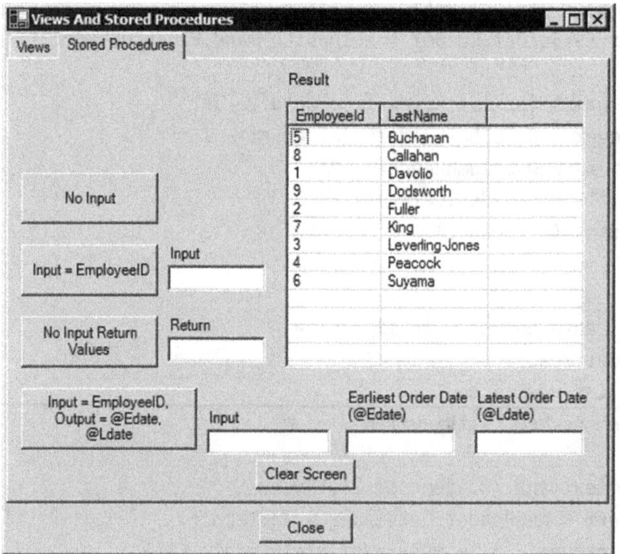

Figure 14-15. *Executing a stored procedure with no arguments*

How It Works

We'll explain only the code relevant to executing the stored procedure. The rest should be familiar by now.

You created a command a bit differently, specifying the `CommandType` property and using the stored procedure name rather than an SQL string as `CommandText`.

```
' Create Command
Dim NoInputCommand As SqlCommand = SqlConnection1.CreateCommand()
NoInputCommand.CommandType = CommandType.StoredProcedure
NoInputCommand.CommandText = "Select_AllEmployees"
```

Since the stored procedure has no parameters, nothing more is required. You know that this stored procedure returns a dataset, so you use a data reader to access it. Not all stored procedures, of course, return datasets; some return just a return value, and others return output parameters. Let's see how to deal with these cases.

You'll call a procedure that accepts one input argument and returns a result set.

Try It Out: Executing a Stored Procedure with One Input Parameter from VB .NET

You'll call the `Orders_ByEmployeeId` stored procedure, supplying the employee ID in a text box and displaying the result set in the list view.

1. Copy the code for the No Input button click handler, and add it to the click event handler for the `Input = Employee ID` button. Make the changes marked in bold:

```
Private Sub cmdInput_Click(ByVal sender As System.Object, _
   ByVal e As System.EventArgs) Handles cmdInput.Click
   ' Clear list view control
   lvwRS.Columns.Clear()
   lvwRS.Items.Clear()

   ' Create Command
   Dim OneInputCommand As SqlCommand = SqlConnection1.CreateCommand()
   OneInputCommand.CommandType = CommandType.StoredProcedure
   OneInputCommand.CommandText = "Orders_ByEmployeeId"

   ' Create Input Parameter
   Dim InputParameter As SqlParameter = _
      OneInputCommand.Parameters.Add("@employeeid", SqlDbType.Int)
   InputParameter.Direction = ParameterDirection.Input
   InputParameter.Value = CInt(txtEmployeeId1.Text)

   Try
      ' Open Connection
      SqlConnection1.Open()

      ' Execute Command and Get Data
      Dim NewReader As SqlDataReader = OneInputCommand.ExecuteReader()
```

```
            ' Get column names for list view from data reader
            For i As Integer = 0 To NewReader.FieldCount - 1
               Dim header As New ColumnHeader
               header.Text = NewReader.GetName(i)
               lvwRS.Columns.Add(header)
            Next

            ' Get rows of data and show in list view
            While NewReader.Read()
               ' Create list view item
               Dim NewItem As New ListViewItem

               ' Specify text and subitems of list view
               NewItem.Text = NewReader.GetValue(0).ToString()
               For i As Integer = 1 To NewReader.FieldCount - 1
                  NewItem.SubItems.Add(NewReader.GetValue(i).ToString())
               Next

               ' Add item to list view items collection
               lvwRS.Items.Add(NewItem)
            End While

            ' Close data reader
            NewReader.Close()

         Catch ex As SqlException
            ' Display error message
            MessageBox.Show("Could not create the view. " & _
               ex.Message)
         Catch ex As Exception
            ' Display error message
            MessageBox.Show("An application error occurred." & _
               ex.ToString())
         Finally
            ' Close Connection
            SqlConnection1.Close()
         End Try
      End Sub
```

2. Now, build and run the solution with Ctrl+F5. In the Input text box, type **2** to get the list of all orders placed by employee 2. Click the Input = Employee ID button to see results as shown in Figure 14-16.

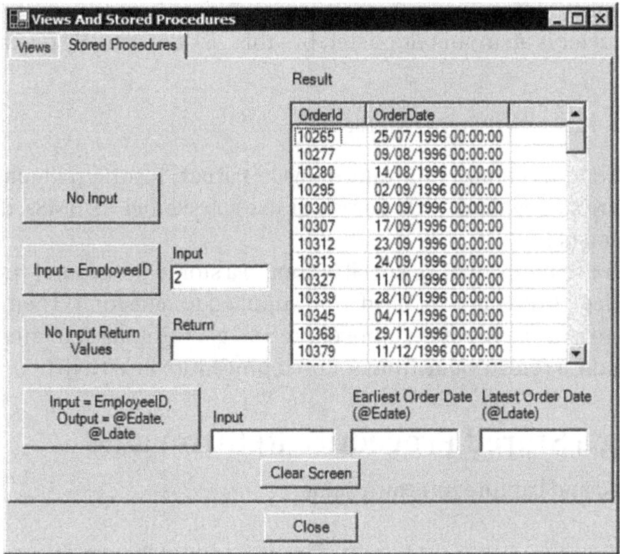

Figure 14-16. *Executing a stored procedure with an input argument*

You can now experiment with different employee IDs.

How It Works

In this example, an employee ID is passed as a parameter. As in the previous example, the only significant change is in configuring the command. You specify that it's for a stored procedure as in the previous example.

```
' Create Command
Dim OneInputCommand As SqlCommand = SqlConnection1.CreateCommand()
OneInputCommand.CommandType = CommandType.StoredProcedure
OneInputCommand.CommandText = "Orders_ByEmployeeId"
```

Then you create a command parameter (an instance of `SqlParameter`) so you can supply the input argument to the command. Each command has a collection named `Parameters`. You create command parameters by adding to this collection (there is no public constructor for `SqlParameter`), providing the parameter's name (note that they *aren't* case sensitive) as the first argument and its data type as the second. Once the command parameter has been created, you specify its direction and value.

```
' Create Input Parameter
Dim InputParameter As SqlParameter = _
   OneInputCommand.Parameters.Add("@employeeid", SqlDbType.Int)
InputParameter.Direction = ParameterDirection.Input
InputParameter.Value = CInt(txtEmployeeId1.Text)
```

Note that you use a member of the System.Data.ParameterDirection enumeration to explicitly state that the parameter is an input parameter, but this was not actually necessary since the default is Input.

```
InputParameter.Direction = ParameterDirection.Input
```

The ParameterDirection enum can take four values: Input, Output, InputOutput, and ReturnValue. The meanings are self-evident. (SQL Server, unlike some other RDBMSs, doesn't support input/output parameters.)

Let's summarize what you've done here. To specify input to a stored procedure, you used a SqlParameter object, specified its direction as Input, and supplied a value for it. Then you simply called ExecuteReader to execute the stored procedure and get the dataset it returns.

Now let's see how to handle a return value from a stored procedure in VB .NET.

Try It Out: Handling a Stored Procedure Return Value

You'll call Orders_MoreThan100 and capture its return value.

1. Add the following code to the click event handler for the No Input Return Values button (cmdReturn):

```
Private Sub cmdReturn_Click(ByVal sender As System.Object, _
   ByVal e As System.EventArgs) Handles cmdReturn.Click
   ' Create Command
   Dim ReturnCommand As SqlCommand = SqlConnection1.CreateCommand()
   ReturnCommand.CommandType = CommandType.StoredProcedure
   ReturnCommand.CommandText = "Orders_MoreThan100"

   ' Create Return Parameter
   Dim ReturnParameter As SqlParameter = _
      ReturnCommand.Parameters.Add("returnvalue", SqlDbType.Int)
   ReturnParameter.Direction = ParameterDirection.ReturnValue

   Try
      ' Open Connection
      SqlConnection1.Open()

      ' Execute Command and Display Return Value
      ReturnCommand.ExecuteScalar()
      txtReturn.Text = _
         ReturnCommand.Parameters("returnvalue").Value.ToString()
```

```
      Catch ex As SqlException
         ' Display error message
         MessageBox.Show("Could not create the view. " & _
            ex.Message)
      Catch ex As Exception
         ' Display error message
         MessageBox.Show("An application error occurred." & _
            ex.ToString())
      Finally
         ' Close Connection
         SqlConnection1.Close()
      End Try
   End Sub
```

2. Build and run with Ctrl+F5. Click the No Input Return Values button and you'll see the display in Figure 14-17. A value of 1 is displayed in the text box adjacent to the button. Remember that this stored procedure returns 1 if there are more than 100 orders placed; otherwise, it returns 2.

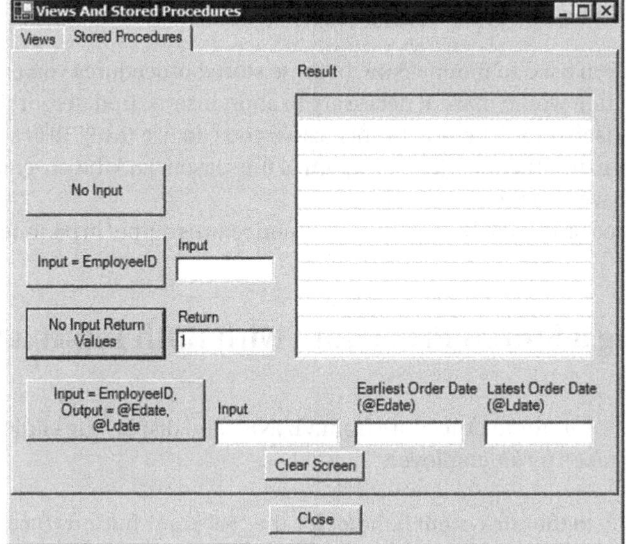

Figure 14-17. *Handling a stored procedure return value*

How It Works

This is similar to the prior example, except you don't need a data reader since no result set is returned. You create a command, and then you add a command parameter to it and configure the parameter to handle a return value.

```
' Create Command
Dim ReturnCommand As SqlCommand = SqlConnection1.CreateCommand()
ReturnCommand.CommandType = CommandType.StoredProcedure
ReturnCommand.CommandText = "Orders_MoreThan100"

' Create Return Parameter
Dim ReturnParameter As SqlParameter = _
   ReturnCommand.Parameters.Add("returnvalue", SqlDbType.Int)
ReturnParameter.Direction = ParameterDirection.ReturnValue
```

Now that you've specified the parameter that will hold the return value, you can execute the stored procedure. Since this stored procedure will return only one value, you call the ExecuteScalar method on the command object.

```
' Execute Command and Display Return Value
ReturnCommand.ExecuteScalar()
```

The return value from the stored procedure will be placed in the Value property of the parReturn command parameter. You convert it to a string and place it in a text box.

```
txtReturn.Text = _
   ReturnCommand.Parameters("returnvalue").Value.ToString()
```

Stored procedures are often used to modify data. In these stored procedures you can check for a certain condition that would make it necessary to abort inserts, updates, or deletes and inform the user of the reason for the failure. In such cases you can use the RETURN statement in the stored procedure to inform the calling program of the reason, and the program can take the appropriate action based on the return value.

The final example is a stored procedure that accepts input and returns output in parameters to the calling program.

Try It Out: Executing a Stored Procedure with Both Input and Output Parameters

You'll call the Dates_ByEmployeeId stored procedure from VB .NET and display the earliest and the latest dates of the orders taken by an employee.

1. Add the following code to the click event handler for the cmdOutput button (Input = EmployeeID, Output = @EDate, @LDate):

```
Private Sub cmdOutput_Click(ByVal sender As System.Object, _
   ByVal e As System.EventArgs) Handles cmdOutput.Click
   ' Create Command
   Dim OutputCommand As SqlCommand = SqlConnection1.CreateCommand()
   OutputCommand.CommandType = CommandType.StoredProcedure
   OutputCommand.CommandText = "Dates_ByEmployeeId"
```

```
        ' Create Input Parameter
        Dim InputParameter As SqlParameter = _
           OutputCommand.Parameters.Add("@employeeid", SqlDbType.Int)
        InputParameter.Direction = ParameterDirection.Input
        InputParameter.Value = CInt(txtEmployeeId2.Text)

        'Create Output Parameters
        Dim OutputParameter1 As SqlParameter = _
           OutputCommand.Parameters.Add("@edate", SqlDbType.DateTime)
        OutputParameter1.Direction = ParameterDirection.Output
        Dim OutputParameter2 As SqlParameter = _
           OutputCommand.Parameters.Add("@ldate", SqlDbType.DateTime)
        OutputParameter2.Direction = ParameterDirection.Output

        Try
           ' Open Connection
           SqlConnection1.Open()

           ' Execute Command and Display Return Values
           OutputCommand.ExecuteNonQuery()
           txtEDate.Text = OutputParameter1.Value.ToString()
           txtLDate.Text = OutputParameter2.Value.ToString()

        Catch ex As SqlException
           ' Display error message
           MessageBox.Show("Could not create the view. " & _
              ex.Message)
        Catch ex As Exception
           ' Display error message
           MessageBox.Show("An application error occurred." & _
              ex.ToString())
        Finally
           ' Close Connection
           SqlConnection1.Close()
        End Try
     End Sub
```

2. Build and run with Ctrl+F5. Enter **3** in the Input text box, and click the button to its left as in Figure 14-18. Observe that the earliest date and latest date of orders taken by employee 3 are then displayed.

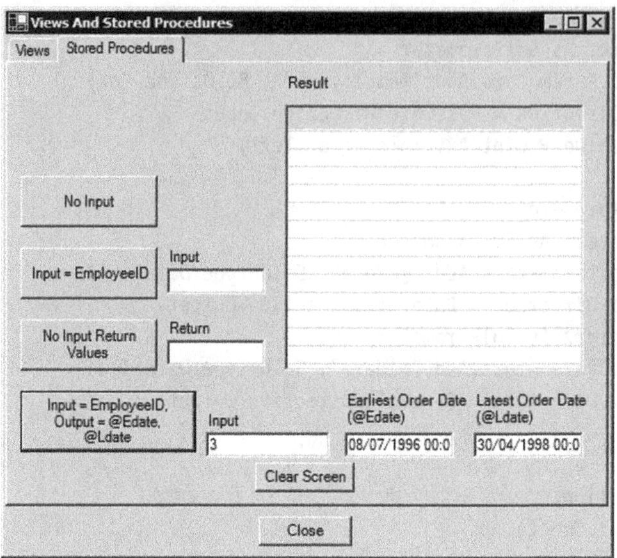

Figure 14-18. *Handling both input and output parameters*

Specify different employee IDs, and observe the results.

How It Works

You specify the `Dates_ByEmployeeId` as the stored procedure to execute.

```
' Create Command
Dim OutputCommand As SqlCommand = SqlConnection1.CreateCommand()
OutputCommand.CommandType = CommandType.StoredProcedure
OutputCommand.CommandText = "Dates_ByEmployeeId"
```

You create a command parameter for `@employeeid` of type `Int` and specify its direction and value.

```
' Create Input Parameter
Dim InputParameter As SqlParameter = _
   OutputCommand.Parameters.Add("@employeeid", SqlDbType.Int)
InputParameter.Direction = ParameterDirection.Input
InputParameter.Value = CInt(txtEmployeeId2.Text)
```

Then you create two output parameters to hold the earliest and latest dates. You call them `OutputParameter1` and `OutputParameter2` and for `@edate` and `@ldate`, respectively, and then specify their direction as `Output`.

```
'Create Output Parameters
Dim OutputParameter1 As SqlParameter = _
   OutputCommand.Parameters.Add("@edate", SqlDbType.DateTime)
OutputParameter1.Direction = ParameterDirection.Output
Dim OutputParameter2 As SqlParameter = _
   OutputCommand.Parameters.Add("@ldate", SqlDbType.DateTime)
OutputParameter2.Direction = ParameterDirection.Output
```

Since this stored procedure doesn't return a result set, you don't use the ExecuteReader method; and since it doesn't return only a return value, you don't use the ExecuteScalar method either. You use ExecuteNonQuery instead.

```
' Execute Command and Display Return Values
OutputCommand.ExecuteNonQuery()
```

You then place the earliest and latest dates in their text boxes.

```
txtEDate.Text = OutputParameter1.Value.ToString()
txtLDate.Text = OutputParameter2.Value.ToString()
```

That's it for the discussion of stored procedures. We could have written an entire book covering how to create and use stored procedures, but these are the essentials you should understand.

Summary

In this chapter you learned about views and stored procedures. First we discussed views, in particular how to create them and use them like tables. You used both Server Explorer and VB .NET to experiment with views.

Most of the chapter was dedicated to stored procedures, the various ways they accept input and produce output, and how to call stored procedures and handle what they return in VB .NET. In particular, you learned how to create appropriate command parameters and when to use the ExecuteReader, ExecuteScalar, and ExecuteNonQuery when dealing with stored procedures.

Along the way you practiced many techniques covered in earlier chapters. We didn't cover handling multiple result sets from stored procedures, because you use the same technique presented in Chapter 7. Applying this to a stored procedure would be an excellent exercise and really test your mastery of the concepts presented in this chapter.

Next we'll return to some database concepts: indexes and constraints.

CHAPTER 15

Using Indexes and Constraints

In the previous chapter, you saw how views and stored procedures allow you to improve the speed and legibility of your queries. In this chapter, you'll learn about two more features of databases that improve a query's performance and consistency. When used properly, indexes can dramatically improve performance, particularly for queries. Constraints enhance data integrity by defining data validation rules in the database itself rather than relying on applications to code them consistently and correctly. You first looked at constraints in Chapter 12, and we'll expand that knowledge here.

In this chapter, we'll cover the following:

- The advantages and disadvantages of indexing
- Choosing the best columns and data types for indexes
- Clustered and nonclustered indexes
- Using constraints to maintain database integrity
- Understanding `UNIQUE`, `CHECK`, `DEFAULT`, and `NOT NULL` constraints

Unlike the previous chapter where the subject of views is fairly straightforward, using both indexes and constraints requires some forethought in order to get the best out of them. Therefore, we'll delve a little deeper into these topics than we might otherwise do in order to give you the best chance of understanding exactly how these work and the different options you have to use them.

Understanding Indexes

Relational databases use indexes to minimize the time it takes to find data. You may not have noticed it in the simple queries you've seen so far, but each query takes some time for the database to run it and return its results. This is more noticeable when running several complex queries against larger tables of data.

Note Neither creating nor dropping indexes requires changes to application code. The database engine uses indexes transparently.

A database engine uses an index in much the same way as a reader uses the index of a book. For example, if you wanted to find all references to INSERT statements in this book, you could begin on page 1 and scan each page of the book, marking each time you found the word until you reach the end of the book. This approach is time consuming and laborious. Alternatively, you can use the index in the back of the book to find the page number for each occurrence of an INSERT statement. This approach produces the same results, but it's much faster and easier.

When a table has no index, the result is similar to the reader who looks at every page; the database engine needs to look at every row. In other words, it performs a *table scan*. This isn't necessarily a problem for small tables, and it's sometimes unavoidable, even with indexes. However, as a table grows to thousands (or even millions) of rows, scans can become prohibitively expensive.

The following query on the Products table of the Northwind database retrieves products in a specific price range:

```
SELECT
   ProductID,
   ProductName,
   UnitPrice
FROM
   Products
WHERE
   (UnitPrice > 12.5) AND (UnitPrice < 14)
```

Currently you have no index on the Product table to help this query, so the database engine performs a table scan and examines each row to see if UnitPrice falls between 12.5 and 14. In Figure 15-1, the database search touches a total of 77 rows to find just three matches.

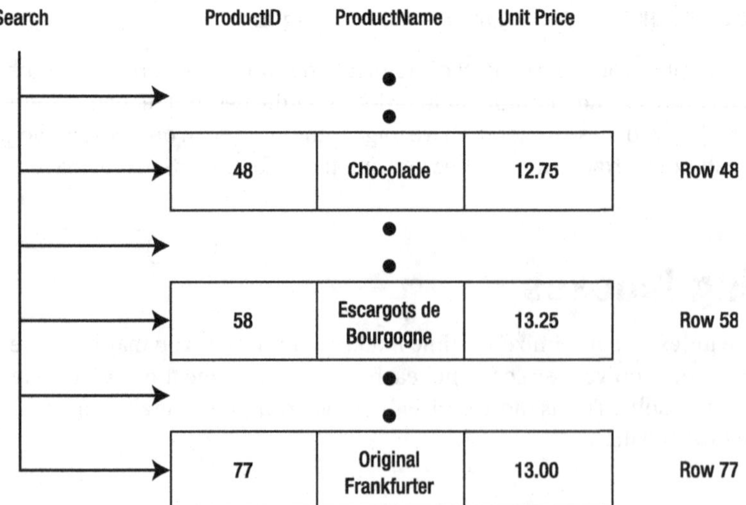

Figure 15-1. *Table scan of* Products

Suppose you created an index on the `UnitPrice` column. The index would contain a copy of each `UnitPrice` value and a reference (much like a page number in a book's index) to each row containing the value. The database keeps the index entries in ascending order and can quickly find the three rows to satisfy the query, without scanning every row in the table.

■ **Caution** In the "Try It Out" sections of this chapter, we'll use some features available only in the Architect and Professional versions of Visual Studio .NET. We'll also present the SQL you can use to produce the same results without these versions of Visual Studio.

Try It Out: Creating a Simple Index

To create a simple index, follow these steps:

1. In Server Explorer, open the entry for the `Northwind` database, right-click the `Products` table, and select Design Table. The window shown in Figure 15-2 appears.

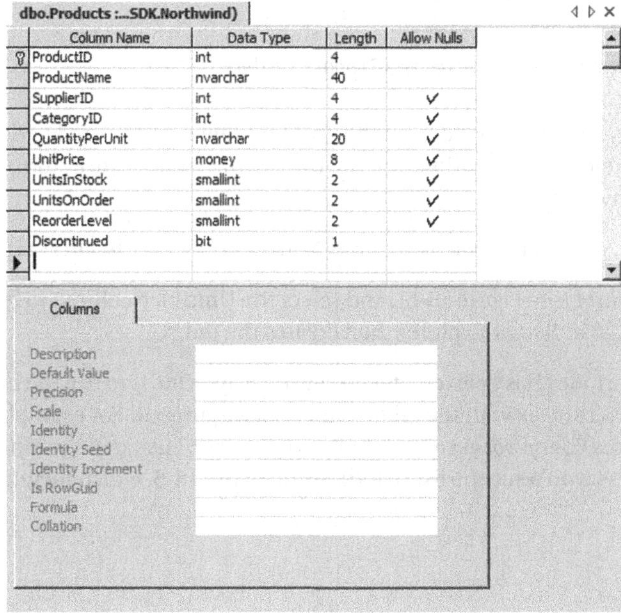

Figure 15-2. *`Products` Design view*

2. Click the Manage Indexes and Keys icon from the Table toolbar (highlighted in Figure 15-3) to open the Property Pages dialog box for the `Products` table (see Figure 15-4).

Figure 15-3. *The Manage Keys and Indexes icon highlighted*

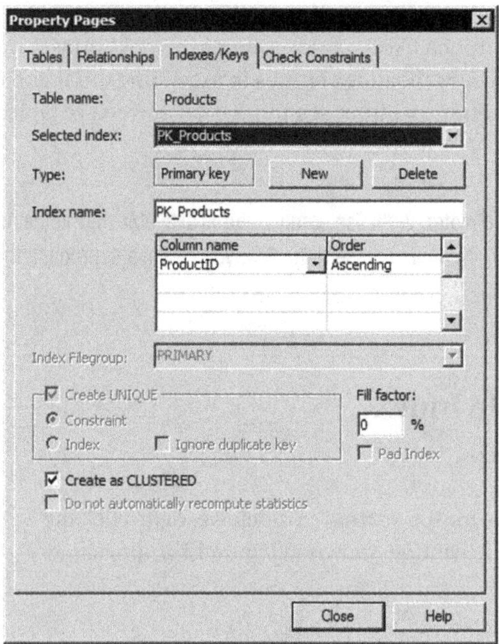

Figure 15-4. *Property Pages dialog box for the `Products` table*

The dialog box displays an existing index on the `Products` table: the `PK_Products` index. In the "Maintaining Uniqueness" section, you'll see how primary keys are automatically indexed to enforce uniqueness.

3. Click the New button, and then replace the Index Name entry with `IDX_UnitPrice`.

4. Expand the column entry (see Figure 15-5), and select the UnitPrice column to include it in the index. Click Close. Server Explorer then creates the index.

5. You can check that the index has been created in several ways. One is to run the built-in stored procedure `sp_helpindex` with the table name as its argument. For example, if you executed it with the `QueryProcessor` you built in Chapter 13 using the command `sp_helpindex products`, you'd see the list of indexes in Figure 15-6, which includes `IDX_UnitPrice`.

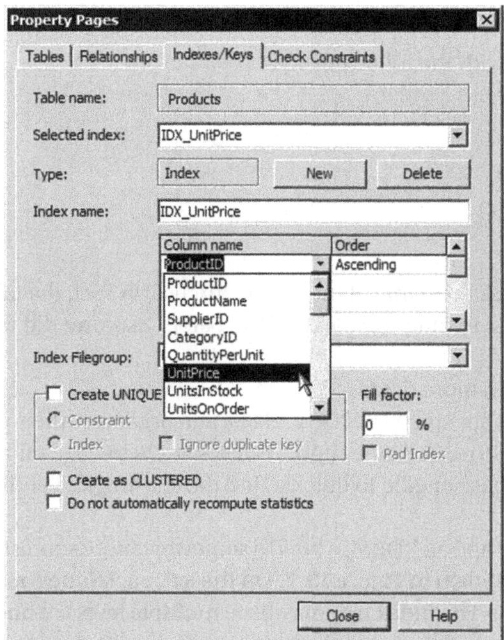

Figure 15-5. *Selecting index columns*

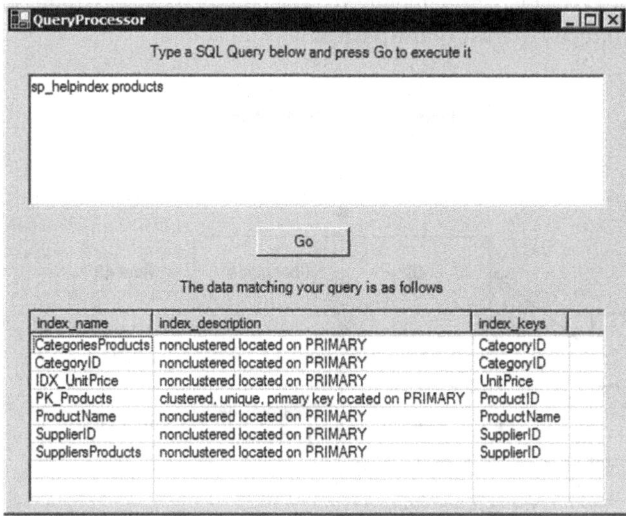

index_name	index_description	index_keys
CategoriesProducts	nonclustered located on PRIMARY	CategoryID
CategoryID	nonclustered located on PRIMARY	CategoryID
IDX_UnitPrice	nonclustered located on PRIMARY	UnitPrice
PK_Products	clustered, unique, primary key located on PRIMARY	ProductID
ProductName	nonclustered located on PRIMARY	ProductName
SupplierID	nonclustered located on PRIMARY	SupplierID
SuppliersProducts	nonclustered located on PRIMARY	SupplierID

Figure 15-6. *Listing indexes with* `sp_helpindex`

How It Works

You could have created the same index with the following SQL:

```
CREATE INDEX IDX_UnitPrice
ON Products
(
   UnitPrice
)
```

The `CREATE INDEX` statement specifies the name of the index (`IDX_UnitPrice`), the table to be indexed (`Products`), and the column(s) to index on (`UnitPrice`). Server Explorer did this for you, and SQL Server created the index.

Let's take a look at what happened in more detail.

The database takes the key columns specified in `CREATE INDEX` and organizes their values into a special data structure known as a *B-tree*. A B-tree supports fast searches with a minimum amount of disk reads, allowing the database engine to quickly find the starting and ending points for a query.

Conceptually (physically, SQL Server and all RDBMSs build a somewhat more sophisticated structure), you can think of an index as shown in Figure 15-7. On the left, each index *node* contains the index key (`UnitPrice`) value. The index tree may have multiple levels of nodes, since each node has a maximum size and nodes *split* as the number of index entries increases. (B-trees split in a balanced way so that the number of levels is kept to a minimum in order to minimize input/output [I/O] in traversing the tree.) At the bottom level, *leaf nodes* have pointers to base table rows for a specific key value. Consequently, data can be accessed with minimal I/Os: to the index nodes and then directly to rows of the base table.

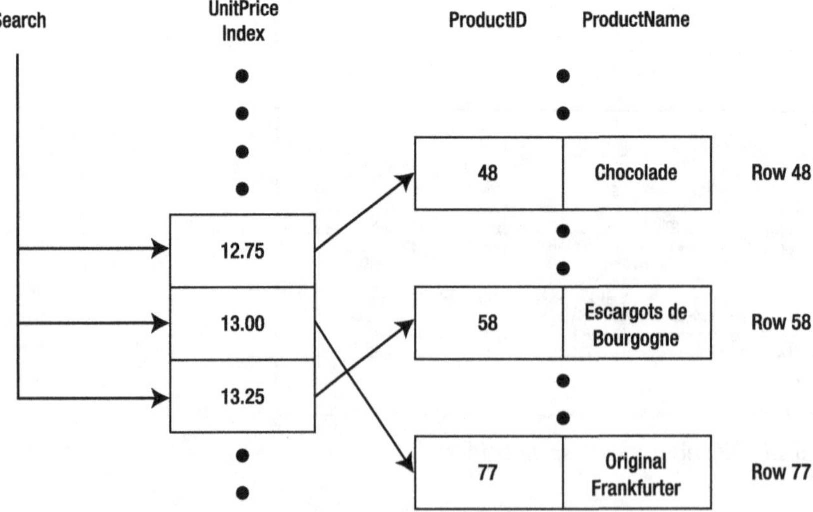

Figure 15-7. *Logical structure of a two-level B-tree index*

Note Although all indexes are conceptually similar to the previous description, they can be configured (both logically and physically) in a variety of ways, and each RDBMS offers its own variations. Consult your database documentation to learn what your RDBMS provides, so you can wisely determine how best to define—and exploit—indexes.

Given this sketch of how indexes work, let's look at some scenarios to examine the benefits they provide.

Taking Advantage of Indexes

The database engine uses indexes to boost performance, often dramatically. All major RDBMSs have a component known as the *query optimizer*. The optimizer's job is to find the fastest and most resource efficient means of executing queries. An important (perhaps the most important) part of this job is selecting the best index or indexes to use. In the following sections, you'll examine the types of queries that typically benefit the most from indexes.

Searching for a Row or Range of Rows

The most obvious use for an index is to find a row or set of rows that satisfies a `WHERE` clause or join (`ON`) predicate. If an index is ordered on the values in a particular column, it can be used to find values within a range as well as for a specific value.

For example, all the following SQL could benefit from an index on `UnitPrice`:

```
DELETE FROM Products
WHERE
   UnitPrice = 1

UPDATE Products
   SET Discontinued = 1
WHERE
   UnitPrice > 15

SELECT
   *
FROM
   Products
WHERE
   UnitPrice BETWEEN 14 AND 16
```

Note that the database engine will use indexes for statements (here, `DELETE` and `UPDATE`) as well as for queries, if applicable.

Sorting Rows

When you ask for a sorted result set, the database will try to find an index to avoid sorting the rows. Sorts most often occur to satisfy the ORDER BY clause, but the DISTINCT keyword and other query components can require internal sorting that may also cause an index to be used.

For example, the following query returns all products sorted by price:

```
SELECT
   ProductName, UnitPrice
FROM
   Products
ORDER BY
   UnitPrice ASC
```

Without an index on UnitPrice, the database must scan the Products table and then sort the rows to process the query. However, even though all rows must be accessed, the optimizer may choose to use the index if it estimates that the resource cost will be less than the combined scan and sort. Note that if only some rather than all rows were to be accessed based on UnitPrice, the probability that the index would be more cost effective would increase and the likelihood that it would be used would be greater.

You can use the same index for the following query, assuming the index is descending (not the case here, since by default SQL Server creates an ascending index), or the RDBMS can scan the index in reverse (SQL Server will but some RDBMSs can't, and some require you to explicitly provide for this when creating the index):

```
SELECT
   ProductName, UnitPrice
FROM
   Products
ORDER BY
   UnitPrice DESC
```

■ **Note** How the optimizer makes its choices depends on many factors. Don't assume that because *you* think an index will be used that the optimizer will agree. The rule of thumb is simple. If no index exists, the optimizer's choices are limited, so it's up to you to make sure that appropriate indexes exist. On the other hand, indexes take up space, and though they can dramatically enhance performance of queries (or any operation that needs to find a subset of rows), they can incur significant overhead since changes to data require indexes to be updated, too. Choose wisely which indexes to create, and the optimizer will be able to make wiser choices; however, never create an index without considering its potential costs as well as benefits.

Grouping Rows

As you saw in Chapter 13, you can use a GROUP BY clause to group rows and aggregate values, for example, counting the number of orders placed by a customer. To process a query with a GROUP BY clause, the database has to sort the rows on the columns on the grouping columns.

The following query counts the number of products by price:

```
SELECT
   COUNT(*),
   UnitPrice
FROM
   Products
GROUP BY
   UnitPrice
```

The database can use the IDX_UnitPrice index to retrieve the prices in order and count the number of products at each price quickly. Indexing a field used in a GROUP BY clause can often speed up a query. As always, whether such an index will be used is up to the optimizer. However, tools such as the query optimizer that comes with the full version of SQL Server can show you which indexes would be used if the query were called.

Maintaining Uniqueness

Columns requiring uniqueness (such as primary keys) must have a *unique index* for the database to enforce this constraint (which we'll discuss soon). You have several methods for establishing a unique constraint. Defining a primary key will automatically (in SQL Server but not in all RDBMSs) cause a unique index to be created for the key. You can also explicitly create unique indexes, in addition to the one for the primary key. Let's do it.

Try It Out: Creating a Unique Index

To create a unique index, follow these steps:

1. In Server Explorer, right-click the Products table and select Design Table. The window in Figure 15-2 appears. Click the Manage Indexes and Keys icon (Figure 15-3) to open the Property Pages dialog box.

2. Click New, name the index IDX_ProductName, select the ProductName column as the key, and then check the Create UNIQUE check box. Click the Index radio button when it becomes enabled (see Figure 15-8). Click Close to create the index and close the dialog box.

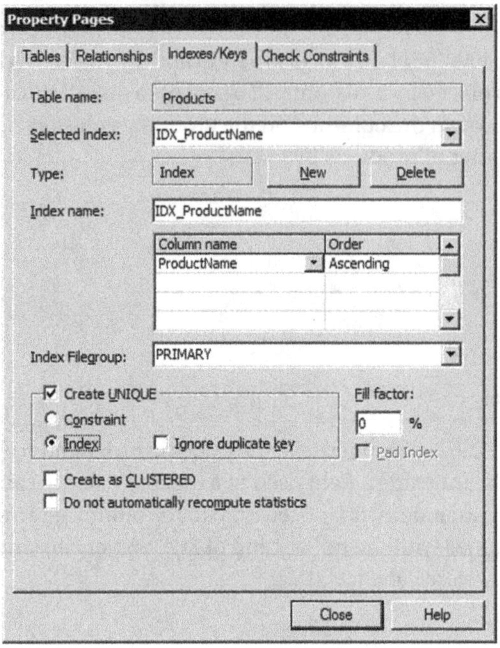

Figure 15-8. *Defining a unique index*

Alternatively, you can create a unique index using the following SQL:

```
CREATE UNIQUE INDEX IDX_ProductName
ON Products
(
   ProductName
)
```

How It Works

The `UNIQUE` keyword specifies that the index will be unique. That doesn't mean the index key is the primary key for the table. Although the index uniquely identifies rows, just like a primary key, a table may have multiple unique indexes but only one primary key.

So far, you've seen why indexes are useful and where they're best applied. Now let's look at some options available when creating an index and some common rules of thumb for designing indexes.

Using Clustered Indexes

Earlier in the chapter we made an analogy between a database index and the index of a book. A book index stores words in order with a reference to the page numbers where the word is located. The corresponding type of index for a database is known as a *nonclustered index*: only the index key and a reference are stored.

In contrast, a *clustered index* maintains base table rows in the same physical sequence as the index key. A phone book is a good analogy. A phone book sorts entries physically in alphabetical order; once you find a name in a phone book, you have immediate access to the rest of the data for the name, such as the phone number and address.

■ **Note** A clustered index determines the physical ordering of the rows in a table. For this reason, a table can have only one clustered index, since it can have only one physical order.

In Figure 15-9, we searched using a clustered index on `UnitPrice`. Note how the rows are stored in index order. The three rows shown are all stored on the same physical database page.

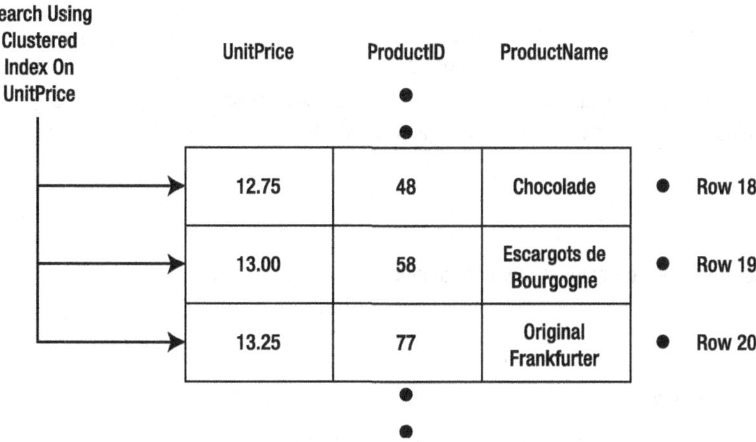

Figure 15-9. *Clustered index data storage*

A clustered index is typically the most important index in terms of performance. Choosing what key to use is often not easy, since a clustered index doesn't need to be unique and several good candidates (often, but not necessarily the primary key) may exist for physical clustering. Almost any large table should be clustered. The performance benefits can be enormous. On the other hand, choosing the clustering key unwisely can lead to disastrous performance.

To create a clustered index, simply use the `CLUSTERED` keyword in the `CREATE INDEX` statement (and note that a clustered index can also be unique, so `CLUSTERED UNIQUE` is valid). For example:

```
CREATE CLUSTERED INDEX IDX_SupplierID
ON Products
(
   SupplierID
)
```

Most of the tables in the Northwind database already have a clustered index. Since there can be only one clustered index per table, if you executed this statement you'd receive an error.

As a general rule of thumb, every table should have a clustered index. If you create only one index for a table, make it clustered. In SQL Server, creating a primary key will automatically create a clustered index (if none already exists) using the primary key as the index key. (Check your RDBMS documentation to see if it automatically defines a clustered index. Some do; others don't.)

Sometimes it's better to use a unique nonclustered index on the primary key and a clustered index on a column or group of columns more commonly used by queries. For example, if the majority of searches are for product price instead of product ID (the primary key), the clustered index could be more effective on the price column.

A DISADVANTAGE OF CLUSTERED INDEXES

If you update a row and change the value of a clustered index key, the database may need to move the row physically to maintain clustering. This essentially turns an UPDATE into a DELETE followed by an INSERT, with an obvious impact on performance. It can also lead to *fragmentation* of storage for base table data, further slowing access and eventually requiring that storage be reorganized, which is often a time-consuming task.

■ **Tip** Don't define a clustered index on columns that are subject to frequent change.

Using Composite Keys

A *composite key* is composed of two or more columns. Both clustered and nonclustered indexes can have composite keys, and composite keys don't necessarily have to be unique. Often, a primary key must be composite because no single column is unique. Sometimes, columns that aren't used to identify rows are included in keys that do, so the database can find data by searching only the index, without accessing the base table itself.

■ **Note** Before designing a composite key that has extra columns, to avoid accessing the base table, read your RDBMS documentation carefully. This may or may not enhance performance at a reasonable cost in extra storage, depending on both your data and your database manager.

Try It Out: Creating an Index with a Composite Key

Suppose the following query is the most popular query executed by your application, and you need to tune the database to support it:

```
SELECT
   ProductName,
   UnitPrice
FROM
   Products
ORDER BY
   UnitPrice
```

You can create a composite index by following these steps:

1. In Server Explorer, right-click the `Products` table and select Design Table. The window in Figure 15-2 appears. Click the Manage Indexes and Keys icon (Figure 15-3) to open the Property Pages dialog box. Give the index the name `IDX_UnitPrice_ProductName`, and specify two columns for the index, `UnitPrice` and `ProductName`, as in Figure 15-10.

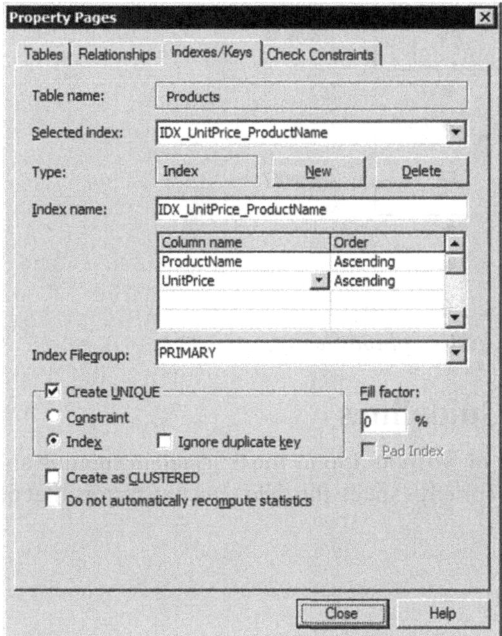

Figure 15-10. *Defining a composite index*

2. Alternatively, you can execute the following equivalent SQL statement:

```
CREATE INDEX IDX_UnitPrice_ProductName
ON Products
(
   UnitPrice,
   ProductName
)
```

How It Works

The index key has two columns. The query can now be satisfied purely from the index since the only columns it needs are in the index key. Figure 15-11 illustrates the index structure. Data from `UnitPrice` and `ProductName` make up the key, and only if you need other data, such as `ProductID`, do you have to access the base table.

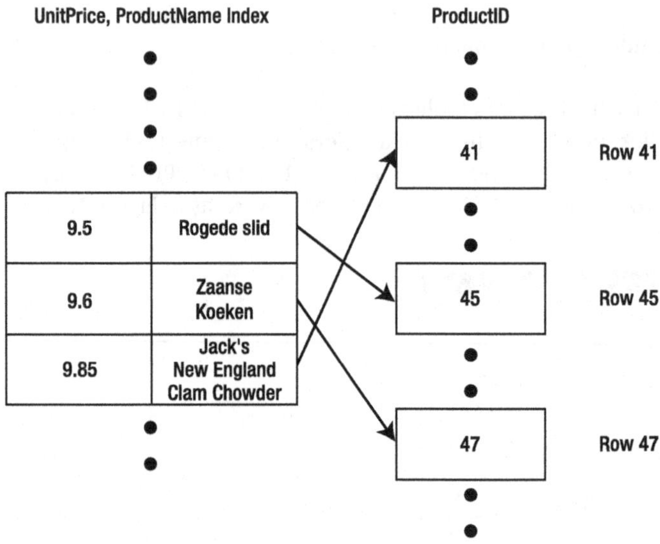

Figure 15-11. *Conceptual view of an index with a composite key*

Learning Additional Index Guidelines

Choosing the correct columns and types for an index is only the first step in creating an effective index. In the following sections, we'll briefly explain the following two factors that deserve consideration:

- Index key length
- Index selectivity

Keeping Index Keys Short

The larger an index key is, the more storage it requires and the harder a database has to work to use the index. As a rule of thumb, limit index keys to as few columns as possible. While composite indexes are useful and can sometimes optimize performance, they're also larger and should be carefully planned before actually implemented. Using a smaller data type for an index key column—for example, a 4-byte rather than an 8-byte integer, or a 10-character fixed-length string rather than a 20-character variable-length one—is often well worth considering.

Finding Distinctive Keys

The most effective indexes are those with a small percentage of duplicate values. Think of having a phone book for a city where 75 percent of the population has the last name Smith. A phone book for this area may be easier to use if the entries were sorted by first name instead of last name. A good index will allow the database to disregard as many rows as possible during a search.

An index with a high percentage of unique values is sometimes called a *selective* index. Obviously, a unique index is the most selective of all, because it has no duplicate values. SQL Server and other RDBMSs can track statistics for indexes and ascertain how selective each index is. The query optimizer utilizes such statistics when selecting the best index to use.

Maintaining Indexes

You can remove indexes with the `DROP INDEX` statement. Since an index is a separate physical structure, dropping an index doesn't affect the data in the underlying base table. Once dropped, an index must be completely re-created. (This can be a relatively expensive process for large tables.)

If an index is dropped, the query optimizer will, of course, have to redetermine the access path to the table and the data rows within it.

Understanding Constraints

The primary purpose of a constraint is to support data integrity. For instance, a foreign key constraint ensuring that all orders reference existing products maintains referential integrity of the data.

Data integrity is so important that relying on users and applications to enforce integrity rules is unwise; you must build these rules into the database. This part of the chapter will show what kinds of rules you can define and how to define them.

Understanding Data Integrity

Data integrity can be classified as follows:

- **Entity integrity**: Each row in a table is uniquely identifiable. You enforce entity integrity with a primary key constraint.
- **Referential integrity**: Relationships between tables are preserved as data is inserted, modified, and deleted. You enforce referential integrity with foreign key constraints.
- **Domain integrity**: Values aren't only of a given data type, but also conform to validity rules (range, format, consistency, and so on) for the real-world entity they represent.

Since we've already covered primary keys and foreign keys, we'll briefly discuss how to define them as constraints and then focus on other constraints that maintain domain integrity.

You can enforce domain integrity using a variety of techniques, including check constraints, unique constraints, and default constraints. These are the techniques we'll cover in this chapter, but other options are available to enforce domain integrity. Even selecting the data type for a column enforces domain integrity to some extent.

The following are some domain integrity constraints you may want to apply to a product table:

- An integer product ID is the primary key.
- A product name must be unique.
- A product name can't be null.
- The unit price must be greater than zero.
- The default unit price is $1.

Defining Constraints

Let's create a table with the previous constraints.

Try It Out: Defining Constraints

To define a constraint, follow these steps:

1. In Server Explorer, right-click Tables for the `Northwind` database, and then click New Table.
2. In the Design grid, define the primary key, `ProductId` as `int` (see Figure 15-12).

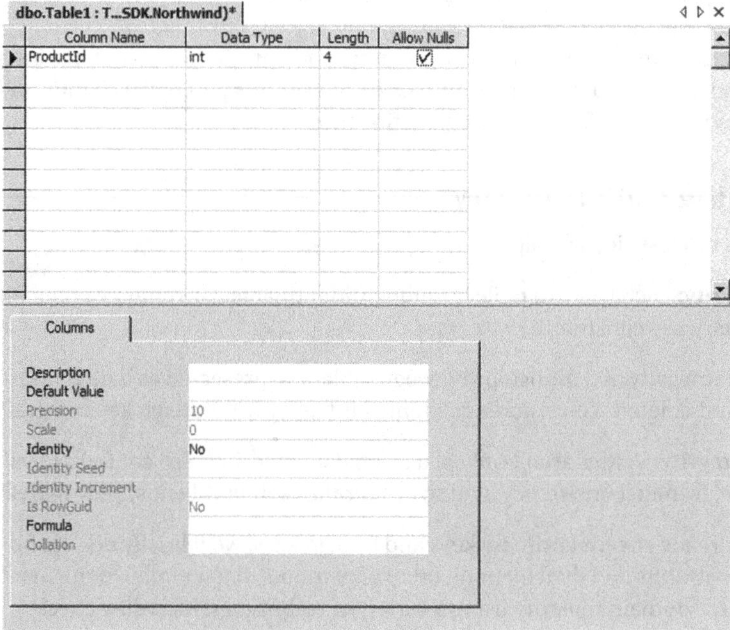

Figure 15-12. *Defining a column*

3. Click the Set Primary Key icon (see Figure 15-13) to designate this column as the primary key. A yellow key appears to the left of the column name to denote this. Note that the Allow Nulls column in the grid is automatically unchecked, since no part of a primary key can be null.

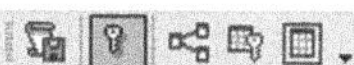

Figure 15-13. *The Set Primary Key icon*

4. Add a ProductName column as `nvarchar` with a length of 40. Uncheck the Allow Nulls column in the grid, as in Figure 15-14. (You'll make it unique later.)

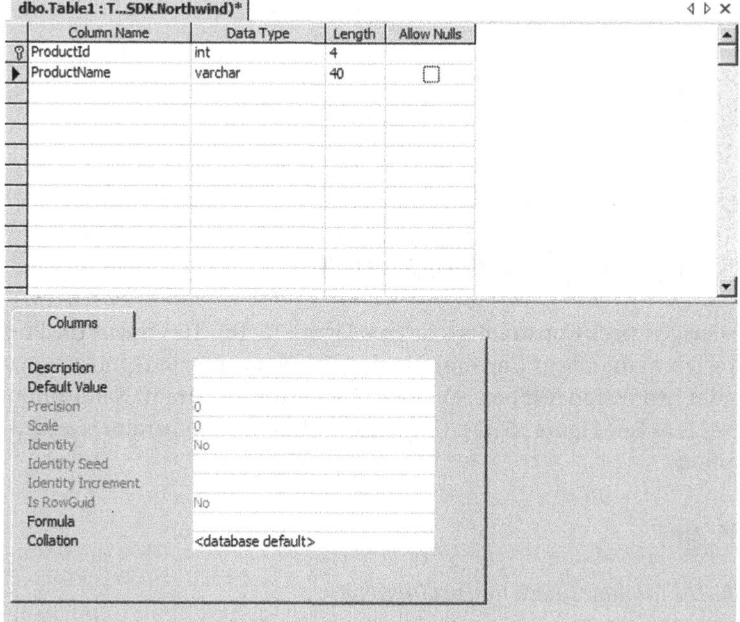

Figure 15-14. *Defining a column as* `NOT NULL`

5. Add a UnitPrice column as `money` and enter **1.00** as the Default Value in the Columns grid, as in Figure 15-15.

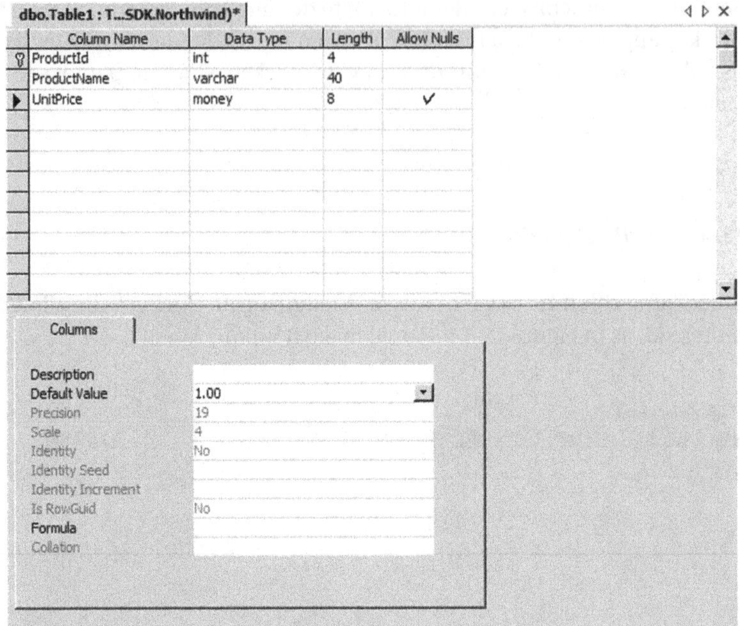

Figure 15-15. *Defining a column with a default value*

6. Click the Manage Check Constraints icon (see Figure 15-16). This opens the Property Pages dialog box at the Check Constraints tab. Click New, enter `unitprice > 0.00` in the Constraint Expression text box, and then change the Constraint Name option to `UnitPriceNotZero` (see Figure 15-17). Click Close. The check constraint is added to the table definition.

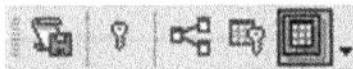

Figure 15-16. *The Manage Check Constraints icon*

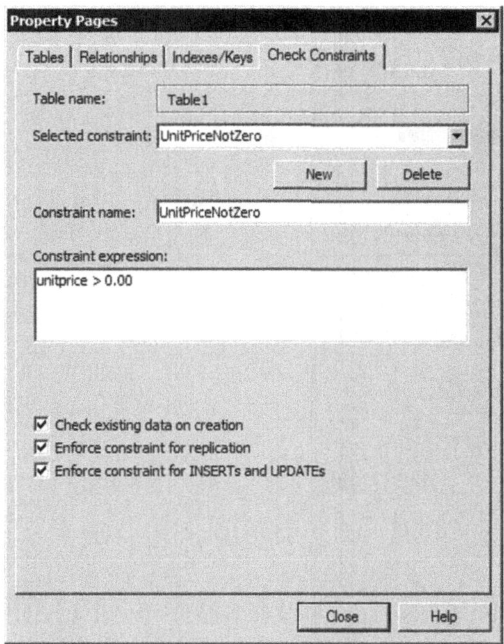

Figure 15-17. *Adding a check constraint*

7. Click the Manage Indexes and Keys icon (Figure 15-3). This opens the Property Pages dialog box at the Indexes/Keys tab (see Figure 15-18). Click New. Change Index name to `IDX_ProductName`. Select the ProductName column as the index key, and check the Create UNIQUE box. Note that when the radio buttons are enabled, you leave the default Constraint selected, unlike Figure 15-9, where you were defining a unique index rather than a unique constraint. Click Close. The unique constraint is added to the table definition.

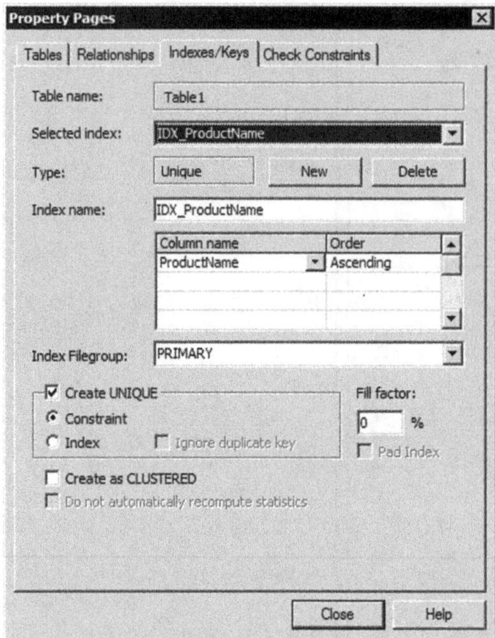

Figure 15-18. *Defining a unique constraint*

8. Click the Save icon, and name the table `ProductsTest` when prompted. Click OK. The new table is created in the `Northwind` database.

9. To see that the constraints have been added, execute the following query in the `QueryProcessor` application from Chapter 13. Widen the columns, and you should see the output as in Figure 15-19.

```
SELECT
   constraint_name,
   constraint_type
FROM
   information_schema.table_constraints
WHERE
   table_name = 'ProductsTest'
```

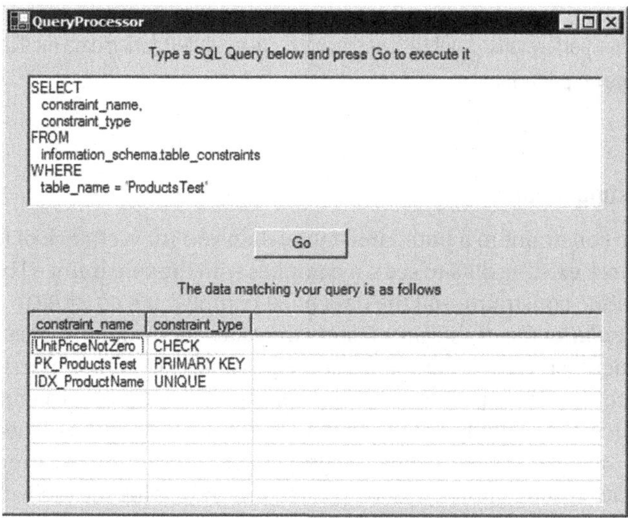

Figure 15-19. *Querying the information schema for table constraints*

How It Works

Defining a table with the help of such a friendly visual tool was easy because it transparently generated a `CREATE TABLE` statement that included all the column and constraint definitions. It even created the primary key index as a clustered index and also a unique index in order to enforce the unique constraint on `ProductName`. The syntactical details are beyond the scope of this book, but rest assured that you could have done the same thing with SQL.

The most important thing to note is that you can define constraints in any order. You could have designated the primary key as your last act rather than doing it immediately after defining the column. (In fact, if the primary key were composite, you would have had to define all the columns for it before designating them as the key.)

Even after you've created a table, you can add constraints (with the `ALTER TABLE` statement, beyond this book's scope—and to be used sparingly and carefully). You'll now look at some of the things that need to be considered when adding constraints, especially if the table isn't empty when the constraint is added.

Using Check Constraints

You use *check constraints* to validate values and formats for a particular column. They're extremely useful for enforcing rules in the database. Check constraints contain an expression, which the database will evaluate when you modify or insert a row. If the expression evaluates to false, the database won't perform the operation.

Defining a check constraint is similar to coding a `WHERE` clause predicate, using relational operators (>, <, <=, >=, <>, =), `BETWEEN`, `IN`, `LIKE`, and `IS NULL`, as well as the `AND` and `OR` logical operators. We specified the check constraint on `UnitPrice` with this predicate:

```
unitprice > 0.00
```

Caution Check constraints have performance implications since they're executed during data modifications. Too many constraints can slow down performance.

Check Constraints and Existing Values

If you add a check or unique constraint to a populated table, then you run a chance of failure, because the database will check existing data to see if it complies with the constraint. (This isn't optional behavior with a unique constraint—all the data must comply.) It's possible to *defer* (SQL Server also calls this *disabling* the constraint) testing the data when adding a check constraint, allowing you to define the constraint and handle possible exceptions later. Load utilities typically use this technique to expedite bulk insertions, particularly when a table has several constraints that would unacceptably slow down the load and for data that's expected to conform to the constraint. However, to ensure data integrity, the constraint should eventually be checked, and most RDBMSs (though not SQL Server) force this by making the table unavailable for processing until the constraint is checked.

It's also possible to defer constraint validation for `INSERT` and `UPDATE` statements and disable specific constraints, using the `ALTER TABLE` statement, but this practice isn't recommended and should be carefully planned beforehand. The various scenarios for enforcing constraints can be quite complicated. Choosing to temporarily not enforce them may be justified for performance but must always be implemented in a way that assures data integrity.

Check Constraints and NULL Values

We've said that the database will stop a data modification only when a check constraint is violated, that is, when the constraint expression evaluates to false. Note that the database allows the modification to take place if the expression is logically unknown because a `NULL` value is involved. For example, suppose you use the following `INSERT` statement on `ProductsTest`:

```
INSERT INTO ProductsTest
(
   ProductId,
   ProductName,
   UnitPrice
)
VALUES (99, 'Product 99', NULL)
```

Even with the constraint that `UnitPrice` must be greater than zero, the `INSERT` is successful. A `NULL` value doesn't allow the database to evaluate the expression as `true` or `false`, making the expression logically unknown.

Restrictions on Check Constraints

Although check constraints are by far the easiest way to enforce domain integrity in a database, they do have some limitations, namely:

- They can't reference a different row in a table.
- They can't reference a column in a different table.

For example, you can't define a check constraint on the `Products` table to test if a product name is unique, since a check constraint can't examine values in rows other than the row currently under examination. For this situation you'd use a unique constraint. Likewise, you can't define a check constraint on the `Products` table to test if a product's `CategoryId` is present in the `Categories` table, as a check constraint can't examine values in other tables. To do this, use a foreign key constraint.

■ **Tip** You can, however, create a check constraint that references more than one column within the same row.

Using NULL Constraints

Although not strictly a constraint, whether to allow `NULL` values in a column is an important part of domain integrity.

When defining a column you can use `NULL` (the default) or `NOT NULL` to specify its *nullability*.

Primary key columns can't be nullable.

Unique constraint key columns can be nullable; however, the constraint checking considers `NULL` values as equal, so only one row may have a `NULL` value for a nullable unique key column. In general, allowing `NULL` values for unique keys isn't a good idea.

Using Default Constraints

Default constraints aren't strictly constraints though some RDBMSs, including earlier versions of SQL Server, allow them to be named like true constraints. They supply a value for a column when an `INSERT` statement doesn't specify one. A default can assign a constant value, the value of a system function, or `NULL` to a column. In SQL Server you can use a default on any column except `IDENTITY` columns and columns of type `timestamp`.

Dropping Constraints

You can permanently remove any constraint from a table with the `DROP CONSTRAINT` clause of the `ALTER TABLE` statement.

Summary

We started this chapter with an explanation of indexes, showing what they are and the advantages and disadvantages of using them. While indexes can increase the performance of some queries, they can slow down the overall process of updating the database. Consequently, you need to think carefully when deciding whether to create an index. You also learned the difference between clustered and nonclustered indexes.

In the second part of the chapter, you learned how various constraints ensure data (entity, referential, and domain) integrity. You saw how to define unique, check, default, and nullability constraints and discussed their implications at runtime.

There's much more to both indexes and constraints, but we've covered the basics you'll use most often. Using them wisely is crucial for successful database operation. Now that you know the fundamentals, study your RDBMS documentation and experiment with various scenarios. Whether an index or a constraint is advisable is often not just a conceptual issue but one best resolved by actually testing one's assumptions.

In the next chapter you'll look at another integrity issue: authenticating and authorizing users.

CHAPTER 16

■ ■ ■

Securing Your Database

You need to ask yourself the following two critical questions about database security:

- *Who* can access the database?
- *What* can they do with the database?

The first question involves *authentication*, which involves determining the identity of the user trying to access the database. The classic authentication approach requires a user name and password to prove the user's identity. The second question involves *authorization*. Users can perform only the actions they're allowed to perform, based on rights granted to them as individuals or groups.

Although many aspects of database security exist and each database system handles it in its own way, you should become familiar with some fundamental concepts and facilities.

In this chapter, we'll cover the following, using SQL Server terminology and techniques:

- Authentication modes
- Login and user management
- Database roles
- How to grant and revoke permissions

Note Security is another area where database terminology is diverse. The SQL standard uses the term *privilege* for the authority granted to a specific user (or group) to perform a specific action on a database object (for example, tables, views, and indexes). Some RDBMSs distinguish between privileges and authorities. SQL Server calls privileges *permissions*.

Although SQL Server provides a visual tool for administering security (called Enterprise Manager), MSDE doesn't. However, it provides a number of stored procedures to view and update security settings. So, we've built our own little utility, AdminHelp, as a visual interface to make using the common stored procedures more convenient. This utility lets you view security-related SQL Server settings. Figure 16-1 shows the utility's main screen.

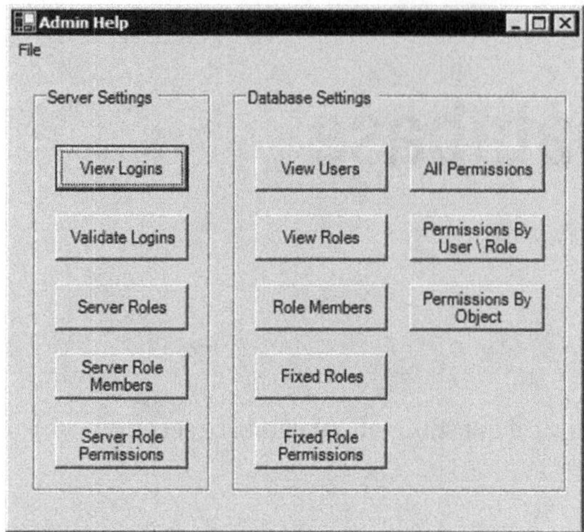

Figure 16-1. *AdminHelp main screen*

This utility is available as a project in the code download for this chapter. Copy the `Chapter16_Examples` directory to your working directory (we used `C:\BegVbNetDb`). Open the solution in Visual Studio, and execute it with Ctrl+F5 to see the screen shown in Figure 16-1. Before you can view any settings, you must connect to a database, which you can do by selecting File ➤ Connect to Database. If you want to use this utility to work with a different database, then simply change the parameters in the connection string for the `thisConnection` object. It's a `SqlConnection` object attached to the form.

Understanding the Security Process

Before we dive into the details of database security, we'll first quickly overview the security process and how it works.

When dealing with Windows security, a system administrator typically places users into one or more groups to ease system management. In addition to built-in groups, such as `Administrators` and `Guests`, an administrator can create new groups.

For example, Joy, Tim, and Amy all work in human resources (HR). All three employees will probably need access to the same resources on a machine or network, such as a spreadsheet of employee salaries. An administrator could create a new group named `HR` and add each user to the group. The administrator then grants permissions for the salary spreadsheet to the group, instead of each user. As employees join or leave the HR department, it's easier to add or remove them from the `HR` group than to comb through each resource and grant or deny privileges at the user level.

Now suppose Joy needs to access an employee database to run a report. The first stage is to log into the database server. As you'll see shortly, the login may be authenticated by the SQL Server instance itself or managed separately by the Windows security system (if Joy has already been authenticated by a Windows domain server). Once the login is authenticated, she is logged into the database server but can't actually do anything. To be able to access a particular database, the login needs to be mapped to one of the user accounts managed by that database.

The database then grants certain permissions to each user, which describe whether they can, for example, view a table or run a stored procedure. This process is known as *authorization*.

As with Windows, it can be difficult to manage all these permissions at the level of the individual user. For a database administrator, groups work equally well. It's likely that everyone in the HR department will need to run reports, so rather than add Joy, Tim, and Amy as individual database user accounts, you can just add the `HR` group as a whole. As employees join and leave the HR group, you wouldn't have to do anything to grant and deny the employees access.

Furthermore, the database supports *roles*, which work at both the server and the individual database level. Rather than grant permissions to individual users, you can add or remove users from roles. You'll see how all this works later in the "Managing Roles" section.

■ **Tip** If you're logged into Windows as an administrator, a lot of this is sorted out under the hood for you, and you'll automatically have full administrative rights over any of the databases on the database server.

Throughout the rest of this chapter, you'll take a closer look at how all this works and at the various stored procedures provided by SQL Server to view and alter the security settings.

Understanding Authentication

The SQL Server database engine operates in one of two authentication modes. In Windows Authentication mode, the engine relies on the operating system to authenticate users. This is the mode we've been using throughout the book, specified by the `Integrated Security=SSPI` (or `Integrated Security=True`) parameter in the connection string.

In Mixed Mode, the database engine can still use Windows Authentication but can also perform authentication itself by verifying a user's login and password credentials using SQL Server Authentication. We'll cover both of these modes in more detail in the following sections.

Windows Authentication

Windows Authentication is the preferred mode for SQL Server because of its tight integration with the more robust and manageable security features of the Windows operating system. Unless you're on a Windows 98 system, Windows Authentication is the default mode for installation.

■ **Tip** Windows 98 doesn't have the strong security system of Windows NT, 2000, and XP, so Windows Authentication isn't available with it. When we use the term *Windows security*, we're referring to Windows NT 4 or later.

In a typical forms-based data access application using Windows Authentication, a user will first log into a Windows machine. The local machine or a domain controller on the network will validate the user name and password supplied by the user. At this point, the user launches the application to connect to an MSDE or SQL Server instance. The connection string includes the following parameter:

```
Integrated Security=SSPI;
```

This parameter instructs the client-side database software to establish a *trusted connection*. This means that the SQL Server instance relies on Windows to authenticate the user who is connecting to the database. The client establishes the connection using a layer of Microsoft software known as the Security Support Provider Interface (SSPI).

■ **Note** Authentication allows a client to connect to an instance of the database engine but doesn't yet grant access to any databases managed by the instance. You'll see how this works in the "User Accounts" section when you learn how to map database user accounts to server logins.

Windows Authentication allows a database administrator to take advantage of the built-in security features of Windows. These features include (but are not limited to) the following:

- **Password expiration**: This forces users to change passwords after a set amount of time.
- **Account lock out**: This helps prevent malicious users from guessing a password by disabling an account after a set number of failed login attempts.
- **Strong passwords**: This prevents guessing passwords by enforcing a minimum length and preventing common words from being used as passwords.

In addition to providing a robust security infrastructure, Windows Authentication allows clients to use the same login and password to access resources on the local machine, the network, and the database server.

Mixed Mode Authentication

In Mixed Mode, the database engine can still perform Windows Authentication over trusted connections, but it also provides a second type of authentication: SQL Server Authentication.

In a typical Mixed Mode scenario, a user logs into a machine and launches a forms-based application that connects to a database. The connection string in this case would include the following parameters:

```
User ID=<a_user_id>;Password=<the_users_password>;
```

This connection string explicitly specifies a user name and password. The client will use a *nontrusted connection*, because no Windows credentials are associated with the connection. The database engine will check that the user ID exists and that the password is valid. The database server carries out the authentication process.

Mixed Mode Authentication places a greater burden on both the database and the database administrator to manage users and passwords. In addition, the security features aren't as robust. For these reasons, Windows Authentication is the preferred authentication mode.

Managing Users

Both of the authentication modes require valid login entries in the database server. To be authorized to access an individual database, however, a login must map to a database-specific user account. Authorization in MSDE revolves around database *users* and database *roles*, which are similar to the users and groups of Microsoft Windows but are specific to each database.

In the following sections, we'll cover how to manage user accounts and roles, but first we'll show how to view server login information and also how to add and remove users.

Database Logins

You can view the list of logins using the `sp_helplogins` stored procedure. When you execute this, it returns the following two result sets:

- The list of available logins
- Detailed information for each login, including the databases for which they're authorized

Although many query windows will show only one result set, you can use our AdminHelp application to view both result sets. Make sure you've established a connection, and then click the View Logins button to get a screen like the one shown in Figure 16-2.

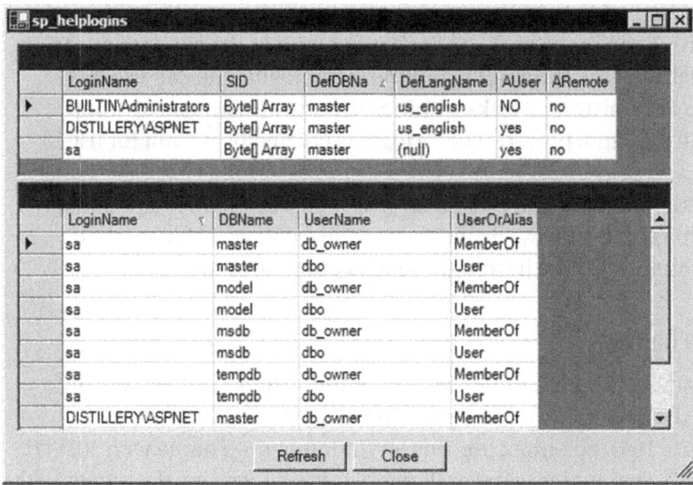

Figure 16-2. *Viewing login information*

■ **Note** Many of the queries in this chapter will return a column with a security identification number (SID). We won't make any special use of SIDs in this chapter. The database uses this number internally to uniquely identify each login name.

For now we want to concentrate on the first column (LoginName) of the first result set. You can see two valid logins for the database engine.

The first row is an entry for a Windows group. Users placed into the Administrators group have additional privileges to perform administrative tasks on a machine. Adding a group as a SQL Server login allows any of the users who are members of the group to log in. When adding a local built-in group such as Administrators, a special prefix (BUILTIN) is used instead of the computer or domain name used for individual users.

■ **Note** By default, installing MSDE and SQL Server adds BUILTIN\Administrators as an available login.

With Windows Authentication, we recommend you manage database logins with groups instead of by individual Windows accounts. As you create database objects (tables, views, stored procedures, and so on), think about how the groups in your organization should be able to access these objects. The second row then seems to contradict this, because you gave the ASPNET account individual permissions to access the Northwind database back in Chapter 9. However, this is a machine account rather than a user's Windows account. Just be careful you don't give it access to everything; malicious users may be able to access all your data through that account.

The final row is a SQL Server login. A client accessing the database using Mixed Mode Authentication can specify this login name as the user ID parameter in the connection string. In fact, the sa login is a special account: the system administrator login. You can use this all-powerful login to perform administrative tasks within SQL Server (members of group BUILTIN\Administrators have the same power). The sa login is created by default for use in Mixed Mode Authentication.

Note that the default password for the sa login is an empty string, which is a potentially disastrous security hole, so you should always explicitly provide a password for sa when installing SQL Server—and carefully secure it from those who don't need to know it.

Adding and Removing Login Entries

The stored procedure sp_grantlogin adds a Windows user or group as a login entry. Only a single argument is required: the user name or group name to add. As shown in the sp_helplogins output in Figure 16-2, you must precede a Windows group name with BUILTIN and a Windows user name with a computer name or domain name, separating the names with a backslash. For example, suppose you really do have a Windows group for human resources named HR. The following command would allow members of the HR group to log in:

```
EXEC sp_grantlogin 'ComputerName\HR'
```

You can grant a login to an individual user with the same stored procedure, like so:

```
EXEC sp_grantlogin 'ComputerName\Joy'
```

To remove a Windows user or group, use the sp_revokelogin stored procedure. This procedure also requires a user or group name in the same format as the previous one. For example, executing the following removes the HR group from the list of valid logins:

```
EXEC sp_revokelogin 'ComputerName\HR'
```

Joy, even if she is a member of the HR group, can still log into the database engine, since she was also added as an individual user with sp_grantlogin. Revoking login permissions for a group doesn't revoke login permissions for users within the group if they already have individual logins. Individual security specifications override those for a group.

As time passes, an administrator may remove users and groups from Windows, but the login permission remains in the database server. You should use the sp_validatelogins stored procedure to see a list of logins granted on the database server with no corresponding entry in Windows. You can also view this list in AdminHelp with the Validate Logins button. These logins should be unusable, so you should revoke them.

SQL Server Logins

Managing logins for SQL Server Authentication requires a different set of stored procedures. To add a SQL Server login, use the sp_addlogin stored procedure. While the only required parameter is a login name, we also recommend you supply a password as the second parameter. The following adds the login name Juan:

```
EXEC sp_addlogin 'Juan', 'Juanpassword'
```

With Windows Authentication, when users change passwords in the operating system, no additional work is required to synchronize a database password. The database relies on the operating system to validate the identity. With SQL Server Authentication, the password is stored in the database, not in Windows. To change a password for a SQL Server login, use the sp_password stored procedure. The parameters are the existing password, the new password, and the login name, like so:

```
EXEC sp_password 'Juanpassword', 'NewJuanpassword', 'Juan'
```

You can use the stored procedure sp_droplogin to remove a SQL Server login. The only parameter for this procedure is the login name. The next command will remove Juan from the list of available logins:

```
EXEC sp_droplogin 'Juan'
```

SQL Server will never confuse a Windows group or user name with a SQL Server login name. Windows groups and usernames always have a backslash (after the computer or domain name). The backslash is an illegal character for SQL Server login names.

It doesn't matter which particular database you're currently using when executing the previous stored procedures. You may be currently using the Northwind database or the master database. In either case, logins apply to the server instance, not to a specific database.

As we mentioned earlier, a login doesn't give a user access to any particular database on the server. For instance, you could apply security settings in the Northwind database that restrict access to administrators only. Other users could still log into the database server and perhaps use other databases. However, only members of the BUILTIN\Administrators group, or users logging in as sa, would have the ability to retrieve information from Northwind.

Special Users

SQL Server has the following two special users:

dbo: dbo is present in every database. This user is the database owner and has permission to perform any activity in a database. You can't delete the dbo user. Note that both the SQL Server sa login and the BUILTIN\Administrators group map to the dbo user in all databases.

guest: By default, the guest user isn't present when you create a new database. You can remove the guest user from a database (except the master and tempdb databases). The guest account allows users to access a database if they have valid logins to the database server but don't have their own user accounts for the database.

Figure 16-3 illustrates the process of mapping logins to user accounts using Windows Authentication. Three members of the HR group—Joy, Tim, and Amy—are using the guest account.

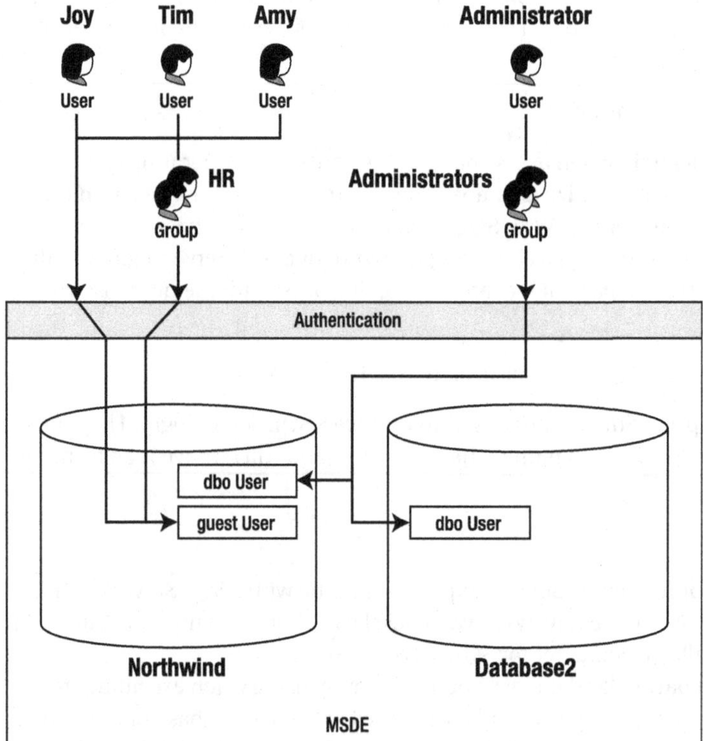

Figure 16-3. *dbo and guest login account mappings*

In this figure, we have logins available for the user Joy, the group HR, and the group BUILTIN\Administrators. The engine maps administrators to the dbo user implicitly. Joy, Tim, and Amy will all log into the Northwind database as the guest user since there's no user account created explicitly for them. In the second database, no explicit user exists for Joy, Tim, and Amy, and a guest account isn't present. The second database isn't available to the members of HR but is available to administrators.

User Accounts

You must map server-level logins to user accounts in each database. Although you could use the guest account to allow access to a database from any login (as shown in Figure 16-3), this isn't best practice. Instead, you should add a user account into each database for every user with a server login that needs to access it. A login can map to different user accounts in different databases; the names don't need to be the same. In the following sections, we'll discuss how to add, delete, and view user accounts.

Adding a User Account

You can map a login to a user account in the current database using the sp_grantdbaccess stored procedure. The first parameter to the stored procedure is the login name, and the second parameter is the name of the user account to create and associate with the login. Assuming you're in the Northwind database as an administrator, you can map the HR login to a user account named HR with the following command:

```
EXEC sp_grantdbaccess 'ComputerName\HR', 'hr'
```

The user account name doesn't need to reflect the login name. For example, you could have also named the user account humanresources. One member of the HR group has her own login: Joy. You can associate Joy with a specific user account as follows:

```
EXEC sp_grantdbaccess 'ComputerName\Joy', 'joy'
```

When Joy logs in, she'll map to the user account specified for her login (joy), even though she's a member of the human resources group and can gain access via the hr user. The engine will always try to match an individual account first, before looking for a group of which the user is a member. You can use this behavior to assign the user different permissions based on the groups in which they belong.

After applying these new changes, you can reexamine the concepts in Figure 16-3. The result is Figure 16-4.

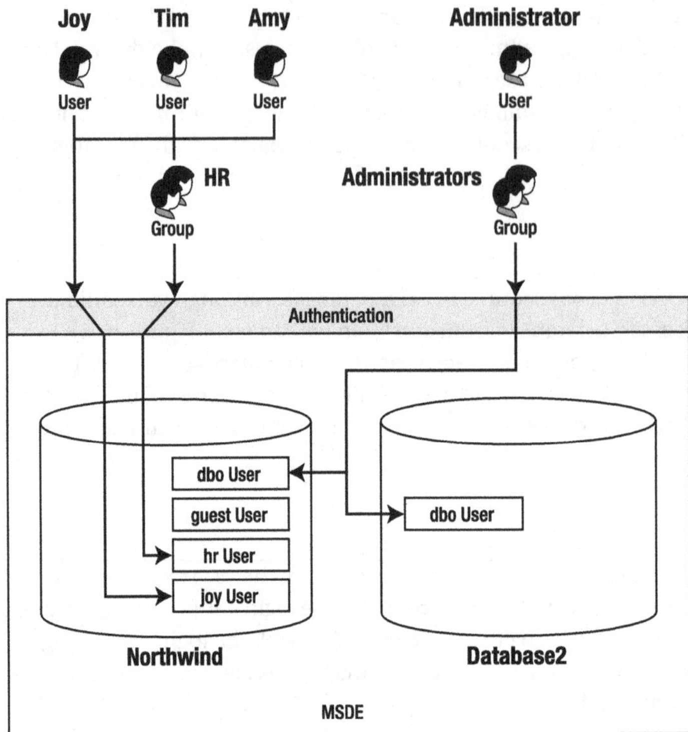

Figure 16-4. *User and group login account mappings*

Viewing User Accounts

You can view all the user accounts in a database using the system stored procedure `sp_helpuser`. The AdminHelp application executes this stored procedure when you click View Users in the main form. The output for the `Northwind` database looks like Figure 16-5.

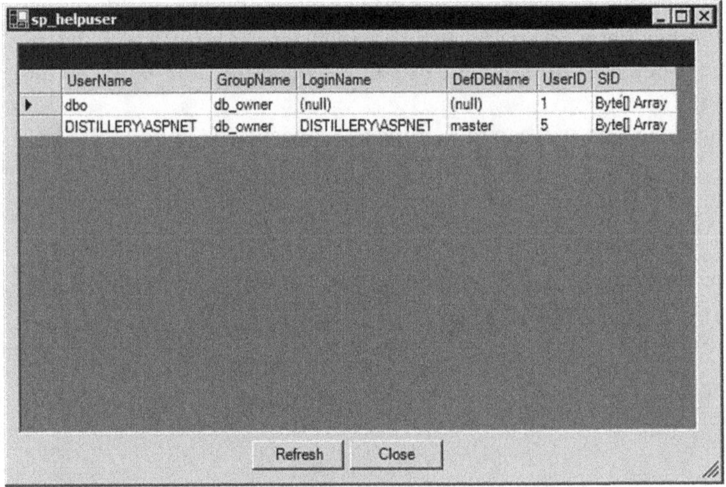

UserName	GroupName	LoginName	DefDBName	UserID	SID
dbo	db_owner	(null)	(null)	1	Byte[] Array
DISTILLERY\ASPNET	db_owner	DISTILLERY\ASPNET	master	5	Byte[] Array

Figure 16-5. *Viewing `Northwind` users*

Removing a User Account

You can remove a user account from a database using the system stored procedure `sp_revokedbaccess`. The only parameter to this procedure is the user name. To remove the user `joy`, you'd issue the following command:

```
EXEC sp_revokedbaccess 'joy'
```

In this case, however, Joy may still be able to log into the database if she is still a member of the `HR` group under Windows.

■ **Tip** As you can see, it makes more sense to handle user authorization at the group level rather than the level of the individual user. If you make changes to a group, then you aren't left with the problem of "dangling users."

Note that you can't remove the `dbo` user, and you can't remove a user who currently owns an object in the database. If you need to revoke access for a user with objects in a database, you can use the `sp_changeobjectowner` stored procedure first to change ownership.

Managing Roles

Database roles are similar to groups in Windows. You can use groups to collect users into a single entity and manage permissions using the collection instead of a single entity. If you're already creating logins based on Windows groups, you're already achieving this behavior. However, database roles add an extra degree of flexibility.

The two types of role are as follows:

- **Fixed server roles**: These are built-in and apply at the server level. They can't be deleted or changed.
- **Database roles**: These apply at the individual database level. A set of fixed database roles is predefined for you, but you can also create your own custom roles.

You'll see in the "Creating Roles" section how to create your own application-specific roles. It's always worth taking a look at the built-in roles first, however, to see if they fit your needs.

We'll also begin to touch upon database permissions; for example, is a given user allowed to create a table or query against a table? Once you have a better understanding of roles, we'll cover specific permissions.

Fixed Server Roles

Adding a user to a fixed server role will grant the user all the permissions associated with the server role. Server roles are *fixed* because you can't add or remove these roles, and you can't modify the permissions assigned to them. Table 16-1 gives the name of each server role and a general description of the permissions associated with the role.

Table 16-1. *Fixed Server Roles*

Fixed Server Role	Users in This Role Are Allowed To...
bulkadmin	Perform bulk inserts to the database.
dbcreator	Add, modify, and remove databases.
diskadmin	Manage the physical disk files used by the server for data storage.
processadmin	Manage processes in the engine and, for example, kill a connection.
securityadmin	Manage logins and change passwords.
serveradmin	Modify configuration settings on the server and shut the server down.
setupadmin	Add and remove remote (linked) servers.
sysadmin	Perform any activity on the server. (The BUILTIN\Administrators group is a member of this role by default. This is the administrative role.)

To view the specific permissions assigned to each fixed server role, execute the sp_srvrolepermission stored procedure. You can use the Server Role Permissions button in AdminHelp to display the results of the stored procedure. The utility will first ask you to select the name of the server role to display. As an example, Figure 16-6 shows the permissions for the dbcreator role.

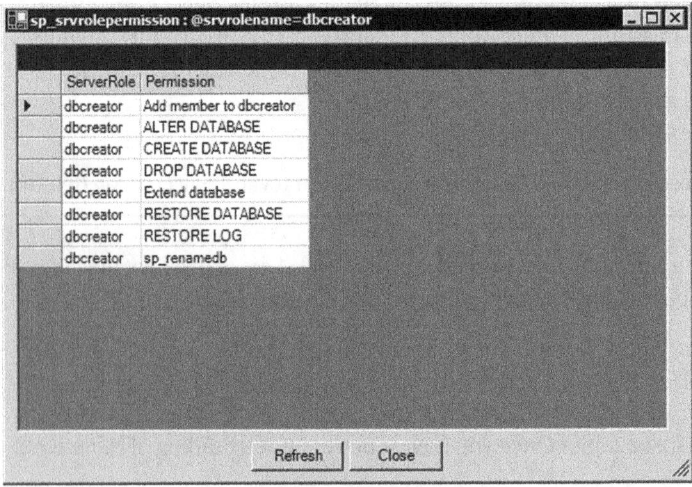

Figure 16-6. *Viewing permissions for role dbcreator*

You can add database users to a fixed server role with the sp_addsrvrolemember stored procedure. Since these are server-level roles, not database roles, you must add a login name, not a user name from a specific database. For example, if Joy still has a valid login, you could make Joy a member of the sysadmin group with the following:

```
EXEC sp_addsrvrolemember 'ComputerName\Joy', sysadmin
```

You can view members in each server role by executing sp_helpsrvrolemember. This is available from AdminHelp by clicking the Server Role Members button. The procedure returns a row for each member in each server role (see Figure 16-7).

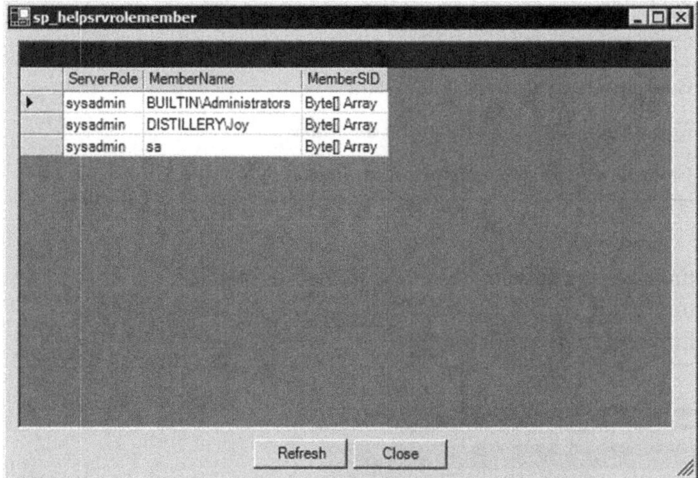

ServerRole	MemberName	MemberSID
sysadmin	BUILTIN\Administrators	Byte[] Array
sysadmin	DISTILLERY\Joy	Byte[] Array
sysadmin	sa	Byte[] Array

Figure 16-7. *Viewing server role members*

To remove a user from the sysadmin server role, execute the sp_dropsrvrolemember procedure, using the login and the role name as parameters, like so:

```
EXEC sp_dropsrvrolemember 'ComputerName\Joy', sysadmin
```

Fixed Database Roles

Adding a user to a fixed database role will grant to the user all the permissions associated with the database role for the given database. These roles are fixed because you can't add or remove them from a database or modify the permissions assigned to them. Table 16-2 summarizes the fixed database roles.

Table 16-2. *Fixed Database Roles*

Fixed Database Role	Description
`db_accessadmin`	Can add or remove users in the database
`db_backupoperator`	Can perform backup and diagnostic operations
`db_datareader`	Can issue `SELECT` queries on any user table in the database
`db_datawriter`	Can modify the data in any user table (using `INSERT`, `UPDATE`, `DELETE` and SQL statements)
`db_ddladmin`	Can issue data definition language commands to create, drop, and alter objects
`db_denydatareader`	Can't select data
`db_denydatawriter`	Can't insert, update, or delete data
`db_owner`	Can perform any activity in the database
`db_securityadmin`	Can manage all permissions, roles, and role memberships

To view the specific permissions assigned to a fixed database role, use the `sp_dbfixedrolepermission` stored procedure, or click the Fixed Role Permissions button in AdminHelp. Figure 16-8 shows sample output for the `db_datawriter` role.

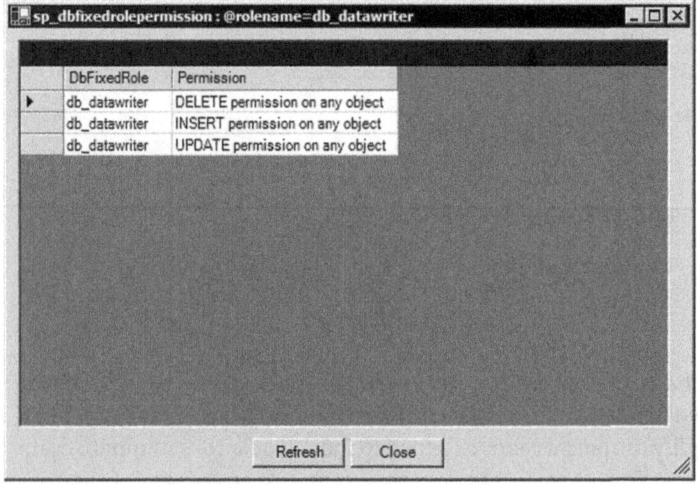

Figure 16-8. *Viewing permissions for fixed database role* `db_datawriter`

A member with the `db_datawriter` role can perform `INSERT`, `UPDATE`, and `DELETE` on any table in the database.

If an existing database role already has the required permission set for a user, the best solution is to use the fixed database role instead of creating a new role. To add a user to a role, execute the `sp_addrolemember` stored procedure, passing the database role and the user name, like so:

```
EXEC sp_addrolemember db_owner, joy
```

You can view a list of the roles and their members using the sp_helprolemember procedure. You can view these in AdminHelp by clicking the Role Members command button.

You can remove a user from a role with the sp_droprolemember procedure, like so:

```
EXEC sp_droprolemember db_owner, joy
```

The Public Role

Every database also contains a fixed role named public. Every user in a database is a member of the public role. You can't remove the public role, and you can't add or remove users from it. The permissions assigned to the public role become the default permissions for the database.

We'll now show how to create your own custom roles.

Creating Roles

You can create a custom role using the sp_addrole stored procedure, passing the role name as follows:

```
EXEC sp_addrole customrole
```

You can create roles only at the database level. The only server roles available are the fixed server roles created by default. Adding a user to a custom role uses the same sp_addrolemember procedure you used earlier.

```
EXEC sp_addrolemember customrole, joy
```

If you now look at the available roles and users for the database through AdminHelp (with the Role Members button), you should see the results in Figure 16-9.

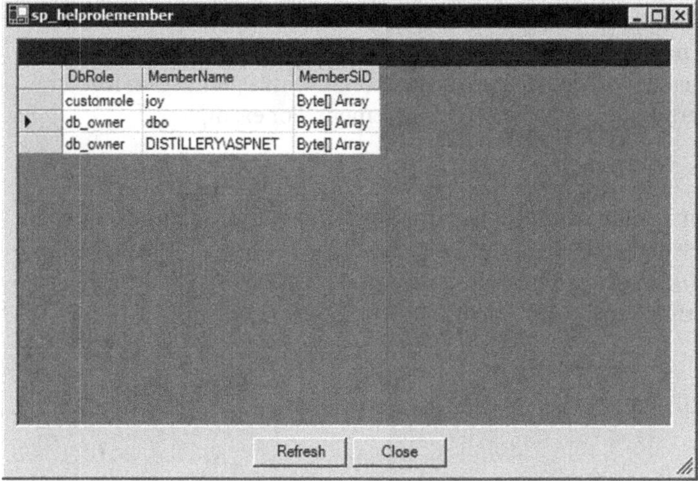

Figure 16-9. *Viewing role members*

The dialog box shows only the roles currently populated with users. Even though other fixed database roles exist in Northwind, they don't have any members. The stored procedure will also not show the members of the public role, since all users (and even the other groups) are members of this role.

To remove a role, execute the sp_droprole stored procedure, passing the name of the role as a parameter. However, you need to remove all members of a role before the procedure returns successfully. You can remove a member from a role with the sp_droprolemember stored procedure, like so:

```
EXEC sp_droprolemember customrole, hr
EXEC sp_droprole customrole
```

With all the users and roles in place, you can finally begin to look at how to assign specific permissions to them.

Managing Permissions

You manage permissions by granting, denying, or revoking them for a user, group, or role. You can grant, revoke, and deny permissions for database objects (such as tables and stored procedures) and even for certain statements (such as CREATE TABLE).

The authority to manage permissions is restricted to a limited number of roles. You need to be a sysadmin, a db_owner, a db_securityadmin, or the owner (or creator) of a database object to manage permissions.

First, we'll cover the differences between granting, denying, and revoking permissions using a simple example. Second, we'll show how to change the authorization for users to select data from the Employees table of the Northwind database.

Revoking Permission

In the Northwind database, the public role has the ability to select from the Employees. Recall that every database user is a member of the public group, so any user has the ability to select from Employees. As the first restriction on Northwind, you'll remove this permission from the public role. You remove a permission with the REVOKE statement. For example:

```
REVOKE SELECT ON employees FROM public
```

The REVOKE statement for a database object (such as a table) requires you to specify the privilege(s) (here, SELECT), the object name (here, Employees), and the user or role (here, the public role) from which you're revoking the privilege. We'll take a closer look at available privileges later in the "Object Permissions" and "Statement Permissions" sections.

After an administrator has executed this REVOKE statement, no public users will be able to retrieve data from the table; however, users in certain fixed roles and the table owner still can. Remember, you can never adjust the permissions of fixed roles, such as the sysadmin and db_owner roles. Users in these roles will always have unrestricted access to objects in a database. However, the hr group has a user account in the database but belongs to no roles other than public. If a member of the hr group attempts to query Employees, they will receive the following error:

```
Msg 229, Level 14, State 5, Server <hostname>\NETSDK, Line 1
SELECT permission denied on object 'Employees', database 'Northwind', owner 'dbo'.
```

■ **Tip** Remember, you mapped the database account hr to the Windows group HR earlier in the chapter with sp_grantdbaccess, so the database user hr is an alias for the Windows group HR.

Granting Permission

Granting a permission enables a user or role to perform some activity. In the following SQL, we grant permission to the hr account to SELECT from the Employee table. The syntax is similar to REVOKE.

```
GRANT SELECT ON Employees TO hr
```

Here, you allow all three members of the HR group (Joy, Tim, and Amy) to select from the Employees table.

Denying Permission

Denying a permission explicitly prohibits a user or role from obtaining it. While REVOKE removes a previous permission, DENY ensures the permission can't be granted. Remember, a user may be a member of multiple groups or roles, and each may be granted different permissions. The only way to ensure a user or role never has a specific permission is to explicitly DENY the permission.

As an example, let's first add Tim as a user to the database, like so:

```
EXEC sp_grantdbaccess 'ComputerName\Tim', 'tim'
```

When Tim accesses the Northwind database, he'll do so as the user tim, instead of the user hr. Remember, the database engine is as selective as possible when mapping a login to a database user. Now explicitly DENY Tim's SELECT access to the Employees table, like so:

```
DENY SELECT ON Employees TO tim
```

Although Tim was granted the permission to SELECT from Employees earlier as a member of the Windows group HR, you've now explicitly denied this privilege to tim, so he no longer has (or can have) this permission.

Note A DENY takes precedence over any permissions a user, group, or role has been granted. Explicitly denying a permission ensures the permission is never inherited from another role or group. However, DENY doesn't work against a fixed server role.

You'll see a specific example of DENY in action in the "Object Permissions" section.

Resolving Permission Conflicts

We've changed a few of the permissions on the database now, so let's quickly review the actions on the Employees table to this point.

- You revoked SELECT from role public.
- You granted SELECT to group hr.
- You denied SELECT to user tim.

Now let's explicitly add Amy (the third member of the HR group) to the database with the following:

```
EXEC sp_grantdbaccess 'ComputerName\Amy', amy
```

Next, revoke Joy's permission to select from the Employees table with the following:

```
REVOKE SELECT ON employees FROM joy
```

At this point you have conflicting permissions. Amy is a member of the HR group, and since you granted this group SELECT permission, Amy can still SELECT from Employees. Then you revoked the permission for Joy. However, she is still a member of the HR group and inherits the permissions of HR. The HR permissions allow Joy to select from Employees. A REVOKE (unlike a DENY) won't take away permissions granted to a user by another role or group. For Tim, on the other hand, you explicitly denied the SELECT permission, and the database won't allow him to inherit this permission from the HR group of which he is a member. Figure 16-10 illustrates the behavior.

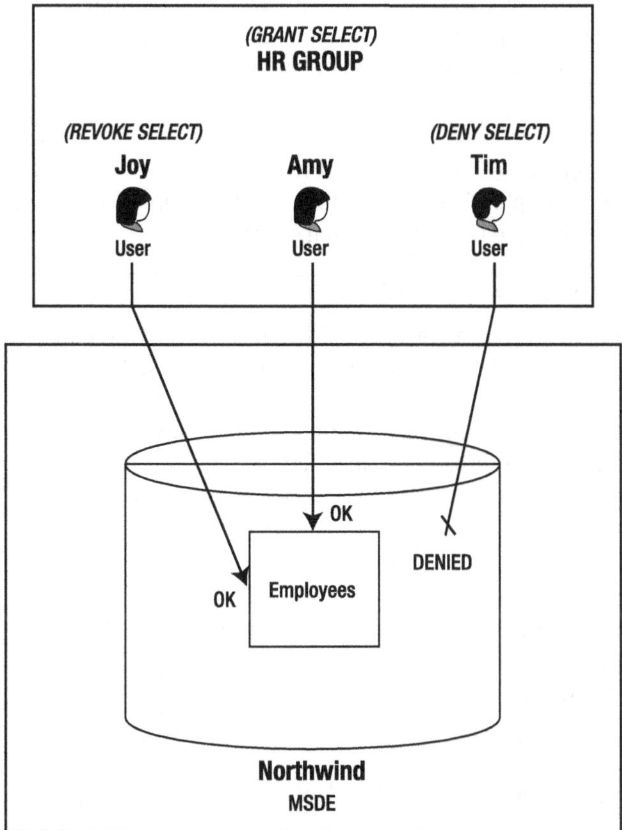

Figure 16-10. *A complex permissions scenario*

With a basic understanding of `GRANT`, `DENY`, and `REVOKE`, you'll now see other permissions you can manage with these statements.

Object Permissions

Object permissions are the permissions you can apply to objects, such as tables or stored procedures. So far, you've been looking at how to work with the `SELECT` permission in these examples. For tables and views, you can grant, deny, or revoke the following permissions:

- `SELECT`
- `INSERT`
- `DELETE`
- `REFERENCES`
- `UPDATE`

You can specify more than one permission in a GRANT, DENY, or REVOKE statement in a comma-separated list. For example, if you wanted to allow hr to retrieve, insert, and update (but not delete) rows in the Employees table, you could use the following:

```
GRANT SELECT, INSERT, UPDATE ON Employees TO hr
```

For SELECT and UPDATE statements, you can grant, deny, or revoke permissions on specific columns instead of the entire table. For example, if you wanted to remove Joy's ability to access the BirthDate and HireDate columns, you could use the following statement:

```
DENY SELECT (BirthDate, HireDate) ON Employees TO joy
```

Notice you need to use a DENY statement instead of a REVOKE, because REVOKE won't take away the GRANT you gave to the HR group, of which Joy is a member. Joy can still update the table with the previous GRANT.

You use the REFERENCES permission to control the placement of foreign key constraints on a table. Foreign key constraints have an obvious impact on INSERT, UPDATE, and DELETE logic for a table, as well as performance implications. You could remove the permission from the public role like this:

```
REVOKE REFERENCES ON Employees FROM public
```

Stored procedures have only one permission: EXECUTE. This permission controls the ability to invoke a stored procedure. You could revoke the permission to execute the CustOrderHist stored procedure from the public role like this:

```
REVOKE EXECUTE ON CustOrderHist FROM public
```

Finally, you can use the following shortcut to modify all permissions for a given object at once, using the ALL keyword:

```
REVOKE ALL ON Employees FROM public
```

This statement removes any permissions the public role has on the Employees table.

Statement Permissions

You also have the ability to grant, deny, or revoke permissions on a select list of statements at the database level. These permissions relate to the kinds of things you can do in terms of the actual structure of the database rather than simply the data it contains. The statements include the following:

- BACKUP DATABASE
- BACKUP LOG
- CREATE DATABASE
- CREATE DEFAULT
- CREATE FUNCTION
- CREATE PROCEDURE

- `CREATE RULE`
- `CREATE TABLE`
- `CREATE VIEW`

By default, only members of the `sysadmin`, `db_owner`, and `ddl_admin` roles have the ability to create a table. You can give Joy the permission to create tables in the `Northwind` database with the following statement:

```
GRANT CREATE TABLE TO joy
```

Notice that many statements aren't in this list (for example, `DROP TABLE` and `ALTER TABLE`). Permissions for these statements are implicitly given to the owner of a database object (and, of course, system administrators and database owners, who have full control). If Joy has permission to create a table, then she is authorized to change or delete any table she creates.

Viewing Permissions

You can view permissions using the stored procedure `sp_helprotect`. This procedure allows you to view all the permission settings in the database or to view just the settings regarding a specific object or user.

The AdminHelp utility provides an interface to the `sp_helprotect` procedure. The All Permissions button will list all the permission settings in the current database. As you can see by the scroll bar in Figure 16-11, listing all the permission settings in a database can produce many rows.

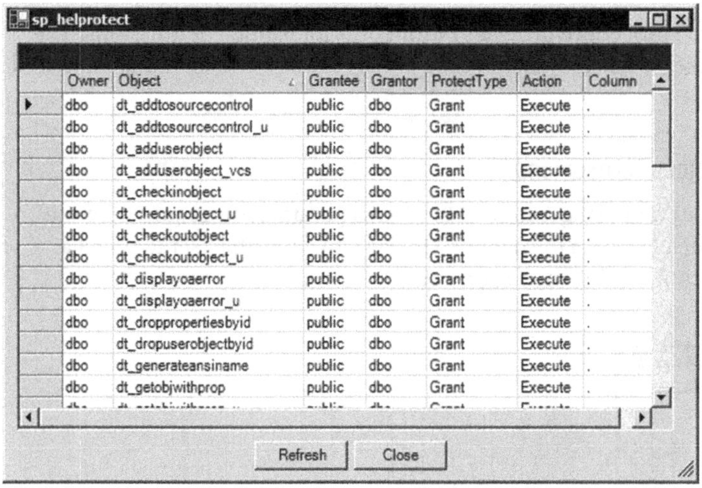

sp_helprotect

Owner	Object	Grantee	Grantor	ProtectType	Action	Column
dbo	dt_addtosourcecontrol	public	dbo	Grant	Execute	.
dbo	dt_addtosourcecontrol_u	public	dbo	Grant	Execute	.
dbo	dt_adduserobject	public	dbo	Grant	Execute	.
dbo	dt_adduserobject_vcs	public	dbo	Grant	Execute	.
dbo	dt_checkinobject	public	dbo	Grant	Execute	.
dbo	dt_checkinobject_u	public	dbo	Grant	Execute	.
dbo	dt_checkoutobject	public	dbo	Grant	Execute	.
dbo	dt_checkoutobject_u	public	dbo	Grant	Execute	.
dbo	dt_displayoaerror	public	dbo	Grant	Execute	.
dbo	dt_displayoaerror_u	public	dbo	Grant	Execute	.
dbo	dt_droppropertiesbyid	public	dbo	Grant	Execute	.
dbo	dt_dropuserobjectbyid	public	dbo	Grant	Execute	.
dbo	dt_generateansiname	public	dbo	Grant	Execute	.
dbo	dt_getobjwithprop	public	dbo	Grant	Execute	.

Refresh Close

Figure 16-11. *Viewing all permissions*

You can also view the permissions assigned to a specific user or role by clicking the Permissions by User/Role button. A dialog box will pop up asking you to select the user or role to view. Figure 16-12 shows sample permissions for `hr`.

sp_helprotect : @username=hr

Owner	Object	Grantee	Grantor	ProtectType	Action	Column
dbo	Employees	hr	dbo	Grant	Insert	.
dbo	Employees	hr	dbo	Grant	Select	(All+New)
dbo	Employees	hr	dbo	Grant	Update	(All+New)

Refresh Close

Figure 16-12. *Permissions for* `hr`

Finally, you can view the permissions assigned to a specific object using the Permissions by Object button. You can then select a table, stored procedure, view, or statement to see the permissions on it. Figure 16-13 shows sample permissions on the `Employees` table.

sp_helprotect : @name=Employees

Owner	Object	Grantee	Grantor	ProtectType	Action	Column
dbo	Employees	hr	dbo	Grant	Insert	.
dbo	Employees	hr	dbo	Grant	Select	(All+New)
dbo	Employees	hr	dbo	Grant	Update	(All+New)
dbo	Employees	joy	dbo	Deny	Select	BirthDate
dbo	Employees	joy	dbo	Deny	Select	HireDate

Refresh Close

Figure 16-13. *Permissions on the* `Employees` *table*

The `sp_helprotect` stored procedure provides output only for explicit permissions. The permissions given to fixed roles (such as `sysadmin` or `db_owner`) are implicit, unchangeable, and not listed in the output.

AdminHelp and Viewing Object Permissions

You've seen a few examples now of using AdminHelp when a parameter is required for the query. In these cases, AdminHelp uses a form named `PickOne` to allow the user to select a parameter from a `ComboBox` control, shown in Figure 16-14.

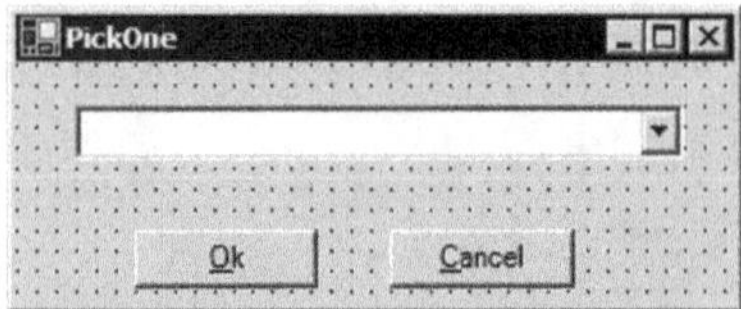

Figure 16-14. `PickOne` *combo box*

The combo box is populated by one of the following overloaded `AppendListContents` methods. The `PickOne` form maintains an `ArrayList` as a data source for the combo box. Items are added to the `ArrayList` from a `SqlDataReader` or from a string array.

```
Public Sub AppendListContents(ByVal dr As SqlDataReader, _
   ByVal fieldName As String)
   While dr.Read()
      list.Add(dr(fieldName))
   End While
   PickList.DataSource = list
End Sub

Public Sub AppendListContents(ByVal items() As String)
   For i As Integer = 0 To items.Length - 1
      list.Add(items(i))
   Next
End Sub
```

The reason you have two methods to populate the ComboBox is that some of the queries build the parameter list from hard-coded values as well as from a database query. For example, the last query we demonstrated called sp_helpprotect to view the permissions on a database object. You want to populate the list with the names of the tables, stored procedures, and views in the database, which you keep in an array.

```
Private Sub btnPermissionsByObject_Click(ByVal sender As System.Object, _
   ByVal e As System.EventArgs) Handles btnPermissionsByObject.Click

   CheckConnection()
   If Not thisConnection Is Nothing Then
      Dim cmd As SqlCommand = GetUserObjectsCommand()
      Dim dr As SqlDataReader = cmd.ExecuteReader()

      Dim po As New PickOne("Select an object or statement")
      po.AppendListContents(dr, "name")
      dr.Close()

      Dim statementPermissions() As String = {"CREATE DATABASE", _
         "CREATE DEFAULT", "CREATE FUNCTION", "CREATE PROCEDURE", _
         "CREATE RULE", "CREATE TABLE", "CREATE VIEW", _
         "BACKUP DATABASE", "BACKUP LOG"}

      po.AppendListContents(statementPermissions)

      If po.ShowDialog() = DialogResult.OK Then
         cmd = GetPermissionsCommand()
         Dim param As New SqlParameter("@name", po.Selected)
         cmd.Parameters.Add(param)

         Dim qf As New QueryForm(cmd)
         qf.ShowDialog()
      End If
   End If
End Sub
```

When the user picks one of the objects or statements from the PickOne dialog box, you add a parameter to the command's Parameter collection and pass the command to QueryForm for execution and display.

Implementing Security

Implementing a security design requires you to analyze how all your users are going to use your databases and applications. Typically, users will fall into one of the following groups (although larger applications and larger organizations may well require more fine-grained control):

- Users who require full control of the database application
- Users who perform a handful of administrative tasks, such as backing up the database
- Typical application users, who can query a majority of the tables but may have restrictions placed on certain objects
- Special application users, who have the all the abilities of typical application users, plus additional rights

Remember, first you need to grant login rights to the server for any users or Windows groups requiring access. For example, imagine you have a customer service forms–based application and the Windows users and groups in Table 16-3.

Table 16-3. *Hypothetical Windows Users and Groups*

Account	Description
APRESS\dbas	Database administrator group
APRESS\netoperations	Network operations, responsible for backups and other maintenance duties
APRESS\customerservice	Customer service employees, who require read and update permission on all the tables with the exception of a few tables and fields with sensitive information
APRESS\Jill	A customer service manager, who will have all the permissions of the customer service group and the additional capability to view and modify sensitive information

You could add the APRESS\dbas group to the sysadmin fixed server role, giving members control over each database on the server. Recall that you also can use the fixed database role, db_owner, if you want to restrict the highest level of control to a single database, instead of all databases on the server.

By adding the APRESS\netoperations group to the db_backupoperator fixed role in the database, you can enable the network operations group to perform backups of the database.

You can grant permissions to nonsensitive database objects directly to the customerservice group and then grant additional permissions to Jill. Ideally, Jill would belong to a Windows group that identifies her as a customer service manager. However, if she doesn't, instead of granting access to sensitive areas of the database directly to Jill, you could create a new role in the database, named managers (for example), assign Jill to the role, and grant the additional permissions to this role. This provides an extra layer of indirection, in case you need to grant new privileges to others.

This is just one example of an application with simple security requirements. More complex applications will require additional planning with additional custom roles. In fact, planning and administering security for an enterprise database system is often a challenging full-time task for a security administrator.

Summary

In this chapter we covered the basic security concepts and facilities for MSDE and SQL Server.

- Using Windows and Mixed Mode Authentication
- Mapping server logins to database accounts
- Grouping users into custom roles, fixed server roles, and fixed database roles
- Setting permissions and granting, revoking, and denying them on database objects and statements

Other RDBMSs provide similar facilities, and all of them support standard SQL's GRANT and REVOKE statements. However, the specifics differ, so consult your database documentation when planning and implementing database security.

CHAPTER 17

Using XML and ADO.NET

XML is a language for organizing data into documents that are readable by humans and have a hierarchical structure. The self-describing nature of XML documents makes them convenient for exchanging information between systems.

The use of XML is so widespread that .NET has from the start provided extensive support for it. In fact, XML is one of the core technologies underlying .NET. While the intent of this chapter isn't to delve deeply into XML, we'll discuss the basics and how you can use XML in VB .NET applications.

Specifically, we'll cover the following topics:

- The advantages and disadvantages of XML
- The structure of an XML document
- ADO.NET support for XML
- Experimentation with XML in VB .NET

The Pros and Cons of XML

XML is a formal standard (called a *recommendation*) of the World Wide Web Consortium (W3C) and has become the de facto industry standard for data exchange. It's easy to use and flexible. Here's an XML snippet that defines a simple XML document:

```
<book>
   <title>Title1</title>
   <author>Author1</author>
   <copyright date=2004 />
</book>
```

This XML document contains four *elements*: `book`, `title`, `author`, and `copyright`. It has the *root element* (also called the *document element*) `book`, which is delimited by a *start tag* (`<book>`) and an *end tag* (`</book>`). This element has content; here, the content is one occurrence of each of the other elements. The `title` and `author` elements also have content, but they contain data rather than other elements. The `copyright` element is *empty*. Note that this is indicated by an *empty-element tag*, which ends with a slash, as opposed to an end tag, which starts with a slash.

The `date=2004` part of the `copyright` tag is called an *attribute*. (Non-empty elements can also have attributes.) This hierarchical structure, where elements nest but never overlap, is required for *well-formed* XML.

You'll examine the structure more in the "Understanding the Structure of an XML Document" section. For now, let's consider some of the important advantages of using XML documents.

- XML is a text-based format containing data and a semantic description of that data. This format is readable by both machines and humans. Its hierarchical structure makes it effective for representing data and relationships.
- XML is a platform-independent standard. This makes it an excellent format for exchanging data between applications, even on different operating systems. This is perhaps the main reason it has been deeply integrated into the .NET Framework.
- XML is at the heart of Web services—a way of programmatically accessing functionality over the Internet. Discovery documents (which are used to locate available Web services, configuration files for Web servers, and many other kinds of information resources) are stored in the XML format.
- XML parsing is well defined and widely implemented, making it possible to retrieve information from XML documents in a variety of environments. Using schemas (themselves a specialized form of XML document), you can validate the structure and meaning of XML data before acceptance and use.
- XML supports the Unicode character encoding, which maps virtually all the characters of all human languages, making it easy to create internationalized documents.
- In SQL Server 2000 (and most other major RDBMSs), you can obtain query results as XML documents.
- You can document VB .NET (and other computer language) source code with XML, and you can easily convert this documentation into an Extensible HTML (XHTML) file for display and distribution.
- You can transfer XML documents via HTTP, so they can pass over the Internet (and through firewalls) more easily than binary data.

Of course, XML has a few drawbacks as well. Its text-based format means the following:

- Data stored as XML will take up more space than the binary representation of the same data.
- XML parsing can be slower than parsing highly optimized binary formats and can require more memory.

XML's flexibility and human readability, as well as that it's an open standard adopted by all major vendors and available on any platform, almost always outweigh its potential disadvantages. Let's now look at the basic structure of an XML document in more detail and create one in Visual Studio .NET.

■ **Tip** You don't need Visual Studio .NET (or any other IDE) to create XML documents. Any text editor will do, since XML documents contain only Unicode text (and ASCII is a subset of Unicode). So, if you don't have Visual Studio, you can use Notepad or WordPad instead. Of course, IDEs are easier to work with, especially for complex or multiple XML documents.

Understanding the Structure of an XML Document

An XML document can be any textual object, a file on disk, a string in memory, or even a stream from some data source. We'll use text files here. Here's a minor variation on the earlier XML document, adding a new first line:

```
<?xml version="1.0" encoding="utf-8" ?>
<book>
  <title>Title1</title>
  <author>Author1</author>
  <copyright date=2004 />
</book>
```

The document begins with the following *XML declaration*:

```
<?xml version="1.0" encoding="utf-8" ?>
```

This specifies the XML version and character encoding of the document. Though not required, the XML declaration is recommended by the W3C XML specification.

Next, the XML document comprises one or more elements. As you saw before, each element has a start tag, content (if any), and an end tag. Elements can contain other elements. In this XML document, the `title` and `author` elements are contained in the `book` element.

Each element can also have attributes. For example, the copyright element has one attribute, `date`, with a *value* of 2004.

```
<copyright date=2004 />
```

XML is called *extensible* because you can define your own tags, as long as they're constructed properly. Properly constructed XML files are well-formed. How do you know if an XML document is well-formed? Well-formedness has many rules, but the following two are always required:

- Every document must have a single root element.
- Elements can't overlap.

A document object model (XML-DOM) accesses the different parts of an XML document. XML-DOM refers to elements, attributes, and textual content as *nodes*. The .NET Framework namespace `System.Xml` contains classes that implement XML-DOM and provides methods for navigating XML documents.

Let's create a simple XML document in Visual Studio .NET. You'll represent two books, their titles, their authors, and the authors' ages. After creating the document, you'll view it and modify it.

Try It Out: Creating an XML Document in Visual Studio .NET

To create an XML document in Visual Studio .NET, follow these steps:

1. Create a new chapter solution, and call it `Chapter17_Examples`.

2. Add a VB .NET Windows application named `XmlDemo`.

3. Right-click the project in Solution Explorer, select Add and Add New Item..., and then select the XML File template. Accept the default filename, `XMLFile1.xml`, as in Figure 17-1. Then click Open.

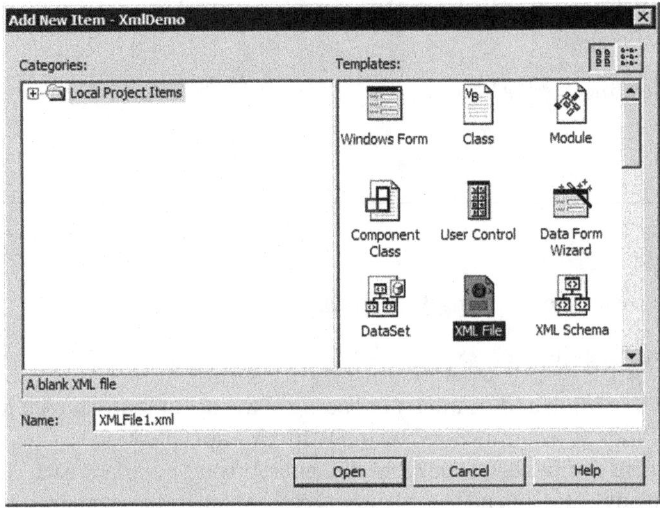

Figure 17-1. *Adding an XML file to a project*

4. If it doesn't open automatically, double-click the file in Solution Explorer to open it in Code view, and then add the following code to it:

```
<books>
  <book>
    <title>Title1</title>
    <author>
      <name>Author1</name>
      <age>34</age>
    </author>
  </book>
  <book>
    <title>Title2</title>
    <author>
      <name>Author2</name>
      <age>24</age>
    </author>
  </book>
</books>
```

5. Right-click in Code view, and select View Data. Even though the XML file is in a hierarchical text format, you can view it in the familiar grid format. You should see the XML data as in Figure 17-2.

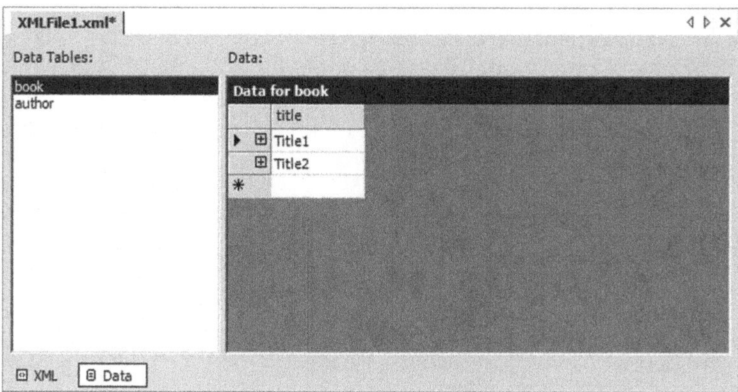

Figure 17-2. *XML data displayed in Visual Studio*

6. Click the plus signs to expand Title1 and Title2, and click the *book author* link to see the author information for each title. As you can see, even though the data was described in a hierarchical XML document, Visual Studio .NET displays it as a table—in fact, as nested tables. You can view the data in either data format by clicking the XML and Data buttons at the bottom of the window.

7. Now let's try to add a new title in Data view and see if the XML source changes to reflect this. Select the row marked with an asterisk below `Title2` and name it `Title3`. Then expand the node, click the *book author* link, and name it `Author3` and `53`, for its name and age, respectively (see Figure 17-3). Make sure you then move the cursor to the next row.

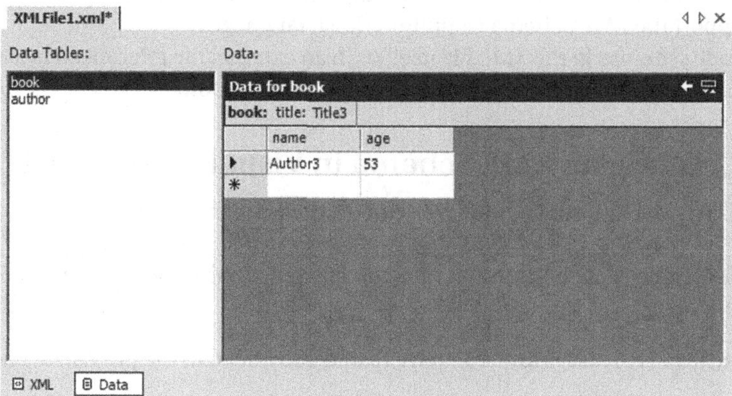

Figure 17-3. *Adding data to an XML document in Data view*

8. Click the XML button at the bottom of the window. You'll see that the XML document has been changed, as in Figure 17-4. Visual Studio .NET automatically updated the XML file with the data you added in Data view.

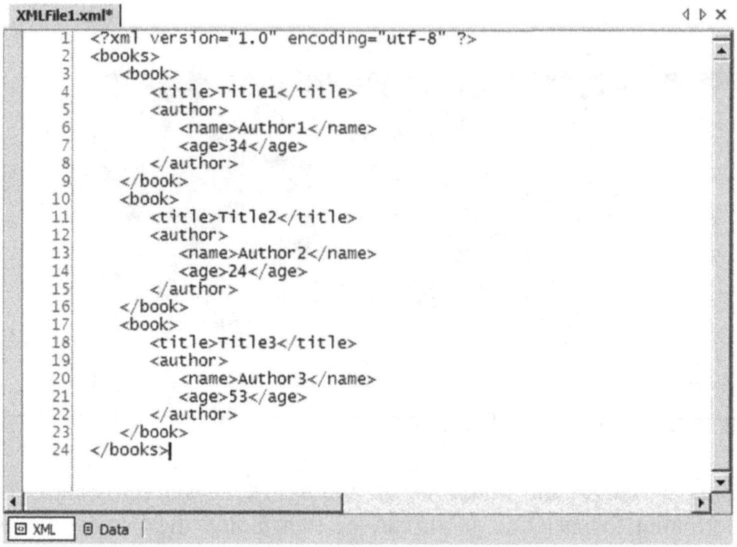

```
<?xml version="1.0" encoding="utf-8" ?>
<books>
   <book>
      <title>Title1</title>
      <author>
         <name>Author1</name>
         <age>34</age>
      </author>
   </book>
   <book>
      <title>Title2</title>
      <author>
         <name>Author2</name>
         <age>24</age>
      </author>
   </book>
   <book>
      <title>Title3</title>
      <author>
         <name>Author3</name>
         <age>53</age>
      </author>
   </book>
</books>
```

Figure 17-4. *XML document changed after changes in Data view*

Understanding Schemas

You can define what elements and attributes are allowed to do in an XML document in two ways: Document Type Definitions (DTDs) and XML Schemas.

DTDs are part of Standard Generalized Markup Language (SGML) from which XML derives, but because they use non-XML syntax, they aren't used much in the .NET Framework. XML Schemas, on the other hand, are XML documents, and .NET provides the `System.Xml.Schema` namespace to support the XML Schema Definition (XSD) language.

You can include schemas in the XML file itself or in an external file referenced by the XML document. Let's create a schema from an XML file using Visual Studio .NET.

Try It Out: Creating an XML Schema in Visual Studio .NET

To create an XML Schema in Visual Studio .NET, follow these steps:

1. In XML view, right-click the `XMLFile1.xml` you created in the previous exercise. Select Create Schema.

2. A file called `XMLFile1.xsd` is immediately created and added to the project, as shown in Figure 17-5.

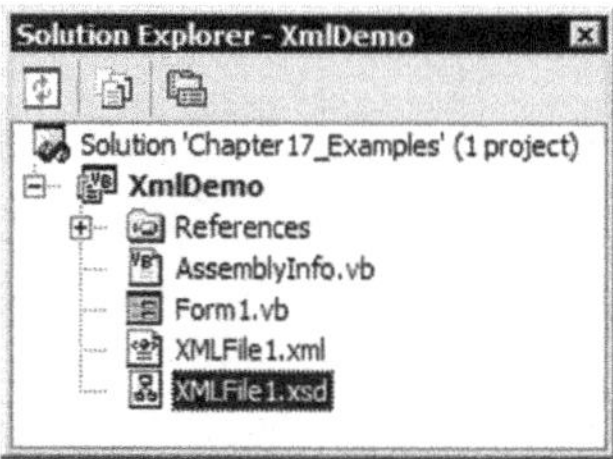

Figure 17-5. *Creating an XML Schema (.xsd file)*

3. In `XMLFile1.xml`, notice that an XML namespace attribute (`xmlns`) has been added to the root element to reference the schema.

```
<books xmlns="http://tempuri.org/XMLFile1.xsd">
```

Now, the XML file is restricted to only the elements defined in the schema. Let's try to violate the schema definition and see what happens.

4. In `XMLFile1.xml`, insert a new element, `salary`, into `Author1`, as in Figure 17-6.

```
XMLFile1.xml*
<?xml version="1.0" encoding="utf-8"?>
<books xmlns="http://tempuri.org/XMLFile1.xsd">
    <book>
        <title>Title1</title>
        <author>
            <name>Author1</name>
            <age>34</age>
            <salary>10000</salary>
        </author>
    </book>
    <book>
        <title>Title2</title>
        <author>
            <name>Author2</name>
            <age>24</age>
        </author>
    </book>
    <book>
        <title>Title3</title>
        <author>
            <name>Author3</name>
            <age>53</age>
        </author>
    </book>
</books>
XML   Data
```

Figure 17-6. *Violating an XML Schema definition*

5. Notice that the editor marks it with a red wavy underline, and the tooltip says that the active schema doesn't support the `salary` element. This warning shows you that the schema specified in the XSD file is controlling the XML document. (Observe that the `salary` element is ignored in Data view.)

6. Double-click `XMLFile1.xsd` in Solution Explorer. You'll see the window in Figure 17-7.

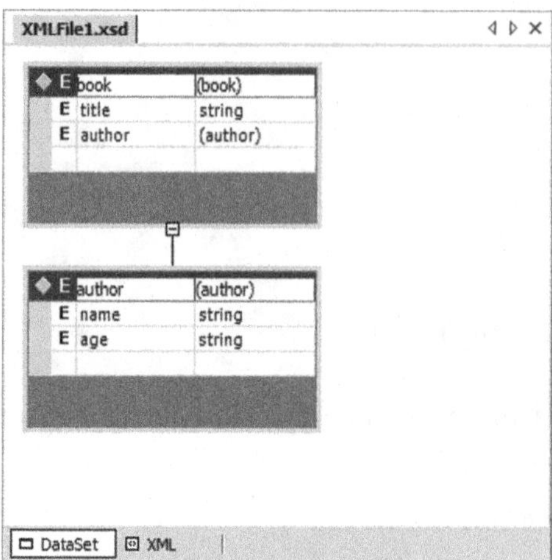

Figure 17-7. *XML Schema graphic display*

7. Notice how the hierarchy (books have `titles` and `authors`; `authors` have names and ages) is represented as though it were composed of two tables. You can see the actual XML code in the XSD file by clicking the XML button (see Figure 17-8).

XMLFile1.xsd

```
<?xml version="1.0"?>
<xs:schema id="books" targetNamespace="http://tempuri.org/XML
  <xs:element name="books" msdata:IsDataSet="true" msdata:Loc
    <xs:complexType>
      <xs:choice maxOccurs="unbounded">
        <xs:element name="book">
          <xs:complexType>
            <xs:sequence>
              <xs:element name="title" type="xs:string" minOc
              <xs:element name="author" minOccurs="0" maxOccu
                <xs:complexType>
                  <xs:sequence>
                    <xs:element name="name" type="xs:string"
                    <xs:element name="age" type="xs:string" m
                  </xs:sequence>
                </xs:complexType>
              </xs:element>
            </xs:sequence>
          </xs:complexType>
        </xs:element>
      </xs:choice>
    </xs:complexType>
  </xs:element>
</xs:schema>
```

DataSet XML

Figure 17-8. *XSD source generated by Visual Studio .NET*

How It Works

XSD is a language of its own, beyond the scope of this book. It's enough for your purposes simply to know how to create an XSD file from an XML file in Visual Studio .NET. In fact, so many facilities of .NET and Visual Studio make using XML transparent that you no longer need to know much at all about XML to be highly productive (though, of course, the more you know, the more you'll understand, and the even more productive you'll be).

Writing Valid XML

An XML file that has an associated schema is considered *valid* when the structure and content of the XML file is consistent with the schema. The elements in the XML document must appear in the structure defined in the schema, and the content of individual elements must conform to the elements and character data specified for them in the schema.

Note that XML documents can be well-formed but not valid. A document that isn't well-formed will raise errors with a parser and can't be validated. A document that's well-formed is valid if it complies with an associated schema (or DTD).

You can use Visual Studio .NET to verify that XML files are both well-formed and valid. Let's try it on `XMLFile1.xml`.

Try It Out: Validating an XML Document

To validate an XML document, follow these steps:

1. Open `XMLFile1.xml` in XML view. (It should still have the `salary` element underlined, as in Figure 17-6. If not, reenter the erroneous line.) Select XML ➤ Validate XML Data. A Task List window will appear as in Figure 17-9, listing errors.

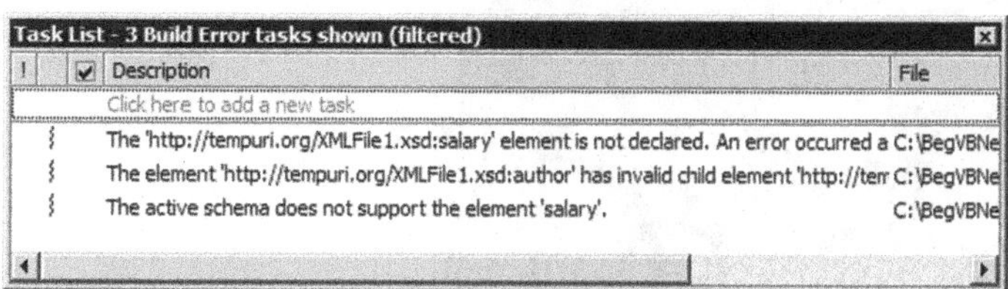

Figure 17-9. *Task List window displaying XML validation errors*

2. Remove the erroneous line, and try again. The status bar at the bottom of the screen should report "No validation errors were found."

Using XML with ADO.NET

You've seen that XML organizes data in a hierarchy. You also know that ADO.NET views data in relational fashion, as tables with rows and columns. The .NET Framework Class Library (FCL) unifies these two models.

XML support (in `System.Xml` and related namespaces) is tightly integrated with ADO.NET (in `System.Data` and related namespaces). The `DataSet` class in `System.Data` represents a relational data source, and the `XmlDocument` class in `System.Xml` represents an XML document and derives from `System.Xml.XmlNode`, which provides methods for using XML-DOM to access the elements of an XML document.

Further, `System.Xml.XmlDataDocument`, derived from `XmlDocument`, maps hierarchical data to `DataSets`, thus transparently unifying ADO.NET and XML for you.

The `System.Data.DataSet` class has extensive support for XML (in fact, the data in data sets is stored internally in XML format), including methods for reading and writing XML data and schemas. The SQL Server data provider supports XML with a variety of methods. For example,

SqlCommand has an ExecuteXMLReader method that creates a System.Xml.XmlReader object that is analogous to relational data reader but accesses XML data instead of database tables.

Let's read data from an XML document into a data set and write data from a data set into an XML document.

Try It Out: Reading an XML Document into a Data Set

To read an XML document into a data set, follow these steps:

1. Rename Form1.vb to XmlDemo.vb, and add three buttons and a data grid to it. Name the buttons btnReadXml, btnWriteXml, and btnConfigXml. Name the data grid XmlGrid. Change the form's caption (the Text property) to XML Demo. The layout should appear as in Figure 17-10.

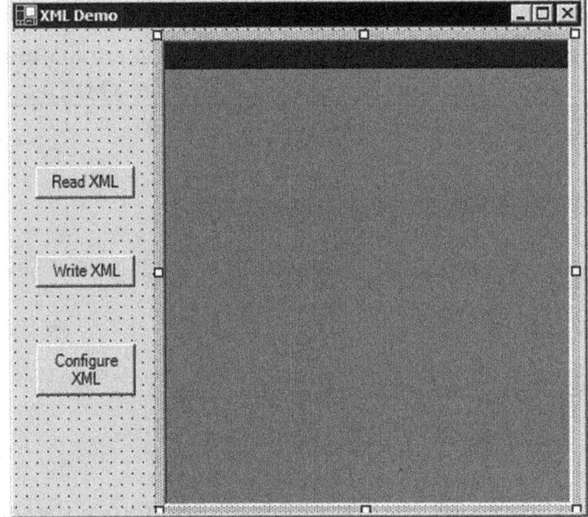

Figure 17-10. *XmlDemo layout*

2. Add the following to the Click event handler for btnReadXml:

```
Private Sub btnReadXml_Click(ByVal sender As System.Object, _
   ByVal e As System.EventArgs) Handles btnReadXml.Click
      Dim ds As New DataSet
      ds.ReadXml("..\XMLFile1.xml", XmlReadMode.InferSchema)
      XmlGrid.SetDataBinding(ds, "book")
End Sub
```

3. Build and run with Ctrl+F5. Click the Read XML button. You'll see that the XML file has been read and the data grid has been populated, as shown in Figure 17-11 (after the title entries have been expanded). You can follow the *book author* links to see name and age.

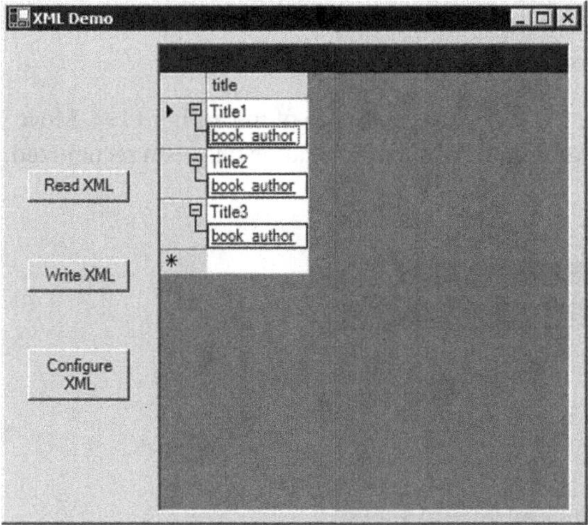

Figure 17-11. *Reading an XML document in an application*

How It Works

First you create a data set.

```
Dim ds As New DataSet
```

Then you call the data set's ReadXML method, passing the file path and XML read mode. The ReadXML method is overloaded and takes several combinations of parameters. The one you use accepts a string, identifying the XML file to read, and accepts a member of the System.Data.XmlReadMode enumeration, indicating how to read the data and schema into the data set. InferSchema means that the schema for this document must be inferred from the XML document itself, not from its XSD file.

```
ds.ReadXml("..\XMLFile1.xml", XmlReadMode.InferSchema)
```

Finally, you bind the table in the DataSet to the data grid. Here, book is the name of the data table, and ds is the data set that contains it.

```
XmlGrid.SetDataBinding(ds, "book")
```

Now let's change the dataset's data and write the changes back to the XML file.

Try It Out: Writing a Data Set to an XML File

To write a data set to an XML file, follow these steps:

1. Add the following to the Click event handler for btnWriteXml:

```
Private Sub btnWriteXml_Click(ByVal sender As System.Object, _
   ByVal e As System.EventArgs) Handles btnWriteXml.Click
      Dim ds As DataSet = CType(XmlGrid.DataSource, DataSet)
      ds.WriteXml("..\XMLFileOut.xml", XmlWriteMode.IgnoreSchema)
End Sub
```

2. Build and run with Ctrl+F5.

3. Click the Read XML button to populate the data grid.

4. Click the *book author* link for `Title2`. Change the age of the author to `44`. Move your cursor to the next line of the grid to make sure the change has been recognized, as shown in Figure 17-12.

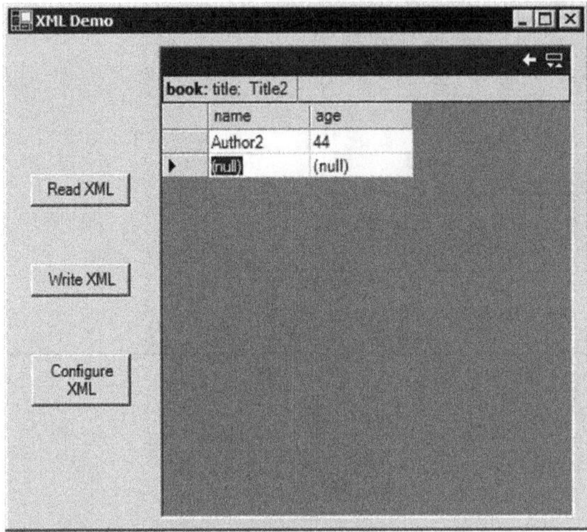

Figure 17-12. *Changing XML data in an application*

5. Click the Write XML button. The `XMLFileOut.xml` file will be created in the `XmlDemo` project folder, but it isn't automatically added to the project. Close the application, and add the file to the project by right-clicking the project in Solution Explorer, selecting Add ➤ Add Existing Item…, selecting All Files (when the dialog box opens), and double-clicking `XMLFileOut.xml`.

6. Double-click the `XMLFileOut.xml` item in Server Explorer to open it in XML view, and observe that the age for `Author2` is 44. Switch to Data view, drill down to the age for `Author2`, and you'll see again that it's 44.

7. Experiment using other values and writing them back out.

How It Works

You first create a `DataSet` object, casting the data grid's data source (of VB .NET `object` type) to the `DataSet` type.

```
Dim ds As DataSet = CType(XmlGrid.DataSource, DataSet)
```

Note that you've already changed the author's age in the data grid, changing the contents of the data set.

Then you call the data set's WriteXML to write the contents of the data set to the file. The XMLWriteMode.IgnoreSchema member of the System.Data.XmlWriteMode enumeration indicates to write the contents of the data set, without an XSD schema.

```
ds.WriteXml("..\XMLFileOut.xml", XmlWriteMode.IgnoreSchema)
```

As you can see, reading and writing XML files is easy thanks to the XML support in ADO.NET. Now let's look at another use of XML: defining application configuration files.

Defining Application Configuration Using XML

Applications typically need some initialization values. For example, database applications need a connection string to connect to the database. Instead of hard-coding this string into the application, if you can store it in a file and read it at runtime, then you can change the connection string (perhaps to point to a backup database should the primary database go down) without changing application source code. You can conveniently store such configuration data in XML files. An application can interrogate the specific section of an XML file where a required item is specified. Prior to XML, configuration files, connection strings and other startup information were generally stored in the Windows registry, but this method wasn't nearly as user-friendly—or robust—as XML configuration files.

The .NET Framework supports the configuration of applications, machine, security settings, and so on, using the System.Configuration namespace. Configuration is a big and complex topic, and a detailed discussion is beyond the scope of this book. You'll learn only how to access a connection string stored in an XML file, but this is a useful thing to know how to do and a good basis for understanding how applications and XML configuration files work together.

XML configuration files have a .config extension, and they must have the same name as the assembly. For example, if chapter17.exe is the name of the executable assembly, then the name of the configuration file must be chapter17.exe.config. The config file must be in the same folder as the assembly or in the Global Assembly Cache. Depending on what you're trying to configure, the config file can implement one of several schemas available—for example, a Startup Settings schema, a Network Setting schema, or a Configuration Sections schema. Each schema has a specific set of elements. The Configuration Sections schema provides XML elements that can be used to specify custom application settings, such as the connection string. So, let's now create an XML file called chapter17.exe.config and access the connection string therein from a VB .NET application.

Try It Out: Creating an Application Configuration File

To create an application configuration file, follow these steps:

1. Right-click the XmlDemo project item in Solution Explorer, select Add ➤ Add New Item..., select Application Configuration File, leave it called app.config, and click Open.

2. Add the following to the config file:

```
<configuration>
  <appSettings>
    <add
      key="cnnorthwind"
      value="
        server = (local)\netsdk;
        integrated security = sspi;
        database = northwind"
    />
  </appSettings>
</configuration>
```

3. Notice that a schema file isn't referenced here. It isn't necessary to do so, because the .NET Framework recognizes the elements you used.

4. In the form, add the following `Imports` directives (for ADO.NET, for accessing the config file, and for working with XML, respectively):

```
Imports System.Data.SqlClient
Imports System.Configuration
Imports System.Xml
```

5. Add the following to the `Click` event handler for `btnConfigXml`:

```
Private Sub btnConfigXML_Click(ByVal sender As System.Object, _
   ByVal e As System.EventArgs) Handles btnConfigXML.Click
   ' Get connection string from config file
   Dim connString As String = ConfigurationSettings.AppSettings("cnnorthwind")

   ' Create connection
   Dim thisConnection As New SqlConnection(connString)

   ' Query string
   Dim sql As String = _
      "SELECT EmployeeId, LastName " & _
      "FROM Employees " & _
      "FOR XML AUTO"

   ' Create Connection
   Dim thisCommand As New SqlCommand(sql, thisConnection)

   Try
      ' Open Connection
      thisConnection.Open()
```

```
            ' Get XML Reader
            Dim reader As XmlReader = thisCommand.ExecuteXmlReader()

            ' Create DataSet
            Dim ds As New DataSet

            ' Reader XMLReader into DataSet
            ds.ReadXml(reader, XmlReadMode.InferSchema)

            ' Bind dataset to datagrid
            XmlGrid.DataSource = ds

        Catch ex As SqlException
            MessageBox.Show(ex.Message)
        Finally
            thisConnection.Close()
        End Try
    End Sub
```

6. Build and run the solution with Ctrl + F5. Now click the Config button. Click the plus button inside the data grid, and then click the *employees* link. You'll see the grid open, as in Figure 17-13.

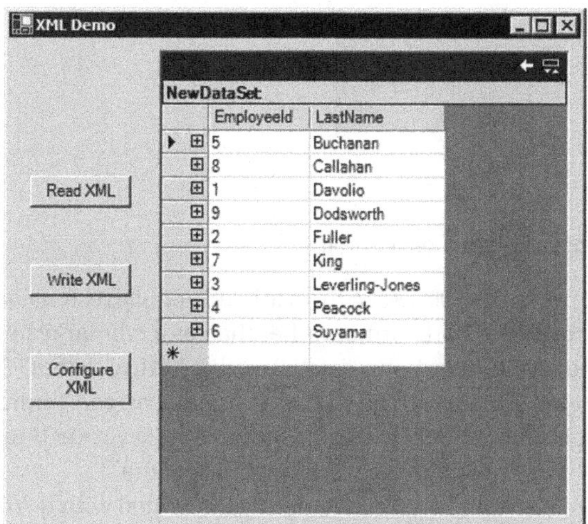

Figure 17-13. *Accessing a database specified in an XML configuration file*

How It Works

In the `XmlDemo.exe.config` file, you use the `appSettings` element to specify the application-specific settings you want for the `configuration`.

```
<configuration>
  <appSettings>
    <add
      key="cnnorthwind"
      value="
        server = (local)\netsdk;
        integrated security = sspi;
        database = northwind"
    />
  </appSettings>
</configuration>
```

Within appSettings, you include an element named add that specifies a key-value pair to include in the application settings. Note that this element is empty. Its related information is given as two attributes: key and value.

You retrieve the connection string from the application settings by using the property's indexer with the key cnnorthwind.

```
' Get connection string from config file
Dim connString As String = ConfigurationSettings.AppSettings("cnnorthwind")
```

After creating a connection using the retrieved connection string, you create a command to retrieve data from the Employees table.

```
' Query string
Dim sql As String = _
   "SELECT EmployeeId, LastName " & _
   "FROM Employees " & _
   "FOR XML AUTO"

' Create Command object
Dim thisCommand As New SqlCommand(sql, thisConnection)
```

Notice that the query has an extra clause. FOR XML AUTO is a Transact-SQL extension that instructs the database to return the results in XML format rather than as a tabular result set. (It's also possible to insert, update, and delete records in a database using XML with the OPENXML Transact-SQL statement.) Since the query will return an XML document, you can't store it in a data reader as you have so far throughout the book. Instead, you use the ExecuteXmlReader method to store the result in an XmlReader object, which is an instance of the System.Xml.XmlReader class, not an ADO.NET class but one tightly integrated with it. You use the ReadXml method to read the contents of the XML reader into a DataSet object.

```
' Get XML Reader
Dim reader As XmlReader = thisCommand.ExecuteXmlReader()

' Create DataSet
Dim ds As New DataSet

' Reader XMLReader into DataSet
ds.ReadXml(reader, XmlReadMode.InferSchema)
```

Finally, you bind the data set to the data grid.

```
' Bind dataset to datagrid
XmlGrid.DataSource = ds
```

Try changing the value properties in the configuration file to an invalid machine or database, and click the buttons to see what error messages result.

Summary

This chapter began with a quick overview of XML and its advantages and disadvantages. Then, after analyzing the basic elements of an XML document, you used Visual Studio .NET to construct an XML document and generate its schema automatically. Next, we discussed support for XML in ADO.NET; you read an XML document into a `DataSet` and wrote an XML document from a `DataSet`. Finally, you looked at application configuration files, an important application of XML in database programs.

XML is a huge topic and we've just skimmed the surface here. But this chapter is a good foundation from which you can develop your experience with this standard for describing and storing data.

In the next chapter, you'll look at handling errors arising from ADO.NET code and the database itself.

CHAPTER 18

Handling Exceptions

Up to now, we've been pretty consistent in our handling of potential database exceptions. Every example has caught any exception that may occur and failed gracefully as a result. Some examples have even differentiated between two types of possible exception so as to deal with them differently.

Robust database applications demand that you pay careful attention to the handling of errors and exceptions, so we'll cover what exceptions can arise when using ADO.NET. We'll focus on the SQL Server data provider, since we're using MSDE, but exception handling isn't RDBMS specific, so the same techniques are applicable to whatever database you use.

Specifically, we'll cover the following:

- Understanding VB .NET exception handling in general
- Handling ADO.NET exceptions
- Handling database exceptions

Let's start with a quick review of VB .NET's exception-handling facilities.

Handling Exceptions with VB .NET

The CLR supports *structured exception handling*. The three basic VB .NET facilities for handling exceptions are as follows:

- The `Try` statement
- `System.Exception` and its derived classes
- The `Throw` statement

The following sections cover each of these techniques briefly.

Using the Try Statement

VB .NET provides the Try statement to support structured exception handling. Its basic syntax is as follows:

```
Try
   ' Code that may throw an exception
Catch ex As <ExceptionType>
   ' Code to handle an exception of a specific type
Finally
   ' Code that always executes after success or failure
End Try
```

The Catch and Finally clauses are optional, but you must use at least one. You can have any number of specific Catch clauses. You must declare them so that derived types appear before base types. You can have at most one general Catch clause—in other words, one that doesn't specify an exception variable. If used, it must be the last Catch clause. You can have at most one Finally clause.

In principle, any code that may throw an exception should be contained in a Try block so that exceptions can be caught. In practice, not every exception necessarily requires handling, but it's always important to make sure you handle all exceptions that can negatively affect your program's performance and reliability.

Sometimes you may want to handle an exception that's thrown internally by executing code that records the exception and then moves forward. Alternatively, you may want to display a useful message to the user. Otherwise, any code that throws an exception will present the user with a gray box of unintelligible error details.

If no exception occurs in the code in the Try block, then execution will move to the Finally block if it exists. It isn't mandatory to provide a Finally block; however, they're useful places for closing connections and other cleanup code. The code in the Finally block will always be executed, regardless of whether a Catch block was entered.

You can also nest Try statements. In this scenario, Catch blocks relate only to the Try statement to which they belong.

If code outside a Try block generates an exception, the runtime will move up the call stack and look for an appropriate Catch clause in a calling method. If none is found, the program will be terminated and a message box displayed that identifies the error. So, at the uppermost level of code, it's important to catch all errors that may arise. The basic idea is prevent users from seeing messages they won't understand. Typically, you can best handle such errors by logging them for later reference and providing users with a polite alert that doesn't leave them wondering what to do next.

Using Class System.Exception

System.Exception is the base class for all exceptions. Two basic kinds of exceptions exist: *system exceptions* (instances of System.SystemException) for CLR-thrown exceptions, and *application exceptions* (instances of System.ApplicationException) for user-defined exceptions. They both provide properties and methods for determining precise information about an exception, and you'll use a variety of them in later examples.

Using the throw Statement

Exceptions are *thrown* with the `Throw` statement. Its syntax is as follows:

```
Throw <object>
```

Any type of object can be thrown, but in practice only. For example, if a method receives an invalid argument, you can throw a `System.ArgumentException` with the following:

```
Throw New System.ArgumentException
```

When this statement is used, the corresponding `Catch` block (if it exists) or a generic `Catch` block will come into play and handle the exception.

Structured exception handling is both elegant and robust. It's of particular importance in database programming, where errors come from three sources: application programs, ADO.NET, and databases. With this in mind, let's look at exceptions thrown by ADO.NET and databases.

Handling ADO.NET Exceptions

Let's first see how to handle exceptions thrown by ADO.NET. In the following example, you'll try to execute a stored procedure without specifying the `CommandText` property. You'll first use no exception handling, and then you'll add it.

Try It Out: Handling an ADO.NET Exception (Part 1)

To handle an ADO.NET exception, follow these steps:

1. Create a new solution named `Chapter18_Examples`.
2. Add a VB .NET Windows application named `AdoNetExceptions`. Rename `Form1.vb` to `Exceptions.vb`.
3. Change the `Text` property of `Form1` to `ADO.NET Exceptions`.
4. Add a tab control to the form. Add a tab page to this, and change its `Text` property to `ADO.NET`. Add a button to the tab page, give it the name `btnADO1`, and change its `Text` property to `ADO.NET Exception 1`. Add a label to the right of this button, and change its `Text` property to `Incorrect ADO.NET code will cause an exception`. Add a second button to the tab page, call it `btnADO2`, and change its `Text` property to `ADO.NET Exception 2`. Add a label to the right of this button, and change its `Text` property to `Accessing a nonexistent column will cause an exception`.
5. Add a second tab page, and change its `Text` property to `Database`. The layout should look like Figure 18-1.

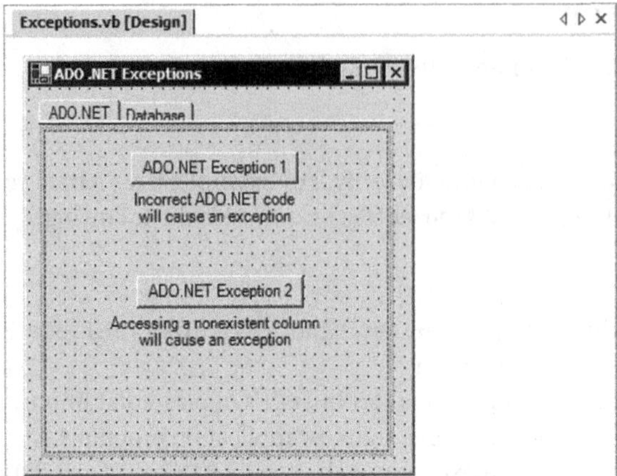

Figure 18-1. *AdoNetExceptions layout*

6. Add the following `Imports` directive for the SQL Server data provider namespace:

```
Imports System.Data.SqlClient
```

7. Return to Design view, and add a `SqlConnection` to the form from the Data tab of the Toolbox. Set its `ConnectionString` property to that for the `Northwind` database.

8. Add the following code to the click event handler for `btnADO1`. This will provide the first exception.

```
Private Sub btnADO1_Click(ByVal sender As System.Object, _
   ByVal e As System.EventArgs) Handles btnADO1.Click
   ' Create SqlCommand Object
   Dim thisCommand As SqlCommand = SqlConnection1.CreateCommand()

   ' Specify that the command is a stored procedure
   thisCommand.CommandType = CommandType.StoredProcedure

   ' Deliberately fail to specify the procedure
   ' thisCommand.CommandText = "Select_AllEmployees"

   ' Open connection
   SqlConnection1.Open()

   ' Run command and get data as a reader
   Dim thisReader As SqlDataReader = thisCommand.ExecuteReader()

   ' Close reader
   thisReader.Close()
```

```
    If SqlConnection1.State = ConnectionState.Open Then
       MessageBox.Show("Finally block closing the connection", "Finally")
       SqlConnection1.Close()
    End If
End Sub
```

9. Run the program with Ctrl+F5. Click the ADO.NET Exception 1 button, and you'll see the message box in Figure 18-2. Click Quit to close the message box and go back to Visual Studio .NET.

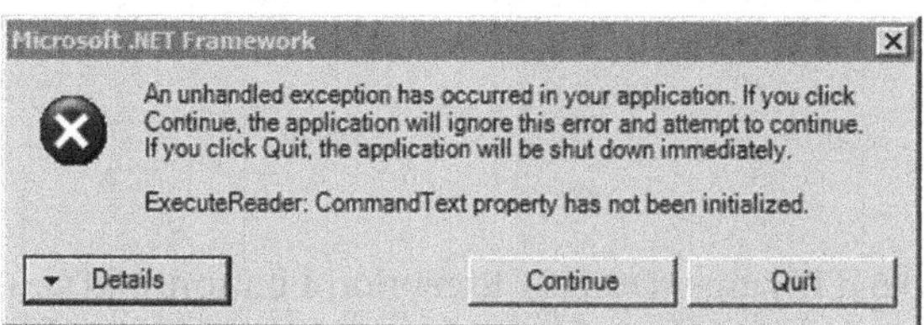

Figure 18-2. *ADO.NET unhandled exception*

10. Modify the btnADO1_Click event handler as shown with the following bold code:

```
Private Sub btnADO1_Click(ByVal sender As System.Object, _
   ByVal e As System.EventArgs) Handles btnADO1.Click
   ' Create SqlCommand Object
   Dim thisCommand As SqlCommand = SqlConnection1.CreateCommand()

   ' Specify that the command is a stored procedure
   thisCommand.CommandType = CommandType.StoredProcedure

   ' Deliberately fail to specify the procedure
   ' thisCommand.CommandText = "Select_AllEmployees"

   Try
      ' Open connection
      SqlConnection1.Open()

      ' Run command and get data as a reader
      Dim thisReader As SqlDataReader = thisCommand.ExecuteReader()

      ' Close reader
      thisReader.Close()

   Catch ex As System.Data.SqlClient.SqlException
      Dim str As String
      str = "Source : " & ex.Source
      str &= ControlChars.NewLine
      str &= "Exception Message : " & ex.Message
      MessageBox.Show(str, "Database Exception")
```

```
      Catch ex As System.Exception
         Dim str As String
         str = "Source : " & ex.Source
         str &= ControlChars.NewLine
         str &= "Exception Message : " & ex.Message
         MessageBox.Show(str, "Non-Database Exception")

      Finally
         If SqlConnection1.State = ConnectionState.Open Then
            MessageBox.Show("Finally block closing the connection", "Finally")
            SqlConnection1.Close()
         End If
      End Try
   End Sub
```

11. Run the program with Ctrl+F5. Click the ADO.NET Exception 1 button, and you'll see the message box in Figure 18-3.

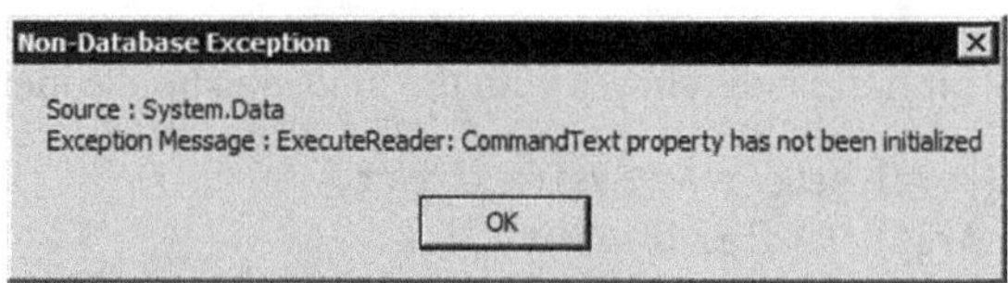

Figure 18-3. *ADO.NET handled exception*

How It Works

It'd be unusual to miss setting the `CommandText` property. However, this was an expedient way to cause an exception. When you call the `ExecuteReader` method, you get an exception, since the stored procedure to call hasn't been specified.

```
' Deliberately fail to specify the procedure
' thisCommand.CommandText = "Select_AllEmployees"

' Open connection
SqlConnection1.Open()

' Run command and get data as a reader
   Dim thisReader As SqlDataReader = thisCommand.ExecuteReader()
```

After seeing what happens without handling the exception, you execute the call from a `Try` block. To catch the exception and prevent the program from crashing, you code two `Catch` clauses.

```
Catch ex As System.Data.SqlClient.SqlException
   Dim str As String
   str = "Source : " & ex.Source
   str &= ControlChars.NewLine
   str &= "Exception Message : " & ex.Message
   MessageBox.Show(str, "Database Exception")

Catch ex As System.Exception
   Dim str As String
   str = "Source : " & ex.Source
   str &= ControlChars.NewLine
   str &= "Exception Message : " & ex.Message
   MessageBox.Show(str, "Non-Database Exception")
```

In the first `Catch` clause, you specify a database exception type. The second `Catch` block, which produced this message box, is a generic block that catches all types of exceptions. Note the caption of the message box in this `Catch` block. It says *Non-Database Exception.* Although you may think that what you've received is a database exception, it's actually a client-side exception; in other words, this error is trapped before it gets to the database server.

When the button is clicked, since the `CommandText` property wasn't specified, an exception is thrown and caught by the second `Catch` clause. Even though a `Catch` clause for `SqlException` was provided, the exception was a `System.InvalidOperationException`, a common exception thrown by the CLR, not a database exception.

The exception message indicates where the problem occurred: in the `ExecuteReader` method. The `Finally` block checks if the connection is open and, if it is, closes it and gives a message.

```
Finally
   If SqlConnection1.State = ConnectionState.Open Then
      MessageBox.Show("Finally block closing the connection", "Finally")
      SqlConnection1.Close()
   End If
End Try
```

Try It Out: Handling an ADO.NET Exception (Part 2)

Let's try another example of an ADO.NET exception. You'll execute a stored procedure and then reference a nonexistent column in the returned dataset. This will throw an ADO.NET exception. This time, you'll use a specific `Catch` clause to trap the exception.

1. You'll use the `Select_AllEmployees` stored procedure you created in Chapter 14. If you haven't already created it, please go to Chapter 14 and follow the steps in the "Try It Out: Creating and Executing a Stored Procedure with No Parameters" section.

2. Replace the code in the body of the btnADO2_Click method with the following code:

```
Private Sub btnADO2_Click(ByVal sender As System.Object, _
   ByVal e As System.EventArgs) Handles btnADO2.Click
   ' Create SqlCommand Object
   Dim thisCommand As SqlCommand = SqlConnection1.CreateCommand()
   thisCommand.CommandType = CommandType.StoredProcedure
   thisCommand.CommandText = "Select_AllEmployees"

   Try
      ' Open connection
      SqlConnection1.Open()

      ' Run command and get data as a reader
      Dim thisReader As SqlDataReader = thisCommand.ExecuteReader()

      ' Access non-existent column
      Dim str As String = thisReader.GetValue(20).ToString()

      ' Close data reader
      thisReader.Close()

   Catch ex As System.InvalidOperationException
      Dim str As String
      str = "Source : " & ex.Source
      str &= ControlChars.NewLine
      str &= "Exception Message : " & ex.Message
      str &= ControlChars.NewLine
      str &= "Stack Trace : " & ex.StackTrace
      MessageBox.Show(str, "Specific Exception")

   Catch ex As System.Data.SqlClient.SqlException
      Dim str As String
      str = "Source : " & ex.Source
      str &= ControlChars.NewLine
      str &= "Exception Message : " & ex.Message
      MessageBox.Show(str, "Database Exception")

   Catch ex As System.Exception
      Dim str As String
      str = "Source : " & ex.Source
      str &= ControlChars.NewLine
      str &= "Exception Message : " & ex.Message
      MessageBox.Show(str, "Generic Exception")
```

```
    Finally
        If SqlConnection1.State = ConnectionState.Open Then
            MessageBox.Show("Finally block closing the connection", "Finally")
            SqlConnection1.Close()
        End If
    End Try
End Sub
```

■ **Tip** Testing whether a connection is open before attempting to close it isn't actually necessary. The `Close` method doesn't throw any exceptions, and calling it multiple times on the same connection, even if it's already closed, causes no errors.

---

3. Run the program with Ctrl+F5. Click the ADO.NET Exception 2 button, and you'll see the message box in Figure 18-4.

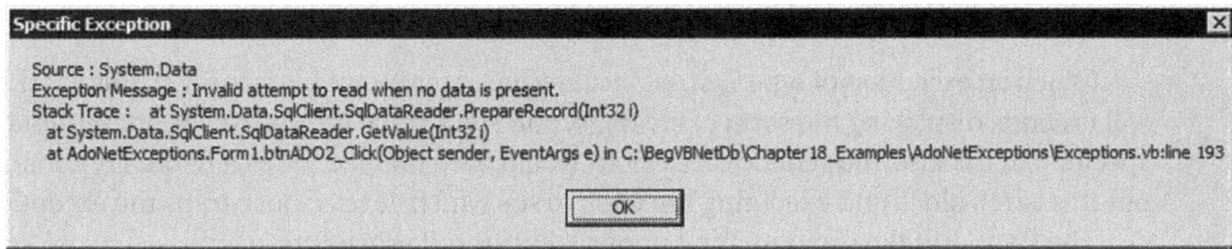

Figure 18-4. *Handling a specific ADO.NET exception*

4. For a quick comparison, we'll now demonstrate a SQL Server exception, an error that occurs within the database. Alter the name of the stored procedure in the code to a name that doesn't exist within the `Northwind` database. For example:

```
' Create SqlCommand Object
Dim thisCommand As SqlCommand = SqlConnection1.CreateCommand()
thisCommand.CommandType = CommandType.StoredProcedure
thisCommand.CommandText = "Select_NoEmployees"
```

5. Run the program with Ctrl+F5. Click the ADO.NET Exception 2 button, and you'll see the message box in Figure 18-5.

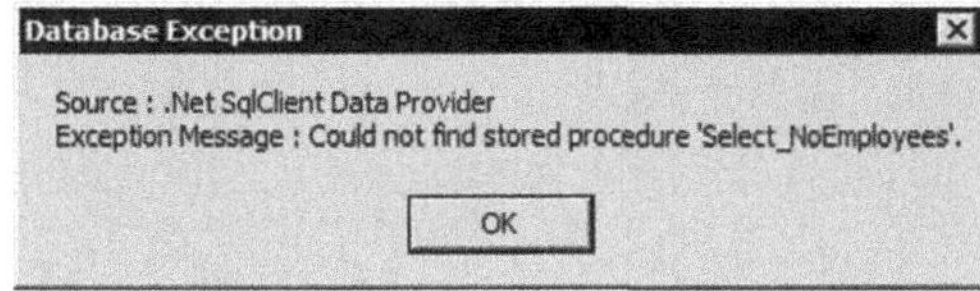

Figure 18-5. *Handling a database exception*

How It Works

First you create the data reader and try to access an invalid column, so an exception is thrown.

```
' Run command and get data as a reader
Dim thisReader As SqlDataReader = thisCommand.ExecuteReader()

' Access non-existent column
Dim str As String = thisReader.GetValue(20).ToString()
```

Here you tried to get the value of column 20, which doesn't exist. You add a new Catch clause to handle this kind of ADO.NET error.

```
Catch ex As System.InvalidOperationException
   Dim str As String
   str = "Source : " & ex.Source
   str &= ControlChars.NewLine
   str &= "Exception Message : " & ex.Message
   str &= ControlChars.NewLine
   str &= "Stack Trace : " & ex.StackTrace
   MessageBox.Show(str, "Specific Exception")
```

When an exception of type System.InvalidOperationException is thrown, this Catch clause will execute, displaying the source, message, and stack trace for the exception. Without this specific Catch clause, the generic Catch block would have trapped the exception. Try commenting out this Catch block and executing the code to see which Catch clause traps the exception.

Next, you run the program for a nonexistent stored procedure.

```
' Create SqlCommand Object
Dim thisCommand As SqlCommand = SqlConnection1.CreateCommand()
thisCommand.CommandType = CommandType.StoredProcedure
thisCommand.CommandText = "Select_AllEmployees"
```

You catch your first database exception with the following:

```
Catch ex As System.Data.SqlClient.SqlException
   Dim str As String
   str = "Source : " & ex.Source
   str &= ControlChars.NewLine
   str &= "Exception Message : " & ex.Message
   MessageBox.Show(str, "Database Exception")
```

This leads into the next topic: handling exceptions thrown by the database manager.

Handling Database Exceptions

An exception of type System.Data.SqlClient.SqlException is thrown when the SQL Server database returns a warning or error. This class is derived from System.SystemException and is sealed so it can't be inherited, but it has several useful members that can be interrogated to obtain valuable information about the exception.

An instance of SqlException is thrown whenever the .NET data provider for SQL Server encounters an error or warning from the database. Table 18-1 describes the properties of this class that provide information about the exception.

Table 18-1. *SqlException Properties*

Property Name	Description
Class	Gets the severity level of the error returned from the SqlClient data provider. The severity level is a numeric code that's used to indicate the nature of the error. Levels 1 to 10 are informational errors; 11 to 16 are user-level errors; 17 to 25 are software or hardware errors. At level 20 or greater, the connection is usually closed.
Errors	Contains one or more SqlError objects that have detailed information about the exception. This is a collection that can be iterated through.
HelpLink	The help file associated with this exception.
InnerException	Gets the exception instance that caused the current exception.
LineNumber	Gets the line number within the Transact-SQL command batch or stored procedure that generated the exception.
Message	The text describing the exception.
Number	The number that identifies the type of exception.
Procedure	The name of the stored procedure that generated the exception.
Server	The name of the computer running the instance of SQL Server that generated the exception.
Source	The name of the provider that generated the exception.
StackTrace	A string representation of the call stack when the exception was thrown.
State	Numeric error code from SQL Server that represents an exception, warning, or "no data found" message. For more information, see SQL Server Books Online.
TargetSite	The method that throws the current exception.

When an error occurs within SQL Server, it uses a Transact-SQL RAISERROR statement to raise an error back to the calling program. A typical error message looks like the following:

```
Server: Msg 2812, Level 16, State 62, Line 1
Could not find stored procedure 'sp_DoesNotExist'
```

In this message, 2812 represents the error number, 16 represents the severity level, and 62 represents the state of the error.

You can also use the RAISERROR statement to display specific messages within a stored procedure. The RAISERROR statement in its simplest form takes three parameters. The first parameter is the message itself that needs to be shown. The second parameter is the severity level of the error. Any users can use severity levels 11 through 16. They represent messages that can be categorized as information, software, or hardware problems. The third parameter is an arbitrary integer from 1 through 127 that represents information about the state or source of the error.

Let's see how a SQL error, raised by a stored procedure, is handled in VB .NET. You'll use the following Transact-SQL to raise an error when the number of orders in the Orders table exceeds ten.

```
IF @orderscount > 10
   RAISERROR (
      'Orders Count is greater than 10 - Notify the Business Manager', 16, 1
   )
```

Note that in this RAISERROR statement, you specify a severity level of 16, an arbitrary state number of 1, and a message string. When a RAISERROR statement that you write contains a message string, the error number is automatically given as 50000. When SQL Server raises errors using RAISERROR, it uses a predefined dictionary of messages to give out the corresponding error numbers. (See SQL Server Books Online to learn how to add your own messages to SQL Server's predefined messages.)

Try It Out: Handling a Database Exception (Part 1): RAISERROR

Follow these steps:

1. Add a button to the Database tab page, name it `btnDB1`, and change its `Text` property to `Database Exception 1 (RAISERROR)`. Add a label underneath this button, and change its `Text` property to `Calls a stored procedure that uses RAISERROR.`

2. Add a second button to the tab page, name it `btnDB2`, and change its `Text` property to `Database Exception-2 (SP Error)`. Add a label to the right of this button, and change its `Text` property to `Calls a stored procedure that encounters an error.`

3. Add a third button to the tab page, name it `btnDB3`, and change its `Text` property to `Database Exception-3 (Errors Collection)`. Add a label to the right of this button, and change its `Text` property to `Multiple SqlError objects created.` The layout should look like Figure 18-6.

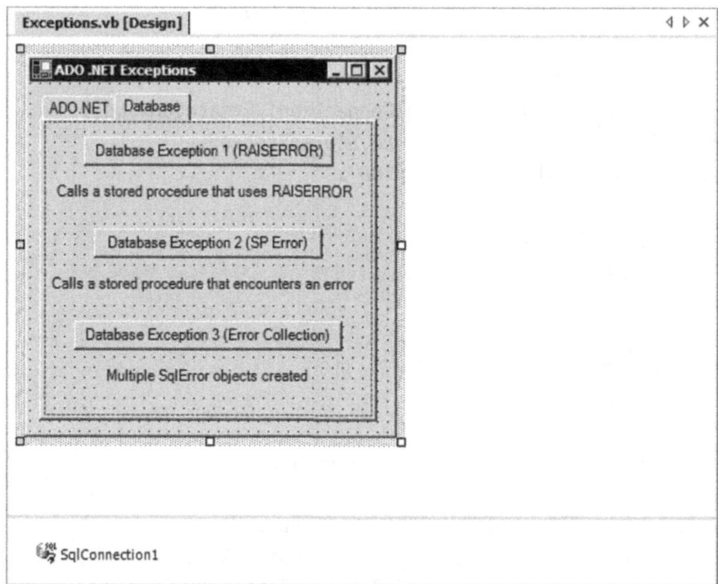

Figure 18-6. *Database tab page layout*

4. Using Server Explorer, create a stored procedure named `DbException_1`, as follows:

```
CREATE PROCEDURE dbo.DbException_1
AS
SET NOCOUNT ON

DECLARE @orderscount int

SELECT
   @orderscount = COUNT(*)
FROM
   ORDERS

IF @orderscount > 10
   RAISERROR (
      'Orders Count is greater than 10 - Notify the Business Manager', 16, 1
   )

RETURN
```

5. Add the following code to the `btnDB1_Click` method:

```
Private Sub btnDB1_Click(ByVal sender As System.Object, _
   ByVal e As System.EventArgs) Handles btnDB1.Click
   ' Create SqlCommand Object
   Dim thisCommand As SqlCommand = SqlConnection1.CreateCommand()
   thisCommand.CommandType = CommandType.StoredProcedure
   thisCommand.CommandText = "DbException_1"

   Try
      ' Open connection
      SqlConnection1.Open()

      ' Run stored procedure
      thisCommand.ExecuteNonQuery()

   Catch ex As System.Data.SqlClient.SqlException
      Dim str As String
      str = "Source : " & ex.Source & ControlChars.NewLine
      str &= "Number : " & ex.Number & ControlChars.NewLine
      str &= "Message : " & ex.Message & ControlChars.NewLine
      str &= "Class : " & ex.Class.ToString() & ControlChars.NewLine
      str &= "Procedure : " & ex.Procedure & ControlChars.NewLine
      str &= "Line number : " & ex.LineNumber.ToString() & _
         ControlChars.NewLine
      str &= "Server : " & ex.Server
      MessageBox.Show(str, "Database Exception")

   Catch ex As System.Exception
      Dim str As String
      str = "Source : " & ex.Source
      str &= ControlChars.NewLine
      str &= "Exception Message : " & ex.Message
      MessageBox.Show(str, "General Exception")

   Finally
      If SqlConnection1.State = ConnectionState.Open Then
         MessageBox.Show("Finally block closing the connection", "Finally")
         SqlConnection1.Close()
      End If
   End Try
End Sub
```

6. Run the program with Ctrl+F5, and then click the RAISERROR button. You'll see the message box in Figure 18-7.

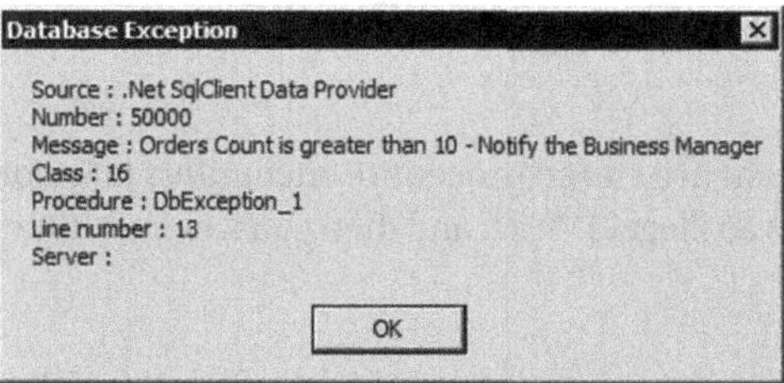

Figure 18-7. *Handling a raised database exception*

Observe the caption and contents of the message box. The source, message, name of the stored procedure, exact line number where the error was found, and name of the machine are all displayed. You obtain this detailed information about the exception from the `SqlException` object.

How It Works

In the `DBException_1` stored procedure, you first find the number of orders in the `Orders` table and store the number in a variable called `@orderscount`. Then, if `@orderscount` is greater than ten, you raise an error using the `RAISERROR` statement.

```
SELECT
   @orderscount = COUNT(*)
FROM
   ORDERS

IF @orderscount > 10
   RAISERROR (
      'Orders Count is greater than 10 - Notify the Business Manager', 16, 1
   )
```

Then within a `Try` block you execute the stored procedure using the `ExecuteNonQuery` method.

```
' Run stored procedure
thisCommand.ExecuteNonQuery()
```

When the stored procedure is executed, the `RAISERROR` statement raises an error. This is trapped by the following `Catch` clause:

```
Catch ex As System.Data.SqlClient.SqlException
   Dim str As String
   str = "Source : " & ex.Source & ControlChars.NewLine
   str &= "Number : " & ex.Number & ControlChars.NewLine
   str &= "Message : " & ex.Message & ControlChars.NewLine
   str &= "Class : " & ex.Class.ToString() & ControlChars.NewLine
   str &= "Procedure : " & ex.Procedure & ControlChars.NewLine
   str &= "Line number : " & ex.LineNumber.ToString() & ControlChars.NewLine
   str &= "Server : " & ex.Server
   MessageBox.Show(str, "Database Exception")
```

Try It Out: Handling a Database Exception (Part 2): Stored Procedure

Now let's see what happens when a statement in a stored procedure encounters an error. You'll now create a stored procedure that attempts an illegal `INSERT`, and then you'll extract information from the `SqlException` object.

1. Using Server Explorer, create a stored procedure named `DbException_2`, as follows:

```
CREATE PROCEDURE dbo.DBException_2
AS
SET NOCOUNT ON

INSERT INTO Employees
(
   EmployeeId,
   FirstName
)
VALUES (50, 'Cinderella')

RETURN
```

2. Copy the code from the `btnDB1_Click` method, and add it to the `btnDB2_Click` method, with the one change shown in bold in the following code to the creation of the `SqlCommand` object:

```
Private Sub btnDB2_Click(ByVal sender As System.Object, _
   ByVal e As System.EventArgs) Handles btnDB2.Click

   ' Create SqlCommand Object
   Dim thisCommand As SqlCommand = SqlConnection1.CreateCommand()
   thisCommand.CommandType = CommandType.StoredProcedure
   thisCommand.CommandText = "DBException_2"

   ...

End Sub
```

3. Run the program with Ctrl+F5, and then click the SP Error button. You'll see the message box in Figure 18-8.

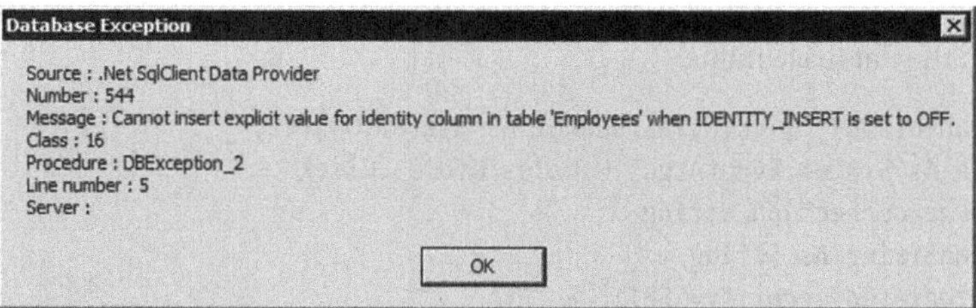

Figure 18-8. *Handling a database exception*

How It Works

The stored procedure tries to insert a new employee into the `Employees` table.

```
INSERT INTO Employees
(
   EmployeeId,
   FirstName
)
VALUES (50, 'Cinderella')
```

However, since the `EmployeeID` column in the `Employees` table is an `IDENTITY` column, you can't explicitly assign a value to it.

■ **Tip** Actually, you can—as the message indicates—if you use `SET IDENTITY_INSERT employees ON` in the stored procedure before you attempt the `INSERT`. This would allow you to insert explicit `EmployeeID` values, but this seldom is, or should be, done.

When this SQL error occurs, the specific `SqlException` `Catch` clause traps it and displays the information. The `Finally` block then closes the connection.

It's possible for stored procedures to encounter several errors. You can trap and debug these using the `SqlException` object, as you'll see next.

Try It Out: Handling a Database Exception (Part 3): Errors Collection

The `SqlException` class has an `Errors` collection property. Each item in the `Errors` collection is an object of type `SqlError`. When a database exception occurs, the `Errors` collection is populated. For the example, let's try to establish a connection to a nonexistent database and investigate the `SqlException`'s `Errors` collection.

1. Add the following code to the btnDB3_Click method. Note that we've intentionally misspelled the database name.

```
Private Sub btnDB3_Click(ByVal sender As System.Object, _
   ByVal e As System.EventArgs) Handles btnDB3.Click
   ' Mistype connection string
   Dim connString As String = _
      "integrated security=SSPI;" & _
      "data source=(local)\NetSDK;" & _
      "initial catalog=Northwnd"

   ' Create Connection
   Dim thisConnection As New SqlConnection(connString)

   ' Create command
   Dim thisCommand As SqlCommand = thisConnection.CreateCommand()
   thisCommand.CommandType = CommandType.StoredProcedure
   thisCommand.CommandText = "DBException_2"

   Try
      ' Open connection
      thisConnection.Open()

      ' Run stored procedure
      thisCommand.ExecuteNonQuery()

   Catch ex As System.Data.SqlClient.SqlException
      Dim str As String = ""
      For i As Integer = 0 To ex.Errors.Count - 1
         str &= ControlChars.NewLine & "Index #" & i & ControlChars.NewLine
         str &= "Exception : " & ex.Errors(i).ToString() & _
            ControlChars.NewLine
         str &= "Number : " & ex.Errors(i).Number.ToString() & _
            ControlChars.NewLine
      Next
      MessageBox.Show(str, "Database Exception")

   Catch ex As System.Exception
      Dim str As String
      str = "Source : " & ex.Source
      str &= ControlChars.NewLine
      str &= "Exception Message : " & ex.Message
      MessageBox.Show(str, "General Exception")
```

```
      Finally
         If thisConnection.State = ConnectionState.Open Then
            MessageBox.Show("Finally block closing the connection", "Finally")
            thisConnection.Close()
         End If
      End Try
   End Sub
```

2. Run the program with Ctrl+F5, and then click the Errors Collection button. You'll see the message box in Figure 18-9.

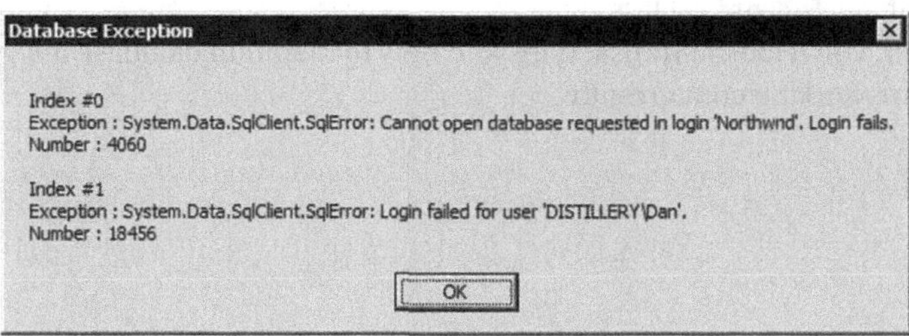

Figure 18-9. *Handling multiple database errors*

Observe that two items are found in the `Errors` collection, and their error numbers are different.

How It Works

In the connection string, you specify a database that doesn't exist on the server; here you misspell `Northwind` as `Northwnd`.

```
' Mistype connection string
Dim connString As String = _
   "integrated security=SSPI;" &_
   "data source=(local)\NetSDK;" &_
   "initial catalog=Northwnd"
```

When you try to open the connection, an exception of type `SqlException` is thrown.

```
Catch ex As System.Data.SqlClient.SqlException
   Dim str As String = ""
   For i As Integer = 0 To ex.Errors.Count - 1
      str &= ControlChars.NewLine & "Index #" & i & ControlChars.NewLine
      str &= "Exception : " & ex.Errors(i).ToString() & ControlChars.NewLine
      str &= "Number : " & ex.Errors(i).Number.ToString() & _
         ControlChars.NewLine
   Next
   MessageBox.Show(str, "Database Exception")
```

You loop through the items of the `Errors` collection and get each `Error` object using its indexer.

This example shows that the `SqlException` object carries detailed information about every SQL error in its `Errors` collection.

Summary

We began this chapter by reviewing VB .NET's structured error handling. Then we discussed the sources of exceptions in ADO.NET database applications.

You saw how to handle exceptions thrown by the CLR and by the database. In particular, you learned how to handle both single and multiple database exceptions with the `System.Data.SqlClient.SqlException` class.

In the next chapter, you'll look at transactions and how to maintain database integrity when multiple users are working concurrently.

CHAPTER 19

Using Transactions

A *transaction* is a group of operations performed in such a way that the operations are guaranteed to succeed or fail as one. Or, in simpler language, a transaction may contain lots of operations but either all the operations are performed successfully in the order they're written in the transaction or when one operation fails, it and those operations carried out before it are reversed so that the database is in the same state it was in before the transaction began.

A common example of a simple transaction is transferring money from a checking account to a savings account. This involves two operations: deducting money from the checking account and adding it to the savings account. Both must succeed together and be *committed* to the accounts, or both must fail together and be *rolled back*, as in Figure 19-1, so that the accounts are maintained in a consistent state. Under no circumstances should money be deducted from the checking account but not added to the savings account (or vice versa). By using a transaction, both operations can be guaranteed to succeed or fail together.

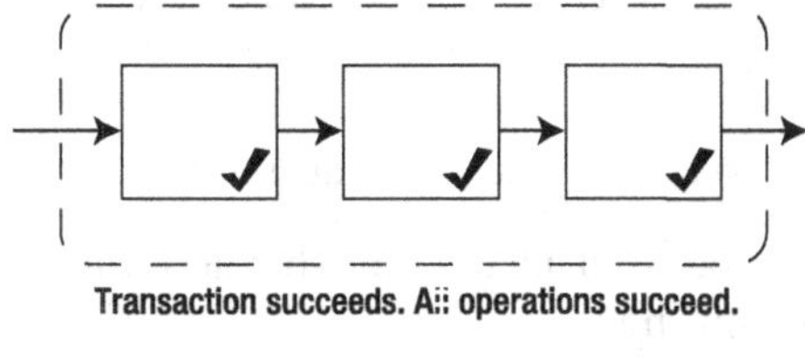

Transaction succeeds. All operations succeed.

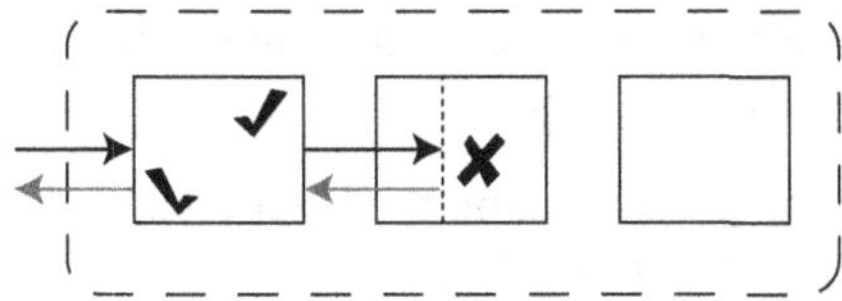

Transaction fails and rolls back.
Operation 1 succeeds. Operation 2 fails.
Operation 2 and then Operation 1 are rolled back.
Database returns to original state before transaction commenced.

Figure 19-1. *Transactions completely succeed, or they roll back.*

Transactions may comprise many individual operations and even other transactions. Transactions are essential for maintaining data integrity, both for multiple related operations and when multiple users update the database *concurrently*.

In this chapter, we'll cover the following topics:

- When to use transactions
- The ACID properties of a transaction
- How to code transactions

When to Use Transactions

You should use transactions when several operations must succeed or fail as a unit. The following are some frequent scenarios where you must use transactions:

- In batch processing, where multiple rows must be inserted or deleted as a single unit
- Whenever a change to one table requires that other tables be kept consistent
- When modifying data in two or more databases, concurrently
- In distributed transactions, where data is manipulated in databases on different machines

When you use transactions, you place locks on data pending permanent change to the database. No other operations can take place on locked data until you lift the lock. You could lock anything from a single row up to the whole database. This is called *concurrency*; that is, concurrency is how the database handles multiple updates at one time. A simple concurrency example works something like this:

1. Transaction 1 (T1) asks a bank database if it can access Jane's bank account.
2. The database sees nothing is accessing her account, so it lets T1 into her account and then locks the door behind it until T1 says it's finished.
3. Transaction 2 (T2) also wants to access Jane's bank account (spends a lot on her Visa, doesn't she?). The database checks, and Jane's account is locked with T1 accessing it, so it puts T2 in a queue to access her account until T1 is finished.
4. T1 finishes, so the database unlocks her account, lets T2 in, and then locks it again in case T3 comes along also looking for Jane's bank account.

In this example, a lock ensured that the two separate transactions didn't access the same account at the same time. If they did, either deposits or withdrawals could be lost. Locks are extremely useful, but they can hinder performance because they exclude any other operation from accessing a database resource (perhaps a table of everyone's bank account details?) until a transaction has finished. It's important to keep transactions pending for the shortest period of time. Too many locks, or locks on frequently accessed resources, can seriously degrade performance. You could also get a situation where two related transactions get stuck because they've each locked out resources that the other needs to finish. This mutual lock can be very problematic.

Understanding the ACID Properties of a Transaction

A transaction is characterized by four properties, often referred to as the *ACID properties*: atomicity, consistency, isolation, and durability.

Atomicity: A transaction is atomic if it's regarded as a single action rather than a collection of separate operations. So then, only when all the separate operations succeed does a transaction succeed and is committed to the database. On the other hand, if a single operation fails during the transaction, everything is considered to have failed and must be undone (rolled back) if it has already taken place. In the case of the order-entry system of the `Northwind` database, when you enter an order into the `Orders` and `Order Details` tables, data will be saved together in both tables, or it won't be saved at all.

Consistency: The transaction should leave the database in a consistent state—whether or not it completed successfully. The data modified by the transaction must comply with all the constraints placed on the columns in order to maintain data integrity. In the case of `Northwind`, you can't have rows in the `Order Details` table without a corresponding row in the `Orders` table, as this would leave the data in an inconsistent state.

Isolation: Every transaction has a well-defined boundary. One transaction shouldn't affect other transactions running at the same time. Data modifications made by one transaction must be isolated from the data modification made by all other transactions. A transaction sees data in the state it was in before another concurrent transaction modified it, or it sees the data after the second transaction has completed, but it doesn't see an intermediate state.

Durability: Data modifications that occur within a successful transaction are kept permanently within the system regardless of what else occurs. Transaction logs are maintained so that should a failure occur, the database can be restored to its original state before the failure. As each transaction is completed, a row is entered in the database transaction log. If you have a major system failure that requires the database to be restored from a backup, you could then use this transaction log to insert (roll forward) any successful transactions that had taken place.

Every database server that offers support for transactions enforces these four properties automatically. All you need to do is create the transactions in the first place, which is what you'll look at next.

How to Code Transactions

The following three statements control transactions in SQL Server:

- **BEGIN TRANSACTION**: This marks the beginning of a transaction.
- **COMMIT TRANSACTION**: This marks the successful end of a transaction. It signals the database to save the work.
- **ROLLBACK TRANSACTION**: This denotes that a transaction hasn't been successful and signals the database to roll back to the state it was in prior to the transaction.

Coding Transactions in SQL

Let's code some simple transactions to see how the transaction control statements work.

Try It Out: Rolling Back a Transaction

This example shows how to safely delete a sales order in the `Northwind` database. As you know, an order has a header row in the `Orders` table and detail rows in the `Order Details` table. When you delete an order, you need to delete both header and details or nothing. You have several ways to achieve this. In this example, you'll do it with a stored procedure.

1. In Server Explorer, expand the Northwind node, right-click the Stored Procedures node, and then click New Stored Procedure.
2. Replace the code with that in Listing 19-1.

Listing 19-1. *TransTest1*

```
CREATE PROCEDURE dbo.TransTest1(@OrderId as integer)
AS
DECLARE @Err int

BEGIN TRANSACTION

-- Delete the order
DELETE FROM Orders
WHERE OrderId = @OrderId

-- Save @@ERROR in local variable @Err
SET @Err = @@ERROR

-- If error number is not zero, roll back
IF @Err <> 0
BEGIN
   ROLLBACK TRANSACTION
   RETURN @Err
END

-- Delete the order details
DELETE [Order Details]
WHERE OrderId = @OrderId

-- Save @@ERROR number in local variable @Err
SET @Err = @@ERROR
```

```
-- If error number is not zero, roll back
IF @Err <> 0
BEGIN
   ROLLBACK TRANSACTION
   RETURN @Err
 END

-- If no error, commit the transaction
COMMIT TRANSACTION
RETURN
```

3. Click the Save icon. This will run the `CREATE PROCEDURE` statement.

4. Before running the stored procedure, you need to make sure that the relationship between `Orders` and `Order Details` doesn't cascade deletes.

   In Server Explorer, right-click the Database Diagrams node, and then click New Diagram. In the Add Table window, select Orders and Order Details, and then click Add. Click Close to view the diagram. Right-click the relationship, and select Property Pages. Select the Relationships tab, and then uncheck the Cascade Delete Related Records check box (see Figure 19-2). Click Close and then Save to make the change in the database.

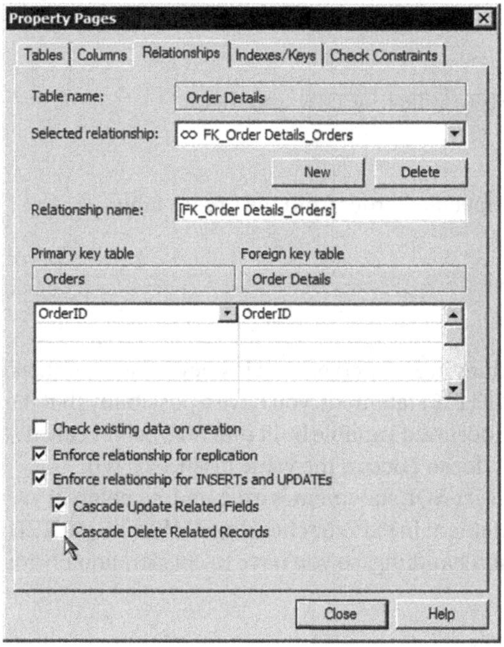

Figure 19-2. *Suppressing cascade deletes*

5. Run the procedure in Server Explorer by right-clicking its node and selecting Run Stored Procedure. When prompted, enter 10261 for @OrderId. You'll see the error message in the output window whose full text is as follows:

```
Running dbo."TransTest1" ( @OrderId = 10261 ).

DELETE statement conflicted with COLUMN REFERENCE constraint
'FK_Order Details_Orders'. The conflict occurred in database 'Northwind',
table 'Order Details', column 'OrderID'.
The statement has been terminated.
No rows affected.
(0 row(s) returned)
@RETURN_VALUE = 547
Finished running dbo."sp_TransTest1".
```

How It Works

You want to delete the rows for a given OrderId from the Orders and Order Details tables in a transaction. You begin by declaring @OrderId as an input parameter for the stored procedure and a local variable @Err, which you use to hold the error number should one occur.

```
CREATE PROCEDURE dbo.TransTest1(@OrderId as integer)
AS
DECLARE @Err int
```

You begin the transaction with the BEGIN TRANSACTION statement.

```
BEGIN TRANSACTION
```

Next you try to delete the row for a specified order from the Orders table.

```
-- Delete the order
DELETE FROM Orders
WHERE OrderId = @OrderId
```

Error handling is important at all times in SQL Server, and it's never more so than inside transactional code. When you issue the DELETE statement, you have a possibility that it may not succeed for whatever reason. If an error occurs, a variable built into SQL Server called @@ERROR will store the error's number. If an error doesn't occur, the value of @@ERROR is 0.

@@ERROR is reset to 0 after every Transact-SQL statement is executed, so before it's reset you store its current value for the DELETE statement in @Err for checking. Unlike VB .NET, Transact-SQL doesn't support structured exception handling, so you have to check manually for each error.

```
-- Save @@ERROR in local variable @Err
SET @Err = @@ERROR
```

If @Err is any value other than 0, an error has occurred, and you must roll back the transaction. You also include PRINT and RAISERROR statements to tell you that a rollback has occurred.

```
-- If error number is not zero, roll back
IF @Err <> 0
BEGIN
   ROLLBACK TRANSACTION
   RETURN @Err
END
```

Note Technically, you didn't need to roll back the transaction since the deletion failed and no data was actually changed in the database.

If all goes well, you try to delete the corresponding rows from `Order Details` for this `@OrderId`. As before, you save `@@ERROR` in the local variable `@Err` and use it to determine if you should roll back the transaction.

```
-- Delete the order details
DELETE [Order Details]
WHERE OrderId = @OrderId

-- Save @@ERROR number in local variable @Err
SET @Err = @@ERROR

-- If error number is not zero, roll back
IF @Err <> 0
BEGIN
   ROLLBACK TRANSACTION
   RETURN @Err
 END
```

If the stored procedure still hasn't encountered any errors, you issue the `COMMIT TRANSACTION` statement to commit the deletions. By default, if no expression is used after `RETURN`, a value of `0` is returned.

```
-- If no error, commit the transaction
COMMIT TRANSACTION
RETURN
```

Try It Out: Committing a Transaction

In this example, you'll modify the stored procedure by flipping the `DELETE` statements so that the `Order Details` rows are deleted before the `Orders` rows.

1. In Server Explorer, expand the Northwind node, right-click the Stored Procedures node, and then click New Stored Procedure.

2. Replace the code with that in Listing 19-2.

Listing 19-2. *dbo.TransTest2*

```
CREATE PROCEDURE dbo.TransTest2(@OrderId as integer)
AS
DECLARE @Err int

BEGIN TRANSACTION

-- Delete the order details
DELETE [Order Details]
WHERE OrderId = @OrderId

-- Save @@ERROR number in local variable @Err
SET @Err = @@ERROR

-- If error number is not zero, roll back
IF @Err <> 0
BEGIN
   ROLLBACK TRANSACTION
   RETURN @Err
 END

-- Delete the order
DELETE FROM Orders
WHERE OrderId = @OrderId

-- Save @@ERROR in local variable @Err
SET @Err = @@ERROR

-- If error number is not zero, roll back
IF @Err <> 0
BEGIN
   ROLLBACK TRANSACTION
   RETURN @Err
END

-- If no error, commit the transaction
COMMIT TRANSACTION
RETURN
```

3. Click the Save icon. This will run the `CREATE PROCEDURE` statement.
4. Run the procedure in Server Explorer by right-clicking its node and selecting Run Stored Procedure. When prompted, enter `10260` for `@OrderId`. You'll see the output window shown in Figure 19-3. No errors occur, and both the order and its details are deleted.

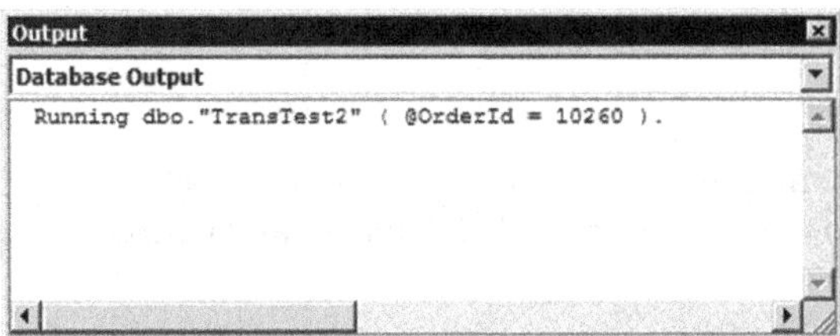

Figure 19-3. *Successful completion of a transaction*

How It Works

The new stored procedure differs from the first only in the order of the `DELETE` statements, which have been reversed. When you execute the stored procedure, a transaction begins, and the rows are deleted from the `Order Details` table first and then from `Orders`. This ensures that the foreign key constraint isn't violated and no error is generated. With both deletions having been successfully carried out, you then commit the transaction.

Understanding ADO.NET Transactions

In ADO.NET, a *transaction* is an instance of a class that implements the interface `System.Data.IDbTransaction`. Like a data reader, a transaction has no constructor of its own but is created by calling another object's method—in this case, a connection's `BeginTransaction` method. Commands are associated with a specific transaction for a specific connection, and any SQL submitted by these commands is executed as part of the same transaction.

Try It Out: Working with ADO.NET Transactions

In this ADO.NET example, you'll code a VB .NET equivalent of `TransTest2`.

1. Create a new solution called `Chapter19_Examples`.
2. Add a VB .NET Windows application named `Transactions`. Rename `Form1.vb` to `Transactions.vb` and the form's `Text` property to `Transactions`.
3. Add a label, a text box (`txtOrderId`), and two buttons (`btnRollback` and `btnCommit`), as shown in Figure 19-4.

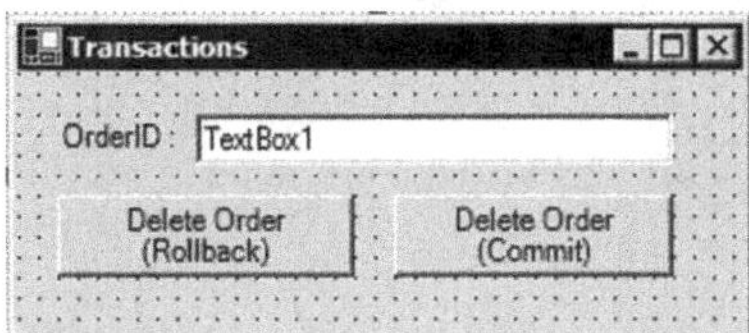

Figure 19-4. `Transactions` *layout*

4. Add the following `Imports` directive to `Transactions.vb`:

```
Imports System.Data.SqlClient
```

5. Add a `SqlConnection` to the form from the Data tab of the Toolbox. Set its `ConnectionString` property to that for the `Northwind` database and its `Name` property to `thisConnection`.

6. Double-click the Delete Order (Roll Back) button, and add the following code to its click event handler:

```
Private Sub btnRollback_Click(ByVal sender As System.Object, _
   ByVal e As System.EventArgs) Handles btnRollback.Click
   ' SQL Delete Command
   Dim sql As String = "DELETE FROM Orders " & _
      "WHERE OrderId = " & txtOrderId.Text

   ' Create command
   Dim thisCommand As New SqlCommand(sql, thisConnection)

   ' Create Transaction
   Dim thisTransaction As SqlTransaction

   Try
      ' Open Connection
      thisConnection.Open()

      ' Begin transaction and attach it to command
      thisTransaction = thisConnection.BeginTransaction()
      thisCommand.Transaction = thisTransaction

      ' Run delete command
      thisCommand.ExecuteNonQuery()

      ' Commit transaction
      thisTransaction.Commit()

      ' Display success
      MessageBox.Show("Transaction Committed. Data Deleted")

   Catch ex As Exception
      ' Roll back transaction
      thisTransaction.Rollback()

      MessageBox.Show("Transaction rolled back : " & ex.Message, "Error")
```

```
    Finally
        ' Close Connection
        thisConnection.Close()
    End Try
End Sub
```

7. Double-click the Delete Order (Commit) button, and add the following code to its click event handler. Apart from the code in bold, it's identical to the code for `btnRollback_Click`, so you could cut and paste from there and then make amendments.

```
Private Sub btnCommit_Click(ByVal sender As System.Object, _
    ByVal e As System.EventArgs) Handles btnCommit.Click
    ' SQL Delete Commands
    Dim sql1 As String = "DELETE FROM [Order Details] " & _
        "WHERE OrderId = " & txtOrderId.Text

    Dim sql2 As String = "DELETE FROM Orders " & _
        "WHERE OrderId = " & txtOrderId.Text

    ' Create command
    Dim thisCommand As New SqlCommand(sql1, thisConnection)

    ' Create Transaction
    Dim thisTransaction As SqlTransaction

    Try
        ' Open Connection
        thisConnection.Open()

        ' Begin transaction and attach it to command
        thisTransaction = thisConnection.BeginTransaction()
        thisCommand.Transaction = thisTransaction

        ' Run first delete command
        thisCommand.ExecuteNonQuery()

        ' Setup and run second delete command
        thisCommand.CommandText = sql2
        thisCommand.ExecuteNonQuery()

        ' Commit transaction
        thisTransaction.Commit()

        ' Display success
        MessageBox.Show("Transaction Committed. Data Deleted")
```

```
        Catch ex As Exception
            ' Roll back transaction
            thisTransaction.Rollback()

            MessageBox.Show("Transaction rolled back : " & ex.Message, "Error")

        Finally
            ' Close Connection
            thisConnection.Close()
        End Try
    End Sub
```

8. Build and run the solution with Ctrl+F5. Enter `10249` for `Order ID`, and click Delete Order (Roll Back). As expected, an error message box appears as in Figure 19-5.

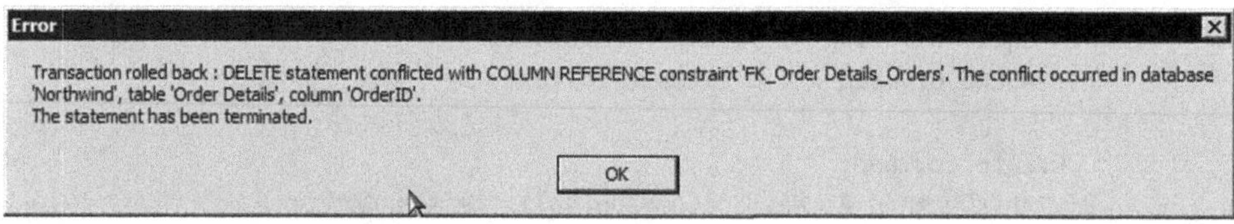

Figure 19-5. *Rolling back a transaction*

9. Now click Delete Order (Commit). As expected, a message box confirming that the transaction is successful appears, as in Figure 19-6.

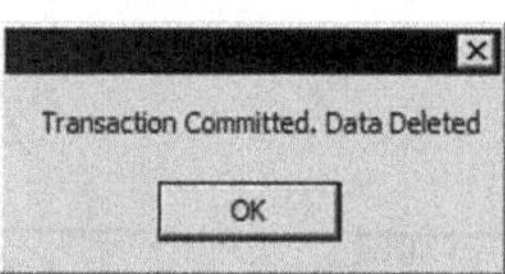

Figure 19-6. *Committing a transaction*

How It Works

Both event handlers work in basically the same way. First you create a command object in the usual way. Then you create a holding variable for a transaction so that it's in scope for both `Try` and `Catch` blocks in the code.

```
' SQL Delete Command
Dim sql As String = "DELETE FROM Orders " & _
   "WHERE OrderId = " & txtOrderId.Text

' Create command
Dim thisCommand As New SqlCommand(sql, thisConnection)

' Create Transaction
Dim thisTransaction As SqlTransaction
```

Now you open the connection and create a transaction for it. Note that transactions are connection specific. You can't create a second transaction for the same connection before committing or rolling back the first one. Though the method implies it begins a transaction, the transaction itself performs no work until the first SQL is executed by a command.

```
Try
   ' Open Connection
   thisConnection.Open()

   ' Begin transaction and attach it to command
   thisTransaction = thisConnection.BeginTransaction()
   thisCommand.Transaction = thisTransaction
```

Now you execute the commands within the transaction. Observe that the first event handler executes only one SQL statement—to delete an order. You then call the transaction's `Commit` method to commit the data. Note that, unlike in the stored procedures, you *don't* execute the `SQL COMMIT` statement. ADO.NET handles transactions differently than SQL does. The details are beyond the scope of this book, but rest assured that both ADO.NET and SQL transactions guarantee all operations will succeed or fail as a unit. Just remember to use `Commit` rather than `COMMIT` in VB .NET programs.

```
' Run delete command
thisCommand.ExecuteNonQuery()

' Commit transaction
thisTransaction.Commit()
```

In the second event handler, you execute two SQL statements—to delete order details before deleting an order. The code for the second `DELETE` statement is assigned to `CommandText` and then submitted to the database with `ExecuteNonQuery`. Only after both statements have executed do you call the transaction's `Commit` method. Had you called `Commit` after the first `DELETE`, the order details would have be deleted and stayed deleted even if the delete of the order failed. `Commit`, just like `COMMIT`, makes changes permanent and ends the current transaction.

```
' Run first delete command
thisCommand.ExecuteNonQuery()

' Setup and run second delete command
thisCommand.CommandText = sql2
thisCommand.ExecuteNonQuery()

' Commit transaction
thisTransaction.Commit()
```

If an error is encountered, a `Catch` block calls the transaction's `Rollback` method. This undoes any changes for all SQL operations performed within the transaction (in other words, since the most recent call to `Commit` or `Rollback`).

```
Catch ex As Exception
   ' Roll back transaction
   thisTransaction.Rollback()

   MessageBox.Show("Transaction rolled back : " & ex.Message, "Error")
```

Suggestions for Further Study

You've seen only the tip of the transaction iceberg in this chapter. Though the basic techniques remain the same and you can write many real-world programs with what you've learned, you have a great deal more to learn about how both ADO.NET and RDBMSs manage transactions. Some important topics that are just too involved to cover here in this introduction include the following:

Isolation levels: Continuing into the topic of concurrency and locking, you can use isolation levels to specify how visible data being modified by a transaction is to another concurrent transaction. What isolation levels are available depends on the RDBMSs. For example, SQL Server supports six isolation levels, DB2 and MySQL support four, and Oracle supports three. The SQL standard itself defines four. Further, the default isolation level is RDBMS specific. Study the documentation for both your database and data provider before choosing an isolation level. The actual choice also depends on just what your program does and what kind of performance it seeks to achieve.

Nested transactions: Transactions can be nested. In general, commits and rollbacks are local to the nested transaction, but, again, consult your RDBMS documentation for specifics.

Savepoints: Savepoints are defined by the SQL standard and supported by most RDBMSs. They allow you to roll back part of a transaction without terminating the entire transaction.

Summary

In this chapter you learned what transactions are and when to use them. You learned about the ACID properties of transactions and that transactions either complete successfully and are committed or fail at some point and are rolled back so the database is left in its original state before the transaction began. You then learned that you can write database transactions in SQL and in VB .NET. You also learned about concurrency and locks; these are key topics in the realm of transactions, as without them you would have no guarantee that information held in databases would remain consistent with the real world.

CHAPTER 20

Working with ADO.NET Events

Just like a Button or any other .NET form control, ADO.NET objects (such as connections and datasets) can fire events when a property has changed. For example, you can make a connection that notifies you when it opens or closes. Similarly, you can create a dataset object that notifies you when a column value is changed or when a row is deleted.

In this chapter, we'll take a from-the-ground-up look at events, starting with exactly how they fit into .NET programming in general and how you work with them. Then we'll cover the following ADO.NET objects and their events:

- The Connection object and its StateChange and InfoMessage events
- The DataAdapter object and its RowUpdating and RowUpdated events

These aren't all the events defined by the ADO.NET objects by a long stretch, but they're some of the most useful when put into an application, as we'll demonstrate in a while.

Understanding Events

An *event* is a class member that enables a class or object to provide notifications by invoking methods on other objects that signal the occurrence of an action. The action could be user interaction, such as mouse clicks, or operations carried out by a program. The object that triggers the event is the *event source*. The object that captures the event and responds to it is the *event consumer* (or *client*). The method that handles the event is the *event handler*.

The event source doesn't care what objects consume its events. The consumers give it delegates; that is, they give it a mapping to methods that the source will execute when the event occurs.

When an event is raised, the code within the event handler is executed. Each event handler provides two parameters that help handle the event correctly. The first parameter, the sender, provides a reference to the object that raised the event. The second parameter is an object specific to the event that's being handled. By referencing the object's properties (and sometimes its methods), you can obtain detailed information about the event. Typically each event has an event handler with a different event-object type for the second parameter.

This event-handling process applies to all events in the .NET Framework. Consequently, ADO.NET objects, such as connections, data adapters, and datasets, all raise events that can be handled using the same process. We'll discuss the events raised by ADO.NET objects in detail throughout this chapter, but for now, let's get a feel for how all the different pieces of this process works.

Connections support two events, InfoMessage and StateChange. If you want to handle these events, you declare that connection using the WithEvents keywords, as follows:

```
Friend WithEvents SqlConnection1 As System.Data.SqlClient.SqlConnection
```

You then use the Handles keyword on the end of a method declaration for the class containing the connection object to denote it's in fact a handler for one of its events. For example, the following skeleton code declares a method that handles the connection's InfoMessage event:

```
Private Sub SqlConnection1_InfoMessage(ByVal sender As Object, _
   ByVal e As System.Data.SqlClient.SqlInfoMessageEventArgs) _
   Handles SqlConnection1.InfoMessage

   ...

End Sub
```

If you use Visual Studio .NET to generate these handlers, their names will default to the form ObjectName_EventName, but you can change this. Note that the second parameter of the event handler changes between most events; it's a good idea to autogenerate handlers with Visual Studio .NET rather than write them out in full yourself. You'll now look at the syntax of adding and removing event handlers.

Adding and Removing Event Handlers

In VB .NET, you specify an event handler by using the Handles keyword. For example, you can bind the StateChange event of the connection object called cn to the StateIsChanging method (which you write yourself). The StateChange event of the connection object fires whenever the connection state changes to open or closed.

```
Private Sub StateIsChanging(ByVal sender As Object, _
   ByVal e As System.Data.StateChangeEventArgs)
   Handles cn.StateChange

...

End Sub
```

You can deactivate the event handler by removing the Handles declaration in bold. Once deactivated, when the StateChange event fires, it won't be handled by the StateIsChanging event handler. You can also set the same method to handle more than one event by presenting a comma-separated list of events for that method to handle after the Handles keyword in the method's declaration. For example, in the following code, StateIsChanging now handles both the Connection object events:

```
Private Sub StateIsChanging(ByVal sender As Object, _
   ByVal e As System.Data.StateChangeEventArgs)
   Handles cn.StateChange, cn.InfoMessage

...

End Sub
```

This process of activating and deactivating an event handler can also take place at runtime using the `AddHandler` command. This takes two arguments: the name of the event to be handled, in the form `objectname.eventname`, and the address of the method doing the handling, in the form `AddressOf methodname`. Note that the two arguments shouldn't be enclosed in parentheses. For example:

```
Sub MiscellaneousMethod()
   AddHandler cn.StateChange, AddressOf StateIsChanging

... do some stuff

   RemoveHandler cn.StateChange, AddressOf StateIsChanging
End Sub
```

In this method, the `StateIsChanging` method is attached as an event handler to the connection object's `StateChange` method by the `AddHandler` method and then detached using the `RemoveHandler` method, which uses the same syntax as `AddHandler`.

Tip It may appear that the `WithEvents`/`Handles` and the `AddHandler`/`RemoveHandler` methods of creating and removing event handlers yield the same results, but actually a subtle difference exists. `WithEvents` ties an event handler to a specific variable, and `AddHandler` ties the handler to a specific object.

In this chapter, we'll discuss the events raised by ADO.NET objects and how to handle them. Although events can be raised and handled by non-ADO.NET objects as well, this chapter pertains only to the ADO.NET objects.

Raising and Handling ADO.NET Events

You can handle the events raised by ADO.NET objects using the appropriate code as discussed previously. These events are raised when a certain property of the object changes. Although these objects raise several events, we'll discuss only a few, because all can be handled in the same fashion. You'll use the `System.Data.SqlClient` .NET data provider, but all data providers handle events in a similar way.

Working with Connection Object Events

The connection object has two events: StateChange and InfoMessage. Let's look at these in more detail.

Using the StateChange Event

The Connection object raises the StateChange event when the state of the connection changes. The event handler receives a StateChangeEventArgs object, which you can examine for detailed information about the event. For example, it has OriginalState and CurrentState properties that you can access to find out the state of the connection before and after a change.

Try It Out: Writing the Connection.StateChange Event

You'll now see how this event is handled. You'll open a connection to the Northwind database, retrieve one row from the Customers table, and close the connection. Then you'll write an event handler to notify you of when the connection state changes.

1. Create a new solution called Chapter20_Examples.
2. Add a VB .NET Windows application named Events, and change Form1.vb to Events.vb.
3. Add four buttons (btnStateChange, btnInfoMessage, btnRowUpdating, and btnMultiple, from top to bottom), a label, and a list box (lbxEventLog) as shown in Figure 20-1.

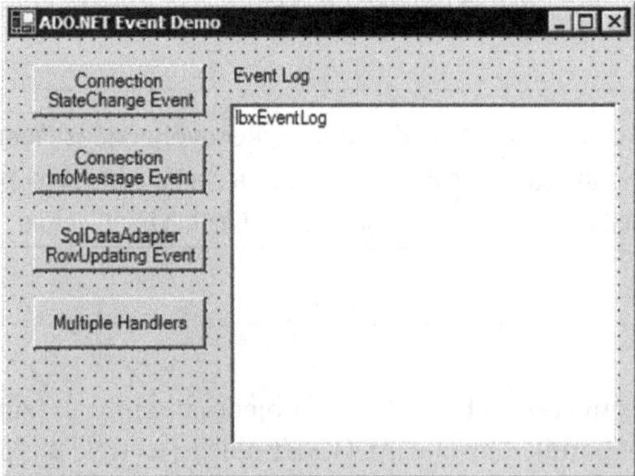

Figure 20-1. *Events layout*

4. Add an Imports directive for the System.Data.SqlClient namespace.
5. Drag a SqlConnection object onto the form from the Data tab of the Toolbox and call it thisConnection. Set its ConnectionString property to that of the Northwind database.
6. In the click event handler for the first button (btnStateChange), add the following code:

```
Private Sub btnStateChange_Click(ByVal sender As System.Object, _
   ByVal e As System.EventArgs)
   Handles btnStateChange.Click
   ' Sql Query
   Dim sql As String = "SELECT TOP 1 " & _
      "CustomerId, CompanyName FROM Customers"

   ' Create command
   Dim thisCommand As New SqlCommand(sql, thisConnection)

   Try
      ' Clear event log
      lbxEventLog.Items.Clear()

      ' Open connection and fire StateChange event
      thisConnection.Open()

      ' Create data reader
      Dim thisReader As SqlDataReader = thisCommand.ExecuteReader()

      ' Display rows in event log
      While thisReader.Read()
         lbxEventLog.Items.Add(thisReader.GetString(0) _
            + "-" + thisReader.GetString(1))
      End While
   Catch ex As SqlException
      MessageBox.Show(ex.Message)
   Finally
      ' Close connection and fire StateChange event
      thisConnection.Close()
   End Try
End Sub
```

7. Add the following method:

```
Private Sub StateIsChanged(ByVal sender As Object, _
   ByVal e As System.Data.StateChangeEventArgs) _
   Handles thisConnection.StateChange
   ' Event handler for the StateChange Event
   lbxEventLog.Items.Add("------------------------------")
   lbxEventLog.Items.Add("Entering StateChange EventHandler")
   lbxEventLog.Items.Add("Sender = " + sender.ToString())
   lbxEventLog.Items.Add("Original State = " + e.OriginalState.ToString())
   lbxEventLog.Items.Add("Current State = " + e.CurrentState.ToString())
   lbxEventLog.Items.Add("Exiting StateChange EventHandler")
   lbxEventLog.Items.Add("------------------------------")
End Sub
```

8. Build and run the solution with Ctrl+F5. Click the Connection StateChange Event button. You'll see the results in Figure 20-2.

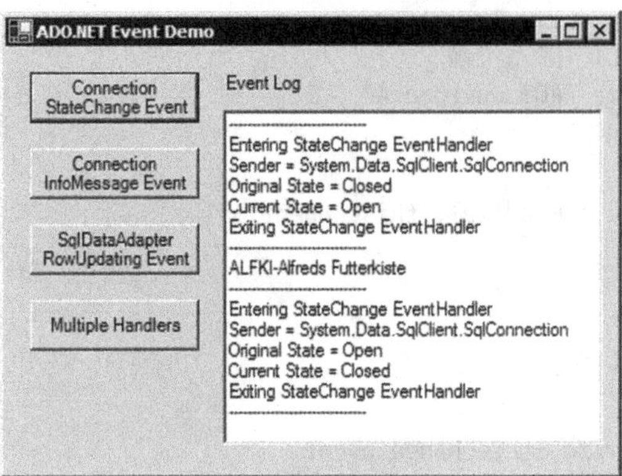

Figure 20-2. *Displaying* `StateChange` *event information*

Notice the values of the `Original State` and `Current State` properties before and after the data displays. This example shows that as the connection state changes the event handler takes over and handles the event.

How It Works

You use a query that selects one row from the `Customers` table.

```
' Sql Query
Dim sql As String = "SELECT TOP 1 " & _
   "CustomerId, CompanyName FROM Customers"
```

By dragging a `SqlConnection` object onto the form from the Toolbox, you had Visual Studio .NET autogenerate a declaration for the object that included the `WithEvents` keyword, as this is the default.

```
Friend WithEvents thisConnection As System.Data.SqlClient.SqlConnection
```

Then you write the event handler. Its declaration must contain both a clause that it `Handles` the `StateChange` event for the connection object and the correct parameter types for that event: an `Object` object and a `StateChangeEventArgs` object. In the background, this matches the signature of the `StateChangeEventHandler` delegate that templates this particular event handler for all data providers. We'll provide more information about this in a minute. (You can also find out more about this online at `http://msdn.microsoft.com/library/en-us/cpref/html/frlrfsystemdatastatechangeeventhandlerclasstopic.asp`.)

```
Private Sub StateIsChanged(ByVal sender As Object, _
   ByVal e As System.Data.StateChangeEventArgs) _
   Handles thisConnection.StateChange
   ' Event handler for the StateChange Event
   lbxEventLog.Items.Add("-----------------------------")
   lbxEventLog.Items.Add("Entering StateChange EventHandler")
   lbxEventLog.Items.Add("Sender = " + sender.ToString())
   lbxEventLog.Items.Add("Original State = " + e.OriginalState.ToString())
   lbxEventLog.Items.Add("Current State = " + e.CurrentState.ToString())
   lbxEventLog.Items.Add("Exiting StateChange EventHandler")
   lbxEventLog.Items.Add("-----------------------------")
End Sub
```

As you can see, the two parameters are a `System.Object` called `sender` and an object of type `StateChangeEventArgs`. The `StateChange` event provides the delegate with these objects, and the delegate gives the event handler these objects so the event handler can handle the event appropriately. That's why `StateIsChanged` has the same parameters as the `StateChangeEventHandler` delegate described previously. You also capture the `sender` object's identity with `sender.ToString()`.

This makes it clear when the execution enters and leaves the event handler. You can also see that the `sender` object is the connection. When the connection is opened, its current state is `Open` and its original state is `Closed`. When the connection is closed, the current state is `Closed` and the original state is `Open`.

This example runs pretty well, and you can see what's happening, but in a real-life application why would users care to be notified if a connection is open or closed? All they need is to see the data. One way to use the `StateChange` event is to keep track of how many times connections are established and keep a running total. Based on this, you can charge users a fee per connection. (Of course, this is a rudimentary way of charging a fee, and you'll have to figure in other factors.) Another way to use this event would be to keep track of how much time a user has had a connection open and charge based on this.

Using the InfoMessage Event

The `InfoMessage` event is raised by the connection when the database gives out information messages. Information messages aren't error messages from the database. They're warning and informational messages issued by the database. In the case of SQL Server, any message with a severity of 10 or less is considered informational and would be captured with the `InfoMessage` event.

The `InfoMessage` event handler receives an `InfoMessageEventArgs` object that contains a collection of the messages from the data source in its `Errors` collection property. The `Error` objects in this collection are of type `SqlError` and can be queried for information such as the number, the source, the message, and the exact line number in the stored procedure where this message originated from, among others. Let's run a query and a Transact-SQL `PRINT` statement. You'll capture this event and query the information in the `Errors` collection.

Try It Out: Writing the Connection.InfoMessage Event

To see the Connection.InfoMessage event in action, follow these steps:

1. In Design view, double-click the Connection InfoMessage Event button (btn_InfoMessage). Cut and paste the code for the btnStateChange_Click handler to the new btnInfoMessage_Click event handler, and add the new code, shown in bold:

```
Private Sub btnInfoMessage_Click(ByVal sender As System.Object, _
   ByVal e As System.EventArgs)
   Handles btnInfoMessage.Click
   ' Sql Query
   Dim sql As String = "SELECT TOP 1 " & _
      "CustomerId, CompanyName FROM Customers"

   ' Create command
   Dim thisCommand As New SqlCommand(sql, thisConnection)

   Try
      ' Clear event log
      lbxEventLog.Items.Clear()

      ' Open connection and fire statechange event
      thisConnection.Open()

      ' Create data reader
      Dim thisReader As SqlDataReader = thisCommand.ExecuteReader()

      ' Display rows in event log
      While thisReader.Read()
         lbxEventLog.Items.Add(thisReader.GetString(0) _
            + "-" + thisReader.GetString(1))
      End While

      ' Close data reader
      thisReader.Close()

      ' execute a PRINT statement
      thisCommand.CommandText = "PRINT 'GET first customer name and id'"
      thisCommand.ExecuteNonQuery()

   Catch ex As SqlException
      MessageBox.Show(ex.Message)

   Finally
      ' Close connection and fire StateChange event
      thisConnection.Close()
   End Try
End Sub
```

2. Add the following method:

```
Private Sub PrintInfoMessage(ByVal sender As Object, _
   ByVal e As System.Data.SqlClient.SqlInfoMessageEventArgs) _
   Handles thisConnection.InfoMessage
   For Each err As SqlError In e.Errors
      lbxEventLog.Items.Add("----------------------------")
      lbxEventLog.Items.Add("Entering InfoMessage Event Handler")
      lbxEventLog.Items.Add("Source- " + err.Source.ToString())
      lbxEventLog.Items.Add("State- " + err.State.ToString())
      lbxEventLog.Items.Add("Number- " + err.Number.ToString())
      lbxEventLog.Items.Add("Procedure- " + err.Procedure)
      lbxEventLog.Items.Add("Server- " + err.Server)
      lbxEventLog.Items.Add("Message- " + err.Message)
      lbxEventLog.Items.Add("Exiting InfoMessage Event Handler")
      lbxEventLog.Items.Add("----------------------------")
   Next
End Sub
```

3. Build and run the solution with Ctrl+F5. Click the Connection InfoMessage Event button. You'll see the results in Figure 20-3, which has been modified a bit to include all the results.

Figure 20-3. *Displaying InfoMessage event information*

How It Works

When the button is clicked, the same SQL SELECT statement is run as before, but then you also execute a PRINT statement against the database. You use the ExecuteNonQuery() method of the command object since the PRINT statement doesn't return any rows.

```
' execute a PRINT statement
thisCommand.CommandText = "PRINT 'GET first customer name and id'"
thisCommand.ExecuteNonQuery()
```

The EventHandler method PrintInfoMessage is written with the same signature as the delegate SqlInfoMessageEventHandler. The two arguments are the sender object and the SqlInfoMessageEventArgs object, which contains information about the event. You then loop through the Errors collection of the object and list several pieces of information about the message itself.

```
Private Sub PrintInfoMessage(ByVal sender As Object, _
   ByVal e As System.Data.SqlClient.SqlInfoMessageEventArgs) _
   Handles thisConnection.InfoMessage
   For Each err As SqlError In e.Errors
      lbxEventLog.Items.Add("----------------------------")
      lbxEventLog.Items.Add("Entering InfoMessage Event Handler")
      lbxEventLog.Items.Add("Source- " + err.Source.ToString())
      lbxEventLog.Items.Add("State- " + err.State.ToString())
      lbxEventLog.Items.Add("Number- " + err.Number.ToString())
      lbxEventLog.Items.Add("Procedure- " + err.Procedure)
      lbxEventLog.Items.Add("Server- " + err.Server)
      lbxEventLog.Items.Add("Message- " + err.Message)
      lbxEventLog.Items.Add("Exiting InfoMessage Event Handler")
      lbxEventLog.Items.Add("----------------------------")
   Next
End Sub
```

Working with Row Update Events

So far you've seen the connection events. ADO.NET supports a wide variety of other events for the purpose of aiding in data validation. For example, a data adapter serves as a bridge between a dataset and a database. When the data adapter is ready to update the changes in the dataset, it raises predefined events. You can code handlers for these events to find more information about the status of the update. Table 20-1 lists some of the common events raised when data is manipulated in ADO.NET objects. The table presents the object that raises the event, the event name, the name of the delegate, and the EventArgs object received by the event handler. The object received by the event handler itself has several properties you can use to take appropriate action.

Table 20-1. *Common ADO.NET Events*

Object	Event	Delegate	Remarks
SqlDataAdapter	RowUpdating	SqlRowUpdatingEventHandler	Raised before the row is updated in the database. The event handler receives a SqlRowUpdatingEventArgs object.
SqlDataAdapter	RowUpdated	SqlRowUpdatedEventHandler	Raised after a row is updated in the database. The event handler receives a SqlRowUpdatedEventArgs object.

Table 20-1. *Common ADO.NET Events (Continued)*

Object	Event	Delegate	Remarks
SqlDataAdapter	FillError	FillErrorEventHandler	Raised when the Fill method is called and an error occurs. The event handler receives a FillErrorEventArgs object.
DataTable	ColumnChanging	DataColumnChangeEventHandler	Raised when the data in a data column is changing. The handler receives a DataColumnChangingEventArgs object.
DataTable	ColumnChanged	DataColumnChangeEventHandler	Raised after value has been changed for the specified data column in a data row. The handler receives a DataColumnChangedEventArgs object.
DataTable	RowChanging	DataRowChangeEventHandler	Raised when a data row is changing. The event handler receives a DataChangeEventArgs object.
DataTable	RowChanged	DataRowChangeEventHandler	Raised after a data row has changed. The event handler receives a DataChangeEventArgs object.
DataTable	RowDeleting	DataRowChangeEventHandler	Raised before a data row is deleted. The event handler receives a DataRowChangeEventArgs object.
DataTable	RowDeleted	DataRowChangeEventHandler	Raised after a data row is deleted. The event handler receives a DataRowchangeEventArgs objects.

Try It Out: Using RowUpdating and RowUpdated Events

Let's experiment with the SQL Server data adapter's RowUpdating and RowUpdated events; in this example, you'll see how they're fired and handled when a value in a dataset changes. You'll also use the AddHandler and RemoveHandler methods to set up the event handlers rather than using the Handles keyword in the handler declaration.

1. In Design view, double-click the SqlDataAdapter RowUpdating Event button (btnRowUpdating). Add the following code to the click event handler:

```
Private Sub btnRowUpdating_Click(ByVal sender As System.Object, _
   ByVal e As System.EventArgs) Handles btnRowUpdating.Click
   ' Sql Query
   Dim sql As String = "SELECT * FROM Customers"

   ' Clear event log
   lbxEventLog.Items.Clear()

   Try
      ' Open connection
      thisConnection.Open()

      ' Create data adapter
      Dim thisAdapter As New SqlDataAdapter(sql, thisConnection)

      ' Create command builder
      Dim cb As New SqlCommandBuilder(thisAdapter)

      ' Create and fill dataset (only first row)
      Dim ds As New DataSet
      thisAdapter.Fill(ds, 0, 1, "Customers")

      ' Add Handlers
      AddHandler thisAdapter.RowUpdating, AddressOf OnRowUpdating
      AddHandler thisAdapter.RowUpdated, AddressOf OnRowUpdated

      ' Modify dataset
      Dim dt As DataTable = ds.Tables("Customers")
      dt.Rows(0)(1) = "The Volcano Corporation"

      ' Update. This fires both events
      thisAdapter.Update(ds, "Customers")

      ' Remove handlers
      RemoveHandler thisAdapter.RowUpdating, AddressOf OnRowUpdating
      RemoveHandler thisAdapter.RowUpdated, AddressOf OnRowUpdated

   Catch ex As SqlException
      MessageBox.Show(ex.Message)
   Finally
      ' Close Connection
      thisConnection.Close()
   End Try
End Sub
```

2. Add the following method to handle the `RowUpdating` event:

```
' Handler for OnRowUpdating
Private Sub OnRowUpdating(ByVal sender As Object, _
   ByVal e As SqlRowUpdatingEventArgs)
   DisplayEventArgs(e)
End Sub
```

3. Add the following method to handle the `RowUpdated` event:

```
' Handler for OnRowUpdated
Private Sub OnRowUpdated(ByVal sender As Object, _
   ByVal e As SqlRowUpdatedEventArgs)
   DisplayEventArgs(e)
End Sub
```

4. Add the following overloaded `DisplayEventArgs` methods:

```
Private Sub DisplayEventArgs(ByVal args As SqlRowUpdatedEventArgs)
   lbxEventLog.Items.Add("OnRowUpdated Event")
   lbxEventLog.Items.Add("Records Affected = " & _
      args.RecordsAffected.ToString())
End Sub

Private Sub DisplayEventArgs(ByVal args As SqlRowUpdatingEventArgs)
   lbxEventLog.Items.Add("OnRowUpdating Event")
   If Not args.Status = UpdateStatus.Continue Then
      lbxEventLog.Items.Add("RowStatus = " & args.Status.ToString())
   End If
End Sub
```

5. Build and run the solution with Ctrl+F5. Click the SqlDataAdapter RowUpdating Event button. You'll see the results in Figure 20-4.

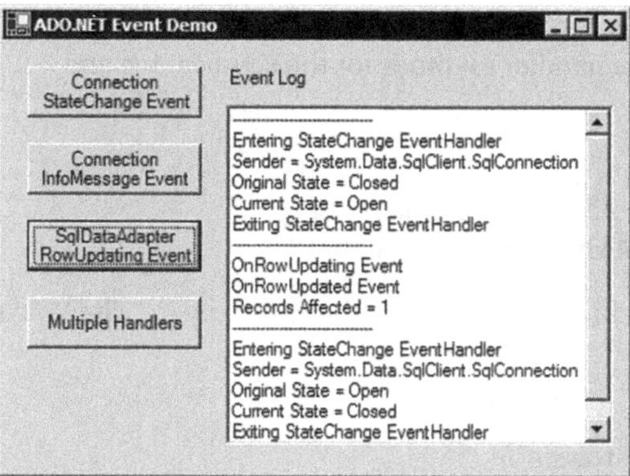

Figure 20-4. *Displaying `RowUpdating` and `RowUpdated` event information*

6. Click the button again. You'll see the results in Figure 20-5.

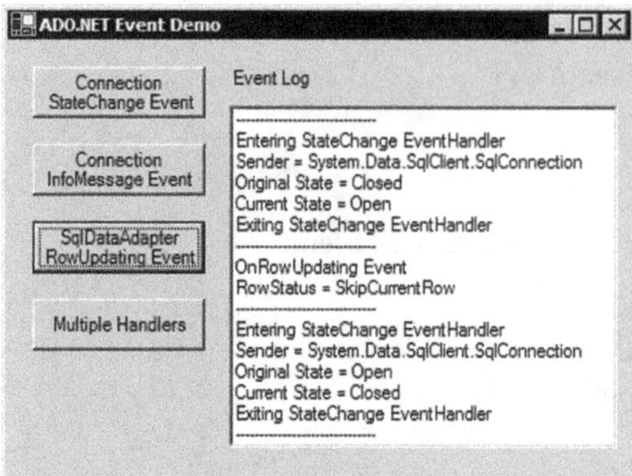

Figure 20-5. *Displaying only `RowUpdating` event information*

How It Works

Note that the first time the button is clicked, the `RowUpdating` and `RowUpdated` events fired. But the second time, the `RowUpdated` event doesn't fire, and the `RowStatus` is `SkipCurrentRow`.

What you've essentially done in this example is retrieve one row from the `Customer` table, update it to get the `RowUpdating` and `RowUpdated` events to fire, and handle the events. You create and initialize a data adapter and a command builder as follows:

```
' Create data adapter
Dim thisAdapter As New SqlDataAdapter(sql, thisConnection)

' Create command builder
Dim cb As New SqlCommandBuilder(thisAdapter)
```

Then you create a dataset and use the `Fill` method to fill it with one row of data.

```
' Create and fill dataset (only first row)
Dim ds As New DataSet
thisAdapter.Fill(ds, 0, 1, "Customers")
```

Then you use `AddHandler` to identify handler methods for the `RowUpdating` and `RowUpdated` events.

```
' Add Handlers
AddHandler thisAdapter.RowUpdating, AddressOf OnRowUpdating
AddHandler thisAdapter.RowUpdated, AddressOf OnRowUpdated
```

You now modify the dataset. You change the name of the company to "The Volcano Corporation."

```
' Modify dataset
Dim dt As DataTable = ds.Tables("Customers")
dt.Rows(0)(1) = "The Volcano Corporation"
```

You now update the database by sending the dataset changes to it. At this moment, the RowUpdating event and the RowUpdated event fire.

```
' Update. This fires both events
thisAdapter.Update(ds, "Customers")
```

Finally, you remove the handlers. It isn't necessary in this example, but we've shown it for demonstration purposes. As mentioned earlier in the chapter, the location in code where handlers are added and removed is important and will affect whether events are handled, even if event handlers are present. These handlers are attached just to this variable rather than any SqlDataAdapter object as the event for the SqlConnection class you wrote in earlier example were. You use RemoveHandler to remove the handlers.

```
' Remove handlers
RemoveHandler thisAdapter.RowUpdating, AddressOf OnRowUpdating
RemoveHandler thisAdapter.RowUpdated, AddressOf OnRowUpdated
```

Both the OnRowUpdating and OnRowUpdated event handlers call a method named DisplayEventArgs. The OnRowUpdating event handler receives the SqlRowUpdatingEventArgs object, and the OnRowUpdated event handler receives the SqlRowUpdatedEventArgs object. As these two events are different, the delegates of these events pass slightly different information to the handler. Note also that neither handler contains the Handles extension to their declarations because they're being linked to events at runtime with AddHandler.

```
' Handler for OnRowUpdating
Private Sub OnRowUpdating(ByVal sender As Object, _
   ByVal e As SqlRowUpdatingEventArgs)
   DisplayEventArgs(e)
End Sub

' Handler for OnRowUpdated
Private Sub OnRowUpdated(ByVal sender As Object, _
   ByVal e As SqlRowUpdatedEventArgs)
   DisplayEventArgs(e)
End Sub
```

The overloaded DisplayEventArgs method adds an item to the list box to indicate that the executing code has entered it. It also uses the argument passed to it and checks Status. Status is an enumeration of type UpdateStatus. If Status isn't UpdateStatus.Continue, the status is written to the list box. When a row is in the process of being updated, if a change has been made to the row, the status of the row will be marked as Continue and the RowUpdated event will fire for the row. If the status isn't UpdateStatus.Continue, then the RowUpdated event won't fire.

```
Private Sub DisplayEventArgs(ByVal args As SqlRowUpdatingEventArgs)
   lbxEventLog.Items.Add("OnRowUpdating Event")
   If Not args.Status = UpdateStatus.Continue Then
      lbxEventLog.Items.Add("RowStatus = " & args.Status.ToString())
   End If
End Sub
```

If the row can be updated, the RowUpdated event will fire, which will be handled by the OnRowUpdated event handler, which in turn will pass the execution to the version of DisplayEventArgs function that takes the SqlRowUpdatedEventArgs object as the parameter. This object carries with it information about how many rows were updated in the RecordsAffected property, which is displayed in the list box.

```
Private Sub DisplayEventArgs(ByVal args As SqlRowUpdatedEventArgs)
   lbxEventLog.Items.Add("OnRowUpdated Event")
   lbxEventLog.Items.Add("Records Affected = " & _
      args.RecordsAffected.ToString())
End Sub
```

The first time the button is clicked, the company name changes to "The Volcano Corporation." This raises both the RowUpdating and the RowUpdated events. The second time the button is clicked, since the company name is already "The Volcano Corporation," only the RowUpdating event is raised, and the row's UpdateStatus is marked as SkipCurrentRow. So the RowUpdated event doesn't fire.

Working with Multiple Handlers

It's also possible to have the same event call multiple handlers. You can do this in two ways. You can individually bind the event to two different event handlers; alternatively, you can use a *multicast delegate* where you specify a list of event handlers, and, when the event is fired, all the listed handlers will be invoked successively. You'll use the first alternative in the following example.

Try It Out: Using Multiple Handlers for the Same Event

Follow these steps:

1. Double-click the Multiple Handlers button (btnMultiple). Cut and paste the code for the btnStateChange_Click handler to the new btnMultiple_Click event handler, and add the following new code, shown in bold:

```
Private Sub btnMultiple_Click(ByVal sender As System.Object, _
   ByVal e As System.EventArgs) Handles btnMultiple.Click
   ' Sql Query
   Dim sql As String = "SELECT TOP 1 " & _
      "CustomerId, CompanyName FROM Customers"

   ' Create command
   Dim thisCommand As New SqlCommand(sql, thisConnection)

   ' Clear event log
   lbxEventLog.Items.Clear()
```

```
      ' Add second handler to StateChange event
      AddHandler thisConnection.StateChange, AddressOf StateIsChanged2

      Try
         ' Open connection and fire two statechange event handlers
         thisConnection.Open()

         ' Create data reader
         Dim thisReader As SqlDataReader = thisCommand.ExecuteReader()

         ' Display rows in event log
         While thisReader.Read()
            lbxEventLog.Items.Add(thisReader.GetString(0) _
               + "-" + thisReader.GetString(1))
         End While
      Catch ex As SqlException
         MessageBox.Show(ex.Message)
      Finally
         ' Remove second handler from StateChange event
         RemoveHandler thisConnection.StateChange, AddressOf StateIsChanged2

      ' Close connection and fire one StateChange event
      thisConnection.Close()
   End Try
End Sub
```

2. Add a second event handler for the StateChange event as follows. This is basically the same as the original handler you wrote for this except for the changes in bold.

```
Private Sub StateIsChanged2(ByVal sender As Object, _
   ByVal e As System.Data.StateChangeEventArgs)
   ' Event handler for the StateChange Event
   lbxEventLog.Items.Add("------------------------------")
   lbxEventLog.Items.Add("Entering Second StateChange EventHandler")
   lbxEventLog.Items.Add("Sender = " + sender.ToString())
   lbxEventLog.Items.Add("Original State = " + e.OriginalState.ToString())
   lbxEventLog.Items.Add("Current State = " + e.CurrentState.ToString())
   lbxEventLog.Items.Add("Exiting Second StateChange EventHandler")
   lbxEventLog.Items.Add("------------------------------")
End Sub
```

3. Build and run the solution with Ctrl+F5. Click the Multiple Handlers button. You'll see the results in Figure 20-6.

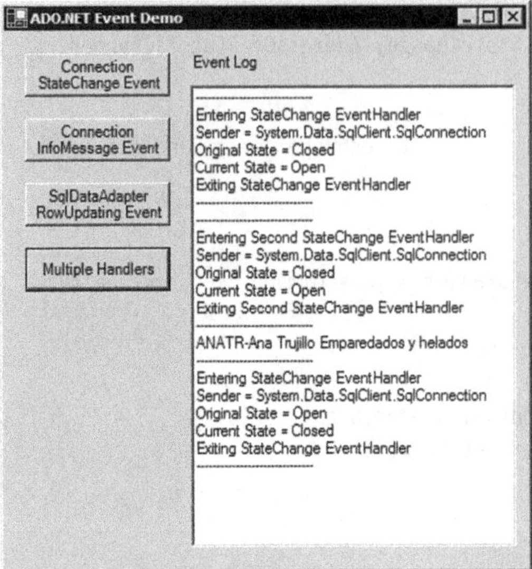

Figure 20-6. *State change events*

Observe that the event log in Figure 20-6 shows that the first `StateChange` event handler was invoked and then the second `StateChange` event handler was invoked when the connection was opened but only the first handler was called when it was closed. You can code these two handlers to perform different actions, of course.

How It Works

In this example, you bound two methods to the same event using the two different methods you learned about at the beginning of the chapter. `StateIsChanged` uses the `Handles` keyword to attach itself to the `SqlConnection` object being used at design time. Meanwhile, `StateIsChanged2` is attached at runtime by calling `AddHandler`. This nicely demonstrates how the two methods can be used together if required.

```
' Add second handler to StateChange event
AddHandler thisConnection.StateChange, AddressOf StateIsChanged2
```

You then open the connection to raise the event and fire the two handlers.

```
Try
   ' Open connection and fire two statechange event handlers
   thisConnection.Open()
```

To prove that `AddHandler` and `RemoveHandler` really work at runtime rather than design time, you remove `StateIsChanged2` as a handler before closing the connection. Sure enough, only the original handler is called.

```
' Remove second handler from StateChange event
RemoveHandler thisConnection.StateChange, AddressOf StateIsChanged2
```

Summary

This chapter discussed the basics of handling ADO.NET events. You saw what events are and how to bind them to event handlers. Specifically, you learned and tried the following features:

- You learned you can bind a handler to an event at design time by declaring a class variable as `WithEvents` and that the handler `Handles` one of that variable's events.
- You learned you can bind and unbind a handler to an event at runtime using the `AddHandler` and `RemoveHandler` methods.
- You learned that a connection's `StateChange` event fires when the state changes from `Open` to `Closed` or from `Closed` to `Open`. You wrote an event handler for this event using the `StateChangeEventHandler` delegate. In the process, you learned that the signature of the event handler must be the same as the signature of the delegate.
- You learned that a connection's `InfoMessage` event fires when the database returns informational messages that aren't errors. You also learned that you can bind any number of events to their respective event handlers from within the same function.
- You then saw how to use a data adapter's `RowUpdating` and `RowUpdated` events to determine the status of a row before and after it's updated.
- You also saw how to bind the same event to more than one event handler. This resulted in each event handler being called and executed.

Several more ADO.NET events exist that you can handle in your applications. Look in Table 20-1 for their names and in the .NET SDK for more information, and then try them.

CHAPTER 21

Working with Text and Binary Data

Some kinds of data have special formats, are very large, or vary greatly in size. Take, for example, a high-resolution image or a Portable Document Format (PDF) file of a 20-page document. Sometimes it's appropriate to store these and other large files in a database table. So then, in this chapter, you'll learn techniques for working with text and binary data, including the following:

- What data types to use
- How to load, retrieve, and display image data
- How to work with headers in binary data
- How to work with data too large to fit easily into memory
- How to retrieve and store text data

This may all sound a bit familiar. We spent the first half of the book teaching you exactly how to work with values stored in a database. How is this any different? Well, images are binary objects, which means that you can't just open them in a text editor or assign them to the `Text` property of some control; if you did, you'd get lots of gobbledygook over your screen. You have to treat them as special cases. Similarly, if you have a piece of text that's too large to store in memory, you can't simply bind it to an object property, or else your machine will run out of memory and either slow down dramatically or just hang. Like images, you have to treat this kind of large data as a special case and use a specific technique to use it. We'll show you how to do that in this chapter. First, though, you need to look at the SQL data types that let you store such large/binary pieces of data in a database in the first place.

Understanding SQL Server Text and Binary Data Types

SQL Server provides the types `CHAR`, `NCHAR`, `VARCHAR`, `NVARCHAR`, `BINARY`, and `VARBINARY` for working with text and binary data. You can use these with text (character) data up to a maximum of 8,000 bytes (4,000 bytes for Unicode data, `NCHAR`, and `NVARCHAR`, which use 2 bytes per character).

For larger data, SQL Server provides the TEXT, NTEXT, and IMAGE data types. TEXT and NTEXT are for large character data (NTEXT is for Unicode characters), and IMAGE is for storing anything else. The SQL Server designers must have decided IMAGE was more intuitive than BLOB, as the most common use for large binary data is pictures. However, IMAGE is usable for any type of binary data—video, sound, documents, or anything else you may store in a file.

■ **Note** DB2, MySQL, Oracle, and the SQL standard call such data types *large objects* (LOBs); specifically, they're binary large objects (BLOBs) and character large objects (CLOBs).

Within your VB .NET program, binary data types map to an array of bytes (byte()), and character data types map to string or character arrays (char()). Table 21-1 summarizes the characteristics of these data types.

Table 21-1. *Large Data Type Mappings*

SQL Server Data Type	VB .NET Data Type	Maximum Size
CHAR, VARCHAR	string, char()	8,000 characters
NCHAR, NVARCHAR	string, char()	4,000 2-byte (Unicode) characters
BINARY, VARBINARY	byte()	8,000 bytes
TEXT	string, char()	2,147,483,647 characters
NTEXT	string, char()	1,073,741,823 2-byte (Unicode) characters
IMAGE	byte()	2,147,483,647 bytes

An alternative to using these data types is to not store the data itself in the database but instead define a column containing a path that points to where the data is actually stored. This can be more efficient for accessing large amounts of data, and it can save resources on the database server by transferring the demand to a file server. It does require more complicated coordination and has the potential for database and data files to get out of sync. We won't use this technique in this chapter.

IMAGE is almost always going to be the best choice for binary data, because it's rare that you can guarantee that the size of a binary data item is always going to be less than 8,000 bytes. Even small pictures or sound files often exceed this size.

IMAGE is stored as a "pointer" within the table that points to another location within the SQL Server database that stores the data, so there's some slight overhead for IMAGE data compared to BINARY and VARBINARY, but for binary data this is typically not a significant performance consideration.

You implement NTEXT and TEXT in a similar way to IMAGE—as pointers to the data. In this case, however, the overhead is worth thinking about in choosing between these types and NVARCHAR or VARCHAR. It depends on your application needs. Many applications have a "notes" or other similar column for text that can be relatively long, but on average you can accommodate 2,000 characters a page for several pages of text in 8,000 characters.

The choice between NTEXT and TEXT depends on whether you want text to be stored as Unicode 2-byte characters or 1-byte ASCII/ANSI characters. The native character type in VB .NET and the .NET Framework is Unicode, so the text will be converted to 2-byte characters when received from a database. If your application will be used internationally, with different languages and character sets, then it makes sense to use Unicode data types. If this isn't the case, then it may be wasteful to double the storage requirement. But storage continually gets cheaper, so flexibility may outweigh this consideration; however, with multimegabyte data, it's worth careful thought.

CHAR, NCHAR, and BINARY are fixed-length data types directly stored in database tables; they always take up the size specified when creating the table, even if the actual size of the data value is shorter. You use this when the data is mostly the same average length close to the specified size. For example, if your table stored icons where the binary size was small and every icon was the same size, then BINARY may well be the best data type to use. Most character data larger than a few hundred characters varies significantly in length, so fixed-length CHAR or NCHAR data types become less appropriate as the data length increases.

NVARCHAR, VARCHAR, and VARBINARY accommodate varying-length data so they don't waste space in the database. Very small bitmaps or sound files that will always be less than 8,000 bytes can be stored as VARBINARY. As mentioned previously, you can store text data a few paragraphs or pages in length and always less than 8,000 bytes in length as VARCHAR or NVARCHAR.

Storing Images in a Database

Let's start by creating a database table for storing images and then loading some images into it. We'll use some images from the ASP.NET QuickStart, located in C:\Program Files\Microsoft Visual Studio .NET 2003\SDK\v1.1\QuickStart\aspplus\images. We'll use small images that can fit in any of the data types we've discussed.

Try It Out: Loading Image Binary Data from Files

In this example, you'll write a program that creates a database table and then stores milk carton images in it.

1. Create a new solution named Chapter21_Examples, and add a VB .NET console application named LoadImages.

2. Rename Module1.vb to LoadImages.vb, and replace its code with the following code. You have a lot of code to add, so we'll show how to do it in steps. First the basics: you'll add the Main subroutine and global declarations in this step.

```
Imports System.IO
Imports System.Data.SqlClient

Namespace LoadImages
   Module LoadImages
```

```
        ' Module-wide variable
        Dim imageFileLocation As String = "C:\Program Files\" & _
           "Microsoft Visual Studio .NET 2003\SDK\v1.1\QuickStart\" & _
           "aspplus\images"
        Dim imageFilePrefix As String = "milk"
        Dim numberOfImageFiles As Integer = 8
        Dim imageFileType As String = ".gif"
        Dim maxImageSize As Integer = 10000
        Dim thisConnection As SqlConnection
        Dim thisCommand As SqlCommand

        Sub Main()
           Try
              ' Create and open connection
              OpenConnection()

              ' Create Command
              CreateCommand()

              ' Create Image Table
              CreateImageTable()

              ' Prepare To Insert Images
              PrepareInsertImages()

              ' Insert Images
              For i As Integer = 1 To numberOfImageFiles
                 ExecuteInsertImages(i)
              Next

           Catch ex As Exception
              Console.WriteLine(ex.ToString())

           Finally
              ' Close Connection
              CloseConnection()
           End Try
        End Sub
     End Module
  End Namespace
```

3. Now you'll add some of the helper functions (within the `Module` declaration). Add the following `Connection` and `Command` helper functions:

```
Sub OpenConnection()
   ' Create Connection object
   thisConnection = New SqlConnection _
      ("server=(local)\netsdk;" & _
       "integrated security=sspi;" & _
       "database=tempdb")

   ' Open Connection
   thisConnection.Open()
End Sub

Sub CloseConnection()
   ' Close connection
   thisConnection.Close()
   Console.WriteLine("Connection Closed")
End Sub

Sub CreateCommand()
   thisCommand = New SqlCommand
   thisCommand.Connection = thisConnection
End Sub

Sub ExecuteCommand(ByVal cmdText As String)
   thisCommand.CommandText = cmdText
   Console.WriteLine("Executing : " & thisCommand.CommandText)
   Dim result As Integer = thisCommand.ExecuteNonQuery()
   Console.WriteLine("ExecuteNonQuery returns {0}", result.ToString())
End Sub
```

4. Now add the methods that actually work with the image files.

```
Sub CreateImageTable()
   ' Sql to create new table to hold images
   Dim sql As String = "CREATE TABLE ImageTable" & - "
      (ImageFile nvarchar(20), ImageData image)"

   ' Run command
   ExecuteCommand(sql)
End Sub
```

```
Sub PrepareInsertImages()
   thisCommand.CommandText = "INSERT INTO ImageTable " & _
      "VALUES (@ImageFile, @ImageData)"
   thisCommand.Parameters.Add("@ImageFile", SqlDbType.NVarChar)
   thisCommand.Parameters.Add("@ImageData", SqlDbType.Image)
End Sub

Sub ExecuteInsertImage(ByVal imageFileNumber As Integer)
   ' Get Filename and Image data
   Dim imageFileName As String = imageFilePrefix & _
      imageFileNumber.ToString() & imageFileType
   Dim imageData() As Byte = LoadImageFile(imageFileName, _
      imageFileLocation, maxImageSize)

   ' Set parameters
   thisCommand.Parameters("@ImageFile").Value = imageFileName
   thisCommand.Parameters("@ImageData").Value = imageData

   ' Run insert command
   ExecuteCommand(thisCommand.CommandText)
End Sub

Function LoadImageFile(ByVal fileName As String, _
   ByVal fileLocation As String, ByVal maxImageSize As Integer) _
   As Byte()
   ' Write state to console window
   Dim fullpath As String = fileLocation & fileName
   Console.WriteLine("Loading file: {0}", fullpath)

   ' Get binary reader to reader image data into variable
   Dim fs As New FileStream(fullpath, FileMode.Open)
   Dim br As New BinaryReader(fs)
   Dim imagebytes() As Byte = br.ReadBytes(maxImageSize)

   ' Write result to console window
   Console.WriteLine("Image has length {0} bytes", _
      imagebytes.GetLength(0))

   Return imagebytes
End Function
```

5. Set the startup object for the project to `Sub Main`, and then run the program with Ctrl+F5. You should see the output in Figure 21-1. It displays the operations performed, their statuses, and the size of each of the eight images.

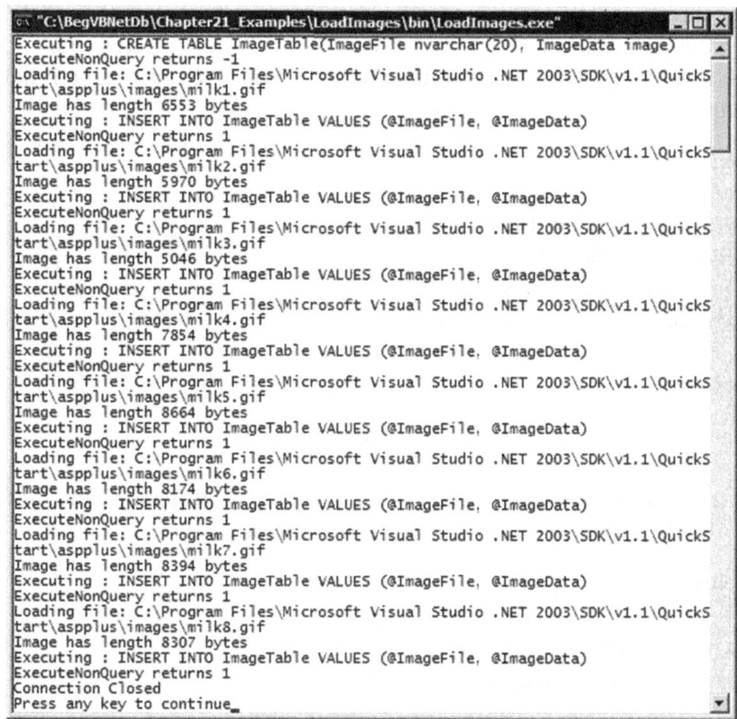

Figure 21-1. *Loading image data*

How It Works

The `Main` method does three major things: it creates a table to hold images, it prepares a command to insert images, and it loops through the image files and inserts them.

```
Sub Main()
...
   ' Create Image Table
   CreateImageTable()

   ' Prepare To Insert Images
   PrepareInsertImages()

   ' Insert Images
   For i As Integer = 1 To numberOfImageFiles
      ExecuteInsertImages(i)
   Next
...
End Sub
```

Note that you connect to tempdb, the temporary database that's created when SQL Server starts. The tables in this database are temporary; that is, they're always deleted when SQL Server stops. This is ideal for these examples, but remember to not use tempdb for any data that needs to be persistent.

```
Sub OpenConnection()
   ' Create Connection object
   thisConnection = New SqlConnection _
      ("server=(local)\netsdk;" & _
       "integrated security=sspi;" & _
       "database=tempdb")

   ' Open Connection
   thisConnection.Open()
End Sub
```

Next, you create the table itself, a simple one containing the image filename and the image. (Note that you use the IMAGE data type for the ImageData column.)

```
Sub CreateImageTable()
   ' Sql to create new table to hold images
   Dim sql As String = "CREATE TABLE ImageTable" & - "
      (ImageFile nvarchar(20), ImageData image)"

   ' Run command
   ExecuteCommand(sql)
End Sub
```

You then configure the command to perform an INSERT statement and map two parameters to the SqlDbType enumeration members that provide an exact match between the VB .NET variables and the database data types.

```
Sub PrepareInsertImages()
   thisCommand.CommandText = "INSERT INTO ImageTable " & _
      "VALUES (@ImageFile, @ImageData)"
   thisCommand.Parameters.Add("@ImageFile", SqlDbType.NVarChar)
   thisCommand.Parameters.Add("@ImageData", SqlDbType.Image)
End Sub
```

The ExecuteInsertImage method accepts an integer to use as a suffix for the image filename, calls LoadImageFile to get a byte array containing the image, assigns the filename and image to their corresponding command parameters, and then executes the command to insert the image.

```
Sub ExecuteInsertImage(ByVal imageFileNumber As Integer)
   ' Get Filename and Image data
   Dim imageFileName As String = imageFilePrefix & _
      imageFileNumber.ToString() & imageFileType
   Dim imageData() As Byte = LoadImageFile(imageFileName, _
      imageFileLocation, maxImageSize)

   ' Set parameters
   thisCommand.Parameters("@ImageFile").Value = imageFileName
   thisCommand.Parameters("@ImageData").Value = imageData

   ' Run insert command
   ExecuteCommand(thisCommand.CommandText)
End Sub
```

The LoadImageFile method reads the image file, displays the number of bytes in the file, and returns the image as a byte array. VB .NET file I/O is beyond the scope of this book, but it's straightforward here, simply reading a file stream in binary mode to fill a byte array.

```
Function LoadImageFile(ByVal fileName As String, _
   ByVal fileLocation As String, ByVal maxImageSize As Integer) _
   As Byte()
   ' Write state to console window
   Dim fullpath As String = fileLocation & fileName
   Console.WriteLine("Loading file: {0}", fullpath)

   ' Get binary reader to reader image data into variable
   Dim fs As New FileStream(fullpath, FileMode.Open)
   Dim br As New BinaryReader(fs)
   Dim imagebytes() As Byte = br.ReadBytes(maxImageSize)

   ' Write result to console window
   Console.WriteLine("Image has length {0} bytes", _
      imagebytes.GetLength(0))

   Return imagebytes
End Function
```

Rerunning the Program

Since the program always creates the imagetable table, you must cycle (stop and restart) SQL Server before rerunning it to re-create an empty tempdb database. (See Chapter 1 if you've forgotten how to stop and start MSDE.)

Using a Different SQL Data Type

To see what happens when you specify a data type with small length restrictions, modify `createImageTable` to use `varbinary(8000)` instead of `image`.

```
Sub CreateImageTable()
   ' Sql to create new table to hold images
   Dim sql As String = "CREATE TABLE ImageTable" & - "
      (ImageFile nvarchar(20), ImageData varbinary(8000))"

   ' Run command
   ExecuteCommand(sql)
End Sub
```

This works for the first couple images, and then an exception appears, as shown in Figure 21-2.

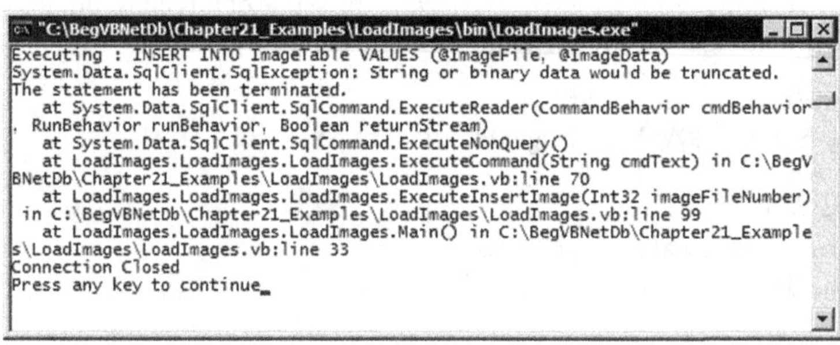

Figure 21-2. *Exceeding column size*

You can see that the size restrictions of `BINARY`/`VARBINARY` aren't adequate, even when working with small images such as these.

Retrieving Images from a Database

Now that you've stored some images, you'll see how to retrieve and display them. Of course, in order to display them, you'll have to switch to a Windows Forms application.

Try It Out: Displaying Stored Images

To display stored images, follow these steps:

1. Add a VB .NET Windows application named `DisplayImages` to your solution. Rename `Form1.vb` to `DisplayImages.vb` and the form's `Text` property to `Display Images`.

2. Add a TextBox (`txtFileName`), Button (`btnNext`), and PictureBox (`pbxImage`) controls to the form as in Figure 21-3.

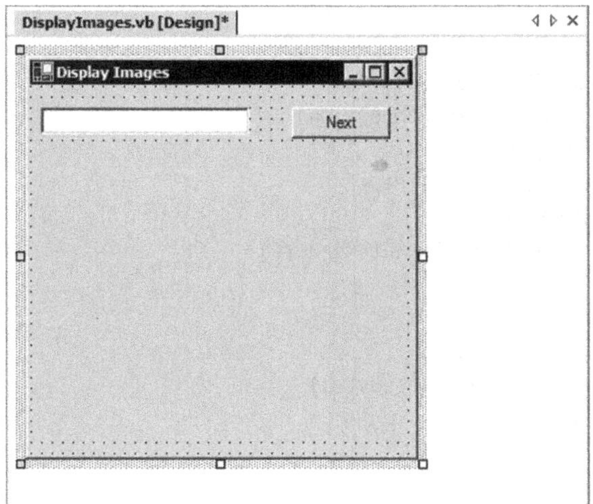

Figure 21-3. *DisplayImages layout*

3. Add a new class named `Images` to the project. Replace the code in `Images.vb` with the code in Listing 21-1.

Listing 21-1. *Images.vb*

```
Imports System
Imports System.Data
Imports System.Data.SqlClient
Imports System.Drawing
Imports System.IO

Namespace DisplayImages
   Public Class Images

      ' Global declarations
      Dim imageFilename As String = ""
      Dim imageBytes() As Byte
      Dim imageConnection As SqlConnection
      Dim imageCommand As SqlCommand
      Dim imageReader As SqlDataReader

      Sub New()
         ' Create connection
         imageConnection = New SqlConnection _
            ("server=(local)\netsdk;" & _
             "integrated security=sspi;" & _
             "database=tempdb")
```

```
            ' Create command
            imageCommand = New SqlCommand _
               ("SELECT ImageFile, ImageData " & _
                "FROM ImageTable", imageConnection)

            ' open connection and create reader
            imageConnection.Open()
            imageReader = imageCommand.ExecuteReader()
         End Sub

         Function GetImage() As Bitmap
            Dim ms As New MemoryStream(imageBytes)
            Dim bmap As New Bitmap(ms)
            Return bmap
         End Function

         Function GetFileName() As String
            Return imageFilename
         End Function

         Function GetRow() As Boolean
            If imageReader.Read() Then
               imageFilename = imageReader.GetValue(0).ToString()
               imageBytes = CType(imageReader.GetValue(1), Byte())
               Return True
            Else
               Return False
            End If
         End Function

         Sub EndImages()
            ' Close reader and connection
            imageReader.Close()
            imageConnection.Close()
         End Sub
      End Class
   End Namespace
```

4. Add an instance variable img of type Images to DisplayImages.vb.

```
Namespace DisplayImages
   Public Class Form1
      Inherits System.Windows.Forms.Form

      Private img As Images
```

5. Expand the Windows Form Designer–generated code region, and add the following bold code to the DisplayImages constructor after the call to InitializeComponent:

```
Public Sub New()
   MyBase.New()

   'This call is required by the Windows Form Designer.
   InitializeComponent()

   'Add any initialization after the InitializeComponent() call
   img = New Images

   If img.GetRow() Then
      Me.txtFileName.Text = img.GetFileName()
      Me.pbxImage.Image = CType(img.GetImage(), Image)
   Else
      Me.txtFileName.Text = "DONE"
      Me.pbxImage.Image = Nothing
   End If
End Sub
```

6. Just to be complete, you should also clean up after yourself in the `Dispose` method by adding the following bold line:

```
Protected Overloads Overrides Sub Dispose(ByVal disposing As Boolean)
   img.EndImages()
   If disposing Then
      If Not (components Is Nothing) Then
         components.Dispose()
      End If
   End If
   MyBase.Dispose(disposing)
End Sub
```

7. Double-click the Next button, and insert the following bold code into the event handler:

```
Private Sub btnNext_Click(ByVal sender As System.Object, _
   ByVal e As System.EventArgs) Handles btnNext.Click
   If img.GetRow() Then
      Me.txtFileName.Text = img.GetFileName()
      Me.pbxImage.Image = CType(img.GetImage(), Image)
   Else
      Me.txtFileName.Text = "DONE"
      Me.pbxImage.Image = Nothing
   End If
End Sub
```

8. Make the project the startup project, and run the program with Ctrl+F5. You should see the output in Figure 21-4. Click Next to see all the milk bottle images; when the end is reached, the word *DONE* will appear in the text box. Since you didn't add an Exit button, just close the window to exit.

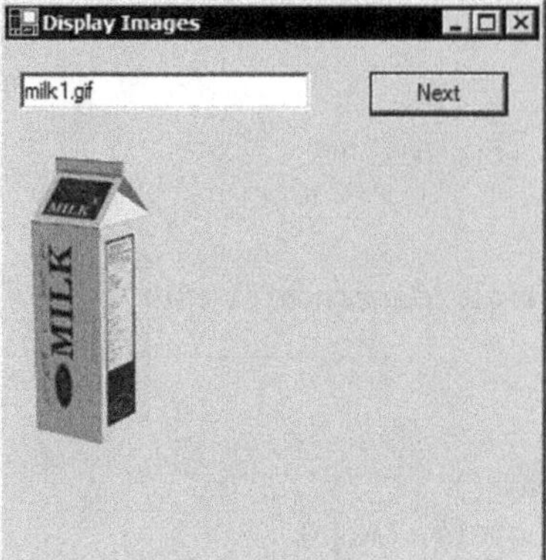

Figure 21-4. *Displaying image data*

How It Works

You declare a type, Images, to access the database and provide methods for the form components to easily get and display images. In its constructor, you connect to the database and create a data reader to handle the result set of a query that retrieves all the images you stored earlier.

```
Sub New()
   ' Create connection
   imageConnection = New SqlConnection _
      ("server=(local)\netsdk;" & _
       "integrated security=sspi;" & _
       "database=tempdb")

   ' Create command
   imageCommand = New SqlCommand _
      ("SELECT ImageFile, ImageData " & _
       "FROM ImageTable", imageConnection)

   ' open connection and create reader
   imageConnection.Open()
   imageReader = imageCommand.ExecuteReader()
End Sub
```

When the form is initialized, the new code creates an instance of Images, looks for an image with GetRow, and, if one is found, assigns the filename and image to the text box and picture box with the GetFilename and GetImage methods, respectively.

```
img = New Images

If img.GetRow() Then
   Me.txtFileName.Text = img.GetFileName()
   Me.pbxImage.Image = CType(img.GetImage(), Image)
```

You use the same if statement in the Next button's click event handler to look for the next image. If none is found, you display the word *DONE* in the text box.

```
Else
   Me.txtFileName.Text = "DONE"
   Me.pbxImage.Image = Nothing
End If
```

You call the EndImages method when the form terminates to close the connection. (Had you used a dataset instead of a data reader, you could have closed the connection in the Images instance immediately after the images were retrieved, which would be a good exercise for you to attempt.)

```
Protected Overloads Overrides Sub Dispose(ByVal disposing As Boolean)
   img.EndImages()
   If disposing Then
      If Not (components Is Nothing) Then
         components.Dispose()
      End If
   End If
   MyBase.Dispose(disposing)
End Sub
```

The image is returned from the database as an array of bytes. The PictureBox control Image property can be a Bitmap, Icon, or Metafile (all derived classes of Image). Bitmap supports a variety of formats including BMP, GIF, and JPG. The getImage method, shown here, returns a Bitmap object:

```
Function GetImage() As Bitmap
   Dim ms As New MemoryStream(imageBytes)
   Dim bmap As New Bitmap(ms)
   Return bmap
End Function
```

Bitmap's constructor doesn't accept a byte array, but it will accept a MemoryStream (which is effectively an in-memory representation of a file), and MemoryStream has a constructor that accepts a byte array. So, you create a memory stream from the byte array and then create a bitmap from the memory stream.

Does this result in a lot of extra memory usage? It does a bit, though you can minimize this by calling the Dispose method on each object as soon as that stage of the conversion is complete. You'll now look at a technique that helps minimize memory usage when reading large text objects.

Working with Text Data

Handling text is similar to handling images except for the data type used for the database column.

Try It Out: Loading Text Data from a File

Follow these steps:

1. Add a VB .NET console application named `LoadText` to the solution.
2. Rename `Module1.vb` to `LoadText.vb`. Like `LoadImages`, we'll split the code up into three segments. The code in this step contains the declarations and `Main` statement.

```
Imports System.Data.SqlClient
Imports System.IO

Namespace LoadText
   Module LoadText

      ' Global Declarations
      Dim FileName As String = _
         "C:\BegVBNetDb\Chapter21_Examples\LoadImages\LoadImages.vb"
      Dim thisConnection As SqlConnection
      Dim thisCommand As SqlCommand

      Sub Main()
         Try
            ' Get Text File
            GetTextFile(FileName)

            ' Open Connection
            OpenConnection()

            ' Build Command
            CreateCommand()

            ' Create Text Table
            CreateTextTable()

            ' Prepare insert command
            PrepareInsertTextFile()

            ' Load Text file
            ExecuteInsertTextFile(FileName)

            ' Display status
            Console.WriteLine("Loaded {0} into table", FileName)
```

```
        Catch ex As Exception
           Console.WriteLine(ex.ToString())

        Finally
           ' Close connection
           CloseConnection()
        End Try
     End Sub
  End Module
End Namespace
```

3. Now you'll add some of the helper functions (within the `Module` declaration). You'll now add the `Connection` and `Command` helper functions. These are actually the same as those for the first example in this chapter.

```
Sub OpenConnection()
   ' Create Connection object
   thisConnection = New SqlConnection _
      ("server=(local)\netsdk;" & _
       "integrated security=sspi;" & _
       "database=tempdb")

   ' Open Connection
   thisConnection.Open()
End Sub

Sub CloseConnection()
   ' Close connection
   thisConnection.Close()
   Console.WriteLine("Connection Closed")
End Sub

Sub CreateCommand()
   thisCommand = New SqlCommand
   thisCommand.Connection = thisConnection
End Sub

Sub ExecuteCommand(ByVal cmdText As String)
   thisCommand.CommandText = cmdText
   Console.WriteLine("Executing : " & thisCommand.CommandText)
   Dim result As Integer = thisCommand.ExecuteNonQuery()
   Console.WriteLine("ExecuteNonQuery returns {0}", result.ToString())
End Sub
```

4. Now you'll add the methods that actually work with the text file.

```
Sub CreateTextTable()
   ExecuteCommand("IF EXISTS( " & _
      "SELECT table_name FROM information_schema.tables " & _
      "WHERE table_name = 'TextTable') " & _
      "DROP TABLE TextTable")

   ExecuteCommand("CREATE TABLE TextTable " & _
      "(TextFile varchar(255), TextData text)")
End Sub

Sub PrepareInsertTextFile()
   thisCommand.CommandText = "INSERT INTO TextTable " & _
      "VALUES (@TextFile, @TextData)"
   thisCommand.Parameters.Add("@TextFile", SqlDbType.NVarChar)
   thisCommand.Parameters.Add("@TextData", SqlDbType.Text)
End Sub

Sub ExecuteInsertTextFile(ByVal textFile As String)
   Dim textData As String = GetTextFile(textFile)
   thisCommand.Parameters("@TextFile").Value = textFile
   thisCommand.Parameters("@TextData").Value = textData
   ExecuteCommand(thisCommand.CommandText)
End Sub

Function GetTextFile(ByVal textFile As String) As String
   ' Display status
   Console.WriteLine("Loading file : {0}", textFile)

   ' Stream text into string
   Dim fs As New FileStream(textFile, FileMode.Open)
   Dim sr As New StreamReader(fs)
   Dim textBytes As String = sr.ReadToEnd()

   ' Display length of file
   Console.WriteLine("File has length {0} bytes", _
      textBytes.Length.ToString())

   ' Close reader and stream
   sr.Close()
   fs.Close()

   Return textBytes
End Function
```

5. Make the project the startup project, make `Sub Main` the startup object for the project, and run the program with Ctrl+F5. You should see the output in Figure 21-5.

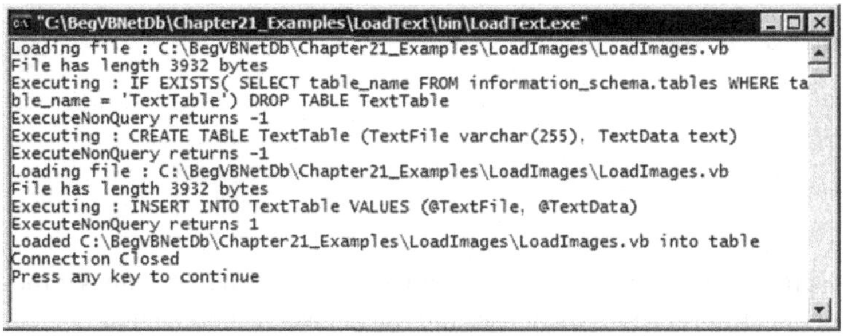

```
"C:\BegVBNetDb\Chapter21_Examples\LoadText\bin\LoadText.exe"
Loading file : C:\BegVBNetDb\Chapter21_Examples\LoadImages\LoadImages.vb
File has length 3932 bytes
Executing : IF EXISTS( SELECT table_name FROM information_schema.tables WHERE ta
ble_name = 'TextTable') DROP TABLE TextTable
ExecuteNonQuery returns -1
Executing : CREATE TABLE TextTable (TextFile varchar(255), TextData text)
ExecuteNonQuery returns -1
Loading file : C:\BegVBNetDb\Chapter21_Examples\LoadImages\LoadImages.vb
File has length 3932 bytes
Executing : INSERT INTO TextTable VALUES (@TextFile, @TextData)
ExecuteNonQuery returns 1
Loaded C:\BegVBNetDb\Chapter21_Examples\LoadImages\LoadImages.vb into table
Connection Closed
Press any key to continue
```

Figure 21-5. *Loading a text file into a database*

How It Works

You simply load the source code for the `LoadImages` program into a table, `TextTable`, that you create in the temporary database.

```
Dim FileName As String = _
   "C:\BegVBNetDb\Chapter21_Examples\LoadImages\LoadImages.vb"


ExecuteCommand("CREATE TABLE TextTable " & _
   "(TextFile varchar(255), TextData text)")
```

The `ExecuteInsertTextFile` method accepts a filename, calls `GetTextFile` to retrieve the text data, assigns the filename and file contents two command parameters, and executes the command to insert a new row.

```
Sub ExecuteInsertTextFile(ByVal textFile As String)
   Dim textData As String = GetTextFile(textFile)
   thisCommand.Parameters("@TextFile").Value = textFile
   thisCommand.Parameters("@TextData").Value = textData
   ExecuteCommand(thisCommand.CommandText)
End Sub
```

Instead of the `BinaryReader` you used for images, `GetTextFile` uses a `StreamReader` (derived from `System.IO.TextReader`) to read the contents of the file into a `string`.

```
Function GetTextFile(ByVal textFile As String) As String
   ' Display status
   Console.WriteLine("Loading file : {0}", textFile)

   ' Stream text into string
   Dim fs As New FileStream(textFile, FileMode.Open)
   Dim sr As New StreamReader(fs)
   Dim textBytes As String = sr.ReadToEnd()
```

```
   ' Display length of file
   Console.WriteLine("File has length {0} bytes", _
      textBytes.Length.ToString())

   ' Close reader and stream
   sr.Close()
   fs.Close()

   Return textBytes
End Function
```

Otherwise, the processing logic is basically the same as you've seen many times throughout the book: open a connection, access a database, and then close the connection.

Now let's retrieve the text you just stored.

Retrieving Data from Text Columns

Retrieving data from TEXT columns is just like retrieving it from the smaller character data types. You'll now write a simple console program to show how this works.

Try It Out: Retrieving Text Data

Follow these steps:

1. Add a VB .NET console application named RetrieveText to the solution.
2. Rename Module1.vb to RetrieveText.vb, and replace the code with that in Listing 21-2.

Listing 21-2. *RetrieveText.vb*

```
Imports System.Data.SqlClient

Namespace RetrieveText
   Module RetrieveText

      ' Global declarations
      Dim textFile As String
      Dim textChars() As Char
      Dim thisConnection As SqlConnection
      Dim thisCommand As SqlCommand
      Dim thisReader As SqlDataReader

      Sub Main()
         ' Create Connection object
         thisConnection = New SqlConnection _
            ("server=(local)\netsdk;" & _
             "integrated security=sspi;" & _
             "database=tempdb")
```

```
      ' Create Command object
      thisCommand = New SqlCommand _
         ("SELECT TextFile, TextData " & _
          "FROM TextTable", _
          thisConnection)

      Try
         ' Open Connection
         thisConnection.Open()

         ' Create data reader
         thisReader = thisCommand.ExecuteReader()

         While GetRow()
            Console.WriteLine("--- End of file {0} ", textFile)
         End While
      Catch ex As Exception
         Console.WriteLine(ex.ToString())

      Finally
         EndRetrieval()

      End Try
   End Sub

   Function GetRow() As Boolean
      Dim textSize As Long
      Dim bufferSize As Integer = 100
      Dim charsRead As Long
      Dim textChars(bufferSize) As Char

      If thisReader.Read() Then
         ' Get File Name
         textFile = thisReader.GetString(0)

         ' Display file info
         Console.WriteLine("--- Start of file {0} ", textFile)
         textSize = thisReader.GetChars(1, 0, Nothing, 0, 0)
         Console.WriteLine("--- Size of file : {0} chars", textSize)

         ' Display piece of file
         charsRead = thisReader.GetChars(1, 0, textChars, 0, 100)
         Console.WriteLine(New String(textChars))
         Console.WriteLine("--- Last 100 characters in text")
         charsRead = thisReader.GetChars _
            (1, textSize - 100, textChars, 0, 100)
         Console.WriteLine(New String(textChars))
```

```
                Return True
             Else
                Return False
             End If
          End Function

          Sub EndRetrieval()
             ' Close Reader and Connection
             thisReader.Close()
             thisConnection.Close()
          End Sub
       End Module
    End Namespace
```

3. Make the project the startup project, and run the program with Ctrl+F5. You should see the output in Figure 21-6.

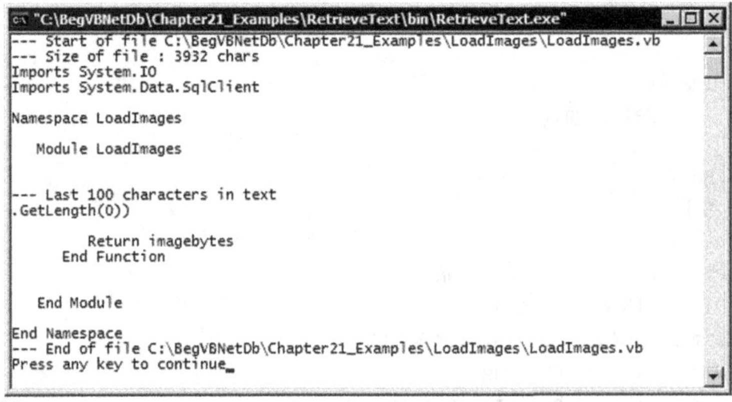

Figure 21-6. *Retrieving text*

How It Works

After querying the database, you get the filename from the table with `GetString` and print it to see which files are displayed. You then call `GetChars` with a null character array to get the size of the `TEXT` column.

```
' Display file info
Console.WriteLine("--- Start of file {0} ", textFile)
textSize = thisReader.GetChars(1, 0, Nothing, 0, 0)
Console.WriteLine("--- Size of file : {0} chars", textSize)
```

Rather than print the whole file, you display the first 100 bytes, using `GetChars` to extract a substring.

```
' Display piece of file
charsRead = thisReader.GetChars(1, 0, textChars, 0, 100)
Console.WriteLine(New String(textChars))
```

You do the same thing with the last 100 characters.

```
Console.WriteLine("--- Last 100 characters in text")
charsRead = thisReader.GetChars _
   (1, textSize - 100, textChars, 0, 100)
Console.WriteLine(New String(textChars))
```

Otherwise, this program is like any other that retrieves and displays character data.

Summary

In this chapter, you learned how to store and retrieve binary and large amounts of text data. You stored such data in a database and then retrieved and displayed it. We've covered the fundamental VB .NET techniques in this chapter that work with any type of database, but it each RDBMS works slightly differently when it comes to dealing with this type of large data. It's a good idea to check in the documentation for the exact name of the types used for storing binary and large text data. Likewise, check to see if any database-specific issues affect performance when working with these data types.

This completes our coverage of VB .NET and databases using ADO.NET 1.1. In the next (and final) chapter, we introduce some of the changes in the forthcoming ADO.NET 2.0.

CHAPTER 22

Using ADO.NET 2.0

As this book goes to press, Microsoft is about to release new versions of ADO.NET, VB .NET, Visual Studio, and SQL Server, all of which are now in beta releases. All these products have been significantly enhanced in many ways, but the changes don't deprecate anything you've learned so far. The majority of changes, particularly to ADO.NET, involves internal and infrastructure issues beyond the scope of this book and largely transparent to all developers.

In this chapter, you'll play with a few new features of ADO.NET that are related to topics we've already covered. You'll see that unless you choose to use new features, no new programming is required. VB .NET programs that use ADO.NET 1.1 will work, without changes, with ADO.NET 2.0. Likewise, VB .NET programs written for .NET Framework 1.1 require no change to run in .NET Framework 2.0. Of course, to use the latest versions of .NET components, you must rebuild your projects with the latest class and runtime libraries.

Many new features offer exciting development and performance benefits. Though you don't have to, you may find it worth the effort to modify programs to take advantage of the new features. We'll show you how to use three of them.

In this chapter, we'll cover the following:

- How to convert ADO.NET 1.1 programs to ADO.NET 2.0
- How to load data tables with data readers
- How to extract XML data more compactly
- How to update data more efficiently

Converting ADO.NET 1.1 Programs to ADO.NET 2.0

Visual Studio 2005 provides a somewhat different interface than Visual Studio 2003. We'll cover it as we prove our assertion that ADO.NET 1.1 programs can run without changes using ADO.NET 2.0. Let's rebuild the `ComplexBinding` project from Chapter 9.

Try It Out: Rebuilding an ADO.NET 1.1 Project for ADO.NET 2.0

To rebuild an ADO.NET 1.1 project for ADO.NET 2.0, follow these steps:

1. Open Visual Studio 2005, and select File ➤ New ➤ Project.... This opens the window in Figure 22-1.

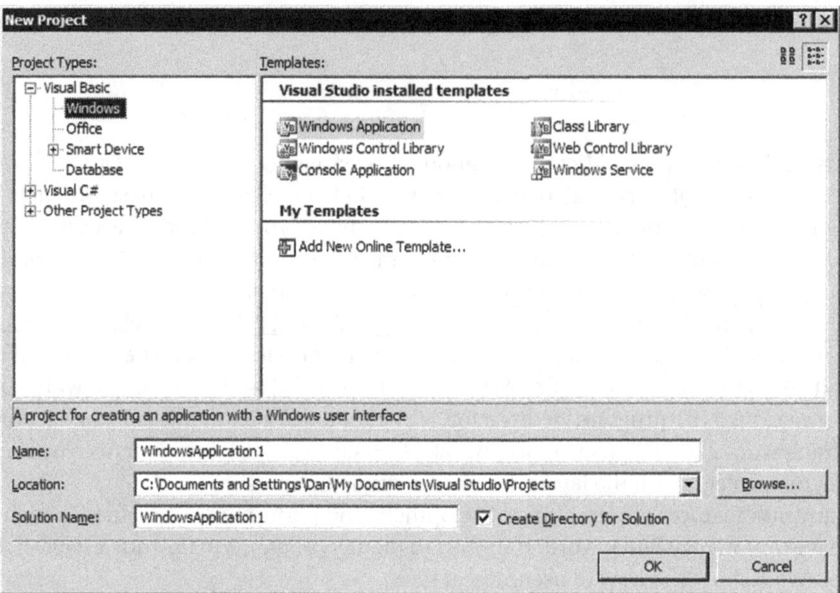

Figure 22-1. *New Project window*

2. Expand the Other Project Types node, and select Visual Studio Solutions. Select Blank Solution, name it `Chapter22_Examples`, and place it in the `C:\BegVBNetDb` directory. Then click OK.

3. In Solution Explorer, right-click the solution and select Add ➤ Existing Project.... When the Add Existing Project window opens, navigate to the `ComplexBinding` project in the `Chapter9_Examples` solution, and then double-click the `ComplexBinding.csproj` file. This starts the Visual Studio Conversion Wizard. Click Next on the opening screen.

4. The next screen (see Figure 22-2) asks if you want to create a backup. After you've decided, click Next. If you create a backup, it will be stored in the `Backup` folder of the solution folder.

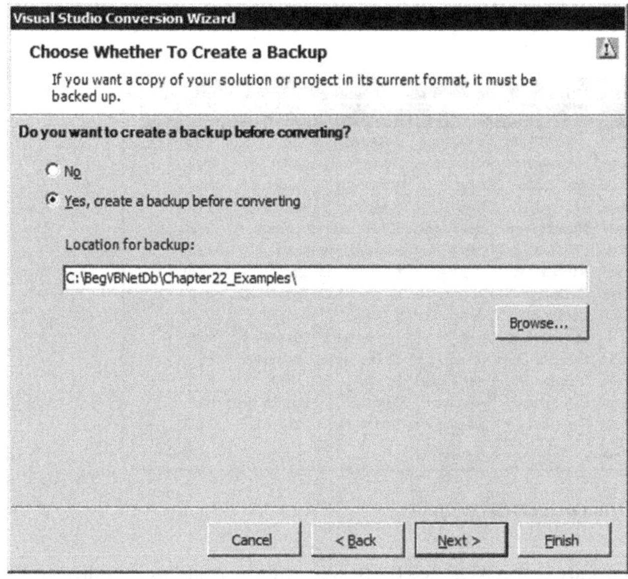

Figure 22-2. *Specifying a backup for a converted project*

5. The next screen summarizes your choices. If you're happy with them, click Finish to start the conversion. If not, click Back and change your choices.

6. If, as it should, all goes well, you'll see the screen in Figure 22-3. Click Close. The `ComplexBinding` project now appears in Solution Explorer.

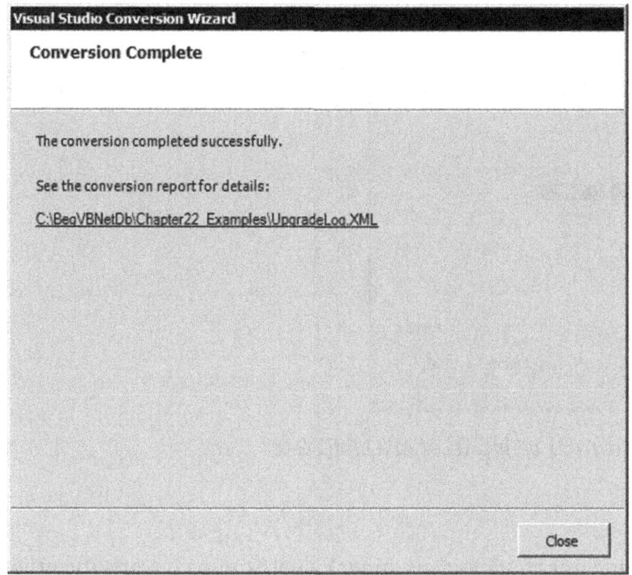

Figure 22-3. *Successful conversion of an existing project*

7. Run the project with Ctrl+F5. Data should appear, as shown in Figure 22-4.

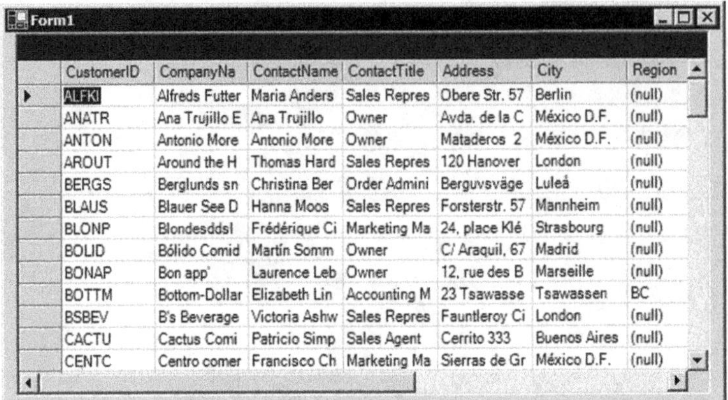

Figure 22-4. *Running the converted project*

8. To prove that you're actually using ADO.NET 2.0, select Show All Files in Solution Explorer, open the References node, right-click `System.Data`, and click Properties. Note that the `Runtime Version` property of the ADO.NET assembly (`System.Data.dll`) is `2.0.40607` (see Figure 22-5). This is the version number for beta 1 of VB .NET 2.0. It will be different if you use beta 2 or the release version.

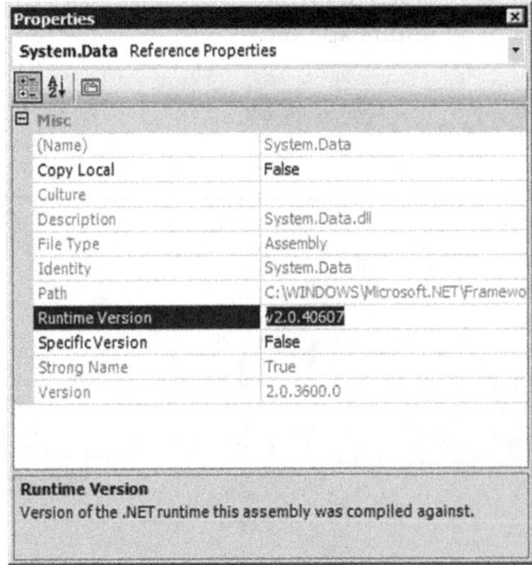

Figure 22-5. *`System.Data.dll` v2 is part of ADO.NET 2.0.*

How It Works

Totally transparently, without your changing anything, Visual Studio converts the original ADO.NET 1.1 project to use ADO.NET 2.0.

Yes, Visual Studio 2005 looks a bit different from Visual Studio 2003, but it still has the Conversion Wizard. All you basically have to do is request the project be added to the solution.

Loading Data Tables with Data Readers

Datasets are powerful but relatively expensive resources. Prior to ADO.NET 2.0, a data table had to be associated with a dataset so it could be loaded with a data adapter. Now, both `System.Data.DataSet` and `System.Data.DataTable` have been enhanced with `Load` methods that use data readers directly instead of relying on data adapters (which use data readers of their own). In cases where you don't need the overhead of a dataset, you can now simply use data tables.

Try It Out: Loading a Data Table with a Data Reader

In this example, you'll modify `ComplexBinding` to use a data table, loaded by a data reader, instead of a dataset loaded by an adapter.

1. Open the `Form1.vb` file in Code view.
2. Select `DataGrid1` from the left drop-down box at the top of the Code view, and then select the `Navigate` event from the right drop-down box. The skeleton code for this event handler is now generated. Add the following bold code to the event handler:

```
Private Sub DataGrid1_Navigate(ByVal sender As Object, _
   ByVal ne As System.Windows.Forms.NavigateEventArgs) _
   Handles DataGrid1.Navigate
   ' Create Connection object
   Dim thisConnection As New SqlConnection _
      ("server=(local)\netsdk;" & _
       "integrated security=sspi;" & _
       "database=northwind")

   ' Create Command Object
   Dim thisCommand As New SqlCommand _
      ("SELECT * FROM Customers", thisConnection)

   ' Create Data Reader
   Dim thisReader As SqlDataReader

   Try
      ' Open Connection
      thisConnection.Open()

      ' Load data table with data reader
      thisReader = thisCommand.ExecuteReader()
      Dim dt As New DataTable("Customers")
      dt.Load(thisReader)

      ' Bind data table to datagrid
      DataGrid1.DataSource = dt
```

```
            ' Close Reader
            thisReader.Close()

         Catch ex As Exception
            MessageBox.Show(ex.Message)
         Finally
            ' Close Connection
            thisConnection.Close()
         End Try
      End Sub
```

3. Replace the code in the Form1_Load method with the following bold code:

```
Private Sub Form1_Load(ByVal sender As System.Object, _
   ByVal e As System.EventArgs) Handles MyBase.Load
   DataGrid1_Navigate(sender, Nothing)
End Sub
```

4. Run it with Ctrl+F5. You should see the same output as in Figure 22-4.

How It Works

The first thing you do is simplify things. The code in Form1_Load would be the same as in dataGrid1_Navigate, so you now call the event handler directly and just change things in only one place.

```
DataGrid1_Navigate(sender, Nothing)
```

In dataGrid1_Navigate, you use the same connection string, query, and connection as before. The big difference comes next, when you replace these three statements:

```
Dim da as New SqlDataAdapter(sql, conn)
Dim ds = new DataSet
da.Fill(ds, "Customers")
```

with the following six statements:

```
' Create Command Object
Dim thisCommand As New SqlCommand _
   ("SELECT * FROM Customers", thisConnection)

' Create Data Reader
Dim thisReader As SqlDataReader

Try
   ' Open Connection
   thisConnection.Open()

   ' Load data table with data reader
   thisReader = thisCommand.ExecuteReader()
   Dim dt As New DataTable("Customers")
   dt.Load(thisReader)
```

Instead of creating a data adapter, passing its constructor the query and connection, you create a command with the same information. Then, since you won't have an adapter to open the connection implicitly when it fills a dataset, you explicitly open the connection. You create a data reader instead of a data adapter, create a data table instead of a dataset, and then load the data table with the data reader by calling its `Load` method and passing the data reader to use.

As in the original program, you bind the data grid to the data table, but instead of using the data grid's `SetDataBinding` method, like so:

```
DataGrid1.SetDataBinding(ds, "customers")
```

you use the data grid's `DataSource` property, like so:

```
' Bind data table to datagrid
DataGrid1.DataSource = dt
```

`SetDataBinding` requires both a dataset and data table, and you don't have (or need) a dataset.

Finally, since you no longer have an adapter to automatically close the connection, you should explicitly close the reader and the connection.

```
      ' Close Reader
      thisReader.Close()
   Finally
      ' Close Connection
      thisConnection.Close()
   End Try
End Sub
```

■ **Note** A `DataTable`'s `Load` method is overloaded. You can optionally specify a member of the `System.Data.LoadOption` enumeration to control how newly retrieved rows will affect the rows in a data table that's already populated. `DataSet`'s `Load` method *always* requires that a load option be specified.

Serializing Data More Compactly

In Chapter 8 you serialized (extracted) a dataset to an XML file. The technique used was appropriate for relatively small amounts of data but produced XML files that weren't as compact as possible. For larger datasets, and especially for data intended to be shared over networks, smaller files can significantly enhance performance. Let's modify the `WriteXml` project from the `Chapter8_Examples` solution to use a more compact ADO.NET 2.0 serialization method.

Try It Out: Serializing a Dataset to a Binary File

To serialize a dataset to a binary file, follow these steps:

1. Following a procedure similar to the earlier "Try It Out: Rebuilding an ADO.NET 1.1 Project for ADO.NET 2.0" section, add the `WriteXML` project from the `Chapter8_Examples` solution to the `Chapter22_Examples` solution.

2. Open the WriteXML.vb file in Code view, and change the folder for the output file as follows:

```
' Extract DataSet to XML file
ds.WriteXml("c:\begvbnetdb\chapter22_examples\productstable.xml")
```

3. Make this the startup project, and run it with Ctrl+F5. It will create a productstable.xml file in the solution directory.

4. The original program doesn't extract much data, so change the query in WriteXML.vb to retrieve all data from the Orders table.

```
' Sql Query
Dim sql As String = _
   "SELECT * FROM Orders"
```

5. Add the following Imports directives:

```
Imports System.IO
Imports System.Runtime.Serialization.Formatters.Binary
```

6. Add the following code after the statement that creates the connection to create an output file for the binary data:

```
' Create file stream
Dim fs As New FileStream _
   ("c:\begvbnetdb\chapter22_examples\orderstable.bin", _
    FileMode.Create)
```

7. Change the name of the XML output file and data table.

```
' Create and fill Dataset
Dim ds As New DataSet
da.Fill(ds, "orders")

' Extract DataSet to XML file
ds.WriteXml("c:\begvbnetdb\chapter22_examples\orderstable.xml")
```

8. Add the following code to the Try block after the call to WriteXml:

```
' Create binary formatter
Dim bf As New BinaryFormatter()

' Specify binary serialization for dataset
ds.RemotingFormat = SerializationFormat.Binary

' Output dataset
bf.Serialize(fs, ds)
```

9. Add the following statement to the Finally block:

```
' Close filestream
fs.Close()
```

10. Make this the startup project, and run it with Ctrl+F5. This creates two files. The file `orderstable.xml` should be about 488 kilobytes (KB) and look like Figure 22-6. The file `orderstable.bin` should be about 138KB and look like Figure 22-7.

orderstable.xml - Notepad

File Edit Format View Help


```
<?xml version="1.0" standalone="yes"?>
<NewDataSet>
  <orders>
    <OrderID>10248</OrderID>
    <CustomerID>VINET</CustomerID>
    <EmployeeID>5</EmployeeID>
    <OrderDate>1996-07-04T00:00:00.0000000+01:00</OrderDate>
    <RequiredDate>1996-08-01T00:00:00.0000000+01:00</RequiredDate>
    <ShippedDate>1996-07-16T00:00:00.0000000+01:00</ShippedDate>
    <ShipVia>3</ShipVia>
    <Freight>32.3800</Freight>
    <ShipName>Vins et alcools Chevalier</ShipName>
    <ShipAddress>59 rue de l'Abbaye</ShipAddress>
    <ShipCity>Reims</ShipCity>
    <ShipPostalCode>51100</ShipPostalCode>
    <ShipCountry>France</ShipCountry>
  </orders>
  <orders>
    <OrderID>10249</OrderID>
```


Figure 22-6. *Text XML document*

orderstable.bin - Notepad

File Edit Format View Help


```
□   ÿÿÿÿ□        □□   QSystem.Data, Version=2.0.3600.0, Culture=neutral,
PublicKeyToken=b77a5c561934e089□□   □System.Data.DataSet"
□DataSet.RemotingVersion□DataSet.RemotingFormat□DataSet.DataSetName□DataSet.Names
pace□DataSet.Prefix□DataSet.CaseSensitive□DataSet.LocaleLCID□DataSet.EnforceConst
raints□DataSet.ExtendedProperties□DataSet.Tables.Count□DataSet.Tables_0□DataTable
_0.Constraints□DataSet.Relations#DataTable_0.DataColumn_0.Expression#DataTable_0.
DataColumn_1.Expression#DataTable_0.DataColumn_2.Expression#DataTable_0.DataColum
n_3.Expression#DataTable_0.DataColumn_4.Expression#DataTable_0.DataColumn_5.Expre
ssion#DataTable_0.DataColumn_6.Expression#DataTable_0.DataColumn_7.Expression#Dat
aTable_0.DataColumn_8.Expression#DataTable_0.DataColumn_9.Expression$DataTable_0.
DataColumn_10.Expression$DataTable_0.DataColumn_11.Expression$DataTable_0.DataCol
umn_12.Expression$DataTable_0.DataColumn_13.Expression□DataTable_0.Rows.Count□Dat
aTable_0.Records.Count□DataTable_0.RowStates□DataTable_0.Records□DataTable_0.Null
Bits□DataTable_0.RowErrors□DataTable_0.ColumnErrors□□□□□   □ □□□□□□□□□□□□□□□□
□□□□□□System.Version□System.Data.SerializationFormat□
□□□□System.Data.PropertyCollection□
□□□System.Collections.ArrayList□System.Collections.ArrayList□□□System.Collections
.BitArray□System.Collections.ArrayList□System.Collections.ArrayList□System.Collec
tions.Hashtable□System.Collections.Hashtable□         □
```


Figure 22-7. *Binary XML document*

How It Works

Though it takes ten steps, you don't really do much work. The first three steps simply convert the original program to ADO.NET 2.0, step 4 changes the query to get more data so that the difference in extracted file size is more obvious, step 5 makes the file I/O and serialization namespaces available, and step 7 just changes the directory for the output file. Let's look at the other steps.

The original program uses the dataset's `WriteXml` method, which implicitly performs I/O to a specified file. However, `WriteXml` doesn't provide for compaction, so you need to explicitly create an output file, and you do so in step 6. Even if you're not familiar with VB .NET file I/O, this is straightforward. You simply create a file stream for the `orderstable.bin` file. The `FileMode.Create` argument means that a new file will be created, overwriting an existing one, if necessary.

```
' Create file stream
Dim fs As New FileStream _
   ("c:\begvbnetdb\chapter22_examples\orderstable.bin", _
    FileMode.Create)
```

In step 8, you add the compaction logic. A binary formatter can serialize or deserialize an object or a collection of related objects. It's not new to .NET 2.0 or part of ADO.NET, but for database applications that pass data over networks, it's often an important alternative to ADO.NET's XML methods. Here, you create a binary formatter, specify that the dataset will be serialized in binary, rather than XML format, and call the binary formatter's `Serialize` method, passing it the file stream to write to and the dataset to format.

```
' Create binary formatter
Dim bf As New BinaryFormatter()

' Specify binary serialization for dataset
ds.RemotingFormat = SerializationFormat.Binary

' Output dataset
bf.Serialize(fs, ds)
```

From an ADO.NET perspective, the second statement is the most interesting. In ADO.NET 2.0, both `DataSet` and `DataTable` have a new property, `RemotingFormat`, which can have one of two values from the new `System.Data.SerializationFormat` enumeration: `Binary` or `Xml`. The default is `SerializationFormat.Xml`, so you set it to `Binary` before serializing the dataset. Unfortunately, though the serialization format for datasets and data tables can now be specified in ADO.NET, somewhat inexplicably, `WriteXml` ignores it, forcing you to use a binary formatter instead to achieve compaction. (Of course, this may be fixed in later betas and the final release of ADO.NET 2.0.)

Step 9 isn't absolutely required, but as with any external resource, you should close open files when done.

```
' Close filestream
fs.Close()
```

Whether you need to use this technique instead of calling `WriteXml` depends on your performance constraints, but it's so easy to do that it may be a good idea to always use it, choosing the `Binary` or `Xml` modes to suit your needs.

■Tip The `Xml` serialization format produces a file somewhat smaller than the text file output by `WriteXml`, but it's not at all as easy for a human to read; therefore, if readability is important, use `WriteXml`.

Updating in Batches

Prior to ADO.NET 2.0, when a data adapter performed updates, it passed every `INSERT`, `UPDATE`, or `DELETE` statement separately to the database manager. This can be quite expensive over network connections, and is still the default behavior, but a new property `UpdateBatchSize` has been added to the data adapters for SQL Server (`System.Data.SqlClient.DataAdapter`) and for the Microsoft-supplied Oracle data provider (`System.Data.OracleClient.DataAdapter`).

Try It Out: Specifying Batch Updates

To specify batch updates, follow these steps:

1. Following a procedure similar to the earlier "Try It Out: Rebuilding an ADO.NET 1.1 Project for ADO.NET 2.0" section, add the `DataGridUpdate` project from the `Chapter9_Examples` solution to the `Chapter22_Examples` solution.

2. Open the `Form1.vb` file in Code view, and add the following bold line of code to the `buttonUpdate_Click` method:

```
Private Sub buttonUpdate_Click(ByVal sender As System.Object, _
   ByVal e As System.EventArgs) Handles buttonUpdate.Click
   da.UpdateBatchSize = 10
   da.Update(DataSet1, "Employees")
End Sub
```

3. Make this the startup project, and run it with Ctrl+F5. The window in Figure 22-8 appears. Change some data, and click Update to test that the program still works.

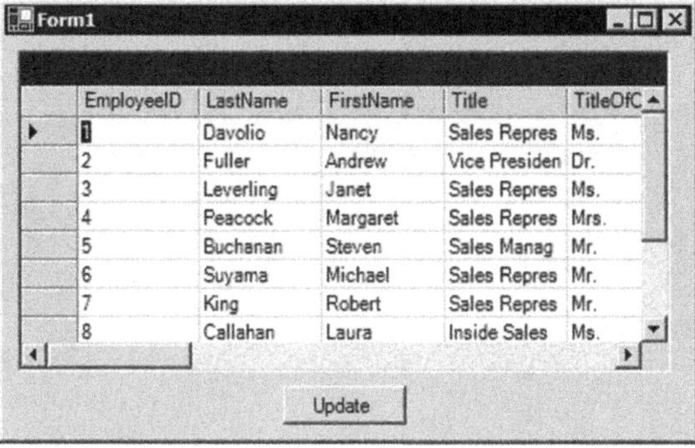

Figure 22-8. *Batch updating*

How It Works

You simply set the data adapter's batch size to a number greater than the default of `1`. That's all there is to it. Just make sure you do it before calling the `Update` method; otherwise you'll use the default.

Summary

In this chapter, you examined a handful of new features of ADO.NET 2.0. It has many more enhancements; in fact, it has so many that several books could probably be written on how best to exploit them, especially in concert with enhancements to SQL Server itself. But the fundamentals of using VB .NET to access databases that you've learned in this book are still the ones you most need to understand.

The ADO.NET architecture has expanded and now offers even more powerful and convenient ways to process database data, but ADO.NET still comes down to connections, commands, and data providers that pass results to data readers either explicitly or implicitly.

Well, that's it. By now you should feel confident and competent in VB .NET database programming. You're no longer just a beginner. We hope you enjoyed our book and found it helpful in your work. Most of all, we hope you'll have as much fun using VB .NET and ADO.NET as we do for real-world programming!

APPENDIX A

Creating the SQL Tool Application

In Chapter 3, we discussed various ways to execute SQL, including using osql and using the Visual Studio .NET SQL tool. You used a custom application to execute queries and statements. Because our tool is a simple VB .NET project to access databases, we're including instructions for how to create it in this appendix.

The utility as implemented here isn't very powerful and doesn't have all the bells and whistles even a small application needs to be ready for production, but you can easily expand it and make it robust enough to suit your needs.

Let's build it!

Try It Out: Building a Custom Query Tool

The tool is a standard VB .NET Windows Forms application, so open Visual Studio .NET and follow these steps:

1. Create a new solution called `AppendixA_Examples`.
2. Create a new VB .NET project within this solution by right-clicking the solution, selecting Add ➤ New Project..., and creating a new VB .NET Windows application called `SqlTool`.
3. Click the form, and set the properties as shown in Table A-1 using the Properties window.

Table A-1. *Form Properties*

Property	**Value**
Text	SQL Tool
WindowState	Maximized

4. Drag and drop a `RichTextBox` control from the Toolbox onto the form.

5. Using the Properties window, set its properties per Table A-2. (Set the font by clicking the (...) button to the right of the `Font` property in the panel and selecting the font name and size.)

Table A-2. *`RichTextBox` Properties*

Property	Value
`(Name)`	`rtfSql`
`Dock`	`Top`
`Text`	`[Clear this property]`
`Font`	`Courier New`
`FontSize`	`10`

6. Drag and drop a `Splitter` control from the Toolbox onto the form. This handy control latches onto the last control placed on a form with a specific value set for the `Dock` property. You want to be able to change the size of the `RichTextBox`, so you just need to change a single property on the splitter (see Table A-3).

Table A-3. *`Splitter` Properties*

Property	Value
`Dock`	`Top`

Your form should now look like Figure A-1.

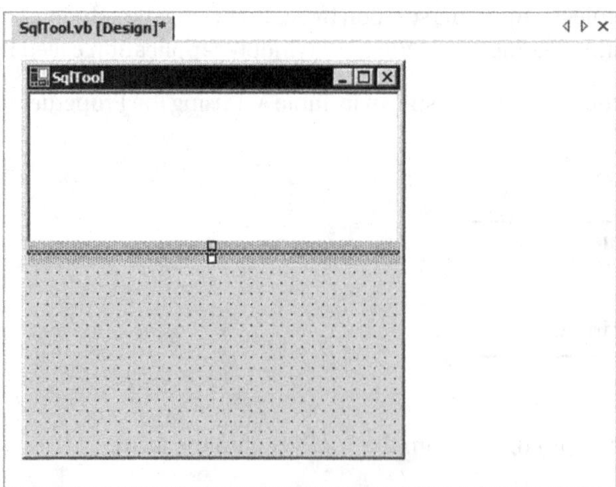

Figure A-1. *Splitter attached to `RichTextBox`*

7. Drag and drop a `ListView` control from the Toolbox onto the form.

8. Set the properties of the list view as in Table A-4.

Table A-4. *List View Properties*

Property	Value
(Name)	listViewResult
Dock	Fill
GridLines	True
View	Details

9. Double-click a `MainMenu` control in the Toolbox. This will place a `mainMenu1` object in the component tray.

10. Create a menu with four items. Click the Type Here box on the form, and then enter the menu name `&Actions`. In the Type Here box beneath it, enter the first menu item name `&Execute` and then the other menu items shown in Table A-5 in each succeeding Type Here box beneath it.

Table A-5. *Menu Item Names*

Property	Value
Text	&Actions
Text	&Execute
Text	&Format Statements
Text	
Text	E&xit

11. The menu items need to have some properties set. Select the `&Execute` item, and set the properties as shown in Table A-6.

Table A-6. *`&Execute` Item Properties*

Property	Value
(Name)	menuItemExecute
Shortcut	F5

12. Select the `&Format statements` item, and set the properties as in Table A-7.

Table A-7. *`&Format statements` Item Properties*

Property	Value
`(Name)`	`menuItemFormat`
`Shortcut`	`F12`

13. Select the `E&xit` item, and set the property as in Table A-8.

Table A-8. *`E&xit` Item Property*

Property	Value
`(Name)`	`menuItemExit`

The form should now look something like Figure A-2.

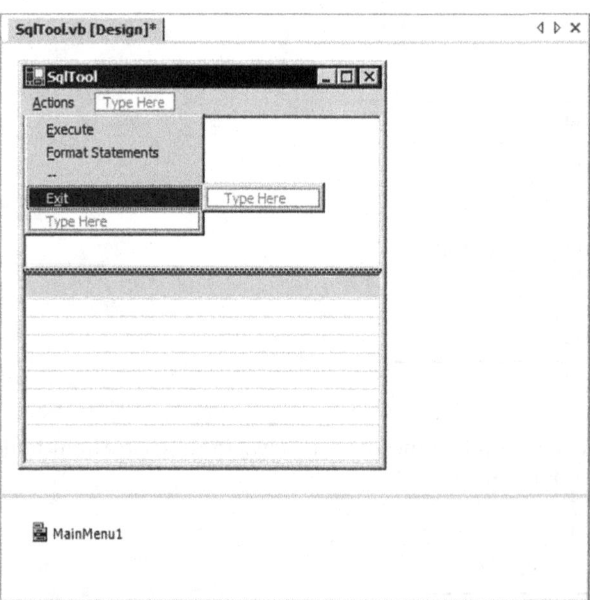

Figure A-2. *Menu and menu items*

14. Right-click the form, and select View Code.

15. Add the following `Imports` directive to include the `SqlClient` data provider classes:

```
Imports System.Data.SqlClient
```

16. Drag a SqlConnection object from the Data tab of the Toolbox onto the form. Name it thisConnection and set its ConnectionString property to that for the Northwind database.

17. Add the following global variable declarations to the Form1 class:

```
' Global Application Variables
Dim thisCommand As SqlCommand
Dim SqlKeywords() As String = _
      {"select", "update", "insert", "into", "delete", "from", _
       "values", "truncate", "table", "join", "on", "where", _
       "create", "drop", "set", "in", "between", "is", "null", _
       "not", "Order by", "asc", "desc"}
```

18. Return to Design view, click the menu, and then double-click the &Execute item. Insert the following lines in bold:

```
Private Sub menuItemExecute_Click(ByVal sender As System.Object, _
   ByVal e As System.EventArgs) Handles menuItemExecute.Click
   ' Get selected text
   Dim selectedText As String = rtfSql.SelectedText

   ' If no text is selected, use all text
   If selectedText.Length = 0 Then
      selectedText = rtfSql.Text
   End If

   ' If SELECT is in the text, treat it as a query
   If selectedText.ToLower().IndexOf("select", 0) >= 0 Then
      ExecuteSelect(selectedText)
   Else
      ExecuteNonQuery(selectedText)
   End If
End Sub
```

19. Now add the two helper functions for the Execute button; one for executing SQL queries and the other for executing SQL statements.

```
Sub ExecuteSelect(ByVal query As String)
   Dim first As Boolean = True
   Dim lvi As ListViewItem
   thisCommand = New SqlCommand(query, thisConnection)

   ' Clear List View
   listViewResult.Items.Clear()
   listViewResult.Columns.Clear()

   Try
      ' Open Connection
      thisConnection.Open()
```

```
            ' Execute Query and get data reader
            Dim thisReader As SqlDataReader = thisCommand.ExecuteReader()

            ' Check data reader was returned
            If thisReader Is Nothing Then
               Return
            End If

            ' Reader valid so create columns in list view
            thisReader.Read()
            For i As Integer = 0 To thisReader.FieldCount - 1
               listViewResult.Columns.Add _
                  (thisReader.GetName(i).ToString(), 100, _
                   HorizontalAlignment.Left)
            Next

            ' Add rows in reader to listview
            Do
               For i As Integer = 0 To thisReader.FieldCount - 1
                  If i = 0 Then
                     lvi = listViewResult.Items.Add _
                        (thisReader.GetValue(i).tostring())
                  Else
                     lvi.SubItems.Add(thisReader.GetValue(i).tostring())
                  End If
               Next
            Loop While thisReader.Read()

         Catch ex As Exception
            MessageBox.Show(ex.Message)

         Finally
            ' Close Connection
            thisConnection.Close()

         End Try
      End Sub

      Sub ExecuteNonQuery(ByVal sql As String)
         Dim rowsAffected As Integer = 0
         Dim lvi As ListViewItem
         thisCommand = New SqlCommand(sql, thisConnection)

         ' Clear List View
         listViewResult.Items.Clear()
         listViewResult.Columns.Clear()
```

```
      Try
         ' Open Connection
         thisConnection.Open()

         ' Execute the Statement
         rowsAffected = thisCommand.ExecuteNonQuery()

         ' Display the number of rows affected
         listViewResult.Columns.Add _
            ("Row Affected", -2, HorizontalAlignment.Left)
         lvi = listViewResult.Items.Add(rowsAffected.ToString())

      Catch ex As Exception
         MessageBox.Show(ex.Message)

      Finally
         ' Close connection
         thisConnection.Close()
      End Try
   End Sub
```

20. Return to Design view, and double-click the `&Format statements` item. Insert the following lines in bold:

```
Private Sub menuItemFormat_Click(ByVal sender As System.Object, _
   ByVal e As System.EventArgs) Handles menuItemFormat.Click
   Dim NotFinishedWordSearch As Boolean

   ' Loop through each keyword in the array
   For i As Integer = 0 To SqlKeywords.Length - 1

      ' Start word search for each keyword
      NotFinishedWordSearch = True

      ' Set start location in text for find routine
      Dim PositionInText As Integer = 0

      ' Check to see if keyword is in the SQL
      While NotFinishedWordSearch

         ' Obtain a location of the search string in richTextBox1.
         Dim indexToText As Integer = rtfSql.Find(SqlKeywords(i), _
            PositionInText, RichTextBoxFinds.WholeWord)

         ' Determine whether the text was found
         If indexToText >= 0 Then
```

```
                ' If text found highlight it and make it upper case
                rtfSql.SelectionColor = Color.Blue
                rtfSql.SelectedText = SqlKeywords(i).ToUpper()

                ' Move search start to next character
                PositionInText += 1
             Else
                ' If text not found, finish search for this word
                NotFinishedWordSearch = False
             End If
          End While
       Next
    End Sub
```

21. Return to Design view, and double-click the `E&xit` item. Insert the following bold line:

```
Private Sub menuItemExit_Click(ByVal sender As System.Object, _
   ByVal e As System.EventArgs) Handles menuItemExit.Click
   Application.Exit()
End Sub
```

22. Run the application. You should get a window that looks like Figure A-3 (after clicking the window's Restore Down box).

Figure A-3. *Application start*

Chapter 3 contains examples using the application.

How It Works

This simple application allows you to enter SQL and send it to a database. You enter the SQL in the `RichTextBox` control at the top of the window and get the results back in the list view below it. You can change the size of the `RichTextBox` and list view by clicking the splitter bar between them and dragging it to the desired position.

Let's look briefly at the code. The first point to note is that if you're using a different database instance/server, you need to change the connection string appropriately.

The next interesting place in the code is the `ExecuteSelect` method. This method is called whenever the SQL contains the word *select*. The code that retrieves the data from the database is as follows:

```
thisCommand = New SqlCommand(query, thisConnection)

Try
   ' Open Connection
   thisConnection.Open()

   ' Execute Query and get data reader
   Dim thisReader As SqlDataReader = thisCommand.ExecuteReader()
```

You first create a command object and instantiate it with the SQL you want to send to the database and the database connection. You then open the connection and call the `ExecuteReader` method on the command object. This method returns another object, which is a `SqlDataReader` that allows you to read data returned from the query.

The following lines of code, down to the `Catch` clause, concern themselves with inserting the data in the list view. The `Catch` and `Finally` clauses are interesting, because you use them to perform two critical tasks: to inform the user of errors and to make absolutely sure that the connection is closed when you leave the method.

```
Catch ex As Exception
   MessageBox.Show(ex.Message)

Finally
   ' Close Connection
   thisConnection.Close()
```

Remember that the `Finally` clause of a `Try` statement is always executed, no matter how the `Try` block is exited.

The other method that's used to pass SQL to the database is `ExecuteNonQuery`. This method sends statements to the database and doesn't return any rows. The method is therefore somewhat less complex than the `ExecuteReader` method. The code that interacts with the database is almost identical to the `ExecuteReader` code.

```
Dim rowsAffected As Integer = 0

Try
   ' Open Connection
   thisConnection.Open()

   ' Execute the Statement
   rowsAffected = thisCommand.ExecuteNonQuery()
```

Note the final line. Instead of calling the `ExecuteReader` method on the command object, you call the `ExecuteNonQuery` method instead. You do so because you're executing a statement instead of a query, so no rows will be returned. `ExecuteNonQuery` returns an integer that indicates how many rows were affected by the statement.

The final method of interest doesn't actually do anything against the database. The method `menuItemFormat_Click` simply runs through the SQL in the `RichTextBox` control, coloring the keywords and changing them to uppercase. (This is entirely cosmetic, and many SQL keywords aren't on the list.)

Summary

We've demonstrated how to develop a simple yet general-purpose database application. Of course, you could enhance the application in many ways, but all we were interested in here was executing SQL. As you progress in VB .NET database programming, modifying this project to perform more sophisticated actions would be a convenient way to practice your new skills.

For example, the tool connects only to the database specified in its hard-coded connection string. Changing it to provide for dynamic database selection would be a straightforward programming exercise. If you really want to stretch yourself, extending it to provide the same features as the `osql` utility would be an ambitious project—and a *very* nice visual tool for the MSDE environment. The only limitations are your time and imagination.

APPENDIX B

XML Primer

Developed in 1996 by the World Wide Web Consortium (W3C), Extensible Markup Language (XML) was first released to the public in 1998. Its most recent version is 1.1, but this offers only minor (albeit important) changes to version 1.0, which is the one we'll discuss since it's the one currently supported by Visual Studio .NET.

A *markup language* provides instructions for humans or machines that read or process them. XML is a subset of the Standard Generalized Markup Language (SGML) developed in the late 1960s and used for complex document definition and publishing. Like SGML, XML is a *meta language* for defining other markup languages. In fact, every time you define an XML document, you're actually defining a small language for formatting and managing it.

XML is much simpler than SGML, but it's an extraordinarily sophisticated and powerful language, with almost all the power of SGML but much less of the complexity. We can't cover every detail here, but XML is essentially straightforward; and since Visual Studio .NET and ADO.NET provide so many facilities for handling XML transparently, most of the time you don't require much beyond basic knowledge of XML. We'll give you enough to be quite effective.

XML has become the single most used and most important data transfer technology in modern computing. It's a core technology that underlies the .NET Framework. Understanding its basics is vital for any .NET programmer.

Understanding XML Documents

Data in XML is contained in *XML documents*. An XML document could be a physical file on your computer, a data stream over a network, or just a string in memory. It has to be complete in itself, however, and must obey certain rules. An XML document basically comprises a hierarchy of *elements* whose names, attributes, and contents are defined with XML to organize data.

XML Elements

XML elements can have *content* (data or other elements) or can be *empty*. An element that has content is delimited by a *start tag* and an *end tag*. An empty element is indicated by an *empty-element tag*.

Tags are formed with angle brackets (< >) and slashes (/). For example:

```
<book>Beginning VB .NET Databases</book>
```

This example defines an element named book, with the start tag <book>, the end tag </book>, and the content Beginning VB .NET Databases. (XML element names are case sensitive, so book isn't the same element as Book.)

A more detailed book element could include a copyright date, and it could be defined as follows (several alternatives exist):

```
<book>
  <title>Beginning VB .NET Databases</title>
  <publisher>Apress</publisher>
  <copyright date="2005" />
</book>
```

In this example, the book element contains three elements instead of data. Its first element, title, contains data, so it's delimited by the start tag <title> and the end tag </title>. Its second element, publisher, also contains data and is delimited by start and end tags (<publisher> and </publisher>). Its third element, copyright, is empty, and it's composed entirely of an empty-element tag.

Note The slash in an empty-element tag comes immediately *before* the closing angle bracket, but the slash in an end tag comes immediately *after* the opening angle bracket.

If you already know some Hypertext Markup Language (HTML) or Extensible HTML (XHTML), you may be thinking that this looks similar—and you're right! In fact, HTML, XHTML, and XML share much of the same syntax. The big difference is that XML doesn't have any predefined elements—you choose the names of your own elements, so there's no limit on the number of elements you can have. The most important point to remember is that XML is a meta language for defining markup languages, each of which has its own distinct vocabulary: a specific set of elements and the structure the elements are allowed to take in a particular document.

XML documents must be *well-formed.* At its simplest, this means that overlapping elements aren't allowed, so you must close all *child* elements before the end tag of their *parent* elements. This means, for example, that you can't do this:

```
<book>
  <title>Beginning VB .NET Databases
     <publisher>Apress
  </title>
     </publisher>
  <copyright date="2005" />
</book>
```

This is illegal syntactically, because the publisher element starts within the title element, but the </title> end tag comes before the </publisher> end tag. It's also wrong semantically, since publisher is supposed to be a child of book, not a child of title, even if the elements didn't overlap.

An alternative syntax for empty elements exists. For example:

```
<copyright date="2005"></copyright>
```

This is equivalent to the following:

```
<copyright date="2005" />
```

Attributes

In addition to content, elements can have attributes, which are defined within the start or empty-element tags. Attributes have the following form, where the value of the attribute must be enclosed in either single or double quotes:

```
name="value"
```

For example:

```
<book title="Beginning VB .NET Databases"></book>
```

And for example:

```
<book title='Beginning VB .NET Databases'></book>
```

These are both legal, but the following isn't:

```
<book title=Beginning VB .NET Databases></book>
```

At this point, you may be wondering why you need both these ways of storing data in XML. Take the following, for instance:

```
<book>
  <title>Beginning VB .NET Databases</title>
</book>
```

What's the difference between it and the following listing?

```
<book title="Beginning VB .NET Databases"></book>
```

Many XML experts argue over this, but no definitive answer exists. Attributes are less favored in general, since the essential purpose of an XML document is to organize data, which is much more flexibly done with elements than with attributes, particularly since a specific attribute may be used only once for a single element. Attributes do consume less bandwidth if the document is sent over a network without compression (with compression there's not much difference). Probably the best course is to consider using elements first, since they map much more easily to relational data. The choice can be subtle (and difficult), and no hard and fast rules exist.

The XML Declaration

Besides elements and attributes, XML documents can have other parts (called *entities*), but most of them are important only if you really need to delve deeply into XML. One part, however, is optional but should be included in almost every XML document. This is the *XML declaration*. If used, it must occur before the first element in an XML document.

The XML declaration is similar in format to an element, but it has question marks immediately next to the angle brackets. It always has the name `xml`, and it always has an attribute named `version`; currently, this has two possible values: `"1.0"` and `"1.1"`. The simplest form of an XML declaration is as follows:

```
<?xml version="1.0" ?>
```

A couple other attributes are defined but aren't required, and you'll usually include only the `version` attribute in your own XML.

Structure of an XML Document

Each XML document has a single *root element* (also called the *document element*), within which all other elements and data are contained. If more than one element exists at the top level of the document, the document isn't well-formed XML. So, the following is a well-formed XML document, since it nests `book` elements within the single `book` root element:

```
<?xml version="1.0" ?>
<books>
  <book>Beginning VB .NET Databases</book>
  <book>Beginning VB .NET Objects</book>
</books>
```

The following, however, isn't, since it has two `book` root elements:

```
<?xml version="1.0" ?>
<book>Beginning VB .NET Databases</book>
<book>Beginning VB .NET Objects</book>
```

Under the root element, you can flexibly structure data in a hierarchical fashion. You can even use XML to structure documents that aren't essentially for data storage, for example. XML has become a popular alternative to both HTML and XHTML for defining Web pages as well as traditional and hypertext documents.

Using XML Namespaces

Just as anyone can define VB .NET classes, anyone can define XML elements. But how do you know which elements belong to which vocabulary? Just as you declare namespaces to organize VB .NET types, you use XML namespaces to declare XML vocabularies. This allows you to include elements from a number of different vocabularies within a single XML document, without the risk of misinterpreting elements, for example, if two different vocabularies define a `customer` element.

XML namespaces can be quite complex, so we won't go into great detail here, but the basic syntax is simple. You associate specific elements or attributes with a specific namespace using a prefix, followed by a colon. For example, `<apress:book>` represents a `book` element that resides in the `apress` namespace. But how do you know what namespace `apress` represents? For this approach to work, you need to be able to guarantee that every namespace is unique. The easiest way to do this is to map the prefixes to something that's already known to be unique. This is exactly what happens: somewhere in the XML document, you need to associate namespace prefixes with a unique identifier. The most common approach is to use a uniform resource identifier (URI). URIs come in several flavors, but the most common type is simply a Web address, such as "http://www.apress.com".

To identify a prefix with a specific namespace, use the xmlns:<prefix> attribute, setting its value to the unique URI that identifies the namespace. You can then use the prefix anywhere within that element, including any nested (child) elements. For example:

```
<?xml version="1.0" ?>
<books>
  <book xmlns:apress="http://www.apress.com">
    <apress:title>Beginning VB .NET Objects</apress:title>
    <apress:author>Jacquie Barker</apress:author>
  </book>
</books>
```

Here you can use the apress: prefix with the title and author elements, because they're within the book element, where the prefix is defined. If you tried to add this prefix to the books element, however, the XML would be illegal, as the prefix isn't defined for this element.

You can also define a default namespace for an element using the xmlns attribute.

```
<?xml version="1.0" ?>
<books>
  <book xmlns="http://www.apress.com">
    <title>Beginning VB .NET Objects</title>
    <author>Jacquie Barker</author>
    <html:img src="begvbnetobj.gif"
      xmlns:html="http://www.w3.org/1999/xhtml" />
  </book>
</books>
```

Here, the default namespace for the book element is "http://www.apress.com". Everything within this element will, therefore, belong to this namespace, unless you explicitly request otherwise by adding a different namespace prefix, as for the img element (we set it to the namespace used by XML-compatible HTML documents).

Understanding Well-Formed and Valid XML

XML distinguishes between two forms of correctness. Documents that obey all the rules required by the XML standard are said to be *well-formed*. If an XML document isn't well-formed, parsers will be unable to interpret it correctly and will reject the document. To be well-formed, a document must at least do the following:

- Have only one root element
- Not have any overlapping elements (all child elements must be fully nested within their parents)
- Enclose all attribute values in quotes

This isn't a complete list by any means, but it highlights the most common pitfalls for programmers who are new to XML.

XML documents can obey all these rules, however, and still not be *valid*. Remember that we said earlier that XML is a meta language for defining markup languages. These languages define specific *document types*. Well-formed XML documents simply comply with the XML standard; to be valid, they also need to conform to any rules specified for the XML application. Not all parsers check whether documents are valid; those that do are called *validating parsers*. To check whether a document complies with an XML document type, you need a way of specifying what the document type is.

Validating XML Documents

XML supports two ways of defining which elements and attributes can be placed in a document and in what order: Document Type Definitions (DTDs) and XML Schemas. DTDs use a non-XML syntax inherited from SGML (the parent of XML) and are gradually being replaced by schemas. DTDs don't allow you to specify the data types of your elements and attributes, so they're relatively inflexible and not used that much in the context of the .NET Framework. Schemas, on the other hand, are flexible. They allow you to specify data types and are written in an XML syntax. However, schemas can be complex, and different formats exist for defining them—even within the .NET world!

Schemas

.NET supports two separate formats for schemas: XML Schema Definition (XSD) language and XML Data Reduced (XDR) schemas. These formats are mutually incompatible, and you really need to be familiar with XML before you attempt to write in either one, so we won't go into great detail here.

You can include schemas either within an XML document or in an external file. Let's look at sample XSD and XDR schemas for the following simple XML document, which contains basic details about an Apress VB .NET book:

```
<?xml version="1.0" ?>
<books>
  <book>
    <title>Beginning VB .NET Databases</title>
    <author>Dan Maharry</author>
    <code>3588</code>
  </book>
</books>
```

XSD Schemas

Elements in XSD schemas must belong to the namespace `"http://www.w3.org/2001/XMLSchema"`. If this namespace isn't included, the schema elements won't be recognized.

To associate the earlier XML document with an XSD schema in another file, you need to use a `schemalocation` element in the root element.

```
<?xml version="1.0" ?>
<books schemalocation="file://C:/BegVbNetDB/XML/books.xsd">
   ...
</books>
```

Now look at the following example XSD schema:

```
<schema xmlns="http://www.w3.org/2001/XMLSchema">
  <element name="books">
    <complexType>
      <choice maxOccurs="unbounded">
        <element name="book">
          <complexType>
            <sequence>
              <element name="title" />
              <element name="author" />
              <element name="code" />
            </sequence>
          </complexType>
        </element>
      </choice>
      <attribute name="schemalocation" />
    </complexType>
  </element>
</schema>
```

The first thing to notice here is that you set the default namespace to the XSD namespace. This tells the parser that all the elements in the document belong to the schema. If you don't specify this namespace, the parser will think that the elements are just normal XML elements and won't realize it needs to use them for validation.

The entire schema is contained within an element called `schema` (with a lowercase *s*—remember, case is important!). Each element that can occur within the document must be represented by an `element` element. This element has a `name` attribute that indicates the name of the element. If the element is to contain nested child elements, you must include the tags for them within a `complexType` element. Inside this, you specify how the child elements must occur. For example, you use a `choice` element to specify that any selection of the child elements can occur, or you use a `sequence` element to specify that the child elements must appear in the same order as they're listed in the schema. If an element can appear more than once (as the `book` element does), you need to include a `maxOccurs` attribute within its parent element. Setting this to `"unbounded"` means that the element can occur as often as you like. Finally, any attributes must be represented by `attribute` elements, including this `schemalocation` attribute, which tells the parser where to find the schema. You place this after the end of the list of child elements.

XDR Schemas

To attach an external XDR schema to an XML document, you specify a namespace for the document with the value `"x-schema:<schema_filename>"`.

```
<?xml version="1.0" ?>
<books xmlns="x-schema:books.xdr">
   ...
</books>
```

The following schema is the XDR equivalent of the XSD schema you just saw. As you can see, it's very different.

```
<Schema xmlns="urn:schemas-microsoft-com:xml-data">
  <ElementType name="title" content="textOnly" />
  <ElementType name="author" content="textOnly" />
  <ElementType name="code" content="textOnly" />
  <ElementType name="book" content="eltOnly">
    <group order="seq">
      <element type="title" />
      <element type="author" />
      <element type="code" />
    </group>
  </ElementType>
  <ElementType name="books" content="eltOnly">
    <element type="book" />
  </ElementType>
</Schema>
```

Again, you set the default namespace to tell the parser that all the elements in the document belong to the schema definition; this time you set it to `"urn:schemas-microsoft-com:xml-data"`. Notice that (unlike XSD schemas), this is a proprietary format, so it won't work with non-Microsoft products. In fact, XDR schemas are particularly useful when working with SQL Server, Microsoft's database server, because it has built-in support for XDR.

This time the root element is `Schema` with a capital *S*. This root element again contains the entire schema definition (remember that XML documents must have a single root element). After this, though, you have a big difference—the elements that will appear in the document are defined *in reverse order*! The reason for this is that each element in the document is represented in the schema by an `ElementType` element, and this contains an `element` element (note the lowercase *e* here) for each child element. Within the `element` tags, you set the `type` attribute to point to an `ElementType` element—and this must already have been declared. If you want to restrict how child elements can appear, you can use a `group` element within the `ElementType` and set its `order` attribute. In the case, you set it to `"seq"` to specify that the elements occur in the same sequence as in the schema—just like the `sequence` element in the XSD schema!

Try It Out: Creating an XML Document in Visual Studio .NET

Now that we've covered the basic syntax of XML, you can create an XML document. Fortunately, Visual Studio .NET does a lot of the hard work for you and will even create an XSD schema based on the XML document, without you having to write a single line of code!

1. Open Visual Studio, and create a new solution called `AppendixB_Examples`. Right-click the solution, select Add ➤ Add New Item..., select XML File, and name it `GhostStories.xml` as in Figure B-1. Then click Open.

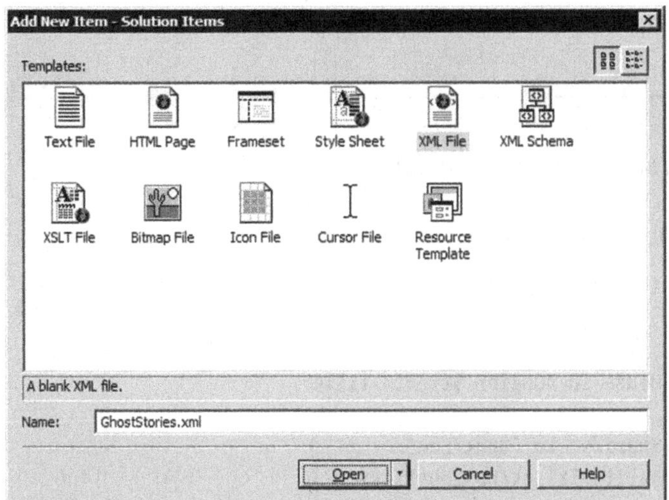

Figure B-1. *Adding an XML file to a solution*

2. Visual Studio opens the file in XML view. Notice how Visual Studio added the XML declaration, complete with an `encoding` attribute (see Figure B-2).

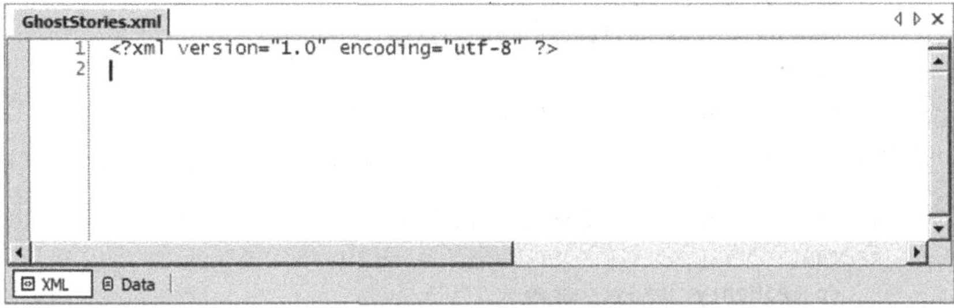

Figure B-2. *XML declaration generated by Visual Studio*

3. Move the cursor to the line underneath the XML declaration, and enter `<stories>`. Notice how Visual Studio automatically generates the end tag as soon as you close the start tag (see Figure B-3).

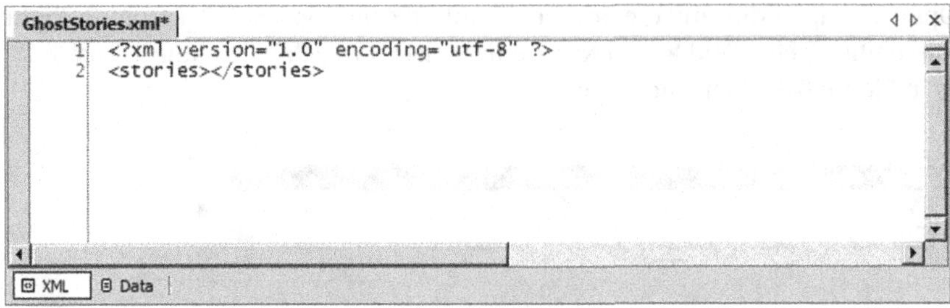

Figure B-3. *Visual Studio generating an end tag*

4. Add the following content to the stories element:

```
<?xml version="1.0" encoding="utf-8" ?>
<stories>
   <story>
      <title>A House in Aungier Street</title>
      <author>
         <name>Sheridan Le Fanu</name>
         <nationality>Irish</nationality>
      </author>
      <rating>eerie</rating>
   </story>
   <story>
      <title>The Signalman</title>
      <author>
         <name>Charles Dickens</name>
         <nationality>English</nationality>
      </author>
      <rating>atmospheric</rating>
   </story>
   <story>
      <title>The Turn of the Screw</title>
      <author>
         <name>Henry James</name>
         <nationality>American</nationality>
      </author>
      <rating>a bit dull</rating>
   </story>
</stories>
```

5. Click the Data tab to switch to Data view, and double-click the separator between title and rating column headings. You should see the display in Figure B-4.

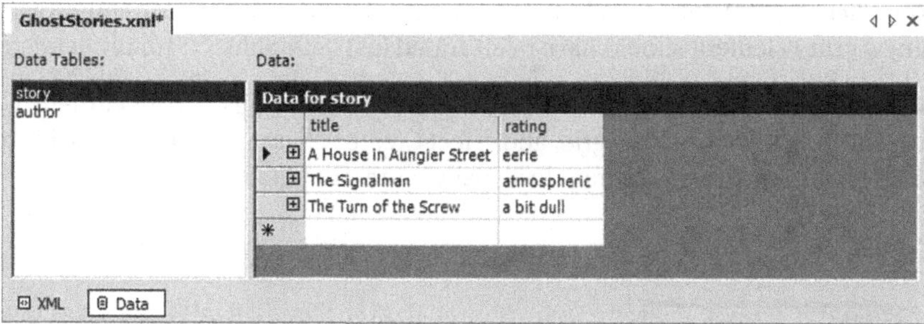

Figure B-4. *XML data displayed*

6. You can actually edit the data in this table, so you can modify your XML document here without even having to type the tags. In the empty row at the bottom of the grid, enter `Number 13` in the `title` column. Now, move to the rating box beside it, and enter `mysterious`. This enters a new story, but you still need to enter the author. To do this, click the plus sign next to the new row. This will open a link (`story author`) for the `author` element (see Figure B-5).

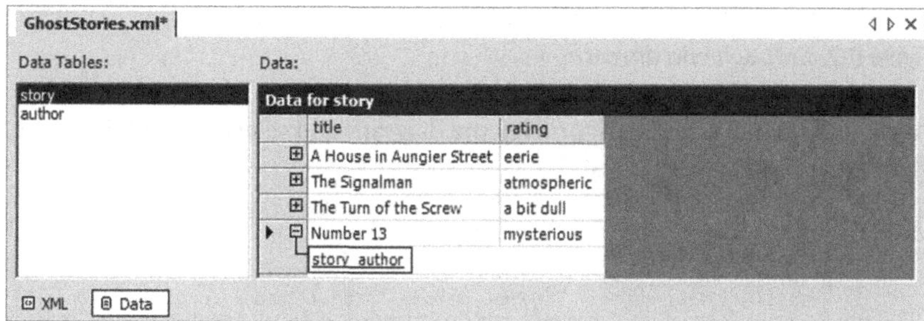

Figure B-5. *Adding an element to an XML file*

7. Click this link, and another table will be displayed so you can enter the name and nationality of the author. Enter `MR James` and `English` in the columns, and then press Enter (see Figure B-6).

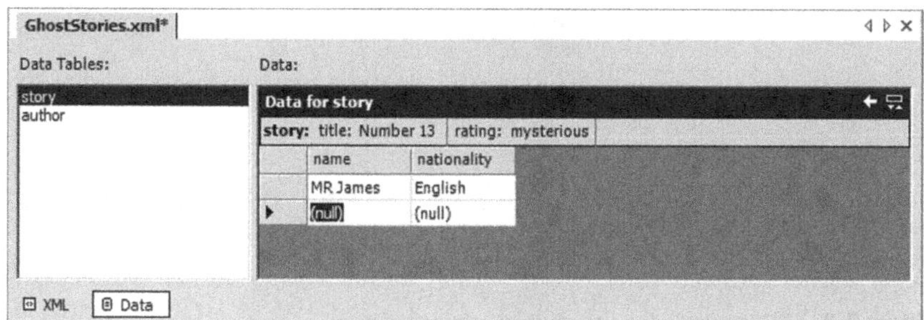

Figure B-6. *Adding nested element information*

8. Now click the XML tab at the bottom of the window to view the XML source again. A new `story` element should have been added just before the `</stories>` end tag.

9. Now you'll get Visual Studio to create an XSD schema for this XML document. Go back to Data view. Right-click the grid, and select Create Schema. Visual Studio will create an XSD schema and also a diagram to visually represent it (see Figure B-7).

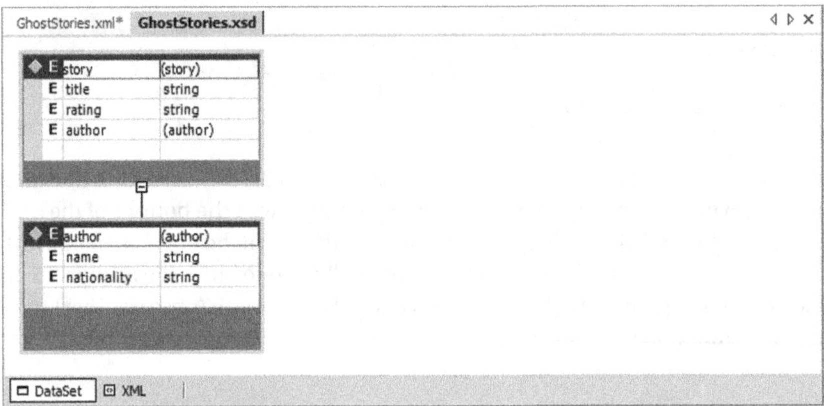

Figure B-7. *XML schema diagram*

10. To view the actual schema, right-click the diagram and select View XML Source (see Figure B-8).

GhostStories.xml* **GhostStories.xsd**

```
<?xml version="1.0"?>
<xs:schema id="stories" targetNamespace="http://tempuri.org/GhostStorie
  <xs:element name="stories" msdata:IsDataSet="true" msdata:Locale="en-
    <xs:complexType>
      <xs:choice maxOccurs="unbounded">
        <xs:element name="story">
          <xs:complexType>
            <xs:sequence>
              <xs:element name="title" type="xs:string" minOccurs="0" /
              <xs:element name="rating" type="xs:string" minOccurs="0"
              <xs:element name="author" minOccurs="0" maxOccurs="unboun
                <xs:complexType>
                  <xs:sequence>
                    <xs:element name="name" type="xs:string" minOccurs=
                    <xs:element name="nationality" type="xs:string" min
                  </xs:sequence>
                </xs:complexType>
              </xs:element>
            </xs:sequence>
          </xs:complexType>
        </xs:element>
      </xs:choice>
    </xs:complexType>
  </xs:element>
</xs:schema>
```

DataSet XML

Figure B-8. *XML schema for the* `stories` *document*

How It Works

Visual Studio provides a convenient environment for editing and maintaining XML source and schemas.

Summary

This appendix is far from a complete guide to XML, but it's a good beginning. We hope you'll be confident about using and creating XML in Visual Studio .NET.

INDEX

Symbols

A

B

D

Q

R

S